MW00649172

Advances in Kernel Methods

Advances in Kernel Methods

Support Vector Learning

edited by
Bernhard Schölkopf
Christopher J.C. Burges
Alexander J. Smola

The MIT Press
Cambridge, Massachusetts
London, England

Printed and bound in the United States of America

Library of Congress Cataloging-in-Publication Data

Advances in kernel methods : support vector learning / edited by Bernhard Schölkopf, Christopher J. C. Burges, Alexander J. Smola.
p. cm.
Includes bibliographical references and index.
ISBN 0-262-19416-3 (alk. paper)
1. Machine learning. 2. Algorithms. 3. Kernel functions
I. Schölkopf, Bernhard. II. Burges, Christopher J. C. III. Smola, Alexander J.
Q325.5.A32 1998
006.3'1–dc21 98–40302
CIP

Contents

Preface ix

1 Introduction to Support Vector Learning 1

2 Roadmap 17

I Theory 23

3 Three Remarks on the Support Vector Method of Function Estimation 25
Vladimir Vapnik

4 Generalization Performance of Support Vector Machines and Other Pattern Classifiers 43
Peter Bartlett & John Shawe-Taylor

5 Bayesian Voting Schemes and Large Margin Classifiers 55
Nello Cristianini & John Shawe-Taylor

6 Support Vector Machines, Reproducing Kernel Hilbert Spaces, and Randomized GACV 69
Grace Wahba

7 Geometry and Invariance in Kernel Based Methods 89
Christopher J. C. Burges

8 On the Annealed VC Entropy for Margin Classifiers: A Statistical Mechanics Study 117
Manfred Opper

9 Entropy Numbers, Operators and Support Vector Kernels 127
Robert C. Williamson, Alex J. Smola & Bernhard Schölkopf

II Implementations **145**

10 Solving the Quadratic Programming Problem Arising in Support Vector Classification **147**
Linda Kaufman

11 Making Large-Scale Support Vector Machine Learning Practical **169**
Thorsten Joachims

12 Fast Training of Support Vector Machines Using Sequential Minimal Optimization **185**
John C. Platt

III Applications **209**

13 Support Vector Machines for Dynamic Reconstruction of a Chaotic System **211**
Davide Mattera & Simon Haykin

14 Using Support Vector Machines for Time Series Prediction **243**
Klaus-Robert Müller, Alex J. Smola, Gunnar Rätsch, Bernhard Schölkopf, Jens Kohlmorgen & Vladimir Vapnik

15 Pairwise Classification and Support Vector Machines **255**
Ulrich Kreßel

IV Extensions of the Algorithm **269**

16 Reducing the Run-time Complexity in Support Vector Machines **271**
Edgar E. Osuna & Federico Girosi

17 Support Vector Regression with ANOVA Decomposition Kernels **285**
Mark O. Stitson, Alex Gammerman, Vladimir Vapnik, Volodya Vovk, Chris Watkins & Jason Weston

18 Support Vector Density Estimation **293**
Jason Weston, Alex Gammerman, Mark O. Stitson, Vladimir Vapnik, Volodya Vovk & Chris Watkins

19 Combining Support Vector and Mathematical Programming Methods for Classification **307**
Kristin P. Bennett

20 Kernel Principal Component Analysis **327**
Bernhard Schölkopf, Alex J. Smola & Klaus-Robert Müller

References 353

Index 373

Preface

Statistical Learning Theory now plays a more active role: after the general analysis of learning processes, the research in the area of synthesis of optimal algorithms was started. These studies, however, do not belong to history yet. They are a subject of today's research activities.

Vladimir Vapnik (1995)

The Support Vector Machine has recently been introduced as a new technique for solving a variety of learning and function estimation problems. During a workshop at the annual Neural Information Processing Systems (NIPS) conference, held in Breckenridge, Colorado in December 1997, a snapshot of the state of the art in Support Vector learning was recorded. A variety of people helped in this, among them our co-organizer Léon Bottou, the NIPS workshop chairs Steve Nowlan and Rich Zemel, and all the workshop speakers and attendees who contributed to lively discussions. After the workshop, we decided that it would be worthwhile to invest some time to have the snapshot printed.

We invited all the speakers as well as other researchers to submit papers for this collection, and integrated the results into the present book. We believe that it covers the full range of current Support Vector research at an early point in time. This is possible for two reasons. First, the field of SV learning is in its early (and thus exciting) days. Second, this book gathers expertise from all contributers, whom we wholeheartedly thank for all the work they have put into our joint effort. Any single person trying to accomplish this task would most likely have failed: either by writing a book which is less comprehensive, or by taking more time to complete the book.

It is our hope that this outweighs the shortcomings of the book, most notably the fact that a collection of chapters can never be as homogeneous as a book conceived by a single person. We have tried to compensate for this by the selection and refereeing process of the submissions. In addition, we have written an introductory chapter describing the SV algorithm in some detail (chapter 1), and added a roadmap (chapter 2) which describes the actual contributions which are to follow in chapters 3 through 20.

Bernhard Schölkopf, Christopher J.C. Burges, Alexander J. Smola

Berlin, Holmdel, July 1998

1 Introduction to Support Vector Learning

The goal of this chapter, which describes the central ideas of SV learning, is twofold. First, we want to provide an introduction for readers unfamiliar with this field. Second, this introduction serves as a source of the basic equations for the chapters of this book. For more exhaustive treatments, we refer the interested reader to Vapnik (1995); Schölkopf (1997); Burges (1998).

1.1 Learning Pattern Recognition from Examples

Training Data

Let us start with the problem of learning how to recognize patterns. Formally, we want to estimate a function $f : \mathbb{R}^N \to \{\pm 1\}$ using input-output training data

$$(\mathbf{x}_1, y_1), \ldots, (\mathbf{x}_\ell, y_\ell) \in \mathbb{R}^N \times \{\pm 1\}, \tag{1.1}$$

Test Data

such that f will correctly classify unseen examples $(\mathbf{x}, y)$, i.e. $f(\mathbf{x}) = y$ for examples $(\mathbf{x}, y)$ that were generated from the same underlying probability distribution $P(\mathbf{x}, y)$ as the training data. If we put no restriction on the class of functions that we choose our estimate f from, however, even a function which does well on the training data, e.g. by satisfying $f(\mathbf{x}_i) = y_i$ for all $i = 1, \ldots, \ell$, need not generalize well to unseen examples. To see this, note that for each function f and any test set $(\bar{\mathbf{x}}_1, \bar{y}_1), \ldots, (\bar{\mathbf{x}}_{\bar{\ell}}, \bar{y}_{\bar{\ell}}) \in \mathbb{R}^N \times \{\pm 1\}$, satisfying $\{\bar{\mathbf{x}}_1, \ldots, \bar{\mathbf{x}}_{\bar{\ell}}\} \cap \{\mathbf{x}_1, \ldots, \mathbf{x}_\ell\} = \{\}$, there exists another function f^* such that $f^*(\mathbf{x}_i) = f(\mathbf{x}_i)$ for all $i = 1, \ldots, \ell$, yet $f^*(\bar{\mathbf{x}}_i) \neq f(\bar{\mathbf{x}}_i)$ for all $i = 1, \ldots, \bar{\ell}$. As we are only given the training data, we have no means of selecting which of the two functions (and hence which of the completely different sets of test outputs) is preferable. Hence, only minimizing the training error (or *empirical risk*),

Empirical Risk

$$R_{emp}[f] = \frac{1}{\ell} \sum_{i=1}^{\ell} \frac{1}{2} |f(\mathbf{x}_i) - y_i|, \tag{1.2}$$

Risk

does not imply a small test error (called *risk*), averaged over test examples drawn from the underlying distribution $P(\mathbf{x}, y)$,

$$R[f] = \int \frac{1}{2} |f(\mathbf{x}) - y| \, dP(\mathbf{x}, y). \tag{1.3}$$

Statistical learning theory (Vapnik and Chervonenkis, 1974; Vapnik, 1979), or VC (Vapnik-Chervonenkis) theory, shows that it is imperative to restrict the class of functions that f is chosen from to one which has a *capacity* that is suitable for the amount of available training data. VC theory provides *bounds* on the test error. The minimization of these bounds, which depend on both the empirical risk and the capacity of the function class, leads to the principle of *structural risk minimization* (Vapnik, 1979). The best-known capacity concept of VC theory is the *VC dimension*, defined as the largest number h of points that can be separated in all possible ways using functions of the given class (cf. chapter 4). An example of a VC bound is the following: if $h < \ell$ is the VC dimension of the class of functions that the learning machine can implement, then for all functions of that class, with a probability of at least $1 - \eta$, the bound

VC dimension

$$R(\alpha) \leq R_{emp}(\alpha) + \phi\left(\frac{h}{\ell}, \frac{\log(\eta)}{\ell}\right) \tag{1.4}$$

holds, where the *confidence term* ϕ is defined as

$$\phi\left(\frac{h}{\ell}, \frac{\log(\eta)}{\ell}\right) = \sqrt{\frac{h\left(\log\frac{2\ell}{h} + 1\right) - \log(\eta/4)}{\ell}}. \tag{1.5}$$

Tighter bounds can be formulated in terms of other concepts, such as the *annealed VC entropy* or the *Growth function*. These are usually considered to be harder to evaluate (cf., however, chapter 9), but they play a fundamental role in the conceptual part of VC theory (Vapnik, 1995). Alternative capacity concepts that can be used to formulate bounds include the *fat shattering dimension*, cf. chapter 4.

The bound (1.4) deserves some further explanatory remarks. Suppose we wanted to learn a "dependency" where $P(\mathbf{x}, y) = P(\mathbf{x}) \cdot P(y)$, i.e. where the pattern $\mathbf{x}$ contains no information about the label y, with uniform $P(y)$. Given a training sample of fixed size, we can then surely come up with a learning machine which achieves zero training error (provided we have no examples contradicting each other). However, in order to reproduce the random labellings, this machine will necessarily require a large VC dimension h. Thus, the confidence term (1.5), increasing monotonically with h, will be large, and the bound (1.4) will *not* support possible hopes that due to the small training error, we should expect a small test error. This makes it understandable how (1.4) can hold independent of assumptions about the underlying distribution $P(\mathbf{x}, y)$: it always holds (provided that $h < \ell$), but it does not always make a nontrivial prediction — a bound on an error rate becomes void if it is larger than the maximum error rate. In order to get nontrivial predictions from (1.4), the function space must be restricted such that the capacity (e.g. VC dimension) is small enough (in relation to the available amount of data).

1.2 Hyperplane Classifiers

To design learning algorithms, one thus needs to come up with a class of functions whose capacity can be computed. Vapnik and Lerner (1963) and Vapnik and

Chervonenkis (1964) considered the class of hyperplanes

$$(\mathbf{w} \cdot \mathbf{x}) + b = 0 \qquad \mathbf{w} \in \mathbb{R}^N, b \in R, \tag{1.6}$$

corresponding to decision functions

$$f(\mathbf{x}) = \mathrm{sgn}((\mathbf{w} \cdot \mathbf{x}) + b), \tag{1.7}$$

and proposed a learning algorithm for separable problems, termed the *Generalized Portrait*, for constructing f from empirical data. It is based on two facts. First, among all hyperplanes separating the data, there exists a unique one yielding the maximum margin of separation between the classes,

Optimal Hyperplane

$$\max_{\mathbf{w},b} \ \min\{\|\mathbf{x} - \mathbf{x}_i\| : \mathbf{x} \in \mathbb{R}^N, (\mathbf{w} \cdot \mathbf{x}) + b = 0, i = 1, \ldots, \ell\}. \tag{1.8}$$

Second, the capacity decreases with increasing margin.

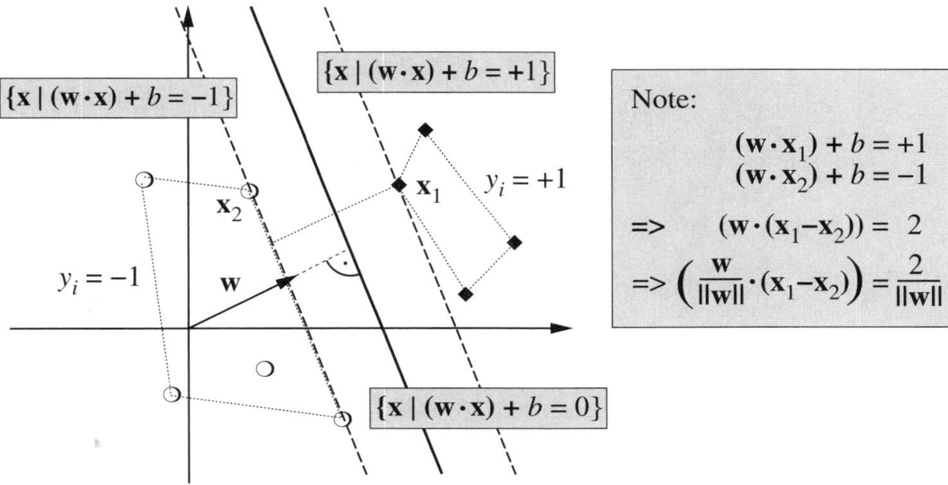

Figure 1.1 A binary classification toy problem: separate balls from diamonds. The *optimal hyperplane* is orthogonal to the shortest line connecting the convex hulls of the two classes (dotted), and intersects it half-way between the two classes. The problem being separable, there exists a weight vector $\mathbf{w}$ and a threshold b such that $y_i \cdot ((\mathbf{w} \cdot \mathbf{x}_i) + b) > 0$ $(i = 1, \ldots, \ell)$. Rescaling $\mathbf{w}$ and b such that the point(s) closest to the hyperplane satisfy $|(\mathbf{w} \cdot \mathbf{x}_i) + b| = 1$, we obtain a *canonical* form $(\mathbf{w}, b)$ of the hyperplane, satisfying $y_i \cdot ((\mathbf{w} \cdot \mathbf{x}_i) + b) \geq 1$. Note that in this case, the *margin*, measured perpendicularly to the hyperplane, equals $2/\|\mathbf{w}\|$. This can be seen by considering two points $\mathbf{x}_1, \mathbf{x}_2$ on opposite sides of the margin, i.e. $(\mathbf{w} \cdot \mathbf{x}_1) + b = 1, (\mathbf{w} \cdot \mathbf{x}_2) + b = -1$, and projecting them onto the hyperplane normal vector $\mathbf{w}/\|\mathbf{w}\|$.

To construct this *Optimal Hyperplane* (cf. figure 1.1), one solves the following optimization problem:

$$\text{minimize} \quad \tau(\mathbf{w}) = \frac{1}{2}\|\mathbf{w}\|^2 \tag{1.9}$$

$$\text{subject to} \quad y_i \cdot ((\mathbf{w} \cdot \mathbf{x}_i) + b) \geq 1, \qquad i = 1, \ldots, \ell. \tag{1.10}$$

Lagrangian

This constrained optimization problem is dealt with by introducing Lagrange multipliers $\alpha_i \geq 0$ and a Lagrangian

$$L(\mathbf{w}, b, \boldsymbol{\alpha}) = \frac{1}{2}\|\mathbf{w}\|^2 - \sum_{i=1}^{\ell} \alpha_i \left(y_i \cdot ((\mathbf{x}_i \cdot \mathbf{w}) + b) - 1 \right). \tag{1.11}$$

The Lagrangian L has to be minimized with respect to the *primal variables* $\mathbf{w}$ and b and maximized with respect to the *dual variables* α_i (i.e. a saddle point has to be found). Let us try to get some intuition for this. If a constraint (1.10) is violated, then $y_i \cdot ((\mathbf{w} \cdot \mathbf{x}_i) + b) - 1 < 0$, in which case L can be increased by increasing the corresponding α_i. At the same time, $\mathbf{w}$ and b will have to change such that L decreases. To prevent $-\alpha_i \left(y_i \cdot ((\mathbf{w} \cdot \mathbf{x}_i) + b) - 1 \right)$ from becoming arbitrarily large, the change in $\mathbf{w}$ and b will ensure that, provided the problem is separable, the constraint will eventually be satisfied. Similarly, one can understand that for all constraints which are not precisely met as equalities, i.e. for which $y_i \cdot ((\mathbf{w} \cdot \mathbf{x}_i) + b) - 1 > 0$, the corresponding α_i must be 0: this is the value of α_i that maximizes L. The latter is the statement of the Karush-Kuhn-Tucker complementarity conditions of optimization theory (Karush, 1939; Kuhn and Tucker, 1951; Bertsekas, 1995).

KKT Conditions

The condition that at the saddle point, the derivatives of L with respect to the primal variables must vanish,

$$\frac{\partial}{\partial b} L(\mathbf{w}, b, \boldsymbol{\alpha}) = 0, \quad \frac{\partial}{\partial \mathbf{w}} L(\mathbf{w}, b, \boldsymbol{\alpha}) = 0, \tag{1.12}$$

leads to

$$\sum_{i=1}^{\ell} \alpha_i y_i = 0 \tag{1.13}$$

and

$$\mathbf{w} = \sum_{i=1}^{\ell} \alpha_i y_i \mathbf{x}_i. \tag{1.14}$$

Support Vector

The solution vector thus has an expansion in terms of a subset of the training patterns, namely those patterns whose α_i is non-zero, called *Support Vectors*. By the Karush-Kuhn-Tucker complementarity conditions

$$\alpha_i \cdot [y_i((\mathbf{x}_i \cdot \mathbf{w}) + b) - 1] = 0, \qquad i = 1, \ldots, \ell, \tag{1.15}$$

the Support Vectors lie on the margin (cf. figure 1.1). All remaining examples of the training set are irrelevant: their constraint (1.10) does not play a role in the optimization, and they do not appear in the expansion (1.14). This nicely captures our intuition of the problem: as the hyperplane (cf. figure 1.1) is completely determined by the patterns closest to it, the solution should not depend on the other examples.

By substituting (1.13) and (1.14) into L, one eliminates the primal variables and arrives at the Wolfe dual of the optimization problem (e.g. Bertsekas, 1995): find multipliers α_i which

Dual Optimization Problem

$$\text{maximize} \quad W(\alpha) = \sum_{i=1}^{\ell} \alpha_i - \frac{1}{2} \sum_{i,j=1}^{\ell} \alpha_i \alpha_j y_i y_j (\mathbf{x}_i \cdot \mathbf{x}_j) \tag{1.16}$$

$$\text{subject to} \quad \alpha_i \geq 0, \quad i = 1, \ldots, \ell, \text{ and } \sum_{i=1}^{\ell} \alpha_i y_i = 0. \tag{1.17}$$

The hyperplane decision function can thus be written as

$$f(\mathbf{x}) = \operatorname{sgn}\left(\sum_{i=1}^{\ell} y_i \alpha_i \cdot (\mathbf{x} \cdot \mathbf{x}_i) + b \right) \tag{1.18}$$

where b is computed using (1.15).

The structure of the optimization problem closely resembles those that typically arise in Lagrange's formulation of mechanics (e.g. Goldstein, 1986). Also there, often only a subset of the constraints become active. For instance, if we keep a ball in a box, then it will typically roll into one of the corners. The constraints corresponding to the walls which are not touched by the ball are irrelevant, the walls could just as well be removed.

Seen in this light, it is not too surprising that it is possible to give a mechanical interpretation of optimal margin hyperplanes (Burges and Schölkopf, 1997): If we assume that each support vector $\mathbf{x}_i$ exerts a perpendicular force of size α_i and sign y_i on a solid plane sheet lying along the hyperplane, then the solution satisfies the requirements of mechanical stability. The constraint (1.13) states that the forces on the sheet sum to zero; and (1.14) implies that the torques also sum to zero, via $\sum_i \mathbf{x}_i \times y_i \alpha_i \cdot \mathbf{w}/\|\mathbf{w}\| = \mathbf{w} \times \mathbf{w}/\|\mathbf{w}\| = 0$.

There are several theoretical arguments supporting the good generalization performance of the optimal hyperplane (Vapnik and Chervonenkis (1974); Vapnik (1979), cf. chapters 3 and 4). In addition, it is computationally attractive, since it can be constructed by solving a quadratic programming problem. But how can this be generalized to the case of decision functions which, unlike (1.7), are nonlinear in the data?

1.3 Feature Spaces and Kernels

To construct SV machines, the optimal hyperplane algorithm had to be augmented by a method for computing dot products in feature spaces nonlinearly related to input space (Aizerman et al., 1964; Boser et al., 1992). The basic idea is to map the data into some other dot product space (called the *feature space*) F via a nonlinear

Feature Space

map

$$\Phi : \mathbb{R}^N \to F, \tag{1.19}$$

and perform the above linear algorithm in F.

For instance, suppose we are given patterns $\mathbf{x} \in \mathbb{R}^N$ where most information is contained in the d-th order products (monomials) of entries x_j of $\mathbf{x}$, i.e. $x_{j_1} \cdot \ldots \cdot x_{j_d}$, where $j_1, \ldots, j_d \in \{1, \ldots, N\}$. In that case, we might prefer to extract these monomial features first, and work in the feature space F of all products of d entries. This approach, however, fails for realistically sized problems: for N-dimensional input patterns, there exist $(N + d - 1)!/(d!(N - 1)!)$ different monomials. Already 16×16 pixel input images (e.g. in character recognition) and a monomial degree $d = 5$ yield a dimensionality of 10^{10}.

This problem can be overcome by noticing that both the construction of the optimal hyperplane in F (cf. (1.16)) and the evaluation of the corresponding decision function (1.18) only require the evaluation of dot products $(\Phi(\mathbf{x}) \cdot \Phi(\mathbf{y}))$, and never the mapped patterns $\Phi(\mathbf{x})$ in explicit form. This is crucial, since in some cases, the dot products can be evaluated by a simple kernel

Mercer Kernel

$$k(\mathbf{x}, \mathbf{y}) = (\Phi(\mathbf{x}) \cdot \Phi(\mathbf{y})). \tag{1.20}$$

For instance, the polynomial kernel

$$k(\mathbf{x}, \mathbf{y}) = (\mathbf{x} \cdot \mathbf{y})^d \tag{1.21}$$

can be shown to correspond to a map Φ into the space spanned by all products of exactly d dimensions of $\mathbb{R}^N$ (Poggio (1975); Boser et al. (1992); Burges (1998); for a proof, see chapter 20). For $d = 2$ and $\mathbf{x}, \mathbf{y} \in \mathbb{R}^2$, e.g., we have (Vapnik, 1995)

$$(\mathbf{x} \cdot \mathbf{y})^2 = (x_1^2, x_2^2, \sqrt{2}\, x_1 x_2)(y_1^2, y_2^2, \sqrt{2}\, y_1 y_2)^\top = (\Phi(\mathbf{x}) \cdot \Phi(\mathbf{y})), \tag{1.22}$$

defining $\Phi(\mathbf{x}) = (x_1^2, x_2^2, \sqrt{2}\, x_1 x_2)$.

By using $k(\mathbf{x}, \mathbf{y}) = (\mathbf{x} \cdot \mathbf{y} + c)^d$ with $c > 0$, we can take into account all product of order up to d (i.e. including those of order smaller than d).

More generally, the following theorem of functional analysis shows that kernels k of positive integral operators give rise to maps Φ such that (1.20) holds (Mercer, 1909; Aizerman et al., 1964; Boser et al., 1992):

Theorem 1.1 (Mercer)
If k is a continuous symmetric kernel of a positive integral operator T, i.e.

$$(Tf)(\mathbf{y}) = \int_{\mathcal{C}} k(\mathbf{x}, \mathbf{y}) f(\mathbf{x})\, d\mathbf{x} \tag{1.23}$$

with

$$\int_{\mathcal{C} \times \mathcal{C}} k(\mathbf{x}, \mathbf{y}) f(\mathbf{x}) f(\mathbf{y})\, d\mathbf{x}\, d\mathbf{y} \geq 0 \tag{1.24}$$

for all $f \in L_2(\mathcal{C})$ ($\mathcal{C}$ being a compact subset of $\mathbb{R}^N$), it can be expanded in a uniformly convergent series (on $\mathcal{C} \times \mathcal{C}$) in terms of T's eigenfunctions ψ_j and positive eigenvalues λ_j,

$$k(\mathbf{x}, \mathbf{y}) = \sum_{j=1}^{N_F} \lambda_j \psi_j(\mathbf{x}) \psi_j(\mathbf{y}), \tag{1.25}$$

where $N_F \leq \infty$ is the number of positive eigenvalues.

Note that originally proven for the case where $\mathcal{C} = [a, b]$ ($a < b \in \mathbb{R}$), this theorem also holds true for general compact spaces (Dunford and Schwartz, 1963).

An equivalent way to characterize Mercer kernels is that they give rise to positive matrices $K_{ij} := k(\mathbf{x}_i, \mathbf{x}_j)$ for all $\{\mathbf{x}_1, \ldots, \mathbf{x}_\ell\}$ (Saitoh, 1988). One of the implications that need to be proven to show this equivalence follows from the fact that K_{ij} is a Gram matrix: for $\boldsymbol{\alpha} \in \mathbb{R}^\ell$, we have $(\boldsymbol{\alpha} \cdot K\boldsymbol{\alpha}) = \| \sum_{i=1}^{\ell} \alpha_i \Phi(\mathbf{x}_i)\|^2 \geq 0$.

From (1.25), it is straightforward to construct a map Φ into a potentially infinite-dimensional l_2 space which satisfies (1.20). For instance, we may use

$$\Phi(\mathbf{x}) = (\sqrt{\lambda_1}\psi_1(\mathbf{x}), \sqrt{\lambda_2}\psi_2(\mathbf{x}), \ldots). \tag{1.26}$$

Rather than thinking of the feature space as an l_2 space, we can alternatively represent it as the Hilbert space $\mathcal{H}_k$ containing all linear combinations of the functions $f(.) = k(\mathbf{x}_i, .)$ ($\mathbf{x}_i \in \mathcal{C}$). To ensure that the map $\Phi : \mathcal{C} \to \mathcal{H}_k$, which in this case is defined as

$$\Phi(\mathbf{x}) = k(\mathbf{x}, .), \tag{1.27}$$

satisfies (1.20), we need to endow $\mathcal{H}_k$ with a suitable dot product $\langle ., . \rangle$. In view of the definition of Φ, this dot product needs to satisfy

$$\langle k(\mathbf{x}, .), k(\mathbf{y}, .)\rangle = k(\mathbf{x}, \mathbf{y}), \tag{1.28}$$

Reproducing Kernel

which amounts to saying that k is a *reproducing kernel* for $\mathcal{H}_k$. For a Mercer kernel (1.25), such a dot product does exist. Since k is symmetric, the ψ_i ($i = 1, \ldots, N_F$) can be chosen to be orthogonal with respect to the dot product in $L_2(C)$, i.e. $(\psi_j, \psi_n)_{L_2(C)} = \delta_{jn}$, using the Kronecker δ_{jn}. From this, we can construct $\langle ., . \rangle$ such that

$$\langle \sqrt{\lambda_j}\psi_j, \sqrt{\lambda_n}\psi_n \rangle = \delta_{jn}. \tag{1.29}$$

Substituting (1.25) into (1.28) then proves the desired equality (for further details, see chapter 6 and Aronszajn (1950); Wahba (1973); Girosi (1998); Schölkopf (1997)).

Besides (1.21), SV practicioners use sigmoid kernels

$$k(\mathbf{x}, \mathbf{y}) = \tanh(\kappa(\mathbf{x} \cdot \mathbf{y}) + \Theta) \tag{1.30}$$

for suitable values of gain κ and threshold Θ (cf. chapter 7), and radial basis function kernels, as for instance (Aizerman et al., 1964; Boser et al., 1992; Schölkopf et al., 1997b)

$$k(\mathbf{x}, \mathbf{y}) = \exp\left(-\|\mathbf{x} - \mathbf{y}\|^2/(2\,\sigma^2)\right), \tag{1.31}$$

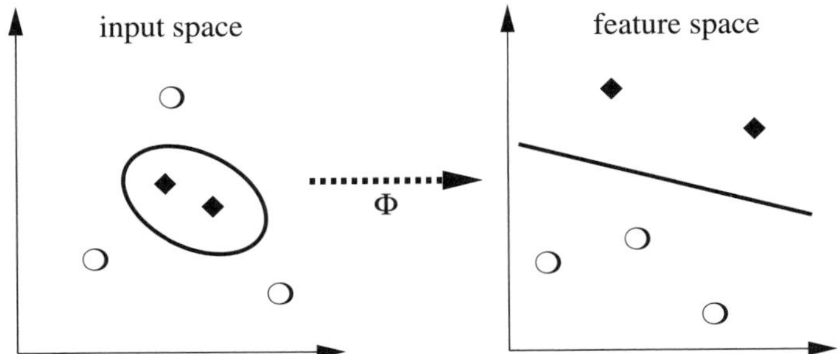

Figure 1.2 The idea of SV machines: map the training data nonlinearly into a higher-dimensional feature space via Φ, and construct a separating hyperplane with maximum margin there. This yields a nonlinear decision boundary in input space. By the use of a kernel function (1.20), it is possible to compute the separating hyperplane without explicitly carrying out the map into the feature space.

with $\sigma > 0$. Note that when using Gaussian kernels, for instance, the feature space $\mathcal{H}_k$ thus contains all superpositions of Gaussians on $\mathcal{C}$ (plus limit points), whereas by definition of Φ (1.27), only single bumps $k(\mathbf{x}, .)$ do have pre-images under Φ.

1.4 Support Vector Machines

To construct SV machines, one computes an optimal hyperplane in feature space. To this end, we substitute $\Phi(\mathbf{x}_i)$ for each training example $\mathbf{x}_i$. The weight vector (cf. (1.14)) then becomes an expansion in feature space, and will thus typically no more correspond to the image of a single vector from input space (cf. Schölkopf et al. (1998c) for a formula how to compute the pre-image if it exists). Since all patterns only occur in dot products, one can substitute Mercer kernels k for the dot products (Boser et al., 1992; Guyon et al., 1993), leading to decision functions of the more general form (cf. (1.18))

Decision Function

$$f(\mathbf{x}) = \operatorname{sgn}\left(\sum_{i=1}^{\ell} y_i\alpha_i \cdot (\Phi(\mathbf{x}) \cdot \Phi(\mathbf{x}_i)) + b\right)$$
$$= \operatorname{sgn}\left(\sum_{i=1}^{\ell} y_i\alpha_i \cdot k(\mathbf{x}, \mathbf{x}_i) + b\right) \tag{1.32}$$

and the following quadratic program (cf. (1.16)):

$$\text{maximize} \quad W(\alpha) = \sum_{i=1}^{\ell} \alpha_i - \frac{1}{2}\sum_{i,j=1}^{\ell} \alpha_i\alpha_j y_i y_j k(\mathbf{x}_i, \mathbf{x}_j) \tag{1.33}$$

$$\text{subject to} \quad \alpha_i \geq 0, \;\; i = 1, \ldots, \ell, \text{ and } \sum_{i=1}^{\ell} \alpha_i y_i = 0. \tag{1.34}$$

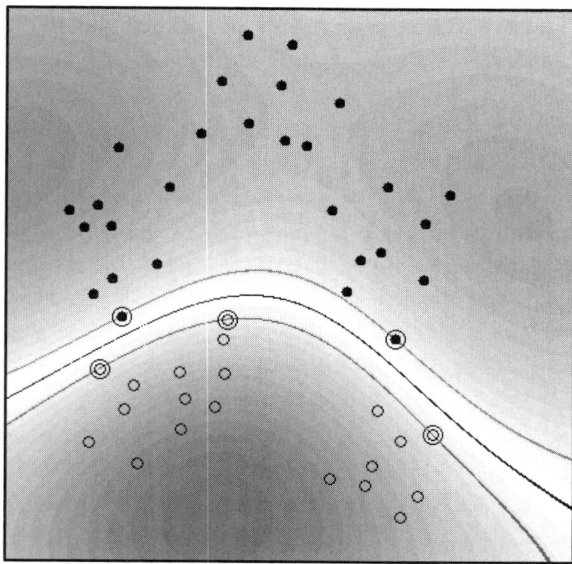

Figure 1.3 Example of a Support Vector classifier found by using a radial basis function kernel $k(\mathbf{x}, \mathbf{y}) = \exp(-\|\mathbf{x} - \mathbf{y}\|^2)$. Both coordinate axes range from -1 to +1. Circles and disks are two classes of training examples; the middle line is the decision surface; the outer lines precisely meet the constraint (1.10). Note that the Support Vectors found by the algorithm (marked by extra circles) are not centers of clusters, but examples which are critical for the given classification task. Grey values code the modulus of the argument $\sum_{i=1}^{\ell} y_i \alpha_i \cdot k(\mathbf{x}, \mathbf{x}_i) + b$ of the decision function (1.32). (From Schölkopf et al. (1996a), see also Burges (1998).)

Soft Margin Hyperplane

In practice, a separating hyperplane may not exist, e.g. if a high noise level causes a large overlap of the classes. To allow for the possibility of examples violating (1.10), one introduces slack variables (Cortes and Vapnik, 1995; Vapnik, 1995)

$$\xi_i \geq 0, \quad i = 1, \ldots, \ell, \tag{1.35}$$

along with relaxed constraints

$$y_i \cdot ((\mathbf{w} \cdot \mathbf{x}_i) + b) \geq 1 - \xi_i, \quad i = 1, \ldots, \ell. \tag{1.36}$$

A classifier which generalizes well is then found by controlling both the classifier capacity (via $\|\mathbf{w}\|$) and the number of training errors, minimizing the objective function

$$\tau(\mathbf{w}, \boldsymbol{\xi}) = \frac{1}{2}\|\mathbf{w}\|^2 + C \sum_{i=1}^{\ell} \xi_i \tag{1.37}$$

subject to the constraints (1.35) and (1.36), for some value of the constant $C > 0$ determining the trade-off. Here and below, we use boldface greek letters as a shorthand for corresponding vectors $\boldsymbol{\xi} = (\xi_1, \ldots, \xi_\ell)$. Incorporating kernels, and rewriting it in terms of Lagrange multipliers, this again leads to the problem of maximizing (1.33), subject to the constraints

$$0 \leq \alpha_i \leq C, \quad i = 1, \ldots, \ell, \text{ and } \sum_{i=1}^{\ell} \alpha_i y_i = 0. \tag{1.38}$$

The only difference from the separable case is the upper bound C on the Lagrange multipliers α_i. This way, the influence of the individual patterns (which could always be outliers) gets limited. As above, the solution takes the form (1.32). The threshold b can be computed by exploiting the fact that for all SVs $\mathbf{x}_i$ with $\alpha_i < C$, the slack variable ξ_i is zero (this again follows from the Karush-Kuhn-Tucker complementarity conditions), and hence

$$\sum_{j=1}^{\ell} y_j \alpha_j \cdot k(\mathbf{x}_i, \mathbf{x}_j) + b = y_i. \tag{1.39}$$

If one uses an optimizer that works with the double dual (e.g. Vanderbei, 1997), one can also recover the value of the primal variable b directly from the corresponding double dual variable.

1.5 Support Vector Regression

The concept of the margin is specific to pattern recognition. To generalize the SV algorithm to regression estimation (Vapnik, 1995), an analogue of the margin is constructed in the space of the target values y (note that in regression, we have $y \in \mathbb{R}$) by using Vapnik's ε-insensitive loss function (figure 1.4)

$$|y - f(\mathbf{x})|_\varepsilon := \max\{0, |y - f(\mathbf{x})| - \varepsilon\}. \tag{1.40}$$

To estimate a linear regression

$$f(\mathbf{x}) = (\mathbf{w} \cdot \mathbf{x}) + b \tag{1.41}$$

with precision ε, one minimizes

$$\frac{1}{2}\|\mathbf{w}\|^2 + C \sum_{i=1}^{\ell} |y_i - f(\mathbf{x}_i)|_\varepsilon. \tag{1.42}$$

Written as a constrained optimization problem, this reads (Vapnik, 1995):

$$\text{minimize} \quad \tau(\mathbf{w}, \boldsymbol{\xi}, \boldsymbol{\xi}^*) = \frac{1}{2}\|\mathbf{w}\|^2 + C \sum_{i=1}^{\ell} (\xi_i + \xi_i^*) \tag{1.43}$$

$$\text{subject to} \quad ((\mathbf{w} \cdot \mathbf{x}_i) + b) - y_i \leq \varepsilon + \xi_i \tag{1.44}$$

$$y_i - ((\mathbf{w} \cdot \mathbf{x}_i) + b) \leq \varepsilon + \xi_i^* \tag{1.45}$$

$$\xi_i, \xi_i^* \geq 0 \tag{1.46}$$

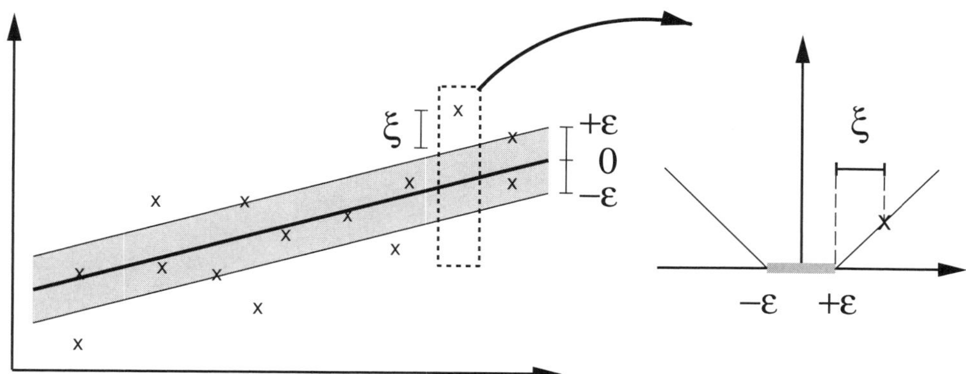

Figure 1.4 In SV regression, a desired accuracy ε is specified a priori. One then attempts to fit a tube with radius ε to the data. The trade-off between model complexity and points lying outside of the tube (with positive slack variables ξ) is determined by minimizing (1.43).

for all $i = 1, \ldots, \ell$. Note that according to (1.44) and (1.45), any error smaller than ε does not require a nonzero ξ_i or ξ_i^*, and hence does not enter the objective function (1.43).

Generalization to nonlinear regression estimation is carried out using kernel functions, in complete analogy to the case of pattern recognition. Introducing Lagrange multipliers, one thus arrives at the following optimization problem: for $C > 0, \varepsilon \geq 0$ chosen a priori,

$$\text{maximize} \quad W(\boldsymbol{\alpha}, \boldsymbol{\alpha}^*) = -\varepsilon \sum_{i=1}^{\ell} (\alpha_i^* + \alpha_i) + \sum_{i=1}^{\ell} (\alpha_i^* - \alpha_i) y_i - \frac{1}{2} \sum_{i,j=1}^{\ell} (\alpha_i^* - \alpha_i)(\alpha_j^* - \alpha_j) k(\mathbf{x}_i, \mathbf{x}_j) \tag{1.47}$$

$$\text{subject to} \quad 0 \leq \alpha_i, \alpha_i^* \leq C, \quad i = 1, \ldots, \ell, \text{ and } \sum_{i=1}^{\ell} (\alpha_i - \alpha_i^*) = 0. \tag{1.48}$$

Regression Function

The regression estimate takes the form

$$f(\mathbf{x}) = \sum_{i=1}^{\ell} (\alpha_i^* - \alpha_i) k(\mathbf{x}_i, \mathbf{x}) + b, \tag{1.49}$$

where b is computed using the fact that (1.44) becomes an equality with $\xi_i = 0$ if $0 < \alpha_i < C$, and (1.45) becomes an equality with $\xi_i^* = 0$ if $0 < \alpha_i^* < C$.

Several extensions of this algorithm are possible. From an abstract point of view, we just need some target function which depends on the vector $(\mathbf{w}, \boldsymbol{\xi})$ (cf. (1.43)). There are multiple degrees of freedom for constructing it, including some freedom how to penalize, or regularize, different parts of the vector, and some freedom how to use the kernel trick. For instance, more general loss functions can be used for

$\boldsymbol{\xi}$, leading to problems that can still be solved efficiently (Smola and Schölkopf, 1998b; Smola et al., 1998a). Moreover, norms other than the 2-norm $\|.\|$ can be used to regularize the solution (cf. chapters 18 and 19). Yet another example is that polynomial kernels can be incorporated which consist of multiple layers, such that the first layer only computes products within certain specified subsets of the entries of $\mathbf{w}$ (Schölkopf et al., 1998d).

Finally, the algorithm can be modified such that ε need not be specified a priori. Instead, one specifies an upper bound $0 \leq \nu \leq 1$ on the fraction of points allowed to lie outside the tube (asymptotically, the number of SVs) and the corresponding ε is computed automatically. This is achieved by using as primal objective function

$$\frac{1}{2}\|\mathbf{w}\|^2 + C\left(\nu\ell\varepsilon + \sum_{i=1}^{\ell} |y_i - f(\mathbf{x}_i)|_\varepsilon\right) \tag{1.50}$$

instead of (1.42), and treating $\varepsilon \geq 0$ as a parameter that we minimize over (Schölkopf et al., 1998a).

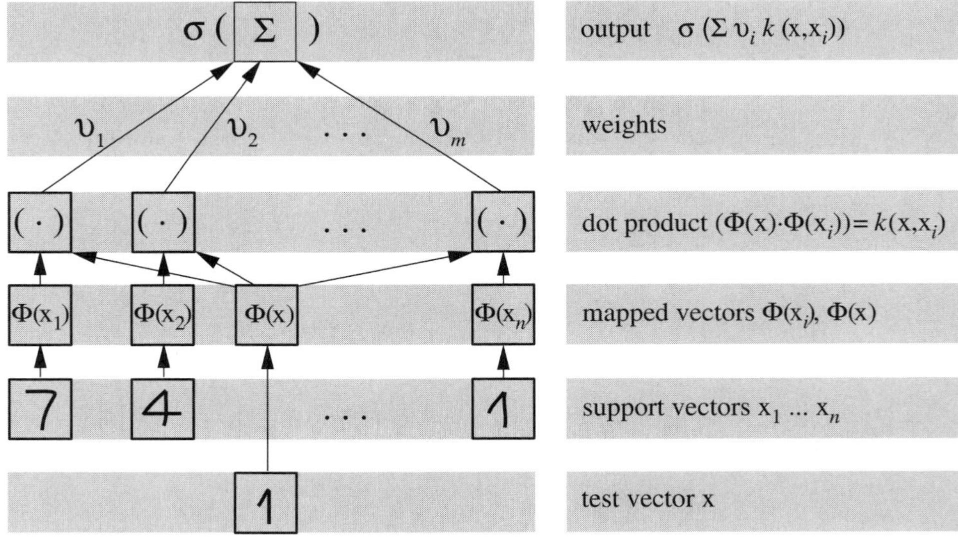

Figure 1.5 Architecture of SV machines. The input $\mathbf{x}$ and the Support Vectors $\mathbf{x}_i$ are nonlinearly mapped (by Φ) into a feature space F, where dot products are computed. By the use of the kernel k, these two layers are in practice computed in one single step. The results are linearly combined by weights υ_i, found by solving a quadratic program (in pattern recognition, $\upsilon_i = y_i\alpha_i$; in regression estimation, $\upsilon_i = \alpha_i^* - \alpha_i$). The linear combination is fed into the function σ (in pattern recognition, $\sigma(x) = \mathrm{sgn}(x + b)$; in regression estimation, $\sigma(x) = x + b$).

1.6 Empirical Results, Implementations, and Further Developments

Having described the basics of SV machines, we now summarize empirical findings and theoretical developments which were to follow. We cannot report all contributions that have advanced the state of the art in SV learning since the time the algorithm was first proposed. Not even the present book can do this job, let alone a single section. Presently, we merely give a concise overview.

By the use of kernels, the optimal margin classifier was turned into a classifier which became a serious competitor of high-performance classifiers. Surprisingly, it was noticed that when different kernel functions are used in SV machines (specifically, (1.21), (1.30), and (1.31)), they lead to very similar classification accuracies and SV sets (Schölkopf et al., 1995). In this sense, the SV set seems to characterize (or *compress*) the given task in a manner which up to a certain degree is independent of the type of kernel (i.e. the type of classifier) used.

Initial work at AT&T Bell Labs focused on OCR (optical character recognition), a problem where the two main issues are classification accuracy and classification speed. Consequently, some effort went into the improvement of SV machines on these issues, leading to the *Virtual SV* method for incorporating prior knowledge about transformation invariances by transforming SVs, and the *Reduced Set* method for speeding up classification. This way, SV machines became competitive with the best available classifiers on both OCR and object recognition tasks (Schölkopf et al., 1996a; Burges, 1996; Burges and Schölkopf, 1997; Schölkopf, 1997). Two years later, the above are still topics of ongoing research, as shown by chapter 16 and (Schölkopf et al., 1998b), proposing alternative Reduced Set methods, as well as by chapter 7 and (Schölkopf et al., 1998d), constructing kernel functions which incorporate prior knowledge about a given problem.

Another initial weakness of SV machines, less apparent in OCR applications which are characterized by low noise levels, was that the size of the quadratic programming problem scaled with the number of Support Vectors. This was due to the fact that in (1.33), the quadratic part contained at least all SVs — the common practice was to extract the SVs by going through the training data in chunks while regularly testing for the possibility that some of the patterns that were initially not identified as SVs turn out to become SVs at a later stage (note that without chunking, the size of the matrix would be $\ell \times \ell$, where ℓ is the number of all training examples). What happens if we have a high-noise problem? In this case, many of the slack variables ξ_i will become nonzero, and all the corresponding examples will become SVs. For this case, a decomposition algorithm was proposed (Osuna et al., 1997a), which is based on the observation that not only can we leave out the non-SV examples (i.e. the $\mathbf{x}_i$ with $\alpha_i = 0$) from the current chunk, but also some of the SVs, especially those that hit the upper boundary (i.e. $\alpha_i = C$). In fact, one can use chunks which do not even contain all SVs, and maximize over the corresponding sub-problems. Chapter 12 explores an extreme case, where the sub-problems are chosen so small that one can solve them analytically. Most of the current implementations use larger subproblems, and employ some quadratic optimizer to solve these problems. Among the optimizers used are LOQO (Vanderbei, 1997), MINOS (Murtagh and Saunders, 1993), and variants of conjugate gradient descent, such as the optimizers of Bottou (cf. Saunders et al., 1998) and Burges (1998). Several public domain SV packages and optimizers are listed on the web page http://svm.first.gmd.de. For more details on the optimization problem, see chapters 10, 11, and 12.

Once the SV algorithm had been generalized to regression, researchers started applying it to various problems of estimating real-valued functions. Very good results were obtained on the Boston housing benchmark (Drucker et al. (1997) and chapter 17), and on problems of times series prediction (see Müller et al. (1997); Mukherjee et al. (1997), as well as chapters 13 and 14). Moreover, the SV method was applied to the solution of inverse function estimation problems (Vapnik et al. (1997); cf. chapters 3 and 18).

On the theoretical side, the least understood part of the SV algorithm initially was the precise role of the kernel, and how a certain kernel choice would influence the generalization ability. In that respect, the connection to regularization theory provided some insight. For kernel-based function expansions, one can show (Smola and Schölkopf, 1998b) that given a regularization operator P mapping the functions of the learning machine into some dot product space, the problem of minimizing the regularized risk

$$R_{reg}[f] = R_{emp}[f] + \frac{\lambda}{2}\|Pf\|^2 \tag{1.51}$$

(with a regularization parameter $\lambda \geq 0$) can be written as a constrained optimization problem. For particular choices of the loss function, it further reduces to a SV type quadratic programming problem. The latter thus is not specific to SV machines, but is common to a much wider class of approaches. What gets lost in the general case, however, is the fact that the solution can usually be expressed in terms of a small number of SVs (cf. also Girosi (1998), who establishes a connection between SV machines and basis pursuit denoising (Chen et al., 1995)). This specific feature of SV machines is due to the fact that the type of regularization and the class of functions that the estimate is chosen from are intimately related (Girosi et al., 1993; Smola and Schölkopf, 1998a; Smola et al., 1998c): the SV algorithm is equivalent to minimizing the regularized risk on the set of functions

$$f(\mathbf{x}) = \sum_i \alpha_i k(\mathbf{x}_i, \mathbf{x}) + b, \tag{1.52}$$

provided that k and P are interrelated by

$$k(\mathbf{x}_i, \mathbf{x}_j) = ((Pk)(\mathbf{x}_i, .) \cdot (Pk)(\mathbf{x}_j, .)) \,. \tag{1.53}$$

To this end, k is chosen as a Green's function of P^*P, for in that case, the right hand side of (1.53) equals $(k(\mathbf{x}_i, .) \cdot (P^*Pk)(\mathbf{x}_j, .)) = (k(\mathbf{x}_i, .) \cdot \delta_{\mathbf{x}_j}(.)) = k(\mathbf{x}_i, \mathbf{x}_j)$. For instance, an RBF kernel thus corresponds to regularization with a functional containing a specific differential operator.

In SV machines, the kernel thus plays a dual role: firstly, it determines the class of functions (1.52) that the solution is taken from; secondly, via (1.53), the kernel determines the type of regularization that is used. The next question, naturally, is what type of regularization (i.e. kernel) we should use in order to get the best generalization performance — this is treated in chapter 9.

We conclude this section by noticing that the kernel method for computing dot products in feature spaces is not restricted to SV machines. Indeed, it has been used in 1996 to develop nonlinear generalizations of algorithms such as PCA (chapter 20), and a number of researchers have followed this example.

1.7 Notation

We conclude the introduction with a list of symbols which are used throughout the book, unless stated otherwise.

$\mathbb{R}$	the set of reals
$\mathbb{N}$	the set of natural numbers
k	Mercer kernel
F	feature space
N	dimensionality of input space
$\mathbf{x}_i$	input patterns
y_i	target values, or (in pattern recognition) classes
ℓ	number of training examples
$\mathbf{w}$	weight vector
b	constant offset (or threshold)
h	VC dimension
ε	parameter of the ε-insensitive loss function
α_i	Lagrange multiplier
$\boldsymbol{\alpha}$	vector of all Lagrange multipliers
ξ_i	slack variables
Q	Hessian of the quadratic program
$(\mathbf{x} \cdot \mathbf{y})$	dot product between patterns $\mathbf{x}$ and $\mathbf{y}$
$\Vert\cdot\Vert$	2-norm (Euclidean distance), $\Vert\mathbf{x}\Vert := \sqrt{(\mathbf{x} \cdot \mathbf{x})}$
ln	logarithm to base e
$\log_2$	logarithm to base 2

2 Roadmap

The overall structure of this collection mirrors the development of SV learning as a field. We start with *theory*, then move on to *implementations*, to *applications*, and conclude with *extensions* of the original algorithm. We now give a brief roadmap of what the respective chapters are about.

2.1 Theory

Just as this collection of chapters should start with the theoretical ones, there is a natural beginning to the theoretical part. We start with Vladimir Vapnik, who can be singled out for his contributions to both the general development of the field and in particular of SV machines. His chapter on **Three Remarks on the Support Vector Method of Function Estimation** gives a concise authoritative account of the conceptual basis of SV machines, and explains an idea for improving generalization ability by taking into account the test points (but not their labels) during training (he calls this method *transduction*). Moreover, he shows how classical problems of statistics, such as conditional density estimation and conditional probability estimation, can be dealt with by treating them as inverse problems to be solved with SV methods. This approach is very much in line with his philosophy to solve the problem that one is interested in directly, rather than trying to solve harder problems as intermediate steps (e.g. by estimating a conditional density as the ratio of two estimated densities).

chapter 3

The seminal work of Vapnik, Chervonenkis and others has sparked a whole research field which studies the generalization ability of learning machines using various capacity concepts and different ways to make predictions about the accuracy of learning machines. Peter Bartlett and John-Shawe-Taylor, two leading researchers in this field, give a comprehensive discussion of the **Generalization Performance of Support Vector Machines and Other Pattern Classifiers**. To this end, they undertook the work of translating a variety of results from the learning theory community into a language that should be comprehensible to the emerging SV community. In particular, they describe the effect of large margins, crucial to SV machines, on the performance of classifiers. The same aspect is discussed by Nello Cristianini and John Shawe-Taylor in their work on **Bayesian Voting Schemes and Large Margin Classifiers**. Their accomplishment lies in the fact that they

chapter 4

chapter 5

have established a potentially very fruitful link to another field of machine learning which has recently attracted considerable attention, namely the field of Bayesian methods.

chapter 6

SV machines, and other kernel based methods, did not emerge in a vacuum. In particular, reproducing kernel Hilbert spaces (RKHS) provide a natural framework for SVMs, and show clearly how SVMs relate to other RKHS approaches, a point emphasized by Grace Wahba in **Support Vector Machines, Reproducing Kernel Hilbert Spaces and the Randomized GACV**. SVMs thus appear naturally when one chooses an appropriate likelihood functional in well known, penalized likelihood methods. In all such approaches, two (additive) terms appear in the objective function: a term that penalizes errors, and one that acts as a regularizer (and which, by the way, is also the norm of a vector in the RKHS). Loosely speaking, the latter is used to control the capacity, or variance, of the resulting learning machine. A critical choice is that of the trade-off between the size of the error penalty term versus that of the regularization ("smoothing") term. The Generalized Approximate Cross Validation technique of Xiang and Wahba (1996) is one such approach. Here, Wahba shows how the GACV method may be adapted to some support vector machines, thus giving one possible answer to some of the questions raised by practicioners (e.g. in chapter 14).

chapter 7

The following paper, Chris Burges's **Geometry and Invariance in Kernel Based Methods**, locks in on the kernel function and studies it in considerable detail. It consists of two parts. The first part explores the geometry of the manifold corresponding to the image of the input space under the kernel mapping. This leads to several interesting results: for example, the manifolds corresponding to homogeneous degree p polynomial kernels, acting on N dimensional data, are flat for $N = 2$ for all p, but have non-vanishing curvature for all $N > 2$ and $p > 1$. In the second part, the problem of adding local invariance to general kernel-based methods is discussed, using translation invariance in pixel images as a concrete example.

chapter 8

As described in the introduction, the VC dimension is the coarsest capacity concept of VC theory. Other concepts, such as the VC entropy or the Growth function, lead to tighter bounds on the generalization error, and could thus lead to more accurate tuning of learning machines. However, these concepts have so far either been believed to be hard to evaluate, or they have been neglected completely. The latter led to the belief that VC theory necessarily only gives bounds which disregard the actual structure of the problem at hand, and that the VC bounds (e.g. (1.4)) are so far from the actual behaviour of learning machines that they are useless. However, the utility of the bounds strongly depends on the capacity concepts used, and on the accuracy with which these concepts can be computed. In his contribution **On the Annealed VC Entropy for Margin Classifiers: A Statistical Mechanics Study**, Manfred Opper has accomplished the technically demanding job of computing a problem-dependent capacity measure for margin classifiers, for Gaussian input distribution. To this end, sophisticated methods from the statistical physics approach to learning theory had to be applied.

The dependence on the underlying distribution can lead to very precise capacity measures. This dependence is thus a strength of Opper's approach; however, his results strictly rely on the assumption of Gaussianity in the space where the hyperplane is constructed, i.e. in the feature space. Now suppose we do not want to make any such assumption, and still want to use a capacity concept which is more accurate than the VC dimension. Then we are essentially left with the Growth function or related concepts derived from taking suprema over covering numbers of function classes. This, again, had previously been considered too hard a quantity to compute. Bob Williamson et al., however, show that by considering the inverse of this quantity, the entropy numbers of suitably defined operators, one can tackle this problem. Crucial in an SV context, their work on **Entropy Numbers, Operators and Support Vector Kernels** takes into account the effect of the kernel, thus marrying the two main ingredients of SV machines — capacity control and the kernel mapping. Their hope is that this will indicate how to select the right kernel for a given problem.

chapter 9

2.2 Implementations

Despite the fact that the perceptron was invented in the sixties, interest in feed forward neural networks only took off in the eighties, due largely to a new training algorithm (actually invented by Werbos (1974), and rediscovered by several authors in the eighties, cf. Müller and Reinhardt (1990)). Backpropagation is conceptually simple and, perhaps more important, easy to implement. We believe that research into Support Vector Machines and related topics has been similarly hampered by the fact that training requires solving a quadratic programming problem, which, unless one happens to have a good QP package available, is a notoriously difficult business. In **Solving the Quadratic Programming Problem Arising in Support Vector Classification**, Linda Kaufman provides a review of the state of the art, and several valuable tips for the budding QP "programmer." A key point is to match the algorithm used to the problem at hand. For example, a largely separable, low noise problem will usually result in few support vectors: it then makes sense to use an algorithm that attempts to keep most of the Lagrange multipliers at zero. For very noisy problems, where most of the training data become support vectors, it makes more sense to consider approaches where most (or all) of the Lagrange multipliers are non-zero, such as interior point methods. One can also take advantage, in the high noise case, of the fact that many multipliers will be at their upper bound: this can be used, for example, to speed up core matrix multiplications.

chapter 10

Thorsten Joachims's contribution on **Making Large-Scale Support Vector Machine Learning Practical** is a hands-on approach to make chunk training work for large-scale real world problems. It builds on the idea of Osuna et al. (1997a) to split up the training set into small chunks and optimize only those variables while keeping the others fixed. The difficulty, however, consists in choosing a good

chapter 11

subset. Joachims gives a selection rule based on a linearization of the objective function similar to the work of Zoutendijk (1970). Yet even more can be gained by effectively restraining the subset of variables which are considered for chunking and taking into account the contribution of the other (then fixed) samples by modifying the overall linear and constant terms of the problem. This is both advantageous for data sets with low noise and data sets containing a large number of errors. An extensive experimental section, including text classification problems (in this domain, SVMs have been reported to exhibit excellent performance, cf. Joachims (1998); Dumais (1998)), backs the effect of these (and other) heuristics. Using tricks like kernel caching, Joachims reports examples where his method performs even faster than John Platt's latest algorithm. In **Fast Training of Support Vector Machines using Sequential Minimal Optimization**, SVMs may have found their backprop. Here is an algorithm that is easy to understand, easy to implement (the chapter even lists pseudocode), and trains an order of magnitude faster (in some cases) than a conjugate-gradient implementation of a QP optimizer. It is our hope that, due to its simplicity and speed, this algorithm will make SVMs accessible to a much larger group of users, and that the encouraging results will withstand the test of a wide range of data sets. Additionally, it seems likely that the algorithm can be modified to handle the case of regression estimation. Note also that it is expected that by using caching of kernel evaluations, it will be possible to further improve the speed of the algorithm.

chapter 12

2.3 Applications

Following these three chapters on SV implementations, we have three interesting papers on applications. Davide Mattera and Simon Haykin use **Support Vector Machines for Dynamic Reconstruction of a Chaotic System**. Also the chapter of Klaus Müller et al., **Using Support Vector Machines for Time Series Prediction**, employs SV regression for reconstruction of a chaotic system and time series prediction. Both works explore the use of different loss functions, most notably ones which are designed in the spirit of Huber's robust statistics (Huber, 1981). The chapters contain thorough experimental analyses on prediction problems, obtaining strong results. Müller et al. compare the SVM approach with that of RBF networks with adaptive centers and widths, a powerful technique for which they also give a useful, self-contained description. The results — a 29% improvement over the best known results on the Santa Fe time series set D benchmark — are clearly a strong endorsement of the approach. However, there are plenty of opportunities for further improvements. For example, how can one make the RBF centers adaptive, in the SVM approach? How can one best choose the SVM error penalty and regression tube sizes? Should one allow different error penalties for different input data (thus weighting different pieces of the time series differently), or allow varying tube sizes? These are all areas of active investigation. The chapters discuss these questions, and propose methods and heuristics for selecting the SV

chapters 13, 14

machine parameters C and ε. Nevertheless, a fair amount of theoretical work remains to be done on these issues.

chapter 15

The following chapter, dealing with **Pairwise Classification and Support Vector Machines**, describes application-oriented work on the optical character recognition (OCR) problem that already served as a testbed in the beginnings of SV research (Cortes and Vapnik, 1995; Schölkopf et al., 1995). In it, Ulrich Kreßel gives an experimental investigation of multi-class pattern recognition by means of pairwise classification. This way, he was able to set a new record on the standard OCR benchmark that he and his colleagues at Daimler-Benz Research had used for a number of years. The question whether this is due to the use of SVMs in general, or due to his specific pairwise approach, cannot be answered conclusively at present. In any case, the pairwise method seems an interesting direction for research, especially on large databases.

2.4 Extensions

chapter 16

For applications where the time it takes to compute a prediction is critical, one needs methods for simplifying the representation of the estimated function. In their contribution on **Reducing the Run-time Complexity in Support Vector Machines**, Edgar Osuna and Federico Girosi describe three such methods. They start by summarizing the so-called reduced set technique, which has been shown to yield substantial speed-ups in OCR applications (Burges, 1996; Burges and Schölkopf, 1997). Following this, they describe two novel methods. First, they propose the use of SV regression to approximate SV expansions using a smaller number of terms. Second, they reformulate the training problem such that it automatically produces expansions which are more sparse, while yielding the same solution. Their methods, which are experimentally validated, are of particular use in situations where many of the Lagrange multipliers hit the upper boundary, such as in noisy applications.

chapter 17

The chapter **Support Vector Regression with ANOVA Decomposition Kernels**, contributed by Mark Stitson et al., considers one particular kernel function, generating the ANOVA decompositions known from classical statistics in an efficient way. Encouraging experimental results on the Boston housing real-world regression problem are reported.

chapter 18

In **Support Vector Density Estimation**, Jason Weston et al. propose SV algorithms for SV density estimation. This is done by considering the problem of density estimation as a problem of solving a linear integral equation: the integral over the density is the distribution function, and the data can be used to give an empirical distribution function. The problem of density estimation differs from the regression problem in several ways, one of them being that the estimated density is required to be positive. These difficulties lead the authors to propose several modifications of the SV algorithm, using linear programming techniques, dictionaries of kernels, and different loss functions.

chapter 19

In **Combining Support Vector and Mathematical Programming Methods for Classification**, Kristin Bennett relates the two domains of Mathematical Programming and Support Vector Classification. By doing so, she is able to construct SV decision trees. Moreover, she analyses a regularization term which is new to the SV field, similar in construction to the one introduced in chapter 18 for density estimation. This is a potentially very fruitful approach as it may lead to linear programming algorithms that could be solved with lower computational cost. The method is extended to multicategory classification, and should be compared to the ones of Weston and Watkins (1998) and chapter 15. The final section presents an extension of the standard SV algorithm to the case of transduction (cf. chapter 3). It is shown empirically that overall optimization of the margin can lead to improved results.

chapter 20

The book concludes with a chapter which uses one of the main ideas of SV learning and transfers it to a rather different domain of learning. Using the kernel trick, Bernhard Schölkopf et al. generalized one of the most widely used algorithms for unsupervised data analysis, linear principal component analysis, to the nonlinear case, obtaining **Kernel Principal Component Analysis**. Experimental results show that this leads to powerful nonlinear feature extractors.

I Theory

3 Three Remarks on the Support Vector Method of Function Estimation

Vladimir Vapnik
AT&T Labs Research
100 Schultz Dr., Red Bank, NJ 07701, USA
vlad@research.att.com
http://www.research.att.com/info/vlad

The Support Vector Machine (SVM) provides non-linear function approximations by mapping the input vectors into high dimensional feature spaces where a special type of hyperplane is constructed. From the theoretical point of view, SVMs possess nice properties of linear machines. This makes it easy to analyze SVMs and to generalize particular existing linear methods to more or less general non-linear methods. In this chapter we use the linear properties of SVM for its analysis, and for the generalization of methods that were originally restricted by linearity in input space. The first generalization of this type was proposed for the extension of the classical (Linear) Principal Component Analysis to Non-Linear Component Analysis, which is described in chapter 20.

3.1 Introduction

The Support Vector (SV) method is a general approach to function estimation problems, i.e. to problems of finding the function $y = f(x)$ given by its measurements y_i with noise at some (usually random) vectors x_i

$$(y_1, x_1), \ldots, (y_\ell, x_\ell). \tag{3.1}$$

It can be applied for pattern recognition (i.e. to estimate indicator functions), for regression (to estimate real-valued functions), and for solving linear operator equations.

The idea behind this method is the following: one maps n-dimensional vectors x of the input space X into high-dimensional (possibly infinite dimensional) vectors

z of the feature space Z, where using the samples

$$(y_1, z_1), \ldots, (y_\ell, z_\ell) \tag{3.2}$$

corresponding to (3.1) one constructs a linear function

$$y = (a \cdot z) + b \tag{3.3}$$

of a special form. In (3.3) we denote by $(a \cdot z)$ an inner product between the two vectors a and z.

Two problems arise with this approach:

1. Which properties should the linear function (3.3) satisfy to approximate well the desired function?

2. How does one construct such a function (in the pattern recognition case: such a hyperplane) in a high-dimensional space?

Two theoretical results made the construction of SV machines possible:

1. The generalization ability of the learning machine depends on the capacity of a set of functions (in particular on the VC dimension of a set of functions) rather than on the dimensionality of a space. Therefore, according to the so called Structural Risk Minimization inductive principle, a function that describes the data well and belongs to a set of functions with low capacity will generalize well regardless of the dimensionality of the space (Vapnik, 1995, 1998).

2. To construct the hyperplane one only needs to evaluate the inner product between vectors of the training data. Since in Hilbert space the general form of the inner product has a kernel representation, the evaluation of the inner product also does not depend on the dimensionality of the space.

The SV method was discovered in the early 1960s for constructing separating hyperplanes for the pattern recognition problem (Vapnik and Lerner, 1963; Vapnik and Chervonenkis, 1964). Then in 1992 – 1995, it was generalized for constructing non-linear separating functions (but linear in feature space) (Boser et al., 1992; Cortes and Vapnik, 1995). In 1995, it was generalized for estimating real-valued functions (Vapnik, 1995). Lastly, in 1996, it was applied for solving linear operator equations (Vapnik et al., 1997).

3.2 The Optimal Hyperplane

3.2.1 Constructing Optimal Hyperplanes

We say that two finite subsets of vectors x from the training set

$$(y_1, x_1), \ldots, (y_\ell, x_\ell), \qquad x \in X^* \subset \mathbb{R}^n, \quad y \in \{-1, 1\}, \tag{3.4}$$

one subset I for which $y = 1$ and another subset II for which $y = -1$, are separable by the hyperplane

$$(x \cdot \mathbf{w}) + b = 0, \tag{3.5}$$

if there exist both a vector $\mathbf{w}$ and a constant b such that the inequalities

$$(x_i \cdot \mathbf{w}) + b > \quad 1, \quad \text{if } x_i \in I, \tag{3.6}$$

$$(x_j \cdot \mathbf{w}) + b < -1, \quad \text{if } x_j \in II \tag{3.7}$$

hold true.

Among all hyperplanes separating the two categories of data, let us consider the one that has maximal distance to the closest vector x from the training data. We call this hyperplane the *optimal hyperplane*.

Optimal Hyperplane

One can show that the optimal hyperplane is defined by the pair consisting of the vector $\mathbf{w}_0$ and the constant b_0 that minimize the quadratic form

$$Q(\mathbf{w}) = (\mathbf{w} \cdot \mathbf{w}) \tag{3.8}$$

subject to constraints

$$y_i[(x_j \cdot \mathbf{w}) + b] \geq 1, \quad i = 1, \ldots, \ell \tag{3.9}$$

We call the hyperplane that minimizes $(\mathbf{w} \cdot \mathbf{w})$ under the constraints (3.9) with $b = 0$ the *optimal hyperplane passing through the origin*.

Support Vector

Using the Lagrange multiplier technique (cf. section 1.2), it is easy to derive that the optimal hyperplane has an expansion on the so-called *support vectors* of the training data $x \in S \subset X^*$

$$(x_i \cdot \mathbf{w}) + b = \sum_{x_i \in S} y_i \alpha_i (x \cdot x_i) + b, \tag{3.10}$$

where the support vectors are those vectors from the training data that satisfy the equation

$$y_i[(x_i \cdot \mathbf{w}) + b] = 1, \tag{3.11}$$

and the coefficients $\alpha_i \geq 0$ of the expansion have to maximize the quadratic form

$$W(\alpha) = \sum_{i=1}^{\ell} \alpha_i - \frac{1}{2} \sum_{i,j=1}^{\ell} y_i y_j \alpha_i \alpha_j (x_i \cdot x_j) \tag{3.12}$$

subject to constraints

$$\alpha_i \geq 0, \quad i = 1, \ldots, \ell, \tag{3.13}$$

$$\sum_{i=1}^{\ell} \alpha_i y_i = 0. \tag{3.14}$$

(In order to construct the optimal hyperplane passing through the origin one has to ignore the last equality.)

In the case where the training data cannot be separated by a hyperplane without errors, our goal is to construct the hyperplane that makes the smallest number of errors.

Generalized Optimal Hyperplane

To get a formal setting of this problem, we introduce the non-negative variables

$$\xi_1, \ldots, \xi_\ell. \tag{3.15}$$

In terms of these variables, the problem of finding the hyperplane that provides the minimal number of training errors has the following formal expression: minimize the functional

$$\Phi(\xi) = C \sum_{i=1}^{\ell} \theta(\xi_i) + (\mathbf{w} \cdot \mathbf{w}) \tag{3.16}$$

subject to the constraints

$$y_i((x_i \cdot \mathbf{w}) + b) \geq 1 - \xi_i, \quad i = 1, \ldots, \ell, \quad \xi_i \geq 0, \tag{3.17}$$

where C is sufficiently large, and $\theta(\xi) = 0$ if $\xi = 0$, $\theta(\xi) = 1$ if $\xi > 0$. It is known that for the non-separable case this optimization problem is NP-complete. Therefore we consider the following approximation to this problem: we would like to minimize the functional

$$\Phi(\xi) = C \sum_{i=1}^{\ell} \xi_i^\sigma + (\mathbf{w} \cdot \mathbf{w}) \tag{3.18}$$

under the constraints (3.17), where $\sigma \geq 0$ is a small value. We will, however, choose $\sigma = 1$, the smallest σ that leads to a simple optimization problem.[1]

Using the Lagrangian technique, one obtains a method for solution of this optimization problem that is almost equivalent to the method of solution of the optimization problem for the separable case: to find the generalized optimal hyperplane

$$\sum_{i=1}^{\ell} \alpha_i y_i (x \cdot x_i) + b = 0, \tag{3.19}$$

one has to maximize the same quadratic form as in the separable case,

$$W(\alpha) = \sum_{i=1}^{\ell} \alpha_i - \frac{1}{2} \sum_{i,j=1}^{\ell} y_i y_j \alpha_i \alpha_j (x_i \cdot x_j), \tag{3.20}$$

under slightly different constraints

$$0 \leq \alpha_i \leq C, \quad i = 1, \ldots, \ell, \tag{3.21}$$

1. The choice $\sigma = 2$ also leads to a simple optimization problem. However, for the pattern recognition problem, this choice does not look attractive. It will be more attractive when we will generalize the results obtained for the pattern recognition problem to the estimation of real-valued functions.

$$\sum_{i=1}^{\ell} \alpha_i y_i = 0. \tag{3.22}$$

As in the separable case, only some of the coefficients $\alpha_i,\ i = 1, \ldots, \ell$ differ from zero (they correspond to the support vectors $S \subset X^*$). They and the corresponding support vectors determine the generalized optimal hyperplane

$$\sum_{x_i \in S} \alpha_i y_i (x_i \cdot x) + b = 0. \tag{3.23}$$

3.2.2 The Support Vector Machine for Pattern Recognition

Let us now define the Support Vector (SV) machine. The SV machine implements the following idea: it maps the input vectors x into the high-dimensional *feature space* Z through some nonlinear mapping, chosen *a priori*. In this space, an Optimal separating hyperplane is constructed.

Example 3.1
To construct a decision surface corresponding to a polynomial of degree two, one can create a feature space Z that has $N = \frac{n(n+3)}{2}$ coordinates of the form

$$\begin{aligned} z^1 &= x^1, \ldots, z^n = x^n\ , && (n \text{ coordinates}) \\ z^{n+1} &= (x^1)^2, \ldots, z^{2n} = (x^n)^2\ , && (n \text{ coordinates}) \\ z^{2n+1} &= x^1 x^2, \ldots, z^N = x^n x^{n-1}\ , && (n(n-1)/2 \text{ coordinates})\ , \end{aligned} \tag{3.24}$$

where $x = (x^1 \ldots, x^n)$. The separating hyperplane constructed in this space is a second degree polynomial in the input space.

Two problems arise in the above approach: a conceptual and a technical one.

(i) *How to find a separating hyperplane that generalizes well?*
(The conceptual problem.)
The dimensionality of the feature space is huge, and a hyperplane that separates the training data does not necessarily generalize well.

(ii) *How to treat such high-dimensional spaces computationally?*
(The technical problem.)
To construct a polynomial of degree 4 or 5 in a 200-dimensional space it is necessary to construct hyperplanes in a billion-dimensional feature space. How can this "curse of dimensionality" be overcome?

3.2.3 Generalization to High-Dimensional Spaces

The conceptual part of this problem can be solved by constructing the Optimal hyperplane.

In section 3.2.5, we shall describe theorems which demonstrate that the generalization ability of the optimal hyperplanes depends on some geometrical characteristics of the training data, but not on the dimensionality of the input space. If these characteristics are appropriate, the expectation of the error will be small, even if the feature space has a high dimensionality.

3.2.4 Hilbert-Schmidt Theory and Mercer's Theorem

However, even if the Optimal hyperplane generalizes well and can theoretically be found, the technical problem of how to treat the high-dimensional feature space remains.

Note, however, that for constructing the Optimal separating hyperplane in the feature space Z, one does not need to consider the feature space in *explicit form*. One only has to calculate the inner products between support vectors and the vectors of the feature space (see (3.19) and (3.20)).

Consider a general property of the inner product in a Hilbert space. Suppose one maps the vector $x \in \mathbb{R}^n$ into a Hilbert space with coordinates

$$z_1(x), \ldots, z_n(x), \ldots \tag{3.25}$$

According to the Hilbert-Schmidt theory, the inner product in a Hilbert space has an equivalent representation

$$(z_1 \cdot z_2) = \sum_{r=1}^{\infty} a_r z_r(x_1) z(x_2) \Longleftrightarrow k(x_1, x_2), \qquad a_r \geq 0 \tag{3.26}$$

Mercer Kernel

where $k(x_1, x_2)$ is a symmetric function satisfying the following conditions

Theorem 3.1 (Mercer)
To guarantee that a continuous symmetric function $k(u, v)$ from $L_2(\mathcal{C})$ has an expansion[2]

$$k(u, v) = \sum_{k=1}^{\infty} a_k z_k(u) z_k(v) \tag{3.27}$$

with positive coefficients $a_k > 0$ (i.e., $k(u, v)$ describes an inner product in some feature space), it is necessary and sufficient that the condition

$$\iint k(u, v) g(u) g(v) \, du \, dv \geq 0 \tag{3.28}$$

be valid for all $g \in L_2(\mathcal{C})$ ($\mathcal{C}$ being a compact subspace of $\mathbb{R}^n$).

The remarkable property of the structure of the inner product in Hilbert space that leads to the construction of the SV machine is that for any kernel function $k(u, v)$ satisfying Mercer's condition, there exists a feature space where this function generates the inner product.

---

2. This means that the right hand side of (3.27) converges to the function $k(u, v)$ uniformly.

Using kernels that satisfy the Mercer condition one can therefore construct a nonlinear separating function of the form

$$f(x) = \sum_{x_i \in S} \alpha_i k(x \cdot x_i) + b, \tag{3.29}$$

that is completely equivalent to a linear function in the corresponding feature space. To find the coefficients α_i of the expansion (3.29), one has to solve the following quadratic optimization problem: maximize the quadratic form

$$W(\alpha) = \sum_{i=1}^{\ell} \alpha_i - \frac{1}{2} \sum_{i,j=1}^{\ell} y_i y_j \alpha_i \alpha_j k(x_i \cdot x_j) \tag{3.30}$$

subject to constraints

$$0 \leq \alpha_i \leq C, \quad i = 1, \ldots, \ell, \tag{3.31}$$

$$\sum_{i=1}^{\ell} \alpha_i y_i = 0. \tag{3.32}$$

This problem is different from the problem of constructing separating hyperplanes only in the calculation of the inner product: we use a kernel representation of the inner product instead of the standard one.

It is important that the nonlinear form of the representation (3.29) has an equivalent linear representation (in some feature space), where one constructs an optimal separating hyperplane. Therefore the analysis of the SV machine is equivalent to the analysis of optimal separating hyperplanes.

3.2.5 Statistical Properties of the Optimal Hyperplane

Definition 3.1 (Canonical Hyperplanes)
Let $X^* = (x_1, \ldots, x_\ell)$ be a set of ℓ vectors in $\mathbb{R}^n$. For any hyperplane

$$(x \cdot \mathbf{w}^*) + b^* = 0 \tag{3.33}$$

Canonical Hyperplane

in $\mathbb{R}^n$, consider the corresponding *canonical hyperplane* defined by the set X^* as follows:

$$\inf_{x \in X^*} |(x \cdot \mathbf{w}) + b| = 1, \tag{3.34}$$

where $\mathbf{w} = c^* \mathbf{w}^*$ and $b = c^* b^*$. Note that the set of canonical hyperplanes coincides with the set of separating hyperplanes. It only specifies the normalization with respect to the given set of data X^*. Note that the method for constructing an optimal hyperplane described in section 3.2.1 constructs canonical hyperplanes.

First let us establish the following important fact.

Theorem 3.2 (VC dimension of canonical hyperplanes)
A subset of canonical hyperplanes defined on $X^* \subset \mathbb{R}^n$, with

$$\max_{x \in X^*} \min_a |x_i - a| \le D, \qquad x_i \in X^*, \tag{3.35}$$

satisfying the constraint

$$|\mathbf{w}| \le A, \tag{3.36}$$

VC dimension bound

has a VC dimension h satisfying

$$h \le \min\left([D^2 A^2], n\right) + 1, \tag{3.37}$$

where $[a]$ denotes the integer part of a.

Note that the norm of the vector coefficients of the canonical hyperplane $\mathbf{w}$ defines the margin

$$\rho\left(\frac{\mathbf{w}}{|\mathbf{w}|}\right) = \frac{\min_{x \in I}\left(x \cdot \frac{\mathbf{w}}{|\mathbf{w}|}\right) - \max_{x \in II}\left(x \cdot \frac{\mathbf{w}}{|\mathbf{w}|}\right)}{2} = \frac{1}{|\mathbf{w}|} \ge \frac{1}{A}. \tag{3.38}$$

It is easy to show that the minimal norm vector $\mathbf{w}$ satisfying the conditions (3.9) is unique, though it can have different expansions on the support vectors. To formulate the next theorems, let us introduce one more concept.

Definition 3.2 (Essential Support Vectors)
We call the support vectors x_i that appear in all possible expansions of the vector $\mathbf{w}$ the *essential support vectors*. In other words, the set of essential support vectors is the intersection of all possible sets of support vectors.

Let

$$(y_1, x_1), \ldots, (y_\ell, x_\ell) \tag{3.39}$$

be the training set. We denote the number of essential support vectors of this training set by

$$\mathcal{K}_\ell = \mathcal{K}((y_1, x_1), \ldots, (y_\ell, x_\ell)). \tag{3.40}$$

We denote by

$$\mathcal{D}_\ell = \mathcal{D}((y_1, x_1), \ldots, (y_\ell, x_\ell)) = \max_i |x_i| \tag{3.41}$$

the maximal norm of essential support vectors from a given training set.

Let n be the dimensionality of the vectors x.

The following four theorems describe the main statistical properties of the Optimal hyperplane.

Theorem 3.3
The following inequality holds true:

$$\mathcal{K}_\ell \le n \tag{3.42}$$

Theorem 3.4
Let

$$ER(\alpha_\ell) = ER(y, x, \alpha(y_1, x_1, \ldots, y_\ell, x_\ell)) \tag{3.43}$$

be the expectation of the probability of error (i.e. of the risk R) for Optimal hyperplanes constructed on the basis of training samples of size ℓ (the expectation taken over both training and test data). Then the inequality

$$ER(\alpha_\ell) \leq \frac{E\mathcal{K}_{\ell+1}}{\ell+1} \tag{3.44}$$

holds true.

Theorem 3.5
For Optimal hyperplanes passing through the origin, the inequality

$$ER(\alpha_\ell) \leq \frac{E\left(\frac{\mathcal{D}_{\ell+1}}{\rho_{\ell+1}}\right)^2}{\ell+1} \tag{3.45}$$

holds true, where $D_{\ell+1}$ and $\rho_{\ell+1}$ are (random) values that for a given training set of size $\ell+1$ define the maximal norm of essential support vectors x and the margin.

One can also prove that the following stronger bound is valid.

Theorem 3.6
Generalization bound

For the Optimal hyperplane passing through the origin the inequality

$$ER(\alpha_\ell) \leq \frac{E\min\left(\mathcal{K}_{\ell+1},\ \left(\frac{\mathcal{D}_{\ell+1}}{\rho_{\ell+1}}\right)^2\right)}{\ell+1} \tag{3.46}$$

is valid.

The proof of these theorems can be found in (Vapnik and Chervonenkis, 1974; Vapnik, 1998).

3.2.6 Remark about the Generalization Ability of SV machines

It is important to compare the bound obtained for the optimal hyperplane with bounds obtained for non-optimal hyperplanes, in particular with bounds for the classical perceptron algorithm. The Perceptron utilizes the following recurrent procedure for constructing a hyperplane passing through the origin,

$$(w \cdot x) = 0, \tag{3.47}$$

(for constructing coefficients $w = (w^1, \ldots, w^n)$) using training data

$$(y_1, x_1), \ldots, (y_\ell, x_\ell). \tag{3.48}$$

Perceptron

(1) At step zero it chooses the function $f(x, 0)$ (with coefficients $w(0) = (0, \ldots, 0)$).

(2) At step t, using the element (y_t, x_t) of the training sequence, it changes the

vector of coefficients $w(t-1)$ in accordance with the rule

$$w(t) = \begin{cases} w(t-1) & \text{if } y_t(w(t-1)\cdot x_t) > 0, \\ w(t-1) + y_t x_t, & \text{if } y_t(w(t-1)\cdot x_t) \leq 0. \end{cases} \tag{3.49}$$

Note that the coefficients $w(t-1)$ change only if the example (y_t, x_t) is misclassified by the hyperplane.

Consider an infinite sequence of examples (in feature space)

$$(y_1, x_1), \ldots, (y_\ell, x_\ell), \ldots \tag{3.50}$$

Suppose that there exists a vector w_0 such that for some $\rho_0 > 0$ the inequality

$$\frac{y_i(w_0 \cdot x_i)}{|w_0|} \geq \rho_0 \tag{3.51}$$

holds true for all vectors of training data. (I.e. the given examples are separable with margin ρ_0.) Then the following theorem holds.

Theorem 3.7 (Novikoff)
Assume that those examples of the training sequence (3.50) where a correction is made satisfy the inequality

$$|x_i| < D. \tag{3.52}$$

Suppose, moreover, that there exists a hyperplane with coefficients w_0 that correctly separates the elements of this subsequence, and satisfies the condition (3.51).

Then the Perceptron constructs a hyperplane which correctly separates all examples of this infinite sequence. To construct such a hyperplane the Perceptron makes at most

$$M = \left[\frac{D^2}{\rho_0^2}\right] \tag{3.53}$$

corrections.

One can see that the number of corrections is bounded by an expression whose structure is analogous to that of the bound on the expectation of error for the optimal hyperplane. Moreover, using a technique analogous to the one that proves the theorem described above, one can prove the following theorem (Vapnik and Chervonenkis, 1974; Vapnik, 1998).

Theorem 3.8
Consider the variant of the perceptron algorithm which, in order to separate a training set of size ℓ, uses the set several times. The expectation of committing an error is bounded according to

$$ER(\alpha_\ell) \leq \frac{E \min\left(M_{\ell+1}, \left(\frac{D_{\ell+1}}{\rho_{\ell+1}}\right)^2\right)}{\ell+1}, \tag{3.54}$$

where $D_{\ell+1}$ is an upper bound on the norm of those vectors of the training data of size $\ell + 1$ where the perceptron committed an error during training, $\rho_{\ell+1}$ is the value of the margin for the corresponding training data, and $M_{\ell+1}$ is the number of corrections for this training set.

Let us compare the bound obtained for the perceptron with the bound obtained for the optimal hyperplane. One can see that in both bounds the values of margin $\rho_{\ell+1}$ are the same.

The difference in the bounds lies in the quantities $D_{\ell+1}$ (for perceptrons) and $\mathcal{D}_{\ell+1}$ (for the optimal hyperplane).

The value $D_{\ell+1}$, for perceptrons, is defined as the largest value of the norm of the vectors where the perceptron makes a correction. The value $\mathcal{D}_{\ell+1}$, on the other hand, is defined as the largest value of norm of essential support vectors. (Note that in both cases, one considers a bound on the norm of those vectors that are used for constructing the hyperplane.)

The difference in the bounds thus lies *not in the value of the margin, but in the geometry of the support vectors.*

This gives a hint that there may exist more advanced models of generalization than that based on maximization of the margin. The bound on the error depends on the expectation of the ratio of two random variables: the radius of the sphere that contains the support vectors, and the margin.

It is quite possible that by minimizing this ratio one can control the generalization better than by maximizing the margin.

Note that in high dimensional feature spaces, where the SV machine constructs hyperplanes, the training set is very sparse and therefore the solution that minimizes this ratio can be quite different from the one that maximizes the margin.

3.3 Transductive Inference Using SV Machines

In order to improve performance on a given test set, a new type of inference, the so-called transductive inference, was introduced (Vapnik and Chervonenkis, 1974; Vapnik, 1998). For the class of linear indicator functions, bounds on the test error were obtained (these bounds generally speaking are better than error rate bounds for inductive inference). In this section we show that using the standard SV technique for transductive inference, one can generalize the technique obtained for linear indicator functions to non-linear indicator functions (which are linear in some feature space).

We considered the following problem: given training data

$$(y_1, x_1), \ldots, (y_\ell, x_\ell), \quad y \in \{-1, 1\} \tag{3.55}$$

and test data

$$x_1^*, \ldots, x_k^*, \tag{3.56}$$

find among all linear functions

$$y = (\mathbf{w} \cdot x) + b \tag{3.57}$$

the one that minimizes the number of errors on the given test set. It was shown that in the separable case, a good solution to this problem provides a classification of the test patterns

$$y_1^*, \ldots, y_k^* \tag{3.58}$$

such that the joint sequence

$$(y_1, x_1), \ldots, (y_\ell, x_\ell), (y_1^*, x_1^*), \ldots, (y_k^*, x_k^*) \tag{3.59}$$

is separated with the maximal margin.

Therefore, we would like to find classifications (3.58) of the test vectors (3.56) for which the *optimal hyperplane*

$$y = (\mathbf{w}_0^* \cdot x) + b_0 \tag{3.60}$$

maximizes the margin when it separates the data (3.59), where $\mathbf{w}_0^*$ denotes the optimal hyperplane satisfying the condition that the test data (3.56) is classified according to (3.58):

$$\mathbf{w}_0^* = \mathbf{w}_0(y_1^*, \ldots, y_k^*). \tag{3.61}$$

Let us write this formally: our goal is to find classifications $y_1^*, \ldots, y_k^*$ such that the inequalities

$$y_i[(x_i \cdot \mathbf{w}^*) + b] \geq 1, \quad i = 1, \ldots, \ell \tag{3.62}$$

$$y_j^*[(x_j^* \cdot \mathbf{w}^*) + b] \geq 1, \quad j = 1, \ldots, k \tag{3.63}$$

are valid, and the functional

$$\Phi(\mathbf{w}_0(y_1^*, \ldots, y_k^*)) = \min_{\mathbf{w}_0^*} \frac{1}{2}|\mathbf{w}^*|^2 \tag{3.64}$$

attains its minimum (over all classifications $y_1^*, \ldots, y_k^*$).

In a more general setting, for the non-separable case, we would like to find classifications $y_1^*, \ldots, y_k^*$ such that the inequalities

$$\begin{array}{rclrcll} y_i[(x_i \cdot \mathbf{w}^*) + b] & \geq & 1 - \xi_i, & \xi_i & \geq & 0, & \text{for } i = 1, \ldots, \ell \\ y_j^*[(x_j^* \cdot \mathbf{w}^*) + b] & \geq & 1 - \xi_j^*, & \xi_j^* & \geq & 0, & \text{for } j = 1, \ldots, k \end{array} \tag{3.65}$$

are valid, and the functional

$$\Phi(y_1^*, \ldots, y_k^*) = \min_{\mathbf{w}^*, \xi, \xi^*} \left[\frac{1}{2}|\mathbf{w}_0^*|^2 + C\sum_{i=1}^{\ell} \xi_i + C^* \sum_{j=1}^{k} \xi_j^* \right] \tag{3.66}$$

(where C and C^* are some given non-negative constants) attains it minimum (over all $y_1^*, \ldots, y_k^*$).

Note that in order to solve this problem, we have to find the optimal hyperplanes for all fixed $y_1^*, \ldots, y_k^*$, and choose the best one. Using the same technique as in the standard support vector method (section 3.2.1), to find the dual representation of the optimal hyperplane for fixed $y_1^*, \ldots, y_k^*$,

$$f(x) = \text{sign}\left[\sum_{i=1}^{\ell} \alpha_i y_i (x \cdot x_i) + \sum_{j=1}^{k} \alpha_i^* y_i^* (x \cdot x_j^*) + b\right] \tag{3.67}$$

one has to maximize the functional

$$W_{y_1^*,\ldots,y_k^*}(\alpha, \alpha^*) = \sum_{i=1}^{\ell} \alpha_i + \sum_{j=1}^{k} \alpha_j^* - \frac{1}{2}\left[\sum_{i,r=1}^{\ell} y_i y_r \alpha_i \alpha_r (x_i \cdot x_r) \right.$$
$$\left. + \sum_{j,r=1}^{k} y_j^* y_r^* \alpha_j^* \alpha_r^* (x_j^* \cdot x_r^*) + 2 \sum_{j=1}^{\ell} \sum_{r=1}^{k} y_j y_r^* \alpha_j \alpha_r^* (x_j \cdot x_r^*)\right] \tag{3.68}$$

subject to constraints

$$0 \le \alpha_i \le C, \tag{3.69}$$

$$0 \le \alpha_j^* \le C^*, \tag{3.70}$$

$$\sum_{i=1}^{\ell} y_i \alpha_i + \sum_{j=1}^{k} y_j^* \alpha_j^* = 0. \tag{3.71}$$

To find the hyperplane for transductive inference, one has to find the minimax solution where the maximum is computed by solving the quadratic optimization problem and the minimum is taken over all admissible classifications of the test set.

Repeating these arguments in feature space, one can formulate a transductive solution which is nonlinear in input space (but linear in some feature space):

Find classifications $y_1^*, \ldots, y_k^*$ such that the functional

$$W(y_1^*, \ldots, y_k^*) = \max_{\alpha,\alpha^*}\left\{\sum_{i=1}^{\ell} \alpha_i + \sum_{j=1}^{k} \alpha_j^* - \frac{1}{2}\left[\sum_{i,r=1}^{\ell} y_i y_r \alpha_i \alpha_r k(x_i, x_r) \right.\right.$$
$$\left.\left. + \sum_{j,r=1}^{k} y_j^* y_r^* \alpha_j^* \alpha_r^* k(x_j^*, x_r^*) + 2 \sum_{j=1}^{\ell} \sum_{r=1}^{k} y_j y_r^* \alpha_j \alpha_r^* k(x_j, x_r^*)\right]\right\} \tag{3.72}$$

attains its minimum subject to constraints

$$0 \le \alpha_i \le C, \tag{3.73}$$

$$0 \le \alpha_j^* \le C^*, \tag{3.74}$$

$$\sum_{i=1}^{\ell} y_i \alpha_i + \sum_{j=1}^{k} y_j^* \alpha_j^* = 0. \tag{3.75}$$

Generally speaking, the exact solution of this minimax problem requires searching over all 2^k possible classifications of the test set. This can be done for a small number of test instances (say 1 – 7). For large numbers of test examples, one can use various heuristic procedures (for example by clustering of the test data and providing the same classification for entire clusters).

Note that the same solution can be suggested for the problem of constructing a decision rule (i.e. not just the classifications $y_1^*, \ldots, y_k^*$) using both labeled (3.55) and unlabeled (3.56) data. Using the parameters α, α^* and b obtained in the transductive solution, one can write down a decision rule

$$y(x) = \text{sign}\left[\sum_{i=1}^{\ell} \alpha_j y_i k(x, x_i) + \sum_{j=1}^{k} \alpha_i^* y_j^* k(x, x_j^*) + b\right] \tag{3.76}$$

that includes information about both data sets.

3.4 Estimation of Conditional Probability and Conditional Density Functions

3.4.1 Conditional Probability Functions

Let us consider the problem of estimating the conditional probability function using data

$$(y_1, z_1), \ldots, (y_\ell, z_\ell), \quad y \in \{-1, 1\} \tag{3.77}$$

as a problem of solving the equation

$$\int_0^z p(y = 1|z) dF(z) = F(y = 1, z) \tag{3.78}$$

in the situation where the distribution functions $F(z)$, $F(y = 1, z)$ are unknown.

To avoid solving the high-dimensional integral equation (3.78) on the basis of data (3.77), in (Vapnik, 1998) the method of estimating the conditional probability function along the line

$$z = z_0 + e(t - t_0) \tag{3.79}$$

passing through a point of interest z_0 was considered, where the unit vector e defines the direction. To estimate the conditional probability along this line, we split the vectors z_i from (3.77) into two components (t_i, u_i), where $t_i = (z_i \cdot e)$ is the projection of the vector z_i onto the given direction e, and u_i is in the orthogonal complement.

For the given direction e, we thus constructed data

$$(y_1, t_1, u_1), \ldots, (y_\ell, t_\ell, u_\ell), \quad y \in \{-1, 1\}, \tag{3.80}$$

which we use to solve the equation

$$\int_0^t p(y=1|t,u_0)dF(t|u_0) = F(y=1,t|u_0). \tag{3.81}$$

In this one dimensional equation (with respect to the parameter t) we have fixed vector u_0. Vector u_0 is defined by the condition that our line passes through some point of interest $z_0 = (t_0, u_0)$. To solve this equation, the approximations

$$F_\ell(t|u_0) = \sum_{i=1}^{\ell} \tau_i(u_0)\theta(t-t_i), \tag{3.82}$$

$$F_\ell(y=1,t|u_0) = \sum_{i=1}^{\ell} \tau_i(u_0)\theta(t-t_i)\delta(y_i), \tag{3.83}$$

$$\tau_i(u_0) = \frac{g_\gamma(|u_i-u_0|)}{\sum_{j=1}^{\ell} g_\gamma(|u_j-u_0|)}, \tag{3.84}$$

were introduced, where $g_\gamma(u)$ is a Parzen kernel (with width parameter γ) and $\delta(y_i)=1$ if $y_i=1$ and zero otherwise.

Using these approximations, and the regularization method of solving stochastic ill-posed problems with approximately defined operators, one can find an approximation of the conditional probability along the line (see Vapnik, 1998).

The problem is how to choose a good direction e. Our goal is to split the space into two subspaces for any point of interest: a one-dimensional subspace that defines the most important direction of change of the conditional probability (conditional density), and the orthogonal complement of this space. In our approximation, we deal especially accurately with the important one-dimensional subspace.

To implement this idea, we use the results of solving the pattern recognition problem (or regression estimation problem) to specify an important direction for solving the desired problem.[3]

First consider the case where a good decision rule is defined by a linear function. In this case it is reasonable to choose as an important direction one that is orthogonal to the separating hyperplane, and as less important the directions that are parallel to the separating hyperplane.

In general, the SV method solves a pattern recognition problem using a hyperplane in feature space, and therefore it is reasonable to choose the direction e defined by the vector that specifies the optimal hyperplane.

---

3. Note that the problem of pattern recognition (regression estimation) is simpler than the problem of conditional probability (conditional density) estimation. Therefore, here we use the solution of a simple problem to solve a more difficult one. Compare this to the classical method of conditional density estimation by first estimating densities, and then estimating a conditional density as the ratio of two densities. In the classical paradigm, the solution of a more simple problem is reduced to the solution of a more difficult one.

It is easy to check that if the inner product of two vectors in feature space Z is defined by the kernel $k(x_i, x_j)$ and α_i, $i = 1, \ldots, \ell$, are coefficients that define the decision rule for a pattern recognition problem

$$f(x) = \theta\left\{\sum_{i=1}^{\ell} y_i\alpha_i k(x_i, x) + b\right\}, \tag{3.85}$$

then the parameters $t_k - t_0$ and $|u_i - t_0|$ for estimating (3.84) can be defined using the corresponding training data in input space

$$(y_1, x_1), \ldots, (y_\ell, x_\ell), \tag{3.86}$$

as follows:

$$t_k - t_0 = \frac{\sum_{i=1}^{\ell} y_i\alpha_i[k(x_i, x_k) - k(x_i, x_0)]}{\sqrt{\sum_{i,j=1}^{\ell} y_i y_j \alpha_i \alpha_j k(x_i, x_j)}}, \tag{3.87}$$

$$|u_k - u_0| = \sqrt{k(x_k, x_k) + k(x_0, x_0) - 2k(x_k, x_0) - (t_k - t_0)^2} \tag{3.88}$$

3.4.2 Conditional Density Functions

Analogously, one can consider the problem of estimating a conditional density function as the problem of solving the integral equation

$$\int_0^y \int_0^z p(y|z)dF(z)dy = F(y, z), \tag{3.89}$$

where y is a real value. To solve this equation in the situation where the distribution functions $F(z)$ and $F(y, z)$ are unknown, but the data

$$(y_1, z_1), \ldots, (y_\ell, z_\ell), \tag{3.90}$$

are given, we use the same idea of estimating the desired conditional density function along a line with a given direction passing through a point of interest. We split the vectors z_i into two elements t_i and u_i, describing the position of the vector on the chosen line and the complement.

To estimate the conditional density function along the line passing through the point of interest $z_0 = (t_0, u_0)$ in a given direction e, we thus solve the equation

$$\int_0^y \int_0^t p(y|t, u_0)dF(t|u_0)dy = F(y, t|u_0). \tag{3.91}$$

As above, we describe the vectors z_i by two components t_i and u_i, thus obtaining the data

$$(y_1, t_1, u_1), \ldots, (y_\ell, t_\ell, u_\ell), \tag{3.92}$$

from which we construct the approximations

$$F_\ell(t|u_0) = \sum_{i=1}^{\ell} \tau_i(u_0)\theta(t - t_i), \tag{3.93}$$

$$F_\ell(y, t|u_0) = \sum_{i=1}^{\ell} \tau_i(u_0)\theta(t - t_i)\theta(y - y_i), \tag{3.94}$$

where $\tau_i(u_0)$ is defined by (3.84).

For estimating a conditional density, it is reasonable to use the direction orthogonal to the linear regression function in feature space.

As in the case of conditional probability, one can use the equivalent support vector representation of the linear regression function,

$$f(x) = \sum_{i=1}^{\ell} y_i \alpha_i k(x_i, x) + b, \tag{3.95}$$

from which, using equation (3.88), one can find the parameters for estimating the approximations (3.93) and (3.94). Using the technique described in (Vapnik, 1998), and the approximations (3.93) and (3.94), one can estimate the conditional density along the desired line in feature space passing through a point of interest.

4 Generalization Performance of Support Vector Machines and Other Pattern Classifiers

Peter Bartlett
Department of Systems Engineering, RSISE, Australian National University
Canberra ACT 0200
Australia
Peter.Bartlett@keating.anu.edu.au
http://wwwsyseng.anu.edu.au/~bartlett/

John Shawe-Taylor
Royal Holloway, University of London
Egham, Surrey TW20 0EX, UK
j.shawe-taylor@dcs.rhbnc.ac.uk
http://www.cs.rhbnc.ac.uk/people/staff/shawe-taylor.shtml

The aim of this chapter is to summarise results that have been obtained for high confidence generalization error bounds for the Support Vector Machine (SVM) and other pattern classifiers related to the SVM. As a by-product of the analysis we argue that the margin and number of support vectors are both estimators of the degree to which the distribution generating the inputs assists identification of the target hyperplane.

4.1 Introduction

Generalization analysis of pattern classifiers is concerned with determining the factors that affect the accuracy of a pattern classifier. Such an analysis requires assumptions to be made about how the data used to train the classifier was gathered and how subsequent data will be generated. One of the most popular assumptions originally championed by Vapnik and Chervonenkis (1971) is to assume that the training and testing data are both generated according to the same probability distribution. The distribution can be viewed as a model of the natural processes which give rise to the observed phenomenon. Since it is usually more difficult to estimate the distribution than to learn the classification function, it is important that no assumptions are made about the distribution, resulting in a so-called distribution-free analysis.

We will consider bounds on the generalization error, that is the probability of misclassifying a randomly chosen example, which hold with high probability over randomly chosen training sets. This type of bound has something of the flavour of a statistical test, in that it allows one to infer that the error is small with the chosen significance level. Such bounds have been described as *PAC* bounds, which stands for Probably (the probability of the bound failing is small) Approximately Correct (when the bound holds the classifier has low error rate).

PAC bounds

The central result of this approach to analysing learning systems relates the number of examples, the training set error and the complexity of the hypothesis space to the generalization error. The appropriate measure for the complexity of the hypothesis space is the Vapnik-Chervonenkis (VC) dimension. (Recall that the VC dimension of a space of $\{-1,1\}$-valued functions is the size of the largest subset of their domain for which the restriction of the space to that subset is the set of all $\{-1,1\}$-valued functions; see Vapnik and Chervonenkis (1971).) For example the following result of Vapnik (in a slightly strengthened version (Shawe-Taylor et al., 1998)) gives a high probability bound on the error of a hypothesis. In this theorem, the training set error $\mathrm{Er}_{\mathbf{x}}(f)$ of a hypothesis $f : X \to \{-1,1\}$ for a sequence $\mathbf{x} = ((x_1,y_1),\ldots,(x_\ell,y_\ell)) \in (X \times \{-1,1\})^\ell$ of ℓ labelled examples is the proportion of examples for which $f(x_i) \neq y_i$. The generalization error of f is the probability that $f(x) \neq y$, for a randomly chosen labelled example $(x,y) \in X \times \{-1,1\}$.

VC dimension

VC upper bound

Theorem 4.1

Let H be a class of functions mapping from a set X to $\{-1,1\}$ and having VC dimension h. For any probability distribution on $X \times \{-1,1\}$, with probability $1-\delta$ over ℓ random examples $\mathbf{x}$, any hypothesis f in H has generalization error no more than

$$2\mathrm{Er}_{\mathbf{x}}(f) + \frac{1}{\ell}\left(4\log\left(\frac{4}{\delta}\right) + 4h\log\left(\frac{2e\ell}{h}\right)\right), \tag{4.1}$$

provided $h \leq \ell$.

The bound is asymptotically close to best possible since there are lower bounds with a similar form. The following result is due to Ehrenfeucht, Haussler, Kearns, and Valiant (1989), and Blumer, Ehrenfeucht, Haussler, and Warmuth (1989). (See, for example, the textbook Anthony and Biggs (1992).)

VC lower bound

Theorem 4.2

Let H be a hypothesis space with finite VC dimension $h \geq 1$. Then for any learning algorithm there exist distributions such that with probability at least δ over ℓ

random examples, the error of f is at least

$$\max\left(\frac{h-1}{32\ell}, \frac{1}{\ell}\log\left(\frac{1}{\delta}\right)\right). \tag{4.2}$$

There is, however, an important difference between the upper and lower bounds. As indicated above, the upper bound theorems hold for all distributions, but the lower bound holds for particular distributions focussed on points which can be shattered by the hypothesis space.

The upper bounds appear in practice to be very loose or in other words overly pessimistic. Several suggestions have been put forward as to why this might be the case. An explanation that we will refer back to later is the possibility that distributions generating real-world data do not behave like the worst case distributions used to prove the lower bounds.

In this chapter, we shall consider classifiers that can be expressed in the form $x \mapsto \text{sgn}(f(x))$, where $f : X \to \mathbb{R}$ is a real-valued function in some function class, and $\text{sgn} : \mathbb{R} \to \{-1, 1\}$ is the function satisfying $\text{sgn}(\alpha) = 1$ iff $\alpha \geq 0$. A key quantity in the generalization analysis of such classifiers is the "margin". The margin of f on a labelled example (x, y) is the quantity $yf(x)$, that is, it is the amount by which the function f is to the correct side of the threshold. It can be thought of as an indication of the confidence with which f classifies the point x.

Margin

Support vector machines (SVMs) are classifiers that can be expressed as the composition of the threshold function with real-valued functions. The SVM algorithm maximises the margin of a linear function on the feature space defined by the mapping Φ, which satisfies $k(\mathbf{x}, \mathbf{y}) = (\Phi(x) \cdot \Phi(y))$; see (1.20). In other words the inner product in the feature space can be computed by the applying the kernel function k to the two input vectors. It is important to note that the mapping Φ is fixed by choosing the kernel function, and though the expression for the linear function expressed in terms of the kernel function does depend on the training set, the mapping Φ does not.

It is well-known that the dimension of the feature space can become very large even for low degree polynomial kernels. Vapnik (1995) gives examples for a character recognition task where with polynomials of degree 3 the dimension is already 1×10^6. This is the VC dimension of the class of hyperplane classifiers (thresholded linear functions) and clearly suggests that learning should not be practical. Indeed, the situation is even worse if we use Gaussian kernels; see (1.31), since in this case the feature space is an infinite dimensional Hilbert space.

4.2 Structural Risk Minimization (SRM) and Data-sensitive SRM

When applying Theorem 4.1 one frequently considers a sequence of hypothesis spaces of increasing complexity and attempts to find a suitable hypothesis from each, for example neural networks with increasing numbers of hidden units. As the complexity increases the number of training errors will usually decrease, but the risk of overfitting the data correspondingly increases. By applying the theorem to each of the hypothesis spaces, we can choose the hypothesis for which the error bound is tightest. The following theorem summarizes this idea. (It follows, for example, from Theorem 2.3 in Shawe-Taylor et al. (1998).)

Theorem 4.3
Let H_i, $i = 1, 2, \ldots$, be a sequence of hypothesis classes mapping X to $\{-1, 1\}$, with $\mathrm{VCdim}(H_i) = h_i$. Let μ be any probability measure on $S = X \times \{-1, 1\}$. Then with probability $1 - \delta$ over ℓ examples $\mathbf{x}$ chosen according to μ, for any $h \leq \ell$ and any hypothesis f in H_i, the generalization error of f is no more than

$$2\mathrm{Er}_{\mathbf{x}}(f) + \frac{1}{\ell}\left(8\log\left(\frac{2\ell}{\delta}\right) + 4h_i \log\left(\frac{2e\ell}{h_i}\right)\right). \tag{4.3}$$

Notice that this result shows that we can obtain generalisation error bounds for functions chosen from any of the hypothesis classes H_i. This is in contrast to Theorem 4.1, in which we needed to fix the class H_i in advance. This approach to trading off empirical error with hypothesis space complexity is known as Structural Risk Minimisation (SRM). It is important to note that in order to apply SRM (using Theorem 4.1) we must define the hierarchy of hypothesis spaces before the data is observed. It is tempting to apply this result to support vector machines, since the following result shows that the VC dimension of large margin hyperplanes need not depend on the dimension of the feature space.

Structural Risk Minimisation

Theorem 4.4 (Vapnik, 1979)
Suppose that X is the ball of radius R in $\mathbb{R}^n$, $X = \{\mathbf{x} \in \mathbb{R}^n : \|\mathbf{x}\| \leq R\}$, and that $X_0 \subset X$. Consider the set

$$\mathcal{F} = \{\mathbf{x} \mapsto \mathbf{w} \cdot \mathbf{x} : \|\mathbf{w}\| \leq 1, \mathbf{x} \in X\}, \tag{4.4}$$

and let $\mathrm{sgn}(\mathcal{F}) = \{\mathbf{x} \mapsto \mathrm{sgn}(f(\mathbf{x})) : f \in \mathcal{F}\}$ be the set of classifiers defined by thresholding functions in $\mathcal{F}$. Let $\mathcal{F}_0$ be the subset of functions in $\mathcal{F}$ that satisfy $|f(\mathbf{x})| \geq \gamma$ for all $\mathbf{x}$ in X_0, i.e. that have margin greater than or equal to γ. Then the restriction of $\mathrm{sgn}(\mathcal{F}_0)$ to the points in X_0 has VC dimension no more than

$$\min\{R^2/\gamma^2, n\} + 1. \tag{4.5}$$

The bound suggests that maximising the margin performs SRM over the hypothesis spaces defined by a sequence of increasing margins, where we would define H_γ to be the space

$$H_\gamma = \{f | f \text{ has margin at least } \gamma \text{ on } X_0\}. \tag{4.6}$$

The problem with this approach is that it violates one of the assumptions made in proving the SRM theorems, namely that the sequence of hypothesis spaces must be chosen before the data arrives. This is not possible, since a particular hyperplane can only be assigned to hypothesis space H_γ once we are able to measure its margin *on the training data.*

Data-dependent SRM

We will present a method for overcoming this problem which amounts to allowing the choice of the hierarchy of spaces to be dependent on the data (Shawe-Taylor et al., 1998). This analysis has been called *data-dependent SRM* for this reason. Intuitively, we may consider that the data is first used to decide which hierarchy to use, and then subsequently to choose the best hypothesis using the inherited measure of quality. For the example of large margins the hierarchies are those determined by the margins of hypotheses to the set of training points, and the inherited quality measure is the observed margin. The approach relies on a generalization of the VC dimension for real valued functions which is known as the fat-shattering dimension.

Fat-shattering dimension

Definition 4.1
Let $\mathcal{F}$ be a set of real valued functions. We say that a set of points X is *γ-shattered by $\mathcal{F}$* if there are real numbers r_x indexed by $x \in X$ such that for all binary vectors b indexed by X, there is a function $f_b \in \mathcal{F}$ satisfying

$$f_b(x) \begin{cases} \geq r_x + \gamma & \text{if } b_x = 1 \\ \leq r_x - \gamma & \text{otherwise} \end{cases} \tag{4.7}$$

The *fat shattering dimension* $\text{fat}_{\mathcal{F}}$ of the set $\mathcal{F}$ is a function from the positive real numbers to the integers which maps a value γ to the size of the largest γ-shattered set, if this is finite, or infinity otherwise.

We may think of the fat-shattering dimension of a set of real-valued functions as the VC dimension obtained by thresholding but requiring that outputs are γ above the threshold for positive classification and γ below for negative. The following theorem shows that the fat-shattering dimension gives generalization error bounds for large margin classifiers. It combines results from Shawe-Taylor et al. (1998) and Bartlett (1998b).

Margin bounds

Theorem 4.5 (Shawe-Taylor et al., 1998; Bartlett, 1998b)
Consider a class $\mathcal{F}$ of real-valued functions. With probability at least $1 - \delta$ over ℓ independently generated examples $\mathbf{x}$, if a classifier $\text{sgn}(f) \in \text{sgn}(\mathcal{F})$ has margin at least γ on $\mathbf{x}$, then the error of $\text{sgn}(f)$ is no more than

$$\frac{2}{\ell}\left(h \log_2\left(\frac{8e\ell}{h}\right) \log_2(32\ell) + \log_2\left(\frac{8\ell}{\delta}\right)\right), \tag{4.8}$$

where $h = \text{fat}_{\mathcal{F}}(\gamma/16)$. Furthermore, with probability at least $1-\delta$, every classifier $\text{sgn}(f) \in \text{sgn}(\mathcal{F})$ has error no more than

$$b/\ell + \sqrt{\frac{2}{\ell}\left(h \log(34e\ell/h) \log_2(578\ell) + \log(4/\delta)\right)}, \tag{4.9}$$

where b is the number of labelled training examples with margin less than γ.

Note that in (Shawe-Taylor et al., 1998) it is shown that when the fat shattering dimension bound is continuous from the right, a scale of $\gamma/8$ can be used for the case where there are no training set errors.

The result can be interpreted as follows. Using the margin γ to measure the performance of a classifier on the training data provides some slack: the relevant measure of complexity of the classifier in this case is the fat-shattering dimension at a scale proportional to γ. The complexity of the class at this scale can be considerably less than its complexity as measured by the VC dimension of $\text{sgn}(\mathcal{F})$, which can be thought of as the complexity at an arbitrarily fine scale. The intuitive explanation for this is that a class with small fat-shattering dimension at a certain value of the accuracy parameter γ can be approximated to that accuracy with a rather simple set of functions. Since the classifier has margin γ on the training data, these approximations reflect the behaviour of functions in $\mathcal{F}$.

Notice that, for zero training error (measured with respect to the margin γ), the error converges to zero at rate $1/\ell$, whereas when the training error is non-zero, it converges at the slower $1/\sqrt{\ell}$ rate. This difference is unavoidable.

In a sense, Theorem 4.5 is an example of a data dependent result, since the margin observed on the training data defines the scale at which we measure the class complexity. In the next section we apply Theorem 4.5 to explain the generalization performance of support vector machines by applying the above results in feature space.

4.3 Support Vector Machines

The following result gives a bound on the fat-shattering dimension for large margin linear classifiers, such as support vector machines in feature space. It has a similar form to the bound of Theorem 4.4 on the VC dimension of certain restrictions of these functions. It improves on a straightforward corollary of Theorem 4.4, and on a result in Gurvits (1997).

Theorem 4.6
Suppose that X is the ball of radius R in a Hilbert space H, $X = \{x \in H : \|x\| \leq R\}$, and consider the set

$$\mathcal{F} = \{\mathbf{x} \mapsto \mathbf{w} \cdot \mathbf{x} : \|\mathbf{w}\| \leq 1, \mathbf{x} \in X\}. \tag{4.10}$$

Then

$$\text{fat}_{\mathcal{F}}(\gamma) \leq \left(\frac{R}{\gamma}\right)^2. \tag{4.11}$$

This result is reminiscent of Theorem 4.4. However, as explained above, Theorem 4.4 cannot be used directly to obtain bounds on generalisation error.

The proof of Theorem 4.6 is related to the proof in Gurvits (1997). It is given in the appendix. Combining Theorems 4.5 and 4.6 gives the following result.

Theorem 4.7
Define the class $\mathcal{F}$ of real-valued functions on the ball of radius R in $\mathbb{R}^n$ as

$$\mathcal{F} = \{\mathbf{x} \mapsto w \cdot \mathbf{x} : \|\mathbf{w}\| \leq 1, \ \|\mathbf{x}\| \leq R\}. \tag{4.12}$$

There is a constant c such that, for all probability distributions, with probability at least $1 - \delta$ over ℓ independently generated training examples, if a classifier $\text{sgn}(f) \in \text{sgn}(\mathcal{F})$ has margin at least γ on all the training examples, then the error of $\text{sgn}(f)$ is no more than

$$\frac{c}{\ell}\left(\frac{R^2}{\gamma^2}\log^2 \ell + \log(1/\delta)\right). \tag{4.13}$$

Furthermore, with probability at least $1 - \delta$, every classifier $\text{sgn}(f) \in \text{sgn}(\mathcal{F})$ has error no more than

$$b/\ell + \sqrt{\frac{c}{\ell}\left(\frac{R^2}{\gamma^2}\log^2 \ell + \log(1/\delta)\right)} \tag{4.14}$$

where b is the number of labelled training examples with margin less than γ.

(With mild conditions on the process generating the random examples, b is the number of support vectors that hit the upper boundary; see chapter 1.) Hence we can bound the generalization error of the SV machine even when the kernel determines an infinite dimensional feature space. There is a particularly simple expression for the margin (see Cortes and Vapnik, 1995).

SV Margin

Lemma 4.1 (Cortes and Vapnik, 1995)
In the standard notation of the SV machine, the margin γ of the optimal hyperplane on a separable training set can be computed from the solution coefficients α_i^0 as

$$\gamma^2 = \left(\sum_{i=1}^{\ell} \alpha_i^0\right)^{-1}. \tag{4.15}$$

Hence, in the generalization error bounds of Theorem 4.7 for SV machines, the factor $1/\gamma^2$ can be replaced by the 1-norm $\|\alpha\|_1$ of the solution coefficients.

We see that in the case of SV machines the underlying VC dimension of the hypothesis space can be infinite and the above bound will still apply. Hence, we have a distribution independent bound on the generalization error of a hypothesis drawn from a space of infinite VC dimension. This appears to contradict the lower bound of Theorem 4.2. The resolution of this apparent paradox lies in the dependence of the lower bound on the choice of particular distributions. Since with high probability both bounds hold, for these distributions with high probability the margin will be sufficiently small to make the bound of Theorem 4.7 greater than the bound of 4.2. This implies that the margin will be very small, rendering the margin based bound ineffective. It is in this sense that we can see that the margin is providing an indicator of how 'benign' the distribution generating the data is. Intuitively, the more the distribution is concentrated away from the decision boundary the fewer examples are required to estimate that boundary to a given accuracy.

Small margin

Hence, although Theorem 4.7 gives a bound for every distribution, it will only be useful for certain classes of distributions. It can thus be viewed as a distribution independent bound of a distribution dependent quantity. This also makes clear that any proof of a generalization error bound in terms of the margin must in some way make use of the distribution generating the data and cannot be a universal type of bound typical for the standard SRM approach.

We now show that the margin is not the only measure that can give information about how benign the input distribution is in relation to the target function. Another measure than can with high confidence place a bound on the generalization error of a consistent hyperplane, is the number of support vectors.

Support vectors

Let MMH be the function that returns the maximal margin hyperplane consistent with a labelled sample. Note that applying the function MMH to the labelled support vectors returns the maximal margin hyperplane of which they are the support vectors.

Theorem 4.8 (Littlestone and Warmuth, 1986)
Let D be any probability distribution on a domain X, c be any $\{-1, 1\}$-valued function on X. Then the probability that ℓ examples drawn independently at random according to D contain a subset of at most h examples that map via MMH to a hypothesis that is both consistent with all ℓ examples and has error larger than ϵ is at most

$$\sum_{i=0}^{h} \binom{\ell}{i} (1-\epsilon)^{\ell-i}. \tag{4.16}$$

The theorem implies that the generalization error of a maximal margin hyperplane with h support vectors among a sample of size ℓ can with confidence $1-\delta$ be bounded by

$$\frac{1}{\ell-h}\left(h \log_2 \frac{e\ell}{h} + \log_2 \frac{\ell}{\delta}\right). \tag{4.17}$$

Note that as with the margin the bound does not depend on the dimension of the space in which the hyperplane is being placed and hence applies to Support Vector Machines, whatever kernel function is being used.

A related result is presented in (Vapnik, 1995), bounding the generalization error in terms of the expected number of support vectors. This result shows that we can obtain such a bound without having to know this number in advance; with high probability, the observed number of support vectors gives enough information.

Since we may have a large number of support vectors with a large margin, as well as a small number of support vectors with a small margin, it is clear that these two measures assess the input distribution according to different criteria, either of which is sufficient to indicate good generalization with high confidence.

4.4 Other Applications

Boosting

This section reviews three other applications of margins analysis. The first is to boosting algorithms, which are techniques for combining classifiers. A result in (Schapire et al., 1998) shows that certain boosting algorithms produce classifiers of the form

$$x \mapsto \operatorname{sgn}\left(\sum_{i=1}^{N} w_i f_i(x)\right) \tag{4.18}$$

that have large margins on the training examples, where $w_i > 0$, $\sum_i w_i = 1$, and f_i are classifiers in some class H. A VC dimension analysis would suggest that the generalization error of these classifiers would increase with N, the number of base hypotheses f_i that are combined. The following result, which follows easily from techniques introduced in (Bartlett, 1998b), shows that the fat-shattering dimension of the class of convex combinations of classifiers is independent of the number of base hypotheses.

Theorem 4.9
There is a constant c so that for all classes H of functions mapping from X to $\{-1, 1\}$, the class of convex combinations of functions from H,

$$\mathcal{F} = \left\{ x \mapsto \sum_{i=1}^{N} w_i f_i(x) : f_i \in H,\, w_i > 0,\, \sum_i w_i = 1 \right\} \tag{4.19}$$

satisfies

$$\operatorname{fat}_{\mathcal{F}}(\gamma) \leq c\frac{h}{\gamma^2}\log(1/\gamma), \tag{4.20}$$

where h is the VC dimension of the class H of base hypotheses.

This result can be combined with the margins analysis technique of Theorem 4.5 to give bounds on generalization error in terms of the margin of the combined classifier. In fact, a more direct argument, from (Schapire et al., 1998), gives the following result, which eliminates a log factor. (Of course, it is trivial to obtain a similar result, without the square root, for the case in which all training examples have margin γ, c.f. Theorem 4.5.)

Theorem 4.10
There is a constant c such that, for the class $\mathcal{F}$ of convex combinations of classifiers from a class H with VC dimension h, for all probability distributions, with probability at least $1 - \delta$ over ℓ independently generated training examples, every classifier $\operatorname{sgn}(f) \in \operatorname{sgn}(\mathcal{F})$ has error no more than

$$b/\ell + \sqrt{\frac{c}{\ell}\left(\frac{h\log^2(\ell/h)}{\gamma^2} + \log(1/\delta)\right)} \tag{4.21}$$

where b is the number of labelled training examples with margin less than γ.

Sigmoid networks

The second application of the margins analysis techniques that we wish to consider here is feed-forward sigmoid networks with small parameters. Define

$$F_0 = \{\mathbf{x} \mapsto x_i : \mathbf{x} = (x_1, \ldots, x_n) \in [-1,1]^n,\ i \in \{1, \ldots, n\}\} \cup \{0, 1\}, \tag{4.22}$$

where 0 and 1 are the identically zero and identically one functions, respectively. For $i \geq 1$, define

$$F_i = \left\{ \sigma\left(\sum_{j=1}^{N} w_j f_j \right) : N \in \mathbb{N},\ f_j \in \bigcup_{k=0}^{i-1} F_k,\ \sum_{j=1}^{N} |w_j| \leq V \right\}, \tag{4.23}$$

where the function $\sigma : \mathbb{R} \to [-1,1]$ satisfies the Lipschitz condition $|\sigma(\alpha_1) - \sigma(\alpha_2)| \leq B|\alpha_1 - \alpha_2|$ for all $\alpha_1, \alpha_2 \in \mathbb{R}$. (For instance, the standard sigmoid function $1/(1+e^{-\alpha})$ satisfies these conditions.) Thus, F_L is the class of functions that can be computed by an L-layer feed-forward network in which each unit has the sum of the magnitudes of its weights bounded by V.

Theorem 4.11 (Bartlett, 1998b)
There is a constant c such that, for $L \geq 1$, the class F_L defined above satisfies

$$\mathrm{fat}_{F_L}(\gamma) \leq \frac{1}{6} \left(\frac{48}{\gamma} \right)^{2L} (2VB)^{L(L+1)} \log(2n+2), \tag{4.24}$$

provided $V \geq 1/(2B)$, and $\gamma \leq 16VB$.

Applying Theorem 4.5 immediately implies a bound on generalization error in terms of the margins behaviour of these neural networks. In practice, neural network classifiers are typically trained using gradient descent algorithms on a squared error criterion. It is easy to see that minimizing squared error at the network output tends to produce a classifier with large margins. In addition, popular heuristics such as weight decay and early stopping tend to give small weights. Experimental results (Loy and Bartlett, 1997) confirm that the relationship between margin behaviour, magnitude of the weight vectors, and generalization performance closely follows that suggested by these results.

Bayes classifier

The generalization performance of the Bayesian posterior classifer has also been related to its margin. This follows from viewing it as a linear functional in a Hilbert space (chapter 5, see also (Cristianini et al., 1998)) given by

$$f(x|D) = \int_w h_w(x) p(w|D) d\mu(w), \tag{4.25}$$

where μ is the prior over the parameters w. If the prior distribution favours hypotheses with low error, it can be shown that the margin of this functional will be large, and a resulting bound on the generalization can be obtained using Theorem 4.7. The bound obtained can benefit from a favourable prior even when the Vapnik-Chervonenkis dimension of the underlying hypothesis class is equal to the sample size. Again we can see that the margin of the posterior function is giving a measure of how well the prior, input distribution and target function are aligned.

4.5 Conclusions

Our aim in this chapter has been twofold. Firstly, we have stated the known results (and some new results) for high confidence bounds on the generalization error of SVMs in terms of the margin and number of support vectors. Secondly, we wanted to highlight that these results can only be obtained from a data-dependent analysis relying as they do on using some measure to estimate how favourable the input distribution is in relation to the target function. This type of analysis is relatively novel (Shawe-Taylor et al., 1998), but we feel that its potential for motivating algorithms that are able to take advantage of collusions between distribution and target is far from being exhausted. Indeed, we believe that this is frequently an ingredient in successful learning systems which has been exploited by accident. By more careful analysis of this phenomenon it may well be possible to motivate key ingredients in the Support Vector arsenal, such as choice of kernel function, the bound used in the soft-margin approach and so on.

We have also given examples to show that the style of analysis is not limited to SVMs but applies to many other learning machines including two of the most effective techniques, boosting and Bayesian methods.

Acknowledgements

John Shawe-Taylor was supported in part by the EPSRC research grant number GR/K70366. Peter Bartlett was supported by the Australian Research Council.

Appendix: Proof of Theorem 4.6

The proof involves two lemmas. The first shows that the sum of any subset of a set shattered by functions from $\mathcal{F}$ is far from the sum of the remainder of that set. The second shows that these sums cannot be too far apart when the norms of the input vectors are small. Comparing the results gives the bound on the fat-shattering dimension.

Lemma 4.2
Let $\mathcal{F} = \{\mathbf{x} \mapsto \mathbf{w} \cdot \mathbf{x} : \|\mathbf{x}\| \leq R, \|\mathbf{w}\| \leq 1\}$. If S is γ-shattered by $\mathcal{F}$, then every subset $S_0 \subseteq S$ satisfies

$$\left\| \sum S_0 - \sum (S - S_0) \right\| \geq |S|\gamma. \tag{4.26}$$

Proof Suppose that $S = \{\mathbf{x}_1, \ldots, \mathbf{x}_h\}$ is γ-shattered by $\mathcal{F}$, witnessed by $r_1, \ldots, r_h \in \mathbb{R}$. Then for all $b = (b_1, \ldots, b_h) \in \{-1, 1\}^h$ there is a $\mathbf{w}_b$ with $\|\mathbf{w}_b\| \leq 1$ such that, for all i, $b_i(\mathbf{w}_b \cdot \mathbf{x}_i - r_i) \geq \gamma$. Fix a subset $S_0 \subseteq S$. We consider two cases: If

$$\sum \{r_i : \mathbf{x}_i \in S_0\} \geq \sum \{r_i : \mathbf{x}_i \in S - S_0\}, \tag{4.27}$$

then fix $b_i = 1$ if and only if $\mathbf{x}_i \in S_0$. In that case we have $\mathbf{w}_b \cdot \mathbf{x}_i \geq r_i + \gamma$ if $\mathbf{x}_i \in S_0$, and $\mathbf{w}_b \cdot \mathbf{x}_i \leq r_i - \gamma$ otherwise. It follows that

$$\mathbf{w}_b \cdot \left(\sum S_0\right) \geq \sum \{r_i : \mathbf{x}_i \in S_0\} + |S_0|\gamma. \tag{4.28}$$

Similarly,

$$\mathbf{w}_b \cdot \left(\sum (S - S_0)\right) \leq \sum \{r_i : \mathbf{x}_i \in S - S_0\} - |S - S_0|\gamma. \tag{4.29}$$

Hence, using (4.27),

$$\mathbf{w}_b \cdot \left(\sum S_0 - \sum (S - S_0)\right) \geq |S|\gamma. \tag{4.30}$$

But since $\|\mathbf{w}\| \leq 1$, by the Cauchy-Schwarz inequality, we must have

$$\left\|\sum S_0 - \sum (S - S_0)\right\| \geq |S|\gamma. \tag{4.31}$$

In the other case (if (4.27) is not satisfied), we fix $b_i = 1$ if and only if $\mathbf{x}_i \in S - S_0$, and use an identical argument. ■

Lemma 4.3
For all $S \subseteq H$ with $\|\mathbf{x}\| \leq R$ for $\mathbf{x} \in S$, some $S_0 \subseteq S$ satisfies

$$\left\|\sum S_0 - \sum (S - S_0)\right\| \leq \sqrt{|S|}R. \tag{4.32}$$

Proof The proof uses the probabilistic method. Suppose $S = \{\mathbf{x}_1, \ldots, \mathbf{x}_h\}$. We choose S_0 randomly, by defining $S_0 = \{\mathbf{x}_i \in S : b_i = 1\}$, where $b_1, \ldots, b_h \in \{-1, 1\}$ are independent and uniform random variables. Then

$$\begin{aligned}
\mathbf{E}\left\|\sum S_0 - \sum (S - S_0)\right\|^2 &= \mathbf{E}\left\|\sum_{i=1}^{h} b_i \mathbf{x}_i\right\|^2 \\
&= \sum_{i=1}^{h} \mathbf{E}\left[(b_i \mathbf{x}_i) \cdot \left(\sum_{j=1}^{h} b_j \mathbf{x}_j\right)\right] \\
&= \sum_{i=1}^{h} \mathbf{E}\left[(b_i \mathbf{x}_i) \cdot \left(\sum_{j \neq i} b_j \mathbf{x}_j + b_i \mathbf{x}_i\right)\right] \\
&= \sum_{i=1}^{h} \left(\sum_{j \neq i} \mathbf{E}\left[(b_i \mathbf{x}_i) \cdot (b_j \mathbf{x}_j)\right] + \mathbf{E}\|b_i \mathbf{x}_i\|^2\right) \\
&= \sum_{i=1}^{h} \mathbf{E}\|b_i \mathbf{x}_i\|^2 \\
&\leq |S|R^2,
\end{aligned}$$

where the last equality follows from the fact that the b_is have zero mean and are independent, so $\mathbf{E}[b_i b_j] = 0$ for $i \neq j$. Since the expected value of the squared norm of the difference between the sums is no more than $|S|R^2$, there must be a set S_0 for which this quantity is no more than $|S|R^2$. ■

5 Bayesian Voting Schemes and Large Margin Classifiers

Nello Cristianini
Department of Engineering Mathematics, University of Bristol
Queen's Building, University Walk, Bristol BS8 1TR, UK
nello.cristianini@bristol.ac.uk
http://zeus.bris.ac.uk/~ennc/nello1.html

John Shawe-Taylor
Royal Holloway, University of London
Egham, Surrey TW20 0EX, UK
j.shawe-taylor@dcs.rhbnc.ac.uk
http://www.cs.rhbnc.ac.uk/people/staff/shawe-taylor.shtml

It is often claimed that one of the main distinctive features of Bayesian Learning Algorithms for neural networks is that they don't simply output one hypothesis, but rather an entire distribution of probability over an hypothesis set: the Bayes posterior.

An alternative perspective is that they output a linear combination of classifiers, whose coefficients are given by Bayes theorem. This can be regarded as a hyperplane in a high-dimensional feature space.

We provide a novel theoretical analysis of such classifiers, based on data-dependent VC theory, proving that they can be expected to be large margin hyperplanes in a Hilbert space, and hence to have low effective VC dimension. This not only explains the remarkable resistance to overfitting exhibited by such classifiers, but also co-locates them in the same class as other systems, such as Support Vector Machines and Adaboost, which have a similar performance.

5.1 Introduction

In recent years, a new method for training neural networks has been proposed and used, mainly due to the work of MacKay and Neal (MacKay, 1992a,b; Neal, 1996).

The systems inspired by this approach are generally know as Bayesian Learning Algorithms and have proven to be quite resistant to overfitting.

They are characterized by the fact that they output an entire distribution of probability over the hypothesis space, rather than a single hypothesis. Such a distribution, the Bayes posterior, depends on the training data and on the prior distribution, and is used to make predictions by averaging the predictions of all the elements of the set, in a weighted majority voting scheme.

Voting Scheme

The posterior is computed according to Bayes' rule, and such a scheme has the remarkable property that — as long as the prior is correct and the computations can be performed exactly — its expected test error is minimal. Typically, the posterior is approximated by combining a gaussian prior and a simplified version of the likelihood (the data-dependent term). Such a distribution is then sampled with a Monte-Carlo method, to form a committee whose composition reflects the posterior probability.

Occam paradox

The classifiers obtained with this method are known to be highly resistant to overfitting. Indeed, neither the committee size nor the network size strongly affect the performance, to such an extent that it is not uncommon — in the Bayesian literature — to refer to "infinite networks" (Neal, 1994; Williams, 1997), meaning by this networks whose number of tunable parameters is much larger than the sample size.

Hyper-plane

The thresholded linear combination of classifiers generated by the Bayesian algorithm can be regarded as a hyperplane in a high dimensional feature space. The mapping from the input to the feature space depends on the chosen hypothesis space (e.g. network architecture).

Large margin

In this chapter we provide a novel description of Bayesian classifiers which makes it possible to perform a margin analysis on them, and hence to apply data-dependent SRM theory (Shawe-Taylor et al. (1998), and chapter 4). In particular, by viewing the posterior distribution as a linear functional in a Hilbert space, the margin can be computed and gives a bound on the generalization error via an *effective* VC dimension which is much lower than the number of parameters. An analogous analysis has been performed in the case of Adaboost by Schapire et al. (1998), whose theorems we will quote for reference.

These results not only explain the remarkable resistance to overfitting observed in Bayesian algorithms, but also provide a surprising unified description of three of the most effective learning algorithms: Support Vector Machines, Adaboost and now also Bayesian classifiers.

Experimental results confirming the predictions of our model are reported in a companion paper (Cristianini et al., 1998).

5.2 Bayesian Learning Theory

The result of Bayesian learning is a probability distribution over the (parameterized) hypothesis space, expressing the degree of belief in a specific hypothesis as an approximation of the target function. This distribution is then used to make predictions.

To start the process of Bayesian learning, one must define a prior distribution $P(\lambda)$ over the parameter space Λ associated to a set of parameterized functions $f(x, \lambda)$, possibly encoding some prior knowledge. In the following we will denote by f_λ the hypothesis associated to the function $f(x, \lambda)$.

After observing the data D, the prior distribution is updated using Bayes' Rule:

$$P(\lambda|D) \propto P(D|\lambda)P(\lambda). \tag{5.1}$$

The posterior distribution so obtained, hence, encodes information coming from the training set (via the likelihood function $P(D|\lambda)$) and prior knowledge.

Bayes classifiers

To predict the label of a new point, Bayesian classifiers integrate the predictions made by every element of the hypothesis space, weighting them with the posterior associated to each hypothesis, obtaining a distribution of probability over the set of possible labels:

$$P(y|x, D) = \int_\lambda f(x, \lambda)p(\lambda|D)dP(\lambda) \tag{5.2}$$

This predictive distribution can be used to minimize the number of misclassifications in the test set; in the 2-class case this is achieved simply by outputting the label which has received the highest vote.

Many practical problems exist in the implementation of such systems, and typically the procedure described above is approximated with numerical methods, by forming a committee sampled from the posterior with a Monte-Carlo simulation.

The likelihood $P(D|\lambda)$, also, needs to be approximated, and generally it is replaced by a function of the kind $e^{-\text{loss}(f_\lambda))}$, meaning by this that hypotheses highly inconsistent with the training set are unlikely to have generated it, and vice-versa. The exact form taken by the likelihood, however, depends on assumptions made about the noise in the data. An introduction to this field can be found in Radford Neal's book (Neal, 1996). The most important fact about Bayesian algorithms is that they turn out to be quite resistant to overfitting (Rasmussen, 1996; Neal, 1996), to the point that it is possible to use networks larger than the number of training example, and to combine them in large committees. They are interesting not only because they work, but also because their behaviour seems to challenge intuition.

5.3 Bayesian Classifiers as Large Margin Hyperplanes

In this section we introduce a rather different view of Bayesian Classifiers, which leads to their reinterpretation as hyperplanes in a high-dimensional Hilbert space. We then study a simplified model of such classifiers, which is easier to analyse but retains all the relevant features of the general case. We wish to understand the properties of their margin, and so of their effective VC dimension. This concept was introduced by Vapnik et al. (1994), though we use the term to mean the fat shattering dimension measured at the scale of the observed margin. Theorem 5.1 below shows that this dimension takes the place of the standard VC dimension in bounds on the generalization error in terms of the margin on the training set.

We first observe that, in the 2-class case examined so far, the predictions are actually performed by a thresholded linear combination of base hypotheses. The coefficients of the linear combinations are the posterior probabilities associated to each element of H, and the thresholding is at zero if the labels are $\{-1, +1\}$.

Convex hull of function space

Hence, the actual hypothesis space used by Bayesian systems is the convex hull of H, $\mathcal{C}(H)$ rather than H, where we have

$$\mathcal{C}(H) = \left\{ F_a \middle| F_a(x) = \int_\lambda a_\lambda f(x,\lambda) dP(\lambda) \text{ where } \int_\lambda a_\lambda dP(\lambda) = 1 \right\}. \tag{5.3}$$

Hence we can view the output hypothesis as a hyperplane, whose coordinates are given by the posterior. In practice the output hypothesis is frequently estimated by a Monte-Carlo sampling of the hypothesis space using the posterior distribution. We will ignore the effect that this has and study the behaviour of the composite hypothesis itself under various assumptions about the underlying function space H and prior $P(\lambda)$. We first give some necessary definitions.

Definition 5.1

Let H be a set of binary valued functions. We say that a set of points X is *shattered by* H if for all binary vectors b indexed by X, there is a function $f_b \in H$ realising b on X. The *Vapnik-Chervonenkis (VC) dimension* $\text{VCdim}(H)$ of the set H is the size of the largest shattered set, if this is finite, or infinity otherwise.

Definition 5.2

Let H be a set of real valued functions. We say that a set of points X is γ-*shattered by* H if there are real numbers r_x indexed by $x \in X$ such that for all binary vectors b indexed by X, there is a function $f_b \in H$ satisfying

$$f_b(x) \begin{cases} \geq r_x + \gamma & \text{if } b_x = 1 \\ \leq r_x - \gamma & \text{otherwise.} \end{cases} \tag{5.4}$$

The *fat shattering dimension* fat_H of the set H is a function from the positive real numbers to the integers which maps a value γ to the size of the largest γ-shattered set, if this is finite or infinity otherwise.

We will make critical use of the following result contained in (Shawe-Taylor et al., 1998) which involves the fat shattering dimension of the space of functions.

Theorem 5.1

Fat VC bound

Consider a real valued function class $\mathcal{H}$ having fat shattering function bounded above by the function $\text{afat} : \Re \to \mathcal{N}$ which is continuous from the right. Fix $\theta \in \Re$. Then with probability at least $1 - \delta$ a learner who correctly classifies ℓ independently generated examples $\mathbf{z}$ with $h = T_\theta(f) \in T_\theta(\mathcal{H})$ such that $\text{er}_{\mathbf{z}}(h) = 0$

and $\gamma = \min|f(\mathbf{x}_i) - \theta|$ will have error of h bounded from above by

$$\epsilon(\ell, k, \delta) = \frac{2}{\ell}\left(k \log_2\left(\frac{8e\ell}{k}\right) \log_2(32\ell) + \log_2\left(\frac{8\ell}{\delta}\right)\right), \tag{5.5}$$

where $k = \mathrm{afat}(\gamma/8)$.

Note how the fat shattering dimension at scale $\gamma/8$ plays the role of the VC dimension in this bound. This result motivates the use of the term effective VC dimension for this value. In order to make use of this theorem, we must have a bound on the fat shattering dimension and then calculate the margin of the classifier. We begin by considering bounds on the fat shattering dimension. The first bound on the fat shattering dimension of bounded linear functions in a finite dimensional space was obtained by Shawe-Taylor et al. (1998). Gurvits (1997) generalised this to infinite dimensional Banach spaces. We will quote an improved version of this bound (slightly adapted for an arbitrary bound on the linear operators) which is contained in this volume (chapter 4).

Theorem 5.2 (chapter 4)
Consider a Hilbert space and the class of linear functions L of norm less than or equal to B restricted to the sphere of radius R about the origin. Then the fat shattering dimension of L can be bounded by

$$\mathrm{fat}_L(\gamma) \leq \left(\frac{BR}{\gamma}\right)^2. \tag{5.6}$$

Linear functions in a Hilbert space

In order to apply Theorems 5.1 and 5.2 we need to bound the radius of the sphere containing the points and the norm of the linear functionals involved. Clearly, scaling by these quantities will give the margin appropriate for application of the theorem.

The Hilbert space we consider is that given by the functions

$$\mathcal{H} = \left\{\mathbf{z} : \Lambda \to \Re \,\middle|\, \text{such that} \int_{\lambda \in \Lambda} \mathbf{z}(\lambda)^2 dP(\lambda) < \infty\right\} \tag{5.7}$$

with the inner product

$$(\mathbf{z}_1 \cdot \mathbf{z}_2) = \int_{\lambda \in \Lambda} \mathbf{z}_1(\lambda)\mathbf{z}_2(\lambda) dP(\lambda). \tag{5.8}$$

There is a natural embedding of the input space X onto the unit sphere of $\mathcal{H}$ given by $\mathbf{x} \mapsto (f(\mathbf{x}, \cdot) \mapsto f(\mathbf{x}, \lambda))$, since

$$\int_{\lambda \in \Lambda} f(\mathbf{x}, \lambda)^2 dP(\lambda) = \int_{\lambda \in \Lambda} dP(\lambda) = 1. \tag{5.9}$$

Hence, the norm of input points is 1 and they are contained in the unit sphere as required. The linear functionals considered are those determined by the posterior distribution. The norm is given by

$$\|a\|^2 = \int_\lambda a_\lambda^2 dP(\lambda). \tag{5.10}$$

Hence,

$$\text{fat}_{\mathcal{C}_B(H)}(\gamma) = \left(\frac{B}{\gamma}\right)^2, \text{ where } \mathcal{C}_B(H) = \left\{F_a \in \mathcal{C}(H) \middle| \|a\|^2 \leq B\right\}. \tag{5.11}$$

Next we consider the margin γ. In order to study the margin of such hyperplanes, we will introduce some simplifications in the general model. We assume that the base hypothesis space, H is sufficiently rich that all dichotomies can be implemented. Further, initially we will assume that the average prior probability over functions in each error shell does not depend on the number of errors.

These are the only assumptions we make, and the second will be relaxed in a later analysis. A natural choice for the evidence function in a Boolean valued hypothesis space is $e^{-\mathbf{r}\sigma}$, which has the required property of giving low likelihood to the predictors which make many mistakes on the training set, and to which the usual Bayesian evidence collapses in the Boolean case. The quantity σ is usually related to the kind of noise assumed to affect the data.

The assumption that all the dichotomies can be implemented with the same probability corresponds to an 'uninformative' prior, where no knowledge is available about the target function. In a second stage we will examine the effect of inserting some knowledge in the prior, by slightly perturbing the uninformative one towards the target hypothesis. We will see that even slightly favourable priors can give a much smaller effective VC dimension than the uninformative one.

5.3.1 The Uninformative Prior

The actual hypothesis space used by Bayesian systems, hence, is the convex hull $\mathcal{C}(H)$, rather than H. The output hypothesis is a hyperplane, whose coordinates are given by the posterior.

In this section we give an expression for the margin of the composite hypothesis, as a function of a parameter related to our model of likelihood. The result is obtained in the case of a uniform prior for the pattern recognition case.

Let us start by stating some simple results and definitions which will be useful in the following.

Definition 5.3

Let $\mathbf{s}_\lambda$ be the number of points whose labeling is incorrectly predicted by the hypothesis f_λ. We define the *balance* of the hypothesis f_λ over a given sample as $B_\lambda = \ell - 2\mathbf{s}_\lambda$, where ℓ is the sample size. Hypotheses having the same value of $\mathbf{s}$ are said to form an *error shell.*

Note that $B_\lambda/\ell = 1 - 2\epsilon_\lambda$, where $\epsilon_\lambda = s_\lambda/\ell$ is the empirical risk of f_λ. During the next proof we will need to know the probability in the prior distribution of hypotheses in our parameter space which have a fixed empirical error. Given that this information is in general not available, we will initially make the simplifying assumption that all behaviours on the training sample can be realised. This implies a hypothesis space with VC dimension greater than or equal to the sample size ℓ.

Neutral prior

We make the further assumption that the prior probability of hypotheses which have empirical risk $\epsilon = r/\ell$ is

$$\frac{1}{2^\ell}\binom{\ell}{r} = \frac{\ell!}{2^\ell(\ell\epsilon)!(\ell-\ell\epsilon)!}, \tag{5.12}$$

in other words that the average prior probability for functions realising different patterns of r errors is $2^{-\ell}$. We will assume that the posterior distribution for a hypothesis which has r training errors is proportional to $e^{-\sigma r} = C^r$, where $C = e^{-\sigma}$. We are now ready to give the main result of this section.

Theorem 5.3
Under the above assumptions the margin of the Bayes Classifier $F(x) \in \mathcal{C}(H)$ is given by

$$1 - \frac{2C}{1+C}. \tag{5.13}$$

Proof Let the set of training examples be $(\mathbf{x}_1, \ldots, \mathbf{x}_\ell)$ with classifications $\mathbf{y} = (y_1, \ldots, y_\ell) \in \{-1,1\}^\ell$ and let the margin M of example i be $M_i = y_i F(\mathbf{x}_i)$. Consider first the average margin

$$\begin{aligned} < M > &= \frac{1}{\ell}\sum_{i\in S} M_i = \frac{1}{\ell}\sum_{i\in S} y_i F(\mathbf{x}_i) = \frac{1}{\ell}\sum_{i\in S} y_i \int_{\lambda\in\Lambda} a_h h(\mathbf{x}_i) dP(h) \\ &= \frac{1}{\ell}\sum_{i\in S} y_i \sum_{j\in J} a_j P_j f_j(\mathbf{x}_i), \end{aligned}$$

where f_j, $j \in J$ are representatives of each possible classification of the sample. We are denoting by P_j the prior probability of classifiers agreeing with f_j. The quantity $a_j P_j$ is the posterior probability of these classifiers, where the coefficient $a_j = Ae^{-\sigma\ell\epsilon_j} = AC^{\ell\epsilon_j}$ is the evidence, which depends only on the empirical error and the normalising constant A. By assumption, we have

$$\sum_{r \text{ error shell}} P_j = \binom{\ell}{r}\frac{1}{2^\ell}.$$

Hence,

$$\begin{aligned} < M > &= \frac{1}{\ell}\sum_{j\in J} a_j P_j \sum_{i\in S} y_i f_j(\mathbf{x}_i), = \frac{1}{\ell}\sum_{j\in J} a_j P_j B_j \\ &= \sum_{j\in J} a_j P_j (1-2\epsilon_j) = 1 - 2\sum_{j\in J} a_j P_j \epsilon_j, \end{aligned} \tag{5.14}$$

by the observation concerning the balance B_j of f_j and the fact that the posterior distribution has been normalised, that is $1 = \int_H a_h dP(h) = \sum_{j\in J} a_j P_j$.

We now regroup the elements of the sum on the right hand side of the above equation by decomposing the hypothesis space into error shells (subsets of H formed by hypotheses with the same error r). Hence, we can write the above sum as

$$\sum_{j\in J} a_j P_j \epsilon_j = \frac{1}{2^\ell}\sum_{r=0}^{\ell} AC^r \binom{\ell}{r}\frac{r}{\ell}. \tag{5.15}$$

Solving for A and substituting, gives

$$\sum_{j\in J} a_j P_j \epsilon_j = \frac{\sum_k C^r \binom{\ell}{r}\frac{r}{\ell}}{\sum_r C^r \binom{\ell}{r}} \tag{5.16}$$

We can now use the equality $\sum_r C^r \binom{\ell}{r} = (1+C)^\ell$, and the observation that $\sum_r C^r \binom{\ell}{r} r$ can be written as $C\frac{d}{dC}\sum_r C^r \binom{\ell}{r} = \ell C(1+C)^{\ell-1}$ to obtain the result for the average margin.

To complete the proof we must show that the average margin is in fact the minimal margin. We will demonstrate this by showing that the margin of all points is equal. Intuitively, this follows from the symmetry of the situation, there being nothing to distinguish between different training points in the structure of the hypothesis.

More formally, note that for every output sequence $\mathbf{z} = (\mathbf{z}_1, \ldots, \mathbf{z}_\ell)$, we can realise the mapping $\mathbf{x}_i \mapsto \mathbf{z}_i, i = 1, \ldots, \ell$, with a function $f_\mathbf{z} \in H$.

Let $s(\mathbf{z})$ be the sequence obtained by swapping the i-th and j-th entries in the sequence $\mathbf{z}$ swapping their signs if the i-th and j-th inputs have opposite classifications according to the training sequence $\mathbf{y}$. Note that s is a bijection of the set of all sequences onto itself. Note also that if a_h is the posterior distribution over the function class H, $a_{f_\mathbf{z}} = a_{f_{s(\mathbf{z})}}$, since the number of errors of the two functions is the same — $f_\mathbf{z}$ is correct on input i precisely when $f_{s(\mathbf{z})}$ is correct on j, that is

$$y_i f_\mathbf{z}(\mathbf{x}_i) = y_j f_{s(\mathbf{z})}(\mathbf{x}_j). \tag{5.17}$$

Now consider the Bayesian posterior function

$$F(x) = \frac{1}{2^\ell}\sum_\mathbf{z} a_{f_\mathbf{z}} f_\mathbf{z}(x). \tag{5.18}$$

The margin of this function on the point $\mathbf{x}_i$ is

$$y_i F(\mathbf{x}_i) = \frac{1}{2^\ell}\sum_\mathbf{z} a_{f_\mathbf{z}} y_i f_\mathbf{z}(\mathbf{x}_i) = \frac{1}{2^\ell}\sum_\mathbf{z} a_{f_\mathbf{z}} y_i f_{s(\mathbf{z})}(\mathbf{x}_i), \tag{5.19}$$

since s is a bijection and weights are unchanged. Hence,

$$y_i F(\mathbf{x}_i) = \frac{1}{2^\ell}\sum_\mathbf{z} a_{f_\mathbf{z}} y_j f_\mathbf{z}(\mathbf{x}_j) = y_j F(\mathbf{x}_j) \tag{5.20}$$

and the margins of the points i and j are equal. Since, i and j are arbitrary all margins are equal and the result is proved. ■

Since the assumption that the underlying hypothesis space can perform any classification of the training set implies that its VC dimension is at least ℓ, we cannot expect that learning is possible in the situation described. Indeed, we have augmented the power of the hypothesis space by taking our functions from the convex hull of H which would appear to make the situation yet worse.

Nonetheless Theorem 5.3 shows that the margin of the Bayes classifier is indeed large under the assumptions we have made, provided a suitable choice of the parameter C is made. A calculation of the effective VC dimension in this case will be made later, though it is too large for any bound on the generalization error to be made. We must make assumptions about the prior in order to be able to learn.

Before proceeding to consider the effect of the prior on the effective VC bound, we will mention two other theorems that might be useful for bounding the generalization error in terms of the margin. We will, however, argue that they are unable to take account of our type of prior that assigns different probabilities to hypotheses. We will quote the theorems from Schapire et al. (1998), though they appear in a more general form in (Bartlett, 1998a).

Following Schapire et al. (1998), let H denote the space from which the base hypotheses are chosen (for example Neural Networks, or Decision Trees). A base hypothesis $f \in H$ is a mapping from an instance space X to $\{-1, +1\}$.

VC bound

Theorem 5.4

Let S be a sample of ℓ examples chosen independently at random according to D. Assume that the base hypothesis space H has VC dimension d, and let be $\delta > 0$. Then, with probability at least $1 - \delta$ over the random choice of the training set S, every weighted average function $f \in \mathcal{C}(H)$ satisfies the following bound for all $\theta > 0$:

$$P_D[yF(x) \leq 0] \leq P_S[yF(x) \leq \theta] + O\left(\frac{1}{\sqrt{\ell}}\left(\frac{d\log^2(\ell/d)}{\theta^2}) + \log(1/\delta\right)^{1/2}\right) \quad (5.21)$$

Finite H bound

Theorem 5.5

Let S be a sample of ℓ examples chosen independently at random according to D. Assume that the base hypothesis space H is finite, and let be $\delta > 0$. Then, with probability at least $1-\delta$ over the random choice of the training set S, every weighted average function $f \in \mathcal{C}(H)$ satisfies the following bound for all $\theta > 0$:

$$P_D[yF(x) \leq 0] \leq P_S[yF(x) \leq \theta] + O\left(\frac{1}{\sqrt{\ell}}\left(\frac{\log^2(\ell)\log|H|}{\theta^2}) + \log(1/\delta\right)^{1/2}\right) \quad (5.22)$$

As observed by the authors, the theorem applies to *every* majority vote method, including boosting, bagging, ECOC, etc.

In order to obtain useful applications of any of the theorems we will need to consider deviations from the most general situation described above. The deviation should not have a significant impact on the margin, while reducing the expressive power of the hypotheses.

In order to apply Theorem 5.5 the number of hypotheses in the base class H must be finite. The logarithm of the number of hypotheses appears in the result. Since we have assumed that all possible classifications of the training set can be performed the number of hypotheses must be at least 2^ℓ making the bound uninteresting. To apply this theorem we must assume that a very large proportion of the hypotheses have zero weight in the prior, while those that have significant weights in the posterior (i.e. have low empirical error) are retained. Making this assumption the bound will become significant. However, we are interested in capturing the effect of non-discrete priors, that is situations where potentially all of the base hypotheses are included, but those with high empirical error have lower prior probability.

In order to apply Theorem 5.4 the underlying hypothesis class H must be assumed to have low VC dimension in such a way that no significant impact is made on the margin. This could be achieved by removing high error functions. Note that the functions would have to be removed, in other words given prior probability 0. Hence, the bound obtained would be no better than a standard VC bound in the original space. A situation where this approach and analysis might be advantageous is where the consistent hypothesis $f_{\mathbf{y}}$ is not included in H. This will reduce the margin by approximately $a_{f_{\mathbf{y}}} 2^{-\ell} = (1+C)^{-\ell}$, since $B_{f_{\mathbf{y}}} = \ell$ (see equation (5.14)). The approximation arises from not adjusting the normalisation to take account of the missing hypothesis and is thus a very small error.

These applications are unable to take into account the prior distribution in a flexible way. In the next section we will present an application of the original approach to show how this can take advantage of a beneficial prior.

5.3.2 The Effect of the Prior Distribution on the Margin Bound

Non neutral prior

We will consider the situation where the prior decays arithmetically with the error shells. In other words the prior on hypotheses with error r is multiplied by ρ^r for some $\rho < 1$. We first repeat the calculations of Theorem 5.3 for this case. The sum (5.15) must take into account that in this case

$$\sum_{r \text{ error shell}} P_j = \rho^r (1+\rho)^{-\ell} \binom{\ell}{r}. \tag{5.23}$$

The factor $(1+\rho)^\ell$ cancels and the factor ρ appears wherever C appears, that is

$$\sum_{j \in J} a_j P_j \epsilon_j = \frac{1}{(1+\rho)^\ell} \sum_{r=0}^{\ell} A C^r \rho^r \binom{\ell}{r} \frac{r}{\ell}, \tag{5.24}$$

while

$$\frac{A}{(1+\rho)^\ell} \sum_{r=0}^{\ell} C^r \rho^r \binom{\ell}{r} = 1. \tag{5.25}$$

Hence, we have shown the following generalization of Theorem 5.3.

Theorem 5.6

Under the above assumptions of a beneficial prior the margin of the Bayes Classifier $F(x) \in \mathcal{C}(H)$ is given by

$$1 - \frac{2\rho C}{1+\rho C}. \tag{5.26}$$

We must further compute the value of $\|a\|$ for the posterior functional in the prior described above. The integral in this case is given by

$$\begin{aligned}\|a\|^2 &= \sum_{j \in J} a_j^2 P_j = \sum_{k=0}^{\ell} A^2 C^{2r} \frac{\rho^r}{(1+\rho)^\ell} \binom{\ell}{r} \\ &= \frac{(1+\rho)^\ell (1+\rho C^2)^\ell}{(1+\rho C)^{2\ell}}.\end{aligned}$$

We can now combine this value with the margin computed above to give the value of the fat shattering dimension from Theorem 5.2 at the appropriate scale. This bound on the effective VC dimension becomes,

$$g(\rho, C) := \frac{(1+\rho)^\ell (1+\rho C^2)^\ell}{(1+\rho C)^{2\ell-2}(1-\rho C)^2}, \tag{5.27}$$

where to keep the formulae simple we have ignored the factor of 64 arising for the scale $\gamma/8$ in Theorem 5.1.

In the rest of this section we will consider how this function behaves for various choices of C and ρ, showing that for careful choices of C, and values of ρ close to 1 can give dimensions significantly lower than ℓ, hence give good bounds on the generalization error. The analysis shows that using this approach it is possible to make use of a beneficial prior. At the same time it suggests a value of C most likely to take advantage of such a prior.

First consider the case when $\rho = 1$, that is the uninformative prior considered in section 5.3.1. Hence,

$$g(1, C) = \frac{2^\ell (1+C^2)^\ell}{(1+C)^{2\ell-2}(1-C)^2}. \tag{5.28}$$

The parameter C can be chosen in the range $[0, 1)$. However, $g(1, C) \underset{C \to 1}{\longrightarrow} \infty$, while $g(1, 0) = 2^\ell$. Clearly, the optimal choice of C needs to be determined if the bound is to be useful. A routine calculation establishes that the value of C which minimises the expression is, $C_0 = (\ell - \sqrt{\ell - 1})/(\ell - 2)$, which gives a value of

$$g(1, C_0) = \ell \left(1 + \frac{1}{\ell - 1}\right)^{\ell - 1} \approx e\ell. \tag{5.29}$$

This confirms that the effective VC dimension is not increased excessively provided C is chosen around $1 - 2/\sqrt{\ell}$, though of course the bound is trivial in this case. The analysis so far can be viewed as a 'sanity check', demonstrating that despite significantly increasing the computational power of the hypothesis class (by moving to $\mathcal{C}(H)$), the increase in the effective VC dimension has been very slight. In order to see how the prior can produce a non-trivial bound, we will study the effect of allowing ρ to move slightly below 1. We will perform a Taylor expansion about $\rho = 1$.

Let $C' = \rho C$ and the function

$$g_1(\rho, C') := g(\rho, C'/\rho) = \frac{(1+\rho)^\ell (1 + C'^2/\rho)^\ell}{(1+C')^{2\ell-2}(1-C')^2}. \tag{5.30}$$

Note that $\left.\frac{\partial g_1(\rho,C')}{\partial C'}\right|_{\rho=1} = 0$, and so $\frac{\partial g(\rho,C_0)}{\partial \rho} = \frac{\partial g_1(\rho,C')}{\partial \rho} + \frac{\partial g_1(\rho,C')}{\partial C'}\frac{dC'}{d\rho}$. Hence,

$$\left.\frac{\partial g(\rho, C_0)}{\partial \rho}\right|_{\rho=1} = \left.\frac{\partial g_1(\rho, C')}{\partial \rho}\right|_{\rho=1}. \tag{5.31}$$

Differentiating gives

$$\left.\frac{\partial g_1(\rho, C')}{\partial \rho}\right|_{\rho=1} = \frac{\ell 2^{\ell-1}(1+C'^2)^{\ell-1}}{(1+C')^{2\ell-3}(1-C')} \tag{5.32}$$

We can now perform a Taylor series expansion of $g(\rho, C_0)$ about $\rho = 1$ to obtain $g(\rho, C_0) \approx e\ell(1 + (\rho-1)\sqrt{\ell-1})$, where we have omitted some routine calculations.

Hence, the bound on the generalization error is (ignoring log factors)

Effect of prior

$$\tilde{O}(1 - (1-\rho)\sqrt{\ell - 1}), \tag{5.33}$$

so that to obtain generalization error of order ϵ, we need

$$\rho \approx 1 - \frac{1 - \epsilon/(e \log \ell)}{\sqrt{\ell - 1}}. \tag{5.34}$$

Hence, for values of ρ very close to 1, the prior can result in improved generalization properties. Note that the value of C used in the calculations is unchanged so that we can take advantage of the prior without any fine tuning of the system. We simply observe the margin, and the value of $\|a\|$ on the Monte-Carlo generated set of hypotheses, to recover a bound on the effective VC dimension and hence an estimate of the generalization error.

5.4 Conclusions

Our theoretical analysis shows that Bayesian Classifiers of the kind described in (Neal, 1996) can be regarded as large margin hyperplanes in a Hilbert space, and consequently can be analysed with the tools of data-dependent VC theory.

The non-linear mapping from the input space to the Hilbert space is given by the initial choice of network architecture, while the coordinates of the hyperplane are given by the Bayes' posterior and hence depend both on the training data and on the chosen prior.

The choice of the prior turns out to be a crucial one, since we have shown how even slightly correctly guessed priors can translate into lower effective VC dimensions of the resulting classifier (and this — coupled with high training accuracy — ensures good generalization). But even with a totally uninformative prior there is at least no harm in using these apparently overcomplex systems.

Unified framework

The main theoretical result of this paper is to co-locate Bayesian Classifiers in the same category of other systems — namely Support Vector Machines and Adaboost — which were motivated by very different considerations but which exhibited very similar behaviours (e.g. with respect to overfitting). A unified analysis of the three systems is now possible, which can make potentially fruitful comparisons and cross-fertilizations much easier.

Experimental results confirming the predictions of the model on some benchmark problems can be found in (Cristianini et al., 1998).

Acknowledgements

Nello Cristianini is funded by EPSRC research grant number GR/L28562. John Shawe-Taylor was supported in part by the EPSRC research grant number GR/K70366.

We wish to thank Chris Williams and Peter Sykacek for many useful discussions about Bayesian Learning Algorithms.

6 Support Vector Machines, Reproducing Kernel Hilbert Spaces, and Randomized GACV

Grace Wahba
Department of Statistics, University of Wisconsin-Madison
1210 W. Dayton St., Madison WI 53706, USA
wahba@stat.wisc.edu
http://www.stat.wisc.edu/~wahba

This chapter is an expanded version of a talk presented in the NIPS 97 Workshop on Support Vector Machines. It consists of three parts: (1) A brief review of some old but relevant results on constrained optimization in Reproducing Kernel Hilbert Spaces (RKHS), and a review of the relationship between zero-mean Gaussian processes and RKHS. Application of tensor sums and products of RKHS including smoothing spline ANOVA spaces in the context of SVMs is also described. (2) A discussion of the relationship between penalized likelihood methods in RKHS for Bernoulli data when the goal is risk factor estimation, and SVM methods in RKHS when the goal is classification. When the goal is classification it is noted that replacing the likelihood functional of the logit (log odds ratio) with an appropriate SVM functional is a natural method for concentrating computational effort on estimating the logit near the classification boundary and ignoring data far away. Remarks concerning the potential of SVMs for variable selection as an efficient preprocessor for risk factor estimation are made. (3) A discussion of how the the GACV (Generalized Approximate Cross Validation) for choosing smoothing parameters proposed in Xiang and Wahba (1996, 1997) may be adapted and implemented in the context of certain convex SVMs.

6.1 Introduction

Several old results in Reproducing Kernel Hilbert Spaces (RKHS) and Gaussian processes are proving to be very useful in the application of support vector machine

(SVM) methods in classification. In section 6.2 of this chapter we very briefly review some of these results. RKHS can be chosen tailored to the problem at hand in many ways, and we review a few of them, including radial basis function and smoothing spline ANOVA spaces.

Girosi (1998); Smola and Schölkopf (1998b); Schölkopf et al. (1997b) and others have noted the relationship between SVMs and penalty methods as used in the statistical theory of nonparametric regression. In section 6.3 we elaborate on this, and show how replacing the likelihood functional of the logit (log odds ratio) in penalized likelihood methods for Bernoulli [yes-no] data, with certain other functionals of the logit (to be called SVM functionals) results in several of the SVMs that are of modern research interest. The SVM functionals we consider more closely resemble a "goodness-of-fit" measured by classification error than a "goodness-of-fit" measured by the comparative Kullback-Leibler distance, which is frequently associated with likelihood functionals. This observation is not new or profound, but it is hoped that the discussion here will help to bridge the conceptual gap between classical nonparametric regression via penalized likelihood methods, and SVMs in RKHS. Furthermore, since SVMs can be expected to provide more compact representations of the desired classification boundaries than boundaries based on estimating the logit by penalized likelihood methods, they have potential as a prescreening or model selection tool in sifting through many variables or regions of attribute space to find influential quantities, even when the ultimate goal is not classification, but to understand how the logit varies as the important variables change throughout their range. This is potentially applicable to the variable/model selection problem in demographic medical risk factor studies as described, for example in Wahba et al. (1994, 1995b).

When using SVM functionals to produce classification boundaries, typically a tradeoff must be made between the size of the SVM functional and the 'smoothness' or complexity of the logit function. This tradeoff is in the first instance embodied in smoothing parameters. In section 6.4 we discuss how the GACV for choosing smoothing parameters proposed in Xiang and Wahba (1996, 1997) may be adapted to some support vector machines.

6.2 Some Facts About RKHS

6.2.1 The Moore-Aronszajn Theorem

Let $\mathcal{T}$ be a set, for example, $\mathcal{T} = \{1, 2, \cdots, N\}, \mathcal{T} = [0, 1]$, or $\mathcal{T} = E^d$, (Euclidean d-space), or $\mathcal{T} = \mathcal{S}_d$, (the d-dimensional sphere). A real symmetric function $K(s,t), s,t \in \mathcal{T}$ is said to be positive definite on $\mathcal{T} \times \mathcal{T}$ if for every $n = 1, 2, \cdots$, and every set of real numbers $\{a_1, a_2, \cdots, a_n\}$ and $t_1, t_2, \cdots t_n,\ t_i \in \mathcal{T}$, we have $\sum_{i,j=1}^{n} a_i a_j K(t_i, t_j) \geq 0$. We have the famous

Moore-Aronszajn Theorem

Theorem 6.1 (Moore-Aronszajn, Aronszajn (1950))
To every positive definite function K on $\mathcal{T} \times \mathcal{T}$ there corresponds a unique RKHS $\mathcal{H}_K$ of real valued functions on $\mathcal{T}$ and vice versa.

The proof is trivial. We just suggest how to construct $\mathcal{H}_K$ given K. Let $K_t(s)$ be the function of s obtained by fixing t and letting $K_t(s) \doteq K(s,t)$. $\mathcal{H}_K$ consists of all finite linear combinations of the form $\sum_{\ell=1}^{L} a_\ell K_{t_\ell}$ with $t_\ell \in \mathcal{T}$ and limits of such functions as the t_ℓ become dense in $\mathcal{T}$, in the norm induced by the inner product

$$< K_s, K_t >_{\mathcal{H}_K} = K(s,t). \tag{6.1}$$

See Wahba (1990) for further details on most of the material in this section. The positive definiteness of K guarantees that (6.1) defines a bona fide inner product. (Furthermore strong limits here imply pointwise limits.[1]) The function $K_t(\cdot)$ is the so-called representer of evaluation at t in $\mathcal{H}_K$ - i.e.: For any $f \in \mathcal{H}_K$ and fixed t

$$< f, K_t >_{\mathcal{H}_K} = f(t), \tag{6.2}$$

where $< \cdot, \cdot >_{\mathcal{H}_K}$ is the inner product in $\mathcal{H}_K$. If $K(s,t)$ has a representation of the form

$$K(s,t) = \sum_{\nu} \lambda_\nu \Psi_\nu(s) \Psi_\nu(t) \tag{6.3}$$

with $\int_{\mathcal{T}} \Psi_\xi(s)\Psi_\eta(s)d\mu(s) = 1$ if $\xi = \eta$, and 0 otherwise, where μ is some measure on $\mathcal{T}$, then $< f, g >_{\mathcal{H}_K} = \sum_\nu \frac{f_\nu g_\nu}{\lambda_\nu}$ where $f_\nu = \int \Psi_\nu(s) f(s) d\mu(s)$ and similarly for g_ν. In particular $< \Psi_\xi, \Psi_\eta >_{\mathcal{H}_K} = \frac{1}{\lambda_\xi}$ if $\xi = \eta$ and 0 otherwise. Examples of μ include Lebesgue measure on [0,1] and counting measure on $\{1, 2, \cdots, N\}$. $K(\cdot, \cdot)$ is known as the reproducing kernel (RK) for $\mathcal{H}_K$, due to the 'reproducing property' (6.1).

Reproducing Kernel

6.2.2 The Representer Theorem

Let $\mathcal{T}$ be an index set, $\mathcal{H}_K$ be an RKHS of real valued functions on $\mathcal{T}$ with RK $K(\cdot, \cdot)$. Let $\{y_i, t_i, i = 1, 2, \cdots n\}$ be given (the "training set"), with t_i (the "attribute vector") $\in \mathcal{T}$. y_i is the "response" (usually a real number, but may be more general, see Wahba (1992)). Let $\{\phi_\nu\}_{\nu=1}^{M}$ be M functions on $\mathcal{T}$ [2] with the property that the $n \times M$ matrix T with $i\nu$th entry $\phi_\nu(t_i)$ is of rank M. ("Least squares regression on *span* $\{\phi_\nu\}$ is unique.") Let $g_i(y_i, f)$ be a functional of f which depends on f only through $f(t_i) \doteq f_i$, that is, $g_i(y_i, f) \doteq g_i(y_i, f_i)$. Then we have:

Representer Theorem

Theorem 6.2 (Representer Theorem, Kimeldorf and Wahba (1971))
Any solution to the problem: find $f \in span\ \{\phi_\nu\} + h$ with $h \in \mathcal{H}_K$ to minimize

$$\frac{1}{n}\sum_{i=1}^{n} g_i(y_i, f_i) + \lambda \|h\|^2_{\mathcal{H}_K} \tag{6.4}$$

1. i.e. $\|f_n - f\| \to 0 \Rightarrow |f_n(t) - f(t)|$, every $t \in \mathcal{T}$.
2. Sufficient conditions on the $\{t_i\}$ for existence are being assumed.

has a representation of the form

$$f(\cdot) = \sum_{\nu=1}^{M} d_\nu \phi_\nu(\cdot) + \sum_{i=1}^{n} c_i K(t_i, \cdot). \tag{6.5}$$

Remark 1 This theorem is explicitly stated in Kimeldorf and Wahba (1971) only for $g_i(y_i, f_i) = (y_i - f_i)^2$ and (letting $y_i = (y_{i1}, y_{i2})$) for $g_i(y_i, f_i) = 0, y_{i1} \leq f_i \leq y_{i2}, = \infty$ otherwise. However, the extension to general g_i is obvious from the argument there (and has appeared in various places, see, for example Cox and O'Sullivan (1990)). One of the most popular support vector machines corresponds to the case $M = 1$, $\phi_1(t) \equiv 1$ and $g_i(y_i, f_i) = V_\epsilon(y_i - f_i)$, where V_ϵ, Vapnik's ϵ-insensitive loss function, is given by $V_\epsilon(u) = max\{0, |u| - \epsilon\}$. f of the form (6.5) is substituted back into (6.4), resulting in an optimization problem in the unknown d_1 and $c = (c_1, \cdots, c_n)'$. Details concerning how this optimization problem is converted to the familiar SVM QP may be found, e.g. in Girosi (1998), see also Vapnik (1995).

Remark 2 Probably the best known example of this problem is the case $\mathcal{T} = [0, 1], M = 2, \|h\|^2_{\mathcal{H}_K} = \int_0^1 (h''(u))^2 du, \phi_1(t) = 1, \phi_2(t) = t$. Then f is a cubic spline with knots at the data points, see Kimeldorf and Wahba (1971); Wahba (1990) for details. Reproducing kernels for $\|h\|^2_{\mathcal{H}_K} = \int_0^1 [(L_m f)(u)]^2 du$ where L_m is a differential operator with a null space spanned by a Tchebychev system are found in Kimeldorf and Wahba (1971) and involve Green's functions for $L_m{*}L_m$. Typically ϕ_1 is a constant function and the ϕ_νs are linear or low degree polynomials. Under certain circumstances a large λ in (6.4) will force the minimizer into $span\{\phi_\nu\}$. In Kimeldorf and Wahba (1971); Wahba (1990) this theorem is stated for $f \in \mathcal{H}_{\tilde{K}}$ where $\mathcal{H}_K$ is a subspace of $\mathcal{H}_{\tilde{K}}$ of codimension M orthogonal to $span\{\phi_\nu\}$.

Remark 3 Let $'$ denote transpose. If we make some assumptions a simple proof exists that the coefficient vector c of any minimizer satisfies $T'c = 0$. First, note that

$$\begin{pmatrix} f_1 \\ \vdots \\ f_n \end{pmatrix} = Kc + Td, \tag{6.6}$$

where $d = (d_1, \cdots d_M)'$ and (with some abuse of notation) we are letting K be the $n \times n$ matrix with i, jth entry $K(t_i, t_j)$ (where it will be clear from the context that we mean K is an $n \times n$ matrix rather than an RK). Similarly, note that $\|\sum_{i=1}^n c_i K_{t_i}\|^2_{\mathcal{H}_K} = c'Kc$. The vectors c and d are found as the minimizers of

$$\frac{1}{n} \sum_{i=1}^{n} g_i(y_i, f_i) + \lambda c' K c. \tag{6.7}$$

Assuming that we can differentiate g_i with respect to f_i, differentiating (6.7)with respect to c and d gives

$$\frac{1}{n}K\frac{\partial g}{\partial f} = -2\lambda K c \tag{6.8}$$

$$\frac{1}{n}T'\frac{\partial g}{\partial f} = 0 \tag{6.9}$$

where $\frac{\partial g}{\partial f} = (\frac{\partial g_1}{\partial f_1}, \cdots, \frac{\partial g_n}{\partial f_n})'$, and, assuming K is of full rank, and multiplying (6.8) by K^{-1} and substituting the result into (6.9) gives the result.

Remark 4 If the matrix K is not of full rank, as would happen if, for example, $K(\cdot, \cdot)$ is of the form

$$K(s,t) = \sum_{\mu=1}^{N} \Psi_\mu(s)\Psi_\mu(t) \tag{6.10}$$

with $N < n$ then c is not uniquely determined by the setup in (6.8), (6.9). Here $\mathcal{H}_K$ contains at most N linearly independent functions. Letting X be the $n \times N$ matrix with i, μ th entry $\Psi_\mu(t_i)$ then $K = XX'$, and if c is a minimizer of (6.7), then $c + \delta$, where δ is orthogonal to the column span of X will also be a minimizer. We may substitute $c = X\gamma$ where γ is an N vector into (6.7), then Kc becomes $X\tilde{\gamma}$ and $c'Kc$ becomes $\tilde{\gamma}'\tilde{\gamma}$, where $\tilde{\gamma} = X'X\gamma$. For uniqueness we also need that if $f(t) = \sum_{\nu=1}^{M} d_\nu \phi_\nu(t)$, then $argmin_d \sum_{i=1}^{n} g_i(y_i, f_i)$ is unique. If the g_i are strictly convex functions of f_i this will be true whenever T is of full column rank. However, the strict convexity will be violated in some of the cases we consider later.

Remark 5 Characterization of isotropic RKs on E^d may be found in Skorokhod and Yadrenko (1973) and some examples along with their RKHS norms are given in the slides for my NIPS 96 workshop talk available via my home page. Characterization of isotropic RKs on the sphere may be found in Schoenberg (1942) and some examples along with their RKHS norms may be found in Wahba (1981, 1982b). $K(s,t)$ of the form $\int_{u \in \mathcal{U}} G(t,u)G(s,u)du$ will always be positive definite if the integral exists.

Remark 6 If $R_1(u_1, v_1), u_1, v_1 \in \mathcal{T}^{(1)}$ and $R_2(u_2, v_2), u_2, v_2 \in \mathcal{T}^{(2)}$ are positive definite functions on $\mathcal{T}^{(1)} \otimes \mathcal{T}^{(1)}$ and $\mathcal{T}^{(2)} \otimes \mathcal{T}^{(2)}$ respectively, then both the tensor product and the tensor sum of R_1 and R_2 are positive definite. That is, letting $\mathcal{T} = \mathcal{T}^{(1)} \otimes \mathcal{T}^{(2)}$, $s = (u_1, u_2) \in \mathcal{T}, t = (v_1, v_2) \in \mathcal{T}$, we have that $K(s,t) = R_1(u_1, v_1)R_2(u_2, v_2)$ and $K(s,t) = R_1(u_1, v_1) + R_2(u_2, v_2)$ are both positive definite on $\mathcal{T} \otimes \mathcal{T}$.

Remark 7 Re: Smoothing Spline ANOVA Spaces: Let $\mathcal{H}_K^\alpha$ be an RKHS of functions on $\mathcal{T}^{(\alpha)}$, for $\alpha = 1, \cdots, d$, and suppose $\mathcal{H}_K^\alpha$ has an orthogonal decomposition

$$\mathcal{H}_K^\alpha = [1^{(\alpha)}] \oplus \mathcal{H}_K^{(\alpha)} \tag{6.11}$$

where $[1^{(\alpha)}]$ is the one-dimensional space of constants on $\mathcal{T}^{(\alpha)}$, and let $R_\alpha(s^\alpha, t^\alpha)$ be the RK for $\mathcal{H}_K^{(\alpha)}$. Examples may be found in Wahba et al. (1994, 1995b) and Gu and Wahba (1993). A Smoothing Spline ANOVA space $\mathcal{H}_K$ of functions on

$\mathcal{T} = \mathcal{T}^{(1)} \otimes \cdots \otimes \mathcal{T}^{(d)}$ may be constructed by defining $\mathcal{H}_K$ as

$$\mathcal{H}_K = \prod_{\alpha=1}^{d} [[1^{(\alpha)}] \oplus \mathcal{H}_K^{(\alpha)}] \tag{6.12}$$

which then has the RK

$$K(s,t) = \prod_{\alpha=1}^{d} [1 + R_\alpha(s^\alpha, t^\alpha)] \tag{6.13}$$

$$= 1 + \sum_{\alpha=1}^{d} R_\alpha(s^\alpha, t^\alpha) + \sum_{\alpha<\beta} R_\alpha(s^\alpha, t^\alpha) R_\beta(s^\beta, t^\beta) + \ldots + \prod_{\alpha=1}^{d} R_\alpha(s^\alpha, t^\alpha) \tag{6.14}$$

Ordinarily the series in (6.14) is truncated somewhere and the direct sum of the corresponding subspaces in the corresponding expansion in (6.12) (which are orthogonal in this construction) constitute the 'model space.' Multiple smoothing parameters can be arranged by multiplying each of the individual RKs which remain in (6.14) after truncation, by $\theta_\alpha, \theta_{\alpha\beta}, \cdots$, and so forth. See Wahba (1990); Wahba et al. (1995b) for details. The so-called main effects spaces, which involve only one t^α at a time are particularly popular, see Hastie and Tibshirani (1990).

Remark 8 The Smoothing Spline ANOVA spaces can be built up including conditionally positive definite functions (Micchelli, 1986), leading to thin plate spline components (Gu and Wahba, 1993), we omit the details.

6.2.3 Gaussian Processes, The Isometric Isomorphism Theorem

The relationship between conditional expectations on Gaussian processes and solutions to variational problems in RKHS has been known for a long time, see Wahba (1990); Kimeldorf and Wahba (1970, 1971); Wahba (1978). This is not a coincidence. Let $X(t), t \in \mathcal{T}$ be a zero mean Gaussian stochastic process with $EX(s)X(t) = K(s,t)$. The Hilbert space $\mathcal{X}_K$ spanned by this stochastic process can be defined as all finite linear combinations of all random variables of the form $\sum_{\ell=1}^{L} a_\ell X(t_\ell)$ with $t_\ell \in \mathcal{T}$ and limits of such functions in the norm induced by the inner product

Gaussian Process

$$EX(s)X(t) = K(s,t). \tag{6.15}$$

Then we have

Isometric Isomorphism Theorem

Theorem 6.3 (Isometric Isomorphism Theorem, Parzen (1962, 1970))

To every RKHS $\mathcal{H}_K$ there corresponds a zero mean Gaussian stochastic process $X(t), t \in \mathcal{T}$ with covariance $K(s,t)$. There is an isometric isomorphism [one-one inner product preserving map] between $\mathcal{X}_K$, the Hilbert space spanned by this stochastic process, and $\mathcal{H}_K$, whereby the random variable $X(t) \in \mathcal{X}_K$ corresponds to the representer $K_t \in \mathcal{H}_K$.

The proof is trivial, details may be found in Wahba (1990). We note that sample functions of $X(t), t \in \mathcal{T}$ are not in $\mathcal{H}_K$ (with probability 1) if $\mathcal{H}_K$ is infinite dimensional. One may understand why this should be true by considering the case where K has a representation of the form (6.3). Then X has a Karhunen-Loeve expansion, namely

$$X(t) = \sum_\nu \xi_\nu \Psi_\nu(t) \tag{6.16}$$

where the ξs are independent, zero mean Gaussian random variables with variance λ_ν, and a little algebra shows that $EX(s)X(t) = K(s,t)$ and also that the expected value of the RKHS norm if it exists, would be

$$E\|X(\cdot)\|^2_{\mathcal{H}_K} = \sum_\nu E\frac{\xi_\nu^2}{\lambda_\nu} \tag{6.17}$$

but this will be ∞ if $\mathcal{H}_K$ is infinite dimensional. This has consequences for how one might choose smoothing and other parameters, see, for example Wahba (1985a).

6.3 From Soft Classification to Hard Classification to SVMs

6.3.1 Hard Classification

Let $\mathcal{T}$ be a set as before, one observes n instances, $\{y_i, t_i\}, i = 1, \cdots, n, y_i \in \{+1, -1\}$ [the training set], where $t_i \in \mathcal{T}$ and $y_i = +1$ if the ith instance is member of class $\mathcal{A}$ and $y_i = -1$ if it is in class $\mathcal{B}$. Consider a random model for $\{y, t\}$:

$$Prob\{y = +1|t\} = p(t) \tag{6.18}$$
$$Prob\{y = -1|t\} = 1 - p(t) \tag{6.19}$$

Log Odds Ratio

Let $f(t) = \ln(p(t)/(1-p(t))$ be the logit [also called the log odds ratio]. Assuming that the cost of misclassification is the same for both kinds of misclassification, then the optimal strategy for generalization, [minimization of expected loss], if one knew f, would be to classify as $\mathcal{A}$ if $f(t) > 0$ and $\mathcal{B}$ if $f(t) < 0$. Thus, letting $[f]_* = 1$ if $f > 0$ and 0 otherwise, one really wants to know sign f, equivalently it is desired to estimate $[-f(t)]_*$ from the training set $\{y_i, t_i\}, i = 1, \cdots, n$. This particular formulation is convenient, because we note that if $\hat{f}$ is used for classification, then the number of misclassifications on the training set will just be $\sum_{i=1}^n [-y_i \hat{f}(t_i)]_*$.

6.3.2 Soft Classification

If, on the other hand one's goal is not simply classification, but to understand how the relative risk $[e^{f(t)}]$ of $\mathcal{A}$ to $\mathcal{B}$, varies with t, as is frequently the case in demographic and environmental studies, then one is interested in estimating the actual value of f for all t in a region of $\mathcal{T}$, for which one is likely to have future observations. See, for example, Wahba et al. (1994, 1995b). In this latter case one might estimate f from the training set by the methods of penalized log likelihood, that is, one finds f in $\{span\ \phi_\nu\} \oplus \mathcal{H}_K$ to minimize

$$\frac{1}{n}\sum_{i=1}^{n} \mathcal{L}(y_i, f_i) + \lambda \|h\|^2_{\mathcal{H}_K}. \tag{6.20}$$

Here, $f_i \doteq f(t_i)$ and $\mathcal{L}(y_i, f_i)$ is the negative log likelihood function.[3] In this example the likelihood that $y_i = 1$ is $p(t_i)$, and the likelihood that $y_i = -1$ is $(1 - p(t_i))$. Thus $\mathcal{L}(y_i, f_i) \doteq l(y_i f_i)$ where $l(\tau) = ln(1 + e^{-\tau})$. To see this, let $p_i \doteq p(t_i)$ and note that

$$\begin{array}{rcccl} \mathcal{L}(1, f_i) & = & -\ln(\frac{e^{f_i}}{1+e^{f_i}}) & = & -\ln p_i \\ \mathcal{L}(-1, f_i) & = & -\ln(\frac{1}{1+e^{f_i}}) & = & -\ln(1 - p_i) \end{array} \tag{6.21}$$

Thus, we may rewrite (6.20) as

$$\frac{1}{n}\sum_{i=1}^{n} l(y_i f_i) + \lambda \|h\|^2_{\mathcal{H}_K} \tag{6.22}$$

where $l(\tau) = \ln(1 + e^{-\tau})$. $l(\tau)$ is plotted in figure 6.1 as ln(1+exp(-tau)).

Note that $l(\tau)$ is strictly convex. We know that $h = \sum_{i=1}^n c_i K_{t_i}$, $\|h\|^2_{\mathcal{H}_K} = c'Kc, f = (f_1, \cdots, f_n)' = Kc + Td$ and, if K is of full rank, $T'c = 0$, with the modifications noted if K is not of full rank. c and d are substituted into (6.22) and, if K is of full rank or the dimension of c is reduced appropriately, a strictly convex optimization problem with readily accessible gradient and Hessian results. A natural target for choosing λ is then to minimize the comparative Kullback-Leibler distance $CKL(\lambda) \doteq CKL(f_{true}, f_\lambda)$ between f_{true} and f_λ.[4] Here f_λ is the minimizer of (6.22) and f_{true} is the logit of the 'true' distribution p_{true} which generated the data. $CKL(\lambda)$ in this case becomes $E_{true} \sum_{i=1}^n l(y_i f_{\lambda i})$, see (Xiang and Wahba, 1996) for more details. Later we will turn to the randomized GACV method for estimating a computable proxy for $CKL(\lambda)$ (Xiang and Wahba (1996, 1997); Lin and Wahba, in preparation).

Kullback-Leibler Distance

6.3.3 Back to Hard Classification

Section 6.3.1 suggests that we choose $f \in \{span\ \phi_\nu\} + h$ with $h \in \mathcal{H}_K$ to minimize

$$\frac{1}{n}\sum_{i=1}^{n} [\epsilon - y_i f_i]_* + \lambda \|h\|^2_{\mathcal{H}_K}, \tag{6.23}$$

for some fixed $\epsilon > 0$, thereby penalizing the misclassification rate rather than the log likelihood. $[-\tau]_*$ is plotted in figure 6.1 as [-tau]* for comparison with $l(\tau)$. Substituting c and d into (6.23) as before, one seeks to find the minimizers, while choosing λ. It appears that a large λ will force f into $span\{\phi_\nu\}$, thus making f

3. In the statistics literature the usual log likelihood functional is stated for $y = 1$ or 0.
4. Recall that the Kullback-Leibler distance is not really a distance.

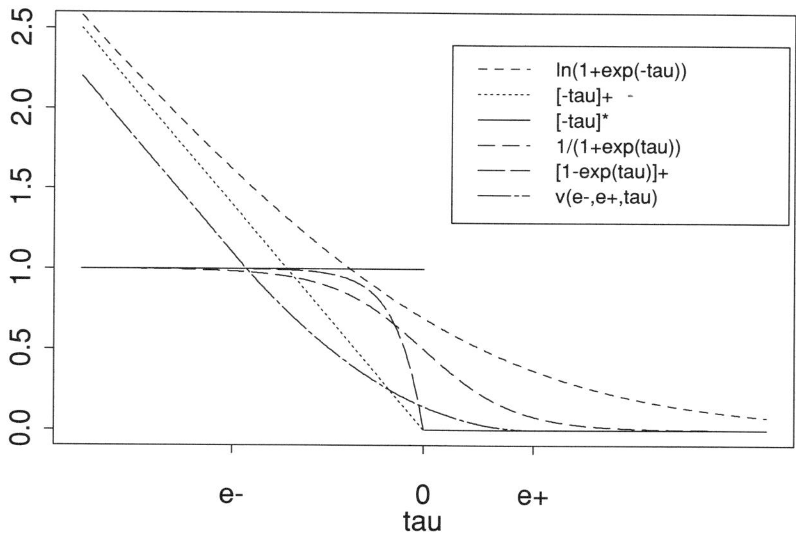

Figure 6.1 Pseudo-distance functions of tau (τ) mentioned in the text.

and (hence the boundaries of the different classification regions) less flexible, while a small λ will allow the classification boundaries to follow the training set more closely. However, if the attribute data is well separated by class, then the minimizer over d of $\sum_{i=1}^{n}[\epsilon - y_i \sum_{\nu=1}^{M} d_\nu \phi_\nu(t_i)]_*$ may not be unique or bounded, so that it will be necessary to further constrain the d_νs. Supposing $\phi_1(t) = 1$, and letting $\phi(t) = \sum_{\nu=2}^{M} d_\nu \phi_\nu(t)$, in what follows we could replace the penalty $\lambda\|h\|^2_{\mathcal{H}_K}$ by $J_\lambda(f)$ where $J_\lambda(f) = \lambda_0\|\phi\|_0^2 + \lambda_1\|h\|^2_{\mathcal{H}_K}$, where $\|\phi\|_0^2$ is some appropriate positive definite quadratic form in $d_2, \cdots, d_M$, for example $\sum_{\nu=2}^{M} d_\nu^2$. Alternatively, the $\{\phi_\nu\}$ could retain their special role by being absorbed into K. In this case, $K(s,t)$ is replaced by $\theta \sum_{\nu=2}^{M} \phi_\nu(s)\phi_\nu(t) + K(s,t)$. Increasing θ forces more of the solution into the $\{\phi_\nu\}$.

Unfortunately the use of $[\epsilon - \tau]_*$ in (6.23) results in a nonconvex optimization problem, with its attendant pitfalls. However, Mangasarian (1994) has recently proposed numerical algorithms in the $\lambda_1 = \infty$ case with $t = (t^1, \cdots, t^d) \in E^d$, $\phi_1(t) = 1, \phi_\alpha(t) = t^\alpha, \alpha = 1, \cdots, d$. Bradley et al. (1995) recently considered problems where the rather nasty function $[-\tau]_*$ is replaced with other more tractable functions including the sigmoidal approximation $1/(1 + e^{a\tau})$ and the function $[1 - e^{a\tau}]_+$, concave for $\tau < 0$. Here, $[x]_+ = x, x > 0, = 0$ otherwise. For comparison, these two functions are also plotted in figure 6.1 with $a = 1$. Bradley *et al.* considered examples with a large number of variables, where the goal was to screen out some non-informative variables for deletion. They penalized the number of variables included and used 10-fold cross validation on the misclassification rate to choose a penalty parameter on the number of variables. See also Bennett and Blue (1997).

6.3.4 Convex Compromises with SVMs

Let $v(\tau) \doteq v_{\epsilon_+,\epsilon_-}(\tau)$ be defined by

$$\begin{aligned} v_{\epsilon_+,\epsilon_-}(\tau) &= [-(\tau - \tfrac{\epsilon_+ + \epsilon_-}{2})]_+ & \tau &< \epsilon_- \\ &= \frac{(\tau-\epsilon_+)^2}{2(\epsilon_+ - \epsilon_-)} & \epsilon_- \leq \tau &\leq \epsilon_+ \\ &= 0 & \epsilon_+ &\leq \tau. \end{aligned} \tag{6.24}$$

For fixed $\epsilon_- < \epsilon_+$, $v_{\epsilon_+,\epsilon_-}(\tau)$ is convex and possesses a continuous first derivative, and a non-negative second derivative everywhere except at ϵ_- and $\epsilon+$, where the second derivative could be defined by assigning it to be continuous from the left, say. $v_{\epsilon_+,\epsilon_-}(\tau)$ is plotted in figure 6.1 as v(e+,e-,tau), along with $v_{0,0}(\tau) \doteq [-\tau]_+$. $v_{\epsilon_+,\epsilon_+}(\tau) \doteq [\epsilon_+ - \tau]_+$. The vs may be thought of as (in some sense) convex approximations to $[\epsilon - \tau]_*$, which for $\epsilon_- < \epsilon_+$ possess a continuous first derivative and non-negative second derivative which could be defined everywhere.

6.4 The Randomized GACV for Choosing λ

So far our discussion has been a relatively straightforward description of bridges between well known results in optimization in RKHS, Gaussian processes, penalized likelihood methods in soft classification (more commonly known as risk factor estimation) and SVM methods. This section is more heuristic and in the nature of work in progress. The goal is to explore to what extent the randomized GACV method in Xiang and Wahba (1996, 1997) for choosing λ in the case $g(\tau) = ln(1 + e^{-\tau})$ may be extended to apply in the context of SVMs. Minimization of the generalized comparative Kullback-Leibler distance (GCKL) of f_λ to the *'true'* f as a function of λ is the target of the GACV. We first describe the GCKL and how it relates in some cases to the expected misclassification rate. Then we describe how the (computable) minimizer of the GACV should be a good estimate of the minimizer of the (not computable) GCKL. The randomized trace method for computing the GACV relatively efficiently is described and the details worked out for a simple case. Finally relations between the the GACV here and its versions in other contexts are noted.

6.4.1 The Generalized Comparative Kullback-Leibler Distance

Suppose unobserved y_is will be generated according to an (unknown) probability model with $p(t) = p_{true}(t)$ being the probability that an instance with attribute vector t is in class $\mathcal{A}$. Let y_j be an (unobserved) value of y associated with t_j. Given f_λ, define the generalized comparative Kullback-Leibler distance (GCKL distance) with respect to g as

$$GCKL(f_{true}, f_\lambda) \doteq GCKL(\lambda) = E_{true}\frac{1}{n}\sum_{j=1}^{n} g(y_j f_{\lambda j}). \tag{6.25}$$

If $g(\tau) = ln(1 + e^{-\tau})$, then $GCKL(\lambda)$ reduces to the usual CKL,[5] averaged over the attribute vectors of the training set. If $g(\tau) = [\epsilon - \tau]_*$, then

$$\begin{aligned} E_{true}[\epsilon - y_j f_{\lambda j}]_* &= p_{[true]j}[\epsilon - f_{\lambda j}]_* + (1 - p_{[true]j})[\epsilon + f_{\lambda j}]_* \\ &= p_{[true]j}, \qquad f_{\lambda j} < -\epsilon \\ &= 1, \qquad -\epsilon \le f_{\lambda j} \le \epsilon \\ &= (1 - p_{[true]j}), \qquad f_{\lambda j} > \epsilon, \end{aligned} \tag{6.26}$$

where $p_{[true]j} = p_{[true]}(t_j)$, so that the $GCKL(\lambda)$ is (a slight over estimate of) the expected misclassification rate for f_λ on unobserved instances if they have the same distribution of t_j as the training set (since the $GCKL$ is assigning 'misclassified' to all $f_{\lambda j} \in [-\epsilon, \epsilon]$.) Similarly, if $g(\tau) = [\epsilon - \tau]_+$, then

$$\begin{aligned} E_{true}[\epsilon - y_j f_{\lambda j}]_+ &= p_{[true]j}(\epsilon - f_{\lambda j}), \qquad f_{\lambda j} < -\epsilon \\ &= \epsilon + (1 - 2p_{[true]j})f_{\lambda j}, \qquad -\epsilon \le f_{\lambda j} \le \epsilon \\ &= (1 - p_{[true]j})(\epsilon + f_{\lambda j}), \qquad f_{\lambda j} > \epsilon, \end{aligned} \tag{6.27}$$

not quite the misclassification rate, but related to it. The misclassification rate would be small if the large negative $f_{\lambda j}$ go with small $p_{[true]j}$ and the large positive $f_{\lambda j}$ go with small $(1 - p_{[true]j})$. We do not, of course, know $p_{[true]}$, so we cannot calculate $GCKL(\lambda)$ directly. However if it were cheap and easy to obtain an estimate of the minimizer of $GCKL(\lambda)$ it would be an appealing method for choosing λ.

Since for $y_i = \pm 1$ and $0 < \epsilon < 1$, $V_\epsilon(y_i, f_i) = max\{0, |1 - y_i f_i| - \epsilon\}$, $g(\tau) = [|1 - \tau| - \epsilon]_+$ corresponds to the 'usual' SVM. Note that this $g(\tau)$ is not monotonic in τ, but is 0 for $\tau \in [1 - \epsilon, 1 + \epsilon]$ and increases outside of this interval linearly as τ goes away from the interval in either direction. The relation of the GCKL to the misclassification rate in this example is not quite so direct, but it still may still be useful.

5. The usual CKL (comparative Kullback-Leibler distance) is the Kullback-Leibler distance plus a term which depends only on $p_{[true]}$.

6.4.2 A Computable Proxy for the $GCKL$

6.4.2.1 *Approximate Cross Validation*

Xiang and Wahba (1996, 1997) proposed the randomized GACV method for estimating a proxy for $CKL(\lambda)$. By a proxy for $CKL(\lambda)$ is meant a computable function whose minimizer is a good estimate for the minimizer of $CKL(\lambda)$. Define

$$I_\lambda(f, Y) = \frac{1}{n}\sum_{i=1}^{n} g(y_i f_i) + J_\lambda(f), \tag{6.28}$$

where $J_\lambda(f)$ is a quadratic penalty on f depending on λ. In this section we follow the derivation in Xiang and Wahba (1996) to find a computable proxy for $GCKL(\lambda)$, in the case that I_λ is strictly convex. In the SVM cases we are interested in, I_λ is generally convex but not strictly convex. However, the end result, below at (6.61) is well defined and plausible, even though some of the steps to get there are heuristic. The derivation proceeds by describing a leaving-out-one cross validation procedure for the GCKL and a series of approximations to get an approximate proxy for the GCKL. Then we describe a randomization procedure for computing this proxy efficiently. We emphasize that we do not actually do leaving-out-one, the randomization technique is a Monte Carlo estimate of a quantity approximating what we would expect to get if we actually did leaving-out-one.

Let $f_\lambda^{[-i]}$ be the solution to the variational problem: find $f \in \{span\ \phi_\nu\} \oplus \mathcal{H}_K$ to minimize

$$\frac{1}{n}\sum_{\substack{j=1\\ j\neq i}}^{n} g(y_j f_j) + J_\lambda(f). \tag{6.29}$$

Then the leaving-out-one function $V_0(\lambda)$ is defined as

$$V_0(\lambda) = \frac{1}{n}\sum_{i=1}^{n} g(y_i f_{\lambda i}^{[-i]}). \tag{6.30}$$

Since $f_{\lambda i}^{[-i]}$ does not depend on y_i but is (presumably) on average close to $f_{\lambda i}$, we may consider $V_0(\lambda)$ a proxy for $GCKL(\lambda)$, albeit one that is not generally feasible to compute in large data sets. Now let

$$V_0(\lambda) = OBS(\lambda) + D(\lambda), \tag{6.31}$$

where $OBS(\lambda)$ is the observed match of f_λ to the data,

$$OBS(\lambda) = \frac{1}{n}\sum_{i=1}^{n} g(y_i f_{\lambda i}) \tag{6.32}$$

and

$$D(\lambda) = \frac{1}{n}\sum_{i=1}^{n}[g(y_i f_{\lambda i}^{[-i]}) - g(y_i f_{\lambda i})]. \tag{6.33}$$

Using a first order Taylor series expansion gives

$$D(\lambda) \approx -\frac{1}{n}\sum_{i=1}^{n} \frac{\partial g}{\partial f_{\lambda i}}(f_{\lambda i} - f_{\lambda i}^{[-i]}). \tag{6.34}$$

Next we let $\mu(f)$ be a 'prediction' of y given f. Here we let

$$\mu_i = \mu(f_i) = \sum_{y \in \{+1,-1\}} \frac{\partial}{\partial f_i} g(y_i f_i). \tag{6.35}$$

When $g(\tau) = ln(1+e^{-\tau})$ then $\mu(f) = 2p - 1 = E\{y|p\}$. For $g(\tau) = v_{\epsilon_+,\epsilon_-}(\tau)$, $\mu(f) = -1, f < min\{\epsilon_+, -\epsilon_-\}$, $\mu(f) = +1, f > max\{\epsilon_+, -\epsilon_-\}$, and varies in a non-decreasing piecewise linear fashion in between. $\mu(f)$ is plotted in figure 6.2 for both these cases. For $g(\tau) = \frac{1}{2}[|1-\tau| - \epsilon]_+$, $\mu(f)$ is a nondecreasing step function with $\mu(-(1+\epsilon)) = -1$, $\mu(1+\epsilon) = +1$.

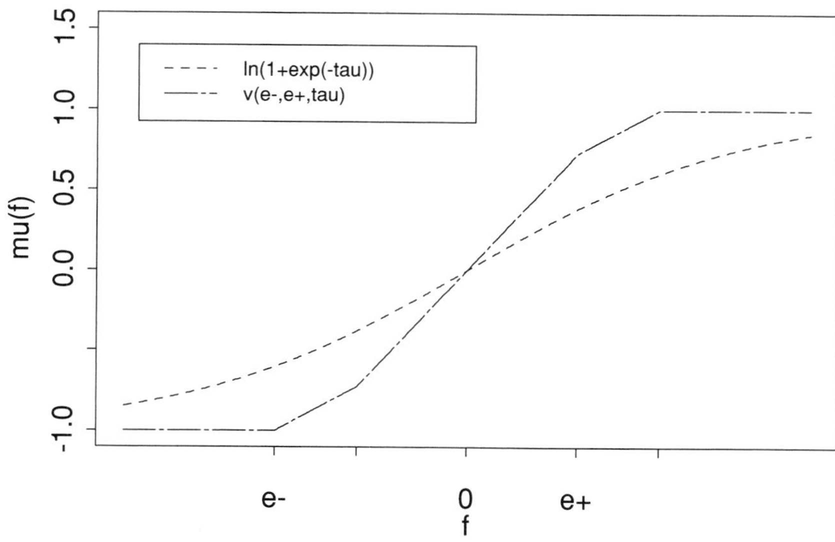

Figure 6.2 Prediction functions $\mu(f)$ defined in the text for $g(\tau) = ln(1+e^{-\tau})$ and $g(\tau) = v_{\epsilon_+,\epsilon_-}(\tau)$.

Letting $\mu_{\lambda i} = \mu(f_{\lambda i})$ and $\mu_{\lambda i}^{[-i]} = \mu(f_{\lambda i}^{[-i]})$, we may write (ignoring, for the moment, the possibility of dividing by 0),

$$D(\lambda) \approx -\frac{1}{n}\sum_{i=1}^{n} \frac{\partial g}{\partial f_{\lambda i}} \frac{(f_{\lambda i} - f_{\lambda i}^{[-i]})}{(y_i - \mu_{\lambda i}^{[-i]})}(y_i - \mu_{\lambda i}^{[-i]}) \tag{6.36}$$

$$\equiv -\frac{1}{n}\sum_{i=1}^{n} \frac{\partial g}{\partial f_{\lambda i}} \frac{(f_{\lambda i} - f_{\lambda i}^{[-i]})}{(y_i - \mu_{\lambda i}^{[-i]})} \frac{(y_i - \mu_{\lambda i})}{(1 - \frac{\mu_{\lambda i} - \mu_{\lambda i}^{[-i]}}{y_i - \mu_{\lambda i}^{[-i]}})}. \tag{6.37}$$

Next, approximate $\mu_{\lambda i} - \mu_{\lambda i}^{[-i]}$ as

$$\mu_{\lambda i} - \mu_{\lambda i}^{[-i]} = \mu(f_{\lambda i}) - \mu(f_{\lambda i}^{[-i]}) \approx \frac{\partial \mu}{\partial f_{\lambda i}}(f_{\lambda i} - f_{\lambda i}^{[-i]}). \tag{6.38}$$

Making the definitions

$$g_i' = \frac{\partial g}{\partial f_{\lambda i}} \tag{6.39}$$

$$\mu_i' = \frac{\partial \mu}{\partial f_{\lambda i}} \tag{6.40}$$

$$h_{ii} = \frac{f_{\lambda i} - f_{\lambda i}^{[-i]}}{y_i - \mu_{\lambda i}^{[-i]}} \tag{6.41}$$

in (6.37) gives, finally

$$D(\lambda) \approx -\frac{1}{n}\sum_{i=1}^{n} g_i' h_{ii} \frac{y_i - \mu_{\lambda i}}{1 - \mu_i' h_{ii}}. \tag{6.42}$$

Now $g_i, \mu_{\lambda i}$ and μ_i' depend only on $f_{\lambda i}$, which presumably, is at hand if the original variational problem has been solved. It remains to find an approximation for the right hand side of (6.41) to use for h_{ii}. The Leaving Out One Lemma will help.

6.4.3 The Leaving Out One Lemma

Let $g(\tau)$ be convex, and let $\mu = \mu(f)$ be a nondecreasing function of f with $\mu(-\infty) = -1$ and $\mu(\infty) = +1$, and let $f^\dagger(\mu)$ be any function of μ such that $\mu(f^\dagger(\mu)) = \mu$. Thus if $\mu(f)$ is a strictly monotone function of f then $f^\dagger$ is uniquely defined and $f^\dagger(\mu) = f(\mu)$. Suppose that

$$g(\mu(f) f^\dagger(\mu(f))) \leq g(\mu(f) f*) \tag{6.43}$$

for any $f*$ for which $\mu(f*) \neq \mu(f)$. It can be shown that $g = l$ and $g = v_{\epsilon_+,\epsilon_-}$ with the 'prediction functions' μ as in figure 6.2 have property (6.43). Then we have the **Leaving-Out-One Lemma**:

Leaving-Out-One

Lemma 6.1 (Craven and Wahba (1979); Xiang and Wahba (1996)) Let $f_\lambda^{[-i]}$ be the minimizer of (6.29) as before. Then $f_\lambda^{[-i]}$ is also the minimizer of

$$\frac{1}{n}\sum_{i=1}^{n} g(y_i f_i) + J_\lambda(f) \tag{6.44}$$

if $\{y_1, \cdots, y_n\}$ is replaced by the data

$$Y^{[-i]} = \{y_1, \cdots, y_{i-1}, \mu(f_{\lambda i}^{[-i]}), y_{i+1}, \cdots, y_n\}. \tag{6.45}$$

A proof is in the Appendix.

This lemma says that if we leave out the ith data point, use the prediction function $\mu(f_\lambda^{[-i]})$ to 'predict' (or impute) y_i, and then solve the variational problem with $\mu(f_{\lambda i}^{[-i]})$ substituted in for y_i, we will get $f_\lambda^{[-i]}$ back for the solution.

6.4.4 An Approximation for $h_{ii} = \frac{f_{\lambda i} - f_{\lambda i}^{[-i]}}{y_i - \mu_{\lambda i}^{[-i]}}$

With some abuse of notation, in this subsection we let f be a vector of function values, at $t_1, \cdots, t_n$ rather than a function, as we have been doing. That is, here

$$f_\lambda = (f_{\lambda 1}, \cdots, f_{\lambda n})' \tag{6.46}$$

$$f_\lambda^{[-i]} = (f_{\lambda 1}^{[-i]}, \cdots f_{\lambda n}^{[-i]})' \tag{6.47}$$

and let

$$Y = (y_1, \cdots, y_n)' \tag{6.48}$$

$$Y^{[-i]} = (y_1, \cdots, y_{i-1}, \mu(f_{\lambda i}^{[-i]}), y_{i+1}, \cdots, y_n)'. \tag{6.49}$$

Recalling the definition of I_λ from (6.28), it can be shown that I_λ depends only on f through the values of f at (some of) the data points $t_1, \cdots, t_n$. We don't need to know this relationship explicitly here, however. Details have been worked out for the strictly convex case in Xiang and Wahba (1996). Expanding the vector $\frac{\partial I_\lambda}{\partial f}$ in a Taylor series about f_λ and Y gives

$$\begin{aligned}\frac{\partial I_\lambda}{\partial f}(f_\lambda^{[-i]}, Y^{[-i]}) = \frac{\partial I_\lambda}{\partial f}(f_\lambda, Y) &+ \frac{\partial^2 I_\lambda}{\partial f \partial f'}(f_\lambda, Y)(f_\lambda^{[-i]} - f_\lambda) \\ &+ \frac{\partial^2 I_\lambda}{\partial f_\lambda \partial Y'}(Y^{[-i]} - Y) + \ldots\end{aligned} \tag{6.50}$$

Now since f_λ is a minimizer of $I_\lambda(f, Y)$ and, by the Leaving Out One Lemma, $f_\lambda^{[-i]}$ is a minimizer of $I_\lambda(f, Y^{[-i]})$, we have

$$\frac{\partial I_\lambda}{\partial f}(f_\lambda^{[-i]}, Y^{[-i]}) = \frac{\partial I_\lambda}{\partial f}(f_\lambda, Y) = 0 \tag{6.51}$$

and, from (6.50),

$$H_{ff}(f_\lambda - f_\lambda^{[-i]}) \approx -H_{fY}(Y - Y^{[-i]}) \tag{6.52}$$

where $H_{ff} = \frac{\partial^2 I_\lambda}{\partial f \partial f'}$ and $H_{fy} = \frac{\partial^2 I_\lambda}{\partial f \partial Y'}$. If H_{ff} were invertible, we could write

$$h_{ii} \equiv \frac{f_{\lambda i} - f_{\lambda i}^{[-i]}}{y_i - \mu_{\lambda i}^{[-i]}} \approx -(H_{ff}^{-1} H_{fY})_{ii} = \tilde{h}_{ii}, \tag{6.53}$$

say, where $(H_{ff}^{-1} H_{fY})_{ii}$ is the iith entry of $H_{ff}^{-1} H_{fY}$. Here $H_{ff} = W + \Sigma_\lambda$ where W is the diagonal matrix with iith entry $w_{ii} = \frac{\partial^2}{\partial f_{\lambda i}^2} g(y_i f_{\lambda i})$, Σ_λ is the Hessian matrix of J_λ with respect to the $f_{\lambda i}$ and H_{fY} is the diagonal matrix with iith entry $\frac{\partial^2}{\partial f_{\lambda i} \partial y_i} g(y_i f_{\lambda i})$. Setting

$$\tilde{h}_{ii} = -(H_{ff}^{-1} H_{fY})_{ii} \tag{6.54}$$

gives our approximate cross validation function $ACV(\lambda)$ as an approximation to $V_0(\lambda)$, the leaving-out-one function of (6.30):

$$ACV(\lambda) = \frac{1}{n} \sum_{i=1}^{n} g(y_i f_{\lambda i}) - \frac{1}{n} \sum_{i=1}^{n} g_i' \tilde{h}_{ii} \frac{y_i - \mu_{\lambda i}}{1 - \mu_i' \tilde{h}_{ii}}. \tag{6.55}$$

$ACV(\lambda)$ can be shown to be equivalent to the $ACV_2(\lambda)$ of Xiang and Wahba (1996), p.689, after suitable modification for the setup here.

6.4.4.1 The Randomized Trace Estimate of $GACV(\lambda)$ for $g(\tau) = [\epsilon - \tau]_+$

Next, we consider $g(\tau) = v_{\epsilon,\epsilon-\delta}(\tau)$ and $\lim_{\delta \to 0} v_{\epsilon,\epsilon-\delta}(\tau) = [\epsilon - \tau]_+$. Table 6.1 gives the ingredients of $D(\lambda)$ other than $\tilde{h}_{ii}$ for $g(\tau) = [\epsilon - \tau]_+$. Note that as we take the above limit certain derivatives used in the derivation of (6.55) do not exist at $\tau = \pm\epsilon$. Nevertheless we proceed. Assuming that we need not be concerned at exactly the degenerate points $y_i f_i = \pm\epsilon$, we have, substituting the entries from table 6.1 into (6.42),

	$y_i f_i < -\epsilon$	$-\epsilon < y_i f_i < \epsilon$	$\epsilon < y_i f_i$
$g(y_i f_i)$	$\epsilon - y_i f_i$		0
$\frac{\partial g}{\partial f_i}$	$-y_i$		0
$\frac{\partial^2 g}{\partial f_i \partial y_i}$	-1		0
$\frac{\partial g}{\partial f_i}(y_i - \mu_i)$	-2	-1	0
	$f_i < -\epsilon$	$-\epsilon < f_i < \epsilon$	$\epsilon < f_i$
$\mu(f_i)$	-1	0	1
$\frac{d\mu}{df_i}$	0	0	0

Table 6.1 Ingredients of $D(\lambda)$ for $g(\tau) = [\epsilon - \tau]_+$.

$$D(\lambda) \approx \frac{1}{n} \sum_{y_i f_{\lambda i} < -\epsilon} 2\tilde{h}_{ii} + \frac{1}{n} \sum_{-\epsilon < y_i f_{\lambda i} < \epsilon} \tilde{h}_{ii}. \tag{6.56}$$

If H_{ff} were invertible, we would have the simple expression

$$D(\lambda) \approx -\frac{2}{n} \text{trace}\, E_\epsilon H_{ff}^{-1} H_{fY}, \tag{6.57}$$

where E_ϵ is the diagonal matrix with 1 in the iith position if $y_i f_i < -\epsilon$, with $\frac{1}{2}$ in the iith position if $-\epsilon < y_i f_i < \epsilon$, and 0 otherwise. We now give a heuristic argument for the randomized trace estimation of $D(\lambda)$ for $g(\tau) = [\epsilon - \tau]_+$, based on a perturbation of the data, and not requiring H_{ff} strictly positive definite. Let $Z = (z_1, \cdots, z_n)'$, where the z_is will be generated by a random number generator with $Ez_i = 0$ and $Ez_i z_j = \sigma_Z^2, i = j, = 0$ otherwise. Let $f_\lambda \equiv f_\lambda^Y$[6] be the minimizer of $I_\lambda(f, Y)$ as before and let f_λ^{Y+Z} be the minimizer of $I_\lambda(f, Y + Z)$. That is, we are perturbing the response vector Y by adding a (small) random perturbation Z. Note that in what follows $y_i + z_i$ does not have to be in $\{-1, 1\}$, and in general the variational problems here do not require the responses to be in that set. Using the Taylor series expansion (6.50) with $(f_\lambda^{Y+Z}, Y + Z)$ replacing $(f_\lambda^{[-i]}, Y^{[-i]})$ gives, assuming that Z is a small perturbation,

$$H_{ff}(f_\lambda^{Y+Z} - f_\lambda^Y) \approx -H_{fY} Z. \tag{6.58}$$

If H_{ff} were invertible we could write

$$f_\lambda^{Y+Z} - f_\lambda^Y \approx -H_{ff}^{-1} H_{fY} Z. \tag{6.59}$$

Then, observing that for any $n \times n$ matrix A, that $EZ'AZ = \sigma_Z^2 \text{trace}\, A$, we would have that

$$\frac{2}{n} \frac{1}{\sigma_z^2} Z' E_\epsilon (f_\lambda^{Y+Z} - f_\lambda^Y) \tag{6.60}$$

is an estimate of $-\frac{2}{n} \text{trace}\, E_\epsilon H_{ff}^{-1} H_{fY}$. For $g(\tau) = [\epsilon - \tau]_+$ generally H_{ff} will not be invertible at f_λ since f_λ does not depend on the inactive data points, that is, those y_i for which $y_i f_{\lambda i} > \epsilon$. However, we argue heuristically that the restriction of the argument above (and thus the restriction of H_{ff}) to just the active data points does make sense. (Recall that we will be limiting ourselves to I_λ with unique solutions.) Thus we conjecture that (6.60) will provide a reasonable randomized estimate of $D(\lambda)$ of (6.56). The end result is the randomized GACV function for $g(\tau) = [\epsilon - \tau]_+$ defined as

$$ranGACV(\lambda) = \frac{1}{n} \sum_{y_i f_{\lambda i} < \epsilon} [\epsilon - y_i f_{\lambda i}^Y]_+ + \frac{2}{n} \frac{1}{\sigma_z^2} Z' E_\epsilon (f_\lambda^{Y+Z} - f_\lambda^Y). \tag{6.61}$$

We conjecture that the minimizer of $ranGACV(\lambda)$, under suitable assumptions (in particular, fairly large sample sizes) should be a good estimate of the minimizer of

---

6. Again, with some abuse of notation, we are letting f stand for a function, when convenient, and for the vector of its values at $t_1, \cdots, t_n$ when convenient.

$GCKL(\lambda)$ of (6.25). Note that the reasonableness of the result (6.61) is independent of *how* the solutions to the variational problem are found. The minimizer of I_λ with $g(\tau) = [\epsilon - \tau]_+$ will be found via a mathematical programming algorithm, whereas the case with $g(\tau) = l(\tau)$ (with its corresponding $GACV$ function) is typically found using a descent algorithm which uses the Hessian.

Note that the same Z should be used for all λ, however it is possible to compute several replicates of $D(\lambda)$ and take a suitable average, see Xiang (1996) who examined this question in the log likelihood case. It is to be expected that $D(\lambda)$ in the $[\epsilon - \tau]_+$ case will be 'bumpy' considered as a function of λ as instances move in and out of the active constraint set as λ varies, see Wahba (1982a); Villalobos and Wahba (1987) for related examples involving linear inequality constraints.

6.4.5 Discussion of *ranGACV*

Using the fact that for $g(\tau) = l(\tau)$ it can be shown that $-g_i' = \frac{1}{2}(y_i - \mu_i)$, then, (as noted before) (6.55) corresponds to the formula ACV_2 in Xiang and Wahba (1996), p.689. In that paper a slightly different leaving out one was used in the setup $y_i = 1$ or $y_i = 0$ with probability p_i and $(1 - p_i)$ respectively. Then the negative log likelihood can be written as $-yf + b(f)$ where $b(f) = \ln(1 + e^f)$.[7] In that paper we used the same argument as described here starting with the leaving out one in the form $-y_i f_{\lambda i}^{[-i]} + b(f_{\lambda i})$, that is, we did not leave out one in the b term. The end result, called ACV there (which is based on $y_i \in \{0, 1\}$) resulted in

$$D(\lambda) = \sum_{i=1}^{n} \frac{y_i \tilde{h}_{ii}(y_i - \mu_{\lambda i})}{(1 - \mu_i' \tilde{h}_{ii})} \tag{6.62}$$

In that paper we replaced D by D_{GACV} defined by

$$D_{GACV}(\lambda) = \bar{h} \frac{\sum_{i=1}^{n} y_i(y_i - \mu_{\lambda i})}{1 - (\overline{\mu' h})} \tag{6.63}$$

where $\bar{h} = \frac{1}{n}\sum_{i=1}^{n} \tilde{h}_{ii}$, $\overline{\mu' h} = \frac{1}{n}\sum_{i=1}^{n} \mu_i' \tilde{h}_{ii}$ and demonstrated that the resulting $GACV(\lambda)$ provided an excellent proxy for the CKL in the examples tried. In Xiang and Wahba (1997) and Lin and Wahba (in preparation) randomized versions of the GACV were tried and proved to be essentially as good as the exact version calculated via matrix decompositions.

The problem of choosing smoothing parameters in the log likelihood case with Gaussian response data with unknown noise variance has been extensively studied. In that case $f_i = Ey_i$ and $l(f) = \sum_{i=1}^{n}(y_i - f_i)^2$. In that case it can be shown (Craven and Wahba, 1979) that

$$(y_i - f_{\lambda i}^{[-i]})^2 = \frac{(y_i - f_{\lambda i})^2}{(1 - h_{ii})^2} \tag{6.64}$$

---

7. This is the usual formulation in the Statistics literature for the log likelihood for a member of an exponential family.

which gave rise to the GCV estimate $V(\lambda)$

$$V(\lambda) = \frac{\frac{1}{n}\sum_{i=1}^{n}(y_i - f_{\lambda i})^2}{(1-\bar{h})^2}, \tag{6.65}$$

which is known to have various theoretically optimum properties (see Li (1986); Wahba (1990)). The randomized trace version of it can be found in Girard (1991, 1998), who showed that the randomized version was essentially as good as the exact version for large data sets, Hutchinson (1989), who used Bernoulli data for the perturbations, Wahba et al. (1995a) who further compared exact and randomized versions of GCV, Gong et al. (1998) where it was applied to a complex variational problem with multiple smoothing parameters, Golub and von Matt (1997), who did extensive simulations. Wahba (1982a, 1985b) and Villalobos and Wahba (1987) considered variational problems in RKHS with Gaussian data and linear inequality constraints as side conditions, where a GCV function adapted to inequality constraints was used. It can be seen in Wahba (1982a) how $GCV(\lambda)$ has jumps as data points move in and out of the active constraint set as λ varies.

Acknowledgements

I would like to thank the organizers of the NIPS 97 SVM Workshop for inviting me to speak. I would especially like to thank Chris Burges for graciously providing me with some unpublished numerical results of his on estimating the misclassification rate, and for Olvi Mangasarian for some very helpful comments and for providing pointers to some important references. A lively dinner discussion with Trevor Hastie and Jerry Friedman at NIPS 96 contributed to the ideas in this chapter. I am grateful to David Callan for his patient help as a sounding board and in producing this document, and to Fangyu Gao for the plots. This work was partly supported by NSF under Grant DMS-9704758 and NIH under Grant R01 EY09946.

Appendix: Proof of the Leaving Out One Lemma

The hypotheses of the Lemma give

$g(\mu(f_{\lambda i}^{[-i]})f^{\dagger}(\mu(f_{\lambda i}^{[-i]}))) \leq g(\mu(f_{\lambda i}^{[-i]})f_*)$

for any f_* for which $\mu(f_*) \neq \mu(f_{\lambda i}^{[-i]})$. and, in particular

$g(\mu(f_{\lambda i}^{[-i]})f_{\lambda i}^{[-i]}) \leq g(\mu(f_{\lambda i}^{[-i]})f_*)$

for any f_* for which $\mu(f_*) \neq \mu(f_{\lambda i}^{[-i]})$. Thus, letting $J(f) = \|h\|^2_{\mathcal{H}_K}$ (in an obvious notation), we have

$$g(\mu(f_{\lambda i}^{[-i]})f_i) + \sum_{j \neq i} g(y_j f_j) + n\lambda J(f)$$
$$\geq g(\mu(f_{\lambda i}^{[-i]})f_{\lambda i}^{[-i]}) + \sum_{j \neq i} g(y_j f_j) + n\lambda J(f)$$
$$\geq g(\mu(f_{\lambda i}^{[-i]})f_{\lambda i}^{[-i]}) + \sum_{j \neq i} g(y_j f_{\lambda j}^{[-i]}) + n\lambda J(f_{\lambda}^{[-i]})$$

giving the result.

7 Geometry and Invariance in Kernel Based Methods

Christopher J.C. Burges
Bell Laboratories, Lucent Technologies
101 Crawford's Corner Road, Holmdel, NJ 07733-3030, USA
burges@lucent.com
http://svm.research.bell-labs.com

We explore the questions of (1) how to describe the intrinsic geometry of the manifolds which occur naturally in methods, such as support vector machines (SVMs), in which the choice of kernel specifies a nonlinear mapping of one's data to a Hilbert space; and (2) how one can find kernels which are locally invariant under some given symmetry. The motivation for exploring the geometry of support vector methods is to gain a better intuitive understanding of the manifolds to which one's data is being mapped, and hence of the support vector method itself: we show, for example, that the Riemannian metric induced on the manifold by its embedding can be expressed in closed form in terms of the kernel. The motivation for looking for classes of kernels which instantiate local invariances is to find ways to incorporate known symmetries of the problem into the model selection (i.e. kernel selection) phase of the problem. A useful by-product of the geometry analysis is a necessary test which any proposed kernel must pass if it is to be a support vector kernel (i.e. a kernel which satisfies Mercer's positivity condition); as an example, we use this to show that the hyperbolic tangent kernel (for which the SVM is a two-layer neural network) violates Mercer's condition for various values of its parameters, a fact noted previously only experimentally. A basic result of the invariance analysis is that directly imposing a symmetry on the class of kernels effectively results in a preprocessing step, in which the preprocessed data lies in a space whose dimension is reduced by the number of generators of the symmetry group. Any desired kernels can then be used on the preprocessed data. We give a detailed example of vertical translation invariance for pixel data, where the binning of the data into pixels has some interesting consequences. The chapter comprises two parts: Part 1 studies the geometry of the kernel mapping, and Part 2 the incorporation of invariances by choice of kernel.

PART 1

7.1 Overview

A Support Vector Machine, whether for pattern classification, regression estimation, or operator inversion, uses a device called *kernel mapping* (Boser et al., 1992; Vapnik, 1995; Burges, 1998) to map the data to a Hilbert space F ("feature space") in which the problem becomes linear (i.e. an optimal separating hyperplane for the pattern recognition case, and a linear regression for the regression and operator inversion cases). If the original data lies in a d-dimensional space, the mapped data will lie in an at most d-dimensional surface $\mathcal{S}$ in F. In Part 1 we explore the intrinsic geometry of these surfaces. Our main motivation is simply to gain a better intuitive understanding of the geometry underlying the support vector approach; however, some useful results will follow. We will show that the surface has an induced Riemannian metric which can be expressed solely in terms of the kernel, and that a given metric is generated by a class of kernels. We derive the volume element in the surface for dot product kernels, and show that positivity of the metric gives some simple necessary tests for whether a proposed kernel is indeed a support vector kernel (i.e. whether it satisfies Mercer's condition: see also Smola et al. (1998a)). Note that the kernel mapping device is beginning to find applications beyond support vector machines (Schölkopf et al., 1998e,f); the work presented here applies to all such algorithms.

In the following, bold typeface will indicate vector or matrix quantities; normal typeface will be used for vector and matrix components and for scalars. Repeated indices are assumed summed.

7.2 The Kernel Mapping

We briefly remind the reader of the kernel mapping used by the support vector approach (Boser et al., 1992; Vapnik, 1995; Burges, 1998). Suppose one has data $\mathbf{x}_i \in \mathbb{R}^{d_L}, \quad i = 1, \cdots, l$ (we do not need to consider the labels $y_i \in \{\pm 1\}$ for the pattern recognition case here). For any symmetric, continuous function $k(\mathbf{x}, \mathbf{y})$ satisfying Mercer's condition, there exists a Hilbert space F, a map $\Phi : \mathbb{R}^{d_L} \mapsto F$, and positive numbers λ_n such that (Courant and Hilbert, 1953):

$$k(\mathbf{x}, \mathbf{y}) = \sum_{n=1}^{d_F} \lambda_n \Phi_n(\mathbf{x}) \Phi_n(\mathbf{y}) \tag{7.1}$$

where d_F is the dimension of F (note that one can add points to give a complete space if necessary). Mercer's condition requires that

Mercer's Condition

$$\int_C k(\mathbf{x}, \mathbf{y}) g(\mathbf{x}) g(\mathbf{y}) d\mathbf{x} d\mathbf{y} \geq 0, \tag{7.2}$$

for any square integrable function $g(\mathbf{x})$, and where $\mathcal{C}$ is some compact subset of $\mathbb{R}^{d_L}$. For the purposes of this work, we absorb the λ_n into the definition of Φ, so that Eq. (7.1) becomes a dot product (in fact, an expansion (7.1) can still be found if a finite number of the λ_n are negative (Courant and Hilbert, 1953)). Below, following Stewart (1978), we will call a continuous symmetric function which satisfies Eq. (7.2) a *positive semidefinite kernel.*

Positive Semidefinite Kernel

7.2.1 Smoothness Assumptions

We make explicit the assumptions we will need. Label the subset of $\mathbb{R}^{d_L}$ on which the data lives $\mathcal{L}$ (we assume that the data is continuous). Given a positive semidefinite kernel with eigenfunctions $\Phi_n,\ \ n = 1, \cdots, d_F$, we assume that some subset $\mathcal{L}_s \in \mathcal{L}$ exists on which the Φ_n are C^3 (i.e. have up to third derivatives defined and continuous), and on which the rank of the mapping Φ is some fixed number m (we usually encounter the case $m = d_L$). We will use $\mathcal{S}$ to denote the image of $\mathcal{L}_s$ under Φ. Thus $\mathcal{S}$ is a m-dimensional surface in F.

Differentiable Manifold

It is instructive to consider under what conditions $\mathcal{S}$ will be a manifold, and under what conditions a differentiable (C^∞) manifold. In order for $\mathcal{S}$ to be a manifold of dimension m, it must be (i) Hausdorff,[1] (ii) locally Euclidean of dimension m, and (iii) have a countable basis of open sets (Boothby, 1986). Condition (i) follows automatically (every Hilbert space is a normal space, hence a metric space, hence Hausdorff (Kolmogorov and Fomin, 1970)). Condition (iii) certainly follows if F is separable, since a Hilbert space has a countable basis of open sets if and only if it is separable, and $\mathcal{S}$, if itself an open set, can inherit the countable basis from F. Condition (ii) will hold whenever the map Φ is of some fixed rank m everywhere. In order for $\mathcal{S}$ to be a differentiable manifold, it is necessary and sufficient that all derivatives of the map Φ exist and are continuous, and that Φ be of rank m everywhere.

Note that the requirement that $\mathcal{S}$ be a differentiable manifold is stronger than we need. In general we need only consider C^3 manifolds, and we allow singularities. The C^3 condition will enable us to define the Riemannian curvature for the surface.

7.3 Measures of Distance on $\mathcal{S}$

There are three measures of distance on $\mathcal{S}$ that spring to mind. They are shown schematically in figure 7.1. There, the embedded surface is represented by a curve, and two points in the surface by P_1 and P_2. In case I, one considers the intrinsic distance measured along the surface itself. This distance is the distance function generated by a Riemannian metric on $\mathcal{S}$. In case II, one considers the Euclidean

1. Recall that a space $\mathcal{S}$ is Hausdorff if and only if, for any pair of distinct points $p_1, p_2 \in \mathcal{S}$, two open sets $S_1, S_2 \in \mathcal{S}$ can be found such that $p_1 \in S_1,\ p_2 \in S_2,\ S_1 \cap S_2 = \emptyset$.

distance measured between the two points in F. In this case, the line joining P_1 and P_2 will in general leave the surface $\mathcal{S}$. In case III, one considers projections of the position vectors of P_1 and P_2 along some vector $\mathbf{w} \in F$. This is an affine distance function (for example, distances can be positive or negative) and it is the distance measure used in the support vector expansion (i.e. the decision rule, for the pattern recognition case, or the approximation to the function, in the regression case).

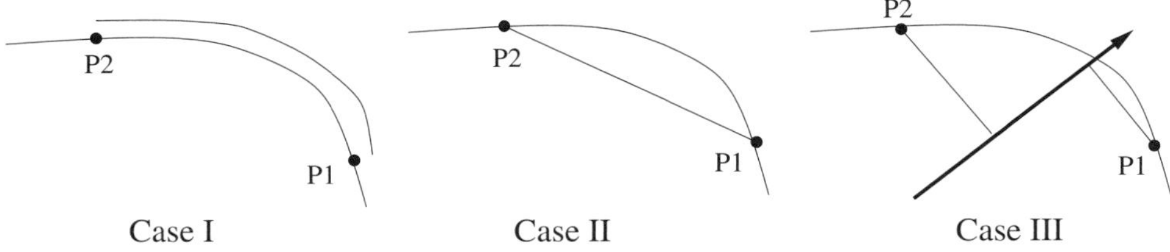

Figure 7.1 Measures of distance on $\mathcal{S}$.

Metric

Recall that in order for a finite real valued function $d(\mathbf{x}, \mathbf{y})$, $\mathbf{x}$, $\mathbf{y} \in \mathbb{R}^{d_L}$ to earn the name "metric", it must satisfy the following conditions[2]:

$$d(\mathbf{x}, \mathbf{y}) = d(\mathbf{y}, \mathbf{x}) \geq 0 \tag{7.3}$$

$$d(\mathbf{x}, \mathbf{y}) = 0 \iff \mathbf{x} = \mathbf{y} \tag{7.4}$$

$$d(\mathbf{x}, \mathbf{y}) + d(\mathbf{y}, \mathbf{z}) \geq d(\mathbf{z}, \mathbf{x}) \tag{7.5}$$

Riemannian Metric

A "Riemannian metric," on the other hand, is a symmetric, positive definite, bilinear form defined on a manifold, and if a manifold admits such a form, it is termed a "Riemannian manifold" (Boothby, 1986). A Riemannian metric defines a metric, such that the distance between two points $\mathbf{x}(t_0)$ and $\mathbf{x}(t_1)$, along a path lying in $\mathcal{S}$ and parameterized by $t \in [t_0, t_1]$, is given by the path integral below, where the expression under the square root in the integrand is the double contraction of the metric form with the tangent vector to the given path. Thus the $g_{\mu\nu}$ are the components (in a given coordinate system) of the metric tensor (Boothby, 1986).

$$\rho(t_0, t_1) = \int_{x(t_0)}^{x(t_1)} \left(g_{\mu\nu} \frac{\partial x^\mu}{\partial t} \frac{\partial x^\nu}{\partial t} \right)^{\frac{1}{2}} dt \tag{7.6}$$

Now consider the metric induced on $\mathcal{S}$ by the Euclidean metric on F, i.e. case II above. This is not a Riemannian metric, since the distances cannot be expressed in the form of Eq. (7.6) (suppose otherwise, and consider some path in $\mathcal{S}$ joining three points P_1, P_2 and P_3; then $d(P_1, P_2) + d(P_2, P_3)$ can in general be greater than $d(P_1, P_3)$, but Eq. (7.6) requires that the distance along the path from P_1 to

2. Note that Eqs. (7.3) in fact follow from Eqs. (7.4) and (7.5) (Copson, 1968).

P_2 plus that along the path from P_2 to P_3 equal the distance along the path from P_1 to P_3). Since in this work we are only interested in the intrinsic geometry of the surface $\mathcal{S}$, we will consider only case I.

7.4 From Kernel to Metric

For any positive kernel, and subset of the data, satisfying the assumptions listed above, the image $\mathcal{S}$ of the associated mapping will be a Riemannian manifold. We can easily find the induced Riemannian metric on $\mathcal{S}$. The line element on $\mathcal{S}$ can be written (here and below, Roman indices will run from 1 to d_F, and Greek from 1 to d_L, unless otherwise stated):

$$\begin{aligned} ds^2 &= g_{ab} d\Phi^a(\mathbf{x}) d\Phi^b(\mathbf{x}), \\ &= g_{\mu\nu} dx^\mu dx^\nu, \end{aligned} \tag{7.7}$$

where $g_{\mu\nu}$ is the induced metric, and the surface $\mathcal{S}$ is parameterized by the x_μ. Letting $d\mathbf{x}$ represent a small but finite displacement, we have

$$\begin{aligned} ds^2 &= \|\Phi(\mathbf{x} + d\mathbf{x}) - \Phi(\mathbf{x})\|^2 \\ &= k(\mathbf{x} + d\mathbf{x}, \mathbf{x} + d\mathbf{x}) - 2k(\mathbf{x}, \mathbf{x} + d\mathbf{x}) + k(\mathbf{x}, \mathbf{x}) \\ &= \left((1/2)\partial_{x_\mu}\partial_{x_\nu} k(\mathbf{x}, \mathbf{x}) - \partial_{y_\mu}\partial_{y_\nu} k(\mathbf{x}, \mathbf{y})\right)_{\mathbf{y}=\mathbf{x}} dx^\mu dx^\nu \\ &= g_{\mu\nu} dx^\mu dx^\nu \end{aligned}$$

Metric Tensor

Thus we can read off the components of the metric tensor:

$$g_{\mu\nu} = (1/2)\partial_{x_\mu}\partial_{x_\nu} k(\mathbf{x}, \mathbf{x}) - \{\partial_{y_\mu}\partial_{y_\nu} k(\mathbf{x}, \mathbf{y})\}_{\mathbf{y}=\mathbf{x}} \tag{7.8}$$

Let's illustrate this with some very simple examples.

Circle: Suppose Φ is the map from the line segment onto the circle of radius r: $\Phi : [0, 2\pi) \mapsto S^1$, i.e.

$$\Phi : \theta \mapsto \begin{pmatrix} r\cos\theta \\ r\sin\theta \end{pmatrix}, \quad r \text{ fixed} \tag{7.9}$$

Then

$$k(\theta, \theta') = r^2(\cos\theta\cos\theta' + \sin\theta\sin\theta') = r^2\cos(\theta - \theta') \tag{7.10}$$

and

$$ds^2 = \{(1/2)\partial_\theta^2 k(\theta, \theta) - \partial_{\theta'}\partial_{\theta'} k(\theta, \theta')\}_{\theta=\theta'} d\theta^2 \tag{7.11}$$

$$= r^2 d\theta^2 \tag{7.12}$$

2-Sphere: Here Φ maps $[0,\pi] \times [0, 2\pi) \mapsto S^2$:

$$\Phi : \{\theta, \psi\} \mapsto \begin{pmatrix} r\sin\theta\cos\psi \\ r\sin\theta\sin\psi \\ r\cos\theta \end{pmatrix} \tag{7.13}$$

Letting ξ be the vector with components θ, ψ,

$$k(\xi_1, \xi_2) = r^2 \sin\theta_1 \cos\psi_1 \sin\theta_2 \cos\psi_2 \tag{7.14}$$
$$+r^2 \sin\theta_1 \sin\psi_1 \sin\theta_2 \sin\psi_2 \tag{7.15}$$
$$+r^2 \cos\theta_1 \cos\theta_2 \tag{7.16}$$

which gives

$$g_{\mu\nu} = \begin{pmatrix} r^2 & 0 \\ 0 & r^2 \sin^2\theta \end{pmatrix} \tag{7.17}$$

A Fourier Sum: The Dirichlet kernel,

$$k(x_1, x_2) = \frac{\sin((N + \frac{1}{2})(x_1 - x_2))}{2\sin((x_1 - x_2)/2)}, \quad x_1,\ x_2 \in \mathbb{R}, \tag{7.18}$$

corresponds to a mapping Φ into a space F of dimension $2N + 1$, where for any $\mathbf{a} \in \mathbb{R}^{2N+1}$, $\mathbf{a} \cdot \Phi(x)$ may be viewed as a Fourier expansion cut off after N terms, with coefficients a_i, $, i = 1, \ldots, 2N + 1$ (Vapnik, 1995; Vapnik et al., 1997; Burges, 1998). As we shall see below, all kernels $k(\mathbf{x}, \mathbf{y})$ which take the form $k(\mathbf{x} - \mathbf{y})$ result in flat manifolds. The above kernel gives line element

$$ds^2 = \frac{1}{6} N(2N + 1)(N + 1) dx^2 \tag{7.19}$$

7.5 From Metric to Kernel

One might want to start with a chosen metric $g_{\mu\nu}$ on the data (for example, one that separates different classes according to some chosen criterion), and ask: is there a Mercer kernel for which the metric induced on $\mathcal{S}$, by its embedding in F, is $g_{\mu\nu}$? By using such a kernel, for example, in a support vector machine, one would be explicitly controlling the intrinsic shape of the embedded surface $\mathcal{S}$. As we will see below, the answer is yes: any Riemannian manifold can be isometrically embedded in a Euclidean space (Nash, 1956). The above analysis shows that the corresponding kernel k must then be a solution to the differential equation (7.8). However, construction of such a kernel, given a metric, may not be straightforward. Although it is guaranteed that there is at least one positive symmetric (and continuous) kernel which satisfies (7.8), in general there will be solutions to (7.8) that are not positive, or that are not symmetric, or both. Note, however, that if one can find a positive symmetric solution to Eq. (7.8) (which will also, by construction, be continuous), then we know how to construct the embedding explicitly: by Mercer's theorem the expansion (7.1) exists, and the embedding is simply given by the eigenfunctions of the found solution, i.e. the Φ in Eq. (7.1).

7.6 Dot Product Kernels

One commonly used class of kernels are the dot product kernels (Vapnik, 1995; Burges and Schölkopf, 1997), where $k(\mathbf{x}, \mathbf{y}) = k(\mathbf{x} \cdot \mathbf{y})$. Using Eq. (7.8) one finds a general expression for the corresponding Riemannian metric:

$$g_{\mu\nu} = \delta_{\mu\nu} k'(\|\mathbf{x}\|^2) + x_\mu x_\nu k''(\|\mathbf{x}\|^2), \tag{7.20}$$

where the prime denotes the derivative with respect to the argument $\|\mathbf{x}\|^2$. A simple example is given by the identity map, where $\Phi_\mu(\mathbf{x}) = x_\mu$, $k(\mathbf{x}, \mathbf{y}) = \mathbf{x} \cdot \mathbf{y}$, $g_{\mu\nu} = \delta_{\mu\nu}$.

Christoffel Symbols

Recall that the Christoffel symbols of the second kind are defined by

$$\Gamma^\alpha_{\beta\gamma} \equiv g^{\alpha\mu} \Gamma_{\beta\gamma\mu} = \frac{1}{2} g^{\alpha\mu} (\partial_\beta g_{\gamma\mu} - \partial_\mu g_{\beta\gamma} + \partial_\gamma g_{\mu\beta}) \tag{7.21}$$

where $g^{\alpha\mu}$ is the inverse of the matrix $g_{\alpha\mu}$ and ∂_α is shorthand for $\frac{\partial}{\partial x^\alpha}$. Note that the Christoffel symbols of the first kind have a particularly simple representation (for any positive semidefinite kernel):

$$\Gamma_{\alpha\beta\gamma} = \sum_{n=1}^{d_F} (\partial_\alpha \partial_\beta \Phi_n(\mathbf{x})) \partial_\gamma \Phi_n(\mathbf{x}) \tag{7.22}$$

The Riemannian metric given above has the form of a projection operator, and its contravariant components are therefore easily found:

$$g^{\mu\nu} = \frac{\delta_{\mu\nu}}{k'} - x_\mu x_\nu \frac{k''/k'}{k' + \|\mathbf{x}\|^2 k''} \tag{7.23}$$

Having the above closed form for $g^{\mu\nu}$ in terms of the kernel greatly facilitates the computation of several other quantities of interest. In the next section we will use it to derive the curvature for homogeneous dot product kernels in arbitrary numbers of dimensions and for polynomials of arbitrary degree. We end this section by noting that it immediately leads to a closed form for the Christoffel symbols of the second kind (for dot product kernels):

$$\Gamma^\rho_{\mu\nu} = \frac{k''}{k'} (x_\mu \delta_{\rho\nu} + x_\nu \delta_{\mu\rho}) + \frac{x_\mu x_\nu x_\rho}{k' + \|\mathbf{x}\|^2 k''} (k''' - 2(k'')^2/k') \tag{7.24}$$

7.6.1 The Curvature for Polynomial Maps

We can gain some insight into the nature of the corresponding surfaces by computing the curvature. We remind the reader that the intrinsic curvature is completely specified by the Riemann tensor (Dodson and Poston, 1991), with components:

Riemann Tensor

$$R_{\nu\alpha\beta}{}^{\mu} = \partial_\alpha \Gamma^\mu_{\beta\nu} - \partial_\beta \Gamma^\mu_{\alpha\nu} + \Gamma^\rho_{\alpha\nu} \Gamma^\mu_{\beta\rho} - \Gamma^\rho_{\beta\nu} \Gamma^\mu_{\alpha\rho} \tag{7.25}$$

For homogeneous polynomial kernels $k(\mathbf{x}, \mathbf{y}) = (\mathbf{x} \cdot \mathbf{y})^p$ (for which Φ is a polynomial map), the metric is

$$g_{\mu\nu} = \delta_{\mu\nu} p(\|\mathbf{x}\|^2)^{p-1} + x_\mu x_\nu p(p-1)(\|\mathbf{x}\|^2)^{p-2} \tag{7.26}$$

and, using Eq. (7.24), we find

$$\Gamma^\rho_{\mu\nu} = \frac{p-1}{\|\mathbf{x}\|^2}\left(x_\mu \delta_{\rho\nu} + x_\nu \delta_{\mu\rho} - \frac{x_\mu x_\nu x_\rho}{\|\mathbf{x}\|^2}\right) \tag{7.27}$$

For $d_L = 2$, we find that these manifolds are flat, for all powers p. For $p = 2$ and $d_L = 2$, we can plot the surface, as shown below (Burges, 1998):

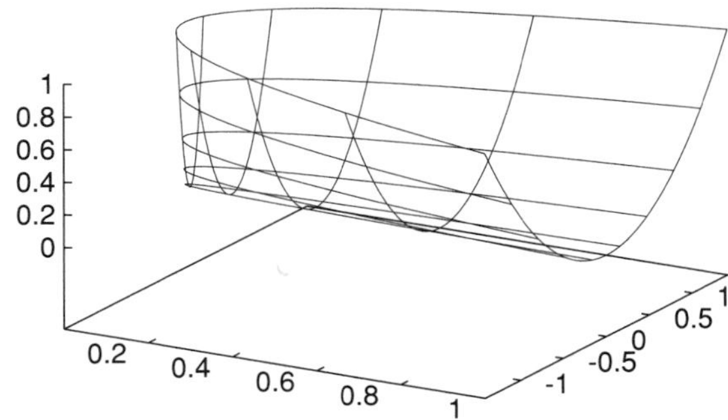

Figure 7.2 Image, in F, of the square $[-1, 1] \times [-1, 1] \in \mathbb{R}^2$ under the mapping Φ.

We use figure 7.2 to emphasize that we are dealing with the intrinsic curvature of the surface. A geometer living on this surface would conclude that the surface is flat because parallel transport of vectors around closed geodesic loops would not give any resulting displacement. Alternatively, one can bend a flat sheet of paper into the surface shown in figure 7.2, without stretching it.

Ricci Tensor

Scalar Curvature

For $d_L \geq 3$, the manifold is not flat. Recalling that the Ricci tensor is defined by $R_{\mu\nu} = R_{\mu\alpha\nu}{}^{\alpha}$, and the scalar curvature by $R = R_\mu{}^\mu$, for general dimension d_L and power p, we have (note the singularity at $\mathbf{x} = 0$):

$$\begin{aligned} R_{\mu\nu\rho}{}^{\sigma} &= \frac{(p-1)}{\|\mathbf{x}\|^2}(\delta_{\rho\nu}\delta_{\sigma\mu} - \delta_{\rho\mu}\delta_{\sigma\nu}) \\ &- \frac{(p-1)}{\|\mathbf{x}\|^4}(x_\nu x_\rho \delta_{\mu\sigma} - x_\mu x_\rho \delta_{\sigma\nu} + x_\sigma x_\mu \delta_{\rho\nu} - x_\sigma x_\nu \delta_{\rho\mu}) \end{aligned} \tag{7.28}$$

$$R_{\mu\rho} = \frac{(p-1)(2-d_L)}{\|\mathbf{x}\|^2}\left(\delta_{\mu\rho} - \frac{x_\mu x_\rho}{\|\mathbf{x}\|^2}\right) \tag{7.29}$$

$$R = \frac{(p-1)(2-d_L)(d_L-1)}{p(\|\mathbf{x}\|^2)^p} \tag{7.30}$$

7.6.2 The Volume Element

The volume element of the mapped surface is of interest for several reasons. For example, one might expect poor generalization performance in the two-class pattern recognition case if some portion of the input space, containing data from both classes, gets mapped to a volume in $\mathcal{S}$ which is very small compared to the volume occupied by the rest of the mapped training data.[3] Secondly, given a probability density $p(\mathbf{x})$ for the data in input space, knowing the volume element, $dV = G(\mathbf{x})d\mathbf{x}$, immediately yields the density $\bar{p}(\mathbf{x})$ of the mapped data in $\mathcal{S}$ (assuming that the mapping is 1-1, and again treating the $\mathbf{x}$ in the latter case as a parameterization of the surface), since then $p(\mathbf{x})d\mathbf{x} = \bar{p}(\mathbf{x})G(\mathbf{x})d\mathbf{x}$.

For the case of dot product kernels we can explicitly compute the volume element $dV = \sqrt{(\det g_{\mu\nu})}dx_1 \dots dx_{d_L}$. Defining the matrix (all quantities are functions of $\|\mathbf{x}\|^2$)

$$A_{\mu\nu} \equiv x_\mu x_\nu (k''/k')) \tag{7.31}$$

and using the identity $\det(1+A) = e^{Tr \ln(1+A)}$, we find

$$dV = (k')^{\frac{d_L}{2}} \sqrt{\left(1 + \|\mathbf{x}\|^2 \frac{k''}{k'}\right)} dx_1 \dots dx_{d_L} \tag{7.32}$$

7.7 Positivity

It is straightforward to check that the induced metric is in general positive definite: combining Eqs. (7.1) and (7.8) gives

$$g_{\mu\nu} = \sum_{n=1}^{d_F} (\partial_{x_\mu} \Phi_n(x))(\partial_{x_\nu} \Phi_n(x)) \tag{7.33}$$

so for any vector $\mathbf{v} \in \mathbb{R}^{d_L}$, $\mathbf{v}^T g \mathbf{v} = \sum_{n,\mu} (v_\mu \partial_{x_\mu} \Phi_n(x))^2 > 0$. (If $d_F = \infty$, we must also require that the the sum on the right hand side be uniformly convergent, and that the derivatives be continuous, in order to be able to take the derivatives underneath the summation sign).

We can use the fact that any Riemannian metric must be positive definite to derive conditions that any prospective kernel must satisfy. Using Eq. (7.20), we can easily find the eigenvectors $\mathbf{V}$ of the metric for the general dot products kernels

3. One might also expect poor generalization performance if some data from both classes is mapped to a subset of the manifold with high curvature.

discussed above:

$$g_{\mu\nu}V_\nu = V_\mu k'(\|\mathbf{x}\|^2) + x_\mu(\mathbf{x}\cdot\mathbf{V})k''(\|\mathbf{x}\|^2)$$
$$= \lambda V_\mu \tag{7.34}$$

Thus the eigenvectors are (i) all $\mathbf{V}$ orthogonal to $\mathbf{x}$ ($d_L - 1$ of them), with eigenvalues $k'(\|\mathbf{x}\|^2)$, and (ii) $\mathbf{V} = \mathbf{x}$, with eigenvalue $k' + \|\mathbf{x}\|^2 k''$. Hence we arrive at the following

Proposition 7.1
Three necessary conditions for a dot product kernel, $k(\mathbf{x}, \mathbf{y}) = k(\mathbf{x}\cdot\mathbf{y})$, to be a positive semidefinite kernel, are:

$$k(\|\mathbf{x}\|^2) \geq 0 \tag{7.35}$$
$$k'(\|\mathbf{x}\|^2) \geq 0 \tag{7.36}$$
$$k'(\|\mathbf{x}\|^2) + \|\mathbf{x}\|^2 k''(\|\mathbf{x}\|^2) \geq 0 \tag{7.37}$$

where the prime denotes derivative with respect to $\|\mathbf{x}\|^2$. The first condition follows directly from Eq. (7.2) (choose a square integrable $g(\mathbf{x})$ which is strongly peaked around some point $\mathbf{x}$, and which falls rapidly to zero elsewhere: see Courant and Hilbert (1953)), the last two from the requirement that the metric have positive eigenvalues.

The kernel $k(\mathbf{x}, \mathbf{y}) = \tanh(a\mathbf{x}\cdot\mathbf{y} + b)$ has been noted as generating a support vector machine which is equivalent to a particular two-layer neural network (Boser et al., 1992; Vapnik, 1995). However it is also known that this only holds for certain values of the parameters a, b: for others, it was noted experimentally that Mercer's condition is violated (Vapnik, 1995). Proposition 7.1 shows that a, b must satisfy

$$b \geq 0 \tag{7.38}$$

$$a \geq 0 \tag{7.39}$$

$$1 - 2a\|\mathbf{x}\|^2 \tanh(a\|\mathbf{x}\|^2 + b) \geq 0 \tag{7.40}$$

Eq. (7.38) follows from (7.35), with the assumption that $\|\mathbf{x}\|^2$ can be chosen to be arbitrarily small; Eq. (7.39) follows from (7.36). The proposition also shows immediately that some proposed kernels, such as $e^{-\mathbf{x}\cdot\mathbf{y}}$, are in fact not Mercer kernels. Note that the proposition gives necessary but not sufficient conditions. However Mercer's condition is often not easy to verify (Eq. (7.2) must hold for *any* square integrable g), so such tests can be very useful.

Clearly, conditions (7.36) and (7.37) must also follow from Mercer's condition. In fact condition (7.37) can be derived by choosing $g(\mathbf{x}) = \delta(\mathbf{x} - \mathbf{x}_0) - \delta(\mathbf{x} - \mathbf{x}_0 - \epsilon)$ in Eq. (7.2) and letting ϵ approach zero (δ is the Dirac delta function).[4]

---

4. A rigorous proof of this assertion would require using suitably peaked L_2 functions,

For kernels of the form $k(\mathbf{x}, \mathbf{y}) = k(\|\mathbf{x} - \mathbf{y}\|^2)$, requiring positivity of the metric gives the following proposition:

Proposition 7.2
Given a function k with first derivatives defined and continuous, two necessary conditions for $k(\|\mathbf{x} - \mathbf{y}\|^2)$ to be a positive definite kernel are

$$k(0) > 0 \tag{7.41}$$

$$k'(0) < 0 \tag{7.42}$$

Here the prime denote derivative with respect to $\|\mathbf{x} - \mathbf{y}\|^2$. The first condition is a direct consequence of Mercer's condition, as before. The second condition follows by noting that the metric is simply $g_{\mu\nu} = -2\delta_{\mu\nu}k'(0)$.

7.8 Nash's Theorem: An Equivalence Class of Kernels

The following theorem holds (Nash, 1956):

Theorem 7.1
Every compact Riemannian d_L-manifold is realizable as a sub-manifold of Euclidean $(d_L/2)(3d_L + 11)$ space. Every non-compact Riemannian d_L-manifold is realizable as a sub-manifold of Euclidean $(d_L/2)(d_L + 1)(3d_L + 11)$ space.

The dimensions of the embedding spaces have since been further tightened (Greene, 1970), but theorem 7.1 alone raises the following puzzle. Support vector machines can map to spaces whose dimension exceeds those in the theorem. For example:

$$k(\mathbf{x}, \mathbf{y}) = e^{-\|\mathbf{x}-\mathbf{y}\|^2/2\sigma^2} \qquad d_F = \infty \tag{7.43}$$

$$k(\mathbf{x}, \mathbf{y}) = (\mathbf{x} \cdot \mathbf{y})^p \qquad d_F = C_p^{p+d_L-1} \tag{7.44}$$

and in the latter case, for $(d_L = 2)$-dimensional data,

$$C_p^{p+d_L-1} > (d_L/2)(3d_L + 11) \quad \text{for} \quad p = 17. \tag{7.45}$$

The explanation is that the map of kernels to metrics is many to one. In the left panel of figure 7.3, the data, which lives in $\mathcal{L}$, maps via positive semidefinite kernel k (and associated mapping Φ) to $\mathbb{R}^{d_F}$ (the left hand side of the panel). This induces a metric on $\mathcal{L}$. Nash's theorem tells us that there exists a space $\mathbb{R}^d$, in which the induced metric is the same as that induced by the support vector mapping (the right hand side of the panel), and where d may be less than d_F. A concrete example is given in the right hand panel. There, one can construct a kernel implementing the identity map, which maps some subset of $\mathbb{R}^2$ to itself. In this case the metric is the (flat) Euclidean metric and the dimension of the embedding space is 2. However, a different kernel can be chosen which maps the data onto some subset of the cylinder,

---

such as Gaussians, instead of Dirac delta functions, since the latter are not in L_2.

or to some subset of a cone (with vertex removed). In the latter two cases, the metric is still the Euclidean metric, but the minimal embedding space has dimension 3. Thus a given kernel may have an associated mapping Φ which maps to a space of higher dimension than that of the minimal dimension Euclidean space in which the input space $\mathcal{L}$, with metric arising from the kernel, can be isometrically embedded.

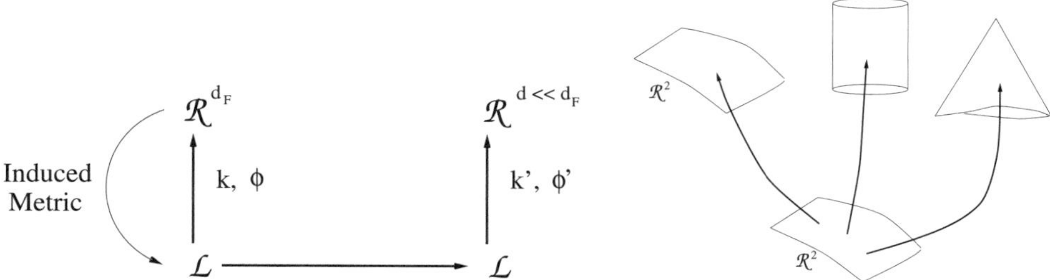

Figure 7.3 The kernels-to-metrics mapping is many-to-one.

Thus in a sense the kernel is more fundamental than the metric. An equivalence class of kernels which generate the same metric can be found by adding functions Ψ to a given kernel, where Ψ is symmetric, continuous and satisfies

$$\{\partial_{x_\mu}\partial_{x_\nu}((1/2)\Psi(\mathbf{x},\mathbf{x}) - \Psi(\mathbf{x},\mathbf{y}))\}_{\mathbf{y}=\mathbf{x}} = 0 \tag{7.46}$$

Note that, if k is a positive semidefinite kernel and $\bar{k} = k+\Psi$, for $\bar{k}$ to be also positive semidefinite, it is sufficient, but not necessary, that Ψ be positive semidefinite (sufficiency follows immediately from the linearity of Mercer's condition; as a counterexample to necessity, consider $k(\mathbf{x},\mathbf{y}) = (\mathbf{x}\cdot\mathbf{y})^p + 1$; then one can choose $\Psi = -1$, which satisfies the conditions, generates positive semidefinite $\bar{k}$, but is not itself positive semidefinite).

7.9 The Metric for Positive Definite Functions

A positive definite function $f(\mathbf{x})$ is defined as any function for which, for any n and any $c_i,\ c_j \in \mathbb{R}$ (Stewart, 1978),

$$\sum_{i,j=1}^{n} c_i c_j f(\mathbf{x}_i - \mathbf{x}_j) > 0. \tag{7.47}$$

It is known that any positive definite function is also a Mercer kernel, by letting $k(\mathbf{x}_i,\mathbf{x}_j) = f(\mathbf{x}_i - \mathbf{x}_j)$ (see Aronszajn (1950); Stewart (1978) and also Smola et al. (1998a)). Further, it is straightforward to show that any positive definite function f satisfies $f(0) \geq f(\mathbf{x})$ for all $\mathbf{x}$ (Stewart, 1978).

Thus Equation (7.42) is in concordance with known properties of positive definite functions.[5]

It seems odd at first that the induced metric should take such a simple form. For example, for Gaussian Radial Basis Function kernels, $k = e^{-\|\mathbf{x}-\mathbf{y}\|^2/2\sigma^2}$, the metric tensor becomes $g_{\mu\nu} = \delta_{\mu\nu}/\sigma^2$, which is flat. One simple consistency check is that, given two points P_1, P_2 in $\mathcal{S}$, the length of the shortest path (geodesic) in $\mathcal{S}$ which joins them must be greater than or equal to the "direct" Euclidean distance between P_1 and P_2 in F. Let $s^2 \equiv \|\mathbf{x}-\mathbf{y}\|^2$ for two data points $\mathbf{x},\ \mathbf{y} \in \mathcal{L}$. Then the squared geodesic distance between $\Phi(\mathbf{x})$ and $\Phi(\mathbf{y})$ in $\mathcal{S}$ is s^2/σ^2. The Euclidean squared distance between $\Phi(\mathbf{x})$ and $\Phi(\mathbf{y})$ is

$$\|\Phi(x) - \Phi(y)\|^2 = 2(1 - e^{-s^2/2\sigma^2}) \tag{7.48}$$

Using the identity

$$1 - e^{-z} < z \quad \forall z \in (0, \infty] \tag{7.49}$$

with $z = s^2/2\sigma^2$, we see that the distances do at least satisfy this consistency check. As usual in infinite dimensional spaces, our intuition is unreliable: the surface $\mathcal{S}$ looks like a sphere (or a subset thereof), since $\|\Phi(\mathbf{x})\|^2 = 1\ \forall\ \mathbf{x} \in \mathcal{L}$, and the manifold $\mathcal{S}$ is a d_L-manifold, but $\mathcal{S}$ is certainly not a d_L-sphere (or a subset thereof).

7.10 A Note on Geodesics

Since support vector machines construct hyperplanes in F, it is interesting to consider the relation between the intersection of hyperplanes with $\mathcal{S}$ and geodesics on $\mathcal{S}$. Here we offer a cautionary note: the intersection of a plane with a surface does not necessarily generate a geodesic on that surface, and the geodesics of a surface are not necessarily generated by the intersections of planes with that surface. An example shown in figure 7.4 illustrates these two points. The geodesics on the right circular cylinder are the generating lines, the circles, and the helices. The former two are generated by the intersection of planes with the cylinder, the latter is not. On the other hand, the intersection of a plane with a right circular cylinder can generate an ellipse, which is not a geodesic.

7.11 Conclusions and Discussion

We have shown how, for a given positive kernel, the image of the data under the associated mapping is a Riemannian manifold (under some very general assumptions on the data and mapping), and have shown how the Riemannian metric can

5. Thanks to F. Girosi for pointing this out.

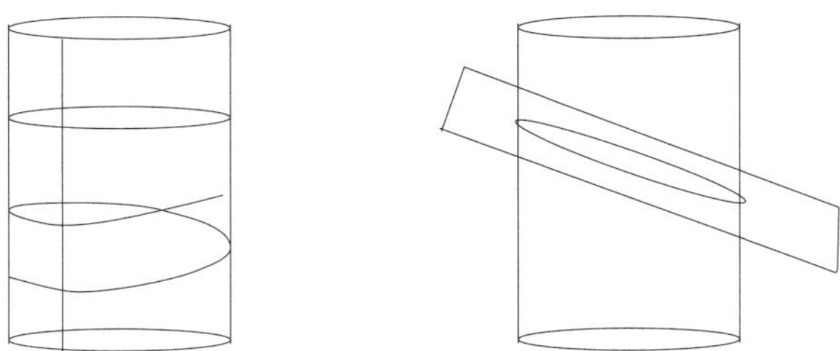

Figure 7.4 Hyperplanes may or may not generate geodesics.

be computed in closed form in terms of the kernel. We have pointed out that the kernel is a more fundamental quantity than the metric, in the sense that a given metric can be generated by a large class of kernels. While the intent was to gain geometrical understanding of the kernel mapping used by the support vector and other algorithms, a useful by-product was found in the requirement that the metric be positive definite, since this gives a simple test that any proposed Mercer kernel must satisfy. A worker may wish to choose a metric on her data, and then find a Mercer kernel which generates that metric: we pointed out that there always exists such a kernel, and gave the differential equation that it must satisfy. It is hoped that the tools described here may prove useful in understanding the intrinsic geometry of the mapping associated with any positive kernel.

While here we have studied the intrinsic geometry of the manifolds to which the data is mapped, it will likely also be useful to consider the extrinsic geometry of these manifolds (i.e. the geometry arising from the particular embedding in F). For example, even though the surface in figure 7.2 has vanishing intrinsic curvature, the extrinsic curvature is nonzero, and one would certainly expect the extrinsic geometry to play a role in the behaviour of an SVM for which F is the feature space. This will also be true for higher dimensions. However, care should be taken not to depend on properties of the embedding which do not depend on the kernel (for example, the kernel corresponding to figure 7.2 is equally well represented by a map to 4 instead of 3 dimensions (Burges, 1998), with correspondingly different extrinsic geometry). One way to accomplish this is to ensure that any quantities one arrives at depend on the mapping Φ only through the kernel.

PART 2

7.12 Overview

We turn now to the question of how to incorporate known invariances of the problem into the particular kernel-based method one is using. The basic idea is as follows: given a data point $\mathbf{x}$, suppose $\mathbf{x}'$ is the result of applying a small transformation to $\mathbf{x}$, corresponding to a known symmetry of the problem (for example, translation invariance in the image classification problem). (See Smola and Schölkopf (1998b) for further discussion on the kinds of symmetries one can consider). One would like one's decision function (or regression function) to give the same result on $\mathbf{x}$ and $\mathbf{x}'$, i.e., to be invariant under local (small) transformations of the data under the known symmetry. One could attempt to approach this problem by building on the metric analysis of the previous sections: that is, by choosing kernels such that $\Phi(\mathbf{x})$ and $\Phi(\mathbf{x}')$ are close, where by "close" we mean, for example, that the geodesic distance[6] joining the two transformed points is small. This could be achieved by looking for kernels whose metrics have the desired isometries.

However, the geometric analysis assumes positivity of the kernels, and many methods are not so restricted. Furthermore, even in SVM-like algorithms, the decision (or regression) function is a projected affine distance (Case III in figure 7.1), not an intrinsic distance measured in the manifold to which the data is mapped. We will therefore instead consider the much more general problem of how to build invariances directly into the (otherwise arbitrary, and in particular, not necessarily Mercer) kernels themselves. Specifically, we consider methods that approximate some unknown function $\mathcal{G}(\mathbf{x})$ by $F(\mathbf{x})$, where $F(\mathbf{x})$ has the form:

$$F(\mathbf{x}) = \sum_q w_q k(\mathbf{p}_q, \mathbf{x}) + b, \quad w_q, b \in \mathbb{R}^1, \quad \mathbf{x} \in \mathbb{R}^n, \quad \mathbf{p}_q \in \mathbb{R}^{n'} \tag{7.50}$$

where $\mathbf{p}_q$, the weights w_q, and the threshold b are parameters that are to be determined from empirical data by a training procedure, and where the form of the kernel k is usually chosen in advance. Additive models (Hastie and Tibshirani, 1990), Radial Basis Functions (Powell, 1987; Girosi et al., 1995; Bishop, 1995), and Support Vector Machines (Cortes and Vapnik, 1995; Vapnik, 1995) are examples of such methods. Pattern recognition, regression estimation, density estimation, and operator inversion are examples of problems tackled with these approaches (Vapnik, 1995). Thus for example in the density estimation case, $\mathbf{x}$ would be a point (in a vector space) at which the probability density is required, and $F(\mathbf{x})$ would be the approximation to that density; for the classification case, $\mathbf{x}$ would be a test pattern to be classified, and $\text{sgn}(F(\mathbf{x}))$ would give the corresponding label.

---

6. Of course, we mean the smallest geodesic distance here (e.g. two points on a 2-sphere are connected by two geodesics, which together make up the great circle on which the points lie).

One can also view the problem as that of model selection: given a task, how can one find a family of kernels that is best suited to that task? While results are known for some particular kernel based methods (for example, for SVMs, model selection based on VC bounds has been investigated by Schölkopf et al. (1995), and more recently, Schölkopf et al. (1998d) describe some methods for incorporating prior knowledge in SVMs), it is of interest to ask how one might restrict the class of models, using the prior knowledge of a known symmetry of the problem, for arbitrary kernel-based methods.

Section 7.13 describes the general approach. In section 7.14, we take the example of vertical translation invariance in images to perform a detailed analysis for a particular case.

7.13 Incorporating Local Invariances

Given two test points $\mathbf{x}$ and $\mathbf{y}$, equation (7.50) defines a distance function

$$\rho(\mathbf{x},\mathbf{y}) = \sum_q w_q(k(\mathbf{p}_q,\mathbf{x}) - k(\mathbf{p}_q,\mathbf{y})). \tag{7.51}$$

Note that $\rho(\mathbf{x},\mathbf{y})$ is an affine distance, in that it can take positive or negative values. For example, ρ can be thought of as counting contours between patterns in the pattern recognition case.

We would like to choose a class of kernels so that $\rho(\mathbf{x},\mathbf{y})$ is close to zero if $\mathbf{y}$ is a transform of $\mathbf{x}$ along some symmetry direction. If $\mathbf{y} = \mathbf{x} + d\mathbf{x}$, then

$$d\rho = \sum_{q,i} w_q dx^i \partial_i k(\mathbf{p}_q,\mathbf{x}) \tag{7.52}$$

Local Invariance

where we define $\partial_i \equiv \partial/\partial x_i$. Requiring that this be zero for all w_q gives:

$$\sum_i dx^i \partial_i k(\mathbf{p}_q,\mathbf{x}) = 0. \tag{7.53}$$

Note that for a particular problem, for which the w_q are known to satisfy certain constraints, equation (7.53) may be more restrictive than is necessary to ensure that $d\rho = 0$, but in this work we will make no assumptions about the w_q.

We write a general one-parameter transformation as:

$$x_i' = x_i + \alpha f_i(\mathbf{x}), \;\; \alpha \in R^1 \tag{7.54}$$

for which, in the limit as $\alpha \to 0$, Eq. (7.53) takes the form:

$$\sum_i f_i(\mathbf{x})\partial_i k(\mathbf{p}_q,\mathbf{x}) \equiv \mathcal{O}k(\mathbf{p}_q,\mathbf{x}) = 0 \tag{7.55}$$

which defines the operator $\mathcal{O}$. Henceforth we will not explicitly write the parameter vector $\mathbf{p}_q$ in k.

7.13.1 Operator Invariance for the Linear Case

We prove two simple propositions for the case in which the transformation (7.54) is both linear and invertible.

Proposition 7.3
For linear, invertible transformations (7.54), the operator $\mathcal{O}$ is itself invariant under the transformation.

Proof Let $\mathbf{U}$ denote the unit matrix, T denote transpose, and ∂ denote the vector with components $\partial_i \equiv \partial/\partial x_i$. Denote the transformation by

$$\mathbf{x}' = (\mathbf{U} + \alpha\mathbf{M})\mathbf{x}. \tag{7.56}$$

Then the operator $\mathcal{O}$ in Eq. (7.55) is given by:

$$\mathcal{O} = \mathbf{x}^T\mathbf{M}^T\partial \tag{7.57}$$

and

$$\mathcal{O}' = \mathbf{x}'^T\mathbf{M}^T\partial' = \sum_{i,j,k} M_{ij}(U + \alpha M)_{jk}x_k(U + \alpha M)^{-1}_{mi}\partial_m = \mathbf{x}^T\mathbf{M}^T\partial = \mathcal{O} \tag{7.58}$$

■

Proposition 7.4
For linear, invertible transformations (7.54), denoting the argument of $k()$ by its components x_i, if $k(x_i)$ satisfies (7.55), then so does $k(x_i + \alpha f_i(\mathbf{x}))$, for *finite* α.

Proof We have

$$\mathcal{O}k(x_i) = 0 = \mathcal{O}'k(x_i + \alpha f_i(\mathbf{x})) = \mathcal{O}k(x_i + \alpha f_i(\mathbf{x})), \tag{7.59}$$

since $\mathcal{O}$ is an invariant by the above theorem. ■

7.13.2 Multiple Symmetries

For a set of M symmetries, there will be M simultaneous equations of the form (7.55):

$$\mathcal{O}_m u(x_0, \ldots, x_{n-1}) = 0, \quad m = 1, \ldots, M \tag{7.60}$$

where $\{\mathcal{O}_m\}$ is a set of linear differential operators, each of which takes the general form

$$\mathcal{O}_m = \sum_i f_{mi}(\mathbf{x})\partial_i. \tag{7.61}$$

Thus in order to find the set of kernels which are simultaneously invariant under multiple symmetries, we need to find all the non-trivial integrals of (7.60). Following Chester (1971), we have:

Complete Operators

Definition 7.1
A system of operators $\{\mathcal{O}_i\}$ is called *complete* if all commutators take the form

$$[\mathcal{O}_i, \mathcal{O}_j] = \sum_k c_{ijk}\mathcal{O}_k, \quad c_{ijk} \in \mathbb{R}^1 \tag{7.62}$$

Note that, from their definition, the c_{ijk} are skew symmetric in i, j and satisfy the Jacobi identity, so they are in fact the structure constants of a Lie algebra (Olver, 1986).

Complete Equations

Definition 7.2
A system of equations (7.60) is called *complete* if the corresponding operators form a complete set (Chester, 1971).

Theorem 7.2
Any complete system of $r < n$ independent equations, of the form (7.60), has exactly $n - r$ independent integrals (Chester, 1971).

Thus, non-trivial integrals u will only exist if the number of operators r in the complete set is less than n, and if so, there will be $n - r$ of them. In the latter case, the general solution of the system (7.60) will have the form

$$F(u_0(x_0, \ldots, x_{n-1}), \ldots, u_{n-r-1}(x_0, \ldots, x_{n-1})) \tag{7.63}$$

where F is any C^1 function. Note that in order to find the complete set of operators one simply generates new operators by computing all the commutators in (7.62). If the number of independent operators thereby found is less than n, one has a complete set; otherwise there exists no non-trivial solution.

Imposing constraints on the kernel functions may thus be viewed as a form of capacity control, where the number of degrees of freedom in the problem is explicitly reduced by the dimension of the Lie algebra in Eq. (7.62).

7.13.3 Building Locally Invariant Kernels

Given the general solution to the system (7.60), we can now easily construct locally invariant kernels, since although the functions F must be differentiable, they are otherwise arbitrary. Henceforth, we will use $\mathcal{I}$ ("input") to label the space $\mathbb{R}^n$ in which the data are elements, and $\mathcal{P}$ ("preprocessed") to label the space $\mathbb{R}^{n-r}$, in which the independent integrals $\mathbf{u}$ may be viewed as coordinates. Thus one can view the mapping from $\mathcal{I}$ to $\mathcal{P}$ as a preprocessing step, after which a known family of kernels may be applied. Note that the kernels may have further constraints placed on them by the particular method being used (for example, their dependence on the parameter set $\mathbf{p}_q$), but that this is easily dealt with, since any of the original set of kernels can be used (but on the preprocessed data).

For example, for support vectors machines, the kernels take the form $k(\mathbf{s}_q, \mathbf{x})$, $\mathbf{s}_q$, $\mathbf{x} \in \mathbb{R}^n$, where the $\mathbf{s}_q$ are the support vectors. The kernels must be symmetric, $k(\mathbf{x}, \mathbf{y}) = k(\mathbf{y}, \mathbf{x}) \;\; \forall \;\; \mathbf{x}, \mathbf{y} \in \mathbb{R}^n$, and continuous, and they must satisfy Mercer's constraint, Eq. (7.2). Now suppose that some number of symmetries have been imposed, resulting in a complete set of size $r < n$, so that the number of independent integrals (and hence, the dimension of $\mathcal{P}$) is $n - r$. Thus, the solutions have the general form (7.63) above. We can then simply choose F to have the form of a kernel function which is known to satisfy the constraints, but which takes $n - r$ arguments instead of n. For example, we might take degree p polynomial kernels, for which the F will have the form

$$F(\mathbf{u}, \mathbf{v}) = (\mathbf{u} \cdot \mathbf{v} + 1)^p, \quad \mathbf{u}, \mathbf{v} \in \mathbb{R}^{n-r} \tag{7.64}$$

Since such kernels are symmetric, continuous and satisfy Mercer's condition, all the desired constraints are satisfied. What was a polynomial support vector machine has become a polynomial support vector machine acting on preprocessed data. However, the functional form that the overall kernels take, when considered as functions of the input data $\mathbf{x}$, will no longer in general be polynomial. However it may be necessary to use kernels other than those which give good performance on data in $\mathcal{I}$, as we shall see below.

7.14 A Detailed Example: Vertical Translation Invariance

Let us use the example of vertical translation invariance for the pattern recognition problem in order to explore in detail where the ideas of the previous section lead. We consider an image of n rows and one column, and we impose cyclic boundary conditions. We do this because solving this problem amounts to solving the general n_1 by n_2 problem: an n_1 by n_2 image can be converted to an $n_1 n_2$ by 1 image by pasting the top of each column of pixels to the bottom of the previous column. Finally, we consider transformations corresponding to shifts of up to one pixel. (To make the cyclic boundary conditions a realistic assumption, a border of one blank pixel could be added to the top and bottom of the original image.) In this case the transformations (7.54) take the form:

$$x_i{}' = (1 - \alpha)x_i + \alpha x_{(i+1)}, \quad i = 0, \ldots, N-1, \quad \alpha \in [0, 1] \tag{7.65}$$

Note that here and below we adopt the convention that indices i, j, k are to be taken modulo n. Eq. (7.55) becomes:

$$\sum_{i=0}^{n-1} \{(x_{i+1} - x_i)\partial_i\} u(\mathbf{x}) = 0 \tag{7.66}$$

7.14.1 The Relation to Group Action

We start by exploring the relation of the transformations (7.65) to a group action. Since pixels are an approximation to a continuous function which can be considered as a representation of the group of translations, let us first make the connection between pixels and the continuous case. Let $I(z)$ represent the original image field for which the n-pixel column is an approximation. Thus

$$x_i = I(i), \ i = 0, \dots, n-1 \tag{7.67}$$

Translating by a distance α means replacing $I(z)$ by $I'(z) = I(z - \alpha)$. The new pixel values become

$$x'_i = I'(i) = I(i - \alpha) \approx I(i) - \alpha(\partial_z I)(i) \tag{7.68}$$

Approximating $(\partial_z I)(i)$ by $I(i) - I(i-1)$ then gives equation (7.65).

However, the binning of the data into a vector has the consequence that Eq. (7.65), for finite α, is not a group action, although it does constitute the desired transformation. We illustrate this point with a simple specific case, namely vertical translation invariance for a column of three pixels, whose values we label by x, y, z. Then (7.65) for x becomes:

$$x' = g_\alpha x \equiv x(1 - \alpha) + \alpha y \tag{7.69}$$

where g_α is the operator instantiating the transformation. Then

$$(g_\beta \circ g_\alpha)x = x(1-\alpha)(1-\beta) + y(\alpha + \beta - 2\alpha\beta) + z\alpha\beta \tag{7.70}$$

so there exists no γ such that $g_\gamma = g_\beta \circ g_\alpha$. However, to first order in α, β, the above transformations do form a group, with $g_\alpha^{-1} = g_{-\alpha}$. Thus, the action may be viewed as of a group only for infinitesimal values of the parameters (Olver, 1986). Despite this fact, the transformation (7.69) does constitute a translation of the binned data for finite values of α (in fact for any $\alpha \in [0, 1]$).

Infinitesimal Group Action

But if the action is a group action for infinitesimal values of the parameters, then the corresponding differential operators are necessarily generators for a one-parameter Lie group. However the representation of that group for finite values of α does not coincide with (7.65). One can find what the representation is by exponentiating the generator corresponding to Eq. (7.65) acting on a particular point, for example:

Generators

$$\begin{aligned} e^{\{\alpha((y-x)\partial_x + (z-y)\partial_y + (x-z)\partial_z)\}}x = x + (y-x)h_1 + (x - 2y + z)h_2 + \\ +(y-z)h_3 + (x + y - 2z)h_4 + (x-z)h_5 + (-2x + y + z)h_6 \end{aligned} \tag{7.71}$$

where the h_i are functions of α alone. This only corresponds to the transformation (7.69) to first order in α. To summarize, the transformation (7.69) coincides with that of a Lie group only for infinitesimal values of the parameters; for finite values, it is no longer a group, but it is still the desired transformation.

7.14.2 A Simple Example: 4 Pixels

Let us find the complete solution for the next simplest case: an image which consists of just 4 pixels. Eq. (7.66) becomes:

$$\{(x_1 - x_0)\partial_{x_0} + (x_2 - x_1)\partial_{x_1} + (x_3 - x_2)\partial_{x_2} + (x_0 - x_3)\partial_{x_3}\}u(\mathbf{x}) = 0. \tag{7.72}$$

The general solution to this is:

$$f(x_0, x_1, x_2, x_3) = F(u_0, u_1, u_2) \tag{7.73}$$

where

$$u_0 = x_0 + x_1 + x_2 + x_3 \tag{7.74}$$

$$u_1 = \ln\left(\frac{x_0 - x_1 + x_2 - x_3}{(x_0 - x_2)^2 + (x_3 - x_1)^2}\right) \tag{7.75}$$

$$u_2 = \arctan\left(\frac{x_3 - x_1}{x_0 - x_2}\right) + +\frac{1}{2}\ln((x_0 - x_2)^2 + (x_3 - x_1)^2) \tag{7.76}$$

where F is any C^1 function. Thus to use this solution in a kernel based method, one would replace F by one's choice of kernel, but it would be a function of the three variables u_0, u_1, u_2 instead of the four x_i.

This solution has two properties to which we wish to draw attention: First, u_0, and only u_0, is "globally" invariant (invariant for any of the allowed values of α in Eq. (7.65); u_0 corresponds to the "total ink" in the image); second, all three independent integrals have a property which we call "additive invariance."

7.14.2.1 Additive Invariance

Recalling that the transformed variables are denoted with a prime (Eq. (7.65)), we define an "additive invariant" integral to be one that has the property:

$$u_j(\mathbf{x}') = u_j(\mathbf{x}) + f_j(\alpha), \quad j = 0, \ldots, 2 \tag{7.77}$$

for some functions f_j. Clearly, by construction, $f_j(\alpha)$ is $O(\alpha^2)$.

Additive invariance reduces the number of degrees of freedom in the problem in the following sense: consider two points in input space $\mathcal{I}$ which are related by a vertical translation. They will map into two points in $\mathcal{P}$, whose difference is independent of the original data, and which depends only on the transformation parameter α. Thus to learn that two images are translates of each other, the learning machine, acting on $\mathcal{P}$, has only to learn a vector valued function of one parameter ($f_j(\alpha)$), *where that parameter is independent of the original data* (i.e. independent of the pixel values of the original image). Note that the original data does not have this property: for pixel data, the difference between two translated images depends on the original image. If we were able to find solutions with $f_j(\alpha) = 0$, we would have a global invariance. However, we shall prove below that, for the symmetry and boundary conditions considered, there is only one globally invariant solution, for arbitrary dimension n; thus, in the absence of a family of globally invariant solutions, additive invariance appears to be a desirable property for the solutions to have.

Note that the solution of a PDE has a large degree of arbitrariness in the independent integrals found. For the above example, we could equally well have taken u_j^2 instead of the u_j as the integrals. The former do not have the additive invariance property. Thus for a general problem, we can only hope to find particular additive invariant integrals, rather than prove that all integrals will be additive invariant.

Note also that additive invariance only strictly holds if the two images $\mathbf{x}$ and $\mathbf{x}'$ being compared have values of the arctan in (7.76) which do not lie on opposite sides of a cut line. If this does not hold, then there will be an additional 2π in $u_2(\mathbf{x}) - u_2(\mathbf{x}')$. While this extra term does not depend continuously on the data, it is nevertheless a dependence.

Finally, we point out that u_0 and u_1 above are also solutions of the corresponding differential equations for vertical translation invariance in the opposite direction. Since the two operators commute, by theorem 7.2 we know that there will be a total of two independent integrals, so we know that u_0 and u_1 constitute the full solution, and this solution is clearly additive invariant. This example also illustrates a property of invariances in binned data which differs from that for continuous data: for continuous data, vertical translations compose a one-parameter, Abelian group. For binned data, translating "down" gives different generators from translating "up," which will give different generators from translating up by 2 pixels instead of 1, and so forth. Each of these imposed symmetries will reduce the dimensionality of $\mathcal{P}$ by one.

The example given in this section raises the following questions for the case of arbitrarily sized images: first, assuming that the general solution can be found, will we still only be able to find one *globally* invariant independent integral (analogous to u_0 above)? If so, additive invariant solutions will perhaps be useful. Second, can one construct solutions so that all independent integrals are additively invariant? The answers to both of these questions is yes, as we shall now show.

7.14.3 The n-Pixel Case

As mentioned above, in order to answer the above questions for an arbitrarily sized image, we only need consider the case of an n-pixel stack, and we must then solve Eq. (7.66). We start, however, by answering the first question above.

7.14.3.1 A No-Go Theorem

We have the following

Theorem 7.3
Any solution of (7.66), which is also invariant under the transformation (7.65) for any $\alpha \in [0,1]$, has the form $F(\sum_i x_i)$, where $F \in C^1$.

The proof is given in the Appendix. This theorem demonstrates that we cannot hope to find globally invariant solutions of Eq. (7.66), other than $F(\sum_i x_i)$. Thus, we will need to search for "second best" solutions, such as additive invariant ones.

7.14.3.2 The General Solution

We now derive the general solution for the n-pixel case. Eq. (7.66) may be viewed as the dot product of the gradient of an unknown function u with a vector field in n dimensions, and to find the general solution one must solve the set of ODE's which describe the characteristic surfaces, which are themselves parameterized by some $t \in \mathbb{R}^1$ (Zachmanoglou and Thoe, 1986):

$$\frac{d\mathbf{x}}{dt} = \mathbf{A}\mathbf{x} \tag{7.78}$$

where

$$A_{ij} = -\delta_{ij} + \delta_{i,j+1}. \tag{7.79}$$

$\mathbf{A}$ has determinant zero and eigenvalues λ_k given by

$$1 + \lambda_k = e^{2\pi ik/n}, \quad k = 0, \cdots, n-1 \tag{7.80}$$

Here and for the remainder, we reserve the symbol i for $\sqrt{-1}$. By inspection we can construct the eigenvectors $\mathbf{z}$ of the matrix $\mathbf{A}$

$$z_{k,j} = e^{2\pi ijk/n}, \quad j, k = 0, \cdots, n-1 \tag{7.81}$$

where the first index k labels the eigenvector, and the second j its components. Let $\mathbf{S}$ be the matrix whose columns are the eigenvectors $\mathbf{z}$. Then $\mathbf{S}$ diagonalizes $\mathbf{A}$:

$$\mathbf{S}^{-1}\mathbf{A}\mathbf{S} = \text{diag}(\lambda_i) \tag{7.82}$$

One can confirm by multiplication that the inverse of $\mathbf{S}$ is given by $(1/n)\mathbf{S}^{\dagger}$ (where $\dagger$ denotes hermitian conjugate). Thus introducing $\mathbf{y} \equiv \mathbf{S}^{-1}\mathbf{x}$, the solutions of equations (7.78) are given by

$$y_0 = c_0 \tag{7.83}$$

$$t = \frac{1}{e^{2\pi ik/n} - 1} \ln(\frac{y_k}{c_k}), \quad k = 1, \cdots, n-1 \tag{7.84}$$

where the c_k are constants of integration. One can then easily show that expressions (7.83) and (7.84) constitute only $n-1$ independent equations.

We can now write the explicit solution to (7.66), which we do for n even (the solution for n odd is similar). Again, let F be any C^1 function. The general solution may be written

$$f(x_0, \cdots, x_{n-1}) = F(u_0, \cdots, u_{n-2}) \tag{7.85}$$

where

$$u_0 = \sum_i x_i \tag{7.86}$$

$$u_{2k-1} = (1/\phi_t)\arctan(\phi_s/\phi_c) + (1/2)\ln(\phi_c^2 + \phi_s^2) \tag{7.87}$$

$$u_{2k} = (1/2)\ln(\phi_c^2 + \phi_s^2) - \phi_t \arctan(\phi_s/\phi_c) - \ln T \tag{7.88}$$

and where $k = 1, \cdots, (n/2) - 1$, and we have introduced

$$\phi_s(n, k, \mathbf{x}) \equiv \sum_{j=0}^{n-1} \sin(2\pi kj/n)x_j \tag{7.89}$$

$$\phi_c(n, k, x) \equiv \sum_{j=0}^{n-1} \cos(2\pi kj/n)x_j \tag{7.90}$$

$$\phi_t(n, k) \equiv \frac{\sin(2\pi k/n)}{\cos(2\pi k/n) - 1} \tag{7.91}$$

and

$$T \equiv \sum_{j=0}^{n-1}(-1)^j x_j = \phi_c(n, n/2, \mathbf{x}). \tag{7.92}$$

7.14.3.3 Additive Invariance

We now show that all the independent integrals in the above solution have the additive invariance property, up to factors of 2π which result from the cut line of the arctan function. Clearly u_0 is additive invariant (in fact it is invariant). The $u_k, \ \ k > 0$ in (7.85) were all obtained by taking real and imaginary parts of linear combinations of equations (7.84), i.e. of

$$t = \frac{1}{e^{2\pi k/n} - 1} \ln\{(1/nc_k)\sum_j e^{-2\pi ikj/n}x_j\}, \quad k > 0 \tag{7.93}$$

Transforming the $\mathbf{x}$ according to (7.65) gives the transform of t:

$$t_\alpha = \left(\frac{1}{e^{2\pi k/n} - 1}\right) \ln(1 - \alpha + \alpha e^{2\pi ik/n}) + t, \quad k > 0 \tag{7.94}$$

Thus taking linear combinations of these equations will always give equations which separate into the sum of an α-dependent part and an $\mathbf{x}$-dependent part. Hence all solutions in (7.87), (7.88) (and (7.86)) are additive invariant.

7.15 The Method of Central Moments

It is interesting to compare the method described above, for the case of translation invariance, with the method of central moments, in which translation invariant features are constructed by taking moments with respect to coordinates which are relative to the center of mass of the image. From these moments, rotation and scale invariant moments can also be constructed. For example, for continuous data, one can construct the translation invariant moments (Schalkoff, 1989):

$$\mu_{pq} = \int_{-\infty}^{\infty}\int_{-\infty}^{\infty} (x - \hat{x})^p(y - \hat{y})^q I(x, y)dxdy, \tag{7.95}$$

where x, y are the coordinates of points in the image, $\hat{x}$, $\hat{y}$ are the coordinates of the center of mass, and $I(x, y)$ is the corresponding image intensity. To apply this to pixel data one must replace (7.95) by an approximate sum, which results in features which are only approximately translation invariant (although as the number of pixels increases, the approximation improves). However, for binary data, $I \in \{0, 1\}$, it is possible to construct moments from the pixel data which are exactly invariant:

$$\mu_{pq} = \sum_{j,k \neq 0} (j - \hat{j})^p (k - \hat{k})^q I(j, k) \tag{7.96}$$

where the sum is over only non-zero values of i and j.

How does the existence of these invariants relate to the above theorem on the existence of only one globally invariant integral for vertical translation invariance with cyclic boundary conditions? The μ_{pq} in Eq. (7.95) are globally invariant, but there the data must be not binned, and are continuous; the μ_{pq} in Eq. (7.96) are also globally invariant, but there the data must be binned, and discrete. Thus our theorem (for binned, continuous data) addresses the case lying between these two extremes. (However, it is an open question whether theorem 7.3 holds also for other choices of boundary conditions).

The method of central moments, compared to the approach described above, has the advantage that the features are likely to be less sensitive to motions in the symmetry directions, especially when the number of pixels is very large. However, it is not clear how many moments, and which moments, are needed to give good generalization performance for a given problem. Furthermore, the problem of which kernels to use on the preprocessed data remains, and is critical, as we see below.

7.16 Discussion

We have explored a very general approach to incorporating known symmetries of the problem in kernel-based methods, by requiring that the kernels themselves be invariant (at least locally) under that set of transformations under which one expects the function (Eq. (7.50)) to be invariant. We have used the case of translation invariance of binned data with cyclic boundary conditions to explore these ideas in detail. For that case, we showed that one cannot hope to construct globally invariant kernels which depend on anything other than the sum of the pixel data. We also showed that the mapping can be chosen to have the property that the difference of two mapped images, which are translates of each other, is independent of the original data. Since the class of globally invariant functions is too small to be of much use, this "additive invariance" would seem to be an attractive property, although to benefit one would have to choose kernels (acting on $\mathcal{P}$), which take advantage of it.

However, experiments done on NIST 28x28 digit data, using polynomial and RBF support vector machines, and also a kernel version of Kth nearest neighbour, acting on data preprocessed according to Eqs. (7.86), (7.87), and (7.88), showed no improvement in generalization performance: in fact, most experiments gave considerably worse results. Since all the original pixel information (minus a degree of freedom due to translation invariance) is still in the preprocessed data, we conclude that these particular kernels, which work well for support vector machines acting on pixel data, are not well suited to the preprocessed data. Perhaps this should not be surprising: after all, a polynomial kernel computes correlations between pixels directly; it is not clear what a polynomial kernel acting on $\mathcal{P}$ is doing. Thus further research is needed regarding how to find suitable kernels for the preprocessed data (in particular, ones which take advantage of additive invariance). But whatever kernels are used, we know that the resulting system will have the desired local invariance.

The theory described above still leaves a great deal of freedom in the form the solutions take. For example in the case studied, the independent integrals, Eqs. (7.86) - (7.88), form the basis for a general solution, but this basis is itself far from unique. It is straightforward to find alternative sets of independent integrals. In one such set, the discrete fourier transform (DFT) character of the transformation can be made explicit, in the sense that if the highest frequency component of the input data is normalized so that $T = 1$ in (7.92), the transformation becomes an exact DFT. Since the DFT has an inverse, this example makes explicit the fact that the effect of preprocessing is to remove just one degree of freedom. The large class of possible solutions raises a similar question to the one above: if one chooses a different set of independent integrals for a given invariance, must one also choose different subsequent kernels to achieve the same generalization performance?

Finally, we have only required that the first derivative of the kernel vanish along a symmetry direction. This is a weak condition: a kernel that satisfies this may still vary significantly when data is transformed, even by small amounts, along that symmetry direction. One could proceed by requiring that higher derivatives also vanish. However, one would still require that the first derivative vanish, so the analysis carried out above would still pertain.

7.17 Appendix

Proof of Theorem 7.3.

We introduce the notation "prm" to denote cyclic permutation of the indices. In the following, indices i, j, k are always to be taken modulo n. By definition, an invariant solution must satisfy $\partial_\alpha u(\mathbf{x}') = 0$, where $\mathbf{x}'$ is the linear function of α defined in (7.65). However,

$$0 = \partial_\alpha u(\mathbf{x}') = (x_1 - x_0)\partial'_0 u(\mathbf{x}') + \text{prm} \tag{7.97}$$

Here we have introduced the notation $\partial_\alpha \equiv \partial/\partial\alpha$ and $\partial'_1 \equiv \partial/\partial x'_1$, etc. We can generate a set of PDEs that u must satisfy by expressing the x_i in terms of the x'_i

in Eq. (7.97). Note first that the transformations (7.65) can be written

$$\mathbf{x}' = \mathbf{M}\mathbf{x} \tag{7.98}$$

where

$$M_{ij} \equiv \delta_{i,j}(1-\alpha) + \delta_{i,j-1}\alpha, \quad i,j = 0,\cdots,n-1 \tag{7.99}$$

Note also that

$$\det(\mathbf{M}) \equiv S = (1-\alpha)^n - (-1)^n\alpha^n. \tag{7.100}$$

One can verify directly, by matrix multiplication, that

$$(M^{-1})_{ij} = (1/S)(\alpha-1)^{i-j-1}\alpha^{j-i}(-1)^{n-1} \tag{7.101}$$

(recall that subexpressions containing i, j, k are to be taken modulo n, so that the exponents in (7.101) only take values between $0,\cdots,n-1$). Thus Eq. (7.98) gives

$$(-1)^{n-1}S(x_1-x_0) = (\alpha^{n-1}-(\alpha-1)^{n-1})x'_0 - \sum_{j=1}^{n-1}(\alpha-1)^{n-j-1}\alpha^{j-1}x'_j \tag{7.102}$$

By using the fact that both $\mathbf{M}$ and $\mathbf{M}^{-1}$ are cyclic matrices, it is straightforward to show that the expression for $x_{i+1}-x_i$ can be obtained from that for x_1-x_0 in Eq. (7.102) by replacing x'_k by x'_{k+i} on the right hand side (and leaving other terms unchanged). We need the following

Lemma 7.1
Extracting the coefficients of powers of α on the right hand side of (7.97) gives the family of PDEs

$$\begin{aligned} ((x'_1-x'_0)\partial'_0 + \text{prm})u(\mathbf{x}') &= 0 \\ ((x'_2-x'_0)\partial'_0 + \text{prm})u(\mathbf{x}') &= 0 \\ &\cdots \\ ((x'_{N-1}-x'_0)\partial'_0 + \text{prm})u(\mathbf{x}') &= 0 \end{aligned} \tag{7.103}$$

Proof The proof is by induction. First we note by inspection that the coefficient of α^0 on the right hand side of (7.102) is $(-1)^n x'_0 - (-1)^{n-2}x'_1$. Thus substituting (7.102) in (7.97) and taking the coefficient of $O(1)$ gives

$$\{(x'_1-x'_0)\partial'_0 + \text{prm}\}u(\mathbf{x}') = 0. \tag{7.104}$$

Equation (7.104) can then be substituted in (7.97) to eliminate terms of order α^0. By repeating the process with coefficients of $O(\alpha)$, one arrives at an equation which one can combine with (7.104) (to eliminate x'_1 in the first term) to get

$$\{(x'_2-x'_0)\partial'_0 + \text{prm}\}u(\mathbf{x}') = 0. \tag{7.105}$$

Now assuming that this works up to α^p (giving the first $p+1$ equations in (7.103)), we must show that it works for α^{p+1} (giving the next equation in (7.103)). The coefficient of ∂'_0 in (7.97) is the right hand side of Eq. (7.102) (we have divided everything by the overall factor $(-1)^{n-1}S$). Using the first $p+1$ equations in (7.103), we can effectively replace x'_1 by x'_0, x'_2 by x'_0 etc., in the first term on the right hand side of Eq. (7.97). Doing this means that the coefficient of ∂'_0 in (7.97) becomes

$$\{\alpha^{n-1} - (\alpha-1)^{n-1} - (\alpha-1)^{n-2} - \alpha(\alpha-1)^{n-3} - \cdots - \alpha^p(\alpha-1)^{n-(p+2)}\}x'_0 - \sum_{j=p+2}^{n-1}(\alpha-1)^{n-j-1}\alpha^{j-1}x'_j \tag{7.106}$$

Using the identity

$$\sum_{i=1}^{p+1} C_i^{n-3-p+i} = C_{p+1}^{n-1} - 1 \tag{7.107}$$

we find that the coefficient of α^{p+1} in (7.106) is $(-1)^{N-p-2}(-x'_0 + x'_{p+2})$. Hence we have generated the $p+2$'th equation in Eq. (7.103). This completes the proof of the lemma. ■

Now note that (7.103) are independent equations, since the matrix of coefficients is of rank $n-1$ for some choices of the x_i. Finally, it is straightforward to check that all the operators appearing in (7.103) commute, so this set of $n-1$ PDEs forms a complete set. Since it is a complete set of $n-1$ PDEs in n dimensions, by theorem 7.2 it has only one integral solution. By substitution it is easily checked that $u(\mathbf{x}) = \sum_i x_i$ is a solution; thus the general solution of (7.97) must take the form $F(\sum_i x_i)$, where $F \in C^1$. This completes the proof of the theorem.

Acknowledgements

I wish to thank P. Knirsch, C.R. Nohl, B. Schölkopf, A. Smola, C. Stenard and V. Vapnik for useful discussions. This work was funded in part by ARPA contract N00014-94-C-0186.

8 On the Annealed VC Entropy for Margin Classifiers: A Statistical Mechanics Study

Manfred Opper
Neural Computing Research Group
Aston University, Birmingham B4 7ET, UK
opperm@aston.ac.uk
http://www.ncrg.aston.ac.uk/

Using techniques from Statistical Physics, the annealed VC entropy for hyperplanes in high dimensional spaces is calculated as a function of the margin for a spherical Gaussian distribution of inputs.

8.1 Introduction

The Vapnik-Chervonenkis (VC) approach to statistical learning theory (Vapnik, 1979, 1995) allows one to express the complexity of a family of statistical predictors in terms of entropic quantities, the so called VC entropies. For the case of a binary classifier, these entropies give the logarithm of the number of different classifications of a set of input points which are realizable by the family of classifiers. Upper bounds on these entropies can be expressed by a single combinatorial quantity, the VC dimension. Classifiers with large VC complexities can have a large deviation between empirical error and generalization error, which for the case of empirical risk minimzation may lead to strong overfitting, when not enough training data are available. For the case of learning in neural networks, the VC approach has been criticized for overestimating the complexities and giving too pessimistic bounds for a practical application in model selection.

effective dimensions

Recently, for margin classifiers and support vector machines it has been shown that if global VC dimensions are replaced by effective, data dependent dimensions (the so called *fat-shattering dimensions* (Alon et al., 1997)), reliable estimates for optimally generalizing models can be obtained (Vapnik, 1995). In these cases, the effective VC dimensions depend on the size of the margin by which positive and negative training inputs can be separated. Aside from general bounds and simulations, such results may be further understood from another approach to computational learning theory which has its origin in statistical mechanics. Using techniques from the theory of disordered systems, a huge variety of results for the typical learning behaviour of large neural networks have been obtained in the last years. For a review see e.g. Watkin et al. (1993), Opper and Kinzel (1996) and Seung et al. (1992). The statistical mechanics approach enables exact calculations for generalization errors and other properties of neural networks (assuming specific 'nice' distributions of examples) in the limit where the dimension of input space and the size of the set of examples are both very large. Although some of these techniques (like many in the field of Theoretical Physics) have not been made fully rigorous so far, this approach yields often new important results on which other, more general methods can be tested.

In the following, I will present a calculation of the *annealed* VC entropy for classifications by hyperplanes (perceptrons) as a function of the margin. The method follows a recent publication (Opper et al., 1997) which aimed at calculating the capacity of a toy neural network. This latter model can be interpreted as a problem of unsupervised learning in a perceptron where the output variables must be chosen in such a way that the margin between positive and negative examples is maximal.

8.2 VC Entropy

Let us assume a training set of ℓ input/output pairs $(\mathbf{x}_1, y_1)\ldots,(\mathbf{x}_\ell, y_\ell)$ for a binary classifier which are drawn independently at random from a fixed distribution. In the following, $\mathbf{x}_1^\ell$ stands for the set of inputs $\mathbf{x}_1,\ldots,\mathbf{x}_\ell$ and y_1^ℓ for the sequence of outputs $y_1,\ldots,y_\ell$. The VC approach enables us to bound the deviations between the training error $E_t(\mathbf{x}_1^\ell, y_1^\ell, c)$ (the number of misclassifications on the training set) and the generalization error $e_g(c)$ (the probability of a misclassification) over a family of classifiers $c \in \mathcal{F}$. E.g., it has been shown (Vapnik, 1995) that

$$\Pr\left(\sup_{c\in\mathcal{F}} |E_t(\mathbf{x}_1^\ell, y_1^\ell, c) - e_g(c)| > \varepsilon\right) \leq 4\exp\left[H_{ann}(2\ell) - \ell\varepsilon^2\right] \tag{8.1}$$

annealed entropy

where the annealed VC entropy is defined as

$$H_{ann}(\ell) = \ln\left\langle \mathcal{N}(\mathbf{x}_1^\ell)\right\rangle, \tag{8.2}$$

and where $\mathcal{N}(\mathbf{x}_1^\ell) \leq 2^\ell$ is the number of classifications (or dichotomies) of ℓ inputs which are realizable by going through the classifiers $c \in \mathcal{F}$, and the brackets $\langle\ldots\rangle$ denote expectations with respect to the distribution of the inputs.

Perceptrons classify inputs $\mathbf{x} \in \mathbb{R}^N$ by hyperplanes via $y = \operatorname{sgn}(\mathbf{w}\cdot\mathbf{x} + b) \in \{-1, +1\}$ (the weight vector $\mathbf{w} \in \mathbb{R}^N$ is normal to the class separating plane and $b \in \mathbb{R}$ is a bias). Throughout this chapter we will be concerned with hyperplanes *through the origin* i.e. $b = 0$ only. For this case, it is well known that

$$\mathcal{N}(\mathbf{x}_1^\ell) = 2\sum_{i=0}^{N-1} \binom{\ell - 1}{i}, \tag{8.3}$$

independently of the position of the inputs $\mathbf{x}_i$ (as long as they are in general position).

For more complicated types of classifiers, exact expressions for the VC entropies are hard to obtain. A remarkable and general combinatorial theorem, proved for the first time by Vapnik and Chervonenkis in the 1960s (Vapnik and Chervonenkis, 1968), however gives the general bound

$$\mathcal{N}(\mathbf{x}_1^\ell) \leq \sum_{i=0}^{h} \binom{\ell}{i}, \tag{8.4}$$

in terms of a single number h, the VC dimension of the family $\mathcal{F}$ of classifiers. This result allows us to obtain distribution independent bounds.

If we restrict the family of perceptrons to the subclass of all those which achieve a margin γ larger than some positive value κ, i.e.

$$\gamma = \max_{||\mathbf{w}||=1} \min_i \; y_i(\mathbf{w} \cdot \mathbf{x}_i) > \kappa, \tag{8.5}$$

VC dimension for margin

the corresponding VC dimension can be much smaller. A bound on the corresponding VC dimension h_κ was given in (Vapnik, 1979)

$$h_\kappa = \min\left(\left[\frac{R^2}{\kappa^2}\right] + 1, N\right), \tag{8.6}$$

where R is the radius of the minimal sphere containing all inputs. It is not directly possible to implement this bound on the VC dimension into the confidence bound (8.1), when the margin is not fixed in advance but taken from a classifier trained on a specific sample. This is because the bound (8.1) requires a fixed, *a priori* chosen (nonrandom) family of classifiers. Somewhat more complicated bounds have been proved recently for the data dependent case (Shawe-Taylor et al., 1996). Nevertheless, we expect that our calculations of the annealed entropy for a fixed margin may also give at least a qualitative picture for the data dependent case.

8.3 The Thermodynamic Limit

We will show that one can obtain exact expressions for the annealed entropy for a fixed margin for the case of a simple spherical distribution, provided we specialize to the so called the 'thermodynamic limit' of large input dimension N, and assume the scaling $\ell, N \to \infty$, keeping $\lambda = \frac{\ell}{N}$ fixed. To see that such a limit makes sense, we set $\lambda_{VC} = \frac{h}{N}$ and apply standard bounds on binomials in terms of binary entropies together with a Laplace approximation on the sum (approximated by an integral) to show that (8.4) yields

$$\lim_{N\to\infty} \frac{1}{N} H_{ann}(\lambda N) \tag{8.7}$$

$$\leq \begin{cases} \lambda \ln(2) & \text{for } \lambda \leq 2\lambda_{VC} \\ -\lambda\left[\frac{\lambda_{VC}}{\lambda}\ln(\frac{\lambda_{VC}}{\lambda}) + (1-\frac{\lambda_{VC}}{\lambda})\ln(1-\frac{\lambda_{VC}}{\lambda})\right] & \text{for } \lambda > 2\lambda_{VC}. \end{cases}$$

This bound becomes an equality for perceptrons without margin. It shows an interesting threshold phenomenon. If $\lambda > 2\lambda_{VC} \doteq \lambda_c$, then only an exponentially small fraction of all $2^{\lambda N}$ classifications can be realized. With probability approaching 1 in the thermodynamic limit, a *random* choice of output labels y_1^ℓ can not be realized by the classifier, when $\lambda > \lambda_c$. This result relates the *capacity* λ_c of the family of classifiers, via $\lambda_c \leq 2\lambda_{VC}$, to its VC dimension. Implemented into (8.1), we also have with probability one, that deviations ε between generalization error and training error larger than $\sqrt{\frac{H_{ann}(2l)}{l}}$ will not occur. Hence, since $\lim_{N\to\infty} \frac{H_{ann}(2\lambda N)}{\lambda N}$ is bounded by a quantity of the order $\frac{\ln\lambda}{\lambda}$ for large λ, the possible deviations ε will become arbitrarily small as λ grows large. For the family of perceptrons through the origin, $h = N$, $\lambda_{VC} = 1$ and the capacity $\lambda_c = 2$.

In the following, we will assume that the inputs are drawn independently from the spherical Gaussian distribution

spherical distribution

$$f(\mathbf{x}) = (2\pi)^{-N/2} e^{-\frac{1}{2}||\mathbf{x}||^2}. \tag{8.8}$$

In this case, we get $||x||^2/N \to 1$ with probability one as $N \to \infty$. Hence, heuristically, we expect that (8.6) applies to this case with $R \approx \sqrt{N}$ so that the capacity λ_c should be bounded by a term which is of the order of $\frac{1}{\kappa^2}$.

8.4 An Expression for the Annealed Entropy

In this section, we present the basic ideas of a calculation for the annealed entropy for classification with a margin. We begin with the obvious fact, that the number of dichotomies can be rewritten in terms of decision variables $\theta(y_1^\ell, \mathbf{x}_1^\ell) \in \{0,1\}$ as

$$\mathcal{N}(\mathbf{x}_1^\ell) = \sum_{y_1^\ell \in \{-1,1\}^\ell} \theta(y_1^\ell, \mathbf{x}_1^\ell), \tag{8.9}$$

where $\theta(y_1^n, \mathbf{x}_1^\ell) = 1$, if the labels are realizable with a margin κ and 0 else. In the next step, we have to average (8.9) over the distribution (8.8). By symmetry, all $2^{\lambda N}$ terms in the sum (8.9) give the same contribution and we can restrict ourselves to the case $y_i = 1$, for all $i = 1, \ldots, \ell$. We will denote the corresponding decision variable by $\theta(\mathbf{x}_1^\ell)$. Our basic idea for a construction of such a decision variable is based on the Kuhn Tucker conditions and the feasibility conditions on the primal/dual quadratic optimization problem which is equivalent to (8.5). These conditions are expressed in terms of Lagrange multipliers α_i and read

$$\mathbf{w} = \sum_i \frac{y_i \alpha_i \, \mathbf{x}_i}{\sqrt{N}} \tag{8.10}$$

$$\frac{y_i}{\sqrt{N}}(\mathbf{w} \cdot \mathbf{x}_i) \geq 1 \tag{8.11}$$

$$\alpha_i \geq 0 \tag{8.12}$$

$$\sum \alpha_i \left(\frac{y_i}{\sqrt{N}}(\mathbf{w} \cdot \mathbf{x}_i) - 1 \right) = 0, \tag{8.13}$$

for $i = 1, \ldots, \ell$. We have rescaled all quantities by $\sqrt{N}$ such that for $N \to \infty$, the typical size of the α_i and the components of $\mathbf{w}$ remain of order 1. The last condition states that positive α_i (corresponding to *support vectors*) satisfy $\frac{y_i}{\sqrt{N}}(\mathbf{w} \cdot \mathbf{x}_i) = 1$. The resulting margin γ is given by

$$\gamma^2 = N/||\mathbf{w}||^2 = N/\sum_i \alpha_i. \tag{8.14}$$

It is useful to introduce auxiliary variables s_i by

$$\alpha_i = s_i \Theta(s_i). \tag{8.15}$$

Inserting the first equation into the second, also setting $y_i = 1$, the set (8.10) - (8.13) can be replaced by the single equation

$$s_i \Theta(-s_i) + \sum_j C_{ij} \alpha_j - 1 = 0 \tag{8.16}$$

with the matrix $C_{ij} = \frac{1}{N}(\mathbf{x}_i \cdot \mathbf{x}_j)$. $\Theta(x)$ is the unit step function which is 1 for $x \geq 0$ and 0 else. Introducing Dirac $\delta-$ distributions for the condition (8.16), we can write

decision variable

$$\theta(\mathbf{x}_1^\ell) = \int_{-\infty}^{\infty} \prod_{i=1}^{\ell} ds_i \, \Theta(1/\kappa^2 - \frac{1}{N} \sum_i \alpha_i) \, \det(A) \times \prod_{i=1}^{\ell} \delta \left(s_i \Theta(-s_i) + \sum_j C_{ij} \alpha_j - 1 \right). \tag{8.17}$$

Obviously, the integral is only different from zero, if the condition (8.16) is fulfilled with a margin above κ. The matrix A guarantees proper normalization and is given by $A_{ij} = C_{ij} \Theta(s_j)$ for $i \neq j$, and $A_{ii} = \Theta(-s_i) + C_{ii} \Theta(s_i)$. Since $C_{ii} \to 1$, with probability one as $N \to \infty$, we may also simply set $A_{ii} = C_{ii}$.

As a result, we have expressed the decision variable $\theta(\mathbf{x}_1^\ell)$ as a high dimensional integral, reminiscent of partition functions in statistical physics.

8.5 Evaluation in the Thermodynamic Limit

The basic strategies employed in the statistical mechanics approach consist in the following steps: Exchanging average and integrations, the average over inputs is performed first. Subsequently, the high dimensional integrations are decoupled by introducing auxiliary (low dimensional) integrations and are carried out. Finally, the low dimensional integrals are performed in the limit $N \to \infty$ by the saddlepoint method. By the fact that we are calculating the annealed average $\langle \mathcal{N}(\mathbf{x}_1^\ell) \rangle$ rather than the *quenched* average $\langle \ln(\mathcal{N}(\mathbf{x}_1^\ell)) \rangle$, more sophisticated methods (such as the 'replica trick') are not needed.

It is convenient to decompose the decision variable $\theta(\mathbf{x}_1^\ell)$ into contributions from the different margins above κ

$$\theta(\mathbf{x}_1^\ell) = \int_0^{1/\kappa^2} Z(q, \mathbf{x}_1^\ell)\, dq \tag{8.18}$$

where now

$$Z(q, \mathbf{x}_1^\ell) = \int_{-\infty}^{\infty} \prod_{i=1}^{\ell} ds_i\, \delta(q - \frac{1}{N} \sum_i \alpha_i)\ \det(A) \times \prod_{i=1}^{\ell} \delta \left(s_i \Theta(-s_i) + \sum_j C_{ij} \alpha_j - 1 \right). \tag{8.19}$$

To average over Z, we perform the expectation over the distribution of $\mathbf{x}_i$ first, before we carry out the integrations over the s_i. We have to average over a product of two terms, the determinant and the part with the $\delta-$ distributions. It is easy to see that $\det(A) = \det(B)$, where B is the submatrix of C, which contains all those elements C_{ij}, for which s_i and s_j are positive, i.e. for which both $\mathbf{x}_i$ and $\mathbf{x}_j$ are support vectors. The dimension of B is $\lambda_s N$, where

$$\lambda_s = \frac{1}{N} \sum_i \Theta(y_i). \tag{8.20}$$

averages

A proper and clean treatment of the determinant would require the introduction of Grassmann variables (Efetov, 1997). This more complicated route will be pursued somewhere else. In this chapter, we will resort to the following simpler heuristic assumption, which was frequently used for the statistical mechanics of similar problems. We argue that the fluctuations of the determinant (to leading order of the exponent in N) can be neglected, and we can thus average both parts independently. In fact, it is more practical to average over $1/\det(B)$ (again neglecting fluctuations), because this has the representation

$$1/\det(B) = \int \prod_{i=1}^{\lambda_s N} dr_i \prod_{i=1}^{\lambda_s N} \delta \left(\sum_j B_{ij} r_j - 1 \right), \tag{8.21}$$

which again is of a similar form as the $\delta-$ distribution part. As an argument, why the fluctuations of the determinant can be neglected, one can use the fact that

$$\lim_{N\to\infty} N^{-1}\langle \ln \det(B)\rangle = -\lim_{N\to\infty} N^{-1} \ln\langle(1/\det(B))\rangle. \tag{8.22}$$

The term on the left can be calculated from the density of eigenvalues of B (Opper, 1989). As a result for the average of (8.21) we get

$$\lim_{N\to\infty} -\frac{1}{N} \ln\langle(1/\det(B))\rangle = -\lambda_s - (1-\lambda_s)\ln(1-\lambda_s). \tag{8.23}$$

For the $\delta-$ distribution part we get

$$\left\langle \prod_{i=1}^{\lambda N} \delta\left(s_i\Theta(-s_i) + \sum_j C_{ij}\alpha_j - 1\right)\right\rangle = \tag{8.24}$$

$$\frac{\exp\left[-\frac{1}{2}\sum_i \frac{(s_i\Theta(-s_i)-1)^2}{2q}\right]}{(2\pi q)^{\lambda N/2}(2\pi Q)^{N/2}} \sqrt{NqQ}\,\frac{\partial}{\partial q}\Omega_N(\sqrt{Nq})$$

where

$$q = \frac{1}{N}\sum_i \alpha_i \tag{8.25}$$

$$Q = \frac{1}{N}\sum_i \alpha_i^2 \tag{8.26}$$

and $\Omega_N(r)$ is the volume of an N dimensional sphere of radius r. These calculations are based on the decomposition

$$\prod_{i=1}^{\lambda N} \delta\left(s_i\Theta(-s_i) + \sum_j C_{ij}\alpha_j - 1\right) \tag{8.27}$$

$$= \int d\mathbf{w}\, \delta\left(\mathbf{w} - \sum_i \frac{\alpha_i\, \mathbf{x}_i}{\sqrt{N}}\right) \prod_{i=1}^{\lambda N} \delta\left(s_i\Theta(-s_i) + \frac{1}{\sqrt{N}}\mathbf{w}\cdot\mathbf{x}_i - 1\right).$$

The average of (8.27) can now be easily calculated from the joint density of the ℓ Gaussian random variables $\frac{1}{\sqrt{N}}\mathbf{w}\cdot\mathbf{x}_i$ and the N dimensional Gaussian vector $\sum_i \frac{\alpha_i\,\mathbf{x}_i}{\sqrt{N}}$.

Since both the conditions (8.25) and (8.26) and (8.20) are of a very simple additive type, the integrals over s_i can be decoupled by introducing their definitions within further δ distributions of the type

$$\delta\left(R - \frac{1}{N}\sum_j f(\alpha_j)\right) = \frac{N}{2\pi}\int d\hat{R}\, \exp\left(iN\hat{R}R - i\hat{R}\sum_j f(\alpha_j)\right). \tag{8.28}$$

decoupling

Note, that here i denotes the imaginary unit. Hence, by using the auxiliary variables $\hat{q}$, $\hat{Q}$, $\hat{\lambda}_s$ and corresponding integrals, the integrations over the s_i factorize and can be carried out. All remains to be done is to perform a 5 dimensional integral which is of the form

$$\langle Z(q, \mathbf{x}_1^{\lambda N})\rangle \propto \int dQ\, d\lambda_s\, d\hat{q}\, d\hat{Q}\, d\hat{\lambda}_s\, \exp[NG(\hat{\lambda}_s, \hat{q}, \hat{Q}, \lambda_s, Q, q)], \tag{8.29}$$

with

$$G(\hat{\lambda}_s, \hat{q}, \hat{Q}, \lambda_s, Q, q) =$$
$$-\lambda_s - (1-\lambda_s)\ln(1-\lambda_s) - \hat{\lambda}_s\lambda_s + \frac{1}{2} + \frac{1}{2}\hat{Q}Q + \frac{1}{2}\ln q + \ln\hat{q} - \hat{q}q - \ln(\hat{q}\sqrt{Q})$$
$$+\alpha\ln\left(\exp\left[-\frac{1}{2q} + \frac{\hat{q}^2}{2\hat{Q}} + \hat{\lambda}_s - \frac{1}{2}\ln q - \ln\hat{q} + \ln(\frac{\hat{q}}{\sqrt{\hat{Q}}})\right]\cdot\phi(-\frac{\hat{q}}{\sqrt{\hat{Q}}}) + \phi(\frac{1}{\sqrt{q}})\right)$$

with $\phi(x) = \int_x^\infty \frac{dt}{\sqrt{2\pi}}\, e^{-t^2/2}$. To leading order in N (8.29) can be evaluated by the saddlepoint method (note, that the integrations over the 'hat' parameters are along the imaginary axis). Hence, $\lim_{N\to\infty}\frac{1}{N}\ln\langle Z(q, \mathbf{x}_1^{\lambda N})\rangle$ equals the function $G(\hat{\lambda}_s, \hat{q}, \hat{Q}, \lambda_s, Q, q)$ evaluated at the values of $\hat{\lambda}_s, \hat{q}, \hat{Q}, \lambda_s, Q$ for which the derivatives of G with respect to these parameters equals zero. One finds that these values satify $Q = 1/\hat{Q}$, $\hat{\lambda}_s = \ln(1-\lambda_s)$ and $q\hat{q} = 1-\lambda_s$. Treating $\hat{q}$ and $r = \frac{\hat{q}}{\sqrt{\hat{Q}}}$ as independent variables, and setting $q = 1/\gamma^2$, the annealed entropy is

$$\lim_{N\to\infty}\frac{1}{N}H_{ann}(\lambda N) = \sup_{\gamma>\kappa} S(\lambda,\gamma) \tag{8.30}$$

where S is given by the expression

$$S(\lambda,\gamma) = \lambda\ln 2 + \lim_{N\to\infty}\frac{1}{N}\ln\langle Z(q = 1/\gamma^2, \mathbf{x}_1^{\lambda N})\rangle =$$
$$\lambda\ln 2 + \ln(\gamma) + \min_r\left\{-\ln r + \alpha\ln\left(e^{-\frac{\gamma^2}{2}+\frac{r^2}{2}+\ln r-\ln\gamma}\phi(-r) + \phi(\gamma)\right)\right\}. \tag{8.31}$$

S is $1/N\times$ log of the average number of dichotomies for which the maximal margin is in a small interval around the value γ

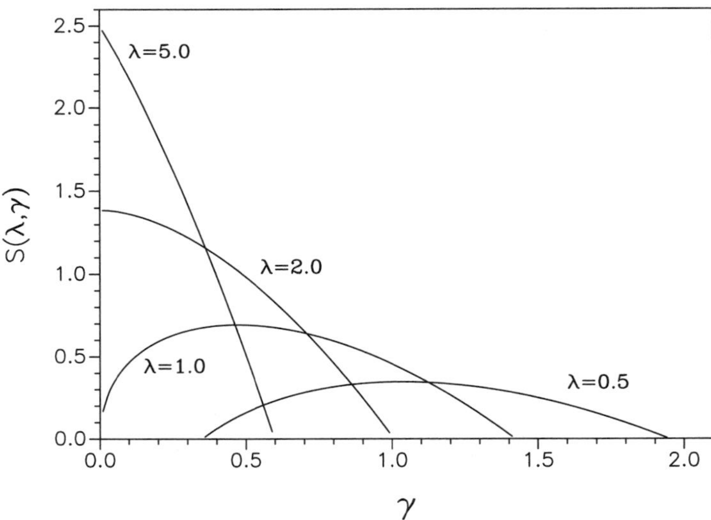

Figure 8.1 Logarithm of number of dichotomies for a maximal margin close to γ.

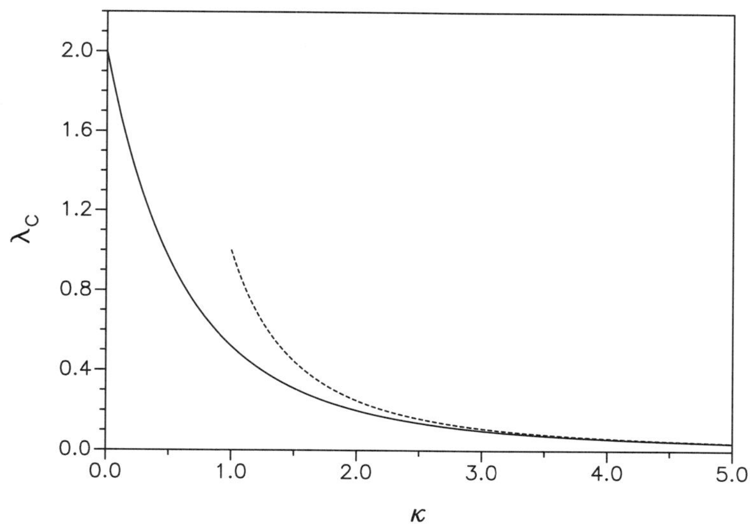

Figure 8.2 Capacity λ_c as a function of the margin κ. The dashed line is $1/\kappa^2$.

8.6 Results and Discussion

The minimization of (8.31) must be done numerically. The resulting function $S(\lambda, \gamma)$ is displayed in figure 8.1 for four values of λ. We have shown the positive part only, but the function extends to negative values as well. For $\lambda < 2$, the maximum of S is achieved for a margin $\gamma > 0$ which can be found by differentiating (8.31) with respect to γ. This results in the equation

$$\lambda \int_{-\gamma}^{\infty} \frac{dt}{\sqrt{2\pi}} e^{-t^2/2}(t+\gamma)^2 = 1. \tag{8.32}$$

capacity

Solving for γ, we also find that for this λ, $S(\lambda, \gamma) = \alpha \ln 2$. This result means that for $\lambda < 2$, almost all $2^{\lambda N}$ dichotomies will be realized with a margin γ given by (8.32). On the other hand, fixing the margin γ, the value of λ given by (8.32) yields the corresponding capacity λ_c. Relation (8.32) (figure 8.2) is a well known result in the statistical mechanics of neural networks, which was first derived by Elizabeth Gardner (1988) using a rather different approach based on the method of replicas. As can be seen, the result is in agreement with the suggested scaling $\lambda_c \sim 1/\gamma^2$ for large margins γ. For $\lambda > 2$, the maximum of $S(\lambda, \gamma)$ is shifted to $\gamma = 0$ and we obtain

$$S(\lambda, \gamma = 0) = \lambda \ln \lambda - (\lambda - 1) \ln(\lambda - 1), \tag{8.33}$$

which gives the correct result (8.7) for the VC entropy with zero margin. In figure 8.3, we have displayed the annealed VC entropy (8.30) as a function of λ/λ_c for three values of κ. While for small κ, the decrease of the annealed entropy (divided by $\lambda ln2$) is similar to the bound (8.7), the decrease becomes faster with

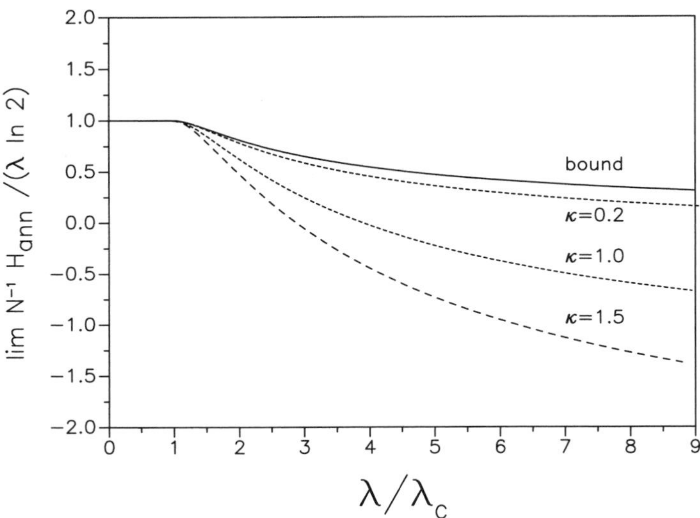

Figure 8.3 Annealed entropy for three different values of margin κ as a function of the number of inputs/capacity. The upper line gives the bound (8.7).

increasing margin κ. In any case, for λ large enough, the annealed entropy also achieves negative values in contrast to the bound (8.7). This should not be too surprising, because it simply means that for too many inputs, there is a nonzero probability, that *none* of the 2^ℓ classifications can be realized with a margin greater than a given κ by hyperplanes through the origin. Our result shows that for sufficiently large margins, the VC complexity of the set of perceptrons is drastically reduced, even stronger than predicted by general bounds. Although it is not trivial to express the generalization error in terms of the annealed entropy (because the data dependent margin is also a random variable) we expect that our results give a further illustration why margin classifiers and support vector machines generalize so well, when the achieved margin κ is large. Although the results have been derived for a spherical Gaussian distribution, one can expect that in the limit $N \to \infty$, by the central limit theorem, any other product distribution for the components of the input vector $\mathbf{x}$ with zero mean and unit variance will lead to the same result. It would be interesting to see if one can proove that our result (by the symmetry of the spherical distribution) may actually give an upper bound on the annealed entropy for any distribution of inputs $\mathbf{x}$ with $||\mathbf{x}||^2 \leq N$. Such a result would be helpful for obtaining sharper bounds on the VC entropy.

Acknowledgements

I would like to thank Peter Kuhlmann and Andreas Mietzner for their pleasant collaboration on (Opper et al., 1997), on which the present calculation is based. I am also grateful to the referees for their helpful comments.

9 Entropy Numbers, Operators and Support Vector Kernels

Robert C. Williamson
Australian National University, Department of Engineering
Canberra, ACT 0200, Australia
Robert.Williamson@anu.edu.au
http://spigot.anu.edu.au/people/williams/home.html

Alexander J. Smola, Bernhard Schölkopf
GMD FIRST
Rudower Chaussee 5, 12489 Berlin, Germany
smola,bs@first.gmd.de
http://www.first.gmd.de/~smola,bs

We derive new bounds for the generalization error of kernel machines, such as support vector machines and related regularization networks by obtaining new bounds on their covering numbers. The proofs make use of a viewpoint that is apparently novel in the field of statistical learning theory. The hypothesis class is described in terms of a linear operator mapping from a possibly infinite dimensional unit ball in feature space into a finite dimensional space. The covering numbers of the class are then determined via the entropy numbers of the operator. These numbers, which characterize the degree of compactness of the operator, can be bounded in terms of the eigenvalues of an integral operator induced by the kernel function used by the machine. As a consequence we are able to theoretically explain the effect of the choice of kernel function on the generalization performance of support vector machines.

9.1 Introduction

In this chapter we give new bounds on the covering numbers for kernel machines. This leads to improved bounds on their generalization performance. Kernel machines perform a mapping from input space into a feature space (see e.g. Aizerman et al. (1964); Nilsson (1965)), construct regression functions or decision boundaries based on this mapping, and use constraints in feature space for capacity control. Support Vector machines are a well known example of this class. We will use SV machines as our model of choice to show how bounds on the covering numbers can be obtained. We outline the relatively standard methods one can then use to hence bound their generalization performance. Our reasoning also applies to similar algorithms such as regularization networks (Girosi et al., 1993) or certain unsupervised learning algorithms (chapter 20, and Schölkopf et al. (1998e)).

Regularization Networks and Kernels

It has been noticed that in SV machines different kernels can be characterized by their regularization properties (Smola et al., 1998c): SV machines are regularization networks minimizing the regularized risk $R_{reg}[f] = R_{emp}[f] + \frac{\lambda}{2}\|Pf\|^2$, (note the similarity to (1.42)) with a regularization parameter $\lambda = \frac{1}{C} \geq 0$, and a regularization operator P, over the set of functions of the form (1.49), provided that k and P are interrelated by $k(\mathbf{x}_s, \mathbf{x}_t) = \langle (Pk)(\mathbf{x}_s, \cdot), (Pk)(\mathbf{x}_t, \cdot)\rangle$. To this end, k is chosen as Green's function of P^*P, where P^* is the adjoint of P.

This provides insight into the regularization properties of SV kernels. However, it does not completely settle the issue of how to select a kernel for a given learning problem, and how using a specific kernel might influence the performance of a SV machine.

Outline of the Chapter.

In the present work, we show that properties of the spectrum of the kernel can be used to make statements about the generalization error of the associated class of learning machines. Unlike in previous SV learning studies, the kernel is no longer merely a means of broadening the class of functions used, e.g. by making a nonseparable dataset separable in a feature space nonlinearly related to input space. Rather, we now view it as a constructive handle by which we can control the generalization error.

Direct Bounds on Covering Number

A key feature is the manner in which we *directly* bound the covering numbers of interest rather than making use of a Combinatorial dimension (such as the VC dimension or the fat-shattering dimension) and subsequent application of a general result relating such dimensions to covering numbers. We bound covering numbers directly by viewing the relevant class of functions as the image of a unit ball under a particular compact operator. A general overview of the method is given in section 9.3.

The remainder of the chapter is organized as follows. We start by introducing notation and definitions (section 9.2). Section 9.4 formulates generalization error bounds in terms of covering numbers. Section 9.5 contains the main result bounding entropy numbers in terms of the spectrum of a given kernel. The results in this chapter rest on a connection between covering numbers of function classes and entropy numbers of suitably defined operators. In particular, we derive an upper bound on the entropy numbers in terms of the size of the weight vector in feature space and the eigenvalues of the kernel used. Section 9.6 shows how to make use of kernels such as $k(x) = e^{-x^2}$ which do not have a discrete spectrum. Section 9.7 presents some results on the entropy numbers obtained for given rates of decay of eigenvalues. The concluding section 9.8 indicates how the various results in the chapter can be glued together in order to obtain overall bounds on the generalization error. Lengthy proofs have been omitted wherever they were not crucial for the understanding of the basic idea — we refer the reader to Williamson et al. (1998a) for the missing details.

We do not present a single master generalization error theorem for three key reasons: 1) the only novelty in the chapter lies in the computation of covering numbers themselves; 2) the particular statistical result one needs to use depends on the specific problem situation; 3) many of the results obtained are in a form which, whilst quite amenable to ready computation on a computer, do not provide much direct insight by merely looking at them, except perhaps in the asymptotic sense, and finally, 4) some applications (such as classification) where further quantities like margins are estimated in a data dependent fashion, need an additional luckiness argument (Shawe-Taylor et al., 1998) to apply the bounds (see also chapter 4).

Thus although our goal has been theorems, we are ultimately forced to resort to a computer to make use of our results. This is not necessarily a disadvantage — it is a both a strength and a weakness of Structural Risk Minimization (SRM) (Vapnik, 1979) that a good generalization error bound is both necessary and sufficient to make the method work well. It is our expectation that the refined (and significantly tighter) covering number bounds obtainable by our methods will be exploitable in SRM algorithms — they could be used for example for model selection. If one is running a computer program anyway, there is little point in expending a large effort to make the generalization error bounds directly consumable in a pencil and paper sense.

9.2 Definitions and Notation

Norms in $\mathbb{R}^d$

We define spaces ℓ_p^d as follows: as vector spaces, they are identical to $\mathbb{R}^d$, in addition, they are endowed with p-norms: for $0 < p < \infty$, $\|\mathbf{x}\|_{\ell_p^d} := \|\mathbf{x}\|_p = \left(\sum_{j=1}^d |x_j|^p\right)^{1/p}$; for $p = \infty$, $\|\mathbf{x}\|_{\ell_\infty^d} := \|\mathbf{x}\|_\infty = \max_{j=1,\ldots,d} |x_j|$. Note that a different normalization of the ℓ_p^d norm is used in some papers in learning theory (e.g. Talagrand (1996)).

Given ℓ points $\mathbf{x}_1, \ldots, \mathbf{x}_\ell \in \ell_p^d$, we use the shorthand $\mathbf{X}^\ell = (\mathbf{x}_1^\top, \ldots, \mathbf{x}_\ell^\top)$.

Suppose $\mathcal{F}$ is a class of functions defined on $\mathbb{R}^d$. The ℓ_∞^d norm *with respect to* $\mathbf{X}^\ell$ of $f \in \mathcal{F}$ is defined as $\|f\|_{\ell_\infty^{\mathbf{X}^\ell}} := \max_{i=1,\ldots,\ell} |f(\mathbf{x}_i)|$.

Given some set $\mathcal{C}$, a measure μ on $\mathcal{C}$, some $1 \leq p < \infty$ and a function $f: \mathcal{C} \to \mathbb{K}$ we define $\|f\|_{L_p(\mathcal{C},\mathbb{K})} := \left(\int |f(x)|^p d\mu(x)\right)^{1/p}$ if the integral exists and $\|f\|_{L_\infty(\mathcal{C},\mathbb{K})} := \operatorname{ess\,sup}_{x\in\mathcal{C}} |f(x)|$. For $1 \leq p \leq \infty$, we let $L_p(\mathcal{C}, \mathbb{K}) := \{f: \mathcal{C} \to \mathbb{K}: \|f\|_{L_p(\mathcal{C},\mathbb{K})} < \infty\}$. We let $L_p(\mathcal{C}) := L_p(\mathcal{C}, \mathbb{R})$.

Let $\mathfrak{L}(E, F)$ be the set of all bounded linear operators T between the normed spaces $(E, \|\cdot\|_E)$ and $(F, \|\cdot\|_F)$, i.e. operators such that the image of the (closed)

Operator Norms

unit ball

$$U_E := \{x \in E \colon \|x\|_E \leq 1\} \tag{9.1}$$

is bounded. The smallest such bound is called the *operator norm*,

$$\|T\| := \sup_{x \in U_E} \|Tx\|_F. \tag{9.2}$$

Entropy Numbers

The nth *entropy number of a set* $M \subset E$, for $n \in \mathbb{N}$, is

$$\epsilon_n(M) := \inf\{\epsilon > 0 \colon \text{there is an } \epsilon\text{-cover for } M \text{ in } E \text{ with } n \text{ or fewer points}\} \tag{9.3}$$

The *entropy numbers of an operator* $T \in \mathfrak{L}(E, F)$ are defined as

$$\epsilon_n(T) := \epsilon_n(T(U_E)). \tag{9.4}$$

Dyadic Entropy Numbers

Note that $\epsilon_1(T) = \|T\|$, and that $\epsilon_n(T)$ certainly is well defined for all $n \in \mathbb{N}$ if T is a *compact operator*, i.e. if $T(U_E)$ is compact. The *dyadic entropy numbers of an operator* are defined by

$$e_n(T) := \epsilon_{2^{n-1}}(T), \qquad n \in \mathbb{N}; \tag{9.5}$$

Covering Numbers

similarly, the dyadic entropy numbers of a set are defined from its entropy numbers. A very nice introduction to entropy numbers of operators is the book of Carl and Stephani (1990). The *ϵ-covering number of $\mathcal{F}$ with respect to the metric d* denoted $\mathcal{N}(\epsilon, \mathcal{F}, d)$ is the size of the smallest ϵ-cover for $\mathcal{F}$ using the metric d.

In this chapter, E and F will always be *Banach spaces*, i.e. complete normed spaces (for instance ℓ_p^d spaces). In some cases, they will be *Hilbert spaces* H, i.e. Banach spaces endowed with a dot product $\langle \cdot, \cdot \rangle_H$ giving rise to its norm via $\|x\|_H = \sqrt{\langle x, x \rangle_H}$. We will map the input data into a feature space via a mapping Φ and let $\tilde{\mathbf{x}} := \Phi(\mathbf{x})$.

9.3 Operator Theory Methods for Entropy Numbers

In this section we briefly explain the new viewpoint implicit in the present chapter. With reference to figure 9.1, consider the traditional viewpoint in statistical learning theory.

One is given a class of functions $\mathcal{F}$, and the generalization performance attainable using $\mathcal{F}$ is determined via the covering numbers of $\mathcal{F}$. More precisely, for some set $\mathcal{C}$, and $\mathbf{x}_i \in \mathcal{C}$ for $i = 1, \ldots, m$, define the *ϵ-Growth function* of the function class $\mathcal{F}$ on $\mathcal{C}$ as

$$\mathcal{N}^\ell(\epsilon, \mathcal{F}) := \sup_{\mathbf{x}_1, \ldots, \mathbf{x}_\ell \in \mathcal{C}} \mathcal{N}(\epsilon, \mathcal{F}, \ell_\infty^{\mathbf{X}^\ell}), \tag{9.6}$$

where $\mathcal{N}(\epsilon, \mathcal{F}, \ell_\infty^{\mathbf{X}^\ell})$ is the ϵ-covering number of $\mathcal{F}$ with respect to $\ell_\infty^{\mathbf{X}^\ell}$. Many generalization error bounds can be expressed in terms of $\mathcal{N}^\ell(\epsilon, \mathcal{F})$. An example is given in the following section.

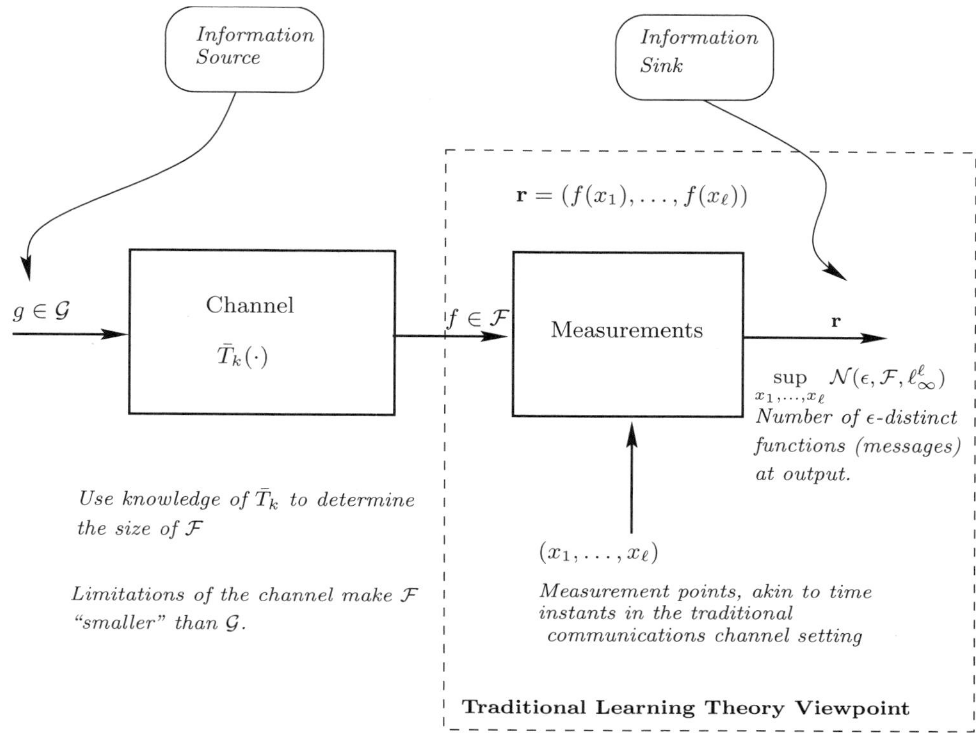

Figure 9.1 Schematic picture of the new viewpoint.

The key novelty in the present work solely concerns the manner in which the covering numbers are computed. Traditionally, appeal has been made to a result such as the so-called Sauer's lemma (originally due to Vapnik and Chervonenkis (1968)). In the case of function learning, a generalization due to Pollard (called the pseudo-dimension), or Vapnik and Chervonenkis (called the VC dimension of real valued functions), or a scale-sensitive generalization of that (called the fat-shattering dimension) is used to bound the covering numbers. These results reduce the computation of $\mathcal{N}^\ell(\epsilon, \mathcal{F})$ to the computation of a single "dimension-like" quantity. An overview of these various dimensions, some details of their history, and some examples of their computation can be found in (Anthony, 1997).

RBF-Networks With Infinite VC Dimension

Note that the 'plain' VC dimension is not appropriate in SV regression at all, as can be seen in the following: Denote r an arbitrary positive number and $C \in \mathbb{R}^n$ a compact set. Consider the class of functions

$$F := \left\{ f : f = \sum_i \alpha_i k(x_i, \cdot) \text{ with } x_i \in C, \sum_{i,j} \alpha_i \alpha_j k(x_i, x_j) \leq r \right\} \tag{9.7}$$

We show that F has infinite VC dimension by showing that any arbitrary set $X =$

$\{x_1, \ldots, x_\ell\} \subset C$ of size ℓ can be shattered. Micchelli (1986) showed that the matrix $(k(x_i, x_j))_{ij}$ has full rank for Gaussian rbf-kernels. For arbitrary $\{y_1, \ldots y_\ell\} \in \{-1, 1\}$ there exists a function $f(\cdot) = \sum_i \alpha_i k(x_i, \cdot)$ with $f(x_i) = y_i$. Rescaling f finally yields some $\tilde{f} \in F$ which proves the statement.

In the present work, we view the class $\mathcal{F}$ as being induced by an operator $\bar{T}_k$ depending on some kernel function k. Thus $\mathcal{F}$ is the image of a "base class" $\mathcal{G}$ under $\bar{T}_k$. The analogy implicit in the picture is that the quantity that matters is the number of ϵ-distinguishable messages obtainable at the information sink. (Recall the equivalence up to a constant factor of packing and covering numbers.) In a typical communications problem, one tries to maximize the number of distinguisable messages (per unit time), in order to maximize the information transmission rate. But from the point of view of the receiver, the job is made easier the *smaller* the number of distinct messages that one needs to be concerned with decoding. The significance of the picture is that the kernel in question is exactly the kernel that is used, for example, in support vector machines. As a consequence, the determination of $\mathcal{N}^\ell(\epsilon, \mathcal{F})$ can be done in terms of properties of the operator $\bar{T}_k$. The latter thus plays a constructive role in controlling the complexity of $\mathcal{F}$ and hence the difficulty of the learning task. We believe that the new viewpoint in itself is potentially very valuable, perhaps more so than the specific results in the chapter. A further exploitation of the new viewpoint can be found in (Williamson et al., 1998b). There are in fact a variety of ways to define exactly what is meant by $\bar{T}_k$, and we have deliberately not been explicit in the picture. We make use of one particular $\bar{T}_k$ in this chapter.

Communication Theory Viewpoint

9.4 Generalization Bounds via Uniform Convergence

The generalization performance of learning machines can be bounded via uniform convergence results as in (Vapnik and Chervonenkis, 1981; Vapnik, 1979). A recent review can be found in (Anthony, 1997). The key thing about these results is the role of the covering numbers of the hypothesis class — the focus of the present chapter. Results for both classification and regression are now known. For the sake of concreteness, we quote below a result suitable for regression which was proved by Alon et al. (1997). See also chapter 4 for results on classification and pattern recognition. Let $P_m(f) := \frac{1}{\ell} \sum_{i=1}^{\ell} f(\mathbf{x}_i)$ denote the *empirical mean* of f on the sample $\mathbf{x}_1, \ldots, \mathbf{x}_\ell$.

Uniform Convergence Bounds

Lemma 9.1 (Alon, Ben-David, Cesa-Bianchi, and Haussler, 1997) Let $\mathcal{F}$ be a class of functions from $\mathcal{C}$ into $[0, 1]$ and let P be a distribution over $\mathcal{C}$. then, for all $\epsilon > 0$ and all $m \geq \frac{2}{\epsilon^2}$,

$$\Pr\left\{\sup_{f \in \mathcal{F}} |P_\ell(f) - P(f)| > \epsilon\right\} \leq 12\ell \cdot \mathbf{E}\left[\mathcal{N}\left(\tfrac{\epsilon}{6}, \mathcal{F}, \ell_\infty^{\bar{\mathbf{X}}^{2\ell}}\right)\right] e^{-\epsilon^2 \ell/36} \tag{9.8}$$

where Pr denotes the probability w.r.t. the sample $\mathbf{x}_1, \ldots, \mathbf{x}_\ell$ drawn i.i.d. from P, and $\mathbf{E}$ the expectation w.r.t. a second sample $\bar{\mathbf{X}}^\ell = (\bar{\mathbf{x}}_1^\top, \ldots, \bar{\mathbf{x}}_{2\ell}^\top)$ also drawn i.i.d. from P.

In order to use this lemma one usually makes use of the fact that for any P,

$$\mathbf{E}\left[\mathcal{N}(\epsilon, \mathcal{F}, \ell_\infty^{\bar{\mathbf{X}}^\ell})\right] \leq \mathcal{N}^\ell(\epsilon, \mathcal{F}). \tag{9.9}$$

The above result can be used to give a generalization error result by applying it to the loss-function induced class. The following Lemma, which is an improved version of (Bartlett et al., 1996, Lemma 17), is useful in this regard:

Lemma 9.2

Denote $\mathcal{F}$ a set of functions from $\mathcal{C}$ to $[a, b]$ with $a < b$, $a, b \in \mathbb{R} \cup \pm\infty$ and $l : \mathbb{R} \to \mathbb{R}_0^+$ a loss function satisfying a Lipschitz-condition

Loss Functions

$$l(\xi) - l(\xi') \leq C|\xi - \xi'| \text{ for all } \xi, \xi' \in [a - b, b - a]. \tag{9.10}$$

Moreover let $\mathbf{z} := (\mathbf{x}_i, y_i)_{j=1}^\ell$, $l_f|_{\mathbf{z}_j} := l(f(\mathbf{x}_j) - y_j)$, $l_f|_{\mathbf{z}} := (l_f|_{\mathbf{z}_j})_{j=1}^\ell$, $l_\mathcal{F}|_{\mathbf{z}} := \{l_f|_{\mathbf{z}} \colon f \in \mathcal{F}\}$ and $\mathcal{N}(\epsilon, l|_{\mathbf{z}}) := \mathcal{N}(\epsilon, l_\mathcal{F}|_{\mathbf{z}}, \ell_\infty^{\mathbf{z}})$. Then the following equation holds:

$$\max_{\mathbf{z} \in (\mathcal{C} \times [a,b])^\ell} \mathcal{N}(\epsilon, l|_{\mathbf{z}}) \leq \max_{\mathbf{x} \in \mathcal{C}^\ell} \mathcal{N}\left(\frac{\epsilon}{C}, \mathcal{F}|_{\mathbf{x}}\right) \tag{9.11}$$

Applying the result above to polynomial loss leads to the following corollary:

Corollary 9.1

Polynomial Loss

Let the assumptions be as above in lemma 9.2. Then for loss functions of type

$$l(\eta) = \frac{1}{p}\eta^p \text{ with } p > 1 \tag{9.12}$$

we have $C = (b - a)^{(p-1)}$, in particular $C = (b - a)$ for $p = 2$ and therefore

$$\max_{\mathbf{z} \in (\mathcal{C} \times [a,b])^\ell} \mathcal{N}(\epsilon, l|_{\mathbf{z}}) \leq \max_{\mathbf{x} \in \mathcal{C}^\ell} \mathcal{N}\left(\frac{\epsilon}{(b - a)^{p-1}}, \mathcal{F}|_{\mathbf{x}}\right) \tag{9.13}$$

One can readily combine the uniform convergence results with the above results to get overall bounds on generalization performance. We do not explicitly state such a result here since the particular uniform convergence result needed depends on the exact set-up of the learning problem. A typical uniform convergence result takes the form

$$P^\ell\{\sup_f |R_{emp}(f) - R(f)| > \epsilon\} \leq c_1(\ell)\mathcal{N}^\ell(\epsilon, \mathcal{F})e^{-\epsilon^\beta \ell / c_2}. \tag{9.14}$$

Even the exponent in (9.14) depends on the setting: In regression β can be set to 1, however in agnostic learning (Kearns et al., 1994) show that in general $\beta = 2$, except if the class is convex in which case it can be set to 1 (Lee et al., 1998). Since our primary interest is in determining $\mathcal{N}^\ell(\epsilon, \mathcal{F})$ we will not try to summarize the large body of work now done on uniform convergence results and generalization error.

Learning Curves

These generalization bounds are typically used by setting the right hand side equal to δ and solving for $\ell = \ell(\epsilon, \delta)$ (which is called the sample complexity). Another way to use these results is as a learning curve bound $\bar{\epsilon}(\delta, \ell)$ where

$$P^\ell\{\sup_f |R_{emp}(f) - R(f)| > \bar{\epsilon}(\delta, \ell)\} \leq \delta. \tag{9.15}$$

We note here that the determination of $\bar{\epsilon}(\delta, \ell)$ is quite convenient in terms of e_n, the dyadic entropy number associated with the covering number $\mathcal{N}^\ell(\epsilon, \mathcal{F})$ in (9.14). Setting the right hand side of (9.14) equal to δ, we have

$$\begin{aligned} \delta &= c_1(\ell)\mathcal{N}^\ell(\epsilon, \mathcal{F}) e^{-\epsilon^\beta \ell / c_2} \\ \Rightarrow \log_2\left(\frac{\delta}{c_1(\ell)}\right) + \frac{\epsilon^\beta \ell}{c_2 \ln 2} &= \log_2 \mathcal{N}^\ell(\epsilon, \mathcal{F}) \\ \Rightarrow e_{\log_2\left(\frac{\delta}{c_1(\ell)}\right) + \frac{\epsilon^\beta \ell}{c_2 \ln 2} + 1} &= \epsilon. \end{aligned} \tag{9.16}$$

Thus $\bar{\epsilon}(\delta, \ell) = \{\epsilon\colon (9.16) \text{ holds}\}$. Thus the use of ϵ_n or e_n (which will arise naturally from our techniques) is in fact a convenient thing to do for finding learning curves.

9.5 Entropy Numbers for Kernel Machines

In the following we will mainly consider machines where the mapping into feature space is defined by Mercer kernels $k(\mathbf{x}, \mathbf{y})$ as they are easier to deal with using functional analytic methods. Such machines have become very popular due to the success of SV machines.

9.5.1 Mercer's Theorem, Feature Spaces and Scaling

Our goal is to make statements about the shape of the image of the input space $\mathcal{C}$ under the feature map $\Phi(\cdot)$. We will make use of Mercer's theorem. For various reasons we need a somewhat stronger statement than theorem 1.1, thus we repeat it as a whole for the sake of completeness. The version stated below is a special case of the theorem proven in (König, 1986, p. 145). In the following we will assume $(\mathcal{C}, \mu)$ to be a finite measure space, i.e. $\mu(\mathcal{C}) < \infty$. As usual, by "almost all" we mean for all elements of $\mathcal{C}^n$ except a set of μ^n-measure zero.

Theorem 9.1 (Mercer)
Suppose $k \in L_\infty(\mathcal{C}^2)$ to be symmetric, i.e. $k(x, x') = k(x', x)$, such that the integral operator $T_k : L_2(\mathcal{C}) \to L_2(\mathcal{C})$,

$$T_k f(\cdot) := \int_{\mathcal{C}} k(\cdot, \mathbf{y}) f(\mathbf{y}) d\mu(\mathbf{y}) \tag{9.17}$$

Bounded and Uniformly Convergent

is positive. Let $\psi_j \in L_2(\mathcal{C})$ be the eigenfunction of T_k associated with the eigenvalue $\lambda_j \neq 0$ and normalized such that $\|\psi_j\|_{L_2} = 1$.

1. $(\lambda_j(T))_j \in \ell_1$.

2. $\psi_j \in L_\infty(\mathcal{C})$ and $\sup_j \|\psi_j\|_{L_\infty} < \infty$.
3. $k(\mathbf{x}, \mathbf{y}) = \sum_{j \in \mathbb{N}} \lambda_j \psi_j(\mathbf{x}) \psi_j(\mathbf{y})$ holds for almost all $(\mathbf{x}, \mathbf{y})$, where the series converges absolutely and uniformly for almost all $(\mathbf{x}, \mathbf{y})$.

We will call a kernel satisfying the conditions of this theorem a *Mercer kernel.* From statement 2 of Mercer's theorem there exists some constant $C_k \in \mathbb{R}^+$ depending on $k(\cdot, \cdot)$ such that

$$|\psi_j(\mathbf{x})| \leq C_k \text{ for all } j \in \mathbb{N} \text{ and } \mathbf{x} \in \mathcal{C}. \tag{9.18}$$

Choice of Coordinate System

(Actually (9.18) holds only for almost all $\mathbf{x} \in \mathcal{C}$, but from here on we gloss over these measure-theoretic niceties in the exposition.) Moreover from statement 3 it follows that $k(\mathbf{x}, \mathbf{y})$ corresponds to a dot product in ℓ_2 i.e. $k(\mathbf{x}, \mathbf{y}) = \langle \Phi(\mathbf{x}), \Phi(\mathbf{y}) \rangle_{\ell_2}$ with

$$\begin{aligned} \Phi : \mathcal{C} &\rightarrow \ell_2 \\ \mathbf{x} &\mapsto (\phi_j(\mathbf{x}))_j := (\sqrt{\lambda_j} \psi_j(\mathbf{x}))_j \end{aligned} \tag{9.19}$$

for almost all $\mathbf{x} \in \mathcal{C}$. In the following we will (without loss of generality) assume the sequence of $(\lambda_j)_j$ be sorted in nonincreasing order. From the argument above one can see that $\Phi(\mathcal{C})$ lives not only in ℓ_2 but in an axis parallel parallelepiped with lengths $2C_k \sqrt{\lambda_j}$.

It will be useful to consider maps that map $\Phi(\mathcal{C})$ into balls of some radius R centered at the origin. The following proposition shows that the class of all these maps is determined by elements of ℓ_2 and the sequence of eigenvalues $(\lambda_j)_j$.

Proposition 9.1 (Mapping $\Phi(\mathbf{x})$ into ℓ_2)
Let S be the diagonal map

$$\begin{aligned} &S : \mathbb{R}^\mathbb{N} \rightarrow \mathbb{R}^\mathbb{N} \\ &S : (x_j)_j \mapsto S(x_j)_j = (s_j x_j)_j. \end{aligned} \tag{9.20}$$

Then S maps $\Phi(\mathcal{C})$ into a ball of finite radius R_S centered at the origin if and only if $(s_j \sqrt{\lambda_j})_j \in \ell_2$.

Proof ($\Leftarrow$) Suppose $(s_j \sqrt{\lambda_j})_j \in \ell_2$ and let $R_S^2 := C_k^2 \|(s_j \sqrt{\lambda_j})_j\|_{\ell_2}^2 < \infty$. For any $\mathbf{x} \in \mathcal{C}$,

$$\|S\Phi(\mathbf{x})\|_{\ell_2}^2 = \sum_{j \in \mathbb{N}} s_j^2 \lambda_j |\psi_j(\mathbf{x})|^2 \leq \sum_{j \in \mathbb{N}} s_j^2 \lambda_j C_k^2 = R_S^2. \tag{9.21}$$

Hence $S\Phi(\mathcal{C}) \subseteq \ell_2$.
($\Rightarrow$) Suppose $(s_j \sqrt{\lambda_j})_j$ is not in ℓ_2. Hence the sequence $(A_n)_n$ with $A_n := \sum_{j=1}^{n} s_j^2 \lambda_j$ is unbounded. Now define

$$a_n(\mathbf{x}) := \sum_{j=1}^{n} s_j^2 \lambda_j |\psi_j(\mathbf{x})|^2. \tag{9.22}$$

Then $\|a_n(\cdot)\|_{L_1(\mathcal{C})} = A_n$ due to the normalization condition on ψ_j. However, as

$\mu(\mathcal{C}) < \infty$, there exists a set $\tilde{\mathcal{C}}$ of nonzero measure such that

$$a_n(\mathbf{x}) \geq \frac{A_n}{\mu(\mathcal{C})} \quad \text{for all } \mathbf{x} \in \tilde{\mathcal{C}}. \tag{9.23}$$

Shape Bound on $\Phi(\mathcal{C})$

Combining the left side of (9.21) with (9.22) we obtain $\|S\Phi(\mathbf{x})\|_{\ell_2}^2 \geq a_n(\mathbf{x})$ for all $n \in \mathbb{N}$ and almost all $\mathbf{x}$. Since $a_n(\mathbf{x})$ is unbounded for a set $\tilde{\mathcal{C}}$ with nonzero measure in $\mathcal{C}$, we can see that $S\Phi(\mathcal{C}) \not\subset \ell_2$. ■

The consequence of this result is that there exists no *axis parallel* ellipsoid $\mathcal{E}$ not completely containing the (also) axis parallel parallelepiped $\mathcal{B}$ of sidelength $(2C_k\sqrt{\lambda_j})_j$, such that $\mathcal{E}$ would contain $\Phi(\mathcal{C})$. More formally

$$\mathcal{B} \subset \mathcal{E} \text{ if and only if } \Phi(\mathcal{C}) \subset \mathcal{E}. \tag{9.24}$$

Hence $\Phi(\mathcal{C})$ contains a set of nonzero measure of elements near the corners of the parallelepiped.

Once we know that $\Phi(\mathcal{C})$ "fills" the parallelepiped described above we can use this result to construct an inverse mapping A from the unit ball in ℓ_2 to an ellipsoid $\mathcal{E}$ such that $\Phi(\mathcal{C}) \subset \mathcal{E}$ as in the following diagram.

(9.25)

Shrinkage Operator

The operator A will be useful for computing the entropy numbers of concatenations of operators. (Knowing the inverse will allow us to compute the forward operator, and that can be used to bound the covering numbers of the class of functions, as shown in the next subsection.) We thus seek an operator $A : \ell_2 \to \ell_2$ such that

$$A(U_{\ell_2}) \subseteq \mathcal{E}. \tag{9.26}$$

We can ensure this by constructing A such that

$$A\colon (x_j)_j \mapsto (R_A a_j x_j)_j \tag{9.27}$$

with $R_A := C_k \|(\sqrt{\lambda_j}/a_j)_j\|_{\ell_2}$. From Proposition 9.1 it follows that all those operators A for which $R_A < \infty$ will satisfy (9.26). We call such scaling (inverse) operators *admissible.*

9.5.2 Entropy Numbers

The next step is to compute the entropy numbers of the operator A and use this to obtain bounds on the entropy numbers for kernel machines like SV machines. We will make use of the following theorem due to Gordon et al. (1987), p. 226, stated in the present form in (Carl and Stephani, 1990, p. 17).

Theorem 9.2
Let $\sigma_1 \geq \sigma_2 \geq \cdots \geq \sigma_j \geq \cdots \geq 0$ be a non-increasing sequence of non-negative numbers and let

$$Dx = (\sigma_1 x_1, \sigma_2 x_2, \ldots, \sigma_j x_j, \ldots) \tag{9.28}$$

Diagonal Operator

for $\mathbf{x} = (x_1, x_2, \ldots, x_j, \ldots) \in \ell_p$ be the diagonal operator from ℓ_p into itself, generated by the sequence $(\sigma_j)_j$, where $1 \leq p \leq \infty$. Then for all $n \in \mathbb{N}$,

$$\sup_{j \in \mathbb{N}} n^{-\frac{1}{j}} (\sigma_1 \sigma_2 \cdots \sigma_j)^{\frac{1}{j}} \leq \epsilon_n(D) \leq 6 \sup_{j \in \mathbb{N}} n^{-\frac{1}{j}} (\sigma_1 \sigma_2 \cdots \sigma_j)^{\frac{1}{j}}. \tag{9.29}$$

We can exploit the freedom in choosing A to minimize an entropy number as the following corollary shows. This will be a key ingredient of our calculation of the covering numbers for SV classes, as shown below.

Corollary 9.2 (Entropy numbers for $\Phi(\mathcal{C})$)

Application to $\Phi(\mathcal{C})$

Let $k: \mathcal{C} \times \mathcal{C} \to \mathbb{R}$ be a Mercer kernel and let A be defined by (9.27). Then

$$\epsilon_n(A: \ell_2 \to \ell_2) \leq \inf_{(a_s)_s: \left(\sqrt{\lambda_s}/a_s\right)_s \in \ell_2} \sup_{j \in \mathbb{N}} 6 C_k \left\| \left(\sqrt{\lambda_s}/a_s\right)_s \right\|_{\ell_2} n^{-\frac{1}{j}} (a_1 a_2 \cdots a_j)^{\frac{1}{j}}. \tag{9.30}$$

This result follows immediately by identifying D and A and exploiting the freedom that we still have in choosing a particular operator A among the class of admissible ones.

As already described in section 9.1 the hypotheses that a SV machine generates can be expressed as $\langle \mathbf{w}, \tilde{\mathbf{x}} \rangle + b$ where both $\mathbf{w}$ and $\tilde{\mathbf{x}}$ are defined in the feature space $\mathcal{S} = \operatorname{span}(\Phi(\mathcal{C}))$ and $b \in \mathbb{R}$. The kernel trick as introduced by Aizerman et al. (1964) was then successfully employed by Boser et al. (1992) and Cortes and Vapnik (1995) to extend the Optimal Margin Hyperplane classifier to what is now known as the SV machine. We deal with the "$+b$" term in section 9.8; for now we consider the class

$$\mathcal{F}_{R_{\mathbf{w}}} := \{\langle \mathbf{w}, \tilde{\mathbf{x}} \rangle : \tilde{\mathbf{x}} \in \mathcal{S}, \|\mathbf{w}\| \leq R_{\mathbf{w}}\} \subseteq \mathbb{R}^{\mathcal{S}}. \tag{9.31}$$

Note that $\mathcal{F}_{R_{\mathbf{w}}}$ depends implicitly on k since $\mathcal{S}$ does.

What we seek are the ℓ_∞^m covering numbers for the class $\mathcal{F}_{R_{\mathbf{w}}}$ induced by the kernel in terms of the parameter $R_{\mathbf{w}}$ which is the inverse of the size of the margin in feature space, or equivalently, the size of the weight vector in feature space as defined by the dot product in $\mathcal{S}$ (see Vapnik and Chervonenkis (1974); Vapnik (1995) for details). In the following we will call such hypothesis classes with length constraint on the weight vectors in feature space *SV classes*. Let T be the operator $T = S_{\tilde{\mathbf{X}}^\ell} R_{\mathbf{w}}$ where $R_{\mathbf{w}} \in \mathbb{R}$ and the operator $S_{\tilde{\mathbf{X}}^\ell}$ is defined by

SV Classes

$$\begin{aligned} S_{\tilde{\mathbf{X}}^\ell} : \ell_2 &\to \ell_\infty^\ell \\ S_{\tilde{\mathbf{X}}^\ell} : \mathbf{w} &\mapsto (\langle \tilde{\mathbf{x}}_1, \mathbf{w} \rangle, \ldots, \langle \tilde{\mathbf{x}}_\ell, \mathbf{w} \rangle). \end{aligned} \tag{9.32}$$

with $\tilde{\mathbf{x}}_j \in \Phi(\mathcal{C})$ for all j. The following theorem is useful to compute entropy numbers in terms of T and A. Originally due to Maurey it was extended by Carl (1985). See (Williamson et al., 1998b) for some extensions and historical remarks.

Maurey's theorem

Theorem 9.3 (Carl and Stephani, 1990, p. 246)
Let $S \in \mathfrak{L}(H, \ell_\infty^\ell)$ where H is a Hilbert space. Then there exists a constant $c > 0$ such that for all $\ell \in \mathbb{N}$, and $1 \leq j \leq \ell$

$$e_n(S) \leq c\|S\| \left(n^{-1} \log_2 \left(1 + \frac{\ell}{n}\right)\right)^{1/2}. \tag{9.33}$$

An alternative proof of this result (given by Williamson et al. (1998b)) provides a small explicit value for the constant: $c = 2(\frac{6}{2-\log_2 3})^{1/2} \leq 5.3771$.

The restatement of Theorem 9.3 in terms of $\epsilon_{2^{n-1}} = e_n$ will be useful in the following. Under the assumptions above we have

$$\epsilon_n(S) \leq c\|S\| \left((\log_2 n + 1)^{-1} \log_2 \left(1 + \frac{\ell}{\log_2 n + 1}\right)\right). \tag{9.34}$$

Now we can combine the bounds on entropy numbers of A and $S_{\mathbf{X}^\ell}$ to obtain bounds for SV classes. First we need the following lemma.

Product Bounds

Lemma 9.3 (Carl and Stephani, 1990, p. 11)
Let E, F, G be Banach spaces, $R \in \mathfrak{L}(F, G)$, and $S \in \mathfrak{L}(E, F)$. Then, for $n, t \in \mathbb{N}$,

$$\epsilon_{nt}(RS) \leq \epsilon_n(R)\epsilon_t(S) \tag{9.35}$$
$$\epsilon_n(RS) \leq \epsilon_n(R)\|S\| \tag{9.36}$$
$$\epsilon_n(RS) \leq \epsilon_n(S)\|R\|. \tag{9.37}$$

Note that the latter two inequalities follow directly from the fact that $\epsilon_1(R) = \|R\|$ for all $R \in \mathfrak{L}(F, G)$.

Theorem 9.4 Bounds for SV classes
Let k be a Mercer kernel, let Φ be induced via (9.19) and let $T := S_{\tilde{\mathbf{X}}^\ell} R_{\mathbf{w}}$ where $S_{\tilde{\mathbf{X}}^\ell}$ is given by (9.32) and $R_{\mathbf{w}} \in \mathbb{R}^+$. Let A be defined by (9.27) and suppose $\tilde{\mathbf{x}}_j = \Phi(\mathbf{x}_j)$ for $j = 1, \ldots, \ell$. Then the entropy numbers of T satisfy the following inequalities:

$$\epsilon_n(T) \leq c\|A\| R_{\mathbf{w}} \log_2^{-1/2} n \log_2^{-1/2} \left(1 + \tfrac{\ell}{\log_2 n}\right) \tag{9.38}$$
$$\epsilon_n(T) \leq 6 R_{\mathbf{w}} C_k \epsilon_n(A) \tag{9.39}$$
$$\epsilon_{nt}(T) \leq 6cC_k R_{\mathbf{w}} \log_2^{-1/2} n \log_2^{-1/2} \left(1 + \tfrac{\ell}{\log_2 n}\right) \epsilon_t(A)$$

where C_k and c are defined as in Corollary 9.2 and Lemma 9.3.

This result gives several options for bounding $\epsilon_n(T)$. The reason for using ϵ_n instead of e_n is that the index only may be integer in the former case (whereas it can be in $[1, \infty)$ in the latter), thus making it easier to obtain tighter bounds. We shall see in examples later that the best inequality to use depends on the rate of decay of the eigenvalues of k. The result gives effective bounds on $\mathcal{N}^\ell(\epsilon, \mathcal{F}_{R_{\mathbf{w}}})$ since

$$\epsilon_n(T\colon \ell_2 \to \ell_\infty^\ell) \leq \epsilon_0 \Rightarrow \mathcal{N}^\ell(\epsilon_0, \mathcal{F}_{R_{\mathbf{w}}}) \leq n. \tag{9.40}$$

Factorization

Proof We will use the following factorization of T to upper bound $\epsilon_n(T)$.

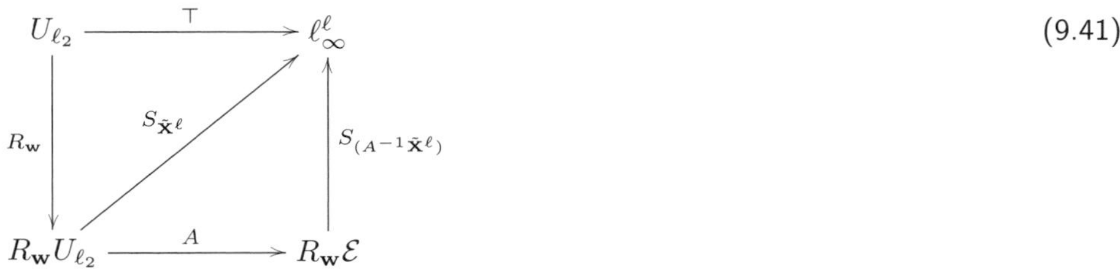

(9.41)

The top left part of the diagram follows from the definition of T. The fact that the diagram commutes stems from the fact that since A is diagonal, it is self-adjoint and so

$$\langle \mathbf{w}, \tilde{\mathbf{x}} \rangle = \langle \mathbf{w}, AA^{-1}\tilde{\mathbf{x}} \rangle = \langle A\mathbf{w}, A^{-1}\tilde{\mathbf{x}} \rangle. \tag{9.42}$$

Instead of computing the covering number of $T = S_{\tilde{\mathbf{X}}^\ell} R_{\mathbf{w}}$ directly, which is difficult or wasteful, as the bound on $S_{\tilde{\mathbf{X}}^\ell}$ does not take into account that $\tilde{\mathbf{x}} \in \mathcal{E}$ but just makes the assumption of $\tilde{\mathbf{x}} \in \rho U_{\ell_2}$ for some $\rho > 0$, we will represent T as $S_{(A^{-1}\tilde{\mathbf{X}}^\ell)} A R_{\mathbf{w}}$. This is more efficient as we constructed A such that $\Phi(\mathcal{C})A^{-1} \in U_{\ell_2}$ filling a larger proportion of it than just $\frac{1}{\rho}\Phi(\mathcal{C})$.

By construction of A and the Cauchy-Schwarz inequality we have $\|S_{A^{-1}\tilde{\mathbf{X}}^\ell}\| = 1$. Thus applying lemma 9.3 to the factorization of T and using Theorem 9.3 proves the theorem. ■

As we shall see in section 9.7, one can give asymptotic rates of decay for $\epsilon_n(A)$. (In fact we give non-asymptotic results with explicitly evaluable constants.) It is thus of some interest to give overall asymptotic rates of decay of $\epsilon_n(T)$ in terms of the order of $\epsilon_n(A)$.

Overall Asymptotic Rates

Lemma 9.4 (Rate bounds on ϵ_n)
Let k be a Mercer kernel and suppose A is the scaling operator associated with it as defined by (9.27).

1. If $\epsilon_n(A) = O(\log_2^{-\alpha} n)$ for some $\alpha > 0$ then

$$\epsilon_n(T) = O(\log_2^{-(\alpha+2)} n). \tag{9.43}$$

2. If $\log_2 \epsilon_n(A) = O(\log_2^{-\beta} n)$ for some $\beta > 0$ then

$$\log_2 \epsilon_n(T) = O(\log_2^{-\beta} n). \tag{9.44}$$

This Lemma shows that in the first case, Maurey's result (theorem 9.3) allows an improvement in the exponent of the entropy number of T, whereas in the second, it affords none (since the entropy numbers decay so fast anyway). The Maurey result may still help in that case though for nonasymptotic n.

Proof From theorem 9.3 we know that $\epsilon_n(S) = O(\log_2^{-2} n)$. Now use (9.35), splitting the index n in the following way:

$$n = n^\tau n^{(1-\tau)} \text{ with } \tau \in (0,1). \tag{9.45}$$

For the first case this yields

Dominant Rates

$$\epsilon_n(T) = O(\log_2^{-2} n^\tau) O(\log_2^{-\alpha} j^{\tau-1}) = \tau^{-2}(1-\tau)^{-\alpha} O(\log_2^{-(\alpha+2)} n). \tag{9.46}$$

In the second case we have

$$\log_2 \epsilon_n(T) = \log_2 \left((\tau^{-2}) O(\log_2^{-2} n) \right) + (1-\tau)^{-\beta} O(\log_2^{-\beta} n) = O(\log_2^{-\beta} n). \tag{9.47}$$

■

In a nutshell we can always obtain rates of convergence better than those due to Maurey's theorem, because we are not dealing with *arbitrary* mappings into infinite dimensional spaces. In fact, for logarithmic dependency of $\epsilon_n(T)$ on n, the effect of the kernel is so strong that it completely dominates the $1/\epsilon^2$ behaviour for arbitrary Hilbert spaces. An example of such a kernel is $k(x,y) = \exp(-(x-y)^2)$; see Proposition 9.4 and also section 9.6 for the discretization question.

9.6 Discrete Spectra of Convolution Operators

The results presented above show that if one knows the eigenvalue sequence $(\lambda_i)_i$ of a compact operator, one can bound its entropy numbers. Whilst it is always possible to assume that the *data* fed into a SV machine have bounded support, the same can not be said of the kernel $k(\cdot,\cdot)$; a commonly used kernel is $k(x,y) = \exp(-(x-y)^2)$ which has noncompact support. The induced integral operator

Integral Operator

$$(T_k f)(x) = \int_{-\infty}^{\infty} k(x,y) f(y) dy \tag{9.48}$$

then has a continuous spectrum (a nondenumerable infinity of eigenvalues) and thus T_k is not compact (Ash, 1965, p.267). The question arises: can we make use of such kernels in SV machines and still obtain generalization error bounds of the form developed above? A further motivation stems from the fact that by a theorem of Widom (1964), the eigenvalue decay of any convolution operator defined on a a compact set via a kernel having compact support can decay no faster than $\lambda_j = O(e^{-j^2})$ and thus if one seeks very rapid decay of eigenvalues (with concomitantly small entropy numbers), one must use convolution kernels with noncompact support.

We will resolve these issues in the present section. Before doing so, let us first consider the case that $\operatorname{supp} k \subseteq [-a,a]$ for some $a < \infty$. Suppose further that the data points $\mathbf{x}_j$ satisfy $\mathbf{x}_j \in [-b,b]$ for all j. If $k(\cdot,\cdot)$ is a convolution kernel (i.e. $k(x,y) = k(x-y)$), then the SV hypothesis $h_k(\cdot)$ can be written

$$h_k(x) := \sum_{j=1}^{m} \alpha_j k(x, \mathbf{x}_j) = \sum_{j=1}^{m} \alpha_j k_v(x, \mathbf{x}_j) =: h_{k_v}(x) \tag{9.49}$$

for $v \geq 2(a+b)$ where $k_v(\cdot)$ is the v-periodic extension of $k(\cdot)$:

$$k_v(x) := \sum_{j=-\infty}^{\infty} k(x - jv). \tag{9.50}$$

We now relate the eigenvalues of T_{k_v} to the Fourier transform of $k(\cdot)$. We do so for the case of $d = 1$ and then state the general case later.

Lemma 9.5

Connection between Spectrum and Fourier Transform

Let $k\colon \mathbb{R} \to \mathbb{R}$ be a symmetric convolution kernel, let $K(\omega) = F[k(x)](\omega)$ denote the Fourier transform of $k(\cdot)$ and k_v denote the v-periodical kernel derived from k (also assume that k_v exists). Then k_v has a representation as a Fourier series with $\omega_0 := \frac{2\pi}{v}$ and

$$\begin{aligned} k_v(x-y) &= \sum_{j=-\infty}^{\infty} \frac{\sqrt{2\pi}}{v} K(j\omega_0) e^{ij\omega_0 x} \\ &= \frac{\sqrt{2\pi}}{v} K(0) + \sum_{j=1}^{\infty} \frac{2}{v} \sqrt{2\pi} K(j\omega_0) \cos(j\omega_0(x-y)). \end{aligned} \tag{9.51}$$

Moreover $\lambda_j = \sqrt{2\pi} K(j\omega_0)$ for $j \in \mathbb{Z}$ and $C_k = \sqrt{\frac{2}{v}}$.

For a proof see (Williamson et al., 1998a). Thus even though T_k may not be compact, T_{k_v} may be (if $(K(j\omega_0))_{j\in\mathbb{N}} \subset \ell_2$ for example). The above lemma can be applied whenever we can form $k_v(\cdot)$ from $k(\cdot)$. Clearly $k(x) = O(x^{-(1+\epsilon)})$ for some $\epsilon > 0$ suffices to ensure the sum in (9.50) converges.

Let us now consider how to choose v. Note that the Riemann-Lebesgue lemma tells us that for integrable $k(\cdot)$ of bounded variation (surely any kernel one would use would satisfy that assumption), one has $K(\omega) = O(1/\omega)$. There is an tradeoff in choosing v in that for large enough ω, $K(\omega)$ is a decreasing function of ω (at least as fast as $1/\omega$) and thus by Lemma 9.5, $\lambda_j = \sqrt{2\pi} K(2\pi j/v)$ is an increasing function of v. This suggests one should choose a small value of v. But a small v will lead to high empirical error (as the kernel "wraps around" and its localization properties are lost) and large C_k. There are several approaches to picking a value of v. One obvious one is to *a priori* pick some $\tilde{\epsilon} > 0$ and choose the smallest v such that $|k(x) - k_v(x)| \leq \tilde{\epsilon}$ for all $x \in [-v/2, v/2]$. Thus one would obtain a hypothesis $h_{k_v}(x)$ uniformly within $C\tilde{\epsilon}$ of $h_k(x)$ where $\sum_{j=1}^{m} |\alpha_j| \leq C$.

Influence of Bandwidth

Finally it is worth explicitly noting how the choice of a different bandwidth of the kernel, i.e. letting $k^{(\sigma)}(\mathbf{x}) := \sigma k(\sigma \mathbf{x})$, affects the eigenspectrum of the corresponding operator. We have $K^{(\sigma)}(\boldsymbol{\omega}) = K(\boldsymbol{\omega}/\sigma)$, hence scaling a kernel by σ means more densely spaced eigenvalues in the spectrum of the integral operator $T_{k^{(\sigma)}}$.

9.7 Covering Numbers for Given Decay Rates

In this section we will show how the asymptotic behaviour of $\epsilon_n(A\colon \ell_2 \to \ell_2)$, where A is the scaling operator introduced before, depends on the eigenvalues of T_k.

A similar analysis has been carried out by Prosser (1966), in order to compute the entropy numbers of integral operators. However all of his operators mapped into $L_2(\mathcal{C}, \mathbb{C})$. Furthermore, whilst our propositions are stated as asympotic results as his were, the proofs actually give non-asympototic information with explicit constants. See (Williamson et al., 1998a) for details.

Note that we need to sort the eigenvalues in a nonincreasing manner because of the requirements in corollary 9.2. If the eigenvalues were unsorted one could obtain far too small numbers in the geometrical mean of $\lambda_1, \ldots, \lambda_j$. Many one-dimensional kernels have nondegenerate systems of eigenvalues in which case it is straightforward to explicitly compute the geometrical means of the eigenvalues as will be shown below. Note that whilst all of the examples below are for convolution kernels, i.e. $k(x, y) = k(x - y)$, there is nothing in the formulations of the propositions themselves that requires this. When we consider the d-dimensional case we shall see that with rotationally invariant kernels, degenerate systems of eigenvalues are generic. This can be dealt with by a slight modification of theorem 9.2 — see Williamson et al. (1998a) for details.

Let us consider the special case where $(\lambda_j)_j$ decays asymptotically with some polynomial or exponential degree. In this case we can choose a sequence $(a_j)_j$ for which we can evaluate (9.30) explicitly. By the eigenvalues of a kernel k we mean the eigenvalues of the induced integral operator T_k.

Laplacian Kernel

Proposition 9.2 (Polynomial Decay)
Let k be a Mercer kernel with eigenvalues satisfying $\lambda_j = \beta^2 i^{-(\alpha+1)}$ for some $\alpha > 0$. Then

$$\epsilon_n(A\colon \ell_2 \to \ell_2) = O\left((\ln n)^{-\frac{\alpha}{2} + O(\ln^{-2} \ln n)}\right) = O(\ln^{-\frac{\alpha}{2}} n). \tag{9.52}$$

An example of such a kernel is $k(x) = e^{-x}$.

Proposition 9.3 (Exponential Decay)
Suppose k is a Mercer kernel with eigenvalues $\lambda_j = \beta^2 e^{-\alpha(j-1)}$ for some $\alpha, \beta > 0$. Then

$$\ln \epsilon_n^{-1}(A\colon \ell_2 \to \ell_2) = O(\ln^{\frac{1}{2}} n) \tag{9.53}$$

An example of such a kernel is $k(x) = \frac{1}{1+x^2}$.

Gaussian Kernel

Proposition 9.4 (Exponential Quadratic Decay)
Suppose k is a Mercer kernel with $\lambda_j = \beta^2 e^{-\alpha(j-1)^2}$ for some $\alpha, \beta > 0$. Then

$$\ln \epsilon_n^{-1}(A\colon \ell_2 \to \ell_2) = O(\ln^{\frac{2}{3}} n). \tag{9.54}$$

An example of such a kernel is the Gaussian $k(x) = e^{-x^2}$. We conclude this section with a general relation between exponential-polynomial decay rates and orders of bounds on $\epsilon_n(A)$.

Proposition 9.5 (Exponential-Polynomial decay)
Suppose k is a Mercer kernel with $\lambda_j = \beta^2 e^{-\alpha j^p}$ for some $\alpha, \beta, p > 0$. Then

$$\ln \epsilon_n^{-1}(A: \ell_2 \to \ell_2) = O(\ln^{\frac{p}{p+1}} n) \tag{9.55}$$

This result is interesting but probably of little theoretical relevance as most practical kernels do not exhibit these rapid decay properties. (Recall the remarks at the beginning of section 9.6.)

Proposition 9.6
The rates given in propositions 9.2, 9.3, 9.4, and 9.5 are tight.

9.8 Conclusions

We have shown how to connect properties known about mappings into feature spaces with bounds on the covering numbers. Our reasoning relied on the fact that this mapping exhibits certain decay properties to ensure rapid convergence and a constraint on the size of the weight vector in feature space. This means that the corresponding algorithms have to restrict exactly this quantity to ensure good generalization performance. This is exactly what is done in Support Vector machines.

The actual application of our results, perhaps for model selection using structural risk minimization, is somewhat involved. Below we outline one possible path. As said before, the viewpoint in this chapter is new, and perhaps there will be refinements soon forthcoming which would make the codification of our existing results into a single generalization bound premature.

9.8.1 A Possible Procedure to use the Results of this Chapter

Choose k and σ The kernel k may be chosen for a variety of reasons, which we have nothing additional to say about here. The choice of σ should take account of the discussion in section 9.6.

Choose the period v of the kernel One suggested procedure is outlined in section 9.6.

Bound $\epsilon_n(A)$ This can be done using Corollary 9.2. Some examples of this sort of calculation are given in section 9.7.

Bound $\epsilon_n(T)$ Using Theorem 9.4.

Standard SV Case

Take account of the "$+b$" The key observation is that given a class $\mathcal{F}$ with known $\mathcal{N}^\ell(\epsilon, \mathcal{F})$, one can bound $\mathcal{N}^\ell(\epsilon, \mathcal{F}^+)$ as follows. (Here $\mathcal{F}^+ := \{f + b : f \in \mathcal{F}, b \in \mathbb{R}\}$.) Suppose V_ϵ is an ϵ-cover for $\mathcal{F}$ and elements of $\mathcal{F}+$ are uniformly bounded by B (this implies a limit on $|b|$ as well as a uniform bound on elements of $\mathcal{F}$). Then

$$V_\epsilon^+ := \bigcup_{j=-B/\epsilon}^{B/\epsilon} V_\epsilon + j\epsilon \tag{9.56}$$

is an ϵ-cover for $\mathcal{F}^+$ and thus $\mathcal{N}^\ell(\epsilon, \mathcal{F}^+) \leq \frac{2B}{\epsilon}\mathcal{N}^\ell(\epsilon, \mathcal{F})$. Observe that this will only be "noticeable" for classes $\mathcal{F}$ with very slowly growing covering numbers (polynomial in $1/\epsilon$).

Take account of the loss function using Lemma 9.2 for example.

Plug into a uniform convergence result See the pointers to the literature and the example in section 9.4.

Classification and Pattern Recognition Together with a stratification of the hypothesis classes in terms of the margin in a data dependent fashion (Shawe-Taylor et al., 1998) the bounds could be used for classification.

Acknowledgements

This work was supported by the Australian Research Council, a grant of the DFG (# Ja 379/71), and NeuroColt II.

II Implementations

10 Solving the Quadratic Programming Problem Arising in Support Vector Classification

Linda Kaufman
Bell Laboratories
700 Mountain Ave, Murray Hill, NJ 07974, USA
lck@research.bell-labs.com
http://cm.bell-labs.com/who/lck/

The support vector technique suggested by Cortes and Vapnik (1995) is designed to solve the classification problem of determining the class of a data point when you are given some characteristics of the point (a vector) and many "training" data of classes and characteristics. This technique has proved rather effective in optical character recognition. As shown by Cortes and Vapnik, the support vector technique leads to a positive semidefinite quadratic programming problem with a dense, structured, positive semidefinite matrix. The number of rows in the matrix equals the number of training data points. Thus for a problem with thousands of training points, just computing the matrix for the quadratic programming problem is expensive and one may not be able to store it. In this chapter we discuss several methods for solving the underlying quadratic programming problem.

10.1 Introduction

In machine learning one is given "training" vectors $\mathbf{x}_i, i = 1, ..., \ell$ of length N and integers $a_i, i = 1, ..., \ell$. which suggest that data $\mathbf{x}_i$ is supposed to be associated with class a_i. From this data one is supposed to create a mechanism by which one can determine for any given data item of length N which class it is in.

As shown in (Vapnik, 1995), central to the support vector technique is a matrix Q where $q_{i,j}$ is a function of $\mathbf{x}_i$ and $\mathbf{x}_j$ and essentially defines the surface that separates the classes. For class m define the vector $\mathbf{y}$ as follows

$$y_i = \begin{cases} 1 & \text{if } a_i = m \\ -1 & \text{otherwise} \end{cases} \tag{10.1}$$

If one wishes the separating surface to be a of polynomial of degree d, for class m one might have

$$q_{i,j} = K(\mathbf{x}_i, \mathbf{x}_j) y_i y_j = ((\mathbf{x}_i^T \mathbf{x}_j + 1)/k)^d y_i y_j. \tag{10.2}$$

Other surfaces are given in (1.30) and (1.31). In general Q is dense and may be positive semidefinite. If ℓ is large, Q might be too big to store.

For each class the support vector technique amounts to solving a quadratic programming (QP) problem: Determine the ℓ vector which minimizes

$$\frac{1}{2}\alpha^{\ T} Q\alpha - \mathbf{e}^T \alpha \tag{10.3}$$

such that

$$0 \le \alpha_i \le C \quad for\ i = 1, ..., n \tag{10.4}$$

and

$$\mathbf{y}^T \alpha = 0. \tag{10.5}$$

If $\boldsymbol{\alpha}$ is the solution of the QP ((10.3)–(10.5)) and $\alpha_i > 0$, then $\mathbf{x}_i$ is considered a support vector. The decision function (1.18) determines whether a new vector $\mathbf{x}$ is in class m.

In section 10.2 we consider properties of the problem that may be important in determining which quadratic programming approach one should use. In particular, in many problems most of the elements in the solution to (10.3)–(10.5) are zero. Ordinarily, computing the gradient of (10.3) requires $\ell^2 + 0(\ell)$ multiplications, but if α has only s nonzeroes, then $\ell s + o(\ell)$ multiplications are necessary and one has to access only s columns of Q. Thus one can decrease the amount of work and storage if one attempts to access only those columns of Q corresponding to nonzero values of α in the final solution. This suggests an active set strategy which starts with $\alpha = 0$.

In section 10.3 we describe several ways of solving the quadratic programming problem. In section 10.4 we consider "chunking" strategies for dealing with the situation when the number of data points is so large that storing the information for the quick use of the Q is impossible. Some experimental results are given in section 10.5. We consider a large problem with $N = 400$ that comes from NIST for recognizing hand written digits, as well as several 2-dimensional problems.

10.2 General Considerations

QP characteristics

The size of the Hessian Q, the structure of that matrix, the nature of the solution, and the structure of the constraints all should be considered when choosing a quadratic programming package to solve (10.3)–(10.5). We begin by listing a few properties of some of the problems we have seen which have influenced our thinking.

(1) For postprocessing it is important to determine which elements of the solution are 0 or at the upper bound C and which are not. Some QP packages, particularly interior point implementations, may return values close to the machine precision rather than at exact zero. One interior point implementation obtained about 30 per cent more support vectors than another because "small" values were misinterpreted.

(2) The constraints are upper and lower bound constraints plus one general equality constraint. Codes that do not make a special provision for bound constraints are probably not useful.

(3) The matrix Q is dense and may be too large to store. We have looked at problems where ℓ is about 10,000 which means that we need to store about 100 million elements just to specify the Q matrix. Some quadratic solvers request the full matrix. Others suggest that the user provide a subroutine which will do matrix by vector multiplication with Q and pick out a row or column of Q. For the support vector problem the latter may be preferable. An algorithm that requires a factorization of the full Q matrix is also space consuming.

(4) The matrix Q can be positive semidefinite. This property eliminates some commercial QP codes.

(5) If N is small or d is 1 or 2 in (10.2), then it is relatively easy to generate the elements of Q from the training vectors each time they are needed. We have seen applications with N=2 where generating an element of $q_{i,j}$ with (10.2) would not be difficult so that with small N if a code does not request a stored Q matrix but asks the user to provide a routine for doing matrix-vector multiplication with Q, the storage problem can be sidestepped easily. Similarly if $d = 1$ in (10.2), let X be the $N \times \ell$ matrix whose i^{th} column is the training vector $\mathbf{x}_i$ and let $\hat{X} = (X : \mathbf{e})$ where $e_i = 1$ for $i = 1, ..., N$. Then to determine $\mathbf{w} = Q\mathbf{v}$ for a given vector $\mathbf{v}$ one proceeds as follows

When $d = 1$

Algorithm $X1$

(1) *Set* $h_j = y_j v_j$ *for* $j = 1, \ldots, \ell$

(2) *Set* $\mathbf{z} = \hat{X}\mathbf{h}$.

(3) *Set* $\mathbf{f} = X^T\mathbf{z}$

(4) *Set* $w_i = (y_i/k) f_i$ *for* $i = 1, \ldots, \ell$

Algorithm $X1$ does not require that Q be formed and costs $2\ell(N+2)$ multiplications vs. ℓ^2 multiplications if one were given Q rather than X . When $\ell = 1000$ and $N = 200$, it is 10 times faster. In the chapter appendix algorithm $X2$ handles

$N = 2$ and requires $0(\ell N^2)$ multiplications. In general one would need $0(\ell N^d)$ multiplications which suggests that if $N^d < \ell$, then not forming all of Q explicitly not only saves space, but also may be cheaper.

(6) For most problems most of the elements of the solution $\boldsymbol{\alpha}$ are 0. Table 10.1 gives an indication of the number of nonzero elements and to which class they belong. One may choose to solve the QP problem as a sequence of smaller problems, in which case, the number of nonzeroes for a particular subproblem may be large, but otherwise the following considerations are relevant:

(a) There will be fewer changes in the zero/nonzero structure of the solution if one begins with a "zero" solution. This fact bodes ill for those interior codes which start with a totally nonzero solution.

(b) Packages that call a subroutine to deliver a column of Q usually require them only for those values of the approximate solution that are nonzero. Thus in this case it may not be necessary to look at all of Q, just the columns that correspond to the nonzero elements in $\boldsymbol{\alpha}$.

(c) Packages that call a subroutine to form $\mathbf{w} = Q\mathbf{v}$ for a given $\mathbf{v}$, are usually trying to form the gradient of the quadratic form and $\mathbf{v}$ will be the current value of $\boldsymbol{\alpha}$. Most of the elements of $\mathbf{v}$ will be 0, and the corresponding columns of Q will not be needed. If there are s nonzeroes, only $s\ell$ multiplications will be needed rather than ℓ^2.

Computing gradient with some elements on boundary

(7) When the upper bound C in (10.4) is too small, the number of nonzero elements in $\boldsymbol{\alpha}$ increases, but many of these extras, will be at C. The significance of this statement is felt in two ways. If one is using a decomposition of the projected Q matrix, one will not see an increase in the size of the projected matrix. Secondly, while doing matrix vector multiplication $Q\mathbf{v}$ one needs only the sum of the columns of the Q matrix corresponding to the elements of $\mathbf{v}$ that equal C, not the elements themselves. For example if

$$\mathbf{v} = (0, C, C, x, C, 0, \ldots, 0) \tag{10.6}$$

then

$$Q\mathbf{v} = \mathbf{q}_4\mathbf{v}_4 + (\mathbf{q}_2 + \mathbf{q}_3 + \mathbf{q}_5)C. \tag{10.7}$$

It would not be unusual if on subsequent iterations, the second, third, and fifth elements of $\mathbf{v}$ would also be at C. Thus if one kept a running total of the sum of the columns of Q at bound, then one would save work on the matrix-vector multiplication and also require less space.

(8) Support vectors of one class will likely be the support vectors of another class. As one changes classes, the Q matrix does not change, but the vector $\mathbf{y}$ in (10.1) definitely changes. That the support vectors are repeated is evident from table 10.1 which used problems from Ho and Kleinberg (1996) and LeCun et al. (1989). For the postal problem only 1567 columns of the Q matrix were needed to solve all 10 quadratic programming problems. If one deleted the columns after each QP

Problem	Tin1	Postal
ℓ	862	7291
N	2	256
classes	4	10
p in polynomial model	5	3
upper bound	10000	128
total number of support vectors all classes	71	2486
number of distinct support vectors	51	1567
total number of support vectors corresponding to class under consideration	31	956
total number at upper bound	22	64

Table 10.1 Characteristics of 2 problems

problem, one would have generated 2486 columns. This suggests that if one has a code that creates and saves columns of the Q matrix, that these columns might be useful while computing the support vectors of another class. Moreover, if one has an opportunity to specify "starting" support vectors, one should choose previously computed columns belonging to the current class.

(9) A large portion of the support vectors for the QP problem of class m, will belong to class m. From table 10.1 we see that for the postal problem that of the 1567 vectors which were support vectors in one or more of the 10 quadratic programming problems, 956 of them appeared as support vectors for their own class. If one can specify starting support vectors, one may wish to choose a large portion from the current class.

10.3 Solving the Quadratic Programming Problem

10.3.1 The Meta Algorithm

Solving the quadratic programming problem (10.3)-(10.5) tends to lead to two subproblems:

(1) Identifying the elements of $\boldsymbol{\alpha}$ which will be at bound, i.e. those that will be "active";

(2) Minimizing (10.3) for the variables not at bound.

These subproblems are not attacked independently. If in the course of minimizing (10.3), it is determined that certain of the variables will violate their bounds, those variables are set at the bound and "activated." Similarly, if it is determined that

(10.3) can be further decreased by releasing some variables from their bounds, then those variables will be "deactivated."

Algorithms differ in their strategy for minimizing (10.3) and for "activating" and "deactivating" constraints. Some strategies tend to work well when most of the variables will be "active"; others in just the opposite situation.

Formally, a sequence of equality constrained problems will be solved. For a particular subproblem assume that the elements of $\boldsymbol{\alpha}$ have been permuted so that the first $\ell - s$ elements of $\boldsymbol{\alpha}$ are to be held at a bound and the last s elements are free to vary. We then wish to minimize

$$f(\alpha) = \frac{1}{2}\alpha^T Q\alpha - \mathbf{e}^T\alpha \tag{10.8}$$

such that

$$A^T\alpha = \mathbf{h}, \tag{10.9}$$

where elements of $\mathbf{h}$ are either 0 or -C, and A^T has the form

$$A^T = \begin{pmatrix} D|0 \\ \tilde{\mathbf{y}}^{\mathbf{T}} \end{pmatrix} \tag{10.10}$$

where $\tilde{\mathbf{y}}$ is a permutation of our $\mathbf{y}$, and D is an $(\ell - s)$ by $(\ell - s)$ diagonal matrix with diagonal elements

$$d_{jj} = \begin{cases} 1 & \alpha_j = 0 \\ -1 & \alpha_j = C \end{cases} \tag{10.11}$$

As the sequence progresses, D will gain and lose rows and columns.

Let $\mathbf{g}(\alpha) = \nabla f(\alpha) = Q\alpha - \mathbf{e}$. The original QP problem (10.3)-(10.5) will be minimized if none of the bound constraints are violated and for $j = \ell - s + 1, \ldots, \ell$

$$g_j = 0 \tag{10.12}$$

and according to the Kuhn Tucker conditions $\mathbf{g}$ can be written as

$$A\mathbf{u} = \mathbf{g} \tag{10.13}$$

where $u_j \geq 0$ for $j = 1, \ldots, \ell - s$.

Because of the form of our constraints and because we are interested in the components of $\mathbf{g}$ which lie in the range of A, the solution $\mathbf{u}$ of (10.13) can be determined rather simply using the equations

$$A^T A\mathbf{u} = A^T\mathbf{g}. \tag{10.14}$$

Denote the first $\ell - s$ elements of $\tilde{\mathbf{y}}$ and $\mathbf{g}$ as $\mathbf{y}_B$ and $\mathbf{g}_B$ respectively and their last s elements as $\mathbf{y}_I$ and $\mathbf{g}_I$ respectively.(The subscript B denotes boundary and the subscript I denotes interior). Then (10.14) is equivalent to solving

$$LL^T = \begin{pmatrix} D\mathbf{g}_B \\ \tilde{\mathbf{y}}^T\mathbf{g} \end{pmatrix}. \tag{10.15}$$

where

$$L = \begin{pmatrix} D & 0 \\ \mathbf{y}_B^T & (\mathbf{y}_I^T \mathbf{y}_I)^{\frac{1}{2}} \end{pmatrix}. \tag{10.16}$$

Solving $L\mathbf{v} = A^T \mathbf{g}$ implies that

$$\mathbf{v} = \begin{pmatrix} \mathbf{g}_B \\ \mathbf{y}_I^T \mathbf{g}_I / (\mathbf{y}_I^T \mathbf{y}_I)^{\frac{1}{2}} \end{pmatrix}. \tag{10.17}$$

KKT criteria

Solving $L^T \mathbf{u} = \mathbf{v}$ yields

$$u_{\ell-s+1} = \mathbf{y}_I^T \mathbf{g}_I / \mathbf{y}_I^T \mathbf{y}_I = \mathbf{y}_I^T \mathbf{g}_I / s. \tag{10.18}$$

for $j = 1, \ldots, \ell - s$

$$u_j = (g_j - u_{\ell-s+1} y_j)/d_{jj}. \tag{10.19}$$

10.3.2 Minimizing f

The variable α in (10.8) can be expressed as

$$\alpha = Z\mathbf{v} + A\mathbf{w} \tag{10.20}$$

Solving the equality constrained QP

where Z spans the null space of A, i.e. $A^T Z = 0$ and Z has rank $s - 1$. The vector $\mathbf{w}$ may be determined by multiplying (10.20) by A giving $A^T A\mathbf{w} = \mathbf{h}$. If all the bound variables are at zero, then $\mathbf{w} = 0$. The significance of the Z matrix in (10.20) is that minimizing (10.8) is equivalent to minimizing

$$\hat{f}(\mathbf{v}) = \frac{1}{2}\mathbf{v}^T Z^T Q Z \mathbf{v} + \mathbf{e}^T Z \mathbf{v}. \tag{10.21}$$

In this section we will present two methods for minimizing (10.21), a Newton approach, which takes 1 step (i.e. one gradient evaluation) to obtain the minimum of the current equality constrained problem, and a conjugate gradient approach, which takes s steps (i.e. s gradient evaluations). The choice of method depends on the representation of Z. The Newton approach requires the explicit storage of Z while the conjugate gradient may use some other representation.

10.3.2.1 A Newton Approach based on the Bunch-Kaufman Algorithm

A Newton approach

Assuming $Z^T Q Z$ is positive definite, the solution α' to the problem of minimizing $f(\alpha)$ is

$$\alpha' = \alpha - Z(Z^T Q Z)^{-1} Z^T \mathbf{g}. \tag{10.22}$$

where $\mathbf{g}$ is the gradient of f at $\boldsymbol{\alpha}$. Obviously the structure of Z will be important to the success of such a Newton approach.

Because of the structure of A in (10.10), the matrix Z will have the structure

$$Z = \begin{pmatrix} 0 \\ Z_2 \end{pmatrix} \tag{10.23}$$

where the first $\ell - s$ rows of Z will be zero. Because of the block of zeros in the Z matrix in (10.23), only $s \times (s-1)$ storage locations are required to store Z and only those rows of Q corresponding to the elements not at bound are needed to form the matrix (Z^TQZ) and α'. Thus only the s columns of Q corresponding to the nonzero elements of $\boldsymbol{\alpha}$ have to be computed. To help solve the linear equations in (10.22) Bunch and Kaufman (1977) choose Z such that

$$Z^TQZ = E \tag{10.24}$$

where E would be diagonal if Q is positive semi-definite. If it is indefinite, it is block diagonal with blocks that are either 1×1 or 2×2. From (10.22) and (10.24)

$$\alpha' = \alpha - ZE^{-1}Z^T\mathbf{g}, \tag{10.25}$$

which means determining $\boldsymbol{\alpha}'$ requires about $2s^2$ multiplications plus of the work required to determine ∇f and Z. Computing Z from scratch each iteration would require $s^3/3 + 0(s^2)$ multiplications, but Bunch and Kaufman (1977) show that if one is solving a sequence of problems where each member of the sequence involves deleting or adding a row or column to A, then updating Z each iteration requires s^2 multiplications when a constraint is activated and $3s^2$ when a constraint is deactivated. When s/ℓ is small, the major work in each iteration is the computation of the gradient.

If α' from (10.22) violates one of original bound constraints, find the first constraint violated along $\mathbf{p} = -ZE^{-1}Z^T\mathbf{g}$. The first is at $\alpha + \gamma\mathbf{p}$ where

$$\gamma = \min(\min_{\substack{i=\ell-s \\ \text{if } p_i < 0}}^{\ell} (-\alpha_i/p_i), \quad \min_{\substack{i=\ell-s \\ \text{if } p_i > 0}}^{\ell} ((C-\alpha_i)/p_i). \tag{10.26}$$

If $\gamma < 1$, which means that a variable now becomes at bound, the Z_2 matrix in (10.23) will lose a row and a column and the decomposition in (10.24) can be updated according to the algorithm given in (Bunch and Kaufman, 1977).

In summary the main disadvantages of the Bunch-Kaufman approach are the storage of Z_2, requiring an $s \times s$ matrix and the cost of computing Z_2 if $s/\ell \approx 1$. It is extremely quick for small values of s.

10.3.2.2 The Conjugate Gradient Algorithm

Another representation for Z is

$$\begin{pmatrix} 0 \\ I - \mathbf{y}_I\mathbf{y}_I^T/\mathbf{y}_I^T\mathbf{y}_I \end{pmatrix} \tag{10.27}$$

where the first $\ell - s$ rows of Z are zero and $\mathbf{y}_I$ is the same vector used in (10.18). Note that $Z^T\mathbf{y} = 0$ and hence $Z^T A = 0$. The advantages of (10.27) are that a 2 dimensional matrix is not necessary to store Z and the application of Z to a vector requires $2s$ multiplications rather than $0(s^2)$. However, (10.27) probably precludes a simple Newton like approach, and one must use an iterative approach, like conjugate gradients.

The conjugate gradient algorithm

For a quadratic function of s variables, the conjugate gradient algorithm is an iterative method guaranteed to converge within s iterations where each iteration requires $0(s^2)$ multiplications. In the conjugate gradient approach, a search direction is a linear combination of the previous search direction and the current gradient. The new direction will be ZQZ orthogonal to all previous search directions for that equality constrained subproblem, and the gradient at the minimum along that direction will be orthogonal to all previous search directions. In contrast the steepest descent algorithm, which follows the gradient, may zig-zag in a narrow valley and may never converge. The key to the conjugate gradient approach is that it uses more than local information; it uses previously gathered information as well.

The conjugate gradient does not need a decomposition of the Hessian matrix Z^TQZ, but requires only that one can multiply a vector by that matrix. The simple representation in (10.27) for Z is ideal. Note that only the rows or columns of Q corresponding to the variables not at bounds have to be formed.

Given $\boldsymbol{\alpha}$, the previous search direction $\hat{\mathbf{p}}$, the current gradient of $f(\alpha)$, $\mathbf{g}$, and the previous gradient, $\hat{\mathbf{g}}$, then the conjugate gradient algorithm to determine the next iterate α' that satisfies $A^T\alpha = \mathbf{h}$ is

Constrained Conjugate Gradient Algorithm

(1) *Compute* $\sigma = \hat{\mathbf{g}}^T Z\hat{\mathbf{g}}/\mathbf{g}^T Z\mathbf{g}$

(2) *Set* $\mathbf{p} = -Z\mathbf{g} + \sigma\hat{\mathbf{g}}$

(3) *Compute* $\tau = \mathbf{g}^T Z\mathbf{g}/\mathbf{p}^{\,T} Q\mathbf{p}$

(4) *Set* $\alpha' = \alpha + \tau\mathbf{p}$

(5) *The new gradient* $\mathbf{g}'$ *is* $\mathbf{g} + \tau Q\mathbf{p}$

The multiplication using Q in step 3 can be reused in step 5 so that only one matrix vector multiplication involving Q is necessary. The gradient in step 5 is the gradient for the last s variables. For the first iteration, σ in step 1 is set to 0.

As with the Newton algorithm in10.3.2.1, if $\boldsymbol{\alpha}$ violates any of the original inequality constraints, one should not take a full step. Essentially, in step 3 set

$$\tau = \min(\mathbf{g}^T Z\mathbf{g}/\mathbf{p}^{\,T} Q\mathbf{p}, \gamma) \tag{10.28}$$

where γ is defined in (10.26), redefine Z and in the next iteration set σ to 0.

Theoretically for each equality constrained problem with s variables not at bound the conjugate gradient algorithm requires s iterations for convergence. One may think of one Newton step as requiring about the same amount of work as five conjugate gradient iterations so that the Newton approach would always be faster. In practice, one may wish to get an approximate solution, like reducing the projected

Training points ℓ interior support points s	400 145	500 182	1000 279
Time to make full Q	8.0	12.7	54.6
Newton including time to make columns needed Initial 0 space — $s^2 + 0(\ell)$	7.9	14.2	53
Conjugate gradient including time to make columns needed Initial 0 space — $s^2 + 0(\ell)$	(6.2) 9.2	(9.7) 15.8	(33.2) 60.5
Conjugate gradient start interior inclding times to make Q	11.7	19.5	86
Snopt with times for forming columns	38.7	57.2	266

Table 10.2 Time (sec.) for finding a "2" in NIST data with different methods

gradient to the square root of the machine precision or greater. Based on (10.19) if a constraint should be deactivated, then the conjugate gradient algorithm should be restarted with a new Z matrix; otherwise the conjugate gradient algorithm should be continued until full convergence is attained. With stopping early for intermediate subproblems, the case for Newton versus conjugate gradient is weakened. Moreover, based on (10.28), constraints are usually activated during the first iteration, so that the overhead associated with "adding" a constraint is much less with conjugate gradient.

Table 10.2 indicates the times required on the SGI Challenge XL with 12 150MHz R4400 processors for the Newton approach and the conjugate gradient method on a problem with $N = 400$. For all strategies the times include that required to form those columns of the Q matrix that are needed for the sequence of equality constraints. The time in parenthesis for the conjugate gradient code starting at 0, is the time spent making the matrix. When $\boldsymbol{\alpha}$ was initially 0 only about 15 percent of the computed columns did not correspond to support vectors of the original problem. For the Newton approach and the two conjugate gradient runs with different starting points, the time required to make Q was greater than all the time spent within the algorithms. The times for the Newton and conjugate gradient algorithms exclusive of the time to construct Q were roughly the same. For the conjugate gradient code, intermediate equality constrained problems were terminated when the projected gradient was less than 10^{-2}, which usually required between 3 and 7 iterations. Lowering this bound increased the time for the conjugate gradient code without adding any benefit.

Most of the work within both the Newton and conjugate gradient approaches involves multiplying the Q matrix by a vector which may have many components set to zero. Any idea, like loop unrolling or improvements in data locality, that make one of the algorithms more efficient would also make the other more efficient. Many manufacturers provide efficient assembly language routines for matrix by vector multiplication, but these do not take account that some of the columns may not be needed. If $s \approx \ell$, ignoring the zeroes and using the manufacturer provided routines is probably the best strategy. Otherwise, it might pay to permute the columns of Q so that those corresponding to the s variables that are free to vary, lie in consecutive columns, and then to call the manufacturer provided routine.

10.3.3 Changing the Equality Constrained Problem

The equality constrained problem is changed whenever a bound constraint is about to be violated. It is also changed when one determines that the minimum (or approximate minimum in the case of conjugate gradients) of the current equality constraint problem has been found and condition (10.19) suggests that a further reduction could be achieved by deactivating one or more constraints.

10.3.3.1 Deactivating Constraints

Moving from boundary

In a conservative approach the constraint with the most negative value of u_i in (10.19) would be deactivated. In a non-conservative approach, all constraints corresponding to negative values of $\mathbf{u}$ would be deactivated. The rationale behind using a non-conservative approach is that time should not be wasted solving equality constrained problems that will probably not be the final equality constrained problem. However, with the non-conservative approach, more constraints are deactivated that will eventually be activated again. If very few of the training points are destined to be support points, then initially a conservative approach is probably worthwhile. Eventually, a less conservative approach might be justified when one has gained a good idea of almost all the support vectors. The cost of obtaining the gradient depends on the approximate number of support vectors and if one overestimates that number then there will be more work per iteration and more columns of Q will have to be computed. In table 10.2, the conservative deactivation strategy was used for the Newton and conjugate gradient approaches.

The difficulties with releasing all those with negative Kuhn-Tucker multipliers is evident if initially $\alpha = 0$, which means that $\mathbf{g} = -\mathbf{e}$. If one had apriori designated at least one corresponding to the prescribed class and one out of the prescribed class as support vectors, then $u_{\ell-s+1} < 1$ in (10.18) and all the remaining training points would be deactivated, which may not be the optimum strategy. If one had prescribed arbitrarily one element to be deactivated, then $u_{\ell-s+1}$ would be either +1 or -1, and either all the members of the class or all the training points not in the class would be activated. In fact in table 10.2, the routine SNOPT (Gill et al., 1997) chose this strategy and the computation times reflect the unfortunate choice for this particular problem.

Of course if one chooses to deactivate more than one constraint, the quantity $u_{\ell-s+1}$ in (10.18) should be recomputed after each constraint is deactivated. If many elements correspond to negative Kuhn-Tucker multipliers, it might be best to use some information about the problem, like preferring training points within the class or training points for which the column of Q is available. One may also wish to incorporate a "sticky" policy, in which if a constraint had once been not at bound and then activated, then it would have low priority for being deactivated (see Burges (1998)).

In theory any bound constraint corresponding to a negative u_i in (10.19) will decrease (10.3). One is not required to actually find the constraint corresponding to the most negative value. Thus there is no need to look at or compute all of the first $(\ell - s)$ elements of $\mathbf{u}$; one needs just enough to find one negative u_i, if one exists. In practice one may compute a subvector of $\mathbf{u}$ and deactivate the one constraint corresponding to the most negative in that subvector. If for that subvector, all elements of $\mathbf{u}$ are positive, then another subvector might be considered. This is called partial pricing in linear programming. One can imagine various algorithms for determining which elements of $\mathbf{u}$ should be considered and how long to stick with the same set of elements. "Chunking" as used in (Boser et al., 1992) or in (Burges, 1998) refers to inspecting the same set of elements of $\mathbf{u}$ until no more constraints can be deactivated. The advantage of not inspecting all of $\mathbf{u}$ is that there is no need to compute those elements of the gradient that are not considered. Since gradient computation is one of the most time consuming portions of each iteration, partial pricing cuts the time per iteration, but it may require more iterations. The chunking strategy of Burges (1998) has the additional feature of delaying the computation of those rows of Q that are not in the present "chunk."

10.3.3.2 Activating Constraints

If one starts with $\boldsymbol{\alpha} = 0$ and uses a very conservative deactivating strategy, few bound constraints will have to be reactivated. However, if one choses to begin in the interior of the domain or the "deactivation" strategy is not conservative enough many constraints may have to be activated or reactivated. If one followed the conjugate gradient approach as given, a gradient computation would be necessary each time a constraint is encountered.

Several suggestion have been proposed to circumnavigate this difficulty (see Bierlaire et al. (1991)) and in general they work with a bent line. In (10.28) let $\theta = \mathbf{g}^T Z\mathbf{g}/\mathbf{p}^T Q\mathbf{p}$. If say $\gamma < \theta/10$, one would change Z to reflect the activation of a new constraint and form $Z\mathbf{p}$ with the new Z and recompute γ. The process would continue until a prescribed maximum number of constraints (like 5 or 10) had been activated, until γ became too large, or the total length of the line became too large. Simply setting the element of $\mathbf{p}$ to 0, corresponding to an activated constraint does not guarantee that the resulting $\boldsymbol{\alpha}$ would satisfy (10.5), and one has to use a new Z. The function and gradient are not computed until the activation is completed. Since there is no guarantee of a function decrease if more than one bound is activated, $\boldsymbol{\alpha}$ corresponding to the activation of the first bound constraint should be saved in case the function increases.

In table 10.2 for the row of the table indicating conjugate gradient with an interior initial point, at each iteration at most 10 bound constraints were activated. The time for this case is greater than those with the initial $\boldsymbol{\alpha}$ at 0 only because the time for creating the full Q matrix is included. If one subtracts off the time to compute all or parts of Q from the computations times, one concludes that the time within the algorithm for the conjugate gradient codes with both starting conditions are very similar. If one had not used a bent line approach for the conjugate gradient code initialized to the interior, the time within that procedure would have been 10 times larger. The row in table 10.2 which starts with an interior point indicates the importance of the initial guess.

10.4 Chunking

If s of the elements of the QP problem are not at bound, the schemes suggested in section 10.3 requires at least ℓs storage locations to store the columns of the Q matrix. If $\ell = 60,000$ and s is about 1000 as in the NIST data set (Bottou et al., 1994), on many machines there will be a storage problem. This problem can be circumvented when either the model is linear, N is small, or the data is binary by generating the elements of Q as they are needed and not storing them for future use. However, in general, regenerating the elements is costly. Another idea, suggested in (Vapnik, 1979) and used in (Boser et al., 1992), involves breaking the problem up into smaller problems and determining the support vectors from the small subproblems. Various alternatives suggest themselves all of which are variations of the theme of incrementing the size of the sample set.

Algorithm A

(1) *Train on some of the vectors.*

(2) *Test the rest of the vectors using* (1.18).

(3) *If there are any testing errors, add the points corresponding to testing errors to the training sample set and return to step (a).*

Algorithm A above must terminate because one is never decreasing the number of points in the sample set and there is a finite number of training points. Because the sample size might be too large, in practice one may not want to add in all the non sample points that are in error or one may have to delete all non support points in the sample. If at least one of the values of u_i in (10.19) is negative, then the objective function for the whole problem will continue to decrease and the algorithm will converge, even if non support points are deleted. However, as we shall see, the algorithm may not converge to the solution on the original QP problem. Only if all the values of u_i in (10.19) are positive do we converge to the solution of the original QP problem.

Table 10.3 gives a typical course of Algorithm A with 10,000 training points in the NIST problem (Bottou et al., 1994) of recognizing digits. The Bunch-Kaufman approach was used to determine a "2" and the initial data set contained a random sample of 500 points with 10 classes. Here $N = 400$, a polynomial model was used with $d = 3$ and C was set to 1000. Our tests were performed on a 4 processor SGI machine. When more points were found in error in step (b) than there were

iteration	1	2	3	4	5
Sample size					
$y_i = 1$	49	321	325	329	330
$y_i = -1$	451	473	685	688	689
Number of support vectors					
$y_i = 1$	39	227	250	254	254
$y_i = -1$	143	217	326	320	319
Number of points in error					
Unrecognized '2'	272	4	4	1	0
Other	22	212	3	1	0
Computation time (sec.)					
generation of Q only	186	312	220	3	3
excluding generation of Q	6	71	208	75	45

Table 10.3 Typical course of Algorithm A on NIST data (10,000 training points).

training set size	time (sec.) with Q creation	time (sec.) Q given	number of support vectors	number of test errors
250	.98	.15	56	165
500	3.9	0.5	67	118
1000	13	1.6	95	89
5000	160	34	234	46

Table 10.4 Influence on number of training points on NIST problem with 10,000 testing points finding "1."

support points, the next iteration was begun with 0. Otherwise, the solution from the previous iteration was used as the initial point. The row labeled "other" are other digits which were erroneously thought to be "2." The table suggests that if the initial training set is sufficiently rich in every class, then the first time through algorithm A, most of the testing errors correspond to members of the class that were not trained on. Adding in these training points moves the margin so that the next time through Algorithm A, most of the errors correspond to testing points outside the prescribed class. From then on there would be very few testing errors. In the second iteration, the number of support vectors with $y_i = -1$, increased by more than the number of sample points added with this property. Thus some of the non-support of the first iteration became support points in the second iteration. The same phenomenom occurs in the third iteration with those training points with $y_i = 1$. Thus points that are not support points may eventually become support points with the criteria in step (b).

training set size	size of original chunk	time (sec.)	number of support vectors	number of test errors
5000	250	95	127	70
5000	500	89	131	56
5000	1000	114	140	57

Table 10.5 Characteristics of different chunking mechanisms on NIST problem with 10,000 testing points finding "1."

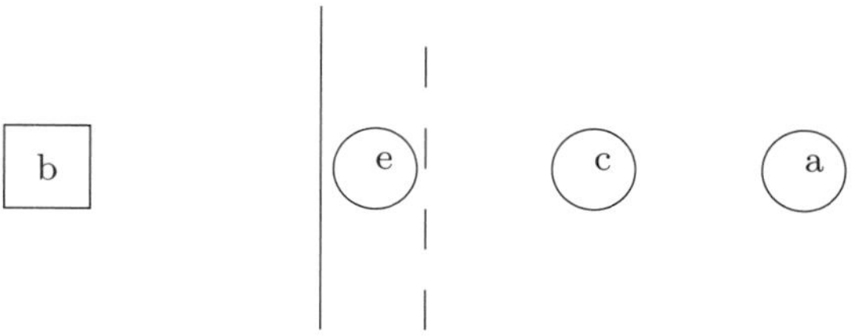

Figure 10.1 Class of squares and circles. Solid line is separating hyperplane for a, b, and c. Dashed line for a and b.

Table 10.4 presents the results of our experimentation with the NIST problem of recognizing a "1" with the Bunch-Kaufman algorithm given in section 10.3.2.1. No element of $\boldsymbol{\alpha}$ was ever at the upper bound and there were no training errors. The table corroborates the idea that with only a small portion of the data one can do rather well. The rate of increase in the number of support points is less than the rate of increase of the number of sample points. Because of the large value of N, the time required to make the columns dwarfed the time actually required by the optimization algorithm itself.

As indicated by table 10.5, Algorithm A can yield different sets of support vectors for different starting conditions. The reason Algorithm A might not lead to the same solution as the original code is indicated in figure 10.1. In that figure one has a "box" class and a "circle" class. Assume point e is a testing point. If one started with points, a, b, and c in the training set and one required a linear separating hyperplane, the solid line would be that hyperplane, and points b and c would be the support points. The test point e would be correctly classified. If, on the other hand, one started with points a and b, these points would be the supporting points and the dashed line would be the separating hyperplane. Now if one tested point c, it would be classified correctly. Thus there would be no need according to the above algorithm to add it to the training sample set. The result would be that point e would obtain the wrong classification. Thus incrementing the training sample set using (1.18) does not lead necessarily to the same support vectors.

method	sequence of added points	time (sec.)	number of support vectors	total test errors	unrecognized "1's"
original		160	234	46	17
A	44,7,1,1	89	131	56	23
B	1203,31,1	172	218	42	16
C	1203	153	219	44	18

Table 10.6 Characteristics of different chunking mechanisms on finding "1" in NIST problem with 5000 training points, initial chunk size of 500, and 10,000 testing points

One way of trying to get around the problem of figure 10.1 is to change the criteria in step (b) to testing the sign of the solution to (10.19). If $u_j < 0$ then we know that if training data j were added to the current chunk, then the new quadratic formed to be minimized could be decreased by deactivating the lower bound constraint on α_j. The test on u_j would dictate that point c in the example above should be added to the training set, which would mean that point e would be classified correctly. The main component of the cost of determining $\mathbf{u}$ in (10.19) is the determination of the gradient $\mathbf{g}$. Since the formula for the gradient involves the product $Q\alpha$, the cost of looking at the signs of the elements of $\mathbf{u}$ is small if one is already computing (1.18) and vice-versa.

Table 10.6 compares several approaches. Because of the results of table 10.5 a chunk size of 500 was chosen. Algorithm B tests the sign of the elements of $\mathbf{u}$ for all iterations. Algorithm C tests $\mathbf{u}$ only the first time and then uses Algorithm A with (1.18) as the test criterion. Table 10.6 suggests that using the solution of (10.19) as a merit function greatly increases the number of sample points added on the first iteration. Theoretically the solution found by Algorithm B should match that determined by the "non-chunking" scheme unless there were duplicate testing points. Each equality subproblem was solved in double precision with no approximation error, but because in Algorithm B some variables were activated then deactivated, a numerical process very susceptible to numerical cancellation error, the solutions differed. Because for this problem the construction of columns of Q is the dominant cost and because some columns of Q were computed and then discarded by Algorithm B, the total computation time for algorithm B is slightly more than for the non-chunking scheme. The number of added points when the merit function is based on (10.19) indicates that for this problem using a non-conservative deactivating scheme discussed in 10.3.3.1 would not be economical. For problems with smaller values of N, using Algorithm A or one of its relatives greatly reduced computational costs.

With the u_i criteria one may delete from the sample set for the next iteration of Algorithm A those vectors that are not support vectors without destroying the ultimate convergence of the algorithm, since one is guaranteed that the function will be decreased. However, after the first few iterations, eliminating non supporting

d	C	time (sec.)	support vectors	support vectors at C	number of testing errors
1	1	19	169	114	564
1	1000	16(11)	124	0	514
2	1	26	212	82	433
2	100	26(14)	199	0	232
3	1	41	272	74	377
3	100	60(26)	284	0	218

Table 10.7 Effect of d and C on NIST data with 1000 data points and 10,000 testing points finding "2."

points from the sample data set tends to delay convergence, since the dropped points often have to be included in later sample sets.

With a chunking mechanism, the solutions to the QP problems may have many nonzeroes and the conditions that predicated our choice of algorithms described in section 10.3 may not hold. When most of the values are nonzero, an interior point method such as (Vanderbei, 1997) may be the method of choice, dependent on the cost of creating Q.

10.5 Computation Experience

We have used the Newton code based on the Bunch-Kaufman updating on a number of examples, some large, with N in the hundreds and some relatively small with N=2. The determination of whether the polynomial model is suitable and, if so, which degree of the polynomial is appropriate is usually the first problem encountered. What has worked with one type of problem usually will work for a similar type of problem. For example, the problem of recognizing digits, whether from the Postal Service (LeCun et al., 1989) or from (Bottou et al., 1994), gave decent results with cubic polynomials and $C = 100$. For problems with $N = 2$ generated by Tin Kam Ho (Ho and Kleinberg, 1996), the radial basis functions are in general preferable. For these problems using a cubic polynomial gives too many test errors.

The second problem is the determination of C, the upper bound. If many variables are hitting the bound, there will probably be some training errors and the probability that the resulting machine will be a good classifier is rather small. Table 10.7 shows the effect of various values of C and d on the NIST data set with 1000 data points and 10000 test points looking for "2." Raising C until all nonzero values were interior to the domain decreased the testing errors as long as $d > 1$. Again computations were performed on the SGI. The computation times include the time to form those columns of Q that were need to solve the QP problem. The times in parenthesis indicate a run where many of the columns of the Q matrix were

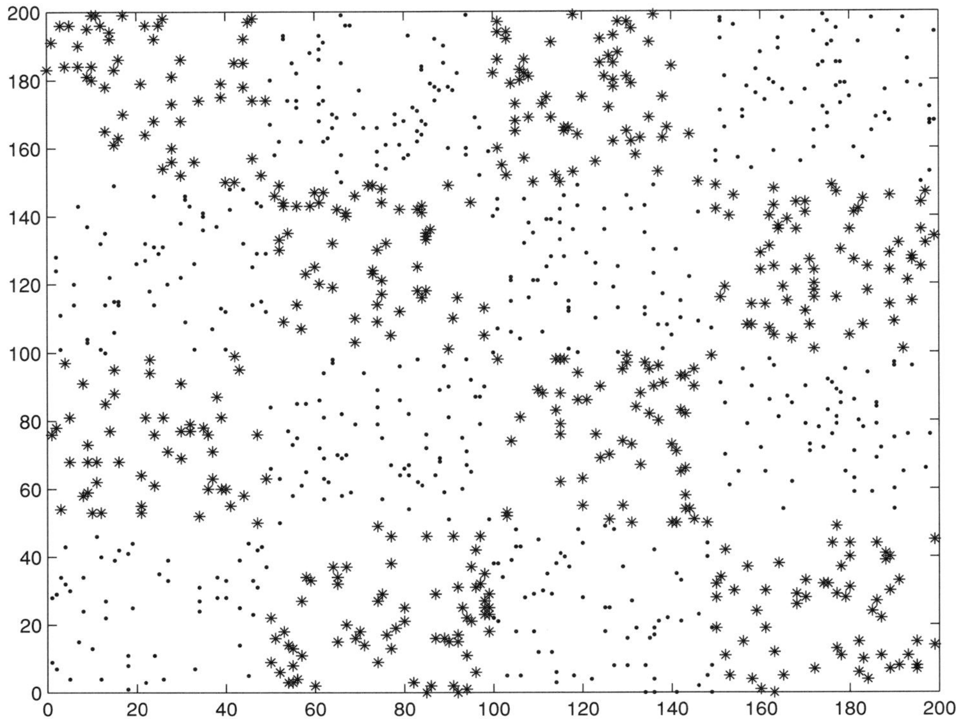

Figure 10.2 Training points for checkerboard pattern

available from the previous quadratic programming problem with the same matrix but a lower value of C. When C was increased, the initial guess for the new problem was the final solution of the previous problem. Thus consecutive runs with changing C cost less than starting from scratch. Note that iterations are rather inexpensive when variable are at the upper bound, because when computing the gradient the trick suggested in (10.6) is used, and the size of the Z matrix is determined by the number of elements of $\boldsymbol{\alpha}$ which are not at their bound. When C is raised the size of Z increases.

In general choosing a huge value of C is a problem only if the variables become huge. If values of α of say 10^{12} are attained, one often is faced with roundoff error problems because of the widely varying scales of the variables.

The author received several 2 dimensional problems from Tin Kam Ho with very sparse input sets. One of these involved 1000 training points in a checkerboard pattern as given in figure 10.2.

When we applied the support vector technique to the checkerboard problem with σ^2 in the radial basis model (1.31) at 0.01 and $C = 10000$ we obtained figure 10.3.

In figure 10.4 we changed the model to a polynomial with $d = 8$. Polynomial models with lower degree were much worse.

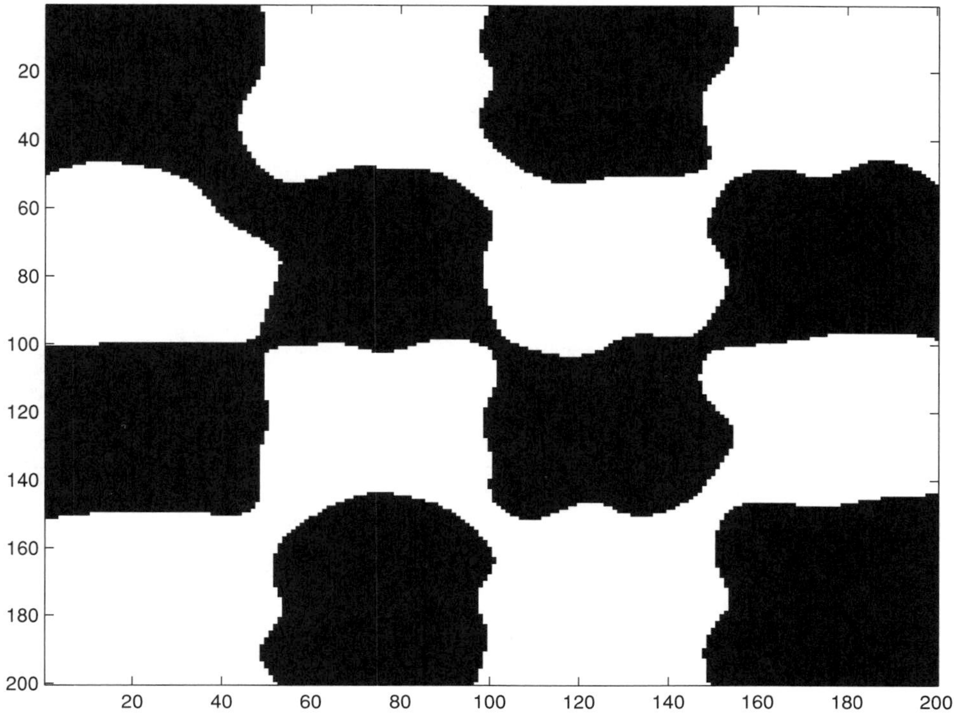

Figure 10.3 A radial basis solution with 1000 training points to a checkerboard

10.6 Conclusions

We have discussed various options for implementing a quadratic programming algorithm and pointed out which options tend to be most amenable to solving the QP problem in support vector machines which have dense large Hessians, bound constraints and one linear equality constraint. The algorithm is viewed as a sequence of equality constrained problems determined by the Kuhn-Tucker conditions. "Chunking" essentially is one way of following these conditions. Solving the equality constrained problem using a Newton approach which updates a factorization of the Hessian takes about the same amount of work as a few steps of the conjugate gradient approach. Thus in general a Newton approach is more efficient than a conjugate gradient algorithm, but it demands s^2 scratch space, where s is the number of support vectors not at bound. We have mentioned that a QP program that allows the user to construct the gradient in a subroutine is more helpful than a QP program that demands that the user give it a full Hessian initially, since those columns of the Hessian corresponding to elements of the solution at zero do not need to be computed.

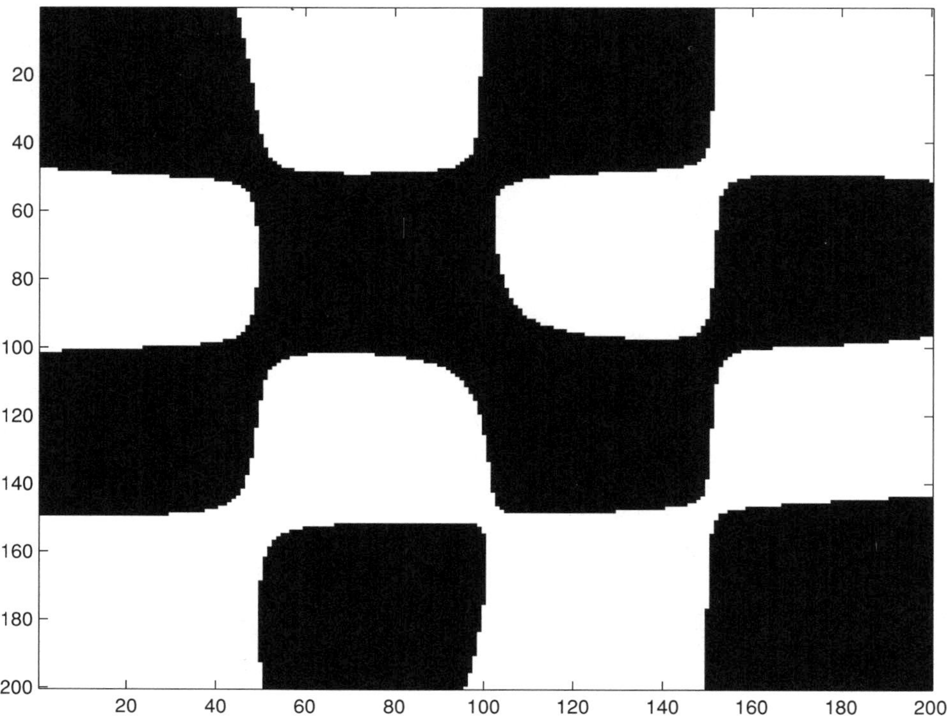

Figure 10.4 A polynomial solution with $d = 8$ to the checkerboard problem

Acknowledgement

I would like to thank Chris Burges for his suggestions on the chunking technique.

Appendix

In this Appendix we will show that if the model (10.2) is quadratic and the training vectors are available, then there is no need to store the Q matrix when doing matrix-vector multiplication with Q. Let us assume that we are given an ℓ vector $\mathbf{v}$ and a $N \times \ell$ matrix X whose columns are the training vectors and we we wish to compute $\mathbf{w} = Q\mathbf{v}$ where

$$q_{ij} = (\mathbf{x}_i^T \mathbf{x}_j)^2. \tag{10.29}$$

Using (10.29) we see that

$$w_i = \sum_{j=1}^{\ell} \sum_{p=1}^{N} x_{pi} x_{pj} \sum_{r=1}^{N} x_{ri} x_{rj} v_j = \sum_{p=1}^{N} \sum_{r=1}^{N} x_{pi} x_{ri} \sum_{j=1}^{\ell} x_{pj} x_{rj} v_j. \tag{10.30}$$

Define a $N \times N$ array U

$$u_{pr} = \sum_{j=1}^{\ell} x_{pj} x_{rj} v_j \qquad for\ p = 1, \ldots, N\ ;\ r = 1, \ldots N. \tag{10.31}$$

Then

$$w_i = \sum_{p=1}^{N} \sum_{r=1}^{N} x_{pi} x_{ri} u_{pr} = \sum_{p=1}^{N} x_{pi} \sum_{r=1}^{N} u_{pr} x_{ri} \tag{10.32}$$

To compute $\mathbf{w} = Q\mathbf{v}$ where H is defined by (10.29), without storing the full U matrix one could proceed as follows:

Algorithm X2

(1) *Set* $\mathbf{w}$ *to* 0.

(2) *For* $p = 1, ..., N$

- *For* $j = 1, ...\ell$

  Set $b_j = x_{pj} v_j$

- *For* $r = 1, ...N$

  Set $u_r = \sum_{j=1}^{\ell} x_{rj} b_j$

- *For* $i = 1, ..., \ell$

  Set $z = \sum_{r=1}^{N} u_r x_{ri}$

  Set $w_i = w_i + z x_{qi}$

The price of Algorithm X2 is $2\ell N^2 + 2\ell N$ multiplications.

Assuming $N = 100$ and $\ell = 10,000$, if the zero structure of $\mathbf{v}$, then computing $\mathbf{w}$ is ignored, the computing requires 2.02×10^8 operations. If Q were available, the cost of computing $\mathbf{w}$ would be 1×10^8 but there would be an initial overhead of $.5 \times 10^{10}$ operations to form Q and require 50 million memory locations. Not until the 25th iteration would one overcome the cost of the initial investment. For $\ell = 10000$, below $N = 71$, Algorithm X2 would always beat the standard approach ignoring the structure of $\mathbf{v}$.

If only s elements of $\mathbf{v}$ are nonzero, then Algorithm X2 requires $(s+\ell)N^2+(s+\ell)N$ multiplications.

11 Making Large-Scale Support Vector Machine Learning Practical

Thorsten Joachims
Universität Dortmund, Informatik, AI-Unit
Baroper Str. 301, 44221 Dortmund, Germany
thorsten@kimo.informatik.uni-dortmund.de
http://www-ai.cs.uni-dortmund.de/PERSONAL/joachims.html

Training a support vector machine (SVM) leads to a quadratic optimization problem with bound constraints and one linear equality constraint. Despite the fact that this type of problem is well understood, there are many issues to be considered in designing an SVM learner. In particular, for large learning tasks with many training examples, off-the-shelf optimization techniques for general quadratic programs quickly become intractable in their memory and time requirements. SVM^{light}[1] is an implementation of an SVM learner which addresses the problem of large tasks. This chapter presents algorithmic and computational results developed for SVM^{light}V2.0, which make large-scale SVM training more practical. The results give guidelines for the application of SVMs to large domains.

11.1 Introduction

Chapter 1 and Vapnik (1995) show how training a support vector machine for the pattern recognition problem leads to the following quadratic optimization problem (QP) OP1.

$$\textbf{(OP1)}\ \text{minimize:} \quad W(\boldsymbol{\alpha}) = -\sum_{i=1}^{\ell} \alpha_i + \frac{1}{2}\sum_{i=1}^{\ell}\sum_{j=1}^{\ell} y_i y_j \alpha_i \alpha_j k(\mathbf{x}_i, \mathbf{x}_j) \tag{11.1}$$

1. SVM^{light} is available at `http://www-ai.cs.uni-dortmund.de/svm_light`

$$\text{subject to:} \quad \sum_{i=1}^{\ell} y_i \alpha_i = 0 \tag{11.2}$$

$$\forall i : 0 \leq \alpha_i \leq C \tag{11.3}$$

The number of training examples is denoted by ℓ. $\boldsymbol{\alpha}$ is a vector of ℓ variables, where each component α_i corresponds to a training example $(\mathbf{x}_i, y_i)$. The solution of OP1 is the vector $\boldsymbol{\alpha}^*$ for which (11.1) is minimized and the constraints (11.2) and (11.3) are fulfilled. Defining the matrix Q as $(Q)_{ij} = y_i y_j k(\mathbf{x}_i, \mathbf{x}_j)$, this can equivalently be written as

$$\text{minimize:} \quad W(\boldsymbol{\alpha}) = -\boldsymbol{\alpha}^T \mathbf{1} + \frac{1}{2} \boldsymbol{\alpha}^T Q \boldsymbol{\alpha} \tag{11.4}$$

$$\text{subject to:} \quad \boldsymbol{\alpha}^T \mathbf{y} = 0 \tag{11.5}$$

$$\mathbf{0} \leq \boldsymbol{\alpha} \leq C\mathbf{1} \tag{11.6}$$

The size of the optimization problem depends on the number of training examples ℓ. Since the size of the matrix Q is ℓ^2, for learning tasks with 10000 training examples and more it becomes impossible to keep Q in memory. Many standard implementations of QP solvers require explicit storage of Q which prohibits their application. An alternative would be to recompute Q every time it is needed. But this becomes prohibitively expensive, if Q is needed often.

One approach to make the training of SVMs on problems with many training examples tractable is to decompose the problem into a series of smaller tasks. SVM^{light}uses the decomposition idea of Osuna et al. (1997c). Thus it splits OP1 in an inactive and an active part — the so called "working set." The main advantage of this decomposition is that it suggests algorithms with memory requirements linear in the number of training examples and linear in the number of SVs. One potential disadvantage is that these algorithms may need a long training time. To tackle this problem, this chapter proposes an algorithm which incorporates the following ideas:

- An efficient and effective method for selecting the working set.
- Successive "shrinking" of the optimization problem. This exploits the property that many SVM learning problems have
  - much less support vectors (SVs) than training examples.
  - many SVs which have an α_i at the upper bound C.
- Computational improvements like caching and incremental updates of the gradient and the termination criteria.

This chapter is structured as follows. First, a generalized version of the decompositon algorithm of Osuna et al. (1997a) is introduced. This identifies the problem of selecting the working set, which is addressed in the following section. In section 11.4 a method for "shrinking" OP1 is presented and section 11.5 describes the computational and implementational approach of SVM^{light}. Finally, experimental results on two benchmark tasks, a text classification task, and an image recognition task are discussed to evaluate the approach.

11.2 General Decomposition Algorithm

This section presents a generalized version of the decomposition strategy proposed by Osuna et al. (1997a). This strategy uses a decomposition similar to those used in *active set* strategies (see Gill et al. (1981)) for the case that all inequality constraints are simple bounds. In each iteration the variables α_i of OP1 are split into two categories.

- the set B of free variables
- the set N of fixed variables

Free variables are those which can be updated in the current iteration, whereas fixed variables are temporarily fixed at a particular value. The set of free variables will also be referred to as the working set. The working set has a constant size q much smaller than ℓ.

The algorithm works as follows:

- `While the optimality conditions are violated`
  - `Select` q `variables for the working set` B`. The remaining` $\ell - q$ `variables are fixed at their current value.`
  - `Decompose problem and solve QP-subproblem: optimize` $W(\boldsymbol{\alpha})$ `on` B`.`
- `Terminate and return` $\boldsymbol{\alpha}$`.`

Optimality Conditions

How can the algorithm detect that it has found the optimal value for $\boldsymbol{\alpha}$? Since OP1 is guaranteed to have a positive-semidefinite Hessian Q and all constraints are linear, OP1 is a convex optimization problem. For this class of problems the following Kuhn-Tucker conditions are necessary and sufficient conditions for optimality. Denoting the Lagrange multiplier for the equality constraint 11.5 with λ^{eq} and the Lagrange multipliers for the lower and upper bounds 11.6 with λ^{lo} and λ^{up}, $\boldsymbol{\alpha}$ is optimal for OP1, if there exist λ^{eq}, λ^{lo}, and λ^{up}, so that (Kuhn-Tucker Conditions, see Werner (1984)):

$$g(\boldsymbol{\alpha}) + (\lambda^{eq}\mathbf{y} - \lambda^{lo} + \lambda^{up}) = \mathbf{0} \tag{11.7}$$

$$\forall i \in [1..n]: \quad \lambda_i^{lo}(-\alpha_i) = 0 \tag{11.8}$$

$$\forall i \in [1..n]: \quad \lambda_i^{up}(\alpha_i - C) = 0 \tag{11.9}$$

$$\lambda^{lo} \geq \mathbf{0} \tag{11.10}$$

$$\lambda^{up} \geq \mathbf{0} \tag{11.11}$$

$$\boldsymbol{\alpha}^T\mathbf{y} = 0 \tag{11.12}$$

$$\mathbf{0} \leq \boldsymbol{\alpha} \leq C\mathbf{1} \tag{11.13}$$

$g(\boldsymbol{\alpha})$ is the vector of partial derivatives at $\boldsymbol{\alpha}$. For OP1 this is

$$g(\boldsymbol{\alpha}) = -\mathbf{1} + Q\boldsymbol{\alpha} \tag{11.14}$$

QP-Subproblems

If the optimality conditions do not hold, the algorithm decomposes OP1 and solves the smaller QP-problem arising from this. The decomposition assures that this will lead to progress in the objective function $W(\boldsymbol{\alpha})$, if the working set B fulfills some minimum requirements (see Osuna et al. (1997c)). In particular, OP1 is decomposed by separating the variables in the working set B from those which are fixed (N). Let's assume $\boldsymbol{\alpha}$, $\mathbf{y}$, and Q are properly arranged with respect to B and N, so that

$$\boldsymbol{\alpha} = \begin{vmatrix} \boldsymbol{\alpha}_B \\ \boldsymbol{\alpha}_N \end{vmatrix} \qquad \mathbf{y} = \begin{vmatrix} \mathbf{y}_B \\ \mathbf{y}_N \end{vmatrix} \qquad Q = \begin{vmatrix} Q_{BB} & Q_{BN} \\ Q_{NB} & Q_{NN} \end{vmatrix} \tag{11.15}$$

Since Q is symmetric (in particular $Q_{BN} = Q_{NB}^T$), we can write

$$\textbf{(OP2)} \text{ minimize: } \quad W(\boldsymbol{\alpha}) = -\boldsymbol{\alpha}_B^T(\mathbf{1} - Q_{BN}\boldsymbol{\alpha}_N) + \frac{1}{2}\boldsymbol{\alpha}_B^T Q_{BB}\boldsymbol{\alpha}_B + \frac{1}{2}\boldsymbol{\alpha}_N^T Q_{NN}\boldsymbol{\alpha}_N - \boldsymbol{\alpha}_N^T\mathbf{1} \tag{11.16}$$

$$\text{subject to: } \quad \boldsymbol{\alpha}_B^T\mathbf{y}_B + \boldsymbol{\alpha}_N^T\mathbf{y}_N = 0 \tag{11.17}$$

$$\mathbf{0} \leq \boldsymbol{\alpha} \leq C\mathbf{1} \tag{11.18}$$

Since the variables in N are fixed, the terms $\frac{1}{2}\boldsymbol{\alpha}_N^T Q_{NN}\boldsymbol{\alpha}_N$ and $-\boldsymbol{\alpha}_N^T\mathbf{1}$ are constant. They can be omitted without changing the solution of OP2. OP2 is a positive semidefinite quadratic programming problem which is small enough to be solved by most off-the-shelf methods. It is easy to see that changing the α_i in the working set to the solution of OP2 is the optimal step on B. So fast progress depends heavily on whether the algorithm can select good working sets.

11.3 Selecting a Good Working Set

When selecting the working set, it is desirable to select a set of variables such that the current iteration will make much progress towards the minimum of $W(\boldsymbol{\alpha})$. The following proposes a strategy based on Zoutendijk's method (see Zoutendijk (1970)), which uses a first-order approximation to the target function. The idea is to find a steepest feasible direction $\mathbf{d}$ of descent which has only q non-zero elements. The variables corresponding to these elements will compose the current working set. This approach leads to the following optimization problem:

$$\textbf{(OP3)} \text{ minimize: } V(\mathbf{d}) = g(\boldsymbol{\alpha}^{(t)})^T\mathbf{d} \tag{11.19}$$

$$\text{subject to: } \quad \mathbf{y}^T\mathbf{d} = 0 \tag{11.20}$$

$$d_i \geq 0 \quad \text{for i: } \alpha_i = 0 \tag{11.21}$$

$$d_i \leq 0 \quad \text{for i: } \alpha_i = C \tag{11.22}$$

$$-\mathbf{1} \leq \mathbf{d} \leq \mathbf{1} \tag{11.23}$$

$$|\{d_i : d_i \neq 0\}| = q \tag{11.24}$$

The objective (11.19) states that a direction of descent is wanted. A direction of descent has a negative dot-product with the vector of partial derivatives $g(\boldsymbol{\alpha}^{(t)})$ at the current point $\boldsymbol{\alpha}^{(t)}$. Constraints (11.20), (11.21), and (11.22) ensure that the direction of descent is projected along the equality constraint (11.5) and obeys the active bound constraints. Constraint (11.23) normalizes the descent vector to make the optimization problem well-posed. Finally, the last constraint (11.24) states that the direction of descent shall only involve q variables. The variables with non-zero d_i are included into the working set B. This way we select the working set with the steepest feasible direction of descent.

11.3.1 Convergence

The selection strategy, the optimality conditions, and the decomposition together specify the optimization algorithm. A minimum requirement this algorithm has to fulfill is that it

- terminates only when the optimal solution is found
- if not at the solution, takes a step towards the optimum

The first requirement can easily be fulfilled by checking the (necessary and sufficient) optimality conditions (11.7) to (11.13) in each iteration. For the second one, let's assume the current $\boldsymbol{\alpha}^{(t)}$ is not optimal. Then the selection strategy for the working set returns an optimization problem of type OP2. Since by construction for this optimization problem there exists a $\mathbf{d}$ which is a feasible direction for descent, we know using the results of Zoutendijk (1970) that the current OP2 is non-optimal. So optimizing OP2 will lead to a lower value of the objective function of OP2. Since the solution of OP2 is also feasible for OP1 and due to the decomposition (11.16), we also get a lower value for OP1. This means we get a strict descent in the objective function of OP1 in each iteration.

11.3.2 How to Solve OP3

The solution to OP3 is easy to compute using a simple strategy. Let $\omega_i = y_i g_i(\boldsymbol{\alpha}^{(t)})$ and sort all α_i according to ω_i in decreasing order. Let's futhermore require that q is an even number. Successively pick the $q/2$ elements from the top of the list for which $0 < \alpha_i^{(t)} < C$, or $d_i = -y_i$ obeys (11.21) and (11.22). Similarly, pick the $q/2$ elements from the bottom of the list for which $0 < \alpha_i^{(t)} < C$, or $d_i = y_i$ obeys (11.21) and (11.22). These q variables compose the working set.

11.4 Shrinking: Reducing the Size of OP1

For many tasks the number of SVs is much smaller than the number of training examples. If it was known a priori which of the training examples turn out as SVs, it would be sufficient to train just on those examples and still get to the same result. This would make OP1 smaller and faster to solve, since we could save time and space by not needing parts of the Hessian Q which do not correspond to SVs.

Similarly, for noisy problems there are often many SVs with an α_i at the upper bound C. Let's call these support vectors "bounded support vectors" (BSVs). Similar arguments as for the non-support vectors apply to BSVs. If it was known a priori which of the training examples turn out as BSVs, the corresponding α_i could be fixed at C leading to a new optimization problem with fewer variables.

During the optimization process it often becomes clear fairly early that certain examples are unlikely to end up as SVs or that they will be BSVs. By eliminating these variables from OP1, we get a smaller problem OP1$'$ of size ℓ'. From OP1$'$ we can construct the solution of OP1. Let X denote those indices corresponding to unbounded support vectors, Y those indexes which correspond to BSVs, and Z the indices of non-support vectors. The transformation from OP1 to OP1$'$ can be done using a decomposition similar to (11.16). Let's assume $\boldsymbol{\alpha}$, $\mathbf{y}$, and Q are properly arranged with respect to X, Y, and Z, so that we can write

$$\boldsymbol{\alpha} = \begin{vmatrix} \boldsymbol{\alpha}_X \\ \boldsymbol{\alpha}_Y \\ \boldsymbol{\alpha}_Z \end{vmatrix} = \begin{vmatrix} \boldsymbol{\alpha}_X \\ C\mathbf{1} \\ \mathbf{0} \end{vmatrix} \qquad \mathbf{y} = \begin{vmatrix} \mathbf{y}_X \\ \mathbf{y}_Y \\ \mathbf{y}_Z \end{vmatrix} \qquad Q = \begin{vmatrix} Q_{XX} & Q_{XY} & Q_{XZ} \\ Q_{YX} & Q_{YY} & Q_{YZ} \\ Q_{ZX} & Q_{ZY} & Q_{ZZ} \end{vmatrix} \tag{11.25}$$

The decomposition of $W(\boldsymbol{\alpha})$ is

$$\text{minimize: } W(\boldsymbol{\alpha}_X) = -\boldsymbol{\alpha}_X^T(\mathbf{1} - (Q_{XY}\mathbf{1}) \cdot C) + \frac{1}{2}\boldsymbol{\alpha}_X^T Q_{XX}\boldsymbol{\alpha}_X + \frac{1}{2}C\mathbf{1}^T Q_{YY} C\mathbf{1} - |Y|C \tag{11.26}$$

$$\text{subject to: } \boldsymbol{\alpha}_X^T \mathbf{y}_X + C\mathbf{1}^T\mathbf{y}_Y = 0 \tag{11.27}$$

$$\mathbf{0} \le \alpha_{\mathbf{X}} \le C\mathbf{1} \tag{11.28}$$

Since $\frac{1}{2}C\mathbf{1}^T Q_{YY} C\mathbf{1} - |Y|C$ is constant, it can be dropped without changing the solution. So far it is not clear how the algorithm can identify which examples can be eliminated. It is desirable to find conditions which indicate early in the optimization process that certain variables will end up at a bound. Since sufficient conditions are not known, a heuristic approach based on Lagrange multiplier estimates is used.

At the solution, the Lagrange multiplier of a bound constraint indicates, how much the variable "pushes" against that constraint. A strictly positive value of a Lagrange multiplier of a bound constraint indicates that the variable is optimal at that bound. At non-optimal points, an estimate of the Lagrange multiplier can be used. Let A be the current set of α_i fulfilling $0 < \alpha_i < C$. By solving (11.7) for λ^{eq} and averaging over all α_i in A, we get the estimate (11.29) for λ^{eq}.

$$\lambda^{eq} = \frac{1}{|A|}\sum_{i \in A}\left[y_i - \sum_{j=1}^{\ell}\alpha_j y_j k(\mathbf{x_i}, \mathbf{x_j})\right] \tag{11.29}$$

Note the equivalence of λ^{eq} and b in (1.18). Since variables α_i cannot be both at the upper and the lower bound simultanously, the multipliers of the bound constraints can now be estimated by

$$\lambda_i^{lo} = y_i \left(\left[\sum_{j=1}^{\ell} \alpha_j y_j k(\mathbf{x_i}, \mathbf{x_j}) \right] + \lambda^{eq} \right) - 1 \tag{11.30}$$

for the lower bounds and by

$$\lambda_i^{up} = -y_i \left(\left[\sum_{j=1}^{\ell} \alpha_j y_j k(\mathbf{x_i}, \mathbf{x_j}) \right] + \lambda^{eq} \right) + 1 \tag{11.31}$$

for the upper bounds. Let's consider the history of the Lagrange multiplier estimates over the last h iterations. If the estimate (11.30) or (11.31) was positive (or above some threshold) at each of the last h iterations, it is likely that this will be true at the optimal solution, too. These variables are eliminated using the decomposition from above. This means that these variables are fixed and neither the gradient, nor the optimality conditions are computed. This leads to a substantial reduction in the number of kernel evaluations.

Since this heuristic can fail, the optimality conditions for the excluded variables are checked after convergence of OP1$'$. If necessary, the full problem is reoptimized starting from the solution of OP1$'$.

11.5 Efficient Implementation

While the previous sections dealt with algorithmic issues, there are still a lot of open questions to be answered before having an efficient implementation. This section addresses these implementational issues.

11.5.1 Termination Criteria

There are two obvious ways to define termination criteria which fit nicely into the algorithmic framework presented above. First, the solution of OP3 can be used to define a necessary and sufficient condition for optimality. If (11.19) equals 0, OP1 is solved with the current $\boldsymbol{\alpha}^{(t)}$ as solution.

SVM^{light} goes another way and uses a termination criterion derived from the optimality conditions (11.7)-(11.13). Using the same reasoning as for (11.29)-(11.31), the following conditions with $\epsilon = 0$ are equivalent to (11.7)-(11.13).

$$\forall i \text{ with } 0 < \alpha_i < C\text{: } \lambda^{eq} - \epsilon \leq y_i - [\textstyle\sum_{j=1}^{\ell} \alpha_j y_j k(\mathbf{x_i}, \mathbf{x_j})] \leq \lambda^{eq} + \epsilon \tag{11.32}$$

$$\forall i \text{ with } \alpha_i = 0\text{:} \quad y_i([\textstyle\sum_{j=1}^{\ell} \alpha_j y_j k(\mathbf{x_i}, \mathbf{x_j})] + \lambda^{eq}) \geq 1 - \epsilon \tag{11.33}$$

$$\forall i \text{ with } \alpha_i = C\text{:} \quad y_i([\textstyle\sum_{j=1}^{\ell} \alpha_j y_j k(\mathbf{x_i}, \mathbf{x_j})] + \lambda^{eq}) \leq 1 + \epsilon \tag{11.34}$$

$$\boldsymbol{\alpha}^T \mathbf{y} = 0 \tag{11.35}$$

The optimality conditions (11.32), (11.33), and (11.34) are very natural since they reflect the constraints of the original optimization problem (1.10). In practice these conditions need not be fulfilled with high accuracy. Using a tolerance of $\epsilon = 0.001$ is acceptable for most tasks. Using a higher accuracy did not show improved generalization performance on the tasks tried, but lead to considerably longer training time.

11.5.2 Computing the Gradient and the Termination Criteria Efficiently

The efficiency of the optimization algorithm greatly depends on how efficiently the "housekeeping" in each iteration can be done. The following quantities are needed in each iteration.

- The vector of partial derivatives $g(\boldsymbol{\alpha}^{(t)})$ for selecting the working set.
- The values of the expressions (11.32), (11.33), and (11.34) for the termination criterion.
- The matrices Q_{BB} and Q_{BN} for the QP subproblem.

Fortunately, due to the decompositon approach, all these quantities can be computed or updated knowing only q rows of the Hessian Q. These q rows correspond to the variables in the current working set. The values in these rows are computed directly after the working set is selected and they are stored throughout the iteration. It is useful to introduce $\mathbf{s}^{(t)}$

$$s_i^{(t)} = \sum_{j=1}^{\ell} \alpha_j y_j k(\mathbf{x_i}, \mathbf{x_j}) \tag{11.36}$$

Knowing $\mathbf{s}^{(t)}$, the gradient (11.14) as well as in the termination criteria (11.32)-(11.34) can be computed very efficiently. When $\boldsymbol{\alpha}^{(t-1)}$ changes to $\boldsymbol{\alpha}^{(t)}$ the vector $\mathbf{s}^{(t)}$ needs to be updated. This can be done efficiently and with sufficient accuracy as follows

$$s_i^{(t)} = s_i^{(t-1)} + \sum_{j \in B} (\alpha_j^{(t)} - \alpha_j^{(t-1)}) y_j k(\mathbf{x}_i, \mathbf{x}_j) \tag{11.37}$$

Note that only those rows of Q are needed which correspond to variables in the working set. The same is true for Q_{BB} and Q_{BN}, which are merely subsets of columns from these rows.

11.5.3 Computational Resources Needed in Each Iteration

Time Complexity

Most time in each iteration is spent on the kernel evaluations needed to compute the q rows of the Hessian. This step has a time complexity of $O(qlf)$, where f is the maximum number of non-zero features in any of the training examples. Using the stored rows of Q, updating $\mathbf{s}^{(t)}$ is done in time $O(ql)$. Setting up the QP subproblem requires $O(ql)$ as well. Also the selection of the next working set, which includes computing the gradient, can be done in $O(ql)$.

Space Complexity

The highest memory requirements are due to storing the q rows of Q. Here $O(ql)$ floating point numbers need to be stored. Besides this, $O(q^2)$ is needed to store Q_{BB} and $O(l)$ to store $\mathbf{s}^{(t)}$.

11.5.4 Caching Kernel Evaluations

As pointed out in the last section, the most expensive step in each iteration is the evaluation of the kernel to compute the q rows of the Hessian Q. Throughout the optimization process, eventual support vectors enter the working set multiple times. To avoid recomputation of these rows, SVM^{light}uses caching. This allows an elegant trade-off between memory consumption and training time.

SVM^{light}uses a least-recently-used caching strategy. When the cache is full, the element which has not been used for the greatest number of iterations, is removed to make room for the current row.

Only those columns are computed and cached which correspond to active variables. After shrinking, the cache is reorganized accordingly.

11.5.5 How to Solve OP2 (QP Subproblems)

Currently a primal-dual interior-point solver (see Vanderbei (1994)) implemented by A. Smola is used to solve the QP subproblems OP2. Nevertheless, other optimizers can easily be incorporated into SVM^{light}as well.

11.6 Related Work

The first approach to splitting large SVM learning problems into a series of smaller optimization tasks was proposed by Boser et al. (1992). It is known as the "chunking" algorithm (see also chapter 10). The algorithm starts with a random subset of the data, solves this problem, and iteratively adds examples which violate the optimality conditions. Osuna et al. (1997c) prove formally that this strategy converges to the optimal solution. One disadvantage of this algorithm is that it is necessary to solve QP-problems scaling with the number of SVs. The decomposition of Osuna et al. (1997a), which is used in the algorithm presented here, avoids this.

Recently, an approach called Sequential Minimal Optimization (SMO) was proposed for SVM training (see Platt (1998) and chapter 12). It can be seen as a special case of the algorithm presented in this chapter, allowing only working sets of size 2. The algorithms differ in their working set selection strategies. Instead of the steepest feasible descent approach presented here, SMO uses a set of heuristics. Nevertheless, these heuristics are likely to produce similar decisions in practice. Another difference is that SMO treats linear SVMs in a special way, which produces a great speedup for training linear separators. Although possible, this is not implemented in SVM^{light}. On the other hand, SVM^{light}uses caching, which could be a valuable addition to SMO.

11.7 Experiments

The following experiments evaluate the approach on four datasets. The experiments are conducted on a SPARC Ultra/167Mhz with 128MB of RAM running Solaris II. If not stated otherwise, in the following experiments the cache size is 80 megabytes, the number of iterations h for the shrinking heuristic is 100, and OP1 is solved up to a precision of $\epsilon = 0.001$ in (11.32)-(11.34).

11.7.1 How Does Training Time Scale with the Number of Training Examples?

11.7.1.1 Income Prediction

This task was compiled by John Platt (see Platt (1998)) from the UCI "adult" data set. The goal is to predict whether a household has an income greater than \$50,000. After discretization of the continuous attributes, there are 123 binary features. On average, there are ≈ 14 non-zero attributes per example.

Table 11.1 and the upper graph in figure 11.1 show training times for an RBF-kernel (1.31) with $\sigma = 10$ and $C = 1$. The results for SMO and Chunking are taken from Platt (1998). When comparing absolute training times, one should keep in mind that SMO and Chunking were run on a faster computer (266Mhz Pentium II).

Both $SVM^{light}$and SMO are substantially faster than the conventional chunking algorithm, whereas $SVM^{light}$is about twice as fast as SMO. The best working set size is $q = 2$. By fitting lines to the log-log plot we get an empirical scaling of $\ell^{2.1}$ for both $SVM^{light}$and SMO. The scaling of the chunking algorithm is $\ell^{2.9}$.

The column "minimum" gives a lower bound on the training time. This bound makes the conjecture that in the general case any optimization algorithms needs to

Examples	SVM^{light}	SMO	Chunking	Minimum	total SV	BSV
1605	7.8	15.8	34.8	4.2	691	585
2265	16.8	32.1	144.7	9.0	1007	849
3185	30.6	66.2	380.5	6.8	1293	1115
4781	68.4	146.6	1137.2	38.4	1882	1654
6414	120.6	258.8	2530.6	70.2	2475	2184
11221	430.8	781.4	11910.6	215.4	4182	3763
16101	906.0	1784.4	N/A	436.2	5894	5398
22697	1845.6	4126.4	N/A	862.8	8263	7574
32562	3850.2	7749.6	N/A	1795.8	11572	10740
Scaling	2.1	2.1	2.9	2.0		

Table 11.1 Training times and number of SVs for the income prediction data.

Examples	SVM^{light}	SMO	Chunking	Minimum	total SV	BSV
2477	18.0	26.3	64.9	3.6	431	47
3470	28.2	44.1	110.4	7.8	571	69
4912	46.2	83.6	372.5	13.2	671	96
7366	102.0	156.7	545.4	27.0	878	138
9888	174.6	248.1	907.6	46.8	1075	187
17188	450.0	581.0	3317.9	123.6	1611	363
24692	843.0	1214.0	6659.7	222.6	1994	506
49749	2834.4	3863.5	23877.6	706.2	3069	948
Scaling	1.7	1.7	2.0	1.7		

Table 11.2 Training times and number of SVs for the Web data.

at least once look at the rows of the Hessian Q which correspond to the support vectors. The column "minimum" shows the time to compute those rows once (exploiting symmetry). This time scales with $\ell^{2.0}$, showing the complexity inherent in the classification task. For the training set sizes considered, $SVM^{light}$is both close to this minimum scaling as well as within a factor of approximately two in terms of absolute runtime.

11.7.1.2 Classifying Web Pages

The second data set — again compiled by John Platt (see Platt (1998)) — is a text classification problem with a binary representation based on 300 keyword features. This representation is extremely sparse. On average there are only ≈12 non-zero features per example.

Table 11.2 shows training times on this data set for an RBF-kernel (1.31) with $\sigma = 10$ and $C = 5$. Again, the times for SMO and Chunking are taken from Platt (1998). $SVM^{light}$is faster than SMO and Chunking on this data set as well, scaling with $\ell^{1.7}$. The best working set size is $q = 2$.

11.7.1.3 Ohsumed Data Set

The task in this section is a text classification problem which uses a different representation. Support vector machines have shown very good generalisation performance using this representation (see Joachims (1998)). Documents are represented as high dimensional vectors, where each dimension contains a (TFIDF-scaled) count of how often a particular word occurs in the document. More details can be found in (Joachims, 1998). The particular task is to learn "Cardiovascular Diseases" category of the Ohsumed dataset. It involves the first 46160 documents from 1991 using 15000 features. On average, there are $\approx$ 63 non-zero features per example. An RBF-kernel with $\sigma = 0.91$ and $C = 50$ is used.

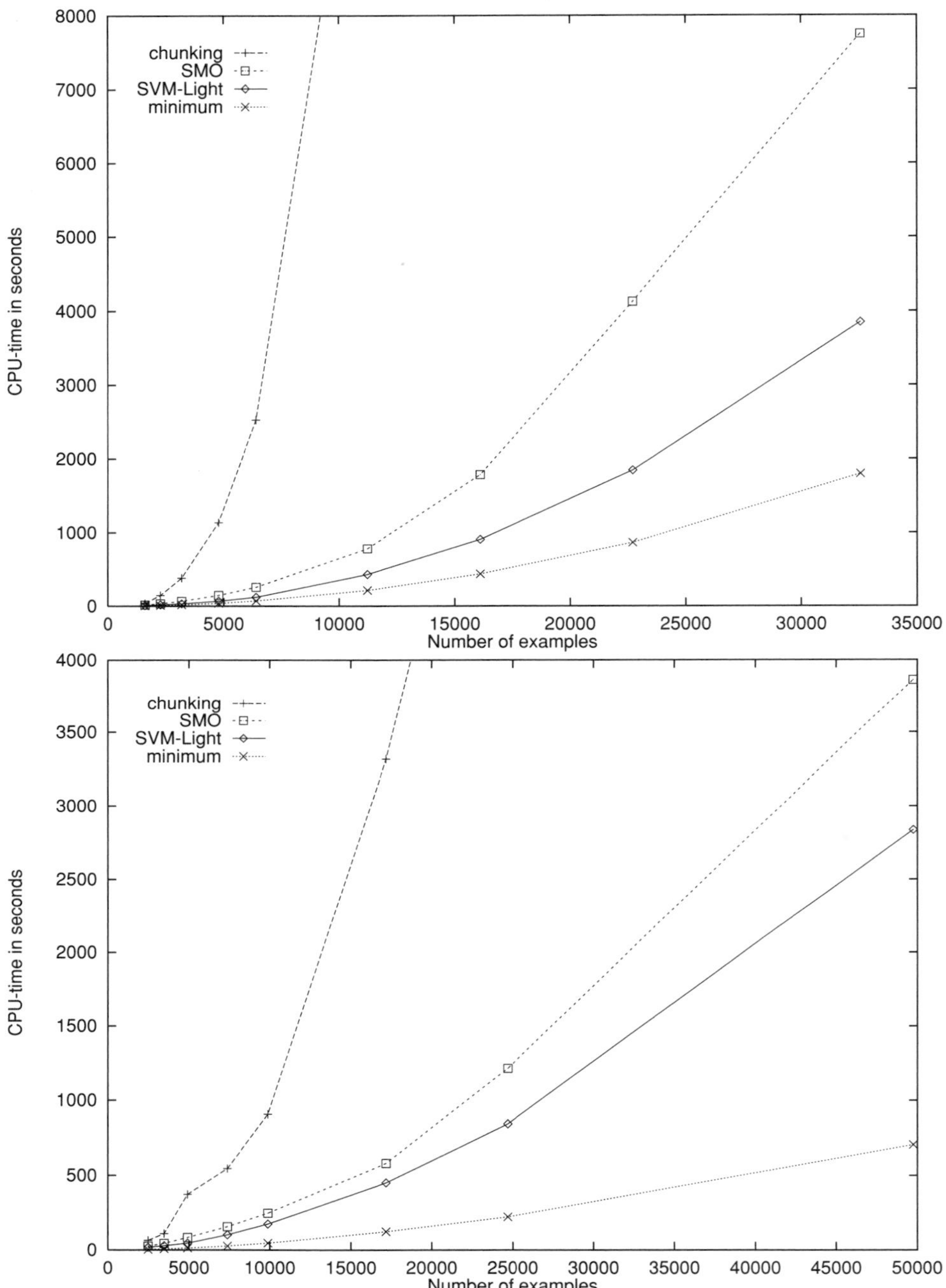

Figure 11.1 Training times from tables 11.1 (top) and 11.2 (bottom) as graphs.

Examples	SVM^{light}	Minimum	total SV	BSV
9337	18.8	7.1	4037	0
13835	46.3	14.4	5382	0
27774	185.7	50.8	9018	0
46160	509.5	132.7	13813	0
Scaling	2.0	1.8		

Table 11.3 Training time (in minutes) and number of SVs for the Ohsumed data.

Examples	SVM^{light}	Minimum	total SV	BSV
512	10.8	8.4	340	0
1025	37.2	31.2	559	0
2050	129.0	111.0	930	0
4100	443.4	381.0	1507	0
8200	1399.2	1170.6	2181	0
Scaling	1.7	1.7		

Table 11.4 Training time and number of SVs for the face detection data.

Table 11.3 shows that this tasks involves many SVs which are not at the upper bound. Relative to this high number of SVs the cache size is small. To avoid frequent recomputations of the same part of the Hessian Q, an additional heuristic is incorporated here. The working set is selected with the constraint that at least for half of the selected variables the kernel values are already cached. Unlike for the previous tasks, optimum performance is achieved with a working set size of $q = 20$. For the training set sizes considered here, runtime is within a factor of 4 from the minimum.

11.7.1.4 Dectecting Faces in Images

In this last problem the task is to classify images according to whether they contain a human face or not. The data set was collected by Shumeet Baluja. The images consist of 20x20 pixels of continuous gray values. So the average number of non-zero attributes per example is 400. An RBF-kernel with $\sigma = 7.1$ and $C = 10$ is used. The working set size is $q = 20$.

Table 11.4 shows the training time (in seconds). For this task, the training time is very close to the minimum. This shows that the working set selection strategy is very well suited for avoiding unnecessary kernel evaluations. The scaling is very close to the optimum scaling. Let us now evaluate how particular strategies of the algorithm influence the performance.

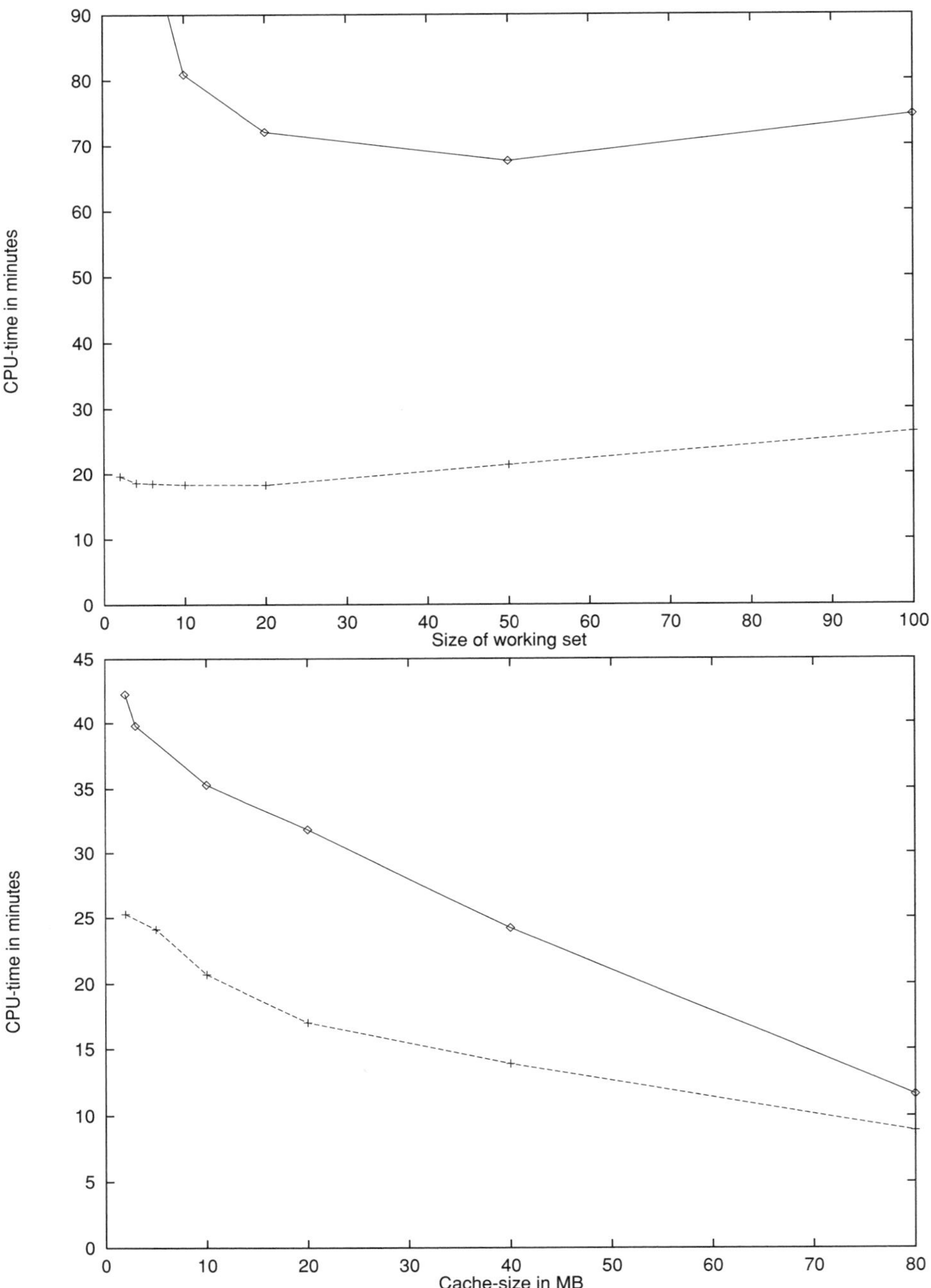

Figure 11.2 Training time dependent on working set size and cache size for the Ohsumed task.

11.7.2 What Is the Influence of the Working Set Selection Strategy?

Working Set Selection

The upper graph of figure 11.2 shows training time dependent on the size of the working set q for the smallest Ohsumed task. The selection strategy from section 11.3 (lower curve) is compared to a basic strategy similar to that proposed in (Osuna et al., 1997b) (upper curve). In each iteration the basic strategy simply replaces half of the working set with variables that do not fulfill the optimality conditions. The graph shows that the new selection strategy reduces time by a factor of more than 3.

11.7.3 What Is the Influence of Caching?

Caching

The curves in the lower graph of figure 11.2 shows that caching has a strong impact on training time. The lower curve shows training time (for an RBF-kernel with $\sigma = 10$ and $C = 50$ on the 9337 examples of the Ohsumed data) dependent on the cache size when shrinking is used. With the cache size ranging from 2 megabytes to 80 megabytes a speedup factor of 2.8 is achieved. The speedup generally increases with an increasing density of the feature vectors $\mathbf{x}_i$.

11.7.4 What Is the Influence of Shrinking?

Shrinking

All experiments above use the shrinking strategy from section 11.4. The upper curve in figure 11.2 (top) shows training time without shrinking. It can be seen that shrinking leads to a substantial improvement when the cache is small in relation to the size of the problem. The gain generally increases the smaller the fraction of unbounded SVs is compared to the number of training examples ℓ (here 2385 unbounded SVs, 110 BSVs, and a total of 9337 examples).

11.8 Conclusions

This chapter presents an improved algorithm for training SVMs on large-scale problems and describes its efficient implementation in SVM^{light}. The algorithm is based on a decomposition strategy and addresses the problem of selecting the variables for the working set in an effective and efficient way. Furthermore, a technique for "shrinking" the problem during the optimization process is introduced. This is found particularly effective for large learning tasks where the fraction of SVs is small compared to the sample size, or when many SVs are at the upper bound. The chapter also describes how this algorithm is efficiently implemented in SVM^{light}. It has a memory requirement linear in the number of training examples and in the number of SVs. Nevertheless, the algorithms can benefit from additional storage space, since the caching strategy allows an elegant trade-off between training time and memory consumption.

Acknowledgements

This work was supported by the DFG Collaborative Research Center on Complexity Reduction in Multivariate Data (SFB475). Thanks to Alex Smola for letting me use his solver. Thanks also to Shumeet Baluja and to John Platt for the data sets.

12 Fast Training of Support Vector Machines Using Sequential Minimal Optimization

John C. Platt
Microsoft Research
1 Microsoft Way, Redmond, WA 98052, USA
jplatt@microsoft.com
http://www.research.microsoft.com/~jplatt

This chapter describes a new algorithm for training Support Vector Machines: Sequential Minimal Optimization, or SMO. Training a Support Vector Machine (SVM) requires the solution of a very large quadratic programming (QP) optimization problem. SMO breaks this large QP problem into a series of smallest possible QP problems. These small QP problems are solved analytically, which avoids using a time-consuming numerical QP optimization as an inner loop. The amount of memory required for SMO is linear in the training set size, which allows SMO to handle very large training sets. Because large matrix computation is avoided, SMO scales somewhere between linear and quadratic in the training set size for various test problems, while a standard projected conjugate gradient (PCG) chunking algorithm scales somewhere between linear and cubic in the training set size. SMO's computation time is dominated by SVM evaluation, hence SMO is fastest for linear SVMs and sparse data sets. For the MNIST database, SMO is as fast as PCG chunking; while for the UCI Adult database and linear SVMs, SMO can be more than 1000 times faster than the PCG chunking algorithm.

12.1 Introduction

SVMs are starting to enjoy increasing adoption in the machine learning (LeCun et al., 1995; Joachims, 1997) and computer vision research communities (Oren et al., 1997; Osuna et al., 1997c). However, SVMs have not yet enjoyed widespread adoption in the engineering community. There are two possible reasons for the limited use by engineers. First, the training of SVMs is slow, especially for large problems. Second, SVM training algorithms are complex, subtle, and sometimes difficult to implement.

This chapter describes a new SVM learning algorithm that is conceptually simple, easy to implement, is often faster, and has better scaling properties than a standard "chunking" algorithm that uses projected conjugate gradient (PCG) (Burges, 1998). The new SVM learning algorithm is called *Sequential Minimal Optimization* (or SMO). Unlike previous SVM learning algorithms, which use numerical quadratic programming (QP) as an inner loop, SMO uses an analytic QP step. Because SMO spends most of its time evaluating the decision function, rather than performing QP, it can exploit data sets which contain a substantial number of zero elements. In this chapter, these data sets are called *sparse*. SMO does particularly well for sparse data sets, with either binary or non-binary input data.

This chapter first reviews current SVM training algorithms in section 12.1.1. The SMO algorithm is then described in detail in section 12.2, which includes the solution to the analytic QP step, heuristics for choosing which variables to optimize in the inner loop, a description of how to set the threshold of the SVM, and some optimizations for special cases. Section 12.3 contains the pseudo-code of the algorithm, while section 12.4 discusses the relationship of SMO to other algorithms. Section 12.5 presents results for timing SMO versus a standard PCG chunking algorithm for various real-world and artificial data sets. Conclusions are drawn based on these timings in section 12.6. Two appendices (sections 12.7 and 12.8) contain the derivation of the analytic optimization and detailed tables of SMO versus PCG chunking timings.

Quadratic Program

For an overview of SVMs, please consult chapter 1. For completeness, the QP problem to train an SVM is shown below:

$$\begin{aligned} \max_{\boldsymbol{\alpha}} W(\boldsymbol{\alpha}) &= \sum_{i=1}^{\ell} \alpha_i - \frac{1}{2}\sum_{i=1}^{\ell}\sum_{j=1}^{\ell} y_i y_j k(\vec{x}_i, \vec{x}_j)\alpha_i\alpha_j, \\ 0 \le \alpha_i &\le C, \quad \forall i, \\ \sum_{i=1}^{\ell} y_i\alpha_i &= 0. \end{aligned} \tag{12.1}$$

The QP problem in equation (12.1) is solved by the SMO algorithm. A point is an optimal point of (12.1) if and only if the Karush-Kuhn-Tucker (KKT) conditions are fulfilled and $Q_{ij} = y_i y_j k(\vec{x}_i, \vec{x}_j)$ is positive semi-definite. Such a point may be a non-unique and non-isolated optimum. The KKT conditions are particularly simple; the QP problem is solved when, for all i:

KKT Conditions

$$\begin{aligned} \alpha_i = 0 &\Rightarrow y_i f(\vec{x}_i) \ge 1, \\ 0 < \alpha_i < C &\Rightarrow y_i f(\vec{x}_i) = 1, \\ \alpha_i = C &\Rightarrow y_i f(\vec{x}_i) \le 1. \end{aligned} \tag{12.2}$$

The KKT conditions can be evaluated one example at a time, which is useful in the construction of the SMO algorithm.

12.1.1 Previous Methods for Training Support Vector Machines

Due to its immense size, the QP problem (12.1) that arises from SVMs cannot easily be solved via standard QP techniques. The quadratic form in (12.1) involves a matrix that has a number of elements equal to the square of the number of training examples. This matrix cannot fit into 128 Megabytes if there are more than 4000 training examples (assuming each element is stored as an 8-byte double precision number).

Chunking

Vapnik (1979) describes a method to solve the SVM QP, which has since been known as "chunking." The chunking algorithm uses the fact that the value of the quadratic form is the same if you remove the rows and columns of the matrix that correspond to zero Lagrange multipliers. Therefore, the large QP problem can be broken down into a series of smaller QP problems, whose ultimate goal is to identify all of the non-zero Lagrange multipliers and discard all of the zero Lagrange multipliers. At every step, chunking solves a QP problem that consists of the following examples: every non-zero Lagrange multiplier from the last step, and the M worst examples that violate the KKT conditions (12.2) (Burges, 1998), for some value of M (see figure 12.1). If there are fewer than M examples that violate the KKT conditions at a step, all of the violating examples are added in. Each QP sub-problem is initialized with the results of the previous sub-problem. The size of the QP sub-problem tends to grow with time, but can also shrink. At the last step, the entire set of non-zero Lagrange multipliers has been identified; hence, the last step solves the large QP problem.

Chunking seriously reduces the size of the matrix from the number of training examples squared to approximately the number of non-zero Lagrange multipliers squared. However, chunking still may not handle large-scale training problems, since even this reduced matrix may not fit into memory. One way to solve this problem is to use sophisticated data structures in the QP method (see, e.g., chapter 10). These data structures avoid the need to store the entire Hessian. The inner loop of such QP methods perform dot products between vectors and rows (or columns) of the Hessian, instead of a full matrix-vector multiply. In this chapter, the chunking benchmarks were implemented using the PCG algorithm, as suggested in the tutorial by Burges (1998).

Decomposition Algorithm

Osuna et al. (1997a) suggested a new strategy for solving the SVM QP problem. Osuna showed that the large QP problem can be broken down into a series of smaller QP sub-problems. As long as at least one example that violates the KKT conditions is added to the examples for the previous sub-problem, each step reduces the overall objective function and maintains a feasible point that obeys all of the constraints. Therefore, a sequence of QP sub-problems that always add at least one violator will asymptotically converge.

Osuna et al. suggest keeping a constant size matrix for every QP sub-problem, which implies adding and deleting the same number of examples at every step (Osuna et al., 1997a) (see figure 12.1). Using a constant-size matrix allows the training of arbitrarily sized data sets. The algorithm given in Osuna's paper (Osuna

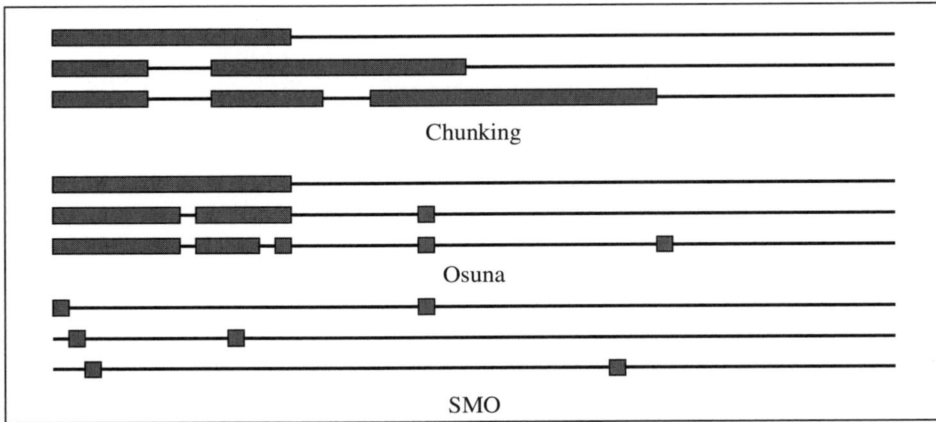

Figure 12.1 Three alternative methods for training SVMs: Chunking, Osuna's algorithm, and SMO. For each method, three steps are illustrated. The horizontal thin line at every step represents the training set, while the thick boxes represent the Lagrange multipliers being optimized at that step. A given group of three lines corresponds to three training iterations, with the first iteration at the top.

et al., 1997a) suggests adding one example and subtracting one example at every step. In practice, researchers add and subtract multiple examples using various techniques (see, e.g., chapter 11). In any event, a numerical QP solver is required for all of these methods. Numerical QP is tricky to get right; there are many numerical precision issues that need to be addressed.

12.2 Sequential Minimal Optimization

Sequential Minimal Optimization (SMO) is a simple algorithm that quickly solves the SVM QP problem without any extra matrix storage and without invoking an iterative numerical routine for each sub-problem. SMO decomposes the overall QP problem into QP sub-problems similar to Osuna's method.

SMO

Unlike the previous methods, SMO chooses to solve the smallest possible optimization problem at every step. For the standard SVM QP problem, the smallest possible optimization problem involves two Lagrange multipliers because the Lagrange multipliers must obey a linear equality constraint. At every step, SMO chooses two Lagrange multipliers to jointly optimize, finds the optimal values for these multipliers, and updates the SVM to reflect the new optimal values (see figure 12.1)[1].

1. It is possible to analytically optimize a small number of Lagrange multipliers that is

The advantage of SMO lies in the fact that solving for two Lagrange multipliers can be done analytically. Thus, an entire inner iteration due to numerical QP optimization is avoided. The inner loop of the algorithm can be expressed in a small amount of C code, rather than invoking an entire iterative QP library routine. Even though more optimization sub-problems are solved in the course of the algorithm, each sub-problem is so fast that the overall QP problem can be solved quickly.

In addition, SMO does not require extra matrix storage (ignoring the minor amounts of memory required to store any 2x2 matrices required by SMO). Thus, very large SVM training problems can fit inside of the memory of an ordinary personal computer or workstation. Because manipulation of large matrices is avoided, SMO may be less susceptible to numerical precision problems.

There are three components to SMO: an analytic method to solve for the two Lagrange multipliers (described in section 12.2.1), a heuristic for choosing which multipliers to optimize (described in section 12.2.2), and a method for computing b (described in section 12.2.3). In addition, SMO can be accelerated using techniques described in section 12.2.4.

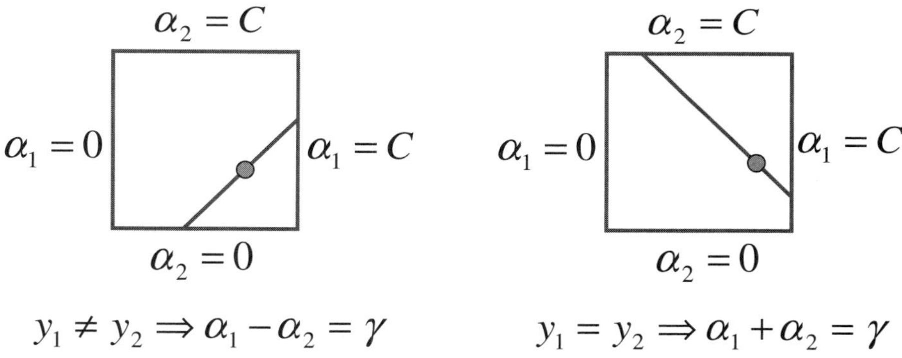

Figure 12.2 The two Lagrange multipliers must fulfill all of the constraints of the full problem. The inequality constraints cause the Lagrange multipliers to lie in the box. The linear equality constraint causes them to lie on a diagonal line. Therefore, one step of SMO must find an optimum of the objective function on a diagonal line segment. In this figure, $\gamma = \alpha_1^{\text{old}} + s\alpha_2^{\text{old}}$, is a constant that depends on the previous values of α_1 and α_2, and $s = y_1 y_2$.

---

greater than 2 (say, 3 or 4). No experiments have been done to test the effectiveness of such a strategy. See chapter 11 for an algorithm that numerically optimizes a small number of multipliers.

12.2.1 Solving for Two Lagrange Multipliers

In order to solve for the two Lagrange multipliers, SMO first computes the constraints on these multipliers and then solves for the constrained maximum. For convenience, all quantities that refer to the first multiplier will have a subscript 1, while all quantities that refer to the second multiplier will have a subscript 2. Because there are only two multipliers, the constraints can easily be displayed in two dimensions (see figure 12.2). The bound constraints in (12.1) cause the Lagrange multipliers to lie within a box, while the linear equality constraint in (12.1) causes the Lagrange multipliers to lie on a diagonal line. Thus, the constrained maximum of the objective function must lie on a diagonal line segment (as shown in figure 12.2). This constraint explains why two is the minimum number of Lagrange multipliers that can be optimized: if SMO optimized only one multiplier, it could not fulfill the linear equality constraint at every step.

Constraints on α_2

The ends of the diagonal line segment can be expressed quite simply. Without loss of generality, the algorithm first computes the second Lagrange multiplier α_2 and computes the ends of the diagonal line segment in terms of α_2. If the target y_1 does not equal the target y_2, then the following bounds apply to α_2:

$$L = \max(0, \alpha_2^{\text{old}} - \alpha_1^{\text{old}}), \qquad H = \min(C, C + \alpha_2^{\text{old}} - \alpha_1^{\text{old}}). \tag{12.3}$$

If the target y_1 equals the target y_2, then the following bounds apply to α_2:

$$L = \max(0, \alpha_1^{\text{old}} + \alpha_2^{\text{old}} - C), \qquad H = \min(C, \alpha_1^{\text{old}} + \alpha_2^{\text{old}}). \tag{12.4}$$

The second derivative of the objective function along the diagonal line can be expressed as:

$$\eta = 2k(\vec{x}_1, \vec{x}_2) - k(\vec{x}_1, \vec{x}_1) - k(\vec{x}_2, \vec{x}_2). \tag{12.5}$$

The next step of SMO is to compute the location of the constrained maximum of the objective function in equation (12.1) while allowing only two Lagrange multipliers to change. The derivation of the maximum location is shown in section 12.7.

Under normal circumstances, there will be a maximum along the direction of the linear equality constraint, and η will be less than zero. In this case, SMO computes the maximum along the direction of the constraint:

Unconstrained Maximum

$$\alpha_2^{\text{new}} = \alpha_2^{\text{old}} - \frac{y_2(E_1 - E_2)}{\eta}, \tag{12.6}$$

where $E_i = f^{\text{old}}(\vec{x}_i) - y_i$ is the error on the ith training example. Next, the constrained maximum is found by clipping the unconstrained maximum to the ends of the line segment:

Constrained Maximum

$$\alpha_2^{\text{new,clipped}} = \begin{cases} H, & \text{if } \alpha_2^{\text{new}} \geq H; \\ \alpha_2^{\text{new}}, & \text{if } L < \alpha_2^{\text{new}} < H; \\ L, & \text{if } \alpha_2^{\text{new}} \leq L. \end{cases} \tag{12.7}$$

α_1 Computation

Now, let $s = y_1 y_2$. The value of α_1 is computed from the new, clipped, α_2:

$$\alpha_1^{\text{new}} = \alpha_1^{\text{old}} + s(\alpha_2^{\text{old}} - \alpha_2^{\text{new,clipped}}). \tag{12.8}$$

Under unusual circumstances, η will not be negative. A zero η can occur if more than one training example has the same input vector $\vec{x}$. In any event, SMO will work even when η is not negative, in which case the objective function W should be evaluated at each end of the line segment. Only those terms in the objective function that depend on α_2 need be evaluated (see equation (12.23)). SMO moves the Lagrange multipliers to the end point with the highest value of the objective function. If the objective function is the same at both ends (within a small ϵ for round-off error) and the kernel obeys Mercer's conditions, then the joint maximization cannot make progress. That scenario is described below.

12.2.2 Heuristics for Choosing Which Multipliers to Optimize

SMO will always optimize two Lagrange multipliers at every step, with one of the Lagrange multipliers having previously violated the KKT conditions before the step. That is, SMO will always alter two Lagrange multipliers to move uphill in the objective function projected into the one-dimensional feasible subspace. SMO will also always maintain a feasible Lagrange multiplier vector. Therefore, the overall objective function will increase at every step and the algorithm will converge asymptotically (Osuna et al., 1997a). In order to speed convergence, SMO uses heuristics to choose which two Lagrange multipliers to jointly optimize.

First Choice Heuristic

There are two separate choice heuristics: one for the first Lagrange multiplier and one for the second. The choice of the first heuristic provides the outer loop of the SMO algorithm. The outer loop first iterates over the entire training set, determining whether each example violates the KKT conditions (12.2). If an example violates the KKT conditions, it is then eligible for immediate optimization. Once a violated example is found, a second multiplier is chosen using the second choice heuristic, and the two multipliers are jointly optimized. The feasibility of the dual QP (12.1) is always maintained. The SVM is then updated using these two new multiplier values, and the outer loop resumes looking for KKT violators.

Outer Loop

To speed training, the outer loop does not always iterate through the entire training set. After one pass through the training set, the outer loop iterates over only those examples whose Lagrange multipliers are neither 0 nor C (the non-bound examples). Again, each example is checked against the KKT conditions, and violating examples are eligible for immediate optimization and update. The outer loop makes repeated passes over the non-bound examples until all of the non-bound examples obey the KKT conditions within ϵ. The outer loop then iterates over the entire training set again. The outer loop keeps alternating between single passes over the entire training set and multiple passes over the non-bound subset until the entire training set obeys the KKT conditions within ϵ. At that point, the algorithm terminates.

The first choice heuristic concentrates the CPU time on the examples that are most likely to violate the KKT conditions: the non-bound subset. As the SMO algorithm progresses, Lagrange multipliers that are at the bounds are likely to stay at the bounds, while Lagrange multipliers that are not at the bounds will change as other examples are optimized. The SMO algorithm will thus iterate over the non-bound subset until that subset is self-consistent, then SMO will scan the entire data set to search for any bound examples that have become KKT-violated due to optimizing the non-bound subset.

Loose KKT Conditions

SMO verifies that the KKT conditions are fulfilled within ϵ. Typically, ϵ can typically be set in the range 10^{-2} to 10^{-3}. Recognition systems typically do not need to have the KKT conditions fulfilled to high accuracy: it is acceptable for examples on the positive margin to have outputs between 0.999 and 1.001. The SMO algorithm (and other SVM algorithms) will not converge as quickly if required to produce very high accuracy output.

Second Choice Heuristic

Once a first Lagrange multiplier is chosen, SMO chooses the second Lagrange multiplier to maximize the size of the step taken during joint optimization. Evaluating the kernel function k is time consuming, so SMO approximates the step size by the absolute value of the numerator in equation (12.6): $|E_1 - E_2|$. SMO keeps a cached error value E for every non-bound example in the training set and then chooses an error to approximately maximize the step size. If E_1 is positive, SMO chooses an example with minimum error E_2. If E_1 is negative, SMO chooses an example with maximum error E_2.

Second Choice Hierarchy

Under unusual circumstances, SMO cannot make positive progress using the second choice heuristic described above. For example, positive progress cannot be made if the first and second training examples share identical input vectors $\vec{x}$, which causes the objective function to become flat along the direction of optimization. To avoid this problem, SMO uses a hierarchy of second choice heuristics until it finds a pair of Lagrange multipliers that can make positive progress. Positive progress can be determined by making a non-zero step upon joint optimization of the two Lagrange multipliers. The hierarchy of second choice heuristics consists of the following: (A) if the above heuristic does not make positive progress, then SMO starts iterating through the non-bound examples, searching for a second example that can make positive progress; (B) if none of the non-bound examples make positive progress, then SMO starts iterating through the entire training set until an example is found that makes positive progress. Both the iteration through the non-bound examples (A) and the iteration through the entire training set (B) are started at random locations in order not to bias SMO towards the examples at the beginning of the training set. In extremely degenerate circumstances, none of the examples will make an adequate second example. When this happens, the first example is skipped and SMO continues with another chosen first example.

12.2.3 The Threshold and the Error Cache

Solving (12.1) for the Lagrange multipliers $\boldsymbol{\alpha}$ does not determine the threshold b of the SVM, so b must be computed separately. After each step, b is re-computed, so that the KKT conditions are fulfilled for both optimized examples. The following threshold b_1 is valid when the new α_1 is not at the bounds, because it forces the output of the SVM to be y_1 when the input is $\vec{x}_1$:

$$b_1 = E_1 + y_1(\alpha_1^{\text{new}} - \alpha_1^{\text{old}})k(\vec{x}_1, \vec{x}_1) + y_2(\alpha_2^{\text{new,clipped}} - \alpha_2^{\text{old}})k(\vec{x}_1, \vec{x}_2) + b^{\text{old}}. \quad (12.9)$$

The following threshold b_2 is valid when the new α_2 is not at the bounds, because it forces the output of the SVM to be y_2 when the input is $\vec{x}_2$:

$$b_2 = E_2 + y_1(\alpha_1^{\text{new}} - \alpha_1^{\text{old}})k(\vec{x}_1, \vec{x}_2) + y_2(\alpha_2^{\text{new,clipped}} - \alpha_2^{\text{old}})k(\vec{x}_2, \vec{x}_2) + b^{\text{old}}. \quad (12.10)$$

When both b_1 and b_2 are valid, they are equal. When both new Lagrange multipliers are at bound and if L is not equal to H, then the interval between b_1 and b_2 are all thresholds that are consistent with the KKT conditions. In this case, SMO chooses the threshold to be halfway in between b_1 and b_2.

Error Cache

As discussed in section 12.2.2, a cached error value E is kept for every example whose Lagrange multiplier is neither zero nor C. When a Lagrange multiplier is non-bound and is involved in a joint optimization, its cached error is set to zero. Whenever a joint optimization occurs, the stored errors for all non-bound multipliers α_k that are not involved in the optimization are updated according to

$$\begin{aligned} E_k^{\text{new}} &= E_k^{\text{old}} + y_1(\alpha_1^{\text{new}} - \alpha_1^{\text{old}})k(\vec{x}_1, \vec{x}_k) \\ &\quad + y_2(\alpha_2^{\text{new,clipped}} - \alpha_2^{\text{old}})k(\vec{x}_2, \vec{x}_k) + b^{\text{old}} - b^{\text{new}}. \end{aligned} \quad (12.11)$$

When an error E is required by SMO, it will look up the error in the error cache if the corresponding Lagrange multiplier is not at bound. Otherwise, it will evaluate the current SVM decision function based on the current $\boldsymbol{\alpha}$ vector.

12.2.4 Speeding Up SMO

A linear SVM can be sped up by only storing a single weight vector, rather than all of the training examples that correspond to non-zero Lagrange multipliers. If the joint optimization succeeds, this stored weight vector must be updated to reflect the new Lagrange multiplier values. The weight vector update is easy, due to the linearity of the SVM:

$$\vec{w}^{\text{new}} = \vec{w}^{\text{old}} + y_1(\alpha_1^{\text{new}} - \alpha_1^{\text{old}})\vec{x}_1 + y_2(\alpha_2^{\text{new,clipped}} - \alpha_2^{\text{old}})\vec{x}_2. \quad (12.12)$$

Because much of the computation time of SMO is spent evaluating the decision function, anything that can speed up the decision function will speed up SMO. If the input data is sparse, then SMO can be sped up substantially.

Normally, an input vector is stored as a vector of floating-point numbers. A sparse input vector is stored as two arrays: `id` and `val`. The `id` array is an integer array that stores the location of the non-zero inputs, while the `val` array is a floating-point array that stores the corresponding non-zero values. The length of both arrays is the number of non-zero inputs.

The dot product for two sparse vectors (`id1, val1`, length = `num1`) and (`id2, val2`, length = `num2`) can be computed quite quickly by scanning through both vectors, as shown in the pseudo-code below:

Sparse Dot Product

```
p1 = 0,  p2 = 0,  dot = 0
while (p1 < num1 && p2 < num2)
{
  a1 = id1[p1],    a2 = id2[p2]
  if (a1 == a2)
  {
    dot += val1[p1]*val2[p2]
    p1++, p2++
  }
  else if (a1 > a2)
    p2++
  else
    p1++;
}
```

The sparse dot product code can be used to compute linear kernels and polynomial kernels directly. Gaussian kernels can also use the sparse dot product code through the use of the following identity:

$$||\vec{x} - \vec{y}||^2 = \vec{x} \cdot \vec{x} - 2\vec{x} \cdot \vec{y} + \vec{y} \cdot \vec{y}. \tag{12.13}$$

For every input, the dot product of each input with itself is pre-computed and stored to speed up Gaussians even further.

Sparse Linear SVM

For a linear SVM, the weight vector is not stored as a sparse array. The dot product of the weight vector `w` with a sparse input vector (`id,val`) can be expressed as

$$\sum_{i=0}^{\text{num}} \texttt{w[id[i]]} * \texttt{val[i]}. \tag{12.14}$$

For binary inputs, storing the array `val` is not even necessary, since it is always 1. In the sparse dot product code, the floating-point multiplication becomes an increment. For a linear SVM, the dot product of the weight vector with a sparse input vector becomes

$$\sum_{i=0}^{\text{num}} \texttt{w[id[i]]}. \tag{12.15}$$

Notice that other code optimizations can be used, such as using look-up tables for the non-linearities or placing the dot products in a cache. Using a dot product cache can substantially speed up many of the SVM QP algorithms, at the expense of added code complexity and memory usage. In chapter 11, using a dot-product cache sped up $SVM^{light}$by a factor of 2.8 in one experiment. Combining SMO with a dot-product cache has not yet been tried.

12.3 Pseudo-Code

The pseudo-code for the overall SMO algorithm is presented below:

```
target = desired output vector
point = training point matrix

procedure takeStep(i1,i2)
  if (i1 == i2) return 0
  alph1 = Lagrange multiplier for i1
  y1 = target[i1]
  E1 = SVM output on point[i1] - y1 (check in error cache)
  s = y1*y2
  Compute L, H
  if (L == H)
    return 0
  k11 = kernel(point[i1],point[i1])
  k12 = kernel(point[i1],point[i2])
  k22 = kernel(point[i2],point[i2])
  eta = 2*k12-k11-k22
  if (eta < 0)
  {
    a2 = alph2 - y2*(E1-E2)/eta
    if (a2 < L) a2 = L
    else if (a2 > H) a2 = H
  }
  else
  {
    Lobj = objective function at a2=L
    Hobj = objective function at a2=H
    if (Lobj > Hobj+eps)
      a2 = L
    else if (Lobj < Hobj-eps)
      a2 = H
    else
      a2 = alph2
  }
  if (|a2-alph2| < eps*(a2+alph2+eps))
    return 0
  a1 = alph1+s*(alph2-a2)
  Update threshold to reflect change in Lagrange multipliers
  Update weight vector to reflect change in a1 & a2, if linear SVM
  Update error cache using new Lagrange multipliers
  Store a1 in the alpha array
```

```
  Store a2 in the alpha array
  return 1
endprocedure

procedure examineExample(i2)
  y2 = target[i2]
  alph2 = Lagrange multiplier for i2
  E2 = SVM output on point[i2] - y2 (check in error cache)
  r2 = E2*y2
  if ((r2 < -tol && alph2 < C) || (r2 > tol && alph2 > 0))
  {
    if (number of non-zero & non-C alpha > 1)
    {
      i1 = result of second choice heuristic
      if takeStep(i1,i2)
        return 1
    }
    loop over all non-zero and non-C alpha, starting at random point
    {
      i1 = identity of current alpha
      if takeStep(i1,i2)
        return 1
    }
    loop over all possible i1, starting at a random point
    {
      i1 = loop variable
      if takeStep(i1,i2)
        return 1
    }
  }
  return 0
endprocedure

main routine:
  initialize alpha array to all zero
  initialize threshold to zero
  numChanged = 0;
  examineAll = 1;
  while (numChanged > 0 | examineAll)
    {
      numChanged = 0;
      if (examineAll)
        loop I over all training examples
          numChanged += examineExample(I)
```

```
        else
          loop I over examples where alpha is not 0 & not C
            numChanged += examineExample(I)
        if (examineAll == 1)
          examineAll = 0
        else if (numChanged == 0)
          examineAll = 1
      }
```

12.4 Relationship to Previous Algorithms

The SMO algorithm is related both to previous SVM and optimization algorithms. SMO can be considered a special case of the Osuna algorithm, where the size of the working set is two and both Lagrange multipliers are replaced at every step with new multipliers that are chosen via good heuristics.

Bregman Methods

SMO is closely related to a family of optimization algorithms called Bregman methods (Bregman, 1967) or row-action methods (Censor, 1981). The classic Bregman method will minimize a function $F(\vec{x})$ subject to multiple constraints $\sum_i \vec{x} \cdot \vec{a}_i \leq b_i$. The Bregman method is iterative and updates an estimate of the optimum, $\vec{p}$. The method defines a function $D(\vec{x}, \vec{y})$:

$$D(\vec{x}, \vec{y}) = F(\vec{x}) - F(\vec{y}) - \nabla F(\vec{y}) \cdot (\vec{x} - \vec{y}). \tag{12.16}$$

The Bregman method iterates through all constraints. For each constraint, it finds the point, $\vec{z}$, that lies on the constraint and minimizes $D(\vec{p}, \vec{z})$. The estimate $\vec{p}$ is then set to $\vec{z}$. Each step is called a D-projection. Given certain conditions on F, including the requirement that the D-projection is unique, the Bregman method will converge (Bregman, 1967; Censor and Lent, 1981).

Unfortunately, the classic Bregman method does not work on an SVM with a threshold b. The input space of the function F must be the joint space $(\vec{w}, b)$. The function F would be the primal objective function τ which minimizes the norm of the weight vector in equation (1.9). In this case,

$$D([\vec{w}_1, b_1], [\vec{w}_2, b_2]) = \frac{1}{2}||\vec{w}_1 - \vec{w}_2||^2; \tag{12.17}$$

and the D-projection is not unique, because it cannot determine b. Hence, the classic Bregman method would not converge. Another way of explaining this outcome is that there is a linear equality constraint in the dual problem caused by b. Row-action methods can only vary one Lagrange multiplier at a time, hence they cannot fulfill the linear equality constraint.

Fixed-b SVMs

It is interesting to consider an SVM where b is held fixed at zero, rather than being a solved variable. A fixed-b SVM would not have a linear equality constraint in (12.1). Therefore, only one Lagrange multiplier would need to be updated at a time and a row-action method can be used. A traditional Bregman method is still not applicable to such SVMs, due to the slack variables ξ_i in equation (1.37). The presence of the slack variables causes the Bregman D-projection to become non-unique in the combined space of weight vectors and slack variables ξ_i.

Fortunately, SMO can be modified to solve fixed-b SVMs. SMO will update individual Lagrange multipliers to be the maximum of $W(\boldsymbol{\alpha})$ along the corresponding dimension. The update rule is

$$\alpha_1^{\text{new}} = \alpha_1^{\text{old}} + \frac{y_1 E_1}{k(\vec{x}_1, \vec{x}_1)}. \tag{12.18}$$

This update equation forces the output of the SVM to be y_1 (similar to Bregman methods or Hildreth's QP method (Hildreth, 1957)). After the new α_1 is computed, it is clipped to the $[0, C]$ interval (unlike previous methods). The choice of which Lagrange multiplier to optimize is the same as the first choice heuristic described in section 12.2.2.

Fixed-b SMO for a linear SVM is similar in concept to the perceptron relaxation rule (Duda and Hart, 1973), where the output of a perceptron is adjusted whenever there is an error, so that the output exactly lies on the margin. However, the fixed-b SMO algorithm will sometimes reduce the proportion of a training input in the weight vector in order to maximize margin. The relaxation rule constantly increases the amount of a training input in the weight vector and hence is not maximum margin.

Fixed-b SMO for Gaussian kernels is also related to the Resource Allocating Network (RAN) algorithm (Platt, 1991). When RAN detects certain kinds of errors, it will allocate a basis function to exactly fix the error. SMO will perform similarly. However SMO/SVM will adjust the height of the basis functions to maximize the margin in a feature space, while RAN will simply use LMS to adjust the heights of the basis functions.

12.5 Benchmarking SMO

The SMO algorithm was tested against a standard PCG chunking SVM learning algorithm (Burges, 1998) on a series of benchmarks. Both algorithms were written in C++, using Microsoft's Visual C++ 5.0 compiler. Both algorithms were run on an unloaded 266 MHz Pentium II processor running Windows NT 4. The CPU time for both algorithms are measured. The CPU time covers the execution of the entire algorithm, including kernel evaluation time, but excluding file I/O time.

The code for both algorithms is written to exploit the sparseness of the input vector and the linearity of the SVM, as described in section 12.2.4.

PCG

The chunking algorithm uses the PCG (Gill et al., 1981) algorithm as its QP solver (Burges, 1998). The chunk size was chosen to be 500. When the PCG code is initialized for a chunk, it assumes that all multipliers that are at bound have active equality constraints. It then releases those multipliers one at a time. This initialization causes the solver to avoid spuriously releasing and re-binding a large number of at-bound multipliers. Furthermore, the chunking algorithm re-uses the Hessian matrix elements from one chunk to the next, in order to minimize the number of extraneous dot products evaluated. In order to limit the amount of memory used by the algorithms, neither the chunking nor the SMO code use kernel caching to evaluate the decision function over the entire training set. Kernel caching for the decision function would favor SMO, because most of the computation time in SMO is spent in computing the decision function.

To further speed up PCG, the computation of the gradient is done sparsely: only those rows or columns of the Hessian that correspond to non-zero Lagrange multipliers are multiplied by the estimated Lagrange multiplier vector (see chapter 10). The computation of the quadratic form in the PCG algorithm is also performed sparsely: the computation is only performed over the active variables.

In order to ensure that the chunking algorithm is a fair benchmark, Burges compared the speed of his PCG chunking code on a 200 MHz Pentium II running Solaris with the speed of the benchmark chunking code (with the sparse dot product code turned off). The speeds were found to be comparable, which indicates that the benchmark chunking code is a reasonable benchmark.

Stopping Criteria

Ensuring that the chunking code and the SMO code attain the same accuracy takes some care. The SMO code and the chunking code will both identify an example as violating the KKT condition if the output is more than 10^{-3} away from its correct value or half-space. The threshold of 10^{-3} was chosen to be an insignificant error in classification tasks. A larger threshold may be equally insignificant and cause both QP algorithms to become faster.

The PCG code has a stopping threshold which describes the minimum relative improvement in the objective function at every step (Burges, 1998). If the PCG takes a step where the relative improvement is smaller than this minimum, the conjugate gradient code terminates and another chunking step is taken. Burges (1998) recommends using a constant 10^{-10} for this minimum, which works well with a KKT tolerance of 2×10^{-2}.

In the experiments below, stopping the PCG at an accuracy of 10^{-10} sometimes left KKT violations larger than 10^{-3}, especially for the very large scale problems. Hence, the benchmark chunking algorithm used the following heuristic to set the conjugate gradient stopping threshold. The threshold starts at 3×10^{-10}. After every chunking step, the output is computed for all examples whose Lagrange multipliers are not at bound. These outputs are computed in order to determine the value for b (see Burges, 1998). Every example suggests a proposed threshold. If the largest proposed threshold is more than 2×10^{-3} above the smallest proposed threshold, then the KKT conditions cannot possibly be fulfilled within 10^{-3}. Therefore, starting at the next chunk, the conjugate gradient stopping threshold is decreased by a factor of 3. This heuristic will optimize the speed of the conjugate gradient; it will only use high precision on the most difficult problems. For most of the tests described below, the threshold stayed at 3×10^{-10}. The smallest threshold used was 3.7×10^{-12}, which occurred at the end of the chunking for the largest web page classification problem.

Experiment	Kernel	Sparse Code Used	Training Set Size	C	% Sparse
Adult Linear Small	Linear	Y	11221	0.05	89%
Adult Linear Large	Linear	Y	32562	0.05	89%
Web Linear	Linear	Y	49749	1	96%
Lin. Sep. Sparse	Linear	Y	20000	100	90%
Lin. Sep. Dense	Linear	N	20000	100	0%
Random Linear Sparse	Linear	Y	10000	0.1	90%
Random Linear Dense	Linear	N	10000	0.1	0%
Adult Gaussian Small	Gaussian	Y	11221	1	89%
Adult Gaussian Large	Gaussian	Y	32562	1	89%
Web Gaussian	Gaussian	Y	49749	5	96%
Random Gaussian Sparse	Gaussian	Y	5000	0.1	90%
Random Gaussian Dense	Gaussian	N	5000	0.1	90%
MNIST	Polynomial	Y	60000	100	81%

Table 12.1 Parameters for various experiments

12.5.1 Experimental Results

The SMO algorithm was tested on the UCI Adult benchmark set, a web page classification task, the MNIST database, and two different artificial data sets. A summary of the experimental results are shown in tables 12.1 and 12.2.

In table 12.2, the scaling of each algorithm is measured as a function of the training set size, which was varied by taking random nested subsets of the full training set. A line was fitted to the log of the training time versus the log of the training set size. The slope of the line is an empirical scaling exponent.

The "N/A" entries in the chunking time column of table 12.2 had matrices that were too large to fit into 128 Megabytes, hence could not be timed due to memory thrashing.

All of the data sets (except for MNIST and the linearly separable data sets) were trained both with linear SVMs and Gaussian SVMs with a variance of 10. For the Adult and Web data sets, the C parameter and the Gaussian variance were chosen to optimize accuracy on a validation set.

UCI Adult Data Set

The first data set used to test SMO's speed was the UCI Adult data set (Merz and Murphy, 1998). The SVM was given 14 attributes of a census form of a household and asked to predict whether that household has an income greater than $50,000. Out of the 14 attributes, eight are categorical and six are continuous. The six continuous attributes were discretized into quintiles, which yielded a total of 123 binary attributes. The full timings for the Adult data set are shown in tables 12.3 and 12.4 in section 12.8. For this data set, the scaling for SMO is approximately one order in the exponent faster than PCG chunking. For the entire Adult training

Experiment	SMO Time (sec)	Chunking Time (sec)	SMO Scaling Exponent	PCG Scaling Exponent
Adult Linear Small	17.0	20711.3	1.9	3.1
Adult Linear Large	163.6	N/A	1.9	3.1
Web Linear	268.3	17164.7	1.6	2.5
Lin. Sep. Sparse	280.0	374.1	1.0	1.2
Lin. Sep. Dense	3293.9	397.0	1.1	1.2
Random Linear Sparse	67.6	10353.3	1.8	3.2
Random Linear Dense	400.0	10597.7	1.7	3.2
Adult Gaussian Small	781.4	11910.6	2.1	2.9
Adult Gaussian Large	7749.6	N/A	2.1	2.9
Web Gaussian	3863.5	23877.6	1.7	2.0
Random Gaussian Sparse	986.5	13532.2	2.2	3.4
Random Gaussian Dense	3957.2	14418.2	2.3	3.1
MNIST	29471.0	33109.0	N/A	N/A

Table 12.2 Timings of SMO versus PCG Chunking on various data sets.

set, SMO is more than 1000 times faster than PCG chunking for a linear SVM and approximately 15 times faster than PCG chunking for the Gaussian SVM. The adult data set shows that, for real-world sparse problems with many support vectors at bound, SMO is much faster than PCG chunking.

Web Page Data Set

Another test of SMO was on text categorization: classifying whether a web page belongs to a category or not. Each input was 300 sparse binary keyword attributes extracted from each web page. The full timings are shown in tables 12.5 and 12.6. For the linear SVM, the scaling for SMO is one order better than PCG chunking. For the non-linear SVM, SMO is between two and six times faster than PCG chunking. The non-linear test shows that SMO is still faster than PCG chunking when the number of non-bound support vectors is large and the input data set is sparse.

MNIST Data Set

Yet another test of SMO was the MNIST database of 60,000 handwritten digits, from AT&T Research Labs (LeCun et al., 1995). One classifier of MNIST was trained: class 8. The inputs are non-binary and are stored as a sparse vector. A fifth-order polynomial kernel, a C of 100, and a KKT tolerance of 0.02 was used to match the AT&T accuracy results. There were 3450 support vectors, with no support vectors at upper bound. Scaling experiments were not done on the MNIST database. However, the MNIST data was trained with both $C = 100$ and $C = 10$. The results for both of these training runs is shown in table 12.7. The MNIST experiment shows that SMO is competitive with PCG chunking for non-linear SVMs trained on moderately sparse data sets with none or very few support vectors at the upper bound.

SMO was also tested on artificially generated data sets to explore the performance of SMO in extreme scenarios. The first artificial data set was a perfectly linearly separable data set. The input data consisted of random binary 300-dimensional vectors, with a 10% fraction of "1" inputs. If the dot product of a stored vector (uniform random in $[-1, 1]$) with an input point was greater than 1, then a positive label was assigned to the input point. If the dot product was less than -1, then a negative label was assigned. If the dot product lay between -1 and 1, the point was discarded. A linear SVM was fit to this data set. The full timing table is shown in table 12.8.

Linearly Separable Data Set

The linearly separable data set is the simplest possible problem for a linear SVM. Not surprisingly, the scaling with training set size is excellent for both SMO and PCG chunking. For this easy sparse problem, therefore, PCG chunking and SMO are generally comparable.

Sparse vs. Non-Sparse

The acceleration of both the SMO algorithm and the PCG chunking algorithm due to the sparse dot product code can be measured on this easy data set. The same data set was tested with and without the sparse dot product code. In the case of the non-sparse experiment, each input point was stored as a 300-dimensional vector of floats. The full timing table for this experiment is shown in table 12.9.

For SMO, use of the sparse data structure speeds up the code by more than a factor of 10, which shows that the evaluation time of the decision function totally dominates the SMO computation time. The sparse dot product code only speeds up PCG chunking by about 6%, which shows that the evaluation of the numerical QP steps dominates the PCG chunking computation. For the linearly separable case, there are absolutely no Lagrange multipliers at bound, which is the worst case for SMO. Thus, the poor performance of non-sparse SMO versus non-sparse PCG chunking in this experiment should be considered a worst case.

The sparse versus non-sparse experiment shows that part of the superiority of SMO over PCG chunking comes from the exploitation of sparse dot product code. Fortunately, real-world problems with sparse input are not rare. Any quantized or fuzzy-membership-encoded problems will be sparse. Also, optical character recognition (LeCun et al., 1995), handwritten character recognition (Bengio et al., 1994), and wavelet transform coefficients of natural images (Oren et al., 1997; Mallat, 1998) can be naturally expressed as sparse data.

Random Data Set

The second artificial data set was generated with random 300-dimensional binary input points (10% "1") and random output labels. Timing experiments were performed for both linear and Gaussian SVMs and for both sparse and non-sparse code. The results of the timings are shown in tables 12.10 through 12.13. Scaling for SMO and PCG chunking is much higher on the second data set both for the linear and Gaussian SVMs. The second data set shows that SMO excels when most of the support vectors are at bound.

For the second data set, non-sparse SMO is still faster than PCG chunking. For the linear SVM, sparse dot product code sped up SMO by about a factor of 6. For the Gaussian SVM, the sparse dot product code sped up SMO by about a factor of 4. In neither case did the PCG chunking code have a noticable speed up. These experiments illustrate that the dot product speed is still dominating the SMO computation time for both linear and non-linear SVMs.

12.6 Conclusions

As can be seen in table 12.2, SMO has better scaling with training set size than PCG chunking for all data sets and kernels tried. Also, the memory footprint of SMO grows only linearly with the training set size. SMO should thus perform well on the largest problems, because it scales very well.

Table 12.2 also shows the effect of sparseness on the speed of SMO. Linear SVMs with 90% sparseness are a factor of 6 to 12 times faster using sparse binary SMO code over standard floating-point array SMO code. Even non-linear SVMs with 90% sparseness are a factor of 4 times faster. These results show that SMO is dominated by decision function evaluation time, and hence benefits from sparseness and binary inputs. In contrast, PCG chunking is dominated by numerical QP time: PCG chunking only speeds up by 6% by exploiting sparse decision function code. These experiments indicate that SMO is well-suited for sparse data sets.

SMO is up to a factor of 1200 times faster for linear SVMs, while up to a factor of 15 times faster for non-linear SVMs. Linear SVMs benefit from the acceleration of the decision function as described in section 12.2.4. Therefore, SMO is well-suited for learning linear SVMs.

Finally, SMO can be implemented without requiring a QP library function, which leads to simplification of the code and may lead to more widespread use of SVMs in the engineering community. While SMO is not faster than PCG chunking for all possible problems, its potential for speed-up should make it a key element in an SVM toolbox.

Acknowledgements

Thanks to Lisa Heilbron for assistance with the preparation of the text. Thanks to Chris Burges for running a data set through his PCG code. Thanks to Leonid Gurvits for pointing out the similarity of SMO with Bregman methods.

12.7 Appendix: Derivation of Two-Example Maximization

Each step of SMO will optimize two Lagrange multipliers. Without loss of generality, let these two multipliers be α_1 and α_2. The objective function from equation (12.1) can thus be written as

$$W(\alpha_1, \alpha_2) = \alpha_1 + \alpha_2 - \frac{1}{2}K_{11}\alpha_1^2 - \frac{1}{2}K_{22}\alpha_2^2 - sK_{12}\alpha_1\alpha_2$$
$$-y_1\alpha_1 v_1 - y_2\alpha_2 v_2 + W_{\text{constant}}, \quad (12.19)$$

where

$$K_{ij} = k(\vec{x}_i, \vec{x}_j), \quad (12.20)$$

$$v_i = \sum_{j=3}^{\ell} y_j \alpha_j^{\text{old}} K_{ij} = f^{\text{old}}(\vec{x}_i) + b^{\text{old}} - y_1 \alpha_1^{\text{old}} K_{1i} - y_2 \alpha_2^{\text{old}} K_{2i}, \tag{12.21}$$

and the variables with "old" superscripts indicate values at the end of the previous iteration. W_{constant} are terms that do not depend on either α_1 or α_2.

Each step will find the maximum along the line defined by the linear equality constraint in (12.1). That linear equality constraint can be expressed as

$$\alpha_1 + s\alpha_2 = \alpha_1^{\text{old}} + s\alpha_2^{\text{old}} = \gamma. \tag{12.22}$$

The objective function along the linear equality constraint can be expressed in terms of α_2 alone:

$$\begin{aligned} W = {} & \gamma - s\alpha_2 + \alpha_2 - \frac{1}{2}K_{11}(\gamma - s\alpha_2)^2 - \frac{1}{2}K_{22}\alpha_2^2 - sK_{12}(\gamma - s\alpha_2)\alpha_2 \\ & -y_1(\gamma - s\alpha_2)v_1 - y_2\alpha_2 v_2 + W_{\text{constant}}. \end{aligned} \tag{12.23}$$

The stationary point of the objective function is at

$$\begin{aligned} \frac{dW}{d\alpha_2} = {} & sK_{11}(\gamma - s\alpha_2) - K_{22}\alpha_2 + K_{12}\alpha_2 - sK_{12}(\gamma - s\alpha_2) \\ & +y_2 v_1 - s - y_2 v_2 + 1 = 0. \end{aligned} \tag{12.24}$$

If the second derivative along the linear equality constraint is positive, then the maximum of the objective function can be expressed as

$$\alpha_2^{\text{new}}(K_{11} + K_{22} - 2K_{12}) = s(K_{11} - K_{12})\gamma + y_2(v_1 - v_2) + 1 - s. \tag{12.25}$$

Expanding the equations for γ and v yields

$$\begin{aligned} \alpha_2^{\text{new}}(K_{11} + K_{22} - 2K_{12}) = {} & \alpha_2^{\text{old}}(K_{11} + K_{22} - 2K_{12}) \\ & +y_2(f(\vec{x}_1) - f(\vec{x}_2) + y_2 - y_1). \end{aligned} \tag{12.26}$$

More algebra yields equation (12.6).

12.8 Appendix: SMO vs. PCG Chunking Tables

This section contains the timing tables for the experiments described in this chapter.

A column labeled "Non-Bound SVs" contains the number of examples whose Lagrange multipliers lie in the open interval $(0, C)$. A column labeled "Bound SVs" contains the number of examples whose Lagrange multipliers exactly equal C. These numbers are produced by SMO: the number of support vector produced by PCG chunking is slightly different, due to the loose KKT stopping conditions.

A column labeled "SMO Iterations" contains the number of successful joint optimizations taken (joint optimizations that do not make progress are excluded). A column labeled "PCG Iterations" contains the number of projected conjugate gradient steps taken, summed over all chunks.

Training Set Size	SMO Time (CPU sec)	PCG Time (CPU sec)	Non-Bound SVs	Bound SVs	SMO Iterations	PCG Iterations
1605	0.4	37.1	42	633	3230	1328
2265	0.9	228.3	47	930	4635	3964
3185	1.8	596.2	57	1210	6950	6742
4781	3.6	1954.2	63	1791	9847	10550
6414	5.5	3684.6	61	2370	10669	12263
11221	17.0	20711.3	79	4079	17128	25400
16101	35.3	N/A	67	5854	22770	N/A
22697	85.7	N/A	88	8209	35822	N/A
32562	163.6	N/A	149	11558	44774	N/A

Table 12.3 SMO and PCG Chunking for a linear SVM on the Adult data set.

Training Set Size	SMO Time (CPU sec)	PCG Time (CPU sec)	Non-Bound SVs	Bound SVs	SMO Iterations	PCG Iterations
1605	15.8	34.8	106	585	3349	1064
2265	32.1	144.7	165	845	5149	2159
3185	66.2	380.5	181	1115	6773	3353
4781	146.6	1137.2	238	1650	10820	5164
6414	258.8	2530.6	298	2181	14832	8085
11221	781.4	11910.6	460	3746	25082	14479
16101	1784.4	N/A	567	5371	34002	N/A
22697	4126.4	N/A	813	7526	51316	N/A
32562	7749.6	N/A	1011	10663	77103	N/A

Table 12.4 SMO and PCG Chunking for a Gaussian SVM on the Adult data set.

Training Set Size	SMO Time (CPU sec)	PCG Time (CPU sec)	Non-Bound SVs	Bound SVs	SMO Iterations	PCG Iterations
2477	2.2	13.1	123	47	25296	1929
3470	4.9	16.1	147	72	46830	2379
4912	8.1	40.6	169	107	66890	4110
7366	12.7	140.7	194	166	88948	7416
9888	24.7	239.3	214	245	141538	8700
17188	65.4	1633.3	252	480	268907	27074
24692	104.9	3369.7	273	698	345736	32014
49749	268.3	17164.7	315	1408	489302	63817

Table 12.5 SMO and PCG Chunking for a linear SVM on the Web data set.

Training Set Size	SMO Time (CPU sec)	PCG Time (CPU sec)	Non-Bound SVs	Bound SVs	SMO Iterations	PCG Iterations
2477	26.3	64.9	439	43	10838	1888
3470	44.1	110.4	544	66	13975	2270
4912	83.6	372.5	616	90	18978	5460
7366	156.7	545.4	914	125	27492	5274
9888	248.1	907.6	1118	172	29751	5972
17188	581.0	3317.9	1780	316	42026	9413
24692	1214.0	6659.7	2300	419	55499	14412
49749	3863.5	23877.6	3720	764	93358	24235

Table 12.6 SMO and PCG Chunking for a Gaussian SVM on the Web data set.

C	SMO (CPU sec)	Chunking (CPU sec)	Non-Bound SVs	Bound SVs
10	25096	29350	3263	149
100	29471	33109	3450	0

Table 12.7 CPU time for MNIST while varying C

Training Set Size	SMO Time (CPU sec)	PCG Time (CPU sec)	Non-Bound SVs	Bound SVs	SMO Iterations	PCG Iterations
1000	15.3	10.4	275	0	66920	1305
2000	33.4	33.0	286	0	134636	2755
5000	103.0	108.3	299	0	380395	7110
10000	186.8	226.0	309	0	658514	14386
20000	280.0	374.1	329	0	896303	20794

Table 12.8 SMO and PCG Chunking for a linear SVM on a linearly separable data set.

Training Set Size	Sparse SMO (CPU sec)	Non-Sparse SMO (CPU sec)	Sparse Chunking (CPU sec)	Non-Sparse Chunking (CPU sec)
1000	15.3	145.1	10.4	11.7
2000	33.4	345.4	33.0	36.8
5000	103.0	1118.1	108.3	117.9
10000	186.8	2163.7	226.0	241.6
20000	280.0	3293.9	374.1	397.0

Table 12.9 Comparison of sparse and non-sparse training time for a linearly separable data set.

Training Set Size	SMO Time (CPU sec)	PCG Time (CPU sec)	Non-Bound SVs	Bound SVs	SMO Iterations	PCG Iterations
500	1.0	6.4	162	263	5697	548
1000	3.5	57.9	220	632	12976	1529
2000	15.7	593.8	264	1476	38107	3720
5000	67.6	10353.3	283	4201	87109	7815
10000	187.1	N/A	293	9034	130774	N/A

Table 12.10 SMO and PCG Chunking for a linear SVM on a random data set.

Training Set Size	Sparse SMO (CPU sec)	Non-Sparse SMO (CPU sec)	Sparse Chunking (CPU sec)	Non-Sparse Chunking (CPU sec)
500	1.0	6.0	6.4	6.8
1000	3.5	21.7	57.9	62.1
2000	15.7	99.3	593.8	614.0
5000	67.6	400.0	10353.3	10597.7
10000	187.1	1007.6	N/A	N/A

Table 12.11 Comparison of sparse and non-sparse training time for linear SVM applied to a random data set.

Training Set Size	SMO Time (CPU sec)	PCG Time (CPU sec)	Non-Bound SVs	Bound SVs	SMO Iterations	PCG Iterations
500	5.6	5.8	22	476	901	511
1000	21.1	41.9	82	888	1840	1078
2000	131.4	635.7	75	1905	3564	3738
5000	986.5	13532.2	30	4942	7815	14178
10000	4226.7	N/A	48	9897	15213	N/A

Table 12.12 SMO and PCG Chunking for a Gaussian SVM on a random problem.

Training Set Size	Sparse SMO (CPU sec)	Non-Sparse SMO (CPU sec)	Sparse Chunking (CPU sec)	Non-Sparse Chunking (CPU sec)
500	5.6	19.8	5.8	6.8
1000	21.1	87.8	41.9	53.0
2000	131.4	554.6	635.7	729.3
5000	986.5	3957.2	13532.2	14418.2
10000	4226.7	15743.8	N/A	N/A

Table 12.13 Comparison of sparse and non-sparse training time for a Gaussian SVM applied to a random data set.

III Applications

13 Support Vector Machines for Dynamic Reconstruction of a Chaotic System

Davide Mattera
Università degli Studi di Napoli Federico II
Dipartimento di Ingegneria Elettronica e delle Telecomunicazioni
Via Claudio 21, I-80125 Napoli, Italy
e-mail: mattera@diesun.die.unina.it
http://diesun.die.unina.it/GruppoTLC/staff.html

Simon Haykin
McMaster University, Communications Research Laboratory
1280 Main St. W, Hamilton, Ontario, Canada, L8S 4K1
e-mail: haykin@synapse.crl.mcmaster.ca
http://www.crl.mcmaster.ca/People/Faculty/Haykin/haykin.html

Dynamic reconstruction is an inverse problem that deals with reconstructing the dynamics of an unknown system, given a noisy time-series representing the evolution of one variable of the system with time. The reconstruction proceeds by utilizing the time-series to build a predictive model of the system and, then, using iterated prediction to test what the model has learned from the training data on the dynamics of the system. In this chapter, we review the details of the theoretical derivation of the Support Vector Machine (SVM); this allows us to derive its close relationship with the regularized radial basis function. The dependence of the SVM performance on the choice of its parameters is investigated both by means of theoretical analysis and numerical experiments performed on the well-known Lorenz system. The results obtained show the effectiveness of the SVM in performing the nonlinear reconstruction; its main advantage consists in the possibility of trading off the required accuracy with the number of Support Vectors.

13.1 Introduction

Dynamic reconstruction is the problem of approximating the unknown function which describes the state evolution of a chaotic system (Abarbanel, 1996). In practice, the state variables and the equations describing its evolution are unknown, only the system output measurements of a single variable are available. However, on the basis of Takens theorem (Takens, 1981) or one of its extensions (Sauer et al., 1991), one can describe the present state of the system by embedding the system output values into a set of lag-vectors. The purpose of the embedding is to create a pseudo-state-space, called the reconstruction space, by which the dynamics of the original chaotic system that created the time series can be reconstructed (according to Takens). The theorem guarantees, under mild conditions, the existence of a diffeomorphism between the trajectory in the reconstructed state-space and the one in the original state-space. The practical implication is that we can use the reconstructed state-space to estimate the global dynamical invariants, such as correlation dimension and Lyapunov exponents, of the chaotic system under study.

Takens Theorem

By utilizing the Takens embedding theorem the problem of dynamic reconstruction can be stated as the problem of approximating an unknown multidimensional function from only a finite number of noisy input-output examples which are available. Neural networks, therefore, are suitable for dynamic reconstruction because they learn directly from the data and they are powerful functional approximators.

Abarbanel, in one of his recent publications (Abarbanel, 1996), revealed the distinction between the dynamic reconstruction and prediction problems. According to him, the capability to solve the prediction problem does not always imply the capability to capture the dynamics of the underlying chaotic systems. Dynamic reconstruction aims at modeling the attractor dynamics (in state-space) while in the prediction problem only the short term prediction capability is of concern. Many of the techniques proposed in the literature for chaotic time-series prediction (see Lillekjendlie et al. (1994) for review) fail in solving the dynamical reconstruction problem (Abarbanel, 1996).

As per the above terminology, the dynamic reconstruction problem may be considered as a system approximation problem, not a function approximation one. This means that the obtained model, though trained in an open loop mode of operation, has to be tested by seeding, at first, its input with a point in the trajectory and, then, feeding back the output to its input to generate recursively the outputs. The reconstructed system should be as close as possible to the original one in terms of its invariants. Two chaotic systems can be considered to be close not only if they present close short-term evolutions from the same initial state but also if their chaotic invariants are sufficiently close. In particular, one cannot consider that a non-chaotic system be a good approximation to a chaotic one.

Closed-Loop Test

After the distinction between dynamical reconstruction and prediction became clear, methods for solving this problem started to appear in the literature. However, at the present point of the research, there is still no method which, in the open loop training, explicitly takes it into account for capturing the required dynamical properties of the approximation. In (Nagayama and Akamatsu, 1994) a four layered feedback neural network (FFBN) trained with the back-propagation algorithm has been utilized for the solution of the dynamical reconstruction problem. Numerical experiments on the Lorenz system showed that the largest Lyapunov exponent of the reconstructed system was very close to zero, so the authors concluded that "FFBN cannot represent chaotic phenomenon well". In (Abarbanel, 1996) and in (Principe and Kuo, 1995) the learning is constrained by a multistep prediction utilizing the structure of the time series as an implicit regularizer. One of the most successful methods (Haykin et al., 1997) employs the regularized radial basis function (RRBF) (Haykin, 1994) with Gaussian kernels. The main limitation of this approach is that the obtained network has a Gaussian kernel on each training example and that the corresponding weights are obtained by inverting a matrix whose dimension is equal to the training set size. Moreover, the influence of the choice of the regularization parameter on the solution is not evident and, therefore, one needs to apply a generalized cross-validation technique.

Previous Works

Since good reconstruction performance was obtained by utilizing a RRBF network which employs a well-founded regularization technique, we tried to solve the same problem by means of the Support Vector Machine. SVM is theoretically well founded, like RRBF, and can, therefore, successfully solve the problem of dynamic reconstruction and allows one to obtain a solution with a smaller number of Support Vectors. The similarity between the performances of SVM and RRBF motivated an investigation into their theoretical derivation.

The important result we present in section 13.3 is the proof that SVMs and RRBFNs (Yee, 1998; Poggio and Girosi, 1990a) can be derived from Vapnik's theory (Vapnik, 1995) and that they only differ in the choice of the cost function. This result is proven by explicitly obtaining the RRBF algorithm in the Vapnik's theory with reference to the classical quadratic cost function instead of the ε-insensitive one. The general relation between the Support Vector (SV) method and regularization theory has been independently discovered by Smola and Schölkopf (1998a): the inclusion of the term $\|\mathbf{w}\|^2$ in the objective function to be minimized constitutes a form of regularization. The explicit relationship that is derived in section 13.3 between the suppport vector machine and the radial basis function network regularized in accordance with Tikhonov's regularization principle is a significant contribution to the theory of support vector machines. Moreover, the influence of the regularization parameter C on the SVM obtained from the training (i.e., to be the maximum value allowed to the weight amplitude) allows one to determine a robust choice which avoids the multiple trainings required by cross-validation techniques or by a rigorous application of the structural risk minimization principle.

The experimental section is mainly dedicated to determine the dependence of the SVM performance on the choice of its parameters. The robustness of the choice proposed in the theoretical section was verified by means of computer simulations on the well-known Lorenz system. The influence of the parameter ε in the cost function on the performance, with respect to different training set sizes and both in presence and in absence of noise, is investigated by means of a theoretical analysis which results in accordance with the experiments we performed on the Lorenz data. The results obtained in this chapter allow one to determine a robust choice for the few parameters that are free in the SVM algorithm; this choice, avoiding the burden of multiple trainings (or, at least, reducing it significantly), increases the advantage of the SVM over other existing neural network methods.

13.2 Nonlinear dynamical reconstruction

Chaos occurs as a feature of orbits $\mathbf{x}(t)$ arising from nonlinear evolution rules which are systems of differential equations of the form

$$\frac{d\mathbf{x}(t)}{dt} = \boldsymbol{F_o}(\mathbf{x}(t)), \tag{13.1}$$

with three or more degrees of freedom or invertible maps of the form

$$\mathbf{x}(k+1) = \boldsymbol{F_o}(\mathbf{x}(k)). \tag{13.2}$$

As a class of observable signals $\mathbf{x}(t)$, chaos lies logically between the well studied domain of predictable, regular or quasi-periodic signals and the totally irregular stochastic signals we call "noise" and which are completely unpredictable (Abarbanel, 1996).

Chaotic Process

The impact of the discovery of chaos lies in the realization that nonlinear systems with few degrees of freedom, while deterministic in principle, can create output signals that look complex, and mimic stochastic signals from the point of view of conventional time-series analysis. The reason for this is that trajectories that have nearly identical initial conditions will separate from one another at an exponentially fast rate (sensitive dependence on initial conditions). This exponential separation causes chaotic systems to exhibit much of the same medium to long-term behavior as stochastic systems.

Takens Theorem

In the common engineering practice, it is seldom the case that all relevant dynamical variables (the components of the vector $\mathbf{x}$) can be measured. A key element in resolving this general class of problems is provided by the Takens embedding theorem (Abarbanel, 1996; Eckmann and Ruelle, 1985; Sauer et al., 1991), as follows:

Given a dynamical system S_1 with observable output $y(k)$ and state $\mathbf{x}(k)$

$$\mathbf{x}(k+1) = \boldsymbol{F_o}(\mathbf{x}(k)), \tag{13.3}$$

$$y(k) = h(\mathbf{x}(k)), \tag{13.4}$$

and the lag-vector

$$\boldsymbol{r}(k) \triangleq [y(k), y(k-T), \ldots, y(k-(d_E-1)T)], \tag{13.5}$$

under quite reasonable conditions on the dynamics $\boldsymbol{F}_o$ of the system and the observation function h, the correspondence $\boldsymbol{D}(\mathbf{x}(k)) \triangleq \boldsymbol{r}(k)$ is a one-to-one smooth correspondence, as long as the embedding dimension d_E is larger than twice the box-counting dimension (Sauer et al., 1991) of the compact finite-dimensional set A of the states $\mathbf{x}(k)$ of the considered system. The one-to-one correspondence determines the existence of the dynamical system S_2

$$\boldsymbol{r}(k+1) = \boldsymbol{D}(\mathbf{x}(k+1)) = \boldsymbol{D}(\boldsymbol{F_o}(\mathbf{x}(k))) = \boldsymbol{D}(\boldsymbol{F_o}(\boldsymbol{D}^{-1}\boldsymbol{r}(k))) = \boldsymbol{F}(\boldsymbol{r}(k)), \tag{13.6}$$

$$y(k) = [\boldsymbol{r}(k)]_1, \tag{13.7}$$

where $[\boldsymbol{r}]_1$ indicates the first component of the vector $\boldsymbol{r}$. The system S_2 has the same output of the original system S_1 (for equivalent initial conditions) and its state is known if the output time-series $y(k)$ can be measured.

This is an important result since, by definition, a point in the phase space carries complete information about the current system state. If the equation, defining the system dynamics, is not known, this phase space is not directly accessible to the observer. A one-to-one correspondence means that the phase-space can be identified by the measurements of the time-series $y(k)$. The smoothness of D and of its image is essential in allowing the demonstration that the dynamical motion of the two systems has the same property, i.e. all the chaotic invariants of the dynamical system S_1 can be evaluated in the reconstructed lag-space with data $\boldsymbol{r}(k)$ as well as in the original space with data $\mathbf{x}(k)$. Therefore, we can think of S_2 as the same dynamical system as S_1 under the coordinate change given by D.

Dynamical Reconstruction as an Approximation Problem

The dynamical reconstruction problem is the problem of approximating the unknown function $\boldsymbol{F}$. Only a certain number of samples of the time-series can be assumed to be known; therefore, we can embed only a certain number of points $\boldsymbol{r}(k)$. The nonlinear reconstruction problem we are facing can be, therefore, stated as the problem of getting an approximation $\hat{\boldsymbol{F}}$ of a function $\boldsymbol{F}$ when only the noisy values assumed by $\boldsymbol{F}$ in a limited number of points are available: it is indeed an inverse problem. Therefore, the statistical learning theory finds a natural application in the problem of dynamical reconstruction.

Takens theorem leaves the embedding parameters d_E and T unspecified. Some results have already been reported in the literature addressing the problem of the choice of d_E and T. They regard, however, the choice of d_E and T in reference to the methods of chaotic parameter estimation. We do not know if such a choice is good also for the dynamical reconstruction, especially in a noisy environment. In (Abarbanel, 1996; Kennel et al., 1992) it has been proposed to determine T as the first minimum T_I of the mutual information of the time-series $y(k)$ and to choose the embedding dimension d_E by the method of global false nearest neighbors.

13.3 The Support Vector Machine

The Support Vector Machine (SVM) is a powerful method to approximate an unknown function by means of some given points or examples. We will present the essence of Vapnik's theory of support vectors machine, with some refinements and extensions to fit into the dynamic reconstruction problem posed in this paper.

13.3.1 Theoretical Background

The method is deeply rooted in the Statistical Learning Theory (Vapnik, 1995). Given a set $\mathcal{F}$ of functions, defined on the set X with values[1] in Y and a probability density[2] $P(\mathbf{x}, y)$ on $X \times Y$, given a function $c(\alpha, \beta)$ that specifies the cost of approximating the value α with β, for each function $f \in \mathcal{F}$ we define the theoretical risk:

$$R(f) \triangleq \int c(y, f(\mathbf{x}))dP(\mathbf{x}, y). \tag{13.8}$$

One of the most remarkable results of the Statistical Learning Theory is a distribution-free upper-bound on the approximation error $R(f)$, valid for each $f \in \mathcal{F}$. Given a set of i.i.d. examples $\{(\mathbf{x}_i, y_i), i = 1, \ldots, \ell\}$ generated according to an unknown probability density, the following bound holds (Vapnik, 1995) with probability $1 - \eta$

Vapnik's Bound

$$R(f) \leq S(\mathcal{F}, c, \ell, \eta) + R_{emp}(f) \text{ for all } f \in \mathcal{F}, \tag{13.9}$$

in which

$$S(\mathcal{F}, c, \ell, \eta) = \phi(\frac{dim(\mathcal{F}^c)}{\ell}, \frac{\ln(\eta/4)}{\ell}), \tag{13.10}$$

where $\mathcal{F}^c$ is the set of functions $\{c(\cdot, f(\cdot)), f \in \mathcal{F}\}$ obtained for f belonging to $\mathcal{F}$ and $dim(\mathcal{F}^c)$ is the Vapnik-Chervonenkis (VC) dimension of this set of functions; R_{emp} is the empirical estimation of the risk on the given examples; it is given by the following formula

$$R_{emp}(f) \triangleq \frac{1}{\ell}\sum_{i=1}^{\ell} c(y_i, f(\mathbf{x}_i)), \tag{13.11}$$

1. The sets X and Y can be very generic but in the view of the applications we are interested in, we can say that X is a subset of $\mathbb{R}^{d_E}$ and Y is the set of real values $\mathbb{R}$.
2. With reference to our application to the problem of nonlinear reconstruction, we can assume that this probability density is the natural density (Eckmann and Ruelle, 1985) of the dynamical systems on which the temporal average are founded. The theory allows us to consider the case in which the joint density on $X \times Y$ is generic; the considered problem is to approximate a conditional density with a deterministic function. For the case of nonlinear reconstruction it is known that a target function does exist and we are trying to get a deterministic approximation of this target function.

and

$$\phi(\alpha, \beta) \triangleq L\sqrt{\alpha \cdot \ln\left(\frac{2}{\alpha} + 1\right) - \beta} \tag{13.12}$$

where L is two times the maximum value of $|c(\cdot, f(\cdot))|$.

If one knows *a priori* a class of functions $\mathcal{F}$ such that both the $\min_{f \in \mathcal{F}} R(f)$ and $\frac{dim(\mathcal{F}^c)}{\ell}$ are sufficiently small, then the minimization of the theoretical risk can be obtained by minimizing directly the empirical risk on the given examples. This approximation principle is usually called Empirical Risk Minimization (ERM) (Vapnik, 1979).

Empirical Risk Minimization

When no *a priori* information is known about the target function, to assure the possibility to achieve a small approximation error we need to consider a class of functions $\mathcal{F}$ with a large value of $\frac{dim(\mathcal{F}^c)}{\ell}$, possibly infinity. In such a case, ERM does not, in general, achieve good approximation results. Nevertheless, the bound (13.9) can be still utilized if a structure is created on the set of function $\mathcal{F}$:

$$\mathcal{F}_1 \subseteq \mathcal{F}_2 \ldots \subseteq \mathcal{F}_{n_s} \subseteq \mathcal{F}, \tag{13.13}$$

$$S(\mathcal{F}_1, c, \ell, \eta) \leq S(\mathcal{F}_2, c, \ell, \eta) \leq \ldots \leq S(\mathcal{F}_{n_s}, c, \ell, \eta) \leq S(\mathcal{F}, c, \ell, \eta), \tag{13.14}$$

where n_s is the number of elements of the structure. In this case it has been suggested (Vapnik, 1979) to determine the approximation function by solving the following minimization problem:

Structural Risk Minimization

$$\min_{j=1,\ldots,n_s} \left[S(\mathcal{F}_j, c, \ell, \eta) + \min_{f \in \mathcal{F}_j} R_{emp}(f) \right]. \tag{13.15}$$

This approximation principle is based on the bound (13.9) and it is usually called Structural Risk Minimization (SRM). It is important to note that better results are obtained if the functions that give better approximation are included in the smallest elements of the structure. The important drawback of (13.15) is that it requires to solve n_s times the problem of minimization of the empirical risk in $\mathcal{F}_j$. Therefore, the value of n_s has to be maintained very low; this limits the performance that one can obtain in practice by applying the SRM on the class of functions $\mathcal{F}$.

13.3.1.1 Modified Structural Risk Minimization

The bound (13.9) and the idea of constructing a structure on the class of functions are very general and can be expressed in similar ways. An alternative statement of the SRM is constituted by the following problem:

$$\min_{f \in \mathcal{F}} \left[R_{emp}(f) + \min_{j : f \in \mathcal{F}_j} S(\mathcal{F}_j, c, \ell, \eta) \right]. \tag{13.16}$$

To the best of our knowledge, this principle has never been explored previously in the literature; we call it the modified Structural Risk Minimization (MSRM). The SVM algorithm was derived as a way that approximately realizes the SRM expression (13.15) and not as a particular realization of the MSRM.

Only one numerical minimization problem needs to be solved for analytically calculating the second term in (13.16). The way in which the second term can be expressed depends on the way in which the structure is built on the class of function $\mathcal{F}$. A typical way in which the structure is built on the set of functions $\mathcal{F} \triangleq \{f(\mathbf{x}, \mathbf{w}) \ : \ \mathbf{w} \in W\}$ is the following:

$$\mathcal{F}_j \triangleq \{f(\mathbf{x}, \mathbf{w}) : p(\mathbf{w}) \leq s_j \text{ and } \mathbf{w} \in W\}, \tag{13.17}$$

where $p(\mathbf{w})$ is a particular function of the parameter $\mathbf{w}$ that defines the class of functions $\mathcal{F}$. When the structure is correctly defined, s_j is equal to $dim(\mathcal{F}_j^c)$ and the following properties are satisfied:

$$S(\mathcal{F}_j, c, \ell, \eta) \triangleq S'(s_j, \ell, \eta), \tag{13.18}$$

$$S'(s_i, \ell, \eta) \leq S'(s_j, \ell, \eta), \text{ for } i \leq j. \tag{13.19}$$

Modified Structural Risk Minimization

With such a structure, (13.16) reduces to

$$\min_{\mathbf{w} \in W} \left[R_{emp}(\mathbf{w}) + S'(int(p(\mathbf{w})), \ell, \eta) \right], \tag{13.20}$$

where $int(a)$ denotes the smallest integer larger than a. One of the important advantages of the MSRM is the large increase of the number of elements in the structure that can be implicitly considered in practice; this better exploits all the possibilities of the considered class of functions $\mathcal{F}$.

13.3.1.2 Specific Class of Functions and Its Structure

The previous results can be applied in practice by introducing a structure on a general class of function. In (Vapnik, 1995) the following class of function $\mathcal{F}$ is considered:

$$\mathcal{F} \triangleq \{f(\mathbf{x}, \mathbf{w}) = (\mathbf{w} \cdot \Phi(\mathbf{x})) + b \text{ with } \mathbf{x} \in X, \mathbf{w} \in \mathbb{R}^{d_c}, b \in \mathbb{R}\}. \tag{13.21}$$

This corresponds to projecting the input vector $\mathbf{x}$ into an intermediate space with d_v components; the final function can, then, be obtained as a linear function in this space. The VC-dimension of $\mathcal{F}$ is equal (Vapnik, 1979) to d_v; therefore, for d_v sufficiently large the class of functions is very general[3] and the bound (13.9) does not allow us to apply the empirical minimization principle. The required structure can be correctly introduced by means of the following choice for $p(\mathbf{w})$ in (13.17):

$$p(\mathbf{w}) = Z^2 \|\mathbf{w}\|^2 + 1, \tag{13.22}$$

3. Many results, the more popular being the Cover's theorem (Cover, 1965), assure us that, increasing d_v, the minimum $\min_{f \in \mathcal{F}} R(f)$ of the approximation error on $\mathcal{F}$ becomes sufficiently small for a generic choice of Φ.

where Z is the radius of smallest hypersphere in R^{d_v} that contains the subset $\{\Phi(\mathbf{x}_1), \ldots, \Phi(\mathbf{x}_\ell)\}$. In fact, the VC-dimension[4] of $\mathcal{F}_j$ in (13.17), (13.21), (13.22) is smaller than $\min(s_j, d_v + 1)$ (see (Vapnik, 1995)). For this class of function the MSRM becomes

$$\min_{\mathbf{w}\in\mathbb{R}^{d_v}, b\in\mathbb{R}} \left[R_{emp}(\mathbf{w}, b) + \phi(\frac{int(Z^2 \cdot \|\mathbf{w}\|^2 + 1)}{\ell}, \frac{\ln(\eta/4)}{\ell}) \right]. \tag{13.23}$$

Here, one can notice an important difference between the statements for SRM (13.15) and MSRM (13.23). For SRM, the quantity ϕ is not involved in the numerical optimization and, therefore, its expression has only to give tight bounds; no particular care of its analytical expression is required. In the MSRM, since the cost function of the numerical problem depends on the analytical expression of ϕ, tight bounds with a simple expression for ϕ are required. Unfortunately, all the existing expression for ϕ are quite complicated to be involved in an analytical specification. Therefore, no better application of this principle can be done than approximating the second term in (13.23) in the following way:

$$\phi\left(\frac{int(Z^2 \cdot \|\mathbf{w}\|^2 + 1)}{l}, \frac{\ln(\eta/4)}{l}\right) \cong \frac{1}{2C\,l}\|\mathbf{w}\|^2, \tag{13.24}$$

where C is a constant that has to be fixed to reduce the error of the approximation. No theoretical result is available in the literature about the dependence of the approximation error on C. With the approximation (13.24) and taking into account (13.11), the MSRM principle suggests that we choose $\mathbf{w}$ by solving the following optimization problem[5]

Basic Optimization Problem

$$\min_{\mathbf{w}\in\mathbb{R}^{d_v}, b\in\mathbb{R}} \frac{1}{2}\|\mathbf{w}\|^2 + C\sum_{i=1}^{\ell} c(y_i, (\mathbf{w} \cdot \Phi(\mathbf{x}_i)) + b). \tag{13.25}$$

We prefer to summarize here the different assumptions that are needed to derive these results:

(1) The bound (13.9) is considered so tight that its minimization implies also the minimization of the actual approximation error; the successive approximation (13.24) of ϕ with a linear function determines (for a suitable choice of the proportionality constant C) an error of the same order of magnitude as other approximations;

(2) The bound on the VC-dimension of the class of nonlinear functions, linear in the parameters vector $\mathbf{w}$, with limited norm $\|\mathbf{w}\|$, is considered so tight to approximate well the actual VC-dimension of this class of functions;

4. One should actually consider the VC dimension of $\mathcal{F}_j^c$, closely related to that of $\mathcal{F}_j$.
5. The learning criterion (13.25) was derived in (Vapnik, 1995) as a way of approximately solving the SRM problem: $\min \sum_{i=1}^{\ell} c(y_i, (\mathbf{w} \cdot \cdot \Phi(\mathbf{x}_i)) + b)$ subject to the condition $\|w\|^2 \leq C_n$. A correct solution of this problem would require to solve the minimization problem for different values of C_n. The SRM principle suggests that we choose the solution which corresponds to the value of C_n for which the bound (13.9) is minimized.

(3) The assumption of independence of training examples under which this result holds is not always satisfied in practice. One can expect the theory to be quite robust to this approximation with respect to the actual natural density of the chaotic time-series. The worst case is constituted by a joint density such that the successive examples are equal to the first one. This worst situation is better approximated for higher sampling rates.

We also note that other existing theories (e.g., regularization theory) suggest to find the approximating function by solving the problem (13.25). Therefore, the Statistical Learning Theory (from whose perspective the SVM was first derived as a particular and important application) can also be substituted by other theories for the derivation of the SVM algorithm.

13.3.1.3 Solving the Minimization Problem: the Dual Method

The choice of the function c defines the theoretical error $R(\mathbf{w})$ that we are trying to minimize. A general form for the function is the following:

$$c(y_i - f(\mathbf{x}_i), \mathbf{x}_i, y_i), \tag{13.26}$$

in which the dependence on the second and third arguments account for the possibility to consider more expensive approximation error in some subsets of the input-output space than in others. However, we simply consider, for sake of clarity, a cost function

$$c(y_i - f(\mathbf{x}_i)). \tag{13.27}$$

We only note here that the parameters that we will subsequently introduce to express the cost function are allowed to assume different values on each training example. The optimization problem (13.25), therefore, becomes

$$\min_{\mathbf{w}\in\mathbb{R}^{d_v}, b\in\mathbb{R}} \left[\frac{1}{2}\|\mathbf{w}\|^2 + C\sum_{i=1}^{\ell} c(y_i - (\mathbf{w}\cdot\Phi(\mathbf{x}_i)) - b) \right]. \tag{13.28}$$

Generalized RBF

For a quadratic loss function $c(\alpha) = \frac{1}{2}\alpha^2$ and for the case in which the threshold b is set to zero, the solution $\mathbf{w}$ is known to be equal to

$$\mathbf{w} = \left(\frac{1}{C}\boldsymbol{I} + \boldsymbol{G}^T\cdot\boldsymbol{G}\right)^{-1}\cdot\boldsymbol{G}^T\cdot\boldsymbol{y}, \tag{13.29}$$

where

$$\boldsymbol{G} \triangleq [\Phi(\mathbf{x}_1), \ldots, \Phi(\mathbf{x}_l)]^T, \tag{13.30}$$

and $\boldsymbol{y} \triangleq [y_1, \ldots, y_l]^T$. This method is usually called Generalized Radial Basis Function (GRBF) and it is usually derived as an application of the regularization theory. This formulation has two main drawbacks: the first one is that the function $\Phi(\boldsymbol{x})$ has to be fixed, the second one is that the complexity of this optimization problem requires that we maintain the value of d_v low. One can solve the optimization problem (13.28) by noticing that it is equivalent to the following one

$$\min_{\mathbf{w}\in\mathbb{R}^{d_v},b\in\mathbb{R},\xi_i^*,\xi_i} \left[\frac{1}{2}\|\mathbf{w}\|^2 + C\sum_{i=1}^{\ell}\Big(c_1(\xi_i^*)+c_2(\xi_i)\Big)\right], \tag{13.31}$$

subject to the following conditions, for each $i \in \{1,\ldots,\ell\}$,

$$\left.\begin{array}{rcl} y_i - (\mathbf{w}\cdot\Phi(\mathbf{x}_i)) - b & \leq & \xi_i^*, \\ -y_i + (\mathbf{w}\cdot\Phi(\mathbf{x}_i)) + b & \leq & \xi_i, \end{array}\right\} \text{ subject to } \xi_i^* \geq a_1,\ \xi_i \geq a_2, \tag{13.32}$$

where $c_1(\xi) \triangleq c(\xi)\Theta(\xi)$ and $c_2(\xi) \triangleq c(-\xi)\Theta(\xi)$ are monotonically increasing functions such that, for $j = 1, 2$, $c_j(\xi) = 0$ if $\xi \leq a_j$ and $c_j(\xi) > 0$ if $\xi > a_j$; $\Theta(\cdot)$ denotes the usual step function. By making use of the Kuhn-Tucker theorem, the optimum solution can be written as $\mathbf{w} = \sum_{i=1}^{\ell}(\alpha_i^* - \alpha_i)\Phi(\mathbf{x})$ where α_i^* and α_i are the solutions of the following problem:[6]

Dual Problem

$$\begin{aligned}\min_{\xi_i^*,\xi_i}\max_{\alpha_i^*,\alpha_i,\gamma_i^*,\gamma_i} & -\frac{1}{2}\sum_{i=1}^{l}\sum_{j=1}^{l}(\alpha_i^*-\alpha_i)(\alpha_j^*-\alpha_j)(\Phi(\mathbf{x}_i)\cdot\Phi(\mathbf{x}_j)) + \sum_{i=1}^{l}(\alpha_i^*-\alpha_i)\ y_i \\ & + \sum_{i=1}^{l}[Cc_1(\xi_i^*) - (\alpha_i^*+\gamma_i^*)\cdot\xi_i^* + a_1\gamma_i^*] \\ & + \sum_{i=1}^{l}[Cc_2(\xi_i) - (\alpha_i+\gamma_i)\cdot\xi_i + a_2\gamma_i],\end{aligned} \tag{13.33}$$

subject to the following conditions, for each $i \in \{1,\ldots,\ell\}$,

$$\sum_{i=1}^{\ell}(\alpha_i^* - \alpha_i) = 0, \tag{13.34}$$

$$C\cdot c_1'(\xi_i^*) - \alpha_i^* - \gamma_i^* = 0, \tag{13.35}$$

$$C\cdot c_2'(\xi_i) - \alpha_i - \gamma_i = 0, \tag{13.36}$$

$$\alpha_i^*,\ \alpha_i,\ \gamma_i^*,\ \gamma_i \geq 0, \tag{13.37}$$

in which c_1' and c_2' are the first derivatives of c_1 and c_2 respectively. It is also known that the following conditions are satisfied, for each $i \in \{1,\ldots,\ell\}$,

$$\alpha_i^*\cdot[y_i - (\mathbf{w}\cdot\Phi(\mathbf{x}_i)) - b - \xi_i^*] = 0, \tag{13.38}$$

$$\alpha_i\cdot[-y_i + (\mathbf{w}\cdot\Phi(\mathbf{x}_i)) + b - \xi_i] = 0, \tag{13.39}$$

$$\gamma_i^*(a_1 - \xi_i^*) = 0, \tag{13.40}$$

$$\gamma_i(a_2 - \xi_i) = 0. \tag{13.41}$$

6. This result has been independently discovered by Smola et al. (1998c).

The obtained approximation function can be expressed as:

$$f(\mathbf{x}) = (\mathbf{w} \cdot \Phi(\mathbf{x})) + b = \left(\left[\sum_{i=1}^{\ell} (\alpha_i^* - \alpha_i) \Phi(\mathbf{x}_i) \right] \cdot \Phi(\mathbf{x}) \right) + b \tag{13.42}$$

$$= \sum_{i=1}^{\ell} (\alpha_i^* - \alpha_i)(\Phi(\mathbf{x}_i) \cdot \Phi(\mathbf{x})) + b = \sum_{i \in S} u_i \cdot k(\mathbf{x}, \mathbf{x}_i) + b,$$

where $k(\mathbf{x}_1, \mathbf{x}_2) \triangleq (\Phi(\mathbf{x}_1) \cdot \Phi(\mathbf{x}_2))$, $u_i \triangleq \alpha_i^* - \alpha_i$ and $S \triangleq \{i : |u_i| > 0\}$. The most important characteristic of this algorithm is that here one does not need to calculate the vector $\Phi(\mathbf{x})$ but only the kernel $k(\mathbf{x}_1, \mathbf{x}_2)$.

To proceed further, we need to specify the cost function c.

13.3.1.4 The ε-insensitive Loss Function

The classical cost function, referring to which the SVM was first defined, has the following form:

$$c(\xi) \triangleq \begin{cases} 0 & \text{for } |\xi| \leq \varepsilon \\ |\xi| - \varepsilon & \text{for } |\xi| \geq \varepsilon. \end{cases} \tag{13.43}$$

This cost function was introduced in (Vapnik, 1995) and it is called the ε-insensitive cost function. For this choice of the class of functions, the problem (13.33) reduces to (1.47) subject to the constraint (1.48)

The task is to solve numerically a quadratic optimization problem with a linear constraint on 2ℓ variables on which there is also the bound constraint. Define the quantities $u_i \triangleq \alpha_i^* - \alpha_i$ and $q_i \triangleq y_i - \sum_{j=1}^{\ell} u_j k(\mathbf{x}_i, \mathbf{x}_j) - b$, from the conditions (13.40), the following implications are valid at the optimal solution:

$$\alpha_i^* \cdot \alpha_i = 0, \tag{13.44}$$

$$u_i = 0 \Rightarrow |q_i| \leq \varepsilon, \tag{13.45}$$

$$0 < |u_i| < C \Rightarrow q_i = \varepsilon \; sign(u_i), \tag{13.46}$$

$$|u_i| = C \Rightarrow |q_i| \geq \varepsilon, \tag{13.47}$$

where $sign(\cdot)$ denotes the signum function. The property (13.46) allows us to calculate the value of the threshold:

$$b = y_i - \sum_{j=1}^{\ell} u_j k(\mathbf{x}_i, \mathbf{x}_j) - \varepsilon \; sign(u_i); \tag{13.48}$$

This equality is valid for any value of i such that $0 < |u_i| < C$. The threshold can also be implicitly taken into account if the function $\mathbf{\Phi}(\mathbf{x})$ is defined having also a component that is constant with respect to $\mathbf{x}$. In this case, the equality constraint in (13.34) is not to be imposed and the numerical problem becomes simpler. How this choice affects the performance has not been studied yet in the literature. These three properties are useful when the implementation problem is addressed.

13.3.1.5 The ε-insensitive Huber Loss Function

Another possible choice for the cost function is the following:

$$c(\xi) \triangleq \begin{cases} 0 & \text{for} \quad |\xi| \leq \varepsilon \\ \frac{(|\xi|-\varepsilon)^2}{2} & \text{for} \quad \varepsilon \leq |\xi| \leq \beta \\ (\beta-\varepsilon)(|\xi|-\varepsilon) - \frac{(\beta-\varepsilon)^2}{2} & \text{for} \quad |\xi| \geq \beta \end{cases} . \tag{13.49}$$

This choice was introduced in (Vapnik, 1995) for $\varepsilon = 0$ and it was called the Huber loss function. The reason for this name is that its minimization constitutes the robust regression estimation for the case in which the density belongs to a class of mixture of two densities, one of which is Gaussian — a result found by Huber. Nevertheless, the role of the parameter ε is very important; we can call the loss function (13.49) ε-insensitive Huber loss function.

For the loss function (13.49), the linear coefficients α_i^* and α_i are the solutions of the following problem (that is obtained from (13.33) for the considered loss function):

$$\max_{\alpha_i^*, \alpha_i} \left\{ -\frac{1}{2} \sum_{i=1}^{\ell} \sum_{j=1}^{\ell} (\alpha_i^* - \alpha_i)(\alpha_j^* - \alpha_j) k(\mathbf{x}_i, \mathbf{x}_j) + \sum_{i=1}^{\ell} (\alpha_i^* - \alpha_i)\, y_i \right. \\ \left. - \sum_{i=1}^{\ell} [\varepsilon(\alpha_i^* + \alpha_i) + \frac{1}{2C}(\alpha_i^{*2} + \alpha_i^2)] \right\}, \tag{13.50}$$

subject to the condition (13.34) and to the following ones, for each $i \in \{1, \ldots, \ell\}$,

$$0 \leq \alpha_i^* \leq C(\beta - \varepsilon) \text{ and } 0 \leq \alpha_i \leq C(\beta - \varepsilon). \tag{13.51}$$

The problem to solve numerically is still a quadratic optimization with a linear constraint on 2ℓ variables on which there is also the bound constraint. The quantities u_i and q_i satisfy the following implication at the optimum solution:

$$\alpha_i^* \cdot \alpha_i = 0, \tag{13.52}$$

$$u_i = 0 \Rightarrow |q_i| \leq \varepsilon, \tag{13.53}$$

$$0 < |u_i| < C(\beta - \varepsilon) \Rightarrow q_i = \left(\frac{|u_i|}{C} + \varepsilon \right) \cdot sign(u_i), \tag{13.54}$$

$$|u_i| = C(\beta - \varepsilon) \Rightarrow |q_i| \geq \beta. \tag{13.55}$$

The property (13.54) allows to calculate the value of the threshold b:

$$b = y_i - \sum_{j=1}^{\ell} u_j k(\mathbf{x}_i, \mathbf{x}_j) - \left(\frac{|u_i|}{C} + \varepsilon \right) \cdot sign(u_i); \tag{13.56}$$

this equality is valid for any value of i such that $0 < u_i < C(\beta - \varepsilon)$.

Making β tend to infinity, the cost function tends to the ε-insensitive quadratic loss function; for this case there is not any upper limit on the size of the coefficients u_i. The classical quadratic loss function is obtained by fixing $\varepsilon = 0$: For this case, the relation (13.54) is valid for any $i \in \{1, \dots, \ell\}$. Therefore, for $\varepsilon = 0$ and $\beta \to \infty$, if the threshold b is set to zero, the coefficient vector $\boldsymbol{u} = [u_1, u_2, \dots, u_\ell]^T$ satisfies the following condition:

Equivalence with RRBF

$$\boldsymbol{u} = \left(\boldsymbol{K} + \frac{1}{C}\boldsymbol{I}\right)^{-1} \cdot \boldsymbol{y}, \tag{13.57}$$

where $\boldsymbol{K} \triangleq \{k(\mathbf{x}_i, \mathbf{x}_j)\}_{i,j=1,\dots,\ell}$ is the classical *strict interpolation condition* imposed in the solution of the regularized RBF networks, utilized in (Haykin et al., 1997) to solve the dynamic reconstruction problem. We can see that, in this case, no limits are imposed on the size of the weights vector $\boldsymbol{u}$ and, therefore, we can have an unacceptable solution from a computational point of view.

This clearly shows that the SVM methods are very general and different kinds of RBF can be viewed as the result of a particular choice of the cost function c or of the kernel function; it constitutes a theoretical answer to the issue of comparing SVM and RBF networks on which the first experimental works on SVM are focussed (Schölkopf et al., 1997b).

13.3.2 Considerations for Implementing the Algorithm

In applying the SV method, one has to solve the problem of finding the minimum of a quadratic function of 2ℓ variables with one linear constraint (13.50). Writing a computer program that solves this problem can be considered to be itself a formidable (at least for large values of ℓ) problem. We will not review the methods that one can use to solve this problem and we will simply attempt to give some specifications about the way in which one can solve the optimization problem that the SVM algorithm specifies. Our suggestion is to utilize one of the existing software packages that can do it. We performed our experiments with the use of a commercial package Minos 5.4 (Murtagh and Saunders, 1993).

One can see that the usual number ℓ of training examples renders the numerical problem quite demanding with respect to the memory requirements: in particular, the storage requirement of the Minos software increases with the square of the number s of nonzero component at the optimum solution. One also needs to calculate a large number of times the objective function of the considered problem and its gradients. The matrix ($\ell \times \ell$) of the quadratic term can be calculated only once and maintained in the memory. The total storage requirement in Megabyte can be approximated by the expression $M(\ell, \varepsilon, d_e) = 4(s^2(\varepsilon, l) + \ell^2))$. Therefore, for a fixed value of the memory available, there would be, by a direct approach, an upper bound $\ell_D(\varepsilon)$ on the training set size for which the problem can be solved in a reasonable time; the dependence of ℓ_D on ε is weak. Fortunately, the problem can still be solved even if $\ell > \ell_D$, making use of a decomposition algorithm.

Generalizing to the continuous functions case, the important method in (Osuna et al., 1997a) relative to the pattern recognition case, we can first fix a subset L_1 of the training set index $L = \{1, \dots, \ell\}$ such that $|L_1| \leq l_D$, where $|L_1|$ is the cardinality of the set L_1; let us call $C_1 \triangleq L - L_1$.

Then, one can solve the minimization problem (1.47) (or, equivalently (13.50)) considering fixed variables with index in C_1. To solve this sub-problem, one needs that $|L_1| \leq l_D$; in fact, the sub-problem remains a quadratic one with a number of variables equal to $|L_1|$. The vector that defines the linear term of the objective function depends on the values of the variables with index in C_1 and requires that the kernel to be evaluated $(l - |L_1|) \cdot |L_1|$ different times for its calculation. This intermediate solution can be the optimal one only if the three implications (13.44), (13.45) and (13.47) (or, equivalently, (13.52), (13.53) and (13.55)) are satisfied for all the training examples. Let us call L_1^* the set of indices of the training examples that do not satisfy one of these three conditions. Let us choose L_2 as a subset of L_1^* such that $|L_2| \leq l_D$, $C_2 \triangleq L - L_2$ and, again, solve the problem of minimizing the objective (1.47) in which only the variables with indices in L_2 are allowed to be optimized and those with indices in C_2 are fixed to the value they had at the end of the previous step. Value of the objective function after the second step will be, obviously, increased with respect to the previous step; this assures one that, after a finite number of steps, the set L_i^* will vanish and, therefore, the optimum solution will be found.

By making use of the decomposition algorithm, one can trade off the memory requirements with the computational time and eliminate the bound on the maximum number of training examples ℓ_D that would exist in a direct approach.

13.3.3 Open Problems: the Choice of the Parameters and of the Kernels

The parameters that are allowed to vary in the SVM are C, ε; also β if the second cost function is chosen. From the theory previously introduced, the kernel is a fixed function and different choices are possible. In the theory we developed, the function Φ and, therefore, the kernel k, have to be fixed before the training process starts and many choices are possible. According to the approximation theory, if no *a priori* knowledge is available, there is no good reason to make *a priori* a kernel choice rather than another, provided that the kernel defines a sufficiently general class of functions. We choose as kernel the following Gaussian function:

Gaussian Kernel

$$F(\mathbf{x}, \boldsymbol{y}) = \exp\left(-\frac{1}{\sigma^2}\|\mathbf{x} - \boldsymbol{y}\|^2\right). \tag{13.58}$$

The value of σ has to be fixed *a priori* or at least an interval of values for σ has to be fixed. We will make this choice with particular reference to the dependence of the dynamical properties of the reconstructed system on σ.

It would be preferable to fix the value of C, ε and σ *a priori*. With reference to the problem of dynamical reconstruction, a robust choice of the values of these parameters can be done *a priori*; however, it is better to tune them to the particular data set under consideration. Two methods exist for tuning the parameters: one method consists of making use of a cross-validation technique[7] on the training set and the other method consists of minimizing a bound on the test error of the SVM introduced by Vapnik; the latter one refers, to the best of our knowledge, to the pattern recognition case. Trying to tune the values of the parameters by these methods can be computationally very intensive since they require that we perform the training (i.e. we solve the minimization problem) several times.[8]

13.3.3.1 Choosing the Value of ε

We start the analysis by considering the influence of the choice of ε on the obtained solution for fixed values of C and σ^2; this choice determines the actual loss function and affects both the approximation error achieved, the training time and the complexity of the solution; the last two depend directly on the number of Support Vectors. A given training example becomes a Support Vector only if (see (13.45) or (13.53)) the approximation error on that example is larger than ε. Therefore, the number of Support Vectors is a decreasing function of ε and a nonzero value of ε is required to utilize, in practice, large training sets. On the other hand, too large values of ε specify a loss-function such that the theoretical risk we are trying to minimize is not a correct measure of the approximation quality. In practice one should ensure that the value of ε be sufficiently small so that the theoretical risk it defines constitutes a reasonable measure of the approximation error. A robust compromise can be to impose the condition that the percentage of Support Vectors be equal to 50%. A larger value of ε can be utilized (especially for very large and/or noisy training sets) trying to reduce the training time and the network complexity; for small increase in the value of ε, the corresponding increase in the approximation error will be sufficiently small.

13.3.3.2 Choosing the Value of C

We next study the effect of the parameter C on the SVM performance; we assume that the ε-insensitive loss function (13.43) has been chosen. Let us suppose that the kernel assumes values in the range $[-1, 1]$. Since C defines the range of the values assumed by linear coefficients u_i, its choice affects the range of the possible output of the SVM. Let us suppose that the output values are in the range $[0, B]$. For a choice of C which is very small compared to B, it would be impossible to obtain a good approximation. For a value of C which is very large compared to

7. The cross-validation technique should take into account both the chaotic-invariants of the reconstructed system and the recursive prediction capability in the cross-validation part of the training set.
8. In this case, it is a good idea to choose, as starting point in the solution of the quadratic optimization problem, the solution of the problem we have solved with close value of the parameters. This choice allows us to reduce the overall training time, especially for larger training set.

B, the eventual increase of the linear coefficients u_i could give rise to numerical instabilities. Therefore, a value of C about equal to B can be considered to be a robust choice. Further increasing the value of C, the relative importance in (13.25) of the empirical error with respect to complexity penalty grows; this implies an increase of the approximation error.

13.3.3.3 Choosing the Value of σ^2

For choosing the parameter σ^2, one has to take into account that the reconstructed system is required to be chaotic. This requirement is not easily satisfied for some choices of σ^2. We illustrate the basic idea with the example of a one-dimensional Gaussian function

$$f(x) = c \cdot \exp\left(-\frac{(x-b)^2}{\sigma^2}\right). \tag{13.59}$$

Let us consider the succession of functions $f^{(k)}(\cdot)$ obtained by recursion by $f(x)$; it can be easily shown[9] that it converges to a constant function if $\sigma > c\sqrt{2/e}$. The convergence can still hold[10] for smaller values of σ. Moreover, also if the function $f(x)$ is not convergent, the function $g(x) = f(f(x))$ can satisfy the conditions for convergence and, therefore, $f^{(k)}(x)$ can be periodic for any x.

In the general d_E dimensional case, the succession of points $\mathbf{x}(n+1) = \hat{\boldsymbol{F}}(\mathbf{x}(n))$ can be convergent[11] or periodic for some choices of σ. The one-dimensional example shows how an incorrect choice of σ can affect the performance. A robust choice for $\frac{\sigma^2}{P \cdot d_E}$, where P is the signal power,[12] is realized by fixing it, once for all, to a value that does not rule out the possibility that the reconstructed system be chaotic. For a time-series normalized such that $P = 1$, a possible choice in accordance with the previous suggestions[13] is $C = 3$ and $\frac{\sigma^2}{d_E} = 0.75$.

---

9. In fact, it is well-known (e.g., (Elden and Wittmeyer-Koch, 1990)) that, if a solution x^* exists to the equation $x = f(x)$ and the absolute value of the derivative of f in the solution is smaller than one, then the succession $x_{n+1} = f(x_n)$ will converge to the solution for any starting point which belongs to an interval around the solution x^* in which the absolute value of the derivative maintains smaller than one. The result follows from the fact that the maximum of the absolute value of the derivative of the function (13.59) is equal to $c/\sigma \cdot \sqrt{2/e}$.
10. It suffices that the derivative at the solution $|f'(x^*)| < 1$.
11. For convergence it suffices that, for any $\mathbf{x}$ in the set S around the solution of the equation $\mathbf{x} = \hat{\boldsymbol{F}}(\mathbf{x})$, the $d_E \times d_E$ matrix $D(\mathbf{x})$ with the partial derivatives of the function $\boldsymbol{f}$ in $\mathbf{x}$ is, for some matrix norm, smaller than one. One should note that the norm of the matrix D is a decreasing function of σ.
12. The power of the time-series $x(k)$ is defined as $\langle x^2(\cdot)\rangle \triangleq \frac{1}{l}\sum_{k=1}^{l} x^2(k)$.
13. We utilized the one-dimensional example to fix the condition $\frac{\sigma^2}{d_E} = 0.75$.

13.4 Applying the SVM to the Nonlinear Reconstruction

Lorenz system

In this section we show the results obtained by applying the SVM to the dynamical reconstruction of the well known Lorenz system (Lorenz, 1963):

$$\begin{aligned} \dot{x} &= \rho(y-x), \\ \dot{y} &= -x\,z + rx - y, \\ \dot{z} &= x\,y - b\,z, \end{aligned} \tag{13.60}$$

with the following values of the parameters: $\rho = 16$, $b = 4$ and $r = 45.92$. We integrated the set of equation (13.60) with a fourth-order Runge-Kutta method and generated 35000 samples at 16-bit resolution with a sampling frequency of 40 Hz and normalized them so that the power of the time-series is equal to one. Let us denote $x(k)$ the obtained time-series which corresponds to the first component. Two other time-series $x_1(k)$ and $x_2(k)$ were generated in which the original data $x(k)$ are disturbed with additive noise:

$$\begin{aligned} x_1(k) &= x(k) + \eta_1(k), \\ x_2(k) &= x(k) + \eta_2(k), \end{aligned} \tag{13.61}$$

where $\eta_1(k)$ is purely stochastic white Gaussian noise generated by a physical mechanism[14] which is added to $x(k)$ to generate $x_1(k)$ with a signal-to-noise ratio (SNR) equal to 20 dB and $\eta_2(k)$ is a colored noise, obtained by filtering a computer-generated time-series uniformly distributed in $[-0.23, 0.23]$ by means of a finite impulse response (FIR) linear filter of order 9 with a cut-off frequency of 10 Hz, which is added to $x(k)$ to generate $x_2(k)$ with SNR equal to 21.5 dB. The last 15000 samples of every time-series were not utilized for training. The short-term predictive capability of any reconstructed system was tested on a fixed set of $M = 2000$ phase-space starting-points $\boldsymbol{r}(k)$ embedded from the last 15000 samples of the non-noisy time-series $x(k)$. We used in our experiments the classical SVM algorithm (1.47) obtained by choosing the ε-insensitive loss function (13.43).

As measures of the short-term prediction performance, we utilized two quantities. The first one is the normalized mean-square prediction error after p steps in dB

$$\mathcal{E}(p \cdot \tau) \triangleq 10 \cdot \log_{10} \frac{\sum\limits_{m=1}^{M} (\hat{x}_m(p) - x_m(p))^2}{\sum\limits_{m=1}^{M} x_m^2(p)}, \tag{13.62}$$

14. The pure white Gaussian noise was generated using a commercially available analog noise generator (NC - 1107A -1, Noise Com. Inc.) coupled with an amplifier and A/D converter. This physical device contains a hermetically-packaged noise diode that has been burned-in for 168 hours and operates in a temperature range of -35 to $+100^o$ C. It produced white Gaussian noise at $+13dBm$ and in a frequency range between $10Hz$ and 100 MHz.

where the $x_m(p) \triangleq x(p + j_m)$ is the output of the actual system, $\hat{x}_m(p)$ is the output of the reconstructed system, the index m refers to M different starting points j_m which the evolution of the reconstructed system is tested from, τ is the sampling period.

Short term Prediction Performance Measures

The second short-term prediction performance measure we utilized in our experiments is the following:

$$t_r(\gamma) \triangleq \frac{1}{M} \sum_{m=1}^{M} t'_m(\gamma), \qquad (13.63)$$

where $t'_m(\gamma)$ is such that

$$\begin{cases} p \cdot \tau & \leq & t'_m(\gamma) & \Rightarrow & |\hat{x}_m(p) - x_m(p)| & \leq & \gamma |x_m(p)| \\ p \cdot \tau & > & t'_m(\gamma) & \Rightarrow & |\hat{x}_m(p) - x_m(p)| & > & \gamma |x_m(p)|. \end{cases} \qquad (13.64)$$

The quantity $t(\gamma)$ is a very severe estimate of the average horizon of iterative prediction actually achieved by the reconstructed system. The severity of the criterion depends on the choice of γ.

13.4.1 The Pure Lorenz Time-Series

In the first part of this section we present the results of the numerical experiments we have performed on the noiseless Lorenz data set $x(k)$ in order to determine the dependence of the performances on the choice of the SVM parameters.

13.4.1.1 Dependence on the Choice of C and σ^2

We first have investigated the dependence of the performances on the choice of the parameters C and σ^2 for a fixed value of $\varepsilon = 0.01$ and $\ell = 400$; the other parameters were fixed[15] as follows: $T = 4$, $d_E = 3$. In table 13.1 the number of Support Vectors, the error $\mathcal{E}(\tau)$ and the largest Lyapunov exponent[16] in nats/sec of the reconstructed system corresponding to different choices for C and $\frac{\sigma^2}{d_E}$ are reported. One should remember that the largest Lyapunov exponent of the original system is 1.52 for the set of parameters chosen. The experimental results agree with the theoretical discussion of the previous section. In fact, one can notice that the choice $C = 3$ and $\sigma^2 = 0.75 \cdot d_E$ is central in the set of values for which the best results are obtained.

15. The values of T and d_E were fixed, respectively, as the first minimum of mutual information and by the false-nearest-neighbors method, as suggested in (Abarbanel, 1996).
16. The largest Lyapunov exponent was estimated from 30000 samples of time-series obtained by iteration of the reconstructed system from a fixed starting point by the method introduced in (Brown et al., 1991); the time-delay and the embedding dimension were fixed, respectively, as the first-minimum of the mutual information (Abarbanel, 1996) and by the false-nearest-neighbors method (Kennel et al., 1992).

13.4.1.2 Dependence on the Training Set Size ℓ and ε

In order to test the dependence of the performances on the values of ε and the training-set size ℓ, we fixed $C = 3$ and $\sigma^2 = 0.75 \cdot d_E$ and the other parameters to the previous values: $T = 4$, $d_E = 3$. In table 13.2 the number of support vectors $s(\varepsilon, \ell)$ and the corresponding values of $\mathcal{E}(\tau)$ are reported.

One can notice that, for a fixed ε, $s(\varepsilon, \ell)$ and $\mathcal{E}(\tau)$ tend to saturate when ℓ increases; this happens when a small percentage of support vectors suffices for approximating the target function within the ε-accuracy requirement, i.e. when the error amplitude is limited, with large probability, by ε. The resulting one-step-ahead approximation error in dB $\mathcal{E}(\tau)$ represents the best result one can achieve with the chosen value of ε and it cannot be reduced by increasing the training set size ℓ; the corresponding error power is a fraction of ε^2. One can also notice that, decreasing ε for a fixed value of ℓ, the approximation error $\mathcal{E}(\tau)$ saturates to best accuracy one can achieve within the class of functions defined by means of the kernels centered in the ℓ available training examples; such an accuracy can be achieved with a percentage of Support Vectors that is quite small.

13.4.2 The Noisy Case

In the next two subsections, the results of the numerical experiments we have performed on the noisy Lorenz data sets, previously introduced, are presented. Our investigations focused on two issues: how the noise influences the dependence of the SVM performances on ε and ℓ and how the performances of the two most popular choices for embedding the phase-space points from the time-series compare between themselves.

13.4.2.1 Dependence on ε and the Training Set Size ℓ

The best choice for the value of ε is not independent of the amount of noise present on the data. In fact, the presence of the noise affects the actual ε-accuracy requirements, i.e. the ε-mask (or ε-tube) imposed on the target function; three cases are possible:

(1) If noise power is very small compared to ε^2, the modification of the mask is very small and the SVM performance is not affected by the presence of the noise;

SVM and Noisy Data

(2) If the noise power is smaller than ε^2, the mask is modified by the presence of the noise and the performance can be expected to increase because the noise-modified mask becomes close to a clean mask defined by a smaller value of ε;

(3) If the noise power is equal or larger to ε^2, the noise-modified mask is no longer a mask or equivalently it becomes close to the clean mask for $\varepsilon = 0$ and, consequently, the percentage of support vectors saturates to one.

The modification of the mask is equivalent to the modification of the signal $\varepsilon + \eta(k)$ with respect to the constant ε. The number of support vectors $s(\varepsilon, \ell)$ depends on the ratio of the noise power and ε^2. We can consider that the mask-shape is preserved if the noise power does not exceed a fraction of ε^2 (say, for example, one half); the points in which the mask-shape is not preserved become support vectors, the others behave similarly to the non-noisy case. The number of support vectors $s(\varepsilon, \ell)$ can, therefore, be approximated by the following expression:

$$s(\varepsilon, \ell) = \ell \cdot Prob\left\{|\eta| \geq \frac{\varepsilon}{\gamma}\right\} + S_r(\varepsilon, \ell) \cdot Prob\left\{|\eta| < \frac{\varepsilon}{\gamma}\right\}, \tag{13.65}$$

where η is the noise present and $S_r(\varepsilon, \ell)$ is a quantity that behaves similarly to the number of Support Vectors in the non-noisy case. The value of γ to get a good approximation is larger than one; in fact, if the noise power is smaller than ε^2, the modification of the ε-mask cannot be considered small; we choose here to consider small modification if the noise power is one half of ε^2 which corresponds to a value of $\gamma = \sqrt{2}$.

As a first trial of the correctness of (13.65), we contaminated the pure Lorenz time-series $x(k)$, considered in the previous sections, with a white computer-generated pseudo-noise time-series uniformly distributed in $[-0.08, 0.08]$ and fixed $\varepsilon = 0.1$. We approximated $S_r(\varepsilon, \ell)$ with the value obtained in the previous section, specifically 31 for $\ell = 1000$, 30 for $\ell = 2000$, 35 for $\ell = 5000$ and 32 for $\ell = 10000$; the number of Support Vectors given by (13.65) is 143.4, 258.5, 611 and 1188 while the numbers resulting from the experiments[17] are 149, 271, 642 and 1266; for $\gamma = 1$, the results given by (13.65) would be completely incorrect.

We performed a series of experiments on three different training sets of size $\ell = 1000$ (with starting points 1, 8001 and 15001) from the time-series $x_1(k)$ contaminated with the white purely-stochastic noise; the other parameters are fixed to the following values: $C = 3$, $\frac{\sigma^2}{d_E} = 0.75$, $T = 4$, $d_E = 5$. The resulting percentages of Support Vectors and $\mathcal{E}(\tau)$ are shown in figures 13.1 and 13.2.

In figure 13.1 the points + are the value obtained by (13.65) with $\gamma = \sqrt{2}$ and the points o with $\gamma = 1$; again, $\gamma = \sqrt{2}$ constitutes a better choice than $\gamma = 1$. In figure 13.2 one can notice that the performances degrade when the percentage of SV goes to one but not very strongly. Moreover, for a fixed value of $\varepsilon = 0.2$ and $\ell = 10^4$, the percentage of Support Vectors is equal to 0.149 which is quite close to the value 0.17 given by (13.65).

We also studied the same issue (i.e, the dependence of the number of Support Vectors and the approximation accuracy on ε and ℓ) for the time series $x_2(k)$ contaminated by colored noise; the training set is constituted by the first ℓ values of the input-output points $(\boldsymbol{r}(k), x(k+1))$. The results are shown in figures 13.3 and 13.4. We notice that in this case the number of Support Vectors is smaller than first term in (13.65) both for $\gamma = \sqrt{2}$ (indicated with +) and for $\gamma = 1$ (indicated

17. The values of the parameters were fixed as follows: $C = 3$, $\frac{\sigma^2}{d_E} = 0.75$, $T = 4$, $d_E = 5$.

with o). One can think that this is due to the fact that the noise, being colored, introduces a milder modification of the ε mask. However, once again, the presence of the noise saturates the percentage of Support Vectors for power of noise larger than $\frac{\varepsilon^2}{2}$. From figure 13.4, one can see again the existence of an optimum value of ε larger than zero and also that the degradation of the performance for ε too small is limited; however, one should also note the increase in the training time and in the complexity of the structure determined by the corresponding increase in the number of Support Vectors. A choice of a value of ε for which the percentage of SV constitutes a considerable percentage of the training set size ℓ (around $40-50\%$) is confirmed to be a robust one.

13.4.2.2 **Dependence on Embedding Dimension d_E and Time Delay T**

In this section, the results of some experiments performed in order to compare the two usual choices for embedding the phase-space vector $\boldsymbol{r}(k)$ are reported.

The first choice[18] consists in fixing $T = T_I$ and $d_E = d_N$ where T_I is the first minimum of the mutual information (Abarbanel, 1996) and d_N is obtained by the global false nearest-neighbors method (Kennel et al., 1992).

The second choice consists in fixing $T = 1$ and d_E to a value around $d_N \cdot T_I$. The second choice utilizes all the past samples of the data in order to smooth the target function. The training time is not affected by this choice while the network complexity is about T_I times larger.

We have considered the time-series $x_1(k)$ contaminated by white noise; for this time-series $T_I = 4$ and $d_E = 5$. We have fixed $\ell = 400$, $C = 3$, $\sigma^2 = 0.75$ and $\varepsilon = 0.1$ and considered different training sets of size 400; this is a difficult situation with respect to both the SNR and the length of the data. This choice was done to magnify the dependence on a correct choice of d_E and T. In table 13.3 the number of support vectors # SV, the one-step-ahead mean square error in dB $\mathcal{E}(\tau)$, the average number of steps of good predictions $\frac{t(0.25)}{\tau}$, the largest Lyapunov

18. In principle, one needs to calculate d_N SVM, one for each component; however, we prefer to utilize the single one that suffices to recursively calculate the evolution of the system when the last $T_I(d_N-1)+1$ samples are given. This is usually a reasonable choice in the case of large training sets.

exponent[19] λ_1 and the correlation dimension[20] d_C of the reconstructed time series results for the first choice $T = T_I = 4$ and $d_E = 5$ for different training sets of size 400 are reported. In table 13.4 the corresponding results are reported for $T = 1$ and $d_E = 15$. We can notice that it is not possible to correctly reconstruct the dynamics of the system for any training set; this is due to the extreme conditions considered for the experiments. However, the results show clearly that the second choice allows us to obtain better results.

For the last two training sets the chaotic dynamics was not captured for both choices. In table 13.5, the results obtained on these training sets for $T = T_I = 4$ and d_E equal to 6 are reported. In table 13.6, the results on the same training sets are reported for the second choice: $T = 1$ and $d_E = 20$. Once again the second choice corresponding to fixing $T = 1$ gives better results.

We performed other experiments on larger training sets from the same time-series $x_1(k)$ and for smaller values of ε; in table 13.7, the results for the first choice $T = 4$ and $d_E = 5$ are reported and in table 13.8 for the second choice $T_E = 1$ and $d_E = 15$. These experiments confirmed the results obtained on the smaller ones. For the first training set $1 - 10^3$, the evolutions for both the two choices from the same starting point equal to 24201 are shown in the figures 13.5 and 13.6 (the first refers to the case $T = 4$). For the larger training set $1 - 10^4$, the evolutions from the starting point 20099 are shown for both cases in figures 13.7 and 13.8 (the first refers to the case $T = 4$). One can notice that the output of the reconstructed system which corresponds to the choice $T = 1$ is, in both cases, closer to the output of the original system than the output corresponding to the second choice for reconstruction. This shows that the larger number of components in the embedding vector $\boldsymbol{r}(k)$, which follows from the choice $T = 1$, specifies an unknown function (which determines the transition of the pseudo-state vector $\boldsymbol{r}(k)$) with a smoother behavior; this allows a better reconstruction, especially when only noisy measurements are available.

19. The largest Lyapunov exponent were estimated from 30000 samples of time-series obtained by iteration of the reconstructed system from a fixed starting point by the method introduced in (Wolf et al., 1985); the time-delay and the embedding dimension were fixed, respectively, as the first-minimum of the mutual information (Abarbanel, 1996) and by the false-nearest-neighbors method (Kennel et al., 1992).

20. The correlation dimension was estimated from 30000 samples of time-series obtained by iteration of the reconstructed system from a fixed starting point by the method introduced in (Schouten et al., 1994); the time-delay and the embedding dimension were fixed, respectively, as the first-minimum of the mutual information (Abarbanel, 1996) and by the false-nearest-neighbors method (Kennel et al., 1992). The correlation dimension for the considered Lorenz system is equal to 2.04.

13.5 Conclusions

This chapter deals with the problem of applying the Support Vector Machine to the problem of dynamical reconstruction of a chaotic process. The main advantage of this technique with respect to the existing regularized RBF networks consists in the possibility of obtaining a similar reconstruction performance with a reduction in the number of centers utilized to represent the solution for a given number of training examples. Moreover, one can trade off the accuracy of the obtained solution with its computational complexity.

The reconstruction performance degradation due to the presence of noise on the time-series measurements has been investigated in detail; the SVM is largely insensitive to the measurement noise if its power is smaller than $\frac{\varepsilon^2}{2}$ but does not allow one to obtain one-step mean square prediction error smaller, in order of magnitude, than the noise power.

C \ $\frac{\sigma^2}{d_E}$	0.1	0.3	0.75	1	1.3	3
0.01	396, -1.7 constant	391, -3.99 constant	393, -5.96 constant	392, -6.06 constant	392, -5.78 constant	395, -4.59 constant
0.05	301, -9.16 periodic	260, -14.1 periodic	302, -16.0 periodic	305, -16.7 periodic	317, -17.8 periodic	366, -17.5 periodic
0.1	240, -13.7 periodic	219, -18.7 periodic	282, -19.6 periodic	297, -19.7 periodic	291, -20.2 periodic	366, -17.5 periodic
0.5	169, -25.1 6	157, -29.3 periodic	383, -11.2 periodic	165, -30.1 3.8	194, -29.2 periodic	218, -26.8 periodic
1	240, -13.7 5.6	219, -18.7 2.1	282, -19.6 1.2	297, -19.7 1.0	291, -20.2 0.6	318, -21.8 periodic
2	145, -26.4 4.0	126, -32.5 1.8	130, -34.7 1.4	121, -34.8 1.3	121, -34.5 1.3	182, -30.7 periodic
5	139, -26.6 4.0	97, -33.2 1.5	67, -37.6 1.2	111, -36.0 1.4	112, -35.7 1.5	177, -32.5 0.68
10	138, -26.4 4.0	92, -33.7 1.4	93, -36.4 1.4	96, -36.3 periodic	105, -36.6 constant	158, -33.8 0.64

Table 13.1 The number of Support Vectors, the one-step ahead mean square error in dB and the estimate of the largest Lyapunov exponent of the reconstructed system for different values of C and $\frac{\sigma^2}{d_E}$.

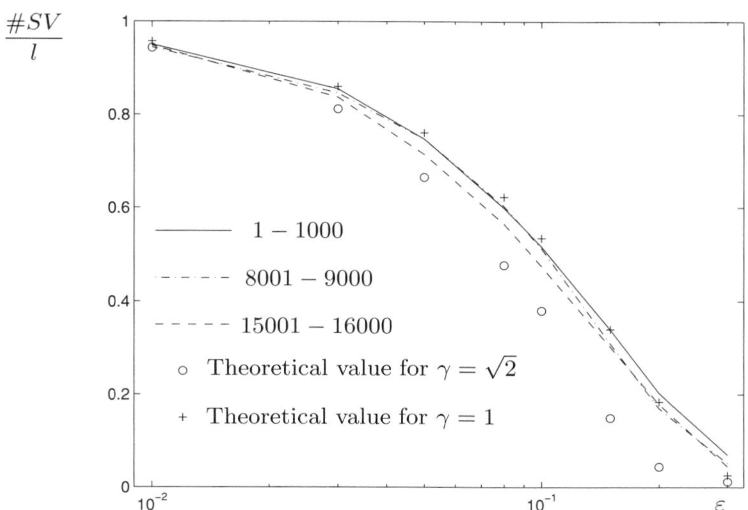

Figure 13.1 The fraction of Support Vectors $\frac{\#SV}{l}$ versus ε for three different training sets of size $l = 1000$ of the time-series contaminated by the purely-stochastic white noise.

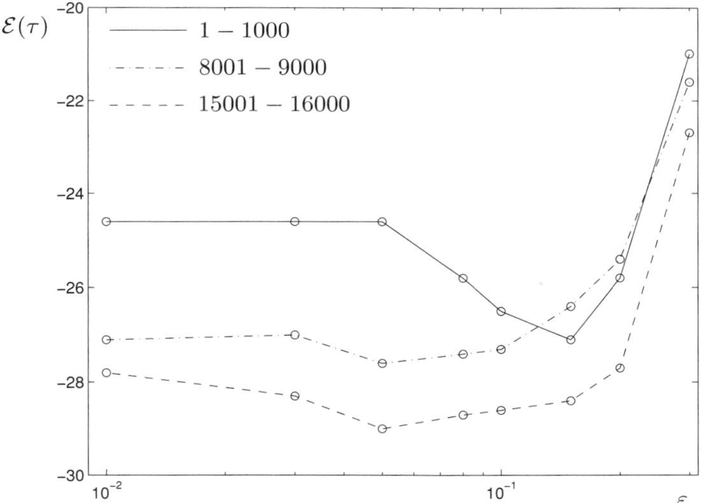

Figure 13.2 The one-step-ahead mean square error in dB $\mathcal{E}(\tau)$ versus ε for three different training sets of size $l = 1000$ of the time-series contaminated by the purely-stochastic white noise.

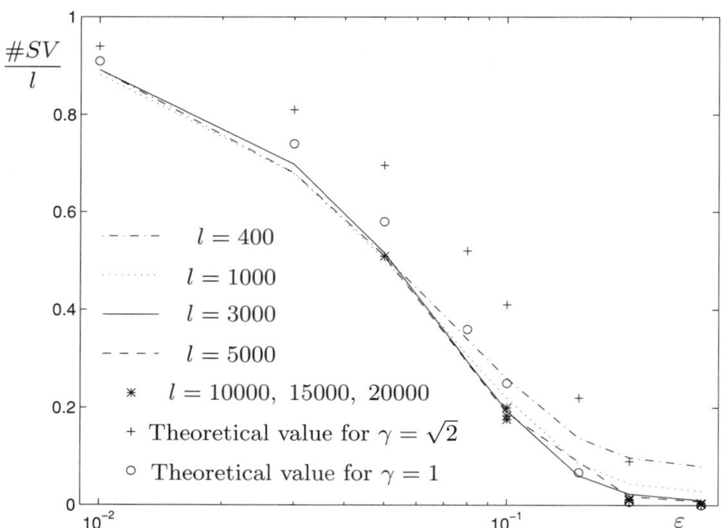

Figure 13.3 The fraction of Support Vectors $\frac{\#SV}{l}$ versus ε for different values of the training set $1 - l$ of the time-series contaminated by 21.5 dB colored noise.

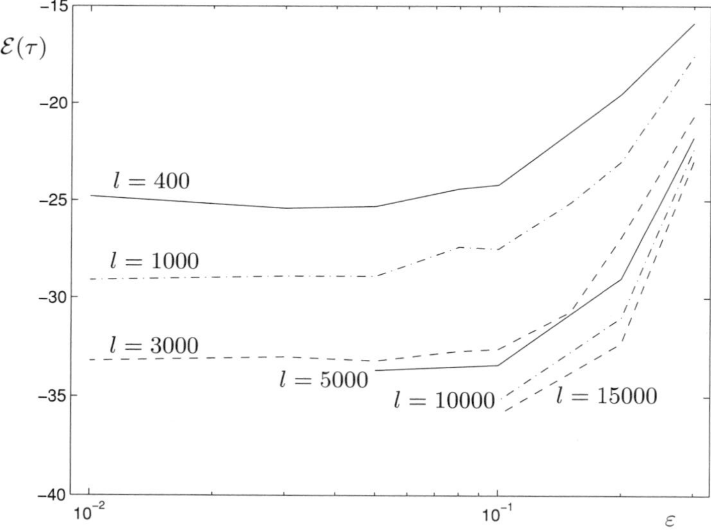

Figure 13.4 The one-step-ahead mean square error in dB $\mathcal{E}(\tau)$ versus ε for different values of the training set $1 - l$ of the time-series contaminated by 21.5 dB colored noise.

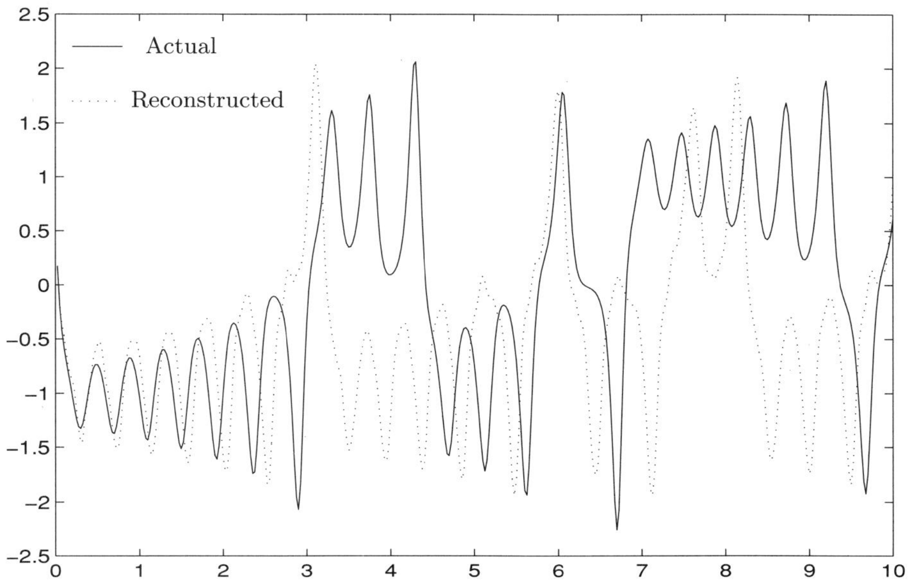

Figure 13.5 The evolution from the starting point 24201 for the choice $T = T_I = 4$ and $d_E = d_N = 5$ and training set $1 - 10^3$.

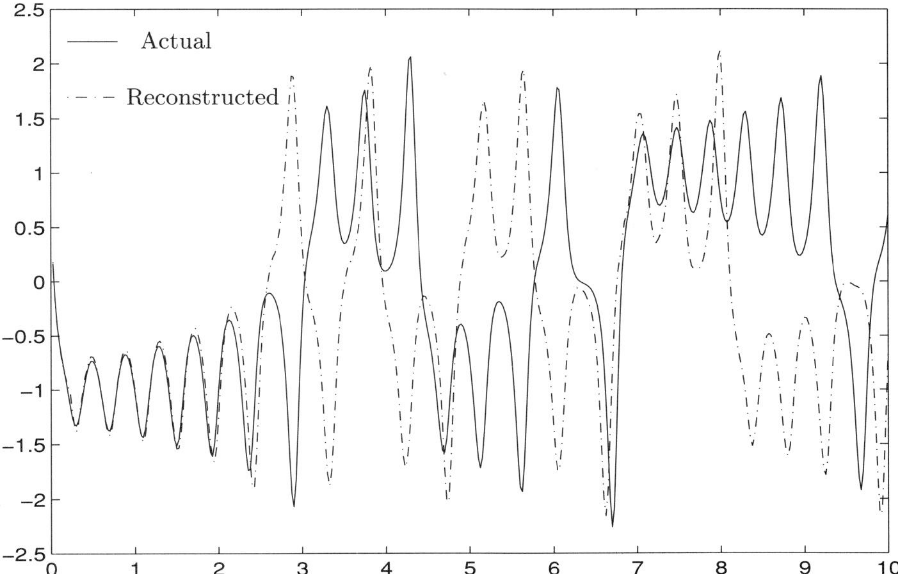

Figure 13.6 The evolution from the starting point 24201 for the choice $T = 1$ and $d_E = 15$ and training set $1 - 10^3$.

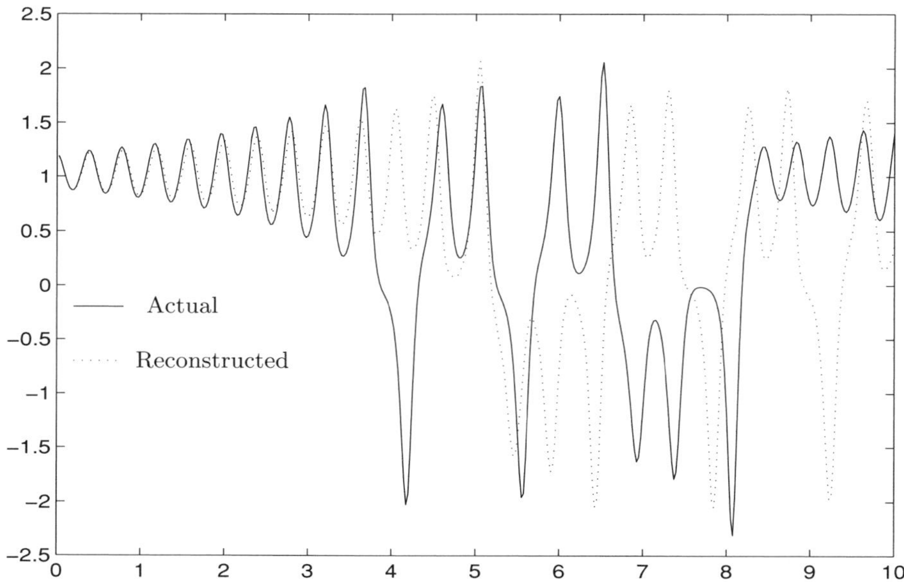

Figure 13.7 The evolution from the starting point 20099 for the choice $T = T_I = 4$ and $d_E = 5$ and training set $1 - 10^4$.

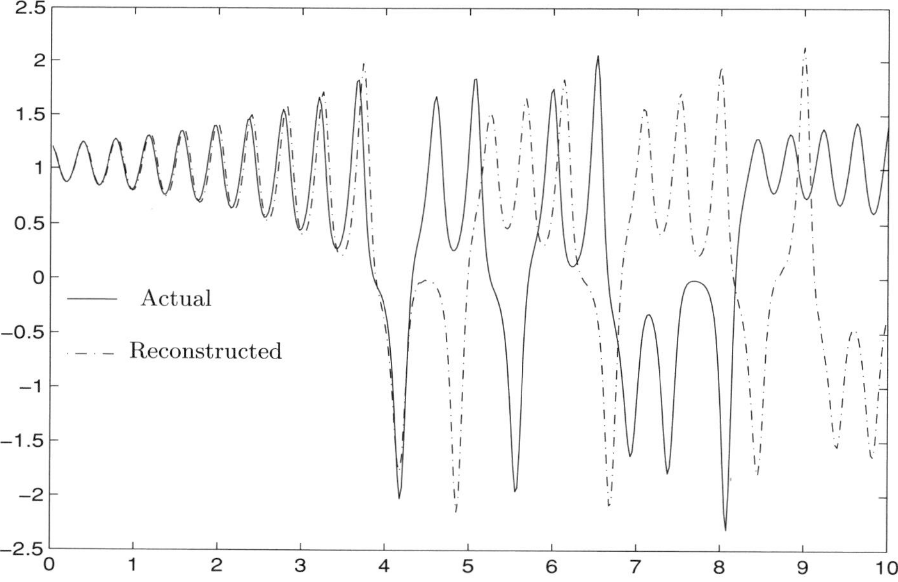

Figure 13.8 The evolution from the starting point 20099 for the choice $T = 1$ and $d_E = 15$ and training set $1 - 10^4$.

ℓ \ ε	0.1		0.05		0.01		0.008	
	SV	$\mathcal{E}(\tau)$	SV	$\mathcal{E}(\tau)$	SV	$\mathcal{E}(\tau)$	SV	$\mathcal{E}(\tau)$
1000	31	-24.4	42	-30.2	185	-38.7	207	-39.3
2000	30	-24.5	47	-30.2	260	-38.7	297	-41.6
3000	36	-24.5	55	-31.2	286	-42.3	337	-43.4
4000	36	-24.5	55	-31.2	314	-42.8	382	-44.0
5000	35	-24.6	57	-31.3	339	-43.2	418	-44.5
6000	35	-24.6	58	-31.3	366	-43.5	456	-44.8
8000	35	-24.5	64	-31.2	436	-43.7	535	-45.2
10000	34	-24.4	70	-31.2	477	-44.1	594	-45.6
20000	34	-24.3	73	-31.1	542	-44.7	772	-46.0

ℓ \ ε	0.005		0.001		0.0008		0.0001	
	SV	$\mathcal{E}(\tau)$	SV	$\mathcal{E}(\tau)$	SV	$\mathcal{E}(\tau)$	SV	$\mathcal{E}(\tau)$
1000	243	-40.0	493	-40.1	534	-40.1	881	-40.0
2000	377	-42.6	946	-42.9	1069	-42.8	1739	-42.7

Table 13.2 The number of Support Vectors $\#SV$ and the one-step ahead mean square error in dB $\mathcal{E}(\tau)$ for different values of ε and of the training set size ℓ.

Training Set	$\mathcal{E}(\tau)$	$\frac{t(0.25)}{\tau}$	λ_1	d_C
1 – 400	−21.2	4.4	CONSTANT	CONSTANT
11001 – 11400	−20.8	3.4	1.2	1.8
15001 – 15400	−24.2	4.7	0.2	1.7
19001 – 19400	−18.7	5.3	0.005	1.0

Table 13.3 The one-step ahead mean-square error $\mathcal{E}(\tau)$ in dB, the effective horizon of prediction $\frac{t(0.25)}{\tau}$, the largest Lyapunov exponent estimate and the correlation dimension of the reconstructed system for the choice $T = T_1 = 4$ and $d_E = d_N = 5$ are reported.

Training Set	$\mathcal{E}(\tau)$	$\frac{t(0.25)}{\tau}$	λ_1	d_C
1 – 400	−24.6	5.4	1.5	1.9
11001 – 11400	−24.5	5.3	1.2	1.9
15001 – 15400	−25.2	5.8	0.03	1.2
19001 – 19400	−26.1	5.4	CONSTANT	CONSTANT

Table 13.4 Results of the same experiments of table 13.3 for the second choice $T = 1$ and $d_E = 15$.

Training Set	$\mathcal{E}(\tau)$	$\frac{t(0.25)}{\tau}$	λ_1	d_C
15001 – 15400	−16.9	3.2	1.1	1.8
19001 – 19400	−19.9	4.4	1.3	1.9

Table 13.5 Results of simulation experiments for $T = T_I = 4$ and $d_E = 6$ on the two training sets for which the learning failed for $d_E = 5$.

Training Set	$\mathcal{E}(\tau)$	$\frac{t(0.25)}{\tau}$	λ_1	d_C
15001 – 15400	−17.9	5.7	1.4	2.0
19001 – 19400	−24.7	5.7	1.3	2.0

Table 13.6 Results of the same experiments of table 13.5 for $T = 1$ and $d_E = 20$.

Training Set	ε	$\mathcal{E}(\tau)$	$\frac{t(0.25)}{\tau}$	λ_1	d_C
15001 – 15400	0.05	-23.0	5.5	1.0	1.7
19001 – 19400	0.2	-28.0	7.7	1.4	2.0

Table 13.7 Results of the simulation experiments on larger training sets for $T = T_I = 4$ and $d_E = 5$.

Training Set	ε	$\mathcal{E}(\tau)$	$\frac{t(0.25)}{\tau}$	λ_1	d_C
15001 – 15400	0.05	-28.6	6.54	1.4	2.0
19001 – 19400	0.2	-32.7	9.5	1.5	2.0

Table 13.8 Results of the same experiments of table 13.7 for $T = 1$ and $d_E = 15$.

14 Using Support Vector Machines for Time Series Prediction

Klaus-Robert Müller, Alexander J. Smola, Gunnar Rätsch, Bernhard Schölkopf, Jens Kohlmorgen
GMD FIRST
Rudower Chaussee 5, 12489 Berlin, Germany.
{klaus,smola,raetsch,bs,jek}@first.gmd.de.
http://candy.first.gmd.de.

Vladimir Vapnik
AT&T Labs Research
100 Schultz Dr., Red Bank, NJ 07701, USA
vlad@research.att.com.
http://www.research.att.com/info/vlad

Support Vector Machines are used for time series prediction and compared to radial basis function networks. We make use of two different loss functions for Support Vectors: training with (i) an ε insensitive loss and (ii) Huber's robust loss function and discuss how to choose the regularization parameters in these models. Two applications are considered: data from (a) a noisy Mackey-Glass system (normal and uniform noise) and (b) the Santa Fe Time Series Competition (set D). In both cases, Support Vector Machines show an excellent performance. In case (b), the Support Vector approach improves the best known result on the benchmark by 29%.

14.1 Introduction

Support Vector Machines have become a subject of intensive study (see e.g. Boser et al. (1992); Vapnik (1995)). They have been applied successfully to classification tasks as OCR (Vapnik, 1995; Schölkopf et al., 1995) and more recently also to regression (Drucker et al., 1997; Vapnik et al., 1997).

In this contribution[1] we use Support Vector Machines in the field of time series prediction and we find that they show an excellent performance.
In the following sections we will give a brief introduction to support vector regression (SVR) and we discuss the use of different types of loss functions. Furthermore, the basic principles of state space reconstruction are introduced in section 14.4. The experimental section considers a comparison of SVR and radial basis function (RBF) networks (introduced in section 14.3) with adaptive centers and variances. Both approaches show similarly excellent performance with an advantage for SVR in the high noise regime for Mackey Glass data. For benchmark data from the Santa Fe Competition (data set D) we get the best result achieved so far, which is 37% better than the winning approach during the competition (Zhang and Hutchinson, 1994) and still 29% better than our previous result (Pawelzik et al., 1996a). A brief discussion concludes the chapter.

14.2 Support Vector Regression

In SVR (section 1.5) the basic idea is to map the data $\mathbf{x}$ into a high-dimensional feature space $\mathcal{F}$ via a nonlinear mapping Φ, and to do linear regression in this space (cf. Boser et al. (1992); Vapnik (1995))

$$f(\mathbf{x}) = (\omega \cdot \Phi(\mathbf{x})) + b \quad \text{with } \Phi : \mathbb{R}^n \to \mathcal{F},\ \omega \in \mathcal{F}, \tag{14.1}$$

where b is a threshold. Thus, *linear* regression in a *high* dimensional (feature) space corresponds to *nonlinear* regression in the *low* dimensional input space $\mathbb{R}^n$. Note that the dot product in (14.1) between $\omega \cdot \Phi(\mathbf{x})$ *would have* to be computed in this high dimensional space (which is usually intractable), if we were not able to use the kernel trick (section 1.3) that eventually leaves us with dot products that can be implicitly expressed in the low dimensional input space $\mathbb{R}^n$. Since Φ is fixed, we determine ω from the data by minimizing the sum of the empirical risk $R_{emp}[f]$ and a complexity term $\|\omega\|^2$, which enforces *flatness* in feature space

$$R_{reg}[f] = R_{emp}[f] + \lambda\|\omega\|^2 = \sum_{i=1}^{l} \mathcal{C}(f(\mathbf{x}_i) - y_i) + \lambda\|\omega\|^2, \tag{14.2}$$

where l denotes the sample size $(\mathbf{x}_1, \ldots, \mathbf{x}_l)$, $\mathcal{C}(.)$ is a loss function and λ is a regularization constant. For a large set of loss functions, (14.2) can be minimized by solving a quadratic programming problem, which is *uniquely* solvable (Smola and Schölkopf, 1998b; Smola et al., 1998c,b). It can be shown that the vector ω can be written in terms of the data points

$$\omega = \sum_{i=1}^{l} (\alpha_i - \alpha_i^*)\Phi(\mathbf{x}_i) \tag{14.3}$$

1. This chapter is an extended version of (Müller et al., 1997).

with α_i, α_i^* being the solution of the aforementioned quadratic programming problem (Vapnik, 1995). α_i, α_i^* have an intuitive interpretation (see Fig. 14.1, bottom) as forces pushing and pulling the estimate $f(\mathbf{x}_i)$ towards the measurements y_i (cf. Burges and Schölkopf (1997)). Taking (14.3) and (14.1) into account, we are able to rewrite the whole problem in terms of dot products in the *low* dimensional input space (a concept introduced by Aizerman et al. (1964))

$$f(\mathbf{x}) = \sum_{i=1}^{l}(\alpha_i - \alpha_i^*)(\Phi(\mathbf{x}_i) \cdot \Phi(\mathbf{x})) + b = \sum_{i=1}^{l}(\alpha_i - \alpha_i^*)k(\mathbf{x}_i, \mathbf{x}) + b. \tag{14.4}$$

In (14.4) we introduced a kernel function $k(\mathbf{x}_i, \mathbf{x}_j) = (\Phi(\mathbf{x}_i) \cdot \Phi(\mathbf{x}_j))$. As explained in section 1.3, any symmetric kernel function k satisfying Mercer's condition corresponds to a dot product in some feature space (see Boser et al. (1992) for details). A common kernel is e.g. a RBF kernel (1.31). For an extensive discussion of kernels, see Smola et al. (1998a).

14.2.1 Vapnik's ε-insensitive Loss Function

For this special loss function the Lagrange multipliers α_i, α_i^* are often sparse, i.e. they result in non-zero values after the optimization (14.2) only if they are on or outside the boundary (see Fig. 14.1, bottom), which means that they fulfill the Karush-Kuhn-Tucker conditions (for more details see Vapnik (1995); Smola and Schölkopf (1998b), and chapter 1). The ε-insensitive loss function is given by

$$\mathcal{C}(f(\mathbf{x}) - y) = \begin{cases} |f(\mathbf{x}) - y| - \varepsilon & \text{for } \ |f(\mathbf{x}) - y| \geq \varepsilon \\ 0 & \text{otherwise} \end{cases} \tag{14.5}$$

(cf. Fig. 14.1, top); the respective quadratic programming problem is defined as

$$\begin{aligned} &\text{minimize} \quad \frac{1}{2}\sum_{i,j=1}^{l}(\alpha_i^* - \alpha_i)(\alpha_j^* - \alpha_j)k(\mathbf{x}_i, \mathbf{x}_j) - \sum_{i=1}^{l}\alpha_i^*(y_i - \varepsilon) - \alpha_i(y_i + \varepsilon) \\ &\text{subject to} \sum_{i=1}^{l}\alpha_i - \alpha_i^* = 0, \quad \alpha_i, \alpha_i^* \in [0, \frac{1}{\lambda}]. \end{aligned} \tag{14.6}$$

Note, that the less noisy the problem, the sparser are the α_i, α_i^* for Vapnik's ε-insensitive loss function. Note, moreover, that the loss from (14.5) introduces a systematic bias, since we tend to underfit if ε is too large, e.g. in the extreme case of very large ε the resulting regression will be a constant.

14.2.2 Huber's Loss Function

Other loss functions like the robust loss function in the sense of Huber (1972) can also be utilized (cf. Fig. 14.1, top) (Smola and Schölkopf, 1998b). This loss function has the advantage of not introducing additional bias (like the ε-insensitive one does), at the expense, however, of sacrificing sparsity in the coefficients α_i, α_i^*.

$$\mathcal{C}(f(\mathbf{x}) - y) = \begin{cases} \varepsilon|f(\mathbf{x}) - y| - \frac{\varepsilon^2}{2} & \text{for } |f(\mathbf{x}) - y| \geq \varepsilon \\ \frac{1}{2}(f(\mathbf{x}) - y)^2 & \text{otherwise} \end{cases} \tag{14.7}$$

The corresponding quadratic programming problem takes the following form

$$\text{minimize } \frac{1}{2}\sum_{i,j=1}^{l}(\alpha_i^* - \alpha_i)(\alpha_j^* - \alpha_j)k(\mathbf{x}_i, \mathbf{x}_j) + \sum_{i=1}^{l}(\alpha_i - \alpha_i^*)y_i + \frac{1}{2\lambda}(\alpha_i^2 + \alpha_i^{*2})$$

$$\text{subject to } \sum_{i=1}^{l}\alpha_i - \alpha_i^* = 0, \quad \alpha_i, \alpha_i^* \in [0, \frac{\varepsilon}{\lambda}]. \tag{14.8}$$

So basically all patterns become support vectors.

14.2.3 How to Compute the Threshold b?

Eqs. (14.6) and (14.8) show how to compute the variables α_k, α_k^*. For the proper choice of b, however, one has to make more direct use of the Karush-Kuhn-Tucker conditions that lead to the quadratic programming problems stated above. The key idea is to pick those values α_k, α_k^* for which the prediction error $\delta_k = f(\mathbf{x}_k) - y_k$ can be determined uniquely. In the ε-insensitive case this means picking points $\mathbf{x}_k$ on the margin, by requiring that one of the corresponding α_k or α_k^* be in the open interval $(0, \frac{1}{\lambda})$. In that case we know the exact value

$$\delta_k = \varepsilon \operatorname{sign}(\alpha_k - \alpha_k^*) \tag{14.9}$$

of the prediction error. Already one $\mathbf{x}_k$ would in principle be sufficient to compute b but for stability purposes it is recommended to take the average over *all points on the margin* with

$$b = \text{average}_k\{\delta_k + y_k - \sum_i(\alpha_i - \alpha_i^*)k(\mathbf{x}_i, \mathbf{x}_k)\}. \tag{14.10}$$

For the Huber case b is computed along the same lines with

$$\delta_k = \lambda(\alpha_k - \alpha_k^*) \tag{14.11}$$

for α_k or $\alpha_k^* \in [0, \frac{\varepsilon}{\lambda})$, i.e. for points where the quadratic part of the loss function is active.

Finally, we note that when we solve the quadratic programming problem with an optimizer which computes the double dual (e.g. Vanderbei (1997)), we can directly recover the value of the primal variable b as the corresponding one of the double dual (Smola et al., 1998c).

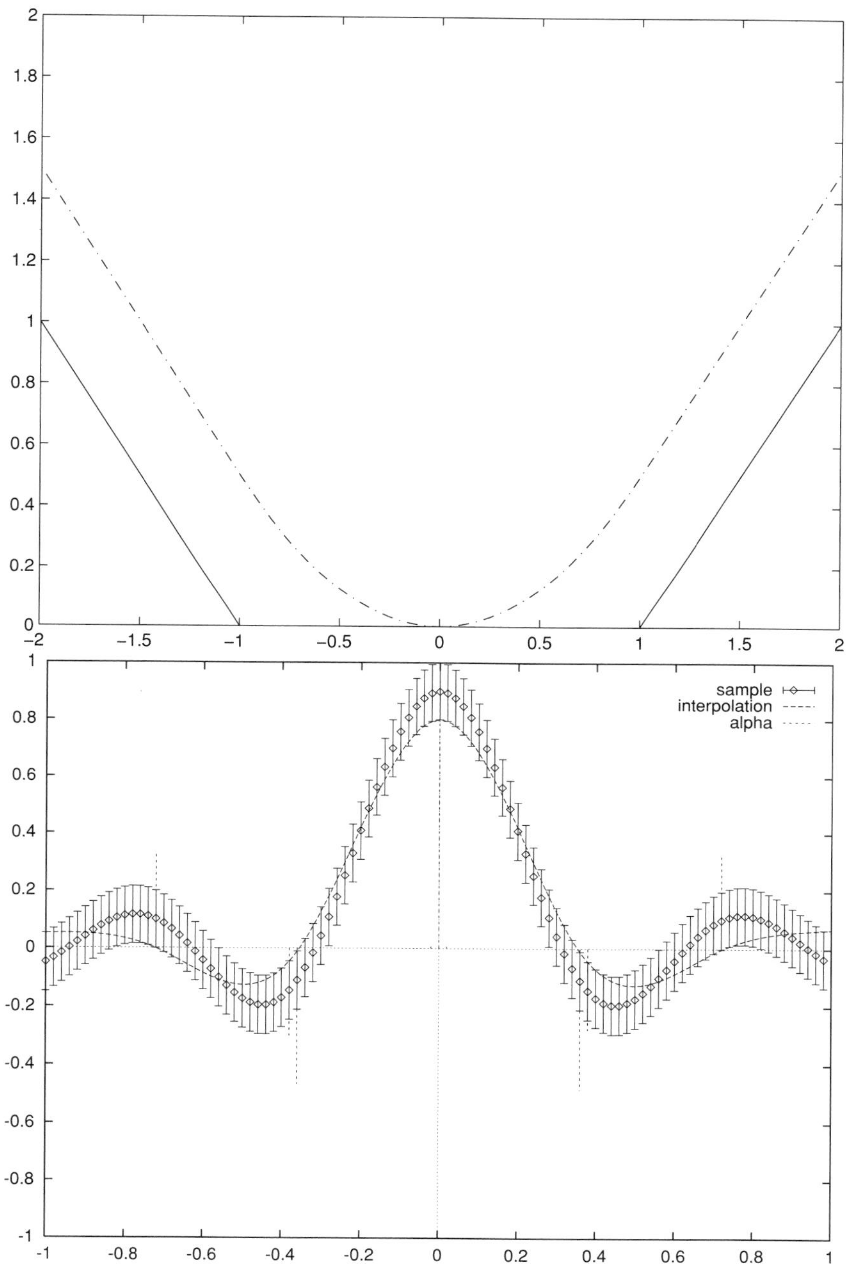

Figure 14.1 *Top:* ε-insensitive and Huber's loss for $\varepsilon = 1$. *Bottom:* The shown regression for the ε-insensitive case (kernel: B-splines (Smola and Schölkopf, 1998b)) of the sinc function is the flattest within the ε tube around the data. α, α^* are drawn as positive and negative forces respectively. All points on the margin, where $f(\mathbf{x}_i) - y_i = \varepsilon \, \text{sign}(\alpha_i - \alpha_i^*)$, are used for the computation of b.

14.3 RBF Networks with Adaptive Centers and Widths

The RBF nets used in the experiments are an extension of the method of Moody and Darken (1989), since centers and variances are also adapted (see also Bishop (1995)). The output of the network is computed as a linear superposition

$$f(\mathbf{x}) = \sum_{k=1}^{K} w_k g_k(\mathbf{x}) , \tag{14.12}$$

where $w_k (k = 1, \ldots, K)$ denotes the weights of the output layer. The Gaussian basis functions g_k are defined as

$$g_k(\mathbf{x}) = \exp\left(-\frac{\|\mathbf{x} - \mu_k\|^2}{2\,\sigma_k^2}\right) , \tag{14.13}$$

where μ_k and σ_k^2 denote means and variances, respectively. In a first step, the means μ_k are initialized with k-means clustering and the variances σ_k are determined as the distance between μ_k and the closest μ_i $(i \neq k)$. Then in the following steps we perform a gradient descent in the regularized error function (weight decay)

$$R_{reg} = \frac{1}{2}\sum_{i=1}^{l}(y_i - f(\mathbf{x}_i))^2 + \frac{\lambda}{2l}\sum_{k=1}^{K}(w_k)^2. \tag{14.14}$$

Note that in analogy to (14.2), we used $\lambda > 0$ to denote the regularization parameter. It is easy to derive the gradients $\partial R_{reg}/\partial\mu_k$ and $\partial R_{reg}/\partial\sigma_k$ (see Appendix). Numerically we minimize (14.14) by a conjugate gradient descent with line search, where we always compute the optimal output weights in every evaluation of the error function during the line search. The optimal output weights $\mathbf{w} = [w_1, \ldots, w_K]^\top$ in matrix notation can be computed in closed form by

$$\mathbf{w} = (G^T G + 2\frac{\lambda}{l}\mathbf{I})^{-1} G^T \mathbf{y}, \quad \text{where} \quad G_{ik} = g_k(\mathbf{x}_i) \tag{14.15}$$

and $\mathbf{y} = [y_1, \ldots, y_l]^\top$ denotes the output vector, and I an identity matrix. For $\lambda = 0$, this corresponds to the calculation of a pseudo-inverse of G.

So, we simultaneously adjust the output weights and the RBF centers and variances (see Appendix for pseudo-code of this algorithm). In this way, the network fine-tunes itself to the data after the initial clustering step, yet, of course, overfitting has to be avoided with careful tuning of the regularization parameter (cf. Bishop (1995)).

14.4 How to Predict?

Let $\{x(t)\}$, $t = 1, \ldots, T$, be a time series that was generated by a dynamical system. For convenience, consider $x(t)$ to be scalar, but note that the treatment of multi-scalar time series is straightforward. We assume that $\{x(t)\}$ is a projection of a dynamics operating in a high-dimensional state space. If the dynamics is deterministic, we can try to predict the time series by reconstructing the state space. A way to reconstruct the state space was introduced by Packard et al. (1980) and mathematically analyzed by Takens (1981). A state vector is defined as

$$\mathbf{x}_t = (x(t),\ x(t-\tau),\ \ldots,\ x(t-(d-1)\tau))\,, \tag{14.16}$$

with time-delay τ and embedding dimension d. If the dynamics runs on an attractor of dimension D, a necessary condition for determining $\mathbf{x}_t$ is

$$d \geq D. \tag{14.17}$$

If the embedding dimension is big enough, such that $\mathbf{x}_t$ unambiguously describes the state of the system at time t, then there exists an equation for points on the attractor, which is of the form

$$x(t+p) = f^*(\mathbf{x}_t). \tag{14.18}$$

In this equation, f^* is a function that allows to predict future values of the time series $\{x(t)\}$ given past values, with p being the prediction horizon. Takens (1981) showed that there is an upper bound

$$d \leq 2D + 1 \tag{14.19}$$

for the embedding dimension d, such that a continuous function f^* can be found within this bound. Regression techniques like SVR or RBF nets can therefore be used to estimate the prediction function on the basis of time-delay coordinates according to (14.16). For stationary dynamical systems the embedding parameters τ and d can be found e.g. by the method of Liebert et al. (1991).

14.5 Experiments

We fix the following experimental setup for our comparison: (a) RBF nets and (b) SVR are trained using a simple cross validation technique. We stop training the RBF networks at the minimum of the one step prediction error measured on a randomly chosen validation set. For SVR the parameters (λ, ε) are also determined at the minimum of the one step prediction error on the same validation set. Other methods, e.g. bootstrap can also be used to assess λ and ε. For SVR we distinguish between a training with Huber loss and ε-insensitive loss. Gaussian kernels with

$$k(\mathbf{x}, \mathbf{y}) = \exp(-\|\mathbf{x} - \mathbf{y}\|^2/(2\sigma^2)) \quad \text{and} \quad \sigma^2 = 0.75 \tag{14.20}$$

are used in the SVR experiments. Note again that the RBF networks employed can adapt their variances σ_k to the data individually. Furthermore, in contrast to SVMs the means μ_k do not need to coincide with data points. As forecasting experiments we consider (i) a toy problem to understand and control the experimental set-up and (ii) a benchmark problem from the Santa Fe Competition (data set D).

14.5.1 Mackey Glass Equation

Our first application is a high-dimensional chaotic system generated by the Mackey-Glass delay differential equation

$$\frac{dx(t)}{dt} = -0.1x(t) + \frac{0.2x(t - t_\Delta)}{1 + x(t - t_\Delta)^{10}}, \tag{14.21}$$

with delay $t_\Delta = 17$. (14.21) was originally introduced as a model of blood cell regulation (Mackey and Glass, 1977) and became quite common as an artificial forecasting benchmark. After integrating (14.21), we added noise to the time series. We obtained training (1000 patterns) and validation (the following 194 patterns) sets using an embedding dimension $d = 6$ and a step size $\tau = 6$. The test set (1000 patterns) is noiseless to measure the true prediction error. We conducted experiments for different signal to noise ratios (SNR) using Gaussian and uniform noise (table 14.1).

We define the SNR in this experiment as the ratio between the variance of the noise and the variance of the Mackey Glass data.

RBF networks and SVR achieve similar results for normal noise. It is to be expected that the method using the proper loss function (squared loss) wins for Gaussian noise, so we would actually expect the RBF nets to perform best followed by SVR trained with Huber loss, which is for large ε close to the squared loss and finally followed by SVR using an ε-insensitive loss. Table 14.1 confirms this intuition partially. For uniform noise, the whole scenario should be reversed, since ε-insensitive loss is the more appropriate noise model (cf. Huber (1972)). This is again confirmed in the experiment. The use of a validation set to assess the proper parameters λ and ε, however, is suboptimal and so the low resolution with which the (λ, ε) space is scanned is partly responsible for table entries that do not match the above intuition.

noise	normal				uniform					
SNR	22.15%		44.3%		6.2%		12.4%		18.6%	
test error	1S	100S	1S	100S	1S	100S	1S	100S	1S	100S
ε-insensitive	0.017	0.218	0.040	0.335	0.006	0.028	0.012	0.070	0.017	0.142
Huber	0.017	0.209	0.040	0.339	0.008	0.041	0.014	0.065	0.019	0.226
RBF	0.018	0.109	0.044	0.266	0.009	0.062	0.014	0.083	0.028	0.282

Table 14.1 1S denotes the 1-step prediction error (RMS) on the test set. 100S is the 100-step iterated autonomous prediction. “SNR” is the ratio between the variance of the respective noise and the underlying time series. E.g. parameter choices for normal noise with SNR 22.15% is $\varepsilon = 0.01$ and $\lambda = 0.56$ for ε-insensitive loss and $\varepsilon = 0.1334$ and $\lambda = 0.0562$ for Huber loss. The respective RBF network uses 30 centers and $\lambda = 0.1$ choosen according to the validation set.

14.5.2 Data Set D from the Santa Fe Competition

Data set D from the Santa Fe competition is artificial data generated from a nine-dimensional periodically driven dissipative dynamical system with an asymmetrical four-well potential and a slight drift on the parameters (Weigend and N. A. Gershenfeld (Eds.), 1994). The system has the property of operating in one well for some time and then switching to another well with a different dynamical behavior. Therefore, we first segment the time series into regimes of approximately stationary dynamics. This is accomplished by applying the *Annealed Competition of Experts* (ACE) method described in (Pawelzik et al., 1996a; Müller et al., 1995) (no assumption about the number of stationary subsystems was made). Moreover, in order to reduce the effect of the continuous drift, only the last 2000 data points of the training set are used for segmentation. After applying the ACE algorithm, the data points are individually assigned to classes of different dynamical modes. We then select the particular class of data that includes the data points at the end of Data Set D as the training set for the RBF networks and the SVR.[2] This allows us to train the RBF networks and the SVR on quasi-stationary data and we avoid having to predict the average over all dynamical modes hidden in the full training set (see also Pawelzik et al. (1996a) for further discussion). However, at the same time we are left with a rather small training set requiring careful regularization, since there are only 327 patterns in the extracted training set. As in the previous section, we use a validation set (50 patterns of the extracted quasi-stationary data) to determine the stopping point and (λ, ε) respectively. The embedding parameters used, $d = 20$ and $\tau = 1$, are the same for all the methods compared in table 14.2.

experiment	ε-ins.	Huber	RBF	ZH	PKM
full set	0.0639	0.0653	0.0677	0.0665	–
segmented set	0.0418	0.0425	0.0569	–	0.0596

Table 14.2 Comparison (under competition conditions) of 25 step iterated predictions (root mean squared errors) on Santa Fe Data set D (*ZH*: Zhang and Hutchinson (1994), *PKM*: (Pawelzik et al., 1996a)). "–" denotes: no prediction available. "Full set" means, that the full training set of set D was used, whereas "segmented set" means that a prior segmentation according to Müller et al. (1995); Pawelzik et al. (1996a) was done as preprocessing.

Table 14.2 shows that our 25 step iterated prediction of the SVR is 37% better than the one achieved by Zhang and Hutchinson (1994), who used a specialized

2. Hereby we assume that the class of data that generated the last points in the training set is the one that is also responsible for the first couple of steps of the iterated continuation that we aim to predict.

network architecture. It is still 29% better than our previous result (Pawelzik et al., 1996a) that used the same ACE preprocessing as above and simple RBF nets (however at that time with non-adaptive centers and variances). As expected, the results are inferior, if we train on the full, non-stationary training set without prior segmentation. However, ε-insensitive SVR is still better than the previous results on the full set.

14.6 Discussion and Outlook

The chapter showed the performance of SVR in comparison to tuned RBF networks. For data from the Mackey-Glass equation we observed that also for SVR it pays to choose the *proper* loss function for the respective noise model (cf. Smola and Schölkopf (1998b); Smola et al. (1998c)). In both SVR cases training consisted in solving a — uniquely solvable — *quadratic optimization* problem, unlike the RBF network training, which requires non-linear optimization with the danger of getting stuck in local minima. Note that a stable prediction is a difficult problem since the noise level applied to the chaotic dynamics was rather high. For the data set D benchmark we obtained excellent results for SVR — 37% above the best result achieved during the Santa Fe competition (Zhang and Hutchinson, 1994). Clearly, this remarkable difference is mostly due to the segmentation used as preprocessing step to get stationary data (Müller et al., 1995; Pawelzik et al., 1996a), nevertheless still 29% improvement remain compared to a previous result using the same preprocessing step (Pawelzik et al., 1996a). This underlines that we need to consider non-stationarities in the time series *before* the actual prediction, for which we can then use SVR or RBF nets (see also Müller et al. (1995); Pawelzik et al. (1996a,b); Kohlmorgen et al. (1998) for discussion).

Our experiments show that SVR methods work particularly well if the data is *sparse* (i.e. we have little data in a high-dimensional space). This is due to their good inherent regularization properties.

Inspecting the RBF network approach more closely, we can see that a variety of individual variances σ_k appear as a result of the learning process. Clearly, in this sense RBF nets are the more flexible model, since multi-scaling information is extracted and taken into account. Of course the higher flexibility must be counter-balanced with a careful regularization. It now appears tempting to keep the principled regularization approach of SVR and to also allow for multiple variance SV kernels in Support Vector machine training. This way we would not to be obliged to determine a single scale to look at the data before learning.[3]

Other things that remain are: determining the proper parameters λ and ε. This is still suboptimal and computationally intensive (if not clumsy). Both, some improved

3. The ability of processing multiscaling information could also be the reason to the often more stable 100 step prediction of RBF nets that was observed in the experiments.

theoretical bounds and/or a simple heuristics to choose them would enhance the usability of SVR, since (λ, ε) are powerful means for *regularization* and *adaptation to the noise in the data.* Bootstrap methods or methods using a validation set are only a first step.

Acknowledgements

Alex J. Smola and Gunnar Rätsch are supported by DFG (# Ja 379/51). We thank Chris Burges for valuable discussions. Moreover, we gratefully acknowledge travel grants from DAAD and NSF.

Appendix

Taking the derivative of (14.14) wrt. to RBF means μ_q and variances σ_q yields

$$\frac{\partial R_{reg}}{\partial \mu_q} = \sum_{i=1}^{l} (f(\mathbf{x}_i) - y_i) \frac{\partial}{\partial \mu_q} f(\mathbf{x}_i), \text{ with } \frac{\partial}{\partial \mu_q} f(\mathbf{x}_i) = w_q \frac{x_i - \mu_q}{(\sigma_q)^2} g_q(\mathbf{x}_i) \tag{14.22}$$

$$\frac{\partial R_{reg}}{\partial \sigma_q} = \sum_{i=1}^{l} (f(\mathbf{x}_i) - y_i) \frac{\partial}{\partial \sigma_q} f(\mathbf{x}_i), \text{ with } \frac{\partial}{\partial \sigma_q} f(\mathbf{x}_i) = w_q \frac{\|\mu_q - \mathbf{x}_i\|^2}{(\sigma_q)^3} g_q(\mathbf{x}_i). \tag{14.23}$$

These two derivatives are employed in the following algorithm (in pseudo-code):

Input:

Sequence of labeled training patterns $\mathbf{Z} = \langle(\mathbf{x}^1, y^1), \cdots, (\mathbf{x}^l, y^l)\rangle$

Number of RBF centers K

Regularization constant λ

Number of iterations T

Initialize:

Run K-means clustering to find initial values for μ_k and determine σ_k (k=1,...,K) as the distance between μ_k and the closest μ_i $(i \neq k)$.

Do for $t = 1 : T$,

1. Compute optimal output weights $\mathbf{w} = \left(G^\top G + \frac{\lambda}{l} I\right)^{-1} G\mathbf{y}^\top$

2a. Compute gradients $\frac{\partial}{\partial \mu_k} R_{reg}$ and $\frac{\partial}{\partial \sigma_k} R_{reg}$ as in (14.23) and (14.22) with optimal $\mathbf{w}$ and form a gradient vector $\mathbf{v}$

2b. Estimate the conjugate direction $\overline{\mathbf{v}}$ with Fletcher-Reeves-Polak-Ribiere CG-Method (Press et al., 1992)

3a. Perform a line search to find the minimizing step size δ in direction $\overline{\mathbf{v}}$; in each evaluation of R_{reg} compute the optimal output weights $\mathbf{w}$ as in line 1

3b. update μ_k and σ_k with $\overline{\mathbf{v}}$ and δ

Output: Optimized RBF net

15 Pairwise Classification and Support Vector Machines

Ulrich H.-G. Kreßel
Daimler-Benz AG, Research and Technology
P.O. Box 2360, 89013 Ulm, Germany
Kressel@DBAG.Ulm.DaimlerBenz.Com

The extension from the binary two-class problem to K classes is an important question for the support vector machine approach. We investigate *pairwise classification* as an alternative to the often used approach 'one class versus all others'. The idea of pairwise classification fits perfectly to the borderline based adaption of the support vector machine. We explain the differences between the both approaches using two-dimensional examples. The advantages of the pairwise classification are quantified for benchmarks based on handwritten digit recognition, showing in many cases not only an improved error rate for the learning and the test set, but also faster adaption and classification times.

15.1 Introduction

Optimal Borderlines

In the area of pattern classification the support vector machine has opened up a new direction of research and applications, as it is based on the *minimization of the number of classification errors* by placing optimal borderlines between classes. This compares well to the least-mean-squares approximation of a posteriori probabilities (Kreßel and Schürmann, 1997; Schürmann, 1996), where the borderlines are defined only as a byproduct, as it is done by most neural networks. Starting from the theoretically convincing idea of the *optimal margin classifier* (Vapnik, 1979), which however needs linearly separable classes, mainly the extensions to *nonlinear kernel functions* (Boser et al., 1992) and to *soft margins with slack variables* (Cortes and Vapnik, 1995) lead to the very successful employment of support vector machines for practical classification tasks.

One problem left (see also chapter 19 in this book) for the support vector machine approach is, however, the extension from the binary two-class problem to classification tasks with K classes. Besides the standard approach to the *K-class problem* by a winner-takes-all like scheme, which is discussed thoroughly in the next section, we investigate *pairwise classification* (Bernhardt, 1983; Friedman, 1996; Schmidt and Gish, 1996) in the third section. The basic idea of pairwise classification is to use $K*(K-1)/2$ classifiers covering all pairs of classes instead of using only K binary classifiers 'one class versus all others'. As we will see, pairwise classification fits perfectly to the characteristics of support vector machines, where the borderlines between two classes are computed directly. Two-dimensional problems are included throughout the discussions, while the real world problem of handwritten digit recognition is used for benchmarking in an extra section.

K-Class Problem

15.2 K-Class Problem

Definition

In the standard approach the two-class decision function of equation 1.1 is extended to K classes by constructing binary decision functions for all classes k as follows:

$$f_k : \mathbb{R}^N \to \{\pm 1\} \quad \begin{cases} +1 & \text{for all samples in class } k, \\ -1 & \text{else.} \end{cases} \tag{15.1}$$

Three Class Example

For a two-dimensional problem with three classes $(+, *, \times)$ the resulting three borderlines of linear support vector machines are drawn at the left hand side in figure 15.1. Each of the three lines separates one class from the both others with only a few errors. Adapting of the support vector machine is done without problems.

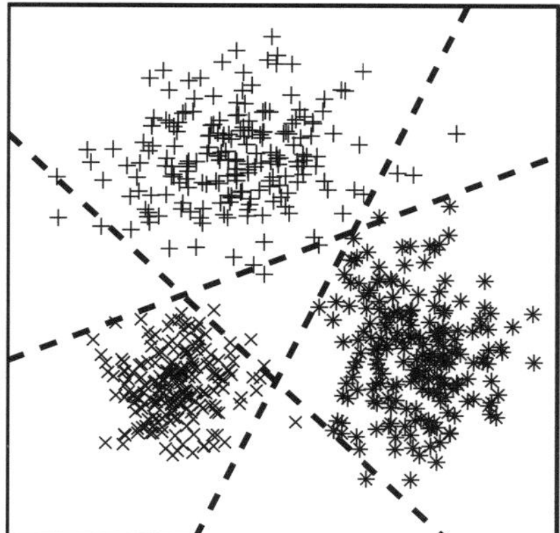

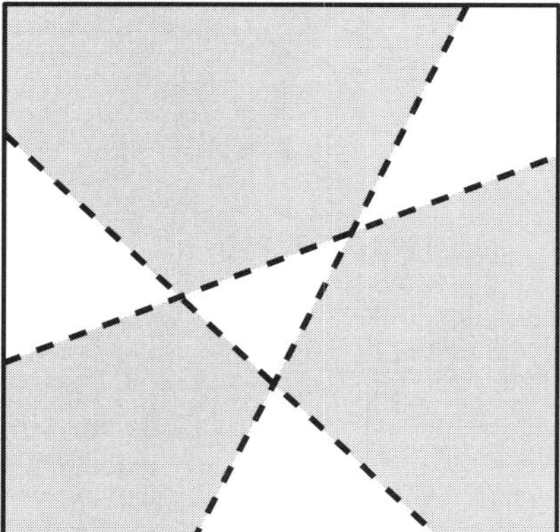

Figure 15.1 Three class example: the resulting three linear borderlines 'one class versus all' are drawn at the left hand side; the right hand side shows, that only for the shaded regions unambiguous decisions are obtained, whereas for the remaining regions either none or two classifiers are active at the same time.

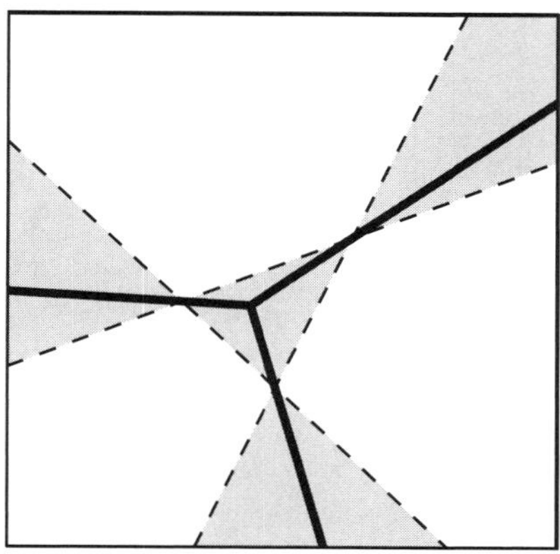
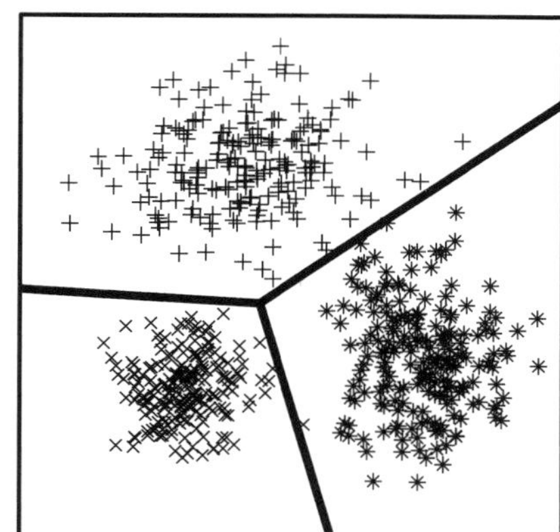

Figure 15.2 Tie breaking by 'winner-takes-all' for the three class example (left hand side) and resulting borderlines together with the learning set samples (right hand side).

Applying, however, the combined support vector machine to new samples, we notice that only in the shaded regions of figure 15.1 (right hand side) exactly one decision function according to equation 15.1 is +1. In the middle of the picture all three decision function respond with −1, hinting that this region belongs to none of the classes. Similar problems arise for the three outer 'triangles', where in each case two decision functions are +1 simultaneously.

Tie Breaking

One usual way to break these tie situations is to neglect the signum operation in the decision functions (see equation 1.18) and to use the real input values to the signum operation instead. Thus, the classification result can be viewed as a discriminant vector $\in \mathbb{R}^K$, where the index of the largest component is chosen as class decision. This approach is called *winner-takes-all*. The according tie breaking is depicted in figure 15.2 at the left hand side and together with the samples of the learning set on the right hand side. While the resulting borderlines are impressively good (only one error remains), we notice that the final borders have only three points in common with the preliminary decision functions calculated by the three support vector machines.

Second Example

Based on the experience gained so far, we can construct another three class example, showing the disadvantages of the standard approach more clearly. In figure 15.3 three classes are approximately aligned along one line. Again the three borderlines are calculated by independently adapting linear support vector machines. Whereas the borderlines for the classes '×' and '+' are adapted easily, it is not possible to linearly separate the class '∗' from the both others. The depicted borderline is the best compromise found by the support vector approach. (This compromise highlights another problem of the approach 'one class versus all others': since very often as in the example all classes have about the same number of samples, the borderline is dominated from the samples of all the other classes rather than by the samples of the class itself. However, this problem (Schmidt and Gish, 1996)

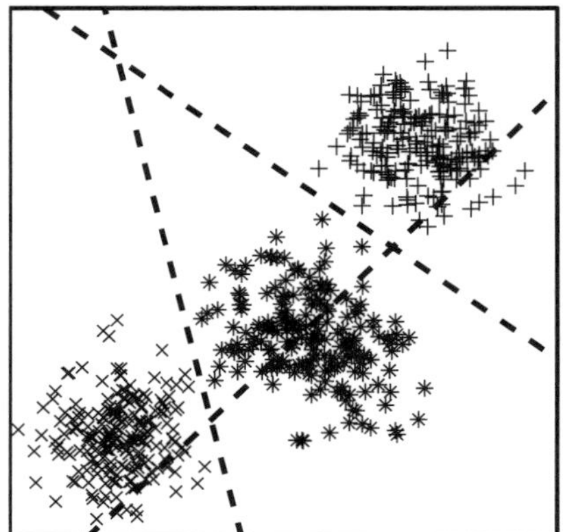
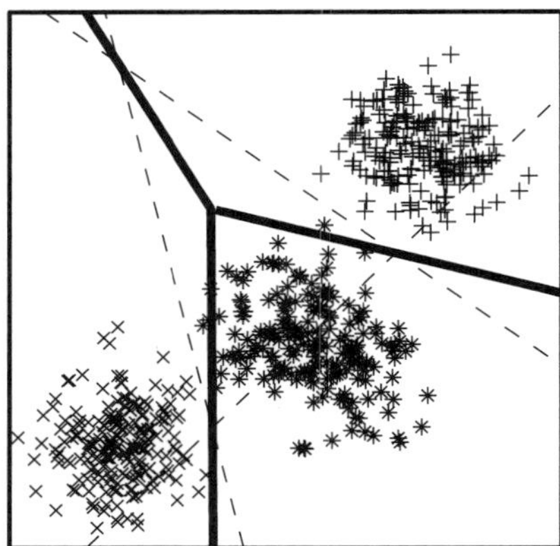

Figure 15.3 Three class example where the classes are approximately aligned along one line: the preliminary three borderlines are drawn at the left hand side and the resulting winner-takes-all borderlines can be seen at the right hand side.

can be tackled by using two different cost values C: one for the addressed class and the second for all remaining classes.)

In figure 15.3 at the right hand side the resulting borderlines after tie breaking are drawn. Even if the number of errors is reduced a lot by the tie breaking, it depicts a rather disappointing situation. Although two 'right' borders have been already found by the support vector machine this good starting point is destroyed by the 'bad' third decision function. (One advantage of the support vector machine compared to the least-mean-squares approach here is that only samples close to the border define the decision boundary; e.g. the boundary between '$\times$' and '$*$' is not influenced by the samples of the class '$+$' and vice versa.)

Both examples of figure 15.2 and 15.3 show, that the heuristic winner-takes-all improves the hard decisions of the single classifiers, but does not yield optimal multicategory decision boundaries, which could be obtained by a simultaneous optimization of all three borders (compare chapter 19 in this book and Weston and Watkins (1998)). Since, however, such a direct approach seems to be computationally rather demanding, we shall in the next section investigate pairwise classification as an intuitive alternative, which fits perfectly to the known characteristics of the support vector machine.

15.3 Pairwise Classification

Definition

For the pairwise classification a decision function f_{kl} is defined for each pair kl of classes. Since the pairwise approach is symmetric, $f_{kl} = -f_{lk}$ follows. For the ease of notation, we further define $f_{kk} = 0$.

$$f_{kl} : \mathbb{R}^N \to \{\pm 1\} \quad \begin{cases} +1 & \text{for all samples in class } k, \\ -1 & \text{for all samples in class } l. \end{cases} \tag{15.2}$$

As known e.g. from the handshakes-at-a-party problem, there exist $\binom{K}{2} = K * (K-1)/2$ different pairwise decision functions. Using the hard decisions given by the signum function, the class decision can be calculated by summing up the according pairwise decision functions: $f_k = \sum_l f_{kl}$. As before, the class decision is given by $\max_k f_k$. If there are no ties — we will discuss tie situations later — the following condition holds: $\max_k f_k = (K-1)$. This equation can be interpreted, that the winner class gets exactly $K-1$ positive votes.

Three Class Example

In figure 15.4 the same example as in figure 15.1 is shown, but this time the decision functions for the pairwise approach are shown at the left hand side. We notice, that all three pairs of classes — for $K = 3$ the number of classes is the same as the number of pairs, for $K > 3$ the number of pairs is larger than the number of classes — are linearly separable. The summing up of the pairwise votes leads easily to the borderlines depicted at the right hand side, which are better compared with figure 15.2. Also all final borderlines are parts of the calculated pairwise decision functions, which was not the case for the standard approach 'one class versus all others'.

Tie Breaking

For the small shaded region in the middle — where '+' wins against '×', and '×' wins against '∗', and '∗' wins against '+' — we need again the real input to the signum function for tie breaking. In this case we have 3 classes with $(K-2) = 1$ positive votes each. For problems with more classes, e.g. for digit recognition with 10 classes, we seldom noticed tie situations with top scores of $(K-2) = 8$ or very seldom even only with $(K-3) = 7$ positive votes. The figure 15.4 gives already

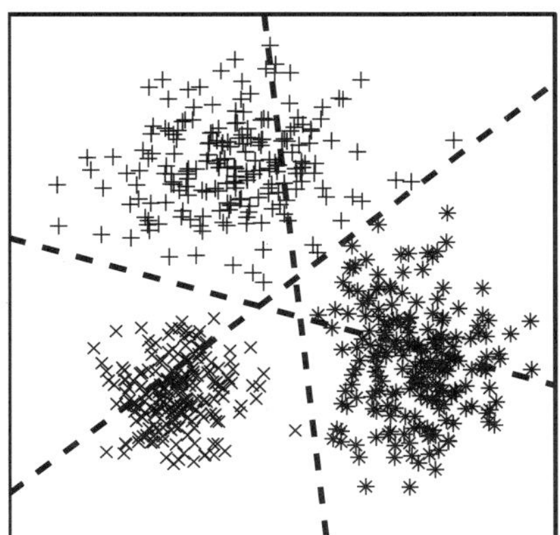

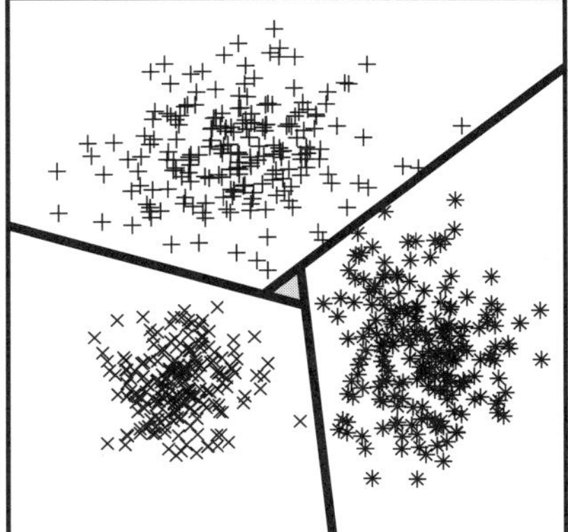

Figure 15.4 Three class example: the three linear decision functions between the pairs are drawn at the left hand side; the resulting borderlines are shown at the right hand side; without tie breaking rules the small shaded region in the middle remains undecided.

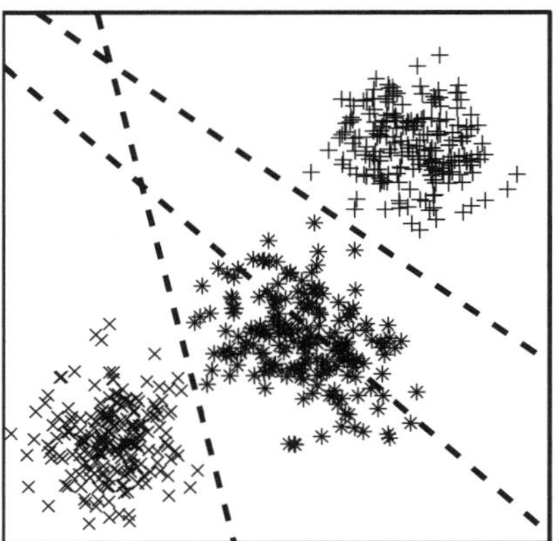

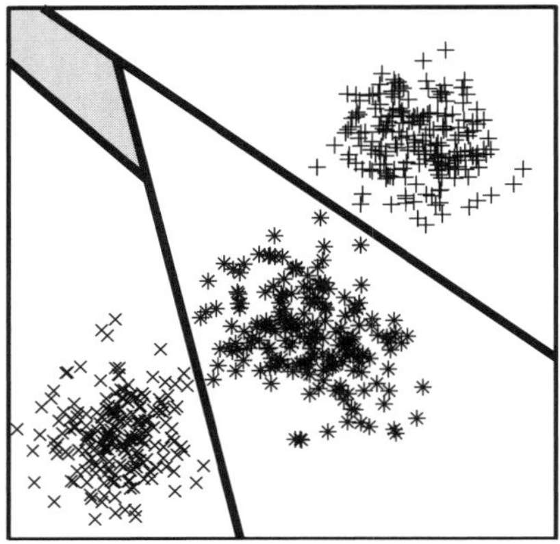

Figure 15.5 Three class example where the classes are approximately aligned along one line (compare figure 15.3): the three linear decision functions between the pairs are drawn at the left hand side; the resulting borderlines are shown at the right hand side; without tie breaking rules the shaded region in the upper left corner remains undecided.

some hints, how tie situations (with top scores less than $K-1$) should be resolved. Each point in the tie region is assigned to the 'closest' class, using the real input to the signum function as distance measure. For the example above we have for each class one positive and one negative vote. The class label in the tie region is assigned according to the (absolute) smallest negative vote. Applying this rule, the shaded area in figure 15.4 is divided by star like borderlines into three regions similar as the middle region in figure 15.2. It should be mentioned, that compared to the standard approach the tie breaking plays only a minor role for the pairwise classification. Probably the best choice is to treat tie regions as rejects.

Second Example

In figure 15.5 the pairwise classifier is applied to the same situation as in figure 15.3. Two borderlines ('$*$' against '$\times$' and '$*$' against '$+$') are identical to the standard support vector machine approach — this would not hold, if least-mean-squares approximation is used — whereas the third decision function ('$\times$' against '$+$') is easy to compute, but not really needed for the final decision. The resulting borderlines are drawn in figure 15.5 at the right hand side and are again parts of the original pairwise decision functions. All three classes are perfectly separated (compare figure 15.3). A tie breaking for the shaded region is possible as described above, but has here no relevance for the class decisions.

Comparison

We can summarize, that compared to the standard approach for the given examples the pairwise classification produces better decision boundaries, which are also intuitively easier to understand. Although the number of decisions functions to compute increases by a factor of $(K-1)/2$, the single decisions functions are faster to adapt (fewer samples and usually fewer overlapping samples) and even sometimes faster to apply, since the number of support vectors for the single decision functions is usually smaller. Often even linear decision functions, as used in the two-dimensional examples, are sufficient to separate the class pairs. The tie breaking, which is heavily relied on in the standard approach (and which does a rather impressive job), plays a minor role for the pairwise classification — most final borderlines are parts of the original decision functions. Therefore, it is easily possible, to use different support vector approaches (different kernel functions or different degrees of the polynomial kernel) for the different class pairs, depending on the difficulty to separate the according pair of classes.

Further Ideas

There are also simple heuristics not to compute the decision functions for all pairs in any case. It is for example possible, to start with a randomly chosen pair of classes and to proceed only with such pairs, where one class has been the winner in the former round. As soon as one class gets $K-1$ positive votes, the process can be stopped. For the ten digits benchmark, on the first view the expense for pairwise classification is larger by a factor of $(K-1)/2 = 4.5$ (not taking into account the simpler decision functions), but can be reduced in the mean to a factor of about 1.5 using the above heuristic. We further made experiments with splitting one class into two or more, if a class had distinguishable appearances, such as the zero written as '0' or as '∅', in order to have the decision boundaries as clear as possible. Numerical results for known benchmarks follow in the next section.

15.4 Benchmarks

Handwritten Digit Classification

For comparison of the proposed algorithms we have chosen two benchmarks from the area of handwritten digit recognition, since we have a long experience in this field. The first set is used in our group since quite a long time (Kreßel, 1991), whereas the second was extracted from the original NIST-competition (Wilkinson et al., 1992; Bottou et al., 1994) and is recently cited more often. Since the first benchmark contains 'only' 10000 samples in the learning set, compared to 60000 samples in the modified NIST learning set, it is faster to conduct many different experiments. Taking into account the powerful classification methods, which are now available, however, the results for the smaller set are not always significantly different.

First Benchmark

Our own benchmark consists of 10000 samples for the learning set and another 10000 samples for the test set. Each digit occurs exactly 1000 times in each set. The samples are preselected from larger sets, such that there is only one basic writing style for each class (e.g. all zeros are written as '∅' and all sevens are written as '7'). The digits are normalized in size to a 16×16 matrix and each gray-valued pixel is coded by a byte representing numbers between 0 and 255. Some samples are given in figure 15.6 as support vectors together with class specific mean vectors and other relevant vectors.

Linear Approach

First we adapt standard and pairwise linear support vector machines as described in the theoretical sections. The only parameter we modify is the cost value C for the slack variables (see equation 1.37). For comparison we also include the results for a least-mean-squares (LMS) approximation of the a posteriori probabilities by

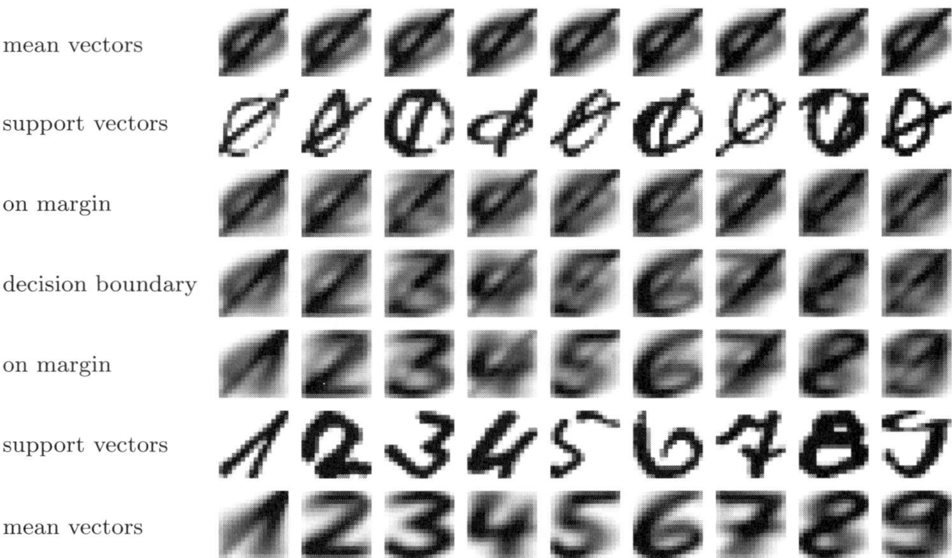

Figure 15.6 Pairwise linear classification of 'zero' against all the other classes. In each column at the top respectively at the bottom the mean vector of the according class is drawn followed by an arbitrary support vector. The center row shows vectors, which lie exactly on the decision boundary between the two classes and on the connecting line between the mean vectors. The remaining two rows are vectors, which lie on the according margin hyperplanes and the connecting line, as described above.

linear functions. The support vector approach (SVM) outperforms the least-mean-squares approximation, however, it is always advantageous to allow some errors on the learning set in order to get a better performance for the test set. It should be mentioned, that using large cost values C for the pairwise classification all class pairs of the learning set are linearly separable, and for the standard approach each of the classes 1, 2, 4, 5, 6, and 7 is linearly separable from all other classes. These facts we did not know before using the support vector approach. The adaption time for the standard support vector approach is about 5 cpu hours, whereas the pairwise adaption needs only about 1 cpu hour in total for all class pairs (on an ALPHA-8200 model 5/300 using MatLab for data handling and linear algebra routines and MINOS 5.4 as the quadratic programming problem solver). One advantage of the linear approach is, that the separating hyperplane can be precomputed out of the support vectors. Therefore, only $(256+1) \times 10 = 2570$ parameters/operations are necessary for the standard approach and $257 \times 45 = 11565$ for the pairwise classification.

Nonlinear Approach

Since our digit benchmark is already pairwise linearly separable, there is on the first view no reason to apply nonlinear support vector machines. However,

adaption	structure	parameter	error rate learning set	error rate test set
LMS	linear		8.61 %	9.98 %
LMS	pairwise linear		1.72 %	3.67 %
SVM	linear	C=100	1.51 %	7.23 %
SVM	linear	C= 10	1.87 %	6.07 %
SVM	linear	C= 1	2.36 %	5.07 %
SVM	linear	C= 0.1	3.40 %	4.66 %
SVM	linear	C= 0.01	4.88 %	5.61 %
SVM	pairwise linear	C= 10	0.00 %	3.30 %
SVM	pairwise linear	C= 1	0.01 %	3.27 %
SVM	pairwise linear	C= 0.1	0.97 %	2.72 %
SVM	pairwise linear	C= 0.01	2.33 %	3.33 %
SVM	quadratic	C= 1	0.00 %	1.51 %
SVM	pairwise quadratic	C= 1	0.00 %	1.71 %
SVM	cubic	C= 1	0.00 %	1.58 %
SVM	pairwise cubic	C= 1	0.00 %	1.97 %
PCA & LMS	quadratic	PCA=40	0.58 %	1.52 %
PCA & LMS	pairwise quadratic	PCA=40	0.00 %	1.20 %
PCA & SVM	quadratic	PCA=40, C=1	0.00 %	1.50 %
PCA & SVM	cubic	PCA=40, C=1	0.00 %	1.20 %
PCA & SVM	degree=4	PCA=40, C=1	0.00 %	1.16 %
PCA & SVM	degree=5	PCA=40, C=1	0.00 %	1.26 %
PCA & SVM	pairwise quadratic	PCA=40, C=1	0.00 %	1.21 %
PCA & SVM	pairwise cubic	PCA=40, C=1	0.00 %	**1.09** %
PCA & SVM	pairwise degree=4	PCA=40, C=1	0.00 %	1.49 %
PCA & SVM	pairwise degree=5	PCA=40, C=1	0.00 %	1.74 %

Table 15.1 Comparison of recognition results for our digit benchmark with 10000 samples for learning and test set each; for further explanations see text.

it is known, that for the digit recognition the cooccurrence of pixels (mainly of pixels which are close by) plays an important role (Kreßel, 1997; Bottou et al., 1994). Therefore, we also adapt a standard and a pairwise quadratic support vector machine. Table 15.1 shows that both methods separate the learning set without errors. The performance on the test set is for both approaches better than for the linear case, confirming the hypothesis of helpful correlations between pixel pairs. On the other hand, however, we notice probably over-adaption for the pairwise classification. Adapting a cubic support vector machine confirms this problem. For the quadratic and the cubic support vector machine it should be mentioned, that the adaption time for the pairwise approach is about half of the time for the standard approach (about 3 versus 6 cpu hours) and also that the total number of different support vectors is less for the pairwise classification (2155 versus 2720 for the quadratic support vector machine and 2038 versus 2827 for the cubic approach). We can reduce the negative effect of overadaption by some kind of regularization (modifying the cost value C did here not improve the generalization performance), such as the principal component analysis (PCA) (Schürmann, 1996). The feature dimension is reduced from $16 \times 16 = 256$ to 40 principal components retaining 84.1 percent of the reconstruction capability, which are then used as input to different nonlinear classifiers. For this size of input it is possible to adapt a polynomial classifier (Schürmann, 1996) by least mean squares (LMS). Compared to the quadratic support vector machine adapted with the original features we see an improvement for the pairwise classifier. Almost the same result as for LMS we get by adapting a quadratic support vector machine with the PCA-transformed features. We see a further improvement using cubic support vector machines, while degree=3 is not possible for the LMS adaption because of limited computing resources. If we increase the degree for the support vector machine further, we get no improvements probably because of overadaption. The result of 1.09 percent errors on the test set is so far the best result we have for this benchmark. Further improvements seem only achievable with larger learning sets or by incorporating problem specific knowledge into the classifiers (Schölkopf et al., 1998d). It should be mentioned, that the adaption times for the pairwise support vector machine using PCA-transformed features are very pleasant (about 1 cpu hour for the quadratic and less than 2 cpu hours for the cubic approach).

Second Benchmark: M-NIST

The modified NIST benchmark was originally set up by the AT&T group (Bottou et al., 1994) and consists of 60000 patterns for the learning and the test set each. All binary images are size-normalized to fit in a 20×20 array, coded by gray-valued pixels in the range between -1 and +1. The aspect ratio, however, is kept as in the original image (for examples see figure 15.7). A slightly different version exists with a dimension of 28×28, which is composed by placing the center of gravity of the 20×20 images into the center of the larger area. In the following we use only the 20×20 images (which are available at `ftp://ftp.mpik-tueb.mpg.de/pub/bs/data/...` or slightly modified at `http://www.research.att.com/~yann/ocr/mnist/`). For learning the full data set of 60000 samples is used, whereas for testing only preselected 10000 samples (numbers 24476–34475) are considered. It should be mentioned, that using preprocessed digits only classifier characteristics can be compared, but not the overall performance of handwritten digit recognition (this includes besides preprocessing — we usually use size, slant and line-thickness normalization — also segmentation).

Linear Approach

As before we adapt different linear classifiers (least-mean-squares adaption and support vector machines in the standard approach and as pairwise classifiers). The adaption times for the LMS approach are 1 cpu hour and 2.5 cpu hours respectively, whereas the adaption of the pairwise support vector machine takes about 1 cpu day. A standard linear support vector machine is not adapted, since we expect too many slack variables (for each class about 10 percent of the learning set of 60000 samples). For a large cost value $C = 1000$ more than 30 of the 45 class pairs are linearly separable. However, such as for the first benchmark, lower values of C show a better generalization performance. If we compare the results of the standard linear classifier (LMS) to published results (Bottou et al., 1994), we notice quite a difference (15.3 percent errors on the test set versus 8.4 percent). The reasons are manifold (see also `http://www.research.att.com/~yann/ocr/mnist/`): First, there the larger 28×28 images were used, second, sometimes special preprocessing (deskewing) was applied.

Nonlinear Approach

This time not all pairs of classes are linearly separable as for the first benchmark and therefore it is certainly reasonable to look at different nonlinear approaches. Since, however, the M-NIST learning set is six times as large as in the first benchmark, we can make only a few selected experiments. The adaption of a one-versus-all-classes support vector machine takes in the mean more than one cpu day per class and needs memory for all 60000 samples. Nevertheless already the standard quadratic support vector machine fully separates the learning set. The

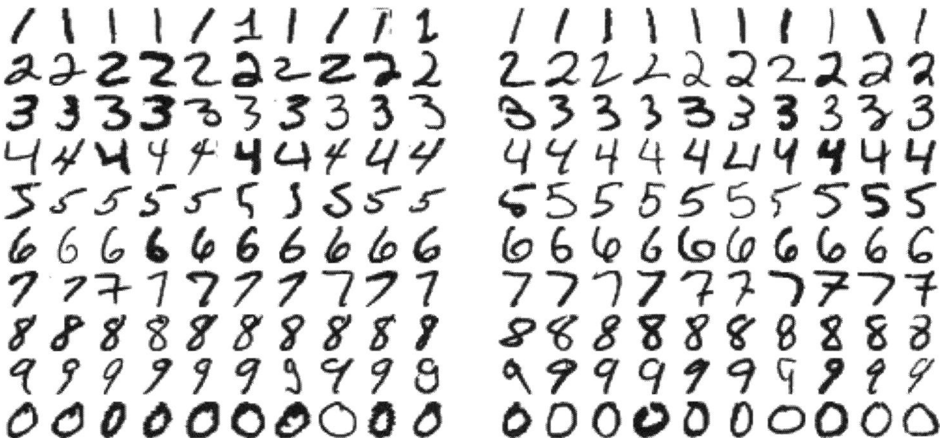

Figure 15.7 Modified NIST benchmark: each digit is given by a 20×20 matrix; at the left hand side the first 10 samples of each class in the learning set are shown and at the right hand side the according images in the preselected test set.

same holds for the pairwise quadratic approach, which has a similar error rate on the test set but needs only 32 cpu hours for adaption of all 45 class pairs and has fewer different support vectors (10092 versus 12152), which speeds up the classification times accordingly. Increasing the degree of the pairwise support vector machine improves the error rate and shows no overfitting as in the first benchmark (the number of different support vectors is 11248 for the pairwise cubic approach, 12820 for degree=4, and 14385 for degree=5). One explanation certainly is, that for the M-NIST benchmark the class distributions are multimodal, whereas in our benchmark only one basic writing style per class is included. As before we use the principal component analysis to reduce the computing requirements and also to have some regularization by reducing the input dimension. Instead of 40 we

adaption	structure	parameter	error rate	
			learning set	test set
LMS	linear		15.55 %	15.29 %
LMS	pairwise linear		6.72 %	7.35 %
SVM	pairwise linear	C=100	1.99 %	7.97 %
SVM	pairwise linear	C= 10	2.20 %	7.49 %
SVM	pairwise linear	C= 1	2.67 %	6.76 %
SVM	pairwise linear	C= 0.1	3.52 %	5.73 %
SVM	pairwise linear	C= 0.01	4.56 %	5.37 %
SVM	pairwise linear	C= 0.001	5.94 %	5.92 %
SVM	quadratic	C= 1	0.00 %	2.13 %
SVM	pairwise quadratic	C= 1	0.00 %	2.20 %
SVM	pairwise cubic	C= 1	0.00 %	1.85 %
SVM	pairwise degree=4	C= 1	0.00 %	1.72 %
SVM	pairwise degree=5	C= 1	0.00 %	1.64 %
PCA & LMS	quadratic	PCA=50	2.92 %	3.22 %
PCA & LMS	pairwise quadratic	PCA=50	0.82 %	1.63 %
PCA & SVM	pairwise quadratic	PCA=50, C=1	0.00 %	2.16 %
PCA & SVM	pairwise cubic	PCA=50, C=1	0.00 %	1.85 %
PCA & SVM	pairwise degree=4	PCA=50, C=1	0.00 %	1.57 %
PCA & SVM	pairwise degree=5	PCA=50, C=1	0.00 %	1.53 %
PCA & SVM	pairwise degree=6	PCA=50, C=1	0.00 %	1.52 %

Table 15.2 Comparison of recognition results for the modified NIST benchmark with 60000 samples for the learning set and with preselected 10000 samples for the test set; for further explanations see text.

selected this time 50 principal components, covering 84.8 percent reconstruction capability. For the reduced input dimension it is possible, to adapt a least-mean-squares classifier, which has for the pairwise case quite a good recognition rate (1.63 percent error rate). This confirms, that the principal component analysis fits well to the least-mean-squares approach. But also the support vector machine profits from the principal component analysis, since the number of support vectors stays about the same (quadratic SVM: 8232 support vectors with PCA compared to 10092 without PCA), while the input dimension is reduced by a factor of $400/50 = 8$. This reduces the memory requirements and speeds up the adaption time (especially if a decomposition algorithm is used) and the classification time. Higher polynomial degrees for the pairwise support vector machine with PCA improve the recognition rates further (the adaption times vary between 12 and 24 cpu hours). Looking at the different numbers, however, one should keep in mind, that the significance is about ± 0.2 percent (i.e. ± 20 errors) for a recognition rate around 99 percent and a test set with 10000 samples, assuming a binomial distribution for the errors and a confidence interval of 95 percent.

15.5 Conclusion

Comparsion

Pairwise classification fits perfectly to the characteristic of the support vector machine to directly determine the borderline between two classes. The multicategory class decision is done by a simple majority voting rule, which can be extended for tie situations. We showed this first intuitively for two-dimensional examples and discussed this later quantitatively for benchmarks based on handwritten digits. One unexpected reward was, that the pairwise classification needed in many cases (much) less adaption time and had comparable many different support vectors — despite the fact that $(K-1)/2$-times as many binary classifiers are used. This fact helps to make the support vector machine even more interesting for large practical problems (compare Schmidt and Gish (1996)). However, the apparently stronger classification performance of the pairwise approach on the learning set, did not lead in all cases to the expected improvements of the generalization error. One reason might be, that the (important) tie breaking of the standard K-class approach already resolves most of the errors of the single classifiers. Another explanation certainly is, that the problem of overfitting is more critical for the pairwise approach (see also the discussion in Friedman (1996)), although it is handled quite robustly by the support vector machine.

Representativity of Learning Set

One drawback for the rather powerful approach of the pairwise support vector machine are the high demands for the representativity of the learning set. For the digit recognition we had quite a few approaches, which all had no errors on the learning set, but significantly different results for the test set. Therefore we need further information, to select good parameters for the cost value C, the polynomial degree d and possibly the length of the principal components. This could be done by some kind of cross validation, such as extra validation sets, which are not yet available for the both benchmarks, but could be easily defined. Adding adequately distorted samples to the sample set or incorporating problem specific knowledge, as it was done e.g. by Schölkopf et al. (1998d), lowers the demands on the learning set and will improve the generalization performance (for the larger 28×28 images and 10000 testing samples the best standard support vector machine with a polynomial degree of 4 has an error rate of 1.1 percent, while using distorted vectors and a support vector machine of degree 9 the error rate can be reduced to 0.8 percent; the best result so far is reported for the boosted LeNet-4 with 0.7 percent error rate; for further scores and details on the modified NIST benchmark see (Bottou et al., 1994) or the web sites mentioned before).

Pairwise Linear Classifiers

But not only the 'high-end' classifiers deserve attention, also the simple linear pairwise support vector machine showed good recognition results with extremely low classification requirements — for the digit recognition the expense compares to a multi-reference euclidean-distance classifier having $(K-1)/2 = 4.5$ reference vectors per class. The linear pairwise support vector machine provides an algorithm to adapt for a given sample set a piecewise linear classifier with at most $K*(K-1)/2$ hyperplanes, which are optimal placed in respect to the error rate. Furthermore, there are relations to a multilayer perceptron with one hidden layer, where the hidden layer represents the pairwise discriminants (Schürmann, 1996).

Further Research

The pairwise support vector machine with its strong discrimination possibilities between class pairs and the ease of combination of these votes allows quite interesting classifier designs, such as using different classifiers depending on the difficulty to separate the given classes or such as pre-classification by a fast (linear) classifier and separation between the top votes by a more elaborate method. Moreover, the relations between the pairwise method and the recently published direct approaches (Bredensteiner and Bennett, 1998; Weston and Watkins, 1998) to multicategory classification need further investigations.

IV Extensions of the Algorithm

16 Reducing the Run-time Complexity in Support Vector Machines

Edgar E. Osuna, Federico Girosi
Center for Biological and Computational Learning
Massachusetts Institute of Technology, E25-201
Cambridge, MA 02139, USA
eosuna,girosi@ai.mit.edu
http://www.ai.mit.edu/people/eosuna,girosi

SVMs are currently considered slower at run-time than other techniques with similar generalization performance. In this chapter we focus on SVM for classification and investigate the problem of reducing its run-time complexity. We present two relevant results: a) the use of SVM itself as a regression tool to approximate the decision surface with a user-specified accuracy; and b) a reformulation of the training problem that yields the exact same decision surface using a smaller number of basis functions. We believe that this reformulation offers great potential for future improvements of the technique. For most of the selected problems, both approaches give reductions of run-time in the 50-95% range, with no system degradation.

16.1 Introduction

Support Vector Machines for pattern recognition classify a new pattern based on the sign of $f(\mathbf{x})$ defined as:

$$f(\mathbf{x}) = \sum_{i=1}^{\ell_s} \alpha_i y_i k(\mathbf{x}_i, \mathbf{x}) + b \qquad (16.1)$$

where ℓ_s is the number of support vectors.

The reduction of the run-time complexity of SVMs can therefore be defined as a series of heuristics or techniques that reduce the computational effort spent in the evaluation or approximation of $f(\mathbf{x})$. The same issue arises in regression SVMs, where $f(\mathbf{x})$ is similarly defined as:

$$f(\mathbf{x}) = \sum_{i=1}^{\ell_s} (\alpha_i^* - \alpha_i) k(\mathbf{x}_i, \mathbf{x}) + b \tag{16.2}$$

In this section we focus on pattern classification with the understanding that the same approaches can be used in regression as well.

The outline of this chapter is as follows: in section 16.2 we introduce the motivation of this problem and comment on possible approaches to its solution; in section 16.3 we summarize the previous work in this topic; in section 16.4 we give an exact description of the properties of the problem we are approaching; in section 16.5 we present a first approach in solving this problem using Support Vector Regression; in section 16.6 we offer a second approach to the solution which involves the reformulation of the training problem; in section 16.7 we present experimental results; and in section 16.8 we comment on the limitations of our two suggested approaches.

16.2 Motivation and Statement of the Problem

The operations described in (16.1) and (16.2) can easily become the bottleneck of any system that performs a massive number of classifications or function evaluations. Examples of this issue arise in our face (Osuna et al., 1997c) and people (Oren et al., 1997) detection systems, where SVMs are used as object-nonobject classifiers exhaustively; in checks and ZIP code readers, where the system can only afford to spend fractions of a second per check or envelope, etc.

In both pattern classification and regression machines, a speedup can be obtained by:

1. Approximating the solution $f(\mathbf{x})$ by:

$$\hat{f}(\mathbf{x}) = \sum_{i=1}^{\ell_s'} \gamma_i k(\mathbf{z}_i, \mathbf{x}) + b \tag{16.3}$$

where $\mathbf{z}_i$ are *synthetic* vectors, which are not necessarily data points anymore, γ_i are weights, and $\ell_s' \ll \ell_s$. This approach, which for radial kernels K resembles the technique of "moving centers" (Moody and Darken, 1989; Poggio and Girosi, 1990b), has been pursued by Burges (1996), but the procedure lacks a principled way for controlling the approximation accuracy.

2. Approximating the solution $f(\mathbf{x})$ by:

$$\hat{f}(\mathbf{x}) = \sum_{i=1}^{\ell_s'} \gamma_i k(\mathbf{x}_i, \mathbf{x}) + b \tag{16.4}$$

where $\mathbf{x}_i$ is still a support vector with weight γ_i, but $\ell_s' \ll \ell_s$. This will be our first approach and it will be described in detail in section 16.5.

3. If possible, rewriting the solution $f(\mathbf{x})$ as:

$$f(\mathbf{x}) = \sum_{i=1}^{\ell'_s} \gamma_i k(\mathbf{x}_i, \mathbf{x}) + b \tag{16.5}$$

where $\mathbf{x}_i$ are still data points (but not necessarily support vectors according to the traditional definition) with weight γ_i, but $\ell'_s \ll \ell_s$. Our hope in this approach is to find an alternative more *efficient* representation of the separating hyperplane in problems where its expansion is not unique. This will be our second approach and it will be described in detail in section 16.6.

All of these heuristics try to approximate $f(\mathbf{x})$ using the kernel operator so that they can establish a meaningful accuracy comparison through the L_2 norm measured in *feature space*. Therefore, they strongly depend on the mapping:

$$\Phi : \mathbb{R}^N \to F, \tag{16.6}$$

where: (1) F can have huge dimensionality, and (2) not very much is known about the characteristics of the mapping itself. These two properties make this problem very hard to approach.

16.3 Previous Work: The Reduced Set Method

As we mentioned in section 16.2, one approach to speedup the test phase of an SVM is to approximate $f(\mathbf{x})$ by:

$$\hat{f}(\mathbf{x}) = \sum_{i=1}^{\ell'_s} \gamma_i k(\mathbf{z}_i, \mathbf{x}) + b \tag{16.7}$$

where $\mathbf{z}_i$ are *synthetic* vectors, γ_i are weights, and $\ell'_s \ll \ell_s$. The purpose of this section is to describe this technique due to Burges (1996), called the *Reduced Set Method*, which is the only piece of previous work in this area.[1]

In order to approximate $f(\mathbf{x})$ with the suggested form, Burges uses the kernel properties that define the dot product in feature space to calculate and minimize the difference between the true decision surface $\mathbf{w}$ and its approximation given by $\hat{\mathbf{w}}$. More formally:

- $\mathbf{w} = \sum_{i=1}^{\ell_s} \alpha_i y_i \mathbf{\Phi}(\mathbf{x}_i)$ is the hyperplane in feature space obtained during the SVM training, and it defines $f(\mathbf{x}) = \mathbf{w}^T \mathbf{\Phi}(\mathbf{x}) + b = \sum_{i=1}^{\ell_s} \alpha_i y_i k(\mathbf{x}_i, \mathbf{x}) + b$.
- $\hat{\mathbf{w}} = \sum_{i=1}^{\ell'_s} \gamma_i \mathbf{\Phi}(\mathbf{z_i})$ is the approximating hyperplane in feature space that we wish to obtain, and it defines $\hat{f}(\mathbf{x}) = \hat{\mathbf{w}}^T \mathbf{\Phi}(\mathbf{x}) + b = \sum_{i=1}^{\ell'_s} \gamma_i k(\mathbf{z}_i, \mathbf{x}) + b$.

1. Experimental results using the *Reduced Set Method* have been reported in (Burges and Schölkopf, 1997).

- The approximation error ρ can be defined as:

$$\begin{aligned}\|\mathbf{w}-\hat{\mathbf{w}}\|^2 &= (\mathbf{w}-\hat{\mathbf{w}})^T(\mathbf{w}-\hat{\mathbf{w}})\\ &= \mathbf{w}^T\mathbf{w}+\hat{\mathbf{w}}^T\hat{\mathbf{w}}-2\mathbf{w}^T\hat{\mathbf{w}}\\ &= \sum_{i,j}^{\ell_s}\alpha_i\alpha_j y_i y_j k(\mathbf{x}_i,\mathbf{x}_j)+\sum_{i,j}^{\ell'_s}\gamma_i\gamma_j k(\mathbf{z}_i,\mathbf{z}_j)-2\sum_i^{\ell_s}\sum_j^{\ell'_s}\alpha_i y_i\gamma_j k(\mathbf{x}_i,\mathbf{z}_j)\end{aligned} \tag{16.8}$$

- By minimizing ρ with respect to the vectors z_i (and its components) and the weights γ_i, we can obtain, for a fixed ℓ'_s, the desired approximation.

The Reduced Set Method can then be stated as an unconstrained minimization of ρ with respect to the synthetic vectors and the corresponding weights. Burges showed that the use of one particular class of kernel, the second degree homogeneous polynomial, allows a closed form solution to this minimization. Next we describe this solution in more detail, since it is used in our face (Osuna et al., 1997c) and people detection (Oren et al., 1997) applications. Our intention is to give some idea of how this particular case behaves. More detail can be found in (Burges, 1996).

Homogeneous Quadratic Polynomials: We consider the case when $k(\mathbf{x}_i,\mathbf{x}_j) = (\mathbf{x}_i^T\mathbf{x}_j)^2$, for $\mathbf{x}_i,\mathbf{x}_j \in \mathbb{R}^N$. To simplify the presentation, we start with the simplest case, that is, when $\ell'_s = 1$. If we introduce the symmetric matrix S, where:

$$S_{\mu\nu} = \sum_{i=1}^{\ell_s}\alpha_i y_i(\mathbf{x}_i)_\mu(\mathbf{x}_i)_\nu \qquad \text{for } \mu,\nu = 1\ldots n \tag{16.9}$$

one can show that to minimize ρ, $\mathbf{z}$ must satisfy:

$$S_{\mu\nu}\mathbf{z}_\nu = \gamma\|\mathbf{z}\|^2\mathbf{z}_\mu \tag{16.10}$$

and that ρ^2 reduces to:

$$\rho^2 = \text{Trace}(S^2) - \gamma^2\|\mathbf{z}\|^4. \tag{16.11}$$

From this expression we obtain that the largest reduction in ρ results when we select $\mathbf{z}$ to be the eigenvector of S with the largest sized absolute eigenvalue, and scale $\mathbf{z}$ so that $\gamma\|\mathbf{z}\|^2$ is that eigenvalue. The factor γ allows the use of negative eigenvalues, and can be chosen accordingly such that $\gamma \in \{-1, 1\}$.

By extending this idea to more vectors (i.e. $\ell'_s > 1$), one can show that the approximation becomes exact (i.e. $\rho = 0$) when $\ell'_s = N$, and that ρ^2 is reduced by:

$$\rho^2 = \text{Trace}(S^2) - \sum_{i=i}^{\ell'_s}\|\mathbf{z}\|^4 \tag{16.12}$$

where $\mathbf{z}_i$ are the eigenvectors of S. In practice, one selects the top ℓ'_s eigenvectors sorted by the absolute value of their corresponding eigenvalue.

We applied this technique to two different databases:

- A set of 1969 support vectors obtained from training our 29 feature vector from the people detection database (see Oren et al. (1997)).
- A set of 964 support vectors obtained from training our 283 pixel vector from the face detection database (see Osuna et al. (1997c)).

As we have stated earlier, exact *compression* to 29 and 283 vectors, respectively, can be achieved without any loss or system degradation. Results obtained when applying this technique can be seen in figures 16.1 and 16.2.

Two interesting issues arise from our experiments:

1. Figure 16.1 shows that in order to get a satisfactory approximation, we must use nearly all of the eigenvectors. This can be contrasted with figure 16.2, which shows that an equally satisfactory approximation can be obtained when using just 30% of the eigenvectors. This is an interesting observation that seems to suggest that the ratio ℓ_s'/n is somewhat dependent on the amount of useful information coded in the input vector. In these particular experiments, the results suggest that nearly all the input components are relevant for the people/non-people discrimination task, whereas not even half are relevant for the face/non-face.

2. Figures 16.1(b) and 16.2(b) show that the MSE, computed as:

$$MSE = \frac{\sum_{i=1}^{\ell_s}(f(\mathbf{x}_i) - \hat{f}(\mathbf{x}_i))^2}{\ell_s} \tag{16.13}$$

is not monotonically decreasing[2] as a function of ℓ_s'. Since the sign of the classification is the sign of $f(\mathbf{x})$, these plots can be used to define a hierarchical classification procedure. This procedure, for example, may approximate $f(\mathbf{x})$ using the first ℓ_{s1} eigenvectors, and continue using up to ℓ_{s2} (with $\ell_{s1} < \ell_{s2}$) eigenvectors if $\hat{f}(\mathbf{x})$ falls within some range of *low confidence.*

16.4 The Class of Problems We Approach

Before characterizing explicitly the kind of problems we are trying to solve, we want to present the following example: training the Ripley data set[3] (250 datapoints, 2 dimensions, not linearly separable) yields roughly 90 support vectors (actually 89 for C=100). This means that the separating hyperplane $\mathbf{w} = \sum_{i=1}^{\ell_s} \alpha_i y_i \mathbf{x}_i$ is defined using 90 non-zero coefficients. Figure 16.3 presents the data set, the support vectors and the separating hyperplane. This representation for $\mathbf{w}$ is strikingly inefficient, as we are using a linear combination of 90 vectors to define a vector $\mathbf{w}$ living in $\mathbb{R}^2$.

2. The threshold b used in $\hat{f}(\mathbf{x})$ for these experiments is the same b as obtained during the SVM training phase. Burges and Schölkopf (1997) present a way to recompute b.
3. Available at ftp://markov.stats.ox.ac.uk/pub/neural/papers/

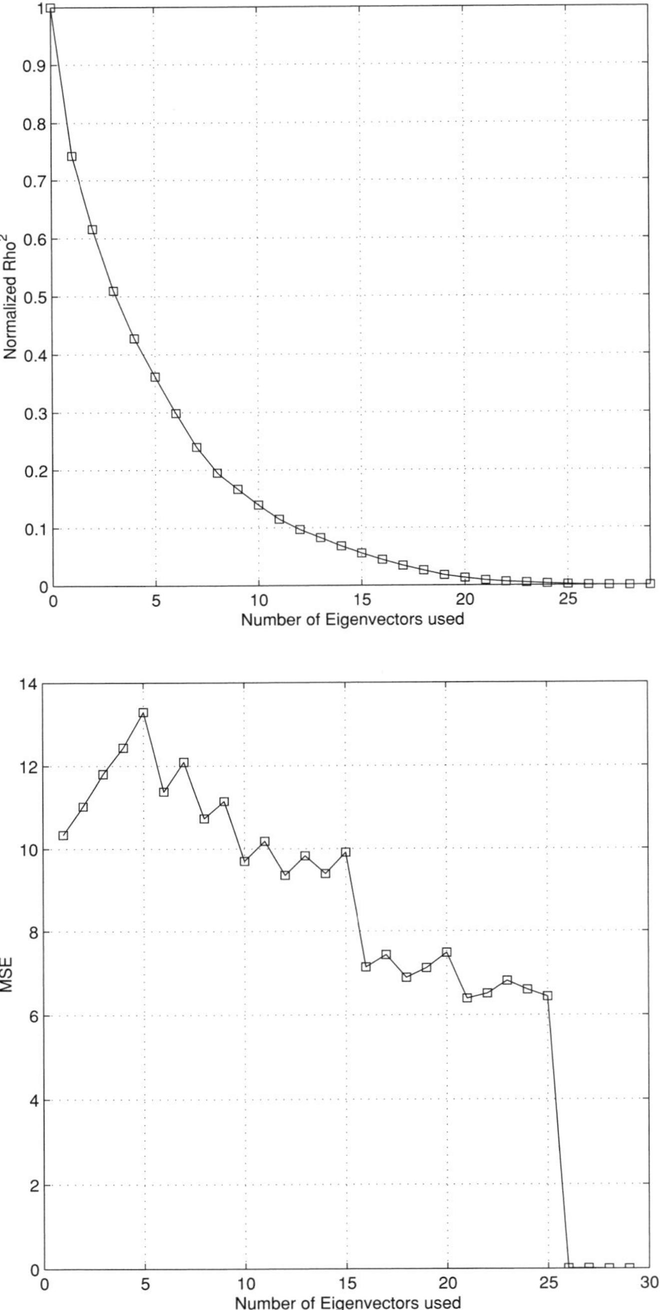

Figure 16.1 The Reduced Set Method applied to the people detection database. (a) Normalized ρ^2 as a function of ℓ'_s (i.e. the number of eigenvectors used in the expansion). (b) MSE from the approximation as a function of ℓ'_s, evaluated over the $\ell_s = 1969$ support vectors originally obtained during training.

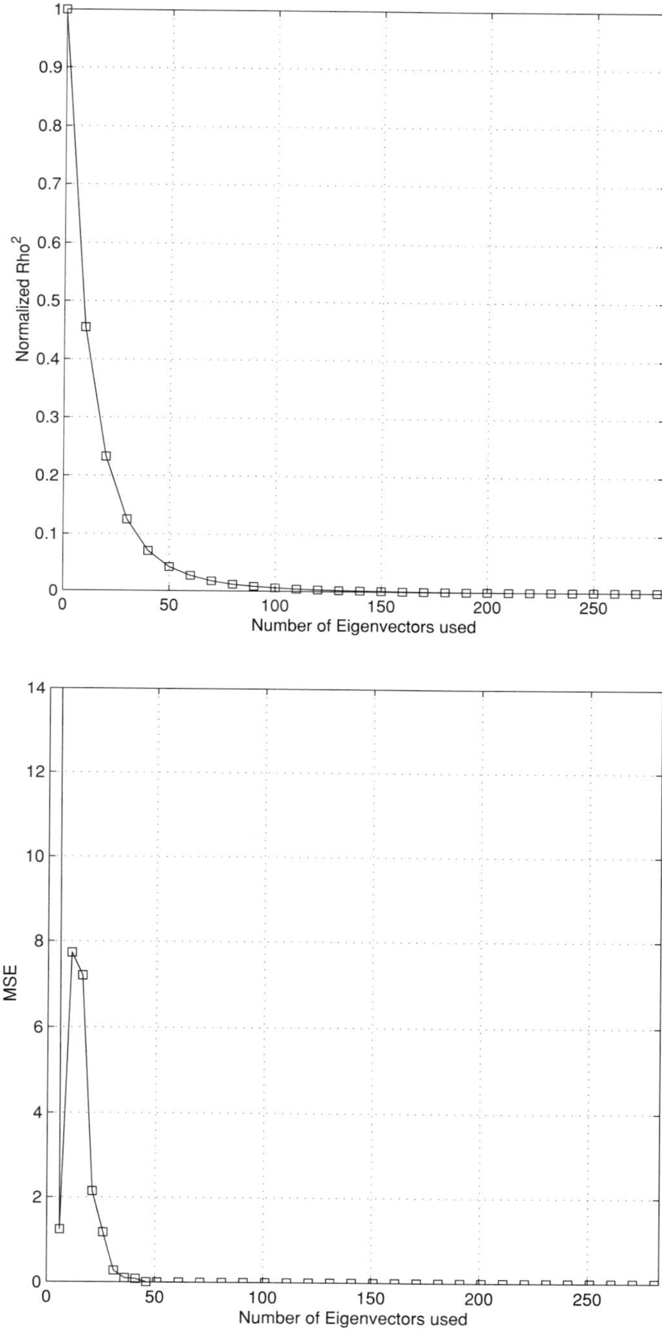

Figure 16.2 The Reduced Set Method applied to the face detection database. (a) Normalized ρ^2 as a function of ℓ'_s (i.e. the number of eigenvectors used in the expansion). (b) MSE from the approximation as a function of ℓ'_s, evaluated over the $\ell_s = 964$ support vectors originally obtained during training.

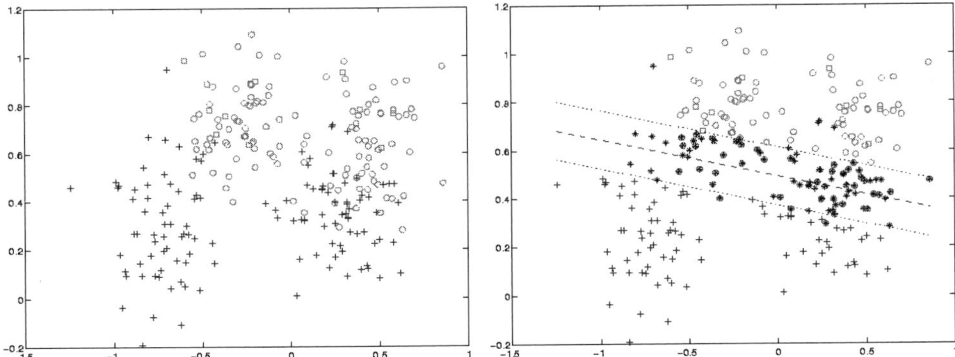

Figure 16.3 (a) The Ripley data set. (b) The optimal separating hyperplane and its support vectors. The dotted lines above and below the hyperplane depict the $\pm$ 1 range around the separating surface.

Although the example given is a simple linear classifier in $\mathbb{R}^2$, it's important to remark that similar behavior will be encountered in other examples involving nonlinear decision surfaces and input spaces with higher dimensionality.

Why is this happening?

1. The Karush-Kuhn-Tucker optimality conditions of the training problem mandate for any misclassified training point[4] to have $\alpha_i = C$.

2. Any non-zero α_i contributes in the expansion of $\mathbf{w}$, and the corresponding example cannot be removed from the training set without affecting the solution.

3. Since the data set is non-separable, all the training errors are present in the expansion.

Moreover, desperate attempts like:

- Removing known errors from the data set before training,
- removing errors from the expansion after training, or
- training, removing the errors from the obtained set of support vectors, and retraining,

will not, in general, give the same separating hyperplane, since some of these errors are actually needed in the expansion of $\mathbf{w}$ and also need to be taken into account when penalizing non-separability. Therefore, we want to approach problems in which the number of support vectors with $\alpha_i = C$ is *excessively* high. This is a problem that appears in particular when the data set is non-separable, and becomes more relevant with the increase of noise, degree of non-separability and sample size.

4. Also points falling within the margin, but correctly classified will have $\alpha_i = C$.

16.5 First Approach: Using SVRM

It has been recently shown (Girosi, 1998) that under certain conditions Support Vector Regression Machines (SVRM) are equivalent to Basis Pursuit De-Noising (BP) (Chen et al., 1995; Chen, 1995). BP is an instance of a *sparse* approximation technique in which a function is reconstructed using the least possible number of basis functions chosen from a large set, which is called a *dictionary*. Having said that, we can think of building a *sparse* approximation of $f(\mathbf{x})$ using as dictionary the implicit mappings given by the kernel function evaluated at the data points.[5]

Given a desired ε-accuracy, we are interested in drawing the least number of basis functions in order to build our approximation.

Which Kernel do we use? At this point we can use any of the valid kernels for SV regression and still obtain a *sparse* approximation. However, by using the same kernel that was used during the initial training, we obtain as by-product three interesting properties:

1. ε-accuracy can be arbitrarily small and a perfect approximation can be achieved, provided that the parameter C is large enough.[6] This is an important property if we consider the approximation quality more important than speed.

2. The error measure $\|\mathbf{w} - \hat{\mathbf{w}}\|^2$ (where $\mathbf{w}$ is the separating hyperplane in feature space and $\hat{\mathbf{w}}$ its approximation) can be computed using the kernel function.

3. Since the kernel used initially during training has already built a linear hyperplane in feature space, using the same kernel takes advantage of that same linearization.

The Algorithm: The formal algorithm can be stated as:

1. Train your SV classifier using the kernel and parameters of your choice. This step defines $f(\mathbf{x}) = \sum_{i=1}^{\ell_s} \alpha_i y_i k(\mathbf{x}_i, \mathbf{x}) + b$.

2. Run SVRM on the data points defined by $(\mathbf{x}, f(\mathbf{x}))$; where $\mathbf{x}$ is a support vector obtained in step 1. Use in this step a high value for the parameter C, the same kernel used in (1), and the desired ε-accuracy.

The results obtained with this approach can be seen in section 16.7.

5. The datapoints are in this case the support vectors obtained during the training of your SV classifier.

6. If C is not big enough, the SVM regression algorithm may *prefer* not to fit a particular data point within ε, and then the desired ε-accuracy will not be satisfied

16.6 Second Approach: Reformulating the Training Problem

Traditionally, the flow of the mathematical derivation for the training problem in SVMs (see the Introduction in this book and Vapnik (1995)) has gone from the easiest problem of linearly separable data sets and linear decision surfaces, to non-linear decision surfaces using kernel functions. During this derivation, a Lagrangian function was introduced as a way to solve the problem and to show how the separating hyperplane $\mathbf{w}$ could be written as a linear combination using Lagrange multipliers as coefficients. This step has somehow (and erroneously) suggested to several researchers that solving a primal version without explicitly incorporating the mapping $\Phi : \mathbb{R}^N \to F$ is impossible. One can easily show that the Wolfe dual of the training problem currently in use corresponds to:

$$\begin{array}{llll} \text{Minimize} & F(\alpha, b, \xi) & = \frac{1}{2}\alpha^T Q\alpha + C\sum_{i=1}^{\ell} \xi_i & \\ \text{subject to} & y_i(\sum_{j=1}^{\ell} \alpha_j y_j k(\mathbf{x}_i, \mathbf{x}_j) + b) & \geq 1 - \xi_i & i = 1 \ldots \ell \\ & \xi_i, \alpha_i & \geq 0 & i = 1 \ldots \ell \\ & b & \textit{free} & \end{array} \quad (16.14)$$

where $Q_{ij} = y_i y_j k(\mathbf{x}_i, \mathbf{x}_j)$.

This problem formulation, which from now on we refer to as the *primal reformulation* has the same initial structure as the original primal formulation, but incorporates the kernel mapping implicitly through the kernel function, and therefore, works also for defining non-linear decision surfaces. Moreover, its interpretation is natural and clear:

- $\alpha^T Q\alpha$ can be shown to be proportional to the inverse of the margin in feature space (and therefore we want to minimize it);
- The constraint $y_i(\sum_{j=1}^{\ell} \alpha_j y_j k(\mathbf{x}_i, \mathbf{x}_j) + b) \geq 1 - \xi_i$ models how well the data point $\mathbf{x}_i$ is classified.[7]
- ξ_i captures for data point i, its *degree of separability*, and *pays* a linear penalty C in the cost function.

One can show that the minimum of this problem gives the same separating surface of the classical approach, but probably with a different expansion for $\mathbf{w}$ (work along these lines has also been done in (Pontil and Verri, 1997)). It is not guaranteed that the new representation of the hyperplane is more sparse than the classical solution. However, experimentally, this approach works very well for two reasons: first, the coefficients are not *forced* to the upper bound for misclassifications, since

7. The slack variables ξ_i were first introduced by Cortes and Vapnik (1995), but only to capture non-separability when using linear separating surfaces.

they are not Lagrange multipliers anymore; and second, starting with $\alpha = \mathbf{0}$ as initial solution helps in keeping at 0 level unnecessary points in the expansion.

16.6.1 Possible Improvements

A clear advantage of this primal reformulation when compared to the training problem typically solved, is that we can include in the cost function certain attractor terms in order to benefit certain type of expansions. For example:

- We can include a small penalty of the form $\sum_{i=1}^{\ell} |\alpha_i|$, which has been used before in other techniques to enforce sparse representations (Chen et al., 1995; Chen, 1995; Girosi, 1998).
- We can include a small penalty for using points that do not meet the separability constraints exactly. This will bring the set of coefficients to be a subset of the support vectors obtained through the current training problem. Since the coefficients are not Lagrange multipliers anymore, the values can be drastically different.
- We can include a small penalty for using errors, etc.

We want to remark that these penalties should be *small* so that the essence of the cost function is altered in a minimal way, that is, these small penalties are just coding a *preference* among all the possible linear combinations. A scheme in which one gradually reduces these penalties to zero is also possible.

The results obtained with this approach can be seen in section 16.7.

16.7 Experimental Results

Three data sets were selected for our experiments, and two different runs were performed with each one of them, using the SVM implementation described in (Osuna et al., 1997a). Each run corresponds to a different kernel and/or parameter setting. The problems selected, the information regarding the kernel parameters, number of support vectors and training performance is given in table 16.1. The training performance (Tr. Perf. = % Correct) is presented to give the reader an idea of the separability of the data.

The results obtained with the SV regression approach can be found in table 16.2. Notice that reduction percentages are above 50% in all runs except electrons (2). Notice also the relationship between the ε-approximation quality and the number of vectors obtained.

The results obtained with the primal reformulation (exactly as presented in equation 16.14, without any additional penalty terms) are shown in table 16.3. As it was the case with the SV regression approach, reduction percentages are above 50% in all runs except electrons (2).

16.8 Limitations and Final Remarks

Although we think that our solutions have been successful for the kind of problem we decided to approach, there are two clear limitations that must be discussed:

1. Neither solution will reduce the run-time complexity of the classifier when all or most of the coefficients are strictly between the bounds (i.e. $0 < \alpha_i < C$). This situation tends to occur when the data is highly (if not totally) separable, and worsens as the dimensionality of the feature space grows. Up to date, the best we can do in cases like this is to use the reduced set method of Burges (1996). In a sense, we see our two new approaches as *complementary* to the reduced set method.

2. Although a delayed column generation algorithm can be devised for decomposing and solving our primal reformulation, memory limitations make it prohibitive for large data sets (beyond 10,000). Alternatives to this problem are still an open area of research.

Database	# Points	Kernel	C	Tr. Perf.	# SVs	# $\alpha_i = C$
skin (1)	1600	pol 2	100	91.94	587	581
skin (2)	1600	pol 5	100	95.81	227	209
electrons (1)	2000	pol 2	100	89.20	611	584
electrons (2)	2000	rbf σ =2	100	91.60	554	481
ripley (1)	250	linear	100	86.40	89	86
ripley (2)	250	rbf σ =1	100	89.60	77	70

Table 16.1 Problems selected for our experiments.

Database	$\varepsilon = 10^{-2}$			$\varepsilon = 10^{-6}$		
	$\frac{\|w-\hat{w}\|}{\|w\|}$	# vec.	Red. %	$\frac{\|w-\hat{w}\|}{\|w\|}$	# vec.	Red. %
skin (1)	1.4×10^{-3}	11	98.13	1.6×10^{-10}	25	95.74
skin (2)	1.2×10^{-3}	10	95.59	6.1×10^{-7}	75	66.96
electrons (1)	6.1×10^{-3}	40	93.45	2.9×10^{-9}	47	92.30
electrons (2)	6.6×10^{-3}	297	46.38	5.1×10^{-7}	554	0.0
ripley (1)	2.6×10^{-5}	3	96.63	2.5×10^{-12}	3	96.63
ripley (2)	4.6×10^{-3}	14	76.82	2.4×10^{-7}	33	57.14

Table 16.2 Results obtained using the SV regression approach. The column denoting "# vec." reflects the number of vectors that are now present in the expansion. This number corresponds with a percentage reduction indicated in the column "Red. %." The performance in corresponding test sets was the same as with the original SV formulation.

Database	# vec.	Red. %
skin (1)	6	98.98
skin (2)	57	74.89
electrons (1)	44	92.80
electrons (2)	521	5.96
ripley (1)	2	97.75
ripley (2)	34	55.84

Table 16.3 Results obtained using the primal reformulation approach. The performance in corresponding test sets was the same as with the original SV formulation.

We feel that both approaches have attacked and solved the problem of excessive number of support vectors with active upper bound (i.e. $\alpha = C$). The SV regression approach is useful since it can be applied as an *after-training* filter, it is not limited by memory requirements, and offers accuracy control of the approximation through the use of the parameter ε. The primal reformulation offers a *one-step* training approach that is not an approximation, but in fact gives exactly the same hyperplane obtained by training the current QP problem. Together with the possible improvements suggested in section 16.6.1, this technique can be made to enforce certain properties of the points used in the linear combination, and in fact, can be made to give a subset of the original support vectors without any loss of accuracy or approximation error. This primal reformulation has a very natural structure and therefore is suitable for improvements in the technique.

As a last comment, we must remark that throughout this section we have only considered reducing the run-time complexity of the SV classifier. The proposed methods can easily be adapted to reducing the complexity of SV regression machines as well.

17 Support Vector Regression with ANOVA Decomposition Kernels

Mark O. Stitson, Alex Gammerman, Vladimir Vapnik, Volodya Vovk, Chris Watkins, Jason Weston
Royal Holloway, University of London
Egham, Surrey, TW20 0EX, UK
M.Stitson@dcs.rhbnc.ac.uk
http://www.dcs.rhbnc.ac.uk/

Support Vector Machines using "ANOVA Decomposition" Kernels (SVAD) are a way of imposing a structure on multi-dimensional kernels which are generated as the tensor product of one-dimensional kernels. This gives more accurate control over the capacity of the learning machine. SVAD uses ideas from ANOVA methods and extends them to generate kernels which directly implement these ideas.

SVAD is used with spline kernels and results show that SVAD performs better than the respective non ANOVA decomposition kernel. The well-known Boston housing data set has been tested on Bagging and Support Vector methods before and these results are compared to the SVAD method.

17.1 Introduction

Support Vector Machines (SVM) (Vapnik, 1995, 1996) can be used for non-linear regression estimation. The class of functions they choose a regression estimate from, is determined by the kernel function (1.20). This chapter reports an experiment with a new kernel, the "ANOVA decomposition" kernel, described in (Vapnik, 1998).

In the next section multiplicative kernels will be briefly reviewed. The idea of ANOVA decomposition, which forms the basis for the ANOVA kernel, is then introduced. Finally experimental results are given and analysed.

17.2 Multiplicative Kernels

The kernel determines the class of functions a SVM can draw its solution from. The choice of kernel significantly affects the performance of a SVM. There are many known kernels and one specific family of kernels is described here.

Kernels, like dot products in $\mathbb{R}^N$, are functions which map from two N-dimensional vectors to a scalar. Multiplicative kernels do this by calculating the product of N identical coordinate-wise one-dimensional kernel functions κ:

$$k(\mathbf{x}, \mathbf{y}) = \prod_{i=1}^{N} \kappa(x^i, y^i) \tag{17.1}$$

where x^i is the ith element of the N-dimensional vector $\mathbf{x}$.

Note that the function $\kappa(x^i, y^i)$ usually is chosen never to be zero, as this would mean certain values in a single coordinate of a vector could make the whole function $k(\mathbf{x}, \mathbf{y})$ equal to zero, that is they would dominate the expression.

The regression estimate using these kernels takes the form (1.49):

$$f(\mathbf{x}) = \sum_{i=1}^{\ell} (\alpha_i^* - \alpha_i) \prod_{j=1}^{N} \kappa(x_i^j, x^j) + b \tag{17.2}$$

where x_i^j is the jth coordinate of $\mathbf{x}_i$, the ith support vector.

There is a potential problem with kernels of this type: if N is large and the multiplicands $\kappa(x_i^j, x^j)$ vary widely in size, then for each $\mathbf{x}$ the sum of the right-hand side may be dominated by a few terms only.

Spline Kernels

Multiplicative kernels include spline kernels, which produce piecewise polynomial approximations of functions. Linear spline kernels with an infinite number of pieces are commonly used and have the form :

$$\kappa(x, y) = \frac{\min(x, y)^3}{3} + \frac{\min(x, y)^2 |x - y|}{2} + 1 + xy \tag{17.3}$$

where $x, y \in \mathbb{R}$ and $x, y \geq 0$. For more information on spline kernels see the appendix or Vapnik et al. (1997).

17.3 ANOVA Decomposition

ANOVA (ANalysis Of VAriance) is a statistical technique to analyse interactions between attributes of data. Lower order interactions are preferred as they provide a less complex explanation of the data.

The "ANOVA decomposition" introduced in (Vapnik, 1998) is motivated by a analogy with ANOVA in classical statistics. The idea is to approximate a function of a vector of N attributes as the sum of functions of smaller numbers of attributes. An order 1 approximation is to use a sum of functions of each attribute separately. An order 2 approximation is to use a sum of functions of all pairs of attributes.

In general an order p approximation is to use a sum of functions of all p-tuples of attributes. That is, the pth order approximation f_p is of the form $f_p(x) = \sum_{1\le k_1<\cdots<k_p\le N} \psi_{k_1,\ldots,k_p}(x^{k_1},\ldots,x^{k_p}) + b$ for some functions $\psi_{k_1,\ldots,k_p}$ that are to be found. Not all functions of N variables can be expressed in this way. For example assume all $\psi_{k_1,\ldots,k_p}$ are differentiable, note that $\frac{\delta}{\delta x^1\ldots\delta x^{p+1}} f_p(\mathbf{x}) = 0$.

17.3.1 ANOVA Decomposition Kernels

The ideas of multiplicative kernels and ANOVA decomposition are combined to form ANOVA kernels (Vapnik, 1998):

$$k_p(\mathbf{x},\mathbf{y}) = \sum_{1\le k_1<\ldots<k_p\le N} \kappa(x^{k_1},y^{k_1}) \times \cdots \times \kappa(x^{k_p},y^{k_p}) \tag{17.4}$$

where maximum size p of the ANOVA subsets is chosen a priori.

The form of the regression estimate from (1.49) then is

$$f_p(\mathbf{x}) = \sum_{i=1}^{\ell}(\alpha_i^* - \alpha_i) \sum_{1\le k_1<\cdots<k_p\le N} \kappa(x_i^{k_1},x^{k_1}) \times \cdots \times \kappa(x_i^{k_p},x^{k_p}) + b \tag{17.5}$$

This form of regression estimate is the sum of a large number of multiplicative terms, where each term is of some low order p.

This estimate may be better behaved than the estimate (17.2), which is the sum of a smaller number of terms of higher order N. The reason is that if N is large, the terms in (17.2) may vary wildly in absolute size and the sum may be dominated by just a few terms. This means that more support vectors may be required to obtain the same level of fit.

Note that it is possible to rewrite the regression estimate in the following way:

$$\begin{aligned} f_p(\mathbf{x}) &= \sum_{i=1}^{\ell}(\alpha_i^* - \alpha_i) \sum_{1\le k_1<\cdots<k_p\le N} \kappa(x_i^{k_1},x^{k_1}) \times \cdots \times \kappa(x_i^{k_p},x^{k_p}) + b \\ &= \sum_{1\le k_1<\cdots<k_p\le N} \sum_{i=1}^{\ell}(\alpha_i^* - \alpha_i)\kappa(x_i^{k_1},x^{k_1}) \times \cdots \times \kappa(x_i^{k_p},x^{k_p}) + b \\ &= \sum_{1\le k_1<\cdots<k_p\le N} \psi_{k_1,\ldots,k_p}(x^{k_1},\ldots,x^{k_p}) + b \end{aligned} \tag{17.6}$$

where $\psi_{k_1,\ldots,k_p}(x^{k_1},\ldots,x^{k_p}) = \sum_{i=1}^{\ell}(\alpha_i^* - \alpha_i)\kappa(x_i^{k_1},x^{k_1}) \times \cdots \times \kappa(x_i^{k_p},x^{k_p})$. This formulation shows that the regressor estimated using an "ANOVA decomposition" kernel is indeed a sum of functions of p-tuples of attributes.

17.3.2 Algorithm

The "ANOVA decomposition" kernel (17.4) is the sum of a possibly large number of terms, but fortunately it is not necessary to compute this sum term by term.

Burges and Vapnik (1995) derived the following efficient recurrent procedure to calculate $k_p(\mathbf{x}, \mathbf{y})$:

Let $k^s(\mathbf{x}, \mathbf{y}) = \sum_{i=1}^{n}(\kappa(x^i, y^i))^s$ and $k_0(\mathbf{x}, \mathbf{y}) = 1$. Then

$$k_p(\mathbf{x}, \mathbf{y}) = \frac{1}{p}\sum_{s=1}^{p}(-1)^{s+1}k_{p-s}(\mathbf{x}, \mathbf{y})k^s(\mathbf{x}, \mathbf{y}) \tag{17.7}$$

There are two ways of using ANOVA decomposition to produce kernels of order p. The first method suggested in (Vapnik, 1998) only includes order p:

$$k(\mathbf{x}, \mathbf{y}) = k_p(\mathbf{x}, \mathbf{y}) \tag{17.8}$$

This method was used to conduct the experiments described below.

A second possibility, which has not yet been tested, includes order p and all lower orders:

$$k(\mathbf{x}, \mathbf{y}) = \sum_{i=1}^{p} k_p(\mathbf{x}, \mathbf{y}) \tag{17.9}$$

The regression estimate for this has the form

$$f(\mathbf{x}) = \sum_{i=1}^{\ell}(\alpha_i^* - \alpha_i)\times \tag{17.10}$$

$$\left(\sum_{1\leq k_1<\cdots<k_m\leq N} \kappa(x_j^{k_1}, x^{k_1}) \times \cdots \times \kappa(x_j^{k_m}, x^{k_m}) + \cdots + \sum_{1\leq k_1<n} \kappa(x_j^{k_1}, x^{k_1})\right) + b \tag{17.11}$$

17.4 Experiments

Boston Housing data

The following experiments were conducted using the Boston housing data from the UCI machine learning repository (Harrison and Rubinfeld, 1978). This has been used as a benchmark data set for non-linear regression estimation.

The data set consists of 506 cases. Each case consists of 13 socio-economic and environmental factors — such as crime rate, nitric oxide concentration, distance to employment centres and age of a property — determining the median house price in a certain area of Boston. The prices lie between \$5,000 and \$50,000 to the nearest \$100. The data set has been used frequently to evaluate regression estimation techniques, for example Bagging (Breiman, 1994) and Polynomial kernel SVM (Drucker et al., 1997).

Breiman (1994) uses his Bagging technique on regression trees. This technique aggregates a set of unstable predictors, generated from subsets of a training set, to form a single more stable predictor with a lower error rate. Drucker et al. (1997) compare SVM using polynomial kernels to Breiman's Bagging.

The Royal Holloway Support Vector Machine was used throughout these experiments (Saunders et al., 1998).

17.4.1 Method

Following Breiman (1994) and Drucker et al. (1997) the data is split into 481 training points and 25 test points randomly 100 times. This gives 100 independent trials on which an average squared error rate is measured.

The ANOVA spline kernel, the spline kernel (17.3) and a polynomial kernel $k(\mathbf{x}, \mathbf{y}) = ((\mathbf{x} \cdot \mathbf{y}) + 1)^d$ (a special case of (1.22)) similar to Drucker et al. (1997) are tested here. These results also include the variance of the average squared error for each trial over the hundred trials, as this gives an indication of the stability of the method.

On each trial the training points were split into a training set of 401 points and a validation set of 80 points. The validation set was used to determine the SVM parameters ε from (1.40) and C from (1.43), and the kernels' parameters (order of the ANOVA decomposition or degree of polynomial d).

Data scaling

The input data was scaled linearly for all kernels, the target values were not scaled. There was no other pre-processing, even though several attributes appeared to be suitable for non-linear re-scaling. Spline kernels require all data to be positive (see the appendix), so for both spline kernels all input values were scaled to lie between 0 and 1. Polynomial kernels generally perform better if the data is centered around 0, so for the polynomial kernel all input values were scaled to lie between -1 and 1.

To find the optimal parameters for the SVM, a set of SVMs was created for each trial for each of the three types of kernels and for each type of kernel the SVM from that set with the lowest error on the validation set was selected. The error rate of the selected SVM was then measured on the test set.

ε insensitivity

For each kernel the tolerance ε is set to \$1,000, \$2,000, \$3,000, \$4,000 and \$5,000 in turn.

Kernel parameters

For the ANOVA kernel the set of SVM is created by choosing the orders 2,4,6,8,10 and 13 in turn with each of the above tolerances ε. C is optimized as described below for each of these 30 SVM.

For the linear spline kernel a SVM is created for each ε above and C is optimized as described below for each of the 5 SVM.

For the polynomial kernel, SVM with kernels of degree $d = 4$ and $d = 5$ are created for each of the above ε and C is optimized for each of the 10 SVM as described below.

Selection of C

C was optimized as follows. The error rate on the validation set computed as a function of C is approximately a convex, but non-smooth function. A heuristic method similar to golden section search was used to find the minimum of this function and thus the optimum value of C.

17.4.2 Results

The error rates are calculated for each trial as the average square error over the test sets:

$$\frac{1}{n}\sum_{i=1}^{n}(y_i - f(\mathbf{x}_i))^2 \tag{17.12}$$

where $n = 25$ is the number of cases in the test set of each trial and the unit for $f(\mathbf{x}_i)$ and y_i is \$1,000, i.e. a deviation of 4 corresponds to \$4,000 and the unit of the average squared error is $(\$1,000)^2$. The average and variance of (17.12) is then calculated over all 100 trials:

Kernel	Avg. Square Error	Variance
Bagging (Breiman, 1994)	11.7	
Polynomial	8.28	24.02
Splines	7.87	12.67
ANOVA Splines	7.56	8.70

Table 17.1 Error rates on the test set

The experiments produced better results for the SVM than for the Bagging results obtained in (Breiman, 1994). Among the three different types of SVM kernel the ANOVA splines performed slightly better than the other kernels; as did the variance of the error rates on the test set, but neither of these effects is statistically significant.[1]

17.5 Conclusion and Further research

A SVM using ANOVA decomposition kernels gave a better result than a SVM using other kernels on the Boston housing data and performed more reliably. The low variance observed also indicates a slightly more stable method than with the other kernels. SVM using ANOVA decomposition kernels also yields results which are better than previously reported results with other regression methods on the same data.

ANOVA decomposition is applicable to many other kernels such as Fourier expansions, Hermite polynomials and Radial Basis Functions.

Further research into the ANOVA decomposition kernels will investigate kernels which include lower order components and better ways of parameter selection using the estimated VC-dimension rather than validation sets.

1. More detailed results can be found in (Stitson et al., 1997).

Appendix: Spline kernels

Splines are piecewise polynomial functions. The pieces are polynomial functions of a certain degree d. The number of pieces $l+1$ is fixed by a given set of $l+1$ knot points $t_0, \ldots, t_l$

$$\text{spline}_d(x) = \sum_{r=0}^{l} \gamma_r (x - t_r)_+^d + \sum_{r=0}^{d} \gamma_r^* x^r \tag{17.13}$$

If $\gamma_r = (y - t_r)_+^d$ and $\gamma_r^* = y^r$, then $\text{spline}_d(x)$ can be re-written as

$$\kappa_d(x, y) = \sum_{r=0}^{l} (x - t_r)_+^d (y - t_r)_+^d + \sum_{r=0}^{d} x^r y^r \tag{17.14}$$

so that $f(x) = \sum_{i=1}^{n} (\alpha_i^* - \alpha_i) \kappa_d(x, x_i)$ defines a spline and $\kappa(x, y)$ can be considered as an inner product.

In general, a sum of terms of this type is needed, as it is not possible to match $\gamma_0, \ldots, \gamma_l$ and $\gamma_0^*, \ldots, \gamma_l^*$ in the original spline using a single value of y.

This has been generalised to deal with an infinite number of nodes on the interval $[0, a]$, $0 < a \leq \infty$ (Vapnik et al., 1997):[2]

$$\text{spline}_d(x) = \int_0^a a(t)(x - t)_+^d \, dt + \sum_{r=0}^{d} \gamma_r^* x^r \tag{17.15}$$

where the unknown values γ_i^*, $i = 0, \ldots, d$, and the unknown function $a(t)$ define the expansion. This leads to the following kernel, which effectively uses the support vectors as knot points:

$$\kappa_d(x, y) = \int_0^{min(x,y)} (x - t)_+^d (y - t)_+^d \, dt + \sum_{r=0}^{d} x^r y^r \tag{17.16}$$

This is equivalent to

$$\kappa_d(x, y) = \sum_{r=0}^{d} \frac{\binom{d}{r}}{2d - r + 1} \min(x, y)^{2d - r + 1} |x - y|^r + \sum_{r=0}^{d} x^r y^r \tag{17.17}$$

where $\binom{d}{r} = \frac{d!}{r!(d-r)!}$.

The experiments in section 17.4 use the linear case ($d = 1$):

$$\kappa_1(x, y) = \frac{\min(x, y)^3}{3} + \frac{\min(x, y)^2 |x - y|}{2} + 1 + xy \tag{17.18}$$

2. This kernel requires all values to be positive, as the knot points are all positive.

18 Support Vector Density Estimation

Jason Weston, Alex Gammerman, Mark O. Stitson, Vladimir Vapnik, Volodya Vovk, Chris Watkins
Royal Holloway, University of London
Egham, Surrey, TW20 0EX, UK
J.Weston@dcs.rhbnc.ac.uk
http://www.dcs.rhbnc.ac.uk/

We describe how the SV technique of solving linear operator equations can be applied to the problem of density estimation and how this method makes use of a special type of problem-specific regularization. We present a new optimization procedure and set of kernels that guarantee the estimate to be a density (be non-negative everywhere and have an integral of 1). We introduce a dictionary of kernel functions to find approximations using kernels of different widths adaptively. A method of SV regression using square loss is introduced and it is shown how this technique is useful for density estimation. Finally, a way of compressing density estimates from classical kernel based methods is described, and all these algorithms are compared to classical kernel density estimates (Parzen's windows).

18.1 The Density Estimation Problem

We wish to approximate the density function $p(x)$ from data where the corresponding distribution function is

$$F(x) = P(X \leq x) = \int_{-\infty}^{x} p(t)dt. \tag{18.1}$$

(If not specified otherwise our densities are with respect to the usual Lebesgue measure.)

Finding the required density means solving the linear operator equation[1]

$$\int_{-\infty}^{\infty} \theta(x-t)p(t)dt = F(x), \tag{18.2}$$

where instead of knowing the distribution function $F(x)$ we are given the iid (independently and identically distributed) data

$$x_1, \ldots, x_\ell \tag{18.3}$$

generated by F.

The problem of density estimation is known to be ill-posed. "Ill-posed" means that when finding p that satisfies the equality $Ap = F$, where A is a linear operator, we can have large deviations in solution p corresponding to small deviations in F. In our terms, a small change in the distribution function of the continuous random variable X can cause large changes in the derivative, the density function. To solve ill-posed problems, regularization techniques can be used.

18.2 SV Method of Estimating Densities

Using the data (18.3) we construct the empirical distribution function

$$F_\ell(x) = \frac{1}{\ell}\sum_{i=1}^{\ell} \theta(x - x_i) \tag{18.4}$$

instead of the right hand side of (18.2), which is unknown. We use the SV method to solve the regression problem of approximating the right hand side, using the data

$$(x_1, F_\ell(x_1)), \ldots, (x_\ell, F_\ell(x_\ell)). \tag{18.5}$$

Applying the SV method of solving linear operator equations (Vapnik et al., 1997) (using $y_i = F_\ell(x_i)$), the parameters of the regression function can then be used to express the corresponding density. Regularization is controlled with the parameters ε and C.

This approach can be refined by further control of the regularization (Vapnik, 1998). For any fixed point x the random value $F_l(x)$ is an unbiased estimate of $F(x)$ and has the standard deviation

$$\sigma = \sqrt{\frac{1}{\ell}F(x)(1 - F(x))} \tag{18.6}$$

so we can characterize the accuracy of our approximation at the data points with

$$\varepsilon_i = \lambda\sigma_i = \lambda\sqrt{\frac{1}{\ell}F_\ell(x_i)(1 - F_\ell(x_i))}, \tag{18.7}$$

1. $\theta(x) = \begin{cases} 1, & x > 0 \\ 0, & \text{otherwise} \end{cases}$

where λ is usually chosen to be 1. Therefore we consider triples

$$(x_1, F_\ell(x_1), \varepsilon_1), \ldots, (x_l, F_l(x_\ell), \varepsilon_\ell). \quad (18.8)$$

We will use a generalization of the usual support vector regression technique (SVR) to allow the value ε_i to define the loss at the training point x_i , $i = 1, \ldots, \ell$; in the usual SV technique $\varepsilon_1 = \ldots = \varepsilon_\ell$.

In the next section we will review how the SV method is used to solve linear operator equations and then use this technique to construct kernels specifically for density estimation.

18.3 SV Density Estimation by Solving the Linear Operator Equation

To solve the density estimation problem we use the SV method for solving linear operator equations

$$Ap(t) = F(x), \quad (18.9)$$

where operator A is a linear mapping from a Hilbert space of functions $p(t)$ to a Hilbert space of functions $F(x)$. We solve a regression problem in the image space $(F(x, \mathbf{w}))$ and this solution, which is an expansion on the support vectors, can be used to describe the solution in the pre-image space $(p(t, \mathbf{w}))$. The method is as follows. Choose a set of density functions $p(t, \mathbf{w})$ to solve the problem in the pre-image space that are linear in the flattening space:

$$p(t, \mathbf{w}) = \sum_{r=0}^{\infty} w_r \phi_r(t) = (\mathbf{w} \cdot \Phi(t)); \quad (18.10)$$

that is, $p(t, \mathbf{w})$ are linear combinations of the functions

$$\Phi(t) = (\phi_0(t), \ldots, \phi_n(t), \ldots). \quad (18.11)$$

Each $p(t, \mathbf{w})$ can be thought of as a hyperplane in this flattening space, where $w = (w_0, \ldots, w_n, \ldots)$ are the coefficients to the hyperplane. The result of the mapping from the pre-image to the image space by the operator A can then be expressed as a linear combination of functions in the image Hilbert space defined thus:

$$F(x, \mathbf{w}) = Ap(t, \mathbf{w}) = \sum_{r=0}^{\infty} w_r \psi_r(x) = (\mathbf{w} \cdot \Psi(x)), \quad (18.12)$$

where $\Psi(x) = (\psi_0(x), \ldots, \psi_n(x), \ldots)$ and ψ_r is the rth function from our set of functions after the linear operator A has been applied, i.e $\psi_r(x) = A\phi_r(t)$.

The problem of finding the required density (finding the vector $\mathbf{w}$ in the pre-image space) is equivalent to finding the vector of coefficients $\mathbf{w}$ in the image space, where $\mathbf{w}$ is an expansion on the support vectors

$$\mathbf{w} = \sum_{i=1}^{\ell} \beta_i \Psi(x_i), \tag{18.13}$$

giving the approximation to the desired density

$$p(t, \mathbf{w}) = \sum_{i=1}^{\ell} \beta_i \Psi(x_i) \Phi(t). \tag{18.14}$$

To find the required density we solve a linear regression problem in the image space by minimizing the same functional we used to solve standard regression problems (Vapnik, 1995; Vapnik et al., 1997). Instead of directly finding the infinite dimensional vector $\mathbf{w}$ which is equivalent to finding the parameters which describe the density function, we use kernel functions to describe the mapping from input space to the image and pre-image Hilbert spaces. We use the kernel

$$k(x_i, x_j) = \sum_{r=0}^{\infty} \psi_r(x_i) \psi_r(x_j) \tag{18.15}$$

to represent the inner product in the image space defined by the set of functions Ψ. We solve the corresponding regression problem in the image space, using the coefficients to define the density function in the pre-image space:

$$p(t, \boldsymbol{\beta}) = \sum_{i=1}^{\ell} \beta_i \mathcal{K}(x_i, t) \tag{18.16}$$

where $\mathcal{K}$ is the so-called cross kernel:

$$\mathcal{K}(x_i, t) = \sum_{r=0}^{\infty} \psi_r(x_i) \phi_r(t). \tag{18.17}$$

18.4 Spline Approximation of a Density

We can look for the solution to equation (18.2) in any set of functions where we can construct a corresponding kernel and cross kernel. For example, consider the set of constant splines with infinite number of nodes, similar to Vapnik et al. (1997). That is we approximate the unknown density by the function:

$$p(t) = \int_0^1 g(\tau) \theta(t - \tau) d\tau + a_0 \tag{18.18}$$

(which is assumed to be concentrated on [0,1]) where function $g(\tau)$ and parameter a_0 are to be estimated. We thus define the regression problem in image space

$$F(x) = \int_0^1 g(\tau) \left[\int_0^x \theta(t - \tau) dt \right] d\tau + \int_0^x a_0 dt = \int_0^1 g(\tau) [(x - \tau)_+] d\tau + a_0 x. \tag{18.19}$$

So the corresponding kernel is

$$k(x_i, x_j) = \int_0^1 (x_i - \tau)_+(x_j - \tau)_+ d\tau + x_i x_j \tag{18.20}$$

$$= (x_i \wedge x_j)^2(x_i \vee x_j) - \frac{1}{2}(x_i \wedge x_j)^3 - \frac{1}{2}(x_i \wedge x_j)^2(x_i \vee x_j) + \frac{1}{3}(x_i \wedge x_j)^3 + x_i x_j \tag{18.21}$$

where we denoted by $(x_i \wedge x_j)$ the minimum and $(x_i \vee x_j)$ the maximum of two values x_i and x_j . The corresponding cross kernel is (notice that $\frac{d}{dt}(t-\tau)_+ = \theta(t-\tau)$)

$$\mathcal{K}(x, t) = \int_0^1 \theta(t-\tau)(x-\tau)_+ d\tau + x \tag{18.22}$$

$$= x(x \wedge t) - \frac{(x \wedge t)^2}{2} + x. \tag{18.23}$$

SV regression with Generalized ε-insensitive Loss Function

Using kernel (18.21) and triples (18.8) we can obtain the support vector coefficients $\beta_i = \alpha_i^* - \alpha_i$, only some of which are non-zero. This is achieved by using the standard SV regression approximation (1.47) (Vapnik et al., 1997) with generalized ε-insensitive loss function, by maximizing the quadratic form

$$W(\boldsymbol{\alpha}^*, \boldsymbol{\alpha}) = -\sum_{i=1}^{\ell} \varepsilon_i(\alpha_i^* + \alpha_i) + \sum_{i=1}^{\ell} y_i(\alpha_i^* - \alpha_i) - \frac{1}{2}\sum_{i,j=1}^{\ell} (\alpha_i^* - \alpha_i)(\alpha_j^* - \alpha_j)k(x_i, x_j) \tag{18.24}$$

subject to the constraints

$$\sum_{i=1}^{\ell} \alpha_i^* = \sum_{i=1}^{\ell} \alpha_i \tag{18.25}$$

$$0 \le \alpha_i^* \le C, \quad i = 1, \ldots, \ell, \tag{18.26}$$

$$0 \le \alpha_i \le C, \quad i = 1, \ldots, \ell. \tag{18.27}$$

For density estimation constraint (18.25) can be removed as the threshold b is not used. These coefficients define the approximation to the density

$$p(t) = \sum_{i=1}^{\ell^0} \beta_i^0 \mathcal{K}(x_i^0, t) \tag{18.28}$$

where x_i^0 are the $\ell^0 \le \ell$ support vectors with corresponding non zero coefficients β_i^0.

18.5 Considering a Monotonic Set of Functions

Unfortunately, the described technique does not guarantee the chosen density will always be positive (recall that a probability is always nonnegative, and the distribution function monotonically increases). This is because the set of functions

$F(x, \mathbf{w})$ from which we choose our regression in the image space can contain non-monotonic functions.

We can choose a set of monotonic regression functions and require that the coefficients β_i, $i = 1, \ldots, \ell$, are positive. However, many sets of monotonic functions expressed with Mercer Kernels are too weak in their expressive power to find the desired regression — for example if we choose from the set of polynomials with only positive coefficients.

Using kernels from classical density estimation theory (for example, see Scott (1992)) in the SV method means solving a regression problem using a non-Mercer Kernel. In the next section we consider a slightly different method of SV regression estimation that allows us to use kernels of this form.

18.6 Linear Programming (LP) Approach to SV Regression Estimation

In the SV approach, regression estimation problems are solved as a quadratic optimization problem (18.27), giving the approximation

$$F(x) = \sum_{i=1}^{\ell^0} \beta_i^0 k(x_i^0, x). \tag{18.29}$$

If we choose as our regularizing term the L_1 norm of $\mathbf{w}$ (in the usual approach we choose the L_2 norm) we are only required to solve a linear program (Vapnik, 1998). In this alternative approach our regularizing term is the sum of the support vector weights. This approach is justified by bounds obtained in the problem of Pattern Recognition that the probability of test error is less than the minimum of three terms, one of which is a function of the number of support vectors.

This gives us the linear program:

$$\min \left(\sum_{i=1}^{\ell} \alpha_i + \sum_{i=1}^{\ell} \alpha_i^* + C \sum_{i=1}^{\ell} \xi_i + C \sum_{i=1}^{\ell} \xi_i^* \right) \tag{18.30}$$

SV Regression with L_1 Norm Regularization

with constraints

$$y_i - \varepsilon - \xi_i \leq \left(\sum_{j=1}^{\ell} (\alpha_j^* - \alpha_j) k(x_i, x_j) \right) + b \leq y_i + \varepsilon + \xi_i^*, \quad i = 1, \ldots, \ell, \tag{18.31}$$

$$\alpha_i \geq 0, \quad \xi_i \geq 0, \quad \alpha_i^* \geq 0, \quad \xi_i^* \geq 0, \quad i = 1, \ldots, \ell. \tag{18.32}$$

Minimizing the sum of coefficients is a (convex) approximation to minimizing the number of support vectors. This regularizing term can be seen as a measure of smoothness in input space; a small number of support vectors will mean a less complex decision function. Note that in this approach $k(x, x')$ does not have to satisfy Mercer's condition. We shall use this freedom to construct kernels to estimate densities from a mixture of Gaussian-like shapes. In general we will consider kernels of the form: $\mathcal{K}(x, x_0)$ is a density function and $k(x, x_0)$ its integral, for any fixed x_0.

18.7 Gaussian-like Approximation of a Density

A common approximation to an unknown density is a mixture of bumps (Gaussian-like shapes). Using the SV method this means approximating the regression in the image space (approximating the unknown distribution function) with a mixture of sigmoidal functions. Considering sigmoids of the form

Sigmoid Kernel

$$k(x, x') = \frac{1}{1 + e^{-\gamma(x-x')}} \tag{18.33}$$

the approximation of the density becomes

$$p(x) = \sum_{i=1}^{\ell} \beta_i \mathcal{K}(x_i, x) \tag{18.34}$$

Gaussian-like Cross Kernel

where

$$\mathcal{K}(x, x') = -\frac{\gamma}{2 + e^{\gamma(x-x')} + e^{-\gamma(x-x')}}. \tag{18.35}$$

The chosen centres for the bumps are defined by the support vectors, and their heights by the size of their corresponding weights. Note that the kernel (18.33) is non-symmetrical and can only be used with the approach to SV regression described in section 18.6.

In fact, we can consider any kernel function from classical density estimation theory (Scott, 1992) (Uniform, Cosine arch,...) which has a known integral in order to construct both kernel and cross kernel functions.

Typically, these kernels have a width parameter which is used to choose the smoothness of the density estimate. We would like to remove this free parameter by considering a set of functions which contains functions of different widths. This can be achieved by considering a dictionary of kernel functions.

18.8 SV Density Estimation Using a Dictionary of Kernels

We would like to estimate the density with kernels of varying widths, allowing the technique to choose the best widths at different training points. This can be achieved by considering a dictionary of κ kernel functions giving the decision function

$$p(x) = \sum_{i=1}^{\ell} (\alpha_i^1 \mathcal{K}_1(x_i, x) + \alpha_i^2 \mathcal{K}_2(x_i, x) + \ldots + \alpha_i^\kappa \mathcal{K}_\kappa(x_i, x)) \tag{18.36}$$

Dictionary of Kernels

where each vector x_i , $i = 1, \ldots, \ell$, has coefficients $\alpha_i^j \geq 0$, $j = 1, \ldots, \kappa$, which are positive to guarantee our density estimate is non-negative everywhere . We then have a corresponding dictionary of κ cross kernels, where $\mathcal{K}_i$ has the width γ_i, for example

$$\gamma_1 = \frac{1}{2}, \quad \gamma_2 = \frac{1}{3}, \ldots \tag{18.37}$$

As usual we want many of these coefficients to be zero. As the sum of coefficients is 1 (to make a density) the regularization described in section 18.6 is not suitable for density estimation. Instead, we choose the regularizer

$$\sum_{i=1}^{\ell}\sum_{n=1}^{\kappa}\frac{1}{\gamma_n}\alpha_i^n \tag{18.38}$$

to penalize kernels with small width. This results in a linear program. It is possible to choose other regularizers, and it is not yet clear whether there exist more appropriate measures of smoothness.

Generalized LP SV Regression With Dictionary of Kernels

We can thus transform the LP SV regression technique (section 18.6) to the following optimization problem:

$$\min\left(\sum_{i=1}^{\ell}\sum_{n=1}^{\kappa}\frac{1}{\gamma_n}\alpha_i^n + C\sum_{i=1}^{\ell}\xi_i + C\sum_{i=1}^{\ell}\xi_i^*\right) \tag{18.39}$$

with constraints

$$y_i - \varepsilon_i - \xi_i \le \sum_{j=1}^{\ell}\sum_{n=1}^{\kappa}\alpha_j^n k_n(x_i, x_j) \le y_i + \varepsilon_i + \xi_i^*, \qquad i = 1, \dots, \ell, \tag{18.40}$$

$$\sum_{i=1}^{\ell}\sum_{n=1}^{\kappa}\alpha_i^n = 1, \tag{18.41}$$

$$\alpha_i^n \ge 0, \quad \xi_i \ge 0, \quad \xi_i^* \ge 0, \qquad i = 1, \dots, \ell, \quad n = 1, \dots, \kappa. \tag{18.42}$$

18.9 One More Method of SV Density Estimation

Densities can also be estimated using square loss instead of absolute loss using a linear regularizer (as introduced in section 18.6). This method gives a quadratic optimization problem:

Square Loss SVR with L_1 Norm Regularization

$$\min\left(\sum_{i=1}^{\ell}\left(y_i - \left[\sum_{j=1}^{\ell}(\alpha_j^* - \alpha_j)k(\mathbf{x}_i, \mathbf{x}_j) + b\right]\right)^2 + \lambda\sum_{i=1}^{\ell}(\alpha_i^* + \alpha_i)\right) \tag{18.43}$$

with constraints

$$\alpha_i \ge 0, \quad \alpha_i^* \ge 0, \quad i = 1, \dots, \ell. \tag{18.44}$$

The sparsity again comes from the regularizing term. Using this method of regression for density estimation with kernels of different width we obtain:

Generalized Square Loss SVR with Dictionary of Kernels

$$\min\left(\sum_{i=1}^{\ell}(y_i - \sum_{j=1}^{\ell}\sum_{n=1}^{\kappa}\alpha_j^n k_n(\mathbf{x}_i, \mathbf{x}_j))^2 + \lambda\sum_{i=1}^{\ell}\sum_{n=1}^{\kappa}\frac{1}{\gamma_n}\alpha_i^n\right) \tag{18.45}$$

with constraint (18.41) and the constraints

$$\alpha_i^n \geq 0, \quad i = 1, \ldots, \ell, \quad n = 1, \ldots, \kappa. \tag{18.46}$$

This solution cannot take advantage of the special regularization that we gained from the ε-insensitive loss function. However, the optimization problem we obtain is more suitable to training with a large number of data points as we can employ decomposition methods (as in Osuna et al. (1997b,a)). This becomes feasible due to the simplicity of the constraints.

18.10 Parzen's Windows

Classical kernel based density estimates use the decision function

$$p_{est}(\mathbf{x}) = \frac{1}{\ell} \sum_{i=1}^{\ell} \mathcal{K}(\mathbf{x}, \mathbf{x}_i; \gamma). \tag{18.47}$$

We choose the kernel

$$\mathcal{K}(\mathbf{x}, \mathbf{x}_i; \gamma) = \frac{1}{\gamma^N} \mathcal{K}\Big(\frac{\mathbf{x} - \mathbf{x}_i}{\gamma}\Big), \mathbf{x} \in \mathbb{R}^N \tag{18.48}$$

where $\mathcal{K}(u)$ is a symmetric unimodal density function. The decision function is an expansion on all ℓ training vectors, rather than just the support vectors. In our experiments we compare density approximations from this classical technique with our techniques.

18.11 Approximating Density Estimates Using SV Regression techniques

The support vector approach can also be used to compress the description of density estimates that are generated by some other method, for example the Parzen's windows estimator. Parzen's windows estimation is an expansion on all of the training data. An approximation to this estimate that has a sparse representation (that uses only some vectors in the training set) can be found using a special kind of regression estimation.

This can be done in the following way: construct the pairs $(\mathbf{x}_1, y_1), \ldots, (\mathbf{x}_\ell, y_\ell)$ where $y_i = p_{est}(\mathbf{x}_i)$, and $\mathbf{x}_i$, $i = 1, \ldots, \ell$, are the original training data. We then approximate this data with a regression function. If we restrict our set of functions to be densities (that are non-negative everywhere and have an integral of 1) we try to find a sparse approximation to the density estimate. Accuracy vs complexity of the approximation is controlled by the regularization. This can be achieved by using the regression techniques described in section 18.8 or section 18.9, replacing the kernel $k(x, y)$ with the set of functions you wish to approximate with, for example the radial basis function (RBF) kernel (18.35).

18.12 Multi-dimensional Density Estimation

To estimate multi-dimensional densities the generalization of the SV method is straightforward. We estimate the density $p(\mathbf{x})$ which has the corresponding distribution function

$$F(\mathbf{x}) = P(X \leq \mathbf{x}) = \int_{-\infty}^{x^1} \cdots \int_{-\infty}^{x^N} p(t)dt \ldots dt \tag{18.49}$$

where $\mathbf{x} = (x^1, \ldots, x^N) \in \mathbb{R}^N$ using the multi-dimensional empirical distribution function

$$F_\ell(\mathbf{x}) = \frac{1}{\ell} \sum_{i=1}^{\ell} \theta(x^1 - x_i^1) \ldots \theta(x^N - x_i^N). \tag{18.50}$$

Multi-dimensional kernels can be chosen to be tensor products of one dimensional kernels, or other kernels can be chosen directly.

18.13 Experiments

We considered a density generated from a mixture of two normal distributions

$$p(x, \mu, \sigma) = \frac{1}{2\sigma\sqrt{(2\pi)}} \exp\left\{-\frac{(x-\mu)^2}{2\sigma^2}\right\} + \frac{1}{2\sqrt{(2\pi)}} \exp\left\{-\frac{x^2}{2}\right\} \tag{18.51}$$

where $\mu = -4$, $\sigma = \frac{1}{2}$. We drew 50 , 75, 100 and 200 examples generated by this distribution, and estimated the density by choosing the best value of parameters for each of the following four techniques:

- Linear Programming SVM with ε-insensitive loss (EL-SVM) (section 18.8). Here $\gamma = 1$ (which fixes ε) and C is a free parameter (although it is typically close to ∞).
- Square loss SVM (SL-SVM) (section 18.9). This has the free parameter λ.
- Approximating Parzen's windows estimates using SV regression (section 18.11). We fixed $C = \infty$ and adjusted the free parameter ε (we do not use different values of ε at different training points in this case).
- Parzen's windows (section 18.10), controlling the kernel width γ.

In all techniques we used the RBF kernel (18.35). In all three SV techniques a dictionary of four kernel widths was used: $\gamma_n = \frac{2\pi}{n}$, $n = 1, \ldots, 4$.

For each method we chose the values of the free parameter(s) which gave the lowest value of ISE (integrated squared error estimated using Simpson's method) given knowledge of the true density. In practice, of course, the true density is unknown and the best parameter(s) cannot be selected; we only use this information to find how close the best case prediction of an estimator can possibly get to the true density.

	EL-SVM		SL-SVM		PE-SVM		Parzen	
pts	SVs	ISE	SVs	ISE	SVs	ISE	SVs	ISE
50	5	0.045	6	0.031	10	0.050	50	0.056
75	7	0.095	6	0.036	13	0.086	75	0.087
100	7	0.105	7	0.064	10	0.079	100	0.091
200	5	0.072	7	0.056	20	0.053	200	0.053

Table 18.1 A comparison of the SV density estimator with ε-insensitive loss (EL-SVM), square loss (SL-SVM), a SV approximation of the Parzen's estimator (PE-SVM) and the Parzen's windows estimator (Parzen). Each estimator was picked with the best possible value of parameters given knowledge of the true density.

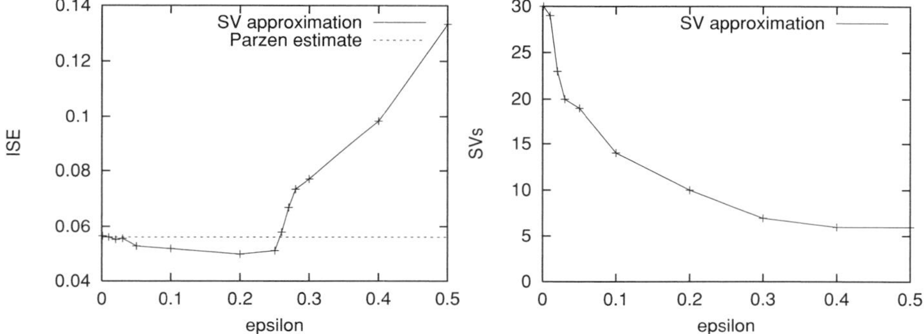

Figure 18.1 Approximating Parzen estimates with the SV method (PE-SVM) gives the same or lower ISE using only a small number of support vectors. Here ε is plotted against ISE (left) and the number of support vectors (right).

The results shown in table 18.1 indicate that all three SV techniques are competitive with the Parzen's estimator, whilst possessing less complex (sparse) decision functions. EL-SVM performed worst but has the advantage of less parameter selection (only C was chosen, and typically $C = \infty$). PE-SVM approximations of Parzen's estimates obtained significantly reduced numbers of support vectors (as Parzen's windows is an expansion on all the training examples) whilst slightly reducing ISE. This reduction is probably due to the decision function being marginally smoother. Trade off between accuracy and complexity when controlling ε in this method can be seen in figure 18.1.

SL-SVM performed best of all, providing functions very close to the true density with small numbers of support vectors. It is worth pointing out this is not because the loss function is square loss instead of absolute loss; setting $\varepsilon = 0$ and controlling the free parameter C in EL-SVM gives as good results (or better) than SL-SVM (results not reported here). However, SL-SVM is better at dealing with a large number of data points (one can employ more efficient decomposition techniques.)

18.14 Conclusions and Further Research

We have described a new SV technique for estimating multi-dimensional densities. Although this results in different optimization problems to normal SVMs, the algorithms have the common feature of possessing sparse decision functions.

We have shown how to solve the density estimation problem as a linear operator equation with a special type of problem-specific regularization using the ε-insensitive loss function.

The integrals of powerful density estimation kernels are not typically symmetrical kernel functions. We show two methods of using non-Mercer kernels with SVM: one with an ε-insensitive loss function and one with square loss. We show how both of these methods can use a dictionary of kernel functions to choose the density estimate from a wide class of functions (for example a mixture of Gaussian-like shapes of different widths).

The results suggest that these methods could obtain good results in real applications. Multi-dimensional problems remain untested; however results in other domains suggest the SV techniques will work well in the multi-dimensional case (the SV kernel regression method is well suited to multi-dimensional problems). Particularly, the square loss method of SV regression is expected to work well as decomposition techniques can be used for dealing with large numbers of training points while using non-Mercer kernels.

Further research lies in the following areas: assessing the performance of the square loss SVM, using dictionaries of kernels in ordinary regression problems and obtaining results in real density estimation applications, in particular in the multi-dimensional case.

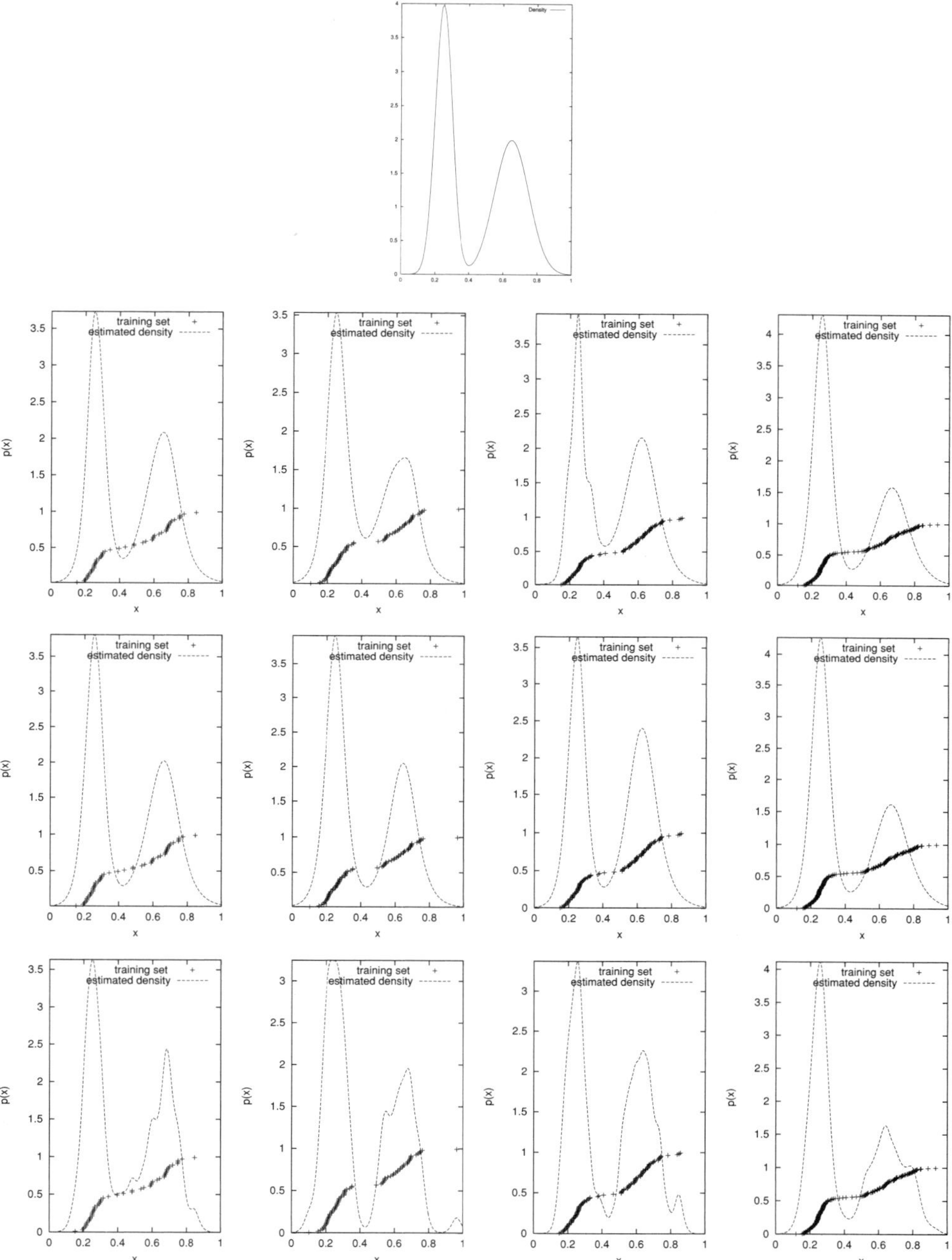

Figure 18.2 The true density (top row) and density estimates by the methods ε-insensitive loss SVM (EL-SVM) (row two), square loss SVM (SL-SVM) (row three), and Parzen's windows estimate (bottom row) generated from (from left to right) 50 , 75 , 100 and 200 points.

19 Combining Support Vector and Mathematical Programming Methods for Classification

Kristin P. Bennett
Mathematical Sciences Department
Rensselaer Polytechnic Institute
Troy, NY 12180, USA
bennek@rpi.edu
http://www.math.rpi.edu/~bennek

We examine the relationship between Support Vector Machines (SVM) for classification and a family of mathematical programming methods (MPM) primarily stemming from Mangasarian's Multisurface Method of Pattern Recognition. MPM and SVM share the same canonical form allowing the two approaches to be easily combined. We show how the dissimilarities of the MPM and SVM approaches have been used to generate two new methods for nonlinear discrimination: support vector decision trees and multicategory learning. Support vector decision trees are decision trees in which each decision is a support vector machine. Multicategory learning is an approach for handing classification problems with more than two classes. In computational studies, altering the original MPM to include principles of statistical learning theory almost always improved generalization. We also show how mathematical programming models and tools allowed us to develop rapidly a practical approach to solving a transduction problem using the theoretical principles of overall risk minimization. The basic of idea of transduction is to predict the class of a given set of unlabeled testing points without first estimating the classification function on the labeled training set. A semi-supervised SVM that includes both labeled training data and unlabeled test data is formulated as a mixed-integer program. Commercial optimization packages are used to solve moderately sized problems. Computational results indicate that the semi-supervised approach did improve generalization on many problems and never performed significantly worse than the baseline supervised SVM.

19.1 Introduction

In this chapter we investigate the relationship between Support Vector Machines (SVM) for classification and a family of mathematical programming methods primarily stemming from Mangasarian's *Multisurface Method of Pattern Recognition* (MSM) (Mangasiarian, 1965; Mangasarian, 1968). We focus on this family of mathematical programming methods (hereafter referred to as MPM) out of the many existing optimization-based classification methods in the literature because they are closely related to SVM. MPM and SVM were developed independently but they share the same canonical form. Thus a great potential exists for interaction between the two approaches. By combining statistical learning theory concepts and SVM ideas, such as kernels, with MPM, potentially many new SVM methods can be derived. Also, model formulation ideas from MPM can be used to develop more rapidly new algorithms based on statistical learning theory.

We begin with an overview of two optimization-based methods for classification: MSM and the *Robust Linear Programming* (RLP) method (Bennett and Mangasarian, 1992). Prior reviews cover how MPM are used for classification, clustering, and function approximation (Mangasarian, 1997; Bradley et al., 1998). Potential for integration of SVM and MPM exists in all these areas. In this chapter we will concentrate on the classification problem only. By starting with the linear classification case, we can see the common roots of MPM and SVM and where the methodologies branched in different directions. By examining dissimilarities, new opportunities for integrated approaches become apparent. Specifically in this chapter we will examine how MPM and SVM can be combined on two problems: nonlinear discrimination via decision trees and multicategory classification. Then we will illustrate how an idea from statistical learning theory on transduction, *Overall Risk Minimization* (Vapnik, 1979), can be quickly converted into a practical algorithm using ideas from MPM. These results are drawn primarily from existing work (Bennett et al., 1998; Bredensteiner and Bennett, 1998; Bennett and Demiriz, 1998). The primary goal of this chapter is to illustrate the current and potential integration of MPM and SVM by making the MPM work accessible in a common format and pointing to future possibilities.

Whenever possible we will use the notation in chapter 1 with a few exceptions. In the original SVM, the separating plane is defined as $\mathbf{w} \cdot \mathbf{x} + b = 0$. To make the notation consistent with MPM literature we will use $\mathbf{w} \cdot \mathbf{x} - \gamma = 0$. The forms are exactly equivalent with $\gamma = -b$. For clarity in some problem formulations, we must divide the training points into their respective classes. For $\Psi \geq 2$ classes, we will denote the classes as A^i, $i = 1, \dots, \Psi$. For example, in the two-class case, the sets are defined as $A^1 := \{\mathbf{x}_i \mid i \in A^1\} := \{\mathbf{x}_i \mid (\mathbf{x}_i, y_i),\ y_i = 1,\ i = 1, \dots, \ell\}$ and $A^2 := \{\mathbf{x}_i \mid i \in A^2\} := \{\mathbf{x}_i \mid (\mathbf{x}_i, y_i),\ y_i = -1,\ i = 1, \dots, \ell\}$. The cardinality of the set A^i is denoted by $\ell_i = |A^i|$.

19.2 Two MPM Methods for Classification

Mangasarian's *Multisurface Method of Pattern Recognition* (Mangasiarian, 1965; Mangasarian, 1968) is very similar in derivation to the Generalized Portrait Method of Vapnik and Chervonenkis (1974). Mangasarian proposed finding a linear discriminant for linearly separable problems by solving the following optimization problem:

$$\begin{aligned} \max_{\mathbf{w},\alpha,\beta} \quad & \alpha - \beta \\ \text{subject to} \quad & \mathbf{w} \cdot \mathbf{x}_i \geq \alpha, \quad i \in A^1 \\ & \mathbf{w} \cdot \mathbf{x}_j \leq \beta, \quad j \in A^2 \\ & \|\mathbf{w}\| = 1 \end{aligned} \tag{19.1}$$

Multisurface Method

The problem constructs two parallel supporting planes, one supporting each class, and then maximizes the separation margin between the planes. The final optimal plane, $\mathbf{w} \cdot \mathbf{x} = \frac{(\alpha+\beta)}{2}$, is the same as that found by the Generalized Portrait Method. Problem (19.1) is difficult to solve as formulated since the constraint, $\|\mathbf{w}\| = 1$, is nonconvex. The SVM formulation (1.9) — (1.10) can be viewed as a transformation of (19.1) in which $\alpha - \beta = 2$ and and $\|\mathbf{w}\|_2$ is minimized. In MSM, Mangasarian proposed using the infinity-norm of $\mathbf{w}$, $\|\mathbf{w}\|_\infty = \max_{i=1,\ldots,n} |\mathbf{w}_i|$, instead of the 2-norm. Then by solving the $2N$ linear programs (LPs), the optimal solution can be found in polynomial time. In each LP one component w_d of the weight vector $\mathbf{w}$ is fixed to either 1 or -1 forcing the constraint $\|\mathbf{w}\|_\infty = 1$ to be satisfied. Thus the first $d = 1, \ldots, N$ linear programs are:

$$\begin{aligned} \max_{\mathbf{w},\alpha,\beta} \quad & \alpha - \beta \\ \text{subject to} \quad & \mathbf{w} \cdot \mathbf{x}_i \geq \alpha, \quad && i \in A^1 \\ & \mathbf{w} \cdot \mathbf{x}_j \leq \beta, \quad && j \in A^2 \\ & -1 \leq \mathbf{w}_i \leq 1, \quad && i = 1, \ldots, N \\ & \mathbf{w}_d = 1 \end{aligned} \tag{19.2}$$

The second set of N LPs consists of Problem (19.2) with $\mathbf{w}_d = -1$ replacing the constraint $\mathbf{w}_d = 1$. The solution to the LP with maximal objective value is the optimal solution of Problem (19.1) with $\|\mathbf{w}\|_\infty = 1$ (Mangasarian et al., 1990).

Unlike the Generalized Portrait Method, MSM also works for the linearly inseparable case. After training, the half-space $\mathbf{w} \cdot \mathbf{x} > \beta$ will contain only training points in A^1; the half-space $\mathbf{w} \cdot \mathbf{x} < \alpha$ will contain only training points in A^2; and the remaining margin may contain a mixture of points from both classes. By using Problem (19.2) recursively on points falling in the margin, MSM constructs a piecewise-linear discriminant function such as in figure 19.1.

Our interest in MSM is primarily historical, because of the similarities to SVM and because MSM set the pattern of how later MPM would address nonlinearly separable problems. While MSM was successfully used in an initial automated breast cancer diagnosis system at the University of Wisconsin-Madison (Wolberg

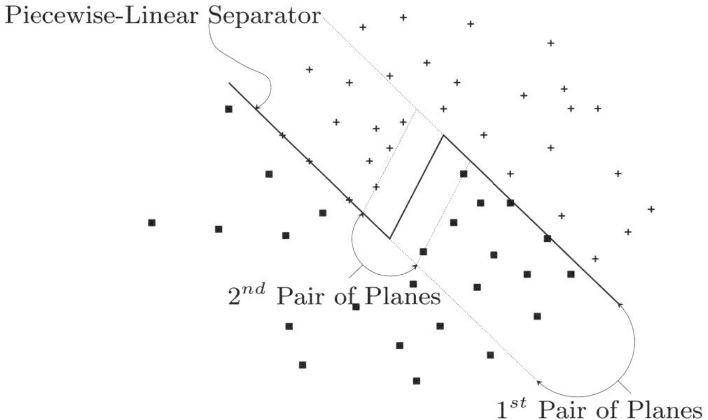

Figure 19.1 Piecewise-linear discriminant constructed by MSM

and Mangasarian, 1990; Mangasarian et al., 1990), the method performs poorly on noisy data sets since it minimizes the largest error in each class. The idea of maximizing the margin of separation was used in both the Generalized Portrait method and MSM, but different norms were used. For the nonlinear case, MSM was applied recursively to yield a piecewise-linear discriminant function. Although Mangasarian did observe that nonlinear discriminants could also be constructed by mapping the input attributes to a higher dimensional space, he made no mention of kernel-based methods.

To make MSM more tolerant of noise, Bennett and Mangasarian proposed the Robust Linear Programming method (RLP) (Bennett and Mangasarian, 1992) using the following linear program:

$$\begin{aligned} \min_{\mathbf{w},\xi,\gamma} \quad & \sum_{i=1}^{l} \delta_i \xi_i \\ \text{subject to} \quad & y_i(w \cdot \mathbf{x}_i - \gamma) + \xi_i \geq 1 \\ & \xi_i \geq 0 \quad i = 1,..,\ell \end{aligned} \tag{19.3}$$

Robust Linear Programming Method

where $\delta_i > 0$ is the fixed misclassification cost associated with point $\mathbf{x}_i$. The original RLP method used $\delta_i = \frac{1}{|A^1|}$ for points in A^1 and $\delta_i = \frac{1}{|A^2|}$ for points in A^2. These choices of δ_i ensure that the meaningless null solution $\mathbf{w} = 0$ is never the unique minimum of Problem (19.3). Smith (1968) proposed Problem (19.3) with $\delta_i = \frac{1}{\ell}$, but $w = 0$ may be the unique optimal solution of the Smith formulation.

Of course RLP is identical to the Soft Margin Hyperplane formulation (1.37) except for the absence of the capacity control term, $\|w\|$, which maximizes the margin of separation. If the 2-norm objective term, $\|w\|_2$, is added to RLP, the result is the original quadratic program for SVM (1.9) — (1.10). From Mangasarian and Meyer (1979) we know that there exists a constant $\bar{C}$ such that for any $C > \bar{C}$, the optimal solution of SVM (1.9) — (1.10) is also an optimal solution of RLP with $\delta_i = 1$. If the solution of RLP is not unique, then the SVM solution with sufficiently large C will be the optimal solution of RLP with the least 2-norm of $\mathbf{w}$. If the 1-norm objective term, $\|\mathbf{w}\|_1$, is added, RLP can be generalized to construct a SVM variation with 1-norm capacity control:

$$\begin{aligned} \min_{\mathbf{w},\gamma,s,\xi} \quad & \lambda \|w\|_1 + (1-\lambda)\sum_{i=1}^{\ell} \delta_i \xi_i \\ \text{subject to} \quad & y_i[\mathbf{w} \cdot \mathbf{x}_i - \gamma] \geq 1 - \xi_i \\ & \xi_i \geq 0, \quad i = 1, \ldots, \ell \end{aligned} \tag{19.4}$$

where $\delta_i > 0$ is a fixed misclassification cost associated with point $\mathbf{x}_i$ and $\lambda \in (0,1)$ is the relative weight on the margin maximization term. If λ is close to 1 more emphasis is placed on obtaining a large margin. If λ is close to 0 then the emphasis is on reducing the misclassification error. This problem is equivalent to following parametric linear program:

Primal RLP with capacity control

$$\begin{aligned} \min_{\mathbf{w},\gamma,s,\xi} \quad & \lambda \sum_{j=1}^{N} s_j + (1-\lambda)\sum_{i=1}^{\ell} \delta_i \xi_i \\ \text{subject to} \quad & y_i[\mathbf{w} \cdot \mathbf{x}_i - \gamma] \geq 1 - \xi_i \\ & \xi_i \geq 0, \quad i = 1, \ldots, \ell \\ & -s_j <= \mathbf{w}_j <= s_j, \quad j = 1, \ldots, N \end{aligned} \tag{19.5}$$

A commercial linear programming package such as CPLEX (CPL, 1994), based on simplex or interior point algorithms, can be used to solve very efficiently the dual RLP problem (Murthy, 1983):

Dual RLP with capacity control

$$\begin{aligned} \min_{\alpha} \quad & \sum_{i=1}^{\ell} \alpha_i \\ \text{subject to} \quad & -(1-\lambda)\mathbf{e} \leq \sum_{i=1}^{\ell} y_i \alpha_i \mathbf{x}_i \leq (1-\lambda)\mathbf{e} \\ & \sum_{i=1}^{\ell} y_i \alpha_i = 0 \\ & 0 \leq \alpha_i \leq \delta_i \lambda, \quad i = 1, \ldots, \ell \end{aligned} \tag{19.6}$$

where $\mathbf{e}$ is an N-dimensional vector of ones. The optimal $\mathbf{w}$ and γ are the Lagrangian multipliers of the constraints of Problem (19.6). Most linear programming packages provide the both the optimal primal and dual solutions.

RLP with 1-norm capacity control has been investigated in several papers (Bennett and Bredensteiner, 1998; Bredensteiner, 1997; Bradley and Mangasarian, 1998a; Bennett et al., 1998). Adding capacity control to RLP has been found empricially to improve generalization. Also there is no empirical evidence that either the 1-norm or 2-norm formulation produces superior generalization. It is an open question what the theoretical generalization differences are. In this chapter, we will refer to the 1-norm form as RLP and the 2-norm form as SVM. Other names, such as Linear Programming Support Vector Machine, have used (Bradley and Mangasarian, 1998a). One benefit of SVM over RLP is that the kernels can easily be introduced into the dual problem in order to make nonlinear discriminants as discussed in chapter 1. But new approaches for incorporating kernels into linear programming based methods are being developed such as those in chapter 18. One major benefit of RLP over SVM is dimensionality reduction. Both RLP and SVM minimize the magnitude of the weights **w**. But RLP forces more of the weights to be 0. This sparsity characteristic of the 1-norm compared to the 2-norm is also used in Basis Pursuit (S. S. Chen, 1996). A second benefit of RLP over SVM is that it can be solved using linear programming instead of quadratic programming. State-of-the-art general-purpose linear program solvers are more efficient, more robust, and capable of solving larger problems than are quadratic program solvers. If the original training data is sparse, the resulting LP formulation will be sparse and typical linear program solvers are constructed to exploit any sparsity. Even for sparse training data, the Hessian of the SVM quadratic program can become very dense. Dense quadratic programs are more difficult. The greater effectiveness of linear versus quadratic programming algorithms is definitely true for general-purpose solvers but optimization methods adapted to SVM problem structure such as the ones discussed in this book and in (Bradley and Mangasarian, 1998b) may help alleviate this difference. Other linear programming formulations such as those of Glover (1990) are also popularly used.

There are many extensions of the basic MSM and RLP methods. The papers (Mangasarian, 1997; Bradley et al., 1998; Bredensteiner, 1997) all contain interesting reviews. For example, two related problems are *feature selection*: constructing the best linear discriminant using the minimum number of attributes; and *misclassification minimization*: explicitly minimizing the number of points misclassified (Bradley and Mangasarian, 1998a; Bradley et al., 1995; Bredensteiner and Bennett, 1997; Bennett and Bredensteiner, 1997). Both problems require minimization of a metric that counts the number of nonzero components of a vector. Both are NP-Hard problems (Amaldi and Kann, 1998, 1995), but approximate answers may be found using nonconvex optimization techniques. Work on maximum feasible subsystems of linear relations can also be applied to these problems (Amaldi and Kann, 1998). These techniques are potentially applicable to SVM-related problems as well.

MPM and SVM have significantly differed in their approach to nonlinear discrimination and multicategory discrimination. For nonlinear discrimination, SVM perform linear discrimination in a higher-dimensional space using kernels to make the problem tractable. Starting with MSM, the primary MPM approach has been to use many linear discriminants to construct piecewise-linear discriminants via a decision tree. In section 19.3 we will investigate how SVM can be combined with the MPM-based decision tree algorithms. Note that there are some MPM that do perform nonlinear mappings into higher dimensional space, most notably the polynomial neural network approaches of Roy et al. (1993, 1995); Roy and Mukhopadhyay (1997). In section 19.4, we examine the SVM and MPM approaches to multicategory discrimination. Multicategory discrimination is the problem of classifying points with more than two classes. The two approaches are combined to yield new methods.

19.3 Nonlinear Separation via Decision Trees

The primary MPM approach for nonlinear separation has been to construct piecewise-linear discriminant functions. These functions are decision trees. This approach can also be used with SVM. The original MSM can be viewed as producing a decision tree with specialized structure. RLP (19.3) has also been successfully used in decision tree algorithms (Bennett, 1992). Here we consider decision trees in which each decision is a support vector machine. Recent results on applying learning theory to decision trees show that there is a tradeoff between the structural complexity of a tree, i.e. the depth and number of nodes, and the complexity of the decisions that are used (Golea et al., 1998; Shawe-Taylor and Cristianini, 1998). We also know that for a given tree structure and empirical risk, decisions with larger margins should produce better generalization (Shawe-Taylor and Cristianini, 1998). So statistical learning theory suggests that using SVM in decision trees is a good idea for generalization. Another benefit is that the decision tree structure provides valuable information about a problem beyond class membership. The decision tree produces potentially interpretable rules, the attributes selected for the decisions indicate which attributes are important, and the leaf nodes cluster the data in potentially meaningful ways. For large data sets, trees with simple decisions based on one attribute can be enormous. Using more powerful decisions, we can construct trees with a much simpler structure. SVM can be regarded as decision trees with one decision but that single decision is largely a black box. By using a linear SVM with 1-norm capacity control (RLP) to construct each decision, a linear rule based on only the necessary attributes will be produced. The 2-norm SVM usually is a function of all the attributes. This attribute reduction is essential in many practical applications. What we want is something in between a very large univariate decision tree and a single nonlinear support vector machine. The ideal decision tree should generalize well, select the only relevant attributes, and provide information about the properties of the underlying data relevant to the application.

Support Vector Decision Trees

In this section we will examine the Support Vector Decision Tree algorithm (SVDT) and its successful application to a database marketing problem. Full details of this work can be found in (Bennett et al., 1998). SVDT uses Dual RLP (19.6) to construct simple decision trees with excellent dimensionality reduction.

SVDT performs top down induction of decision trees (TDIDT) like many other decision tree algorithms including CHAID, CART, MSMT, C4.5, and OC1 (Breiman et al., 1984; Bennett, 1992; Quinlan, 1993; Murthy et al., 1994). The primary distinguishing factors between SVDT and other TDIDT algorithms are the type of decisions used (linear SVM) and the method of constructing the decisions (RLP (19.6)). The basic TDIDT algorithm works as follows:

Algorithm 19.3.1 BASIC TDIDT Alogrithm
Start with the root node.
While a node remains to split

- *Construct decision based on some splitting criterion.*
- *Partition the node into two or more child nodes based on decision.*

Prune the tree if necessary.

In our case the splitting criterion and method is RLP (19.6) solved using the commercial linear programming package CPLEX 5.0 (CPL, 1994).

SVDT has been applied to problems in database marketing. In database marketing problems the primary goal is not testing set accuracy. The primary goal is to produce a good rank ordering of customers. Decision tree algorithms using one attribute per decision are frequently used in database marketing. The problem is that univariate decision tree algorithms can produce very large trees with hundreds of decisions on these large marketing data sets. In SVDT, we use more powerful decisions to produce very compact trees typically with three decisions. By using RLP (19.6) with 1-norm capacity control to construct the decisions, SVDT also performs extensive dimensionality reduction. This is a property of the 1-norm formulation. The primal objective term $\|\mathbf{w}\|_1$ tends to force the weights to zero. For each decision, all of the original attributes are included in the RLP (19.6) model, and then at optimality some of the constraints will be inactive or equivalently not at bound. The Lagrangian multipliers for the constraints are the primal $\mathbf{w}$ variables. Those corresponding to the inactive constraints must be zero due to complementarity in the Karush-Kuhn-Tucker optimality conditions. So the linear program solver will automatically determine which weights/attributes can be eliminated from the problem at that decision.

The SVDT is constructed as part of the customer scoring process. The tradeoffs between training accuracy, dimensionality reduction, and capacity control are controlled by the parameter λ. We tune λ and prune the tree using a validation set. The tuning takes into account the desired goals of the models in database marketing. The customers are ranked based on the response rate of the decision tree nodes and the minimum distance of the points from the decision. The results are reported in gainscharts. The gainscharts are used to compare models for validation, to identify potential customers, and to determine expected utility or profit. In (Bennett et al., 1998) results are given on three business problems. SVDT produced simple, accurate trees that would perform excellent scoring using a small number of attributes. The trees also provide information about the structure of the problem.

On the data set Business I, SVDT produced the tree in figure 19.2. The training data consisted of 2,358 points with 612 attributes and the testing set consisted of 1,006 points. CPLEX produced the root decision in 55 CPU seconds on a Sun Ultra 1/140 with 688 Megabytes of memory. The testing set accuracy of the tree is 77.8% using three linear decisions. For comparison, C4.5 (Quinlan, 1993) produced a tree consisting of 251 univariate decisions with 66% testing set accuracy. C4.5 took 110

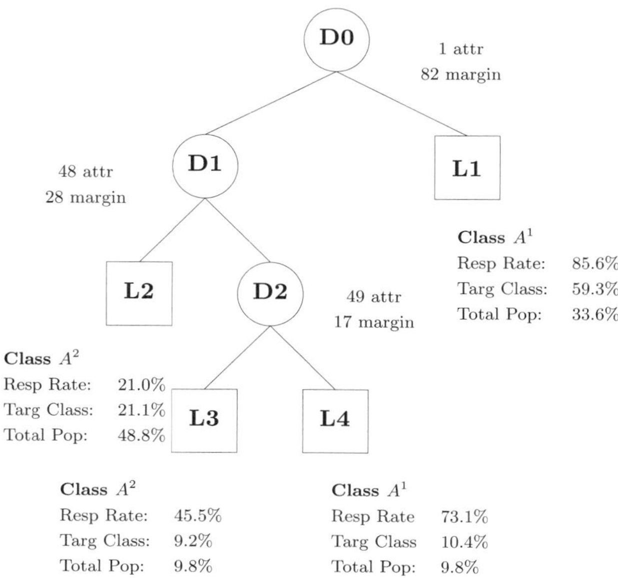

Figure 19.2 Decision tree for Business I test data, target class A^1

minutes to construct the decision tree on the same platform. More accurate SVDT trees exist but their corresponding gainscharts are not significantly different. Recall that the goal is to identify "good" customers, e.g. customers in the target class A^1. The structure of this tree is very interesting. The tree has three internal nodes. A value of $\lambda = .50$ was used at the root node D0 and a value of $\lambda = .25$ for the two subsequent decision nodes D1 and D2. In figure 19.2 each leaf node is labeled with the response rate of the target Class A^1: (|Class A^1 at node|/|all points at node|), the percentage of the target class reached at each node: (|Class A^1 at node|/|Class A^1 in population|), and the percentage of the total population reaching the node: (|all points at node|/|all points in population|). The optimal number of attributes and margin of separation ($\frac{2}{\|\mathbf{w}\|_2}$) is also given for each decision. The optimal number of attributes is the number of attributes at that decision with nonzero optimal weights. Notice that the first decision has only **one** nonzero weight and thus requires only one attribute. This simple decision, using one attribute, produces leaf L1 which reaches 59.3% of the target class with a response rate of 85.8%. Decision D1 uses 48 attributes to produce Leaf L2 that predominately contains points in A^2. The response rate of the target class is only 21.0%, and 48.9% of the total population reaches that node. So in some sense decision D0 identifies the easy points in A^1 and decision D1 separates the points easily identified as being in A^2. The points reaching decision D2 are difficult to classify. The margin of separation in decision D2 is much smaller and the accuracy of the decision is low. But decision D2 still produces useful information for scoring. We can rank customers based on the leaf of the tree that they reach. Our customer preference is L1, L4, L3, and then L2.

Decile	Class A^1 Population	Cumulative Class A^1 Population	Class A^1 Response Rate	Cumulative Response Rate	Lift
1	20.04	20.04	**97.03**	97.03	199.62
2	18.00	38.04	**88.00**	92.54	190.37
3	15.54	53.58	**76.00**	87.04	179.07
4	15.13	68.71	**73.27**	83.58	171.95
5	8.79	77.51	42.57	75.35	155.01
6	7.36	84.87	35.64	68.71	141.35
7	4.50	89.37	22.00	62.07	127.70
8	4.29	93.66	20.79	56.89	117.05
9	3.48	97.14	17.00	52.49	107.98
10	2.86	100.00	13.86	48.61	100.00

Table 19.1 Gainschart for Business I test data.

After the points are ranked, they are sorted and the results displayed in a gainschart. Each line of the gainschart contains one decile (10%) of the population. The deciles appear in order of response rate. For each decile we report the percentage of the total target class population included in that decile, the cumulative percentage of the total target class population, response rate of the target class in that decile, and the cumulative target class response rate. The last column represents lift, a measure of how much better we are doing over choosing customers at random. The lift is defined as 100*(response rate)*|Class A^1 in population|/|Class A^1 in decile|. Deciles with over 50% of Class A^1 are shown in bold. The gainschart for the Business I test data is given in table 19.1.

Once we have the final model, we construct the gainschart using the test data. The testing set response rate by decile is used to estimate the expected business response rate. So for example if we market the top 40% of the customers we could expect a response rate of 83.6% and we would reach approximately 68.7% of all possible target customers in our population. The rule of thumb in database marketing is: if in the fifth decile more than 70% of the target class is reached, then the model is successful. In our gainschart the fifth decile is underlined. We reached 77% of the Class A^1 population at the fifth decile. The testing gainschart combined with a model of expected profitability can be used to determine thresholds for scoring. In the scoring process, potential customers are selected based on the model and the selected threshold (Thomas, 1996; Hughes, 1996).

SVDT was also tested on two other database marketing problems with similar results. The largest data set attempted contained 33.6 megabytes of training data. The largest root decision was solved in 23 minutes by CPLEX on a Sun Ultra 1/140 with 688 megabytes of memory. The interested reader should consult (Bennett et al., 1998) for full details of these experiments.

Other versions of SVDT are possible. The original SVM quadratic program (1.37) approach could be used in a TDIDT algorithm. The catch is that this approach frequently results in only one decision in the tree. Thus alternative SVM-based algorithms that consider and optimize all the decisions in the tree simultaneously have been proposed (Blue, 1998; Bennett and Blue, 1997). The trees found by SVDT on the database marketing problem look very much like the classifiers produced by the original MSM algorithm. So another possibility is to use trees with three-way splits at each decision, the region to the left of the margin, the region in the margin, and the region to the right of the margin. The more popular decision tree algorithms like CART and C4.5 work on attributes that are symbolic. What does the margin mean in the context of symbolic attributes? Can statistical learning theory help in algorithms for problems with symbolic attributes? These are open research topics.

19.4 Multicategory Classification

In this section we focus on the different approaches MPM and SVM have used to solve problems with $\Psi > 2$ classes. The original SVM method for multiclass problems was to find Ψ separate two-class discriminants (Cortes and Vapnik, 1995; Vapnik, 1995). Each discriminant is constructed by separating a single class from all the others. This process requires the solution of Ψ quadratic programs. We will denote this method Ψ-SVM. When applying all Ψ classifiers to the original multicategory data set, multiply classified points or unclassified points may occur. This ambiguity has been avoided by choosing the class of a point corresponding to the classification function that is maximized at that point. The LP approach has been to construct directly Ψ classification functions such that for each point the corresponding class function is maximized (Bennett and Mangasarian, 1993, 1994). The Multicategory Discrimination Method (Bennett and Mangasarian, 1993, 1994) constructs a piecewise-linear discriminant for the Ψ-class problem using a single linear program. We will call this method M-RLP since it is a direction extension of the RLP approach. The Ψ-SVM and M-RLP approaches can be combined to yield two new methods: Ψ-RLP, and M-SVM. We will provide a very brief description of this work. Full details on all the results of this section can be found in (Bredensteiner and Bennett, 1998; Bredensteiner, 1997).

To simplify the equations we introduce some notation. We wish to construct a discriminant function between the elements of the sets, $A^i, i = 1, \ldots, \Psi$, in the N-dimensional real space $\mathbb{R}^N$. Let $\mathbf{A}^i$ be an $\ell_i \times N$ matrix whose rows are the points in A^i. The jth point in A^i and the jth row of $\mathbf{A}^i$ are both denoted $\mathbf{A}^j_i$. Let $\mathbf{e}$ denote a vector of ones of the appropriate dimension. We can express a set of constraints such as $\mathbf{w} \cdot \mathbf{A}^i_j \geq \gamma + 1,\ j = 1, \ldots, \ell_i$ as $\mathbf{A}^i\mathbf{w} \geq (\gamma + 1)\mathbf{e}$.

In the linear case the original MPM and SVM methods both construct a piecewise-linear separator to discriminate between $\Psi > 2$ classes of $\ell^i,\ i = 1, \ldots, \Psi$, points. In Ψ-SVM (Vapnik, 1995; Cortes and Vapnik, 1995) a quadratic program is solved to construct a discriminant function to separate one class from the remaining $\Psi - 1$ classes. This process is repeated Ψ times. In the separable case, the

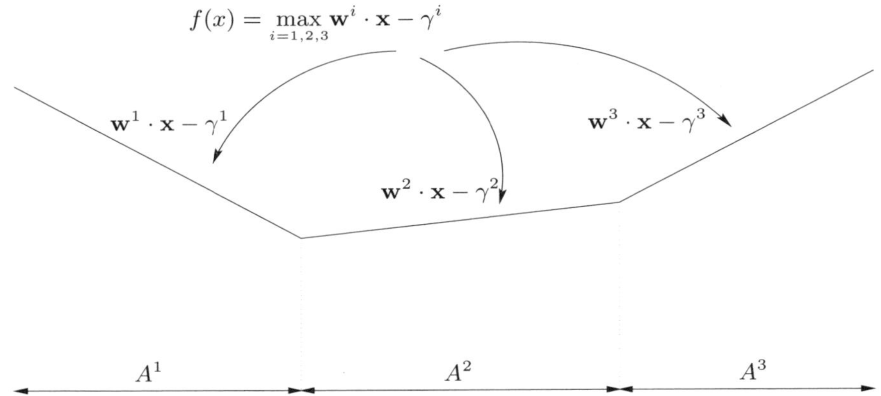

Figure 19.3 Piecewise-linear separation of sets A^1, A^2, and A^3 by the convex piecewise-linear function $f(\mathbf{x})$

Ψ-SVM

linear discriminant for each class must satisfy the following set of inequalities: Find $(\mathbf{w}^1, \gamma^1), \ldots, (\mathbf{w}^\Psi, \gamma^\Psi)$, such that

$$\begin{aligned} A^i\mathbf{w}^i - \gamma^i\mathbf{e} \geq \mathbf{e} \\ -\mathbf{e} \geq A^j\mathbf{w}^i - \gamma^i\mathbf{e}, \quad i,j = 1, \ldots, \Psi, \quad i{\neq}j. \end{aligned} \tag{19.7}$$

For the separable case, solving the Ψ one-class-from-the-rest SVM will yield $(\mathbf{w}^1, \gamma^1), \ldots, (\mathbf{w}^\Psi, \gamma^\Psi)$ if a solution exists.

To classify a new point $\mathbf{x}$, compute $f_i(\mathbf{x}) = \mathbf{w}^i \cdot \mathbf{x} - \gamma^i$. If $f_i(\mathbf{x}) > 0$ for only one i then clearly the point belongs to Class A^i. If more than one $f_i(\mathbf{x}) > 0$ or $f_i(\mathbf{x}) \leq 0$ for all $i = 1, \ldots, \Psi$ then the class is ambiguous. Thus the general rule is that the class of a point $\mathbf{x}$ is determined from $(\mathbf{w}^i, \gamma^i)$, $i = 1, \ldots, \Psi$, by finding i such that

$$f_i(\mathbf{x}) = \mathbf{w}^i \cdot \mathbf{x} - \gamma^i \tag{19.8}$$

is maximized. Figure 19.3 shows a piecewise-linear function $f(x) = \max_{i=1,2,3} f_i(\mathbf{x})$ on R that separates three sets. Note that while $(\mathbf{w}^i, \gamma^i)$, $i = 1 \ldots, \Psi$, are constructed in Ψ separate optimization problems, in the final classification function the problem is not separable into Ψ separate functions.

Note that either SVM (1.37) or RLP can be used to construct the Ψ two-class discriminants depending on the norm desired for capacity control. For clarity, we will call this method used with SVM (1.37), Ψ-SVM. We will denote this method used with RLP (19.6), Ψ-RLP. For both Ψ-SVM and Ψ-RLP to attain perfect training set accuracy using the function (19.8), the following inequalities must be feasible, i.e. there exist $(\mathbf{w}^1, \gamma^1), \ldots, (\mathbf{w}^\Psi, \gamma^\Psi)$ satisfying

$$\mathbf{A}^i\mathbf{w}^i - \gamma^i\mathbf{e} > \mathbf{A}^i\mathbf{w}^j - \gamma^j\mathbf{e}, \quad i,j = 1, \ldots, \Psi, \quad i{\neq}j \tag{19.9}$$

or equivalently

$$\mathbf{A}^i(\mathbf{w}^i - \mathbf{w}^j) - (\gamma^i - \gamma^j)\mathbf{e} \geq \mathbf{e}, \quad i,j = 1,\ldots,\Psi, \quad i{\neq}j \tag{19.10}$$

M-RLP

The M-RLP method[1] proposed and investigated in (Bennett and Mangasarian, 1993, 1994) can be used to find $(\mathbf{w}_i,\ \gamma_i)$, $i = 1,\ldots,\Psi$ satisfying the inequalities (19.10). In the two-class case, M-RLP simplifies to the original RLP method:

$$\min_{\mathbf{w}^i,\gamma^i,\mathbf{z}^{ij}} \left\{ \sum_{i=1}^{\Psi} \sum_{\substack{j=1 \\ j\neq i}}^{\Psi} \frac{e^T \mathbf{z}^{ij}}{\ell^i} \;\middle|\; \begin{array}{c} \mathbf{z}^{ij} \geq -A^i(\mathbf{w}^i - \mathbf{w}^j) + (\gamma^i - \gamma^j)e + e,\ \mathbf{z}^{ij} \geq 0, \\ i,\ j = 1,\ldots,\Psi \quad i \neq j \end{array} \right\} \tag{19.11}$$

where $\mathbf{z}^{ij} \in R^{\ell_i \times 1}$. In M-RLP (19.11), if the optimal objective value is zero, then the data set is piecewise-linearly separable. If the data set is not piecewise-linearly separable, the positive values of the variables $\mathbf{z}_l^{ij}$ are proportional to the magnitude of the misclassified points from the plane $(\mathbf{w}^i - \mathbf{w}^j) \cdot \mathbf{x} = (\gamma^i - \gamma^j) + 1$. M-RLP (19.11) is a linear program. Like the original RLP (19.3), M-RLP does not include any terms for maximizing the margin. So we will now show how M-RLP and SVM can be combined by including margin maximization and generalized inner products into M-RLP.

Intuitively, the "optimal" $(\mathbf{w}^i, \gamma^i)$ should provide the largest margin of separation possible. So in an approach analogous to the two-class SVM approach, we add margin maximization terms to control capacity. The dashed lines in figure 19.4 represent the margins for each piece $(\mathbf{w}^i - \mathbf{w}^j, \gamma^i - \gamma^j)$ of the piecewise-linear separating function. The margin of separation between the classes i and j, i.e. the distance between

$$\begin{aligned} &A^i(\mathbf{w}^i - \mathbf{w}^j) \geq (\gamma^i - \gamma^j)e + e \quad \text{and} \\ &A^j(\mathbf{w}^i - \mathbf{w}^j) \leq (\gamma^i - \gamma^j)e - e, \end{aligned} \tag{19.12}$$

is $\frac{2}{\|\mathbf{w}^i - \mathbf{w}^j\|}$. So, we would like to minimize $\left\|\mathbf{w}^i - \mathbf{w}^j\right\|$ for all $i,j = 1,\ldots,\Psi,\ i \neq j$. Also, we will add the regularization term $\frac{1}{2}\sum_{i=1}^{\Psi}\left\|\mathbf{w}^i\right\|^2$ to the objective. For the piecewise-linearly inseparable problem we get the following:

$$\begin{aligned} \min_{\mathbf{w}^i,\gamma^i,\mathbf{z}^{ij}} \quad & (1-\lambda) \sum_{i=1}^{\Psi} \sum_{\substack{j=1 \\ j\neq i}}^{\Psi} \frac{\mathbf{e}\cdot\mathbf{z}^{ij}}{\ell^i} + \frac{\lambda}{2}\left[\sum_{i=1}^{\Psi}\sum_{j=1}^{i-1} \left\|\mathbf{w}^i - \mathbf{w}^j\right\|^2 + \sum_{i=1}^{\Psi}\left\|\mathbf{w}^i\right\|^2 \right] \\ \text{subject to} \quad & \mathbf{z}^{ij} + \mathbf{A}^i(\mathbf{w}^i - \mathbf{w}^j) - \mathbf{e}(\gamma^i - \gamma^j) - \mathbf{e} \geq 0 \\ & i,j = 1,\ldots,\Psi \quad i \neq j. \end{aligned} \tag{19.13}$$

where $\lambda \in (0,1)$. Note that the misclassification costs of $\frac{1}{\ell^i}$ could be any positive constant. In (Weston and Watkins, 1998) a Ψ-class formulation very similar to Problem (19.13) is proposed except the margin maximization term that minimizes $\|\mathbf{w}^i - \mathbf{w}^j\|^2$ is omitted.

1. The method was originally called Multicategory Discrimination.

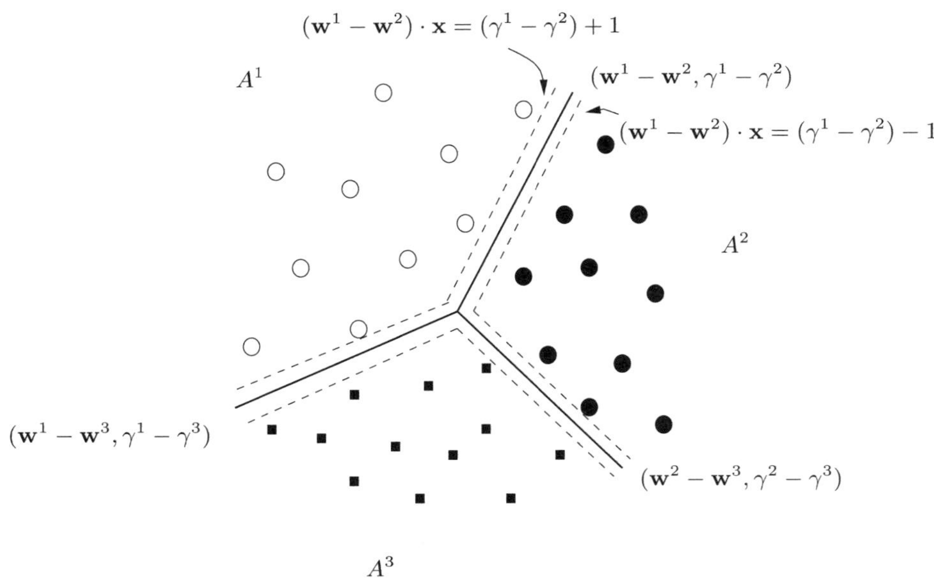

Figure 19.4 Piecewise-linear separator with margins for three classes

As in the two-class case, the dual of the problem can be formulated (see Bredensteiner and Bennett (1998)). Kernels can be easily incorporated into the dual formulation to allow piecewise-nonlinear discriminants. The notion of support vector exists in this formulation. There are $\Psi - 1$ Lagrangian multipliers, $\mathbf{u}$, for each point. The final M-SVM produces a piecewise-nonlinear classification that computes the class of a point $\mathbf{x}$ by finding $i = 1, \ldots, \Psi$ such that the classification function

$$f_i(\mathbf{x}) = \sum_{\substack{j=1 \\ j \neq i}}^{\Psi} \left[\sum_{\mathrm{SV} \in A^i} \mathbf{u}_p^{ij} K(\mathbf{x}, {\mathbf{A}_p^i}^T) - \sum_{\mathrm{SV} \in A^j} \mathbf{u}_p^{ji} K(\mathbf{x}, {\mathbf{A}_p^j}^T) \right] - \gamma^i \tag{19.14}$$

is maximized. Figure 19.5 illustrates the results of M-SVM on a three-class problem in two dimensions.

We summarize some of the computational results comparing M-SVM (19.13), M-RLP (19.11), Ψ-SVM using SVM (1.37), and Ψ-RLP using RLP (19.6). See (Bredensteiner and Bennett, 1998; Bredensteiner, 1997) for full details on the problem formulation and results. The quadratic programming problems for M-SVM and Ψ-SVM were solved using the nonlinear solver implemented in MINOS 5.4 (Murtagh and Saunders, 1993). This solver uses a reduced-gradient algorithm in conjunction with a quasi-Newton method. In M-SVM, Ψ-SVM, and M-RLP, the values for λ are .03, .05, and .03 respectively. Better solutions may result with different choices of λ. Additionally, it is not necessary for the same value of λ to be used for both methods. The kernel function for the piecewise-nonlinear M-SVM and Ψ-SVM methods is $K(x, x_i) = \left(\frac{x \cdot x_i}{n} + 1\right)^d$, where d is the degree of the desired polynomial.

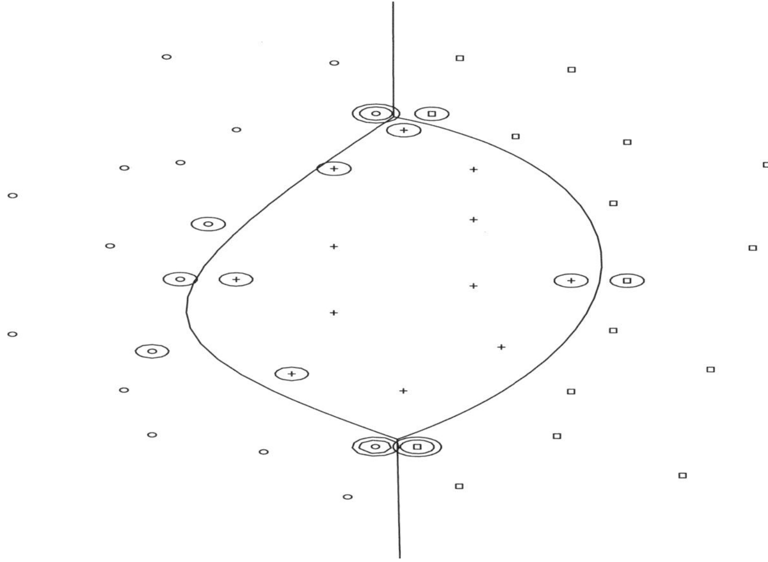

Figure 19.5 Piecewise-polynomial separation of three classes in two dimensions. Support vectors are indicated with large ovals.

We experimented with the United States Postal Service (USPS) Database (LeCun et al., 1989) containing zipcode samples from actual mail. This database is comprised of separate training and testing sets. There are 7291 samples in the training set and 2007 samples in the testing set. Each sample belongs to one of ten classes: the integers 0 through 9. The samples are represented by 256 features. Our experiment was conducted on two subsets of the USPS. Subsets were selected because the M-SVM for the complete formulation was too large for our solver without using decomposition techniques. These data contain handwriting samples of the integers 0 through 9. The objective of this data set is to interpret zipcodes quickly and effectively. This data set has separate training and testing sets, each of which consists of the 10 integer classes. We compiled two individual training subsets from the USPS training data. The first subset contains 1756 examples each belonging to the classes 3, 5, and 8. We call this set USPS-1 training data. The second subset contains 1961 examples each belonging to the classes 4, 6, and 7. We call this set USPS-2 training data. Similarly, two subsets are created from the testing data. In all of these data sets the data values are scaled by $\frac{1}{200}$. Testing set accuracies are reported for all four methods. The total numbers of unique support vectors in the resulting classification functions for the M-SVM and Ψ-SVM methods are given. Reference SVM accuracies on the full 10-class USPS benchmark are 95.8%, using a polynomial kernel, and 97.0%, incorporating prior knowledge by using a local kernel and Virtual SVs (Schölkopf et al., 1998d).

Data	Method	Degree				
		1	2	3	4	5
USPS-1	M-RLP	80.69	-	-	-	-
	Ψ-RLP	91.46	-	-	-	-
	M-SVM	91.26 (415)	91.87 (327)	92.28 (312)	92.07 (305)	92.28 (317)
	Ψ-SVM	91.67 (666)	92.28 (557)	92.89 (514)	92.68 (519)	92.48 (516)
USPS-2	M-RLP	80.66	-	-	-	-
	Ψ-RLP	96.13	-	-	-	-
	M-SVM	94.58 (228)	94.97 (185)	95.36 (167)	94.97 (166)	94.00 (180)
	Ψ-SVM	96.13 (383)	96.52 (313)	96.13 (303)	95.16 (294)	94.58 (289)

Table 19.2 Percent testing set accuracies and (total number of support vectors) for four multicategory discrimination methods

Table 19.2 contains results for the four methods on the USPS data subsets. Both of these data sets are piecewise-linearly separable. The solution that M-RLP has found for each of these data sets tests significantly worse than the other methods. This shows the importance of margin maximization, since M-RLP is the only method lacking capacity control. The Ψ-SVM method generalizes slightly better than M-SVM and is also more computationally efficient. The Ψ-RLP method reports accuracies similar to those of the Ψ-SVM method. Additionally, Ψ-RLP is solving many small linear program rather than one big linear program or quadratic programs, so the computational training time is significantly smaller than that of the other methods. Changing the parameter λ may further improve generalization. The M-SVM method consistently finds classification functions using fewer support vectors than those found by Ψ-SVM. With fewer support vectors, a sample can be classified more quickly since the dot-product of the sample with each support vector must be computed. Thus M-SVM would be a good method to choose when classification time is critical.

The results illustrate the value of combining SVM and MPM approaches. By incorporating margin maximization, the M-RLP method was greatly improved and two new methods Ψ-RLP and M-SVM were constructed. Overall, the one-class-from-the-rest approaches, Ψ-RLP and Ψ-SVM, are best both in terms of generalization and computational time on the problems we tested. Our computational experiments, however, were limited by the capacity of the solver used (MINOS). Decomposition methods such as the ones discussed in this book could be used to make the M-SVM method tractable for larger problems with more classes. Also, 1-norm capacity control and kernels could be added to the M-RLP formulation.

So the best multicategory formulation is still very much an open question both practically and theoretically.

19.5 Overall Risk Minimization and MPM

In this section we show how modeling techniques from mathematical programming can be used to help translate concepts from statistical learning theory into practical algorithms. As a concrete example, we examine the problem of overall risk minimization in transduction. Vapnik briefly presented this problem at the NIPS 1997 Support Vector Machine Workshop (see chapter 3) and it also can be found in chapter 10 of (Vapnik, 1979) and briefly in (Vapnik, 1995). Roughly, the transduction problem is: given a training set of labeled points $(\mathbf{x}_1, y_1), \ldots, (\mathbf{x}_\ell, y_\ell)$, estimate the value of a function $y = f(\mathbf{x})$, at a given unlabeled working set[2] $x_{\ell+1}, \ldots, x_m$. Vapnik distinguishes between this problem of transduction and the induction problem. In induction the goal is to estimate the function f at all possible points. Future testing points are classified using deduction. In transduction, the goal is to estimate the function value at a particular set of testing or working points. In induction, the structural risk is minimized. In transduction, the overall risk is minimized. According to overall risk minimization, by explicitly including the working set data in the problem formulation, we can expect better generalization on problems with insufficient data. We define the semi-supervised support vector machine problem (S^3VM) as: given a training set of points with known class, and a working set of data points with unknown class, construct a SVM to label the working set.

To formulate S^3VM, we start with either the 1-norm RLP or 2-norm SVM formulation, and then add two constraints for each point in the working set. One constraint calculates the misclassification error as if the point were in class A^1 and the other constraint calculates the misclassification error as if the point were in class A^2. The objective function calculates the minimum of the two possible misclassification errors. The final class of the points corresponds to the one that results in the smallest error. Specifically we define the S^3VM as:

Semi-supervised support vector machine

$$\begin{array}{lrl}
\min\limits_{\mathbf{w},\gamma,\xi,z} & (1-\lambda)\left[\sum\limits_{i=1}^{l_1}\delta_i\xi_i + \sum\limits_{j=1}^{l_2}\delta_j z_j + \sum\limits_{i=\ell+1}^{m}\delta_i min(\xi_i, z_i)\right] + \frac{\lambda}{2}\parallel \mathbf{w} \parallel & \\
\text{subject to} & \mathbf{w}\cdot\mathbf{x}_i - \gamma + \xi_i \geq 1 & \xi_i \geq 0 \;\; i \in A^1 \\
& -\mathbf{w}\cdot\mathbf{x}_j + \gamma + z_j \geq 1 & z_j \geq 0 \;\; j \in A^2 \\
& \mathbf{w}\cdot\mathbf{x}_s - \gamma + \xi_s \geq 1 & \xi_s \geq 0 \;\; s \in working\ set \\
& -\mathbf{w}\cdot\mathbf{x}_s + \gamma + z_s \geq 1 & z_s \geq 0
\end{array} \tag{19.15}$$

where $\delta_i > 0$ are fixed misclassification costs. For the experiments reported here we used $\delta_i = 1/m$ and $\lambda = .005$.

2. This set is refered to as the testing set in (Vapnik, 1995).

Integer programming can be used to solve this problem. The basic idea is to add a 0 or 1 decision variable, d_s, for each point $\mathbf{x}_s$ in the working set. This variable indicates the class of the point. If $d_s = 1$ then the point is in class A^1 and if $d_s = 0$ then the point is in class A^2. This results in the following mixed integer program (S^3VM-MIP):

S^3VMMixed Integer Program

$$\min_{\mathbf{w},\gamma,\xi,z,d} \quad (1-\lambda)\left[\sum_{i=1}^{l_1}\delta_i\xi_i + \sum_{j=1}^{l_2}\delta_i z_j + \sum_{i=\ell+1}^{m}\delta_i(\xi_i + z_i)\right] + \frac{\lambda}{2} \parallel \mathbf{w} \parallel_1$$

$$\begin{array}{rll} \text{subject to} \quad \mathbf{w}\cdot x_i - \gamma + \xi_i \geq 1 & \xi_i \geq 0 & i \in A^1 \\ -\mathbf{w}\cdot x_j + \gamma + z_j \geq 1 & z_j \geq 0 & j \in A^2 \\ \mathbf{w}\cdot x_s - \gamma + \xi_s + M(1-d_s) \geq 1 & \xi_s \geq 0 & s \in \mathit{working\ set} \\ -\mathbf{w}\cdot x_s + \gamma + z_s + Md_s \geq 1 & z_s \geq 0 & d_s = \{0,1\} \end{array} \tag{19.16}$$

The constant $M > 0$ is chosen sufficiently large such that if $d_s = 0$ then $\xi_s = 0$ is feasible for any optimal $\mathbf{w}$ and γ. Likewise if $d_s = 1$ then $z_s = 0$.

If the 1-norm is used, this problem can be exactly solved using CPLEX or other commercial integer programming codes (CPL, 1994). CPLEX uses a combination of branch-and-bound and branch-and-cut techniques to produce an enumeration tree. At each node of the tree a continuous relaxation of the integer program is solved using low-cost linear algebra. For problem (19.16) the effectiveness of the algorithm is dependent on the number of integer variables, i.e., the size of the working set, and the effectiveness of the algorithm at pruning the search space. Using the mathematical programming modeling language AMPL (Fourer et al., 1993), we were able to express the problem in approximately thirty lines of code plus a data file and solve it using CPLEX.[3] If the 2-norm is used for margin maximization, then the problem becomes a quadratic integer program. Methods exists for solving these problems but we did not have access to such a solver.

The S^3VM-MIP can be used to solve the transduction problem using overall risk minimization. Consider the simple problem given in figure 20 of (Vapnik, 1979). The results of RLP and SVM-MIP on this problem are shown in figure 19.6. The training set points are shown as transparent triangles and hexagons. The working set points are shown as filled circles. The left picture in figure 19.6 shows the solution found by RLP. Note that when the working set points are added, the resulting separation has a very small margin. The right picture shows the S^3VM-MIP solution constructed using the unlabeled working set. Note that a much larger and clearer separation margin is found. These computational solutions are virtually the same as the solution presented in (Vapnik, 1979).

We also tested S^3VM-MIP on ten real-world data sets from (Murphy and Aha, 1992). S^3VM-MIP tested better on nine of the ten data sets although not always significantly so. On no data set did S^3VM-MIP perform significantly worse. The

3. The AMPL code is available on request from the author at http://www.math.rpi.edu/~bennek.

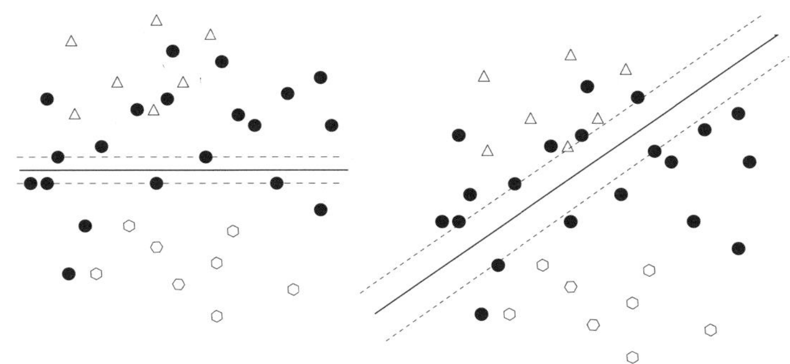

Figure 19.6 Left = solution found by RLP; Right = solution found by S^3VM-MIP

Data Set	Dim	Points	CV-size	RLP	S^3VM-MIP	p-value
Bright	14	2462	50*	0.02	**0.018**	0.343
Cancer	9	699	70	0.036	**0.034**	0.591
Cancer(Prognostic)	30	569	57	0.035	**0.033**	0.678
Dim	14	4192	50*	0.064	**0.054**	0.096
Heart	13	297	30	0.173	**0.160**	0.104
Housing	13	506	51	0.155	**0.151**	0.590
Ionosphere	34	351	35	0.109	**0.106**	0.59
Musk	166	476	48	**0.173**	**0.173**	0.999
Pima	8	769	50*	**0.220**	0.222	0.678
Sonar	60	208	21	0.281	**0.219**	0.045

Table 19.3 RLP vs S^3VM-MIP Average Testing Error

results are given in table 19.3. For each data set, we performed 10-fold cross-validation. For the three starred data sets, our integer programming solver failed due to excessive branching required within the CPLEX algorithm. On those data sets we randomly extracted 50-point working sets for each trial. The same parameters were used for each data set in both the RLP and S^3VM-MIP problems. While the p-values for the paired t-test of the testing set accuracies are not always small, this is not a surprise. Many algorithms have been applied successfully to these problems without incorporating working set information. Thus it was not clear *a priori* that S^3VM would improve generalization on these data sets. For the data sets where no improvement is possible, we would like S^3VM-MIP to not degrade the performance of RLP. Our results are consistant with the statistical learning theory results that incorporating working data improves generalization when insufficient training information is available. In every case, S^3VM-MIP either improved or showed no significant difference in generalization compared to the baseline empirical risk minimization approach RLP. With additional constraints SVM-MIP can be adapted to clustering as well. Other problem formulations for S^3VM that incorporate kernels are being investigated.

19.6 Conclusions

We have shown that the past problem formulations for MPM from the work of Mangasarian share the same canonical form with SVM. These similarities allow MPM and SVM methods to be easily combined. We examined how the dissimilarities of the MPM and SVM approaches can be used to generate new methods for nonlinear discrimination using support vector decision trees and multicategory learning. In almost every case incorporating margin maximization into the MPM resulted in better generalization. We also showed how MPM models and tools allowed us to develop rapidly a practical approach to solving a transduction problem using overall risk minimization. This integer programming approach was able to solve moderately sized problem using commercial software. Our preliminary empirical results support the overall risk minimization theory and indicate that transduction is both a promising and practical research direction for both SVM and MPM. The review here has been solely limited to a few examples from a single family of MPM. There are many extensions of these methods such as those covered in (Bradley et al., 1998; Mangasarian, 1997) that can also be potentially combined with SVM. In addition, there are wide classes of totally unrelated MPM approaches, e.g. Glover (1990); Gochet et al. (1997), that also can be potentially synthesized with SVM. Omission of any method from this paper should not be used as an indication of the quality of the method. The primary weakness of the MPM approaches is that they have not been guided by statistical learning theory. In the problems investigated in this chapter, altering MPM methods to include principles of statistical learning theory almost always improved generalization. Many other optimization-based methods can potentially be improved by similar transformations.

Acknowledgments

Thanks to my collaborators in this work: Leonardo Auslender, Erin Bredensteiner, Ayhan Demiriz, and Donghui Wu and to Scott Vandenberg for his editorial comments. This work was supported by NSF grants IRI-9409427 and IRI-9702306.

20 Kernel Principal Component Analysis

Bernhard Schölkopf, Alexander J. Smola, Klaus-Robert Müller
GMD FIRST
Rudower Chaussee 5, 12489 Berlin, Germany
bs,smola,klaus@first.gmd.de
http://first.gmd.de/~bs,smola,klaus

The idea of implicitly mapping the data into a high-dimensional feature space has been a very fruitful one in the context of SV machines. Indeed, it is this feature which distinguishes them from the Generalized Portrait algorithm which has been known for a long time (Vapnik and Lerner, 1963; Vapnik and Chervonenkis, 1974), and which makes them applicable to complex real-world problems which are not linearly separable. Thus, it was natural to ask the question whether the same idea could prove fruitful in other domains of learning.

The present chapter proposes a new method for performing a nonlinear form of Principal Component Analysis. By the use of Mercer kernels, one can efficiently compute principal components in high-dimensional feature spaces, related to input space by some nonlinear map; for instance the space of all possible 5-pixel products in 16×16 images. We give the derivation of the method and present first experimental results on polynomial feature extraction for pattern recognition.[1]

20.1 Introduction

Principal Component Analysis (PCA) is a powerful technique for extracting structure from possibly high-dimensional data sets. It is readily performed by solving an eigenvalue problem, or by using iterative algorithms which estimate principal components. For reviews of the existing literature, see Jolliffe (1986); Diamantaras and Kung (1996); some of the classical papers are due to Pearson

1. This chapter is an extended version of a chapter from (Schölkopf, 1997), and an article published in *Neural Computation*, Vol. 10, Issue 5, pp. 1299 – 1319, 1998, The MIT Press (Schölkopf et al., 1998e) (First version: (Schölkopf et al., 1996b)).

(1901); Hotelling (1933); Karhunen (1946). PCA is an orthogonal transformation of the coordinate system in which we describe our data. The new coordinate values by which we represent the data are called *principal components*. It is often the case that a small number of principal components is sufficient to account for most of the structure in the data. These are sometimes called *factors* or *latent variables* of the data.

The present work studies PCA in the case where we are not interested in principal components in input space, but rather in principal components of variables, or *features*, which are nonlinearly related to the input variables. Among these are for instance variables obtained by taking arbitrary higher-order correlations between input variables. In the case of image analysis, this amounts to finding principal components in the space of products of input pixels.

To this end, we are computing dot products in feature space by means of kernel functions in input space (cf. chapter 1). Given *any* algorithm which can be expressed solely in terms of dot products, i.e. without explicit usage of the variables themselves, this kernel method enables us to construct different nonlinear versions of it. Even though this general fact was known (Burges, private communication), the machine learning community has made little use of it, the exception being Vapnik's Support Vector machines. In this chapter, we give an example of applying this method in the domain of unsupervised learning, to obtain a nonlinear form of PCA.

In the next section, we will first review the standard PCA algorithm. In order to be able to generalize it to the nonlinear case, we formulate it in a way which uses exclusively dot products. Using kernel representations of dot products (chapter 1), section 20.3 presents a kernel-based algorithm for nonlinear PCA and explains some of the differences to previous generalizations of PCA. First experimental results on kernel-based feature extraction for pattern recognition are given in section 20.4. We conclude with a discussion (section 20.5). Some technical material that is not essential for the main thread of the argument has been relegated to the Appendix.

20.2 Principal Component Analysis in Feature Spaces

Covariance Matrix

Given a set of centered observations $\mathbf{x}_k \in \mathbb{R}^N$, $k = 1, \ldots, M$, $\sum_{k=1}^M \mathbf{x}_k = 0$, PCA diagonalizes the covariance matrix[2]

$$C = \frac{1}{M} \sum_{j=1}^{M} \mathbf{x}_j \mathbf{x}_j^\top . \tag{20.1}$$

2. More precisely, the covariance matrix is defined as the expectation of $\mathbf{x}\mathbf{x}^\top$; for convenience, we shall use the same term to refer to the estimate (20.1) of the covariance matrix from a finite sample.

To do this, one has to solve the eigenvalue equation

$$\lambda \mathbf{v} = C\mathbf{v} \tag{20.2}$$

for eigenvalues $\lambda \geq 0$ and eigenvectors $\mathbf{v} \in \mathbb{R}^N \backslash \{0\}$. As

$$\lambda \mathbf{v} = C\mathbf{v} = \frac{1}{M}\sum_{j=1}^{M}(\mathbf{x}_j \cdot \mathbf{v})\mathbf{x}_j, \tag{20.3}$$

all solutions $\mathbf{v}$ with $\lambda \neq 0$ must lie in the span of $\mathbf{x}_1 \ldots \mathbf{x}_M$, hence (20.2) in that case is equivalent to

$$\lambda(\mathbf{x}_k \cdot \mathbf{v}) = (\mathbf{x}_k \cdot C\mathbf{v}) \text{ for all } k = 1, \ldots, M. \tag{20.4}$$

In the remainder of this section, we describe the same computation in another dot product space F, which is related to the input space by a possibly nonlinear map

$$\Phi : \mathbb{R}^N \to F, \quad \mathbf{x} \mapsto \mathbf{X}. \tag{20.5}$$

Feature Space

Note that the *feature space* F could have an arbitrarily large, possibly infinite, dimensionality. Here and in the following, upper case characters are used for elements of F, while lower case characters denote elements of $\mathbb{R}^N$.

Again, we assume that we are dealing with centered data, $\sum_{k=1}^{M}\Phi(\mathbf{x}_k) = 0$ — we shall return to this point later. In F, the covariance matrix takes the form

$$\bar{C} = \frac{1}{M}\sum_{j=1}^{M}\Phi(\mathbf{x}_j)\Phi(\mathbf{x}_j)^\top. \tag{20.6}$$

Note that if F is infinite-dimensional, we think of $\Phi(\mathbf{x}_j)\Phi(\mathbf{x}_j)^\top$ as a linear operator on F, mapping

$$\mathbf{X} \mapsto \Phi(\mathbf{x}_j)(\Phi(\mathbf{x}_j) \cdot \mathbf{X}). \tag{20.7}$$

We now have to find eigenvalues $\lambda \geq 0$ and eigenvectors $\mathbf{V} \in F\backslash\{0\}$ satisfying

$$\lambda \mathbf{V} = \bar{C}\mathbf{V}. \tag{20.8}$$

Again, all solutions $\mathbf{V}$ with $\lambda \neq 0$ lie in the span of $\Phi(\mathbf{x}_1), \ldots, \Phi(\mathbf{x}_M)$. For us, this has two useful consequences: first, we may instead consider the set of equations

$$\lambda(\Phi(\mathbf{x}_k) \cdot \mathbf{V}) = (\Phi(\mathbf{x}_k) \cdot \bar{C}\mathbf{V}) \text{ for all } k = 1, \ldots, M, \tag{20.9}$$

and second, there exist coefficients α_i $(i = 1, \ldots, M)$ such that

$$\mathbf{V} = \sum_{i=1}^{M}\alpha_i\Phi(\mathbf{x}_i). \tag{20.10}$$

Combining (20.9) and (20.10), we get

$$\lambda\sum_{i=1}^{M}\alpha_i(\Phi(\mathbf{x}_k) \cdot \Phi(\mathbf{x}_i)) = \frac{1}{M}\sum_{i=1}^{M}\alpha_i\left(\Phi(\mathbf{x}_k) \cdot \sum_{j=1}^{M}\Phi(\mathbf{x}_j)(\Phi(\mathbf{x}_j) \cdot \Phi(\mathbf{x}_i))\right) \tag{20.11}$$

for all $k = 1, \ldots, M$. Defining an $M \times M$ matrix K by

$$K_{ij} := (\Phi(\mathbf{x}_i) \cdot \Phi(\mathbf{x}_j)), \tag{20.12}$$

this reads

$$M\lambda K\boldsymbol{\alpha} = K^2\boldsymbol{\alpha}, \tag{20.13}$$

where $\boldsymbol{\alpha}$ denotes the column vector with entries $\alpha_1, \ldots, \alpha_M$. To find solutions of (20.13), we solve the eigenvalue problem

Eigenvalue Problem in F

$$M\lambda\boldsymbol{\alpha} = K\boldsymbol{\alpha} \tag{20.14}$$

for nonzero eigenvalues. In the Appendix, we show that this gives us all solutions of (20.13) which are of interest for us.

Let $\lambda_1 \leq \lambda_2 \leq \ldots \leq \lambda_M$ denote the eigenvalues of K (i.e. the solutions $M\lambda$ of (20.14)), and $\boldsymbol{\alpha}^1, \ldots, \boldsymbol{\alpha}^M$ the corresponding complete set of eigenvectors, with λ_p being the first nonzero eigenvalue (assuming that Φ is not identically 0). We normalize $\boldsymbol{\alpha}^p, \ldots, \boldsymbol{\alpha}^M$ by requiring that the corresponding vectors in F be normalized, i.e.

$$(\mathbf{V}^k \cdot \mathbf{V}^k) = 1 \text{ for all } k = p, \ldots, M. \tag{20.15}$$

By virtue of (20.10) and (20.14), this translates into a normalization condition for $\boldsymbol{\alpha}^p, \ldots, \boldsymbol{\alpha}^M$:

$$\begin{aligned} 1 &= \sum_{i,j=1}^{M} \alpha_i^k \alpha_j^k (\Phi(\mathbf{x}_i) \cdot \Phi(\mathbf{x}_j)) = \sum_{i,j=1}^{M} \alpha_i^k \alpha_j^k K_{ij} \\ &= (\boldsymbol{\alpha}^k \cdot K\boldsymbol{\alpha}^k) = \lambda_k(\boldsymbol{\alpha}^k \cdot \boldsymbol{\alpha}^k) \end{aligned} \tag{20.16}$$

For the purpose of principal component extraction, we need to compute projections onto the eigenvectors $\mathbf{V}^k$ in F ($k = p, \ldots, M$). Let $\mathbf{x}$ be a test point, with an image $\Phi(\mathbf{x})$ in F, then

$$(\mathbf{V}^k \cdot \Phi(\mathbf{x})) = \sum_{i=1}^{M} \alpha_i^k (\Phi(\mathbf{x}_i) \cdot \Phi(\mathbf{x})) \tag{20.17}$$

may be called its nonlinear principal components corresponding to Φ.

In summary, the following steps were necessary to compute the principal components: first, compute the matrix K, second, compute its eigenvectors and normalize them in F; third, compute projections of a test point onto the eigenvectors.[3]

For the sake of simplicity, we have above made the assumption that the observations are centered. This is easy to achieve in input space, but more difficult in

3. Note that in our derivation we could have used the known result (e.g. Kirby and Sirovich, 1990) that PCA can be carried out on the dot product matrix $(\mathbf{x}_i \cdot \mathbf{x}_j)_{ij}$ instead of (20.1), however, for the sake of clarity and extendability (in the Appendix, we shall consider the question how to center the data in F), we gave a detailed derivation.

F, as we cannot explicitly compute the mean of the mapped observations in F. There is, however, a way to do it, and this leads to slightly modified equations for kernel-based PCA (see Appendix).

To conclude this section, note that Φ can be an arbitrary nonlinear map into the possibly high-dimensional space F, for instance, the space of all d-th order monomials in the entries of an input vector. In that case, we need to compute dot products of input vectors mapped by Φ, with a possibly prohibitive computational cost. The solution to this problem, however, is to use kernel functions (1.20) — we *exclusively* need to compute dot products between mapped patterns (in (20.12) and (20.17)); *we never need the mapped patterns explicitly.* Therefore, we can use the kernels described in chapter 1. The particular kernel used then implicitly determines the space F of all possible features. The proposed algorithm, on the other hand, is a mechanism for *selecting* features in F.

20.3 Kernel Principal Component Analysis

The Algorithm. To perform kernel-based PCA (figure 20.1), henceforth referred to as *kernel PCA*, the following steps have to be carried out: first, we compute the matrix $K_{ij} = (k(\mathbf{x}_i, \mathbf{x}_j))_{ij}$. Next, we solve (20.14) by diagonalizing K, and normalize the eigenvector expansion coefficients α^n by requiring $\lambda_n(\boldsymbol{\alpha}^n \cdot \boldsymbol{\alpha}^n) = 1$. To extract the principal components (corresponding to the kernel k) of a test point $\mathbf{x}$, we then compute projections onto the eigenvectors by (cf. Eq. (20.17), figure 20.2),

Feature Extraction

$$(\mathbf{V}^n \cdot \Phi(\mathbf{x})) = \sum_{i=1}^{M} \alpha_i^n k(\mathbf{x}_i, \mathbf{x}). \tag{20.18}$$

If we use a kernel satisfying Mercer's conditions (Proposition 1.1), we know that this procedure exactly corresponds to standard PCA in some high-dimensional feature space, except that we do not need to perform expensive computations in that space.

Properties of Kernel-PCA. For Mercer kernels, we know that we are in fact doing a standard PCA in F. Consequently, all mathematical and statistical properties of PCA (cf. Jolliffe (1986); Diamantaras and Kung (1996)) carry over to kernel PCA, with the modifications that they become statements about a set of points $\Phi(\mathbf{x}_i), i = 1, \ldots, M$, in F rather than in $\mathbb{R}^N$. In F, we can thus assert that PCA is the orthogonal basis transformation with the following properties (assuming that the eigenvectors are sorted in descending order of the eigenvalue size):

- the first q ($q \in \{1, \ldots, M\}$) principal components, i.e. projections on eigenvectors, carry more variance than any other q orthogonal directions
- the mean-squared approximation error in representing the observations by the first q principal components is minimal[4]

4. To see this, in the simple case where the data $\mathbf{z}_1, \ldots, \mathbf{z}_\ell$ are centered, we consider an

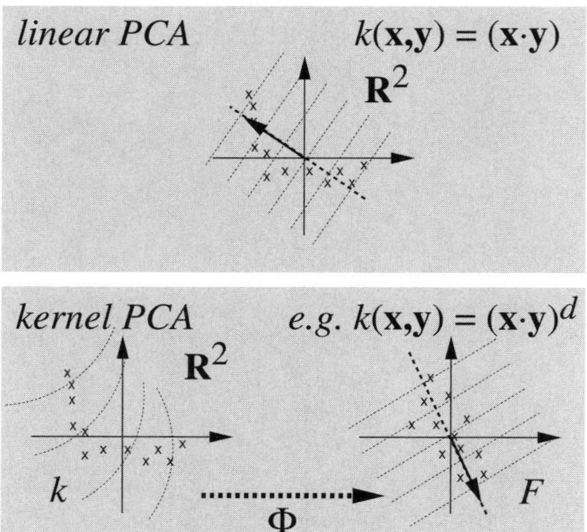

Figure 20.1 The basic idea of kernel PCA. In some high-dimensional feature space F (bottom right), we are performing linear PCA, just as a PCA in input space (top). Since F is nonlinearly related to input space (via Φ), the contour lines of constant projections onto the principal eigenvector (drawn as an arrow) become *nonlinear* in input space. Note that we cannot draw a preimage of the eigenvector in input space, as it may not even exist. Crucial to kernel PCA is the fact that there is no need to perform the map into F: all necessary computations are carried out by the use of a kernel function k in input space (here: $\mathbb{R}^2$).

- the principal components are uncorrelated
- the first q principal components have maximal mutual information with respect to the inputs (this holds under Gaussianity assumptions, and thus depends on the particular kernel chosen and on the data)

---

orthogonal basis transformation W, and use the notation P_q for the projector on the first q canonical basis vectors $\{\mathbf{e}_1, \ldots, \mathbf{e}_q\}$. Then the mean squared reconstruction error using q vectors is

$$\begin{aligned} & \frac{1}{\ell}\sum_i \|\mathbf{z}_i - W^\top P_q W \mathbf{z}_i\|^2 = \frac{1}{\ell}\sum_i \|W\mathbf{z}_i - P_q W \mathbf{z}_i\|^2 = \frac{1}{\ell}\sum_i \sum_{j>q} (W\mathbf{z}_i \cdot \mathbf{e}_j)^2 \\ = \; & \frac{1}{\ell}\sum_i \sum_{j>q} (\mathbf{z}_i \cdot W^\top \mathbf{e}_j)^2 = \frac{1}{\ell}\sum_i \sum_{j>q} (W^\top \mathbf{e}_j \cdot \mathbf{z}_i)(\mathbf{z}_i \cdot W^\top \mathbf{e}_j) = \sum_{j>q} (W^\top \mathbf{e}_j \cdot C W^\top \mathbf{e}_j). \end{aligned}$$

It can easily be seen that the values of this quadratic form (which gives the variances in the directions $W^\top \mathbf{e}_j$) are minimal if the $W^\top \mathbf{e}_j$ are chosen as its (orthogonal) eigenvectors with smallest eigenvalues.

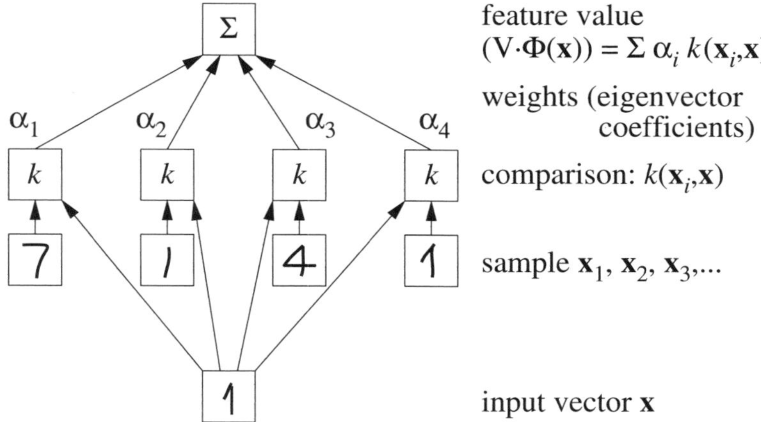

Figure 20.2 Feature extractor constructed by kernel PCA (cf. (20.18)). In the first layer, the input vector is compared to the sample via a kernel function, chosen a priori (e.g. polynomial, Gaussian, or sigmoid). The outputs are then linearly combined using weights which are found by solving an eigenvector problem. As shown in the text, the depicted network's function can be thought of as the projection onto an eigenvector of a covariance matrix in a high-dimensional feature space. As a function on input space, it is nonlinear.

To translate these properties of PCA in F into statements about the data in input space, they need to be investigated for specific choices of a kernels.

Invariance of Polynomial Kernels

We conclude this section with a characterization of kernel PCA with polynomial kernels. In section 1.3, it was explained how using polynomial kernels $(\mathbf{x} \cdot \mathbf{y})^d$ corresponds to mapping into a feature space whose dimensions are spanned by all possible d-th order monomials in input coordinates. The different dimensions are scaled with the square root of the number of ordered products of the respective d pixels (e.g. $\sqrt{2}$ in (1.22)). These scaling factors precisely ensure invariance of kernel PCA under the group of all orthogonal transformations (rotations and mirroring operations). This is a desirable property: it ensures that the features extracted do not depend on which orthonormal coordinate system we use for representing our input data.

Theorem 20.1 (Invariance of Polynomial Kernels)
Up to a scaling factor, kernel PCA with $k(\mathbf{x}, \mathbf{y}) = (\mathbf{x} \cdot \mathbf{y})^d$ is the only PCA in a space of all monomials of degree d which is invariant under orthogonal transformations of input space.

This means that even if we *could* compute all monomials of degree p for the data at hand and perform PCA on the monomials, with the additional requirement of not implying any preferred directions, we would obtain multiples of the results generated by kernel PCA.

Cum grano salis, the theorem applies to all methods which are based on Mercer kernels. In the context of SV machines, it states that the estimated function is the same if the SV optimization is performed on data which is described in a rotated coordinate system.

The proof is given in the appendix.

Computational Complexity. A fifth order polynomial kernel on a 256-dimensional input space yields a 10^{10}-dimensional feature space. For two reasons, kernel PCA can deal with this huge dimensionality. First, as pointed out in Sect. 20.2 we do not need to look for eigenvectors in the full space F, but just in the subspace spanned by the images of our observations $\mathbf{x}_k$ in F. Second, we do not need to compute dot products explicitly between vectors in F (which can be impossible in practice, even if the vectors live in a lower-dimensional subspace), as we are using kernel functions. Kernel PCA thus is computationally comparable to a linear PCA on ℓ observations with an $\ell \times \ell$ dot product matrix. If k is easy to compute, as for polynomial kernels, e.g., the computational complexity is hardly changed by the fact that we need to evaluate kernel functions rather than just dot products. Furthermore, in the case where we need to use a large number ℓ of observations, we may want to work with an algorithm for computing only the largest eigenvalues, as for instance the power method with deflation (for a discussion, see Diamantaras and Kung (1996)). In addition, we can consider using an estimate of the matrix K, computed from a subset of $M < \ell$ examples, while still extracting principal components from all ℓ examples (this approach was chosen in some of our experiments described below). The situation can be different for principal component extraction. There, we have to evaluate the kernel function M times for each extracted principal component (20.18), rather than just evaluating one dot product as for a linear PCA. Of course, if the dimensionality of F is 10^{10}, this is still vastly faster than linear principal component extraction in F. Still, in some cases, e.g. if we were to extract principal components as a preprocessing step for classification, we might want to speed up things. This can be carried out by the reduced set technique (Burges, 1996; Burges and Schölkopf, 1997) used in the context of Support Vector machines. In the present setting, we approximate each eigenvector

Reduced Set

$$\mathbf{V} = \sum_{i=1}^{\ell} \alpha_i \Phi(\mathbf{x}_i) \tag{20.19}$$

(Eq. (20.10)) by another vector

$$\tilde{\mathbf{V}} = \sum_{j=1}^{m} \beta_j \Phi(\mathbf{z}_j), \tag{20.20}$$

where $m < \ell$ is chosen a priori according to the desired speedup, and $\mathbf{z}_j \in \mathbb{R}^N$, $j = 1, \ldots, m$.

This is done by minimizing the squared difference

$$\rho = \|\mathbf{V} - \tilde{\mathbf{V}}\|^2. \tag{20.21}$$

This can be carried out without explicitly dealing with the possibly high-dimensional space F. Since

$$\rho = \|\mathbf{V}\|^2 + \sum_{i,j=1}^{m} \beta_i \beta_j k(\mathbf{z}_i, \mathbf{z}_j) - 2 \sum_{i=1}^{\ell} \sum_{j=1}^{m} \alpha_i \beta_j k(\mathbf{x}_i, \mathbf{z}_j), \tag{20.22}$$

the gradient of ρ with respect to the β_j and the $\mathbf{z}_j$ is readily expressed in terms of the kernel function, thus ρ can be minimized by standard gradient methods. For the task of handwritten character recognition, this technique led to a speedup by a factor of 50 at almost no loss in accuracy (Burges and Schölkopf, 1997).

Finally, we add that although kernel principal component extraction is computationally more expensive than its linear counterpart, this additional investment can pay back afterwards. In experiments on classification based on the extracted principal components, we found when we trained on nonlinear features, it was sufficient to use a linear Support Vector machine to construct the decision boundary. Linear Support Vector machines, however, are much faster in classification speed than nonlinear ones. This is due to the fact that for $k(\mathbf{x}, \mathbf{y}) = (\mathbf{x} \cdot \mathbf{y})$, the Support Vector decision function (1.32) can be expressed with a single weight vector $\mathbf{w} = \sum_{i=1}^{\ell} y_i \alpha_i \mathbf{x}_i$ as $f(\mathbf{x}) = \text{sgn}((\mathbf{x} \cdot \mathbf{w}) + b)$. Thus the final stage of classification can be done extremely fast; the speed of the principal component extraction phase, on the other hand, and thus the accuracy-speed trade-off of the whole classifier, can be controlled by the number of components which we extract, or by the number m (cf. Eq. (20.20)).

Interpretability and Variable Selection. In PCA, it is sometimes desirable to be able to select specific axes which span the subspace into which one projects in doing principal component extraction. This way, it may for instance be possible to choose variables which are more accessible to interpretation. In the nonlinear case, there is an additional problem: some elements of F do not have preimages in input space. To make this plausible, note that the linear span of the training examples mapped into feature space can have dimensionality up to M (the number of examples). If this exceeds the dimensionality of input space, it is rather unlikely that each vector of the form (20.10) has a preimage (cf. Schölkopf et al., 1998c). To get interpretability, we thus need to find directions in input space (i.e. input variables) whose images under Φ span the PCA subspace in F. This can be done with an approach akin to the one described above: we could parametrize our set of desired input variables and run the minimization of (20.22) only over those parameters. The parameters can be e.g. group parameters which determine the amount of translation, say, starting from a set of images.

Dimensionality Reduction, Feature Extraction, and Reconstruction. Unlike linear PCA, the proposed method allows the extraction of a number of principal components which *can* exceed the input dimensionality. Suppose that the number of observations M exceeds the input dimensionality N. Linear PCA, even when it is based on the $M \times M$ dot product matrix, can find at most N nonzero eigenvalues — they are identical to the nonzero eigenvalues of the $N \times N$ covariance matrix. In contrast, kernel PCA can find up to M nonzero eigenvalues — a fact that illustrates that it is impossible to perform kernel PCA directly on an $N \times N$ covariance matrix. Even more features could be extracted by using several kernels. Being just a basis transformation, standard PCA allows the reconstruction of the original patterns $\mathbf{x}_i, i = 1, \ldots, \ell$, from a complete set of extracted principal components $(\mathbf{x}_i \cdot \mathbf{v}_j), j = 1, \ldots, \ell$, by expansion in the eigenvector basis. Even from an incomplete set of components, good reconstruction is often possible. In kernel PCA, this is more difficult: we can reconstruct the image of a pattern in F from its nonlinear components; however, if we only have an approximate reconstruction, there is no guarantee that we can find an exact preimage of the reconstruction in input space. In that case, we would have to resort to an approximation method (cf. (20.22)). First results obtained by using this approach are reported in (Schölkopf et al., 1998c). Alternatively, we could use a suitable regression method for estimating the reconstruction mapping from the kernel-based principal components to the inputs.

Generalizations of PCA

Comparison to Other Methods for Nonlinear PCA. Starting from some of the properties characterizing PCA (see above), it is possible to develop a number of possible generalizations of linear PCA to the nonlinear case. Alternatively, one may choose an iterative algorithm which adaptively estimates principal components, and make some of its parts nonlinear to extract nonlinear features. Rather than giving a full review of this field here, we briefly describe four approaches, and refer the reader to Diamantaras and Kung (1996) for more details.

Hebbian Networks. Initiated by the pioneering work of Oja (1982), a number of unsupervised neural-network type algorithms computing principal components have been proposed (e.g. Sanger, 1989). Compared to the standard approach of diagonalizing the covariance matrix, they have advantages for instance in cases where the data are nonstationary. Nonlinear variants of these algorithms are obtained by adding nonlinear activation functions. The algorithms then extract features that the authors have referred to as nonlinear principal components. These approaches, however, do not have the geometrical interpretation of kernel PCA as a standard PCA in a feature space nonlinearly related to input space, and it is thus more difficult to understand what exactly they are extracting. For a discussion of some approaches, see Karhunen and Joutsensalo (1995).

Autoassociative Multi-Layer Perceptrons. Consider a linear perceptron with one hidden layer, which is smaller than the input. If we train it to reproduce the input values as outputs (i.e. use it in autoassociative mode), then the hidden unit activations form a lower-dimensional representation of the data, closely related to PCA (see for instance Diamantaras and Kung (1996)). To generalize to a nonlinear setting, one uses nonlinear activation functions and additional layers.[5] While this of course can be considered a form of nonlinear PCA, it should be stressed that the resulting network training consists in solving a hard nonlinear optimization problem, with the possibility to get trapped in local minima, and thus with a dependence of the outcome on the starting point of the training. Moreover, in neural network implementations there is often a risk of getting overfitting. Another drawback of neural approaches to nonlinear PCA is that the number of components to be extracted has to be specified in advance. As an aside, note that hyperbolic tangent kernels can be used to extract neural network type nonlinear features using kernel PCA (figure 20.7). The principal components of a test point $\mathbf{x}$ in that case take the form (figure 20.2) $\sum_i \alpha_i^n \tanh(\kappa(\mathbf{x}_i, \mathbf{x}) + \Theta)$.

Principal Curves. An approach with a clear geometric interpretation in input space is the method of principal curves (Hastie and Stuetzle, 1989), which iteratively estimates a curve (or surface) capturing the structure of the data. The data are projected onto (i.e. mapped to the closest point on) a curve, and the algorithm tries to find a curve with the property that each point on the curve is the average of all data points projecting onto it. It can be shown that the only straight lines satisfying the latter are principal components, so principal curves are indeed a generalization of the latter. To compute principal curves, a nonlinear optimization problem has to be solved. The dimensionality of the surface, and thus the number of features to extract, is specified in advance. Some authors (e.g. Ritter et al., 1990) have discussed parallels between the Principal Curve algorithm and self-organizing feature maps (Kohonen, 1982) for dimensionality reduction.

Kernel PCA. Kernel PCA is a nonlinear generalization of PCA in the sense that (a) it is performing PCA in feature spaces of arbitrarily large (possibly infinite) dimensionality, and (b) if we use the kernel $k(\mathbf{x}, \mathbf{y}) = (\mathbf{x} \cdot \mathbf{y})$, we recover the original PCA algorithm. Compared to the above approaches, kernel PCA has the main advantage that no nonlinear optimization is involved — it is essentially linear algebra, as simple as standard PCA. In addition, we need not specify the number of components that we want to extract in advance. Compared to neural approaches, kernel PCA could be disadvantageous if we need to process a very large number of observations, as this results in a large matrix K. Compared to principal curves, kernel PCA is so far harder to interpret in input space; however, at least for polynomial kernels, it has a very clear interpretation in terms of higher-order features.

5. Simply using nonlinear activation functions in the hidden layer would not suffice: already the linear activation functions lead to the best approximation of the data (given the number of hidden nodes), so for the nonlinearities to have an effect on the components, the architecture needs to be changed (see e.g. Diamantaras and Kung (1996)).

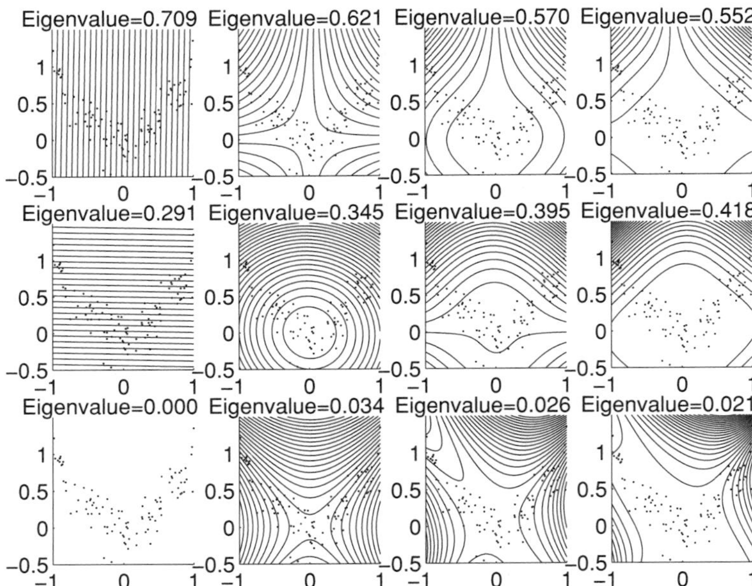

Figure 20.3 Two-dimensional toy example, with data generated in the following way: x-values have uniform distribution in $[-1, 1]$, y-values are generated from $y_i = x_i^2 + \upsilon$, were υ is normal noise with standard deviation 0.2. From left to right, the polynomial degree in the kernel (1.21) increases from 1 to 4; from top to bottom, the first 3 eigenvectors are shown, in order of decreasing eigenvalue size. The figures contain lines of constant principal component value (contour lines); in the linear case, these are orthogonal to the eigenvectors. We did not draw the eigenvectors, as in the general case, they live in a higher-dimensional feature space.

20.4 Feature Extraction Experiments

In this section, we present a set of experiments where we used kernel PCA (in the form taking into account centering in F, as described in the Appendix) to extract principal components. First, we shall take a look at a simple toy example; following that, we describe real-world experiments where we assess the utility of the extracted principal components by classification tasks.

Toy Examples. To provide some insight into how PCA in F behaves in input space, we show a set of experiments with an artificial 2-D data set, using polynomial kernels (cf. (1.21)) of degree 1 through 4 (see figure 20.3). Linear PCA (on the left) only leads to 2 nonzero eigenvalues, as the input dimensionality is 2. In contrast, nonlinear PCA allows the extraction of further components. In the figure, note that nonlinear PCA produces contour lines of constant feature value which reflect the structure in the data better than in linear PCA. In all cases, the first principal component varies monotonically along the parabola which underlies the data. In the nonlinear cases, also the second and the third components show behaviour which is similar for different polynomial degrees. The third component, which comes with small eigenvalues (rescaled to sum to 1), seems to pick up the variance caused by the noise, as can be nicely seen in the case of degree 2. Dropping this component would thus amount to noise reduction.

In figure 20.3, it can be observed that for larger polynomial degrees, the principal component extraction functions become increasingly flat around the origin. Thus, different data points not too far from the origin would only differ slightly in the value of their principal components. To understand this, consider the following example: suppose we have two data points

$$\mathbf{x}_1 = \begin{pmatrix} 1 \\ 0 \end{pmatrix}, \quad \mathbf{x}_2 = \begin{pmatrix} 2 \\ 0 \end{pmatrix}, \tag{20.23}$$

and a kernel $k(\mathbf{x}, \mathbf{y}) := (\mathbf{x} \cdot \mathbf{y})^2$. Then the differences between the entries of $\mathbf{x}_1$ and $\mathbf{x}_2$ get scaled up by the kernel, namely $k(\mathbf{x}_1, \mathbf{x}_1) = 1$, but $k(\mathbf{x}_2, \mathbf{x}_2) = 16$. We can compensate for this by rescaling the individual entries of each vector $\mathbf{x}_i$ by

$$(\mathbf{x}_i)_k \mapsto \operatorname{sign}((\mathbf{x}_i)_k) \cdot |(\mathbf{x}_i)_k|^{\frac{1}{2}}. \tag{20.24}$$

Indeed, figure 20.4, taken from Schölkopf et al. (1997a), shows that when the data are preprocessed according to (20.24) (where higher degrees are treated correspondingly), the first principal component extractors do hardly depend on the degree anymore, as long as it is larger than 1. If necessary, we can thus use (20.24) to preprocess our data. Note, however, that the above scaling problem is irrelevant for the character and object databases to be considered below: there, most entries of the patterns are ± 1.

Further toy examples, using radial basis function kernels (1.31) and neural network type sigmoid kernels (1.30), are shown in figures 20.5 – 20.8. Matlab code for carrying out kernel PCA can be obtained from http://svm.first.gmd.de.

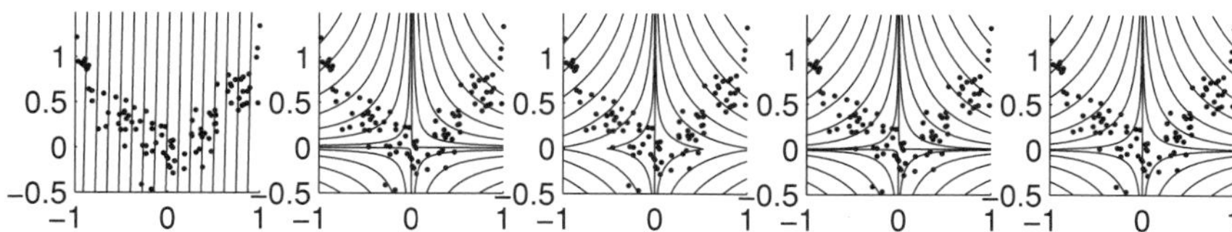

Figure 20.4 PCA with kernel (1.21), degrees $d = 1, \ldots, 5$. 100 points $((x_i)_1, (x_i)_2)$ were generated from $(x_i)_2 = (x_i)_1^2 + v$ (where v is Gaussian noise with standard deviation 0.2); all $(x_i)_j$ were rescaled according to $(x_i)_j \mapsto \operatorname{sgn}((x_i)_j) \cdot |(x_i)_j|^{1/d}$. Displayed are contour lines of constant value of the first principal component. Nonlinear kernels ($d > 1$) extract features which nicely increase along the direction of main variance in the data; linear PCA ($d = 1$) does its best in that respect, too, but it is limited to straight directions.

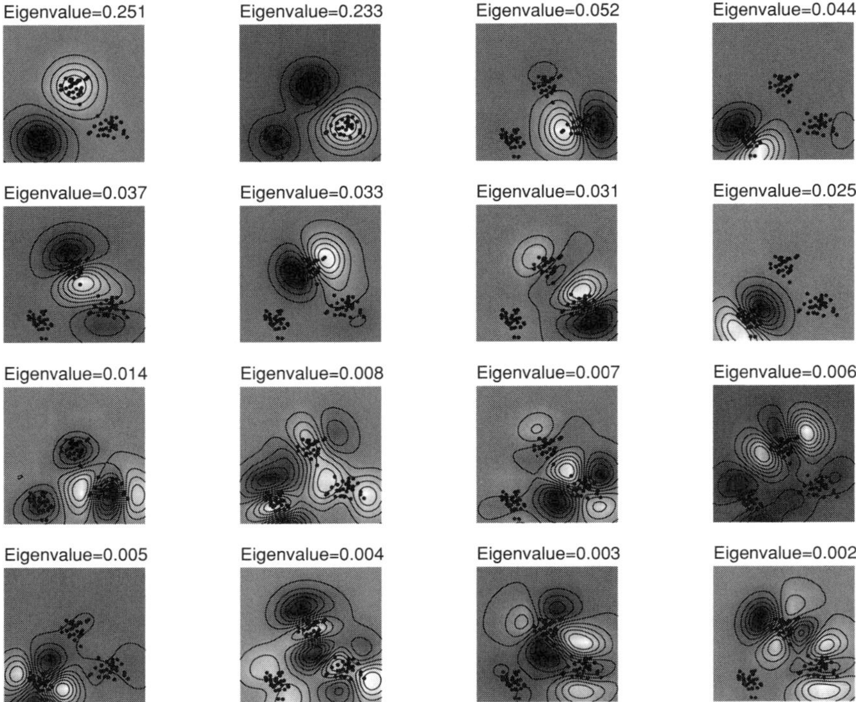

Figure 20.5 Two-dimensional toy example with three data clusters (Gaussians with standard deviation 0.1, depicted region: $[-1, 1] \times [-0.5, 1]$): first 16 nonlinear principal components extracted with $k(\mathbf{x}, \mathbf{y}) = \exp\left(-\|\mathbf{x} - \mathbf{y}\|^2/0.1\right)$. Note that the first 2 principal component (top left), with the largest eigenvalues, nicely separate the three clusters. The components 3 – 5 split up the clusters into halves. Similarly, the components 6 – 8 split them again, in a way orthogonal to the above splits. The higher components are more difficult to describe. They look for finer structure in the data set, identifying higher-order moments.

Object Recognition. In this set of experiments, we used the MPI chair database with 89 training views of 25 different chair models (figure 20.9, Blanz et al. (1996); Schölkopf (1997)). We computed the matrix K from all 2225 training examples, and used polynomial kernel PCA to extract nonlinear principal components from the training and test set. To assess the utility of the components, we trained a soft margin hyperplane classifier on the classification task. This is a special case of Support Vector machines, using the standard dot product as a kernel function. Table 20.1 summarizes our findings: in all cases, nonlinear components as extracted by polynomial kernels (Eq. (1.21) with $d > 1$) led to classification accuracies superior to standard PCA. Specifically, the nonlinear components afforded top test performances between 2% and 4% error; in the linear case we obtained 17%.

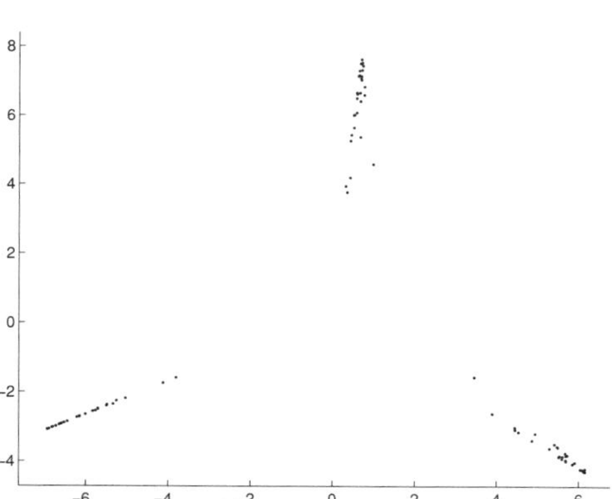

Figure 20.6 A plot of the data representation given by the first two principal components of figure 20.5. The clusters of figure 20.5 end up roughly on separated lines (the left, right, and top region corresponds to the clusters left, top, and right, respectively). Note that already the first component (the horizontal axis) separates the clusters — this cannot be done using linear PCA.

# of components	Test Error Rate for degree						
	1	2	3	4	5	6	7
64	23.0	21.0	17.6	16.8	16.5	16.7	16.6
128	17.6	9.9	7.9	7.1	6.2	6.0	5.8
256	16.8	6.0	4.4	3.8	3.4	3.2	3.3
512	n.a.	4.4	3.6	3.9	2.8	2.8	2.6
1024	n.a.	4.1	3.0	2.8	2.6	2.6	2.4
2048	n.a.	4.1	2.9	2.6	2.5	2.4	2.2

Table 20.1 Test error rates on the MPI chair database for linear Support Vector machines trained on nonlinear principal components extracted by PCA with polynomial kernel (1.21), for degrees 1 through 7. In the case of degree 1, we are doing standard PCA, with the number of nonzero eigenvalues being at most the dimensionality of the space, 256; thus, we can extract at most 256 principal components. The performance for the nonlinear cases (degree > 1) is significantly better than for the linear case, illustrating the utility of the extracted nonlinear components for classification.

Character Recognition. To validate the above results on a widely used pattern recognition benchmark database, we repeated the same experiments on the US postal service database of handwritten digits (figure 20.10, e.g. Simard et al. (1993); LeCun et al. (1989)). This database contains 9298 examples of dimensionality 256; 2007 of them make up the test set. For computational reasons, we decided to use a subset of 3000 training examples for the matrix K. Table 20.2 illustrates two advantages of using nonlinear kernels: first, performance of a linear classifier trained on nonlinear principal components is better than for the same number of linear components; second, the performance for nonlinear components can be further improved by using more components than possible in the linear case. The

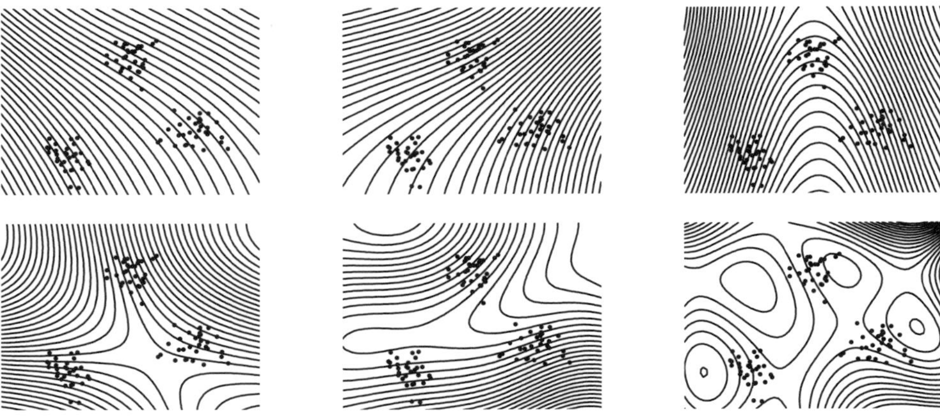

Figure 20.7 Two-dimensional toy example with three data clusters (Gaussians with standard deviation 0.1, depicted region: $[-1,1] \times [-0.5,1]$): first 6 nonlinear principal components extracted with $k(\mathbf{x}, \mathbf{y}) = \tanh(2(\mathbf{x} \cdot \mathbf{y}) - 1)$ (the gain and threshold values were chosen according to the values used in SV machines, cf. Schölkopf et al. (1995)). Note that the first 2 principal components are sufficient to separate the three clusters, and the third and fourth component simultaneously split all clusters into halves.

latter is related to the fact that of course there are many more higher-order features than there are pixels in an image. Regarding the first point, note that extracting a certain number of features in a 10^{10}-dimensional space constitutes a much higher reduction of dimensionality than extracting the same number of features in 256-dimensional input space.

For all numbers of features, the optimal degree of kernels to use is around 4, which is compatible with Support Vector machine results on the same data set (Schölkopf et al., 1995). Moreover, with only one exception, the nonlinear features are superior to their linear counterparts. The resulting error rate for the best of our classifiers (4.0%) is competitive with convolutional 5-layer neural networks (5.0% were reported by LeCun et al. (1989)) and nonlinear Support Vector classifiers (4.0%, Schölkopf et al. (1995)); it is much better than linear classifiers operating directly on the image data (a linear Support Vector machine achieves 8.9%; Schölkopf et al. (1995)). Our results were obtained without using any prior knowledge about symmetries of the problem at hand, explaining why the performance is inferior to Virtual Support Vector classifiers (3.2%, Schölkopf et al. (1996a)), and Tangent Distance Nearest Neighbour classifiers (2.6%, Simard et al. (1993)). We believe that adding e.g. local translation invariance, be it by generating "virtual" translated examples (cf. Schölkopf et al., 1996a) or by choosing a suitable kernel incorporating locality (e.g. as the ones in (Schölkopf et al., 1998d), which led to an error rate of 3.0%), could further improve the results.

USPS Benchmark

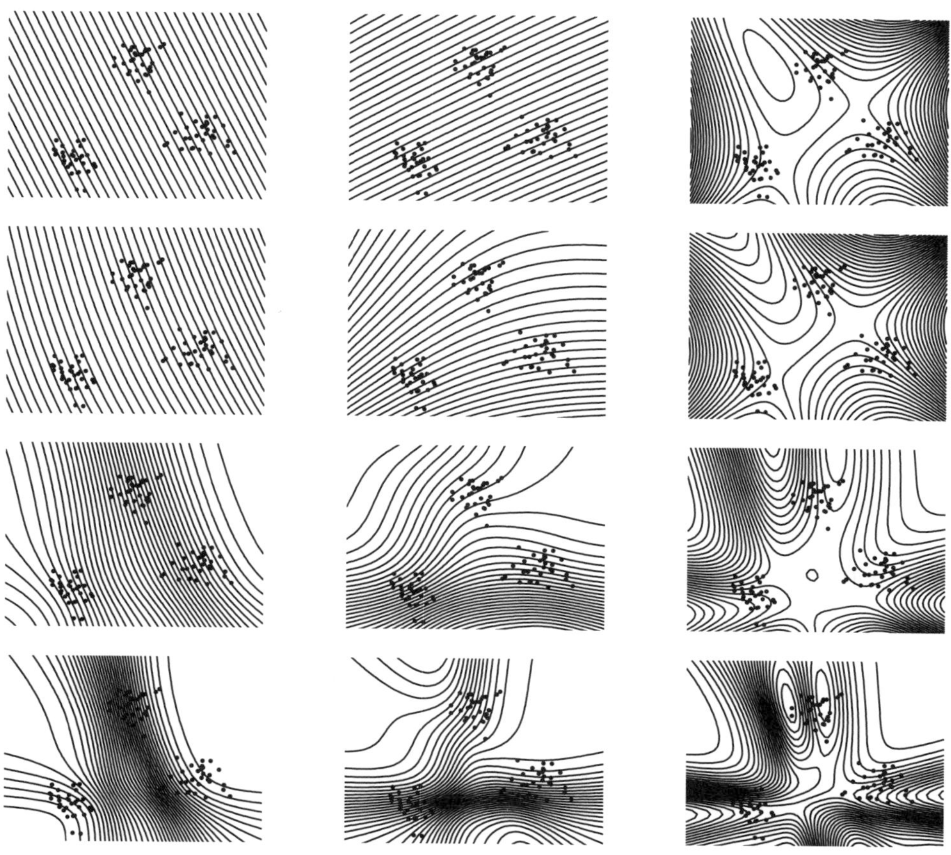

Figure 20.8 A smooth transition from linear PCA to nonlinear PCA is obtained by using hyperbolic tangent kernels $k(\mathbf{x}, \mathbf{y}) = \tanh(\kappa(\mathbf{x} \cdot \mathbf{y}) + 1)$ with varying gain κ: from top to bottom, $\kappa = 0.1, 1, 5, 10$ (data as in the previous figures). For $\kappa = 0.1$, the first two features look like linear PCA features. For large κ, the nonlinear region of the tanh function becomes effective. In that case, kernel PCA can exploit this nonlinearity to allocate the highest feature gradients to regions where there are data points, as can be seen nicely in the case $\kappa = 10$.

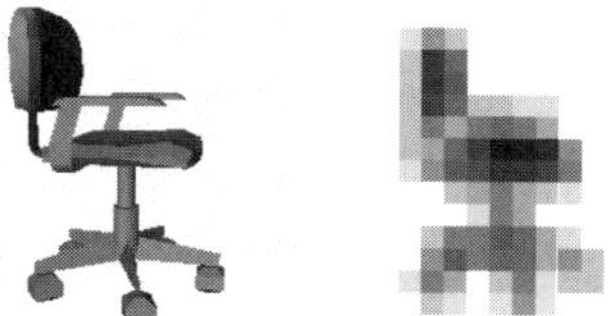

Figure 20.9 *Left*: rendered view of a 3-D model from the MPI chair database; *right*: 16×16 downsampled image, as used in the experiments.

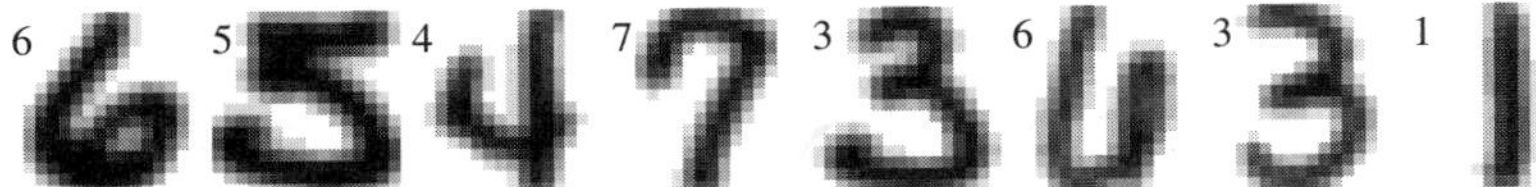

Figure 20.10 The first 8 patterns from the US Postal Service database of handwritten digits, with class labels.

# of components	Test Error Rate for degree						
	1	2	3	4	5	6	7
32	9.6	8.8	8.1	8.5	9.1	9.3	10.8
64	8.8	7.3	6.8	6.7	6.7	7.2	7.5
128	8.6	5.8	5.9	6.1	5.8	6.0	6.8
256	8.7	5.5	5.3	5.2	5.2	5.4	5.4
512	n.a.	4.9	4.6	4.4	5.1	4.6	4.9
1024	n.a.	4.9	4.3	4.4	4.6	4.8	4.6
2048	n.a.	4.9	4.2	4.1	4.0	4.3	4.4

Table 20.2 Test error rates on the USPS handwritten digit database for linear Support Vector machines trained on nonlinear principal components extracted by PCA with kernel (1.21), for degrees 1 through 7. In the case of degree 1, we are doing standard PCA, with the number of nonzero eigenvalues being at most the dimensionality of the space, 256. Clearly, nonlinear principal components afford test error rates which are superior to the linear case (degree 1).

20.5 Discussion

Feature Extraction for Classification. This chapter was devoted to the presentation of a new technique for nonlinear PCA. To develop this technique, we made use of the Mercer kernel method so far only used in supervised learning. Kernel PCA constitutes a mere first step towards exploiting this technique for a large class of algorithms.

In experiments comparing the utility of kernel PCA features for pattern recognition using a linear classifier, we found two advantages of nonlinear kernels: first, nonlinear principal components afforded better recognition rates than corresponding numbers of linear principal components; and second, the performance for nonlinear components can be further improved by using more components than possible in the linear case. We have not yet compared kernel PCA to other techniques for nonlinear feature extraction and dimensionality reduction. We can, however, compare results to other feature extraction methods which have been used in the past by researchers working on the USPS classification problem (cf. section 20.4). Our system of kernel PCA feature extraction plus linear support vector machine for instance performed better than LeNet1 (LeCun et al., 1989). Even though the latter result has been obtained a number of years ago, it should be stressed that LeNet1 provides an architecture which contains a great deal of prior information about the handwritten character classification problem. It uses shared weights to improve transformation invariance, and a hierarchy of feature detectors resembling parts of the human visual system. These feature detectors were for instance used by Bottou and Vapnik (1992) as a preprocessing stage in their experiments in local learning. Note that, in addition, our features were extracted without taking into account that we want to do classification. Clearly, in supervised learning, where we are given a set of labelled observations $(\mathbf{x}_1, y_1), \ldots, (\mathbf{x}_\ell, y_\ell)$, it would seem advisable to make use of the labels not only during the training of the final classifier, but already in the stage of feature extraction.

To conclude this paragraph on feature extraction for classification, we note that a similar approach could be taken in the case of regression estimation, to generalize PCA regression (e.g. Jolliffe, 1986) to the nonlinear case.

Feature Space and the Curse of Dimensionality. We are doing PCA in 10^{10}-dimensional feature spaces, yet getting results in finite time which are comparable to state-of-the-art techniques. In fact, of course, we are not working in the full feature space, but just in a comparably small linear subspace of it, whose dimension equals at most the number of observations. The method automatically chooses this subspace and provides a means of taking advantage of the lower dimensionality — an approach which consisted in explicitly mapping into feature space and then performing PCA would have severe difficulties at this point: even if PCA was done based on an $M \times M$ dot product matrix (M being the sample size) whose diagonalization is tractable, it would still be necessary to evaluate dot products in a 10^{10}-dimensional feature space to compute the *entries* of the matrix in the first place. Kernel-based methods avoid this problem — they do not explicitly compute all dimensions of F (loosely speaking, all possible features), but only work in a relevant subspace of F.

Note, moreover, that we did not get overfitting problems when training the linear SV classifier on the extracted features. The basic idea behind this two-step approach is very similar in spirit to nonlinear SV machines: one maps into a very complex space to be able to approximate a large class of possible decision functions, and then uses a low VC-dimension classifier in that space to control generalization.

Regularization. As kernel PCA belongs to the domain of unsupervised learning, VC-theory methods are not directly applicable to discuss its regularization and generalization properties. It is, however, possible to draw some simple analogies to the standard SV reasoning. The feature extractors (20.18) are linear functions in the feature space F whose regularization properties, as in the SV case, can be characterized by the length of their weight vector. When applied to the training data, the k-th feature extractor generates a set of outputs with variance λ_k. Dividing each weight vector $\boldsymbol{\alpha}^k$ by $\sqrt{\lambda_k}$, we obtain a set of nonlinear feature extractors with unit variance output and the property that out of all such extractors which can be written in the form (20.18), the first k kernel PCA extractors are those with the shortest weight vectors (subject to the condition that they are orthogonal in F). Therefore, kernel PCA can be considered as a method for extracting potentially interesting functions (with unit variance on the data) that have low capacity. The complexity measure used here is identical to the one used in Gaussian processes (Williams, 1998), i.e. it could be interpreted as a Bayesian prior on the space of functions by setting $p(f) \propto \exp(-\frac{1}{2}\|Pf\|^2)$ where P is the regularization operator corresponding to k (see Smola and Schölkopf (1998b) for details). In this view, the first extractor (cf. (20.18)) $f(\mathbf{x}) = \sum_{i=1}^{M} \alpha_i k(\mathbf{x}_i, \mathbf{x})$ is given by

$$f = \operatorname*{argmax}_{\mathrm{Var}(f)=1} \exp\left(-\frac{1}{2}\|Pf\|^2\right), \tag{20.25}$$

where $\mathrm{Var}(f)$ denotes the (estimate of the) variance of $f(\mathbf{x})$ for $\mathbf{x}$ drawn from the underlying distribution.

Conclusion. Compared to other techniques for nonlinear feature extraction, kernel PCA has the advantages that it does not require nonlinear optimization, but only the solution of an eigenvalue problem, and by the possibility to use different kernels, it comprises a fairly general class of nonlinearities that can be used. Clearly, the last point has yet to be evaluated in practice, however, for the support vector machine, the utility of different kernels has already been established. Different kernels (polynomial, sigmoid, Gaussian) led to fine classification performances (Schölkopf et al., 1995). The general question of how to select the ideal kernel for a given task (i.e. the appropriate feature space), however, is an open problem.

We conclude this chapter with a twofold outlook. The scene has been set for using the kernel method to construct a wide variety of rather general and still feasible nonlinear variants of classical algorithms. It is beyond the scope of the present work to explore all the possibilities, including many distance-based algorithms, in detail. In (Schölkopf et al., 1996b), we have proposed and begun to work out several possibilities, for instance kernel-based independent component analysis and nonlinear forms of k-means clustering. The latter has meanwhile been further developed and implemented by Graepel and Obermayer (1998). Other domains where researchers have recently started to investigate the use of Mercer kernels include Gaussian Processes (Williams, 1998).

Linear PCA is being used in numerous technical and scientific applications, including noise reduction, density estimation, image indexing and retrieval systems, and the analysis of natural image statistics. Kernel PCA can be applied to all domains where traditional PCA has so far been used for feature extraction, and where a nonlinear extension would make sense.

Acknowledgements

AS and BS were supported by grants from the Studienstiftung des deutschen Volkes, and thank V. Vapnik for introducing them to kernel representations of dot products during joint work on support vector machines. AS was supported by a grant of the

DFG (JA 379/71). This work profited from discussions with V. Blanz, L. Bottou, C. Burges, H. Bülthoff, P. Haffner, Y. Le Cun, S. Mika, N. Murata, P. Simard, S. Solla, V. Vapnik, and T. Vetter. We are grateful to V. Blanz, C. Burges, and S. Solla for reading a preliminary version of the manuscript, and to L. Bottou, C. Burges, and C. Cortes for parts of the SV training code.

Appendix

The Eigenvalue Problem in the Space of Expansion Coefficients

Being symmetric, K has an orthonormal basis of eigenvectors $(\boldsymbol{\beta}^i)_i$ with corresponding eigenvalues μ_i, thus for all i, we have $K\boldsymbol{\beta}^i = \mu_i\boldsymbol{\beta}^i$ $(i = 1, \ldots, M)$. To understand the relation between Eq. (20.13) and Eq. (20.14), we proceed as follows: first suppose $\lambda, \boldsymbol{\alpha}$ satisfy (20.13). We may expand $\boldsymbol{\alpha}$ in K's eigenvector basis as $\boldsymbol{\alpha} = \sum_{i=1}^{M} a_i\boldsymbol{\beta}^i$. Eq. (20.13) then reads

$$M\lambda \sum_i a_i\mu_i\boldsymbol{\beta}^i = \sum_i a_i\mu_i^2\boldsymbol{\beta}^i, \tag{20.26}$$

or, equivalently, for all $i = 1, \ldots, M$, $M\lambda a_i\mu_i = a_i\mu_i^2$. This in turn means that for all $i = 1, \ldots, M$,

$$M\lambda = \mu_i \quad or \quad a_i = 0 \quad or \quad \mu_i = 0. \tag{20.27}$$

Note that the above are not exclusive *or*-s. We next assume that $\lambda, \boldsymbol{\alpha}$ satisfy (20.14), to carry out a similar derivation. In that case, we find that Eq. (20.14) is equivalent to

$$M\lambda \sum_i a_i\boldsymbol{\beta}^i = \sum_i a_i\mu_i\boldsymbol{\beta}^i, \tag{20.28}$$

i.e. for all $i = 1, \ldots, M$,

$$M\lambda = \mu_i \quad or \quad a_i = 0. \tag{20.29}$$

Comparing (20.27) and (20.29), we see that all solutions of the latter satisfy the former. However, they do not give its full set of solutions: given a solution of (20.14), we may always add multiples of eigenvectors of K with eigenvalue 0 and still satisfy (20.13), with the same eigenvalue.[6] This means that there exist solutions of Eq. (20.13) which belong to different eigenvalues yet are not orthogonal in the space of the $\boldsymbol{\alpha}^k$. It does, however, not mean that the eigenvectors of $\bar{C}$ in F are not orthogonal. Indeed, note that if $\boldsymbol{\alpha}$ is an eigenvector of K with eigenvalue 0, then the corresponding vector $\sum_i \alpha_i\Phi(\mathbf{x}_i)$ is orthogonal to *all* vectors in the span of the $\Phi(\mathbf{x}_j)$ in F, since $(\Phi(\mathbf{x}_j) \cdot \sum_i \alpha_i\Phi(\mathbf{x}_i)) = (K\boldsymbol{\alpha})_j = 0$ for all j, which means that

6. This observation could be used to change the vectors $\boldsymbol{\alpha}$ of the solution, e.g. to make them maximally sparse, without changing the solution.

$\sum_i \alpha_i \Phi(\mathbf{x}_i) = 0$. Thus, the above difference between the solutions of (20.13) and (20.14) is irrelevant, since we are interested in vectors in F rather than vectors in the space of the expansion coefficients of (20.10). We thus only need to diagonalize K to find all relevant solutions of (20.13).

Centering in High-Dimensional Space

Given any Φ and any set of observations $\mathbf{x}_1, \ldots, \mathbf{x}_M$, the points

$$\tilde{\Phi}(\mathbf{x}_i) := \Phi(\mathbf{x}_i) - \frac{1}{M}\sum_{i=1}^{M} \Phi(\mathbf{x}_i) \tag{20.30}$$

are centered. Thus, the assumptions of section 20.2 now hold, and we go on to define covariance matrix and $\tilde{K}_{ij} = (\tilde{\Phi}(\mathbf{x}_i) \cdot \tilde{\Phi}(\mathbf{x}_j))$ in F. We arrive at our already familiar eigenvalue problem

$$\tilde{\lambda}\tilde{\boldsymbol{\alpha}} = \tilde{K}\tilde{\boldsymbol{\alpha}}, \tag{20.31}$$

with $\tilde{\boldsymbol{\alpha}}$ being the expansion coefficients of an eigenvector (in F) in terms of the points (20.30), $\tilde{\mathbf{V}} = \sum_{i=1}^{M} \tilde{\alpha}_i \tilde{\Phi}(\mathbf{x}_i)$. As we do not have the centered data (20.30), we cannot compute $\tilde{K}$ directly; however, we can express it in terms of its non-centered counterpart K. In the following, we shall use $K_{ij} = (\Phi(\mathbf{x}_i) \cdot \Phi(\mathbf{x}_j))$, and the notations $1_{ij} = 1$ for all i, j, $(1_M)_{ij} := 1/M$, to compute $\tilde{K}_{ij} = (\tilde{\Phi}(\mathbf{x}_i) \cdot \tilde{\Phi}(\mathbf{x}_j))$:

$$\begin{aligned}\tilde{K}_{ij} &= \left((\Phi(\mathbf{x}_i) - \frac{1}{M}\sum_{m=1}^{M} \Phi(\mathbf{x}_m)) \cdot (\Phi(\mathbf{x}_j) - \frac{1}{M}\sum_{n=1}^{M} \Phi(\mathbf{x}_n))\right) \\ &= K_{ij} - \frac{1}{M}\sum_{m=1}^{M} 1_{im}K_{mj} - \frac{1}{M}\sum_{n=1}^{M} K_{in}1_{nj} + \frac{1}{M^2}\sum_{m,n=1}^{M} 1_{im}K_{mn}1_{nj} \\ &= (K - 1_M K - K 1_M + 1_M K 1_M)_{ij}.\end{aligned} \tag{20.32}$$

We thus can compute $\tilde{K}$ from K, and then solve the eigenvalue problem (20.31). As in (20.16), the solutions $\tilde{\boldsymbol{\alpha}}^k$ are normalized by normalizing the corresponding vectors $\tilde{\mathbf{V}}^k$ in F, which translates into $\tilde{\lambda}_k(\tilde{\boldsymbol{\alpha}}^k \cdot \tilde{\boldsymbol{\alpha}}^k) = 1$. For feature extraction, we compute projections of centered Φ-images of test patterns $\mathbf{t}$ onto the eigenvectors of the covariance matrix of the centered points,

$$(\tilde{\mathbf{V}}^k \cdot \tilde{\Phi}(\mathbf{t})) = \sum_{i=1}^{M} \tilde{\alpha}_i^k (\tilde{\Phi}(\mathbf{x}_i) \cdot \tilde{\Phi}(\mathbf{t})). \tag{20.33}$$

Consider a set of test points $\mathbf{t}_1, \ldots, \mathbf{t}_L$, and define two $L \times M$ matrices by $K_{ij}^{test} = (\Phi(\mathbf{t}_i) \cdot \Phi(\mathbf{x}_j))$ and $\tilde{K}_{ij}^{test} = \left((\Phi(\mathbf{t}_i) - \frac{1}{M}\sum_{m=1}^{M} \Phi(\mathbf{x}_m)) \cdot (\Phi(\mathbf{x}_j) - \frac{1}{M}\sum_{n=1}^{M} \Phi(\mathbf{x}_n))\right)$. As in (20.32), we express $\tilde{K}^{test}$ in terms of K^{test}, and arrive at

$$\tilde{K}^{test} = K^{test} - 1'_M K - K^{test} 1_M + 1'_M K 1_M, \tag{20.34}$$

where $1'_M$ is the $L \times M$ matrix with all entries equal to $1/M$.

Proof of Theorem 20.1

The proof requires some basic notions from group theory. Denote $\mathrm{O}(N)$ the orthogonal group on $\mathbb{R}^N$, i.e. the group of $N \times N$ matrices with $O^\top O = 1$; with the additional requirement $\det O = 1$, we obtain the special orthogonal group $\mathrm{SO}(N)$. A representation ρ of $\mathrm{SO}(N)$ is a map that preserves the group structure, i.e. $T(O_1 O_2) = T(O_1)T(O_2)$ for all $O_1, O_2 \in \mathrm{SO}(N)$.

Proof ($\Longrightarrow$) Due to the definition of $k(\mathbf{x}, \mathbf{y}) := (\mathbf{x} \cdot \mathbf{y})^d$, it follows immediately that $k(O\mathbf{x}, O\mathbf{y}) = (\mathbf{x} \cdot O^\top O\mathbf{y})^d = (\mathbf{x} \cdot \mathbf{y})^d$ for any $O \in \mathrm{O}(N)$.

($\Longleftarrow$) Define $P(d, N)$ to be the (feature) space given by the evaluation of all possible monomials of order p on $\mathbb{R}^N$, furnished with a Euclidean dot product.[7] Then the map into feature space, $\Phi : \mathbb{R}^N \to P(d, N), \mathbf{x} \to \Phi(\mathbf{x})$, induces a representation ρ of $\mathrm{SO}(N)$ on $P(d, N)$ via $\Phi(O\mathbf{x}) = \rho(O)\Phi(\mathbf{x})$. This is a consequence of (Vilenkin, 1968, chapter IX.2). We have

$$(\Phi(\mathbf{x}) \cdot \Phi(\mathbf{y})) = (\mathbf{x} \cdot \mathbf{y})^d = (O\mathbf{x} \cdot O\mathbf{y})^d = (\rho(O)\Phi(\mathbf{x}) \cdot \rho(O)\Phi(\mathbf{y})). \tag{20.35}$$

What is more, ρ is an orthogonal representation, i.e. $\rho(O)^\top \rho(O) = 1$ for all $O \in \mathrm{SO}(N)$. This follows from $(\Phi(\mathbf{x}) \cdot \Phi(\mathbf{y})) = (\rho(O)\Phi(\mathbf{x}) \cdot \rho(O)\Phi(\mathbf{y}))$ and $\operatorname{span}\Phi(\mathbb{R}^N) = P(d, N)$.

We now prove that any positive diagonal matrix D acting on $P(d, N)$, satisfying the invariance condition

$$(D^{\frac{1}{2}}\Phi(\mathbf{x}) \cdot D^{\frac{1}{2}}\Phi(\mathbf{y})) = (D^{\frac{1}{2}}\rho(O)\Phi(\mathbf{x}) \cdot D^{\frac{1}{2}}\rho(O)\Phi(\mathbf{y})) \tag{20.36}$$

for all $O \in \mathrm{SO}(N)$, is necessarily a multiple of the unit matrix. If that were not true, then $k_D(\mathbf{x}, \mathbf{y}) := (D^{\frac{1}{2}}\Phi(\mathbf{x}) \cdot D^{\frac{1}{2}}\Phi(\mathbf{y})) = k_D(O\mathbf{x}, O\mathbf{y})$ would be a different kernel invariant under $\mathrm{SO}(N)$. Again, as $\operatorname{span}\Phi(\mathbb{R}^N) = P(d, N)$, we may rewrite (20.36) as

$$D = \rho(O)^\top D\rho(O), \text{ i.e. } D\rho(O) = \rho(O)D. \tag{20.37}$$

In componentwise notation (in $P(d, N)$), this reads

$$D_i \rho(O)_{ij} = D_j \rho(O)_{ij}. \tag{20.38}$$

Therefore, we can show that $D_i = D_j$ for all i, j by showing that there exist sufficiently many nonzero $\rho(O)_{ij}$. To this end, consider a rotation $\tilde{O}$ mapping $\mathbf{x}_1 := (1, 0, \ldots, 0)$ into $\mathbf{x}_2 := \frac{1}{\sqrt{N}}(1, \ldots, 1)$. Clearly, $\Phi(\mathbf{x}_1) = (1, 0, \ldots, 0) \in P(d, N)$, whereas $\Phi(\mathbf{x}_2) = \Phi(\tilde{O}\mathbf{x}_1) = \rho(\tilde{O})\Phi(\mathbf{x}_1)$ contains only nonzero entries. Hence also

---

7. It is straightforward to see that the polynomial kernel corresponds to a dot product in the space of all monomials: simply compute $(\mathbf{x} \cdot \mathbf{y})^d = \sum_{j_1, \ldots, j_d = 1}^{N} x_{j_1} \cdot \ldots \cdot x_{j_d} \cdot y_{j_1} \cdot \ldots \cdot y_{j_d} = (C_d(\mathbf{x}) \cdot C_d(\mathbf{y}))$, where C_d maps $\mathbf{x}$ to the vector $C_d(\mathbf{x})$ whose entries are all possible d-th degree ordered products of the entries of $\mathbf{x}$ (Schölkopf, 1997). Identifying the entries which just differ by the ordering of the coordinates, we obtain pre-factors of the form $\sqrt{\frac{d!}{p_1! p_2! \ldots p_N!}} x_1^{p_1} x_2^{p_2} \ldots x_N^{p_N}$, with $\sum_i p_i = p$ (Smola et al., 1998a).

the first row of $\rho(\tilde{O})$ contains only nonzero entries. By (20.38), we conclude that $D_1 = D_i$ for all i, and therefore $D = \lambda 1$.

This completes the argument concerning the invariance of the polynomial kernel. The transfer to the invariance of kernel PCA, i.e. to the invariance of kernel PCA feature extraction for all test and training sets, is straightforward. ∎

Note that the above statement does not hold if we allow D to be an arbitrary matrix of full rank. In particular, due to Schur's lemma (Hamermesh, 1962) one can show that the number of different subspaces that can be scaled separately equals the number of irreducible representations contained in ρ.

Kernels

The remainder of the chapter provides some further material on kernels, partly reprinted from (Schölkopf et al., 1996b).

Kernels Corresponding to Bilinear Forms in Another Space. Mercer's theorem of functional analysis gives conditions under which we can construct the mapping Φ from the eigenfunction decomposition of k (cf. (1.25)) such that $k(\mathbf{x}, \mathbf{y}) = (\Phi(\mathbf{x}) \cdot \Phi(\mathbf{y}))$.
In fact, k does not have to be the kernel of a positive *definite* operator: even if a finite number of eigenvalues λ_i in (1.25) is negative, the expansion (1.25) is still valid. In that case, k corresponds to a Lorentz scalar product in a space with indefinite signature. We can then no longer interpret our method as PCA in some feature space; however, it could still be viewed as a nonlinear factor analysis.[8] For instance, we have used the thin plate spline kernel $k(\mathbf{x}, \mathbf{y}) = \|\mathbf{x} - \mathbf{y}\|^2 \ln \|\mathbf{x} - \mathbf{y}\|$, which is not positive definite (it is conditionally positive definite of order 2, cf. e.g. Smola et al. (1998c)).

Kernels Constructed from Mappings. We stated above that once we have a suitable kernel, we need not worry anymore about exactly which map Φ the kernel corresponds to. For the purpose of constructing kernels, however, it can well be useful to compute the kernels from mappings into some dot product space F, $\Phi : \mathbb{R}^N \to F$. Ideally, we would like to choose Φ such that we can obtain an expression for $(\Phi(\mathbf{x}) \cdot \Phi(\mathbf{y}))$ which can be computed efficiently. Presently, we shall consider mappings into function spaces,

$$\mathbf{x} \mapsto f_{\mathbf{x}}, \tag{20.39}$$

with $f_{\mathbf{x}}$ being a complex-valued function on some measure space. We furthermore

8. The fact that we can use indefinite operators distinguishes this approach from the usage of kernels in the support vector machine: in the latter, the definiteness is necessary for the convex programming.

assume that these spaces are equipped with a dot product

$$(f_{\mathbf{x}} \cdot f_{\mathbf{y}}) = \int f_{\mathbf{x}}(u)\ f_{\mathbf{y}}(u)\ du. \tag{20.40}$$

We can then define kernels of the type

$$k(\mathbf{x}, \mathbf{y}) := (f_{\mathbf{x}} \cdot f_{\mathbf{y}})^d. \tag{20.41}$$

(These kernels can also be used if our observations are already given as functions, as is usually the case for the variant of PCA which is referred to as the Karhunen-Loève-Transformation; see Karhunen (1946)) As an example, suppose the input patterns $\mathbf{x}_i$ are $q \times q$ images. Then we can map them to two-dimensional image intensity distributions $f_{\mathbf{x}_i}$ (e.g. splines on $[0,1]^2$). The corresponding kernel will then approximately equal the original dot product between the images represented as pixel vectors, which can be seen by considering the finite sum approximation to the integral,

$$q^2 \int_0^1 \int_0^1 f_{\mathbf{x}}(u) f_{\mathbf{y}}(u)\ d^2u \approx \sum_{i=1}^{q} \sum_{j=1}^{q} f_{\mathbf{x}} \left(\frac{i-\frac{1}{2}}{q}, \frac{j-\frac{1}{2}}{q} \right) f_{\mathbf{y}} \left(\frac{i-\frac{1}{2}}{q}, \frac{j-\frac{1}{2}}{q} \right). \tag{20.42}$$

Combining Kernels. If k and k' satisfy Mercer's conditions, then so will $k + k'$ and, for $\lambda > 0$, λk. In other words, the admissible kernels form a cone in the space of all integral operators. Clearly, $k + k'$ corresponds to mapping into the direct sum of the respective spaces into which k and k' map. Of course, we could also explicitly do the principal component extraction twice, for both kernels, and decide ourselves on the respective numbers of components to extract. In this case, we would not obtain combinations of the two feature types.

Combining polynomial kernels, we can thus construct admissible kernels by series expansions: given a function f with a uniformly convergent power series expansion $f(x) = \sum_i a_i x_i$, then $k_f(\mathbf{x}, \mathbf{y}) := f((\mathbf{x} \cdot \mathbf{y}))$ is a Mercer kernel. In fact, the latter can be generalized to expansions in terms of Mercer kernels k, i.e. $f(k(\mathbf{x}, \mathbf{y}))$, other than just the usual dot product. This is due to the fact that by an argument similar to the one proving that $(\mathbf{x} \cdot \mathbf{y})^d$ is a Mercer kernel ($d \in \mathbb{N}$), also $k(\mathbf{x}, \mathbf{y})^d$ is a Mercer kernel, since it can be written as $(\Phi(\mathbf{x}) \cdot \Phi(\mathbf{y}))^d$ (Smola et al., 1998c).

Another way of combining kernels is to use different kernels for different parts of the input vectors. In the simplest case, we can define $k(\mathbf{x}, \mathbf{y}) := k_1(\mathbf{x}_1, \mathbf{y}_1) + k_2(\mathbf{x}_2, \mathbf{y}_2)$, where $\mathbf{x} = \mathbf{x}_1 \oplus \mathbf{x}_2$ and $\mathbf{y} = \mathbf{y}_1 \oplus \mathbf{y}_2$, and k_1, k_2 are Mercer kernels on the two lower-dimensional spaces comprising only parts of the input. This method can be useful if the different parts of the input have different meanings and should be dealt with differently.

Iterating Kernels. Given a kernel k, we can construct iterated kernels (e.g. Courant and Hilbert, 1953) by

$$k^{(2)}(\mathbf{x}, \mathbf{y}) := \int k(\mathbf{x}, \mathbf{z}) k(\mathbf{z}, \mathbf{y})\ d\mathbf{z}. \tag{20.43}$$

In fact, $k^{(2)}$ will be positive even if k is not, as can be seen from

$$\int k^{(2)}(\mathbf{x},\mathbf{y})f(\mathbf{x})f(\mathbf{y})\,d\mathbf{x}d\mathbf{y} = \int\int k(\mathbf{x},\mathbf{z})k(\mathbf{z},\mathbf{y})f(\mathbf{x})f(\mathbf{y})\,d\mathbf{z}d\mathbf{x}d\mathbf{y}$$
$$= \int\left(\int k(\mathbf{x},\mathbf{z})f(\mathbf{x})\,d\mathbf{x}\right)^2 d\mathbf{z}. \tag{20.44}$$

This gives us a method for constructing admissible kernels.

Multi-Layer Support Vector Machines

By first extracting nonlinear principal components according to (20.18), and then training a Support Vector machine, we can construct Support Vector type machines with additional layers. The number of components extracted then determines the size of of the first hidden layer. Combining (20.18) with the Support Vector decision function (1.32), we thus get machines of the type

$$f(\mathbf{x}) = \operatorname{sgn}\left(\sum_{i=1}^{\ell}\psi_i k_2(\vec{g}(\mathbf{x}_i)\cdot\vec{g}(\mathbf{x})) + b\right) \tag{20.45}$$

with

$$\vec{g}(\mathbf{x})_j = \left(\mathbf{V}^j\cdot\Phi(\mathbf{x})\right) = \sum_{k=1}^{M}\alpha_k^j k_1(\mathbf{x}_k,\mathbf{x}). \tag{20.46}$$

Here, the expansion coefficients ψ_i are computed by a standard Support Vector Machine. Note that different kernel functions k_1 and k_2 can be used for the different layers. Also note that this could provide an efficient means of building multivariate Support Vector Machines, i.e. q machines mapping $\mathbb{R}^N \to \mathbb{R}^q$, where $q \in \mathbb{N}$. All these machines may share the first preprocessing layer which includes the numerically expensive steps and then use a simple kernel for the second layer. Similar considerations apply for multi-class classification, where often a set of binary classifiers (which could share some preprocessing) is constructed.

References

H. D. I. Abarbanel. *Analysis of Observed Chaotic Data.* Springer Verlag, New York, 1996.

M. Aizerman, E. Braverman, and L. Rozonoer. Theoretical foundations of the potential function method in pattern recognition learning. *Automation and Remote Control*, 25:821 – 837, 1964.

N. Alon, S. Ben-David, N. Cesa-Bianchi, and D. Haussler. Scale–sensitive Dimensions, Uniform Convergence, and Learnability. *Journal of the ACM*, 44(4):615–631, 1997.

E. Amaldi and V. Kann. The complexity and approximability of finding maximum feasible subsystems of linear relations. *Theoretical Computer Science*, 147:181–210, 1995.

E. Amaldi and V. Kann. On the approximability of minimizing nonzero variables or unsatisfied relations in linear systems. *Theoretical Computer Science*, 1998. To appear.

M. Anthony. Probabilistic analysis of learning in artificial neural networks: The PAC model and its variants. *Neural Computing Surveys*, 1:1–47, 1997. http://www.icsi.berkeley.edu/~jagota/NCS.

M. Anthony and N. Biggs. *Computational Learning Theory*, volume 30 of *Cambridge Tracts in Theoretical Computer Science.* Cambridge University Press, 1992.

N. Aronszajn. Theory of reproducing kernels. *Transactions of the American Mathematical Society*, 68:337 – 404, 1950.

R. Ash. *Information Theory.* Interscience Publishers, New York, 1965.

P. L. Bartlett. Pattern classification in neural networks. *IEEE Transactions on Information Theory*, 44(2):525–536, 1998a.

P. L. Bartlett. The sample complexity of pattern classification with neural networks: the size of the weights is more important than the size of the network. *IEEE Transactions on Information Theory*, 44(2):525–536, 1998b.

P. L. Bartlett, P. Long, and R. C. Williamson. Fat–Shattering and the Learnability of Real–Valued Functions. *Journal of Computer and System Sciences*, 52(3):434–452, 1996.

Y. Bengio, Y. LeCun, and D. Henderson. Globally trained handwritten word recognizer using spatial representation, convolutional neural networks and hidden markov models. In J. Cowan, G. Tesauro, and J. Alspector, editors, *Advances in Neural Information Processing Systems*, volume 5, pages 937–944, 1994.

K. P. Bennett. Decision tree construction via linear programming. In M. Evans, editor, *Proceedings of the 4th Midwest Artificial Intelligence and Cognitive Science Society Conference*, pages 97–101, Utica, Illinois, 1992.

K. P. Bennett and J. A. Blue. A support vector machine approach to decision trees. In *Proceedings of IJCNN'98*, pages 2396 – 2401, Anchorage, Alaska, 1997.

K. P. Bennett and E. J. Bredensteiner. A parametric optimization method for machine learning. *INFORMS Journal on Computing*, 9(3):311–318, 1997.

K. P. Bennett and E. J. Bredensteiner. Geometry in learning. In C. Gorini, E. Hart, W. Meyer, and T. Phillips, editors, *Geometry at Work*, Washington, D.C., 1998. Mathematical Association of America. Available http://www.math.rpi.edu/~bennek/geometry2.ps.

K. P. Bennett and A. Demiriz. Semi-supervised support vector machines. Unpublished manuscript based on talk given at Machines That Learn Conference, Snowbird, 1998.

K. P. Bennett and O. L. Mangasarian. Robust linear programming discrimination of two linearly inseparable sets. *Optimization Methods and Software*, 1:23–34, 1992.

K. P. Bennett and O. L. Mangasarian. Multicategory separation via linear programming. *Optimization Methods and Software*, 3:27–39, 1993.

K. P. Bennett and O. L. Mangasarian. Serial and parallel multicategory discrimination. *SIAM Journal on Optimization*, 4(4):722–734, 1994.

K. P. Bennett, D. H. Wu, and L. Auslender. On support vector decision trees for database marketing. R.P.I. Math Report No. 98-100, Rensselaer Polytechnic Institute, Troy, NY, 1998.

L. Bernhardt. Zur Klassifizierung vieler Musterklassen mit wenigen Merkmalen. In H. Kazmierczak, editor, *5. DAGM Symposium: Mustererkennung 1983*, pages 255 – 260, Berlin, 1983. VDE-Verlag.

D. P. Bertsekas. *Nonlinear Programming*. Athena Scientific, Belmont, MA, 1995.

M. Bierlaire, Ph. Toint, and D. Tuyttens. On iterative algorithms for linear least squares problems with bound constraints. *Linear Alebra Appl.*, pages 111–143, 1991.

C. M. Bishop. *Neural Networks for Pattern Recognition.* Clarendon Press, Oxford, 1995.

V. Blanz, B. Schölkopf, H. Bülthoff, C. Burges, V. Vapnik, and T. Vetter. Comparison of view-based object recognition algorithms using realistic 3D models. In C. von der Malsburg, W. von Seelen, J. C. Vorbrüggen, and B. Sendhoff, editors, *Artificial Neural Networks — ICANN'96*, pages 251 – 256, Berlin, 1996. Springer Lecture Notes in Computer Science, Vol. 1112.

J. A. Blue. *A Hybrid of Tabu Search and Local Descent Algorithms with Applications in Artificial Intelligence.* PhD thesis, Rensselaer Polytechnic Institute, 1998.

A. Blumer, A. Ehrenfeucht, D. Haussler, and M. K. Warmuth. Learnability and the Vapnik-Chervonenkis dimension. *Journal of the ACM*, 36(4):929–965, 1989.

W. M. Boothby. *An introduction to differentiable manifolds and Riemannian geometry.* Academic Press, 2nd edition, 1986.

B. E. Boser, I. M. Guyon, and V. N. Vapnik. A training algorithm for optimal margin classifiers. In D. Haussler, editor, *Proceedings of the 5th Annual ACM Workshop on Computational Learning Theory*, pages 144–152, Pittsburgh, PA, 1992. ACM Press.

L. Bottou, C. Cortes, J. S. Denker, H. Drucker, I. Guyon, L. D. Jackel, Y. LeCun, U. A. Müller, E. Säckinger, P. Simard, and V. Vapnik. Comparison of classifier methods: a case study in handwritten digit recognition. In *Proceedings of the 12th International Conference on Pattern Recognition and Neural Networks, Jerusalem*, pages 77 – 87. IEEE Computer Society Press, 1994.

L. Bottou and V. N. Vapnik. Local learning algorithms. *Neural Computation*, 4(6): 888–900, 1992.

P. S. Bradley, U. M. Fayyad, and O. L. Mangasarian. Data mining: Overview and optimization opportunities. Technical Report Mathematical Programming Technical Report 98-01, University of Wisconsin-Madison, 1998. Submitted for publication.

P. S. Bradley and O. L. Mangasarian. Feature selection via concave minimization and support vector machines. Technical Report Mathematical Programming Technical Report 98-03, University of Wisconsin-Madison, 1998a. To appear in ICML-98.

P. S. Bradley and O. L. Mangasarian. Massive data discrimination via linear support vector machines. Technical Report Mathematical Programming Technical Report 98-05, University of Wisconsin-Madison, 1998b. Submitted for publication.

P. S. Bradley, O. L. Mangasarian, and W. N. Street. Feature selection via mathematical programming. Technical Report 95-21, Computer Sciences Department, University of Wisconsin, Madison, Wisconsin, 1995. To appear in *INFORMS Journal on Computing* 10, 1998.

E. J. Bredensteiner. *Optimization Methods in Data Mining and Machine Learning.* PhD thesis, Rensselaer Polytechnic Institute, 1997.

E. J. Bredensteiner and K. P. Bennett. Feature minimization within decision trees. *Computational Optimization and Applications*, 10:110–126, 1997.

E. J. Bredensteiner and K. P. Bennett. Multicategory classification by support vector machines. *Computational Optimization and Applications*, 1998. To appear.

L. M. Bregman. The relaxation method of finding the common point of convex sets and its application to the solution of problems in convex programming. *USSR Computational Mathematics and Mathematical Physics*, 7:200–217, 1967.

L. Breiman. Bagging predictors. Technical Report 421, Department of Statistics, UC Berkeley, 1994. ftp://ftp.stat.berkeley.edu/pub/tech-reports/421.ps.Z.

L. Breiman, J. Friedman, R. Olshen, and C. Stone. *Classification and Regression Trees.* Wadsworth International, California, 1984.

R. Brown, P. Bryant, and H. D. I. Abarbanel. Computing the lyapunov spectrum of a dynamical system from observed time-series. *Phys. Rev. Lett.*, 43(6):2787–2806, 1991.

J. R. Bunch and L. Kaufman. Some stable methods for calculating inertia and solving symmetric linear systems. *Mathematics of Computation*, 31:163–179, 1977.

C. J. C. Burges. Simplified support vector decision rules. In L. Saitta, editor, *Proceedings, 13th Intl. Conf. on Machine Learning*, pages 71–77, San Mateo, CA, 1996. Morgan Kaufmann.

C. J. C. Burges. A tutorial on support vector machines for pattern recognition. *Data Mining and Knowledge Discovery*, 2(2):1–47, 1998.

C. J. C. Burges and B. Schölkopf. Improving the accuracy and speed of support vector learning machines. In M. Mozer, M. Jordan, and T. Petsche, editors, *Advances in Neural Information Processing Systems 9*, pages 375–381, Cambridge, MA, 1997. MIT Press.

C. J. C. Burges and V. Vapnik. A new method for constructing artificial neural networks: Interim technical report, ONR contract N00014-94-c-0186. Technical report, AT&T Bell Laboratories, 1995.

B. Carl. Inequalities of Bernstein-Jackson-type and the degree of compactness of operators in Banach spaces. *Annales de l'Institut Fourier*, 35(3):79–118, 1985.

B. Carl and I. Stephani. *Entropy, compactness, and the approximation of operators.* Cambridge University Press, Cambridge, UK, 1990.

Y. Censor. Row-action methods for huge and sparse systems and their applications. *SIAM Review*, 23(4):444–467, 1981.

Y. Censor and A. Lent. An iterative row-action method for interval convex programming. *J. Optimization Theory and Applications*, 34(3):321–353, 1981.

S. Chen. *Basis Pursuit.* PhD thesis, Department of Statistics, Stanford University, 1995.

S. Chen, D. Donoho, and M. Saunders. Atomic decomposition by basis pursuit. Technical Report 479, Department of Statistics, Stanford University, 1995.

C. R. Chester. *Techniques in Partial Differential Equations.* McGraw Hill, 1971.

E. T. Copson. *Metric Spaces.* Cambridge University Press, 1968.

C. Cortes and V. Vapnik. Support vector networks. *Machine Learning*, 20:273 – 297, 1995.

R. Courant and D. Hilbert. *Methods of Mathematical Physics*, volume 1. Interscience Publishers, Inc, New York, 1953.

T. M. Cover. Geometrical and statistical properties of systems of linear inequalities with applications in pattern recognition. *IEEE Trans. Elect. Comp.*, 14:326–334, 1965.

D. Cox and F. O'Sullivan. Asymptotic analysis of penalized likelihood and related estimators. *Ann. Statist.*, 18:1676–1695, 1990.

CPLEX Optimization Incorporated, Incline Village, Nevada. *Using the CPLEX Callable Library*, 1994.

P. Craven and G. Wahba. Smoothing noisy data with spline functions: estimating the correct degree of smoothing by the method of generalized cross-validation. *Numer. Math.*, 31:377–403, 1979.

N. Cristianini, J. Shawe-Taylor, and P. Sykacek. Bayesian classifiers are large margin hyperplanes in a hilbert space. In J. Shavlik, editor, *Machine Learning: Proceedings of the Fifteenth International Conference*, San Francisco, CA, 1998. Morgan Kaufmann.

K. I. Diamantaras and S. Y. Kung. *Principal Component Neural Networks.* Wiley, New York, 1996.

K. Dodson and T. Poston. *Tensor Geometry.* Springer-Verlag, 2nd edition, 1991.

H. Drucker, C. J. C. Burges, L. Kaufman, A. Smola, and V. Vapnik. Support vector regression machines. In M. Mozer, M. Jordan, and T. Petsche, editors, *Advances in Neural Information Processing Systems 9*, Cambridge, MA, 1997. MIT Press.

R. O. Duda and P. E. Hart. *Pattern Classification and Scene Analysis.* John Wiley & Sons, 1973.

S. Dumais. Using SVMs for text categorization. *IEEE Intelligent Systems*, 13(4), 1998. In: M.A. Hearst, B. Schölkopf, S. Dumais, E. Osuna, and J. Platt: Trends and Controversies — Support Vector Machines.

N. Dunford and J. T. Schwartz. *Linear Operators Part II: Spectral Theory, Self Adjoint Operators in Hilbert Space.* Number VII in Pure and Applied Mathematics. John Wiley & Sons, New York, 1963.

J. P. Eckmann and D. Ruelle. Ergodic theory of chaos and strange attractors. *Rev. Modern Phys.*, 57(3):617–656, 1985.

K. Efetov. *Supersymmetry in Disorder and Chaos.* Cambridge University Press, Cambridge, 1997.

A. Ehrenfeucht, D. Haussler, M. Kearns, and L. Valiant. A general lower bound on the number of examples needed for learning. *Information and Computation*, 82: 247–261, 1989.

L. Elden and L. Wittmeyer-Koch. *Numerical Analysis: An Introduction.* Academic Press, Cambrigde, 1990.

R. Fourer, D. Gay, and B. Kernighan. *AMPL A Modeling Language for Mathematical Programming.* Boyd and Frazer, Danvers, Massachusetts, 1993.

J. H. Friedman. Another approach to polychotomous classification. Technical report, Department of Statistics and Stanford Linear Accelerator Center, Stanford University, 1996.

E. Gardner. The space of interactions in neural networks. *Journal of Physics A*, 21:257–70, 1988.

P. E. Gill, W. Murray, and M. A. Saunders. Snopt: An sqp algorithm for large-scale constrained optimization. Technical Report NA-97-2, Dept. of Mathematics, U.C. San Diego, 1997.

P. E. Gill, W. Murray, and M. H. Wright. *Practical Optimization*. Academic Press, 1981.

D. Girard. Asymptotic optimality of the fast randomized versions of GCV and C_L in ridge regression and regularization. *Ann. Statist.*, 19:1950–1963, 1991.

D. Girard. Asymptotic comparison of (partial) cross-validation, GCV and randomized GCV in nonparametric regression. *Ann. Statist.*, 126:315–334, 1998.

F. Girosi. An equivalence between sparse approximation and support vector machines. *Neural Computation*, 10(6):1455–1480, 1998.

F. Girosi, M. Jones, and T. Poggio. Priors, stabilizers and basis functions: From regularization to radial, tensor and additive splines. A.I. Memo No. 1430, MIT, 1993.

F. Girosi, M. Jones, and T. Poggio. Regularization theory and neural networks architectures. *Neural Computation*, 7(2):219–269, 1995.

F. Glover. Improved linear programming models for discriminant analysis. *Decision Sciences*, 21:771–785, 1990.

W. Gochet, A. Stam, V. Srinivasan, and S. Chen. Multigroup discriminant analysis using linear programming. *Operations Research*, 45(2):213–559, 1997.

H. Goldstein. *Classical Mechanics*. Addison-Wesley, Reading, MA, 1986.

M. Golea, P. L. Bartlett, W. S. Lee, and L. Mason. Generalization in decision trees and DNF: Does size matter? In *Advances in Neural Information Processing Systems 10*, 1998.

G. Golub and U. von Matt. Generalized cross-validation for large-scale problems. *J. Comput. Graph. Statist.*, 6:1–34, 1997.

J. Gong, G. Wahba, D. Johnson, and J. Tribbia. Adaptive tuning of numerical weather prediction models: simultaneous estimation of weighting, smoothing and physical parameters. *Monthly Weather Review*, 125:210–231, 1998.

Y. Gordon, H. König, and C. Schütt. Geometric and probabilistic estimates for entropy and approximation numbers of operators. *Journal of Approximation Theory*, 49:219–239, 1987.

T. Graepel and K. Obermayer. Fuzzy topographic kernel clustering. In W. Brauer, editor, *Proceedings of the 5th GI Workshop Fuzzy Neuro Systems '98*, pages 90 – 97, 1998.

R. E. Greene. *Isometric Embeddings of Riemannian and Pseudo-Riemannian*

Manifolds. American Mathematical Society, 1970.

C. Gu and G. Wahba. Semiparametric analysis of variance with tensor product thin plate splines. *J. Royal Statistical Soc. Ser. B*, 55:353–368, 1993.

L. Gurvits. A note on a scale-sensitive dimension of linear bounded functionals in banach spaces. In *Proceedings of Algorithm Learning Theory, ALT-97*, 1997. Also: NECI Technical Report, 1997.

I. Guyon, B. Boser, and V. Vapnik. Automatic capacity tuning of very large VC-dimension classifiers. In S. J. Hanson, J. D. Cowan, and C. L. Giles, editors, *Advances in Neural Information Processing Systems*, volume 5, pages 147–155. Morgan Kaufmann, San Mateo, CA, 1993.

M. Hamermesh. *Group theory and its applications to physical problems*. Addison Wesley, Reading, MA, 2 edition, 1962. Reprint by Dover, New York, NY.

D. Harrison and D. L. Rubinfeld. Hedonic prices and the demand for clean air. In *J. Environ. Economics & Management*, volume 5, pages 81–102, 1978. Original source of the Boston Housing data, actually from ftp://ftp.ics.uci.com/pub/machine-learning-databases/housing.

T. Hastie and W. Stuetzle. Principal curves. *JASA*, 84:502 – 516, 1989.

T. J. Hastie and R. J. Tibshirani. *Generalized Additive Models*, volume 43 of *Monographs on Statistics and Applied Probability*. Chapman & Hall, London, 1990.

S. Haykin. *Neural Networks : A Comprehensive Foundation*. Macmillan, New York, 1994.

S. Haykin, S. Puthusserypady, and P. Yee. Reconstruction of underlying dynamics of an observed chaotic process. Technical Report 353, Comm. Res. Lab., McMaster University, 1997.

C. Hildreth. A quadratic programming procedure. *Naval Research Logistics Quarterly*, 4:79–85, 1957.

T. K. Ho and E. Kleinberg. Building projectable classifiers for arbitrary complexity. In *Proceedings of the 12th International Conference on Pattern Recognition, Vienna*, pages 880–885, 1996.

H. Hotelling. Analysis of a complex of statistical variables into principal components. *Journal of Educational Psychology*, 24:417–441 and 498–520, 1933.

P. J. Huber. Robust statistics: a review. *Ann. Statist.*, 43:1041, 1972.

P. J. Huber. *Robust Statistics*. John Wiley and Sons, New York, 1981.

A. M. Hughes. *The Complete Database Marketer*. Irwin Prof. Publishing, Chicago, 1996.

M. Hutchinson. A stochastic estimator for the trace of the influence matrix for Laplacian smoothing splines. *Commun. Statist.-Simula.*, 18:1059–1076, 1989.

T. Joachims. Text categorization with support vector machines: Learning with many relevant features. Technical Report 23, LS VIII, University of Dortmund,

1997.

T. Joachims. Text categorization with support vector machines. In *European Conference on Machine Learning (ECML)*, 1998.

I. T. Jolliffe. *Principal Component Analysis.* Springer-Verlag, New York, 1986.

J. Karhunen and J. Joutsensalo. Generalizations of principal component analysis, optimization problems, and neural networks. *Neural Networks*, 8(4):549–562, 1995.

K. Karhunen. Zur Spektraltheorie stochastischer Prozesse. *Ann. Acad. Sci. Fenn.*, 34, 1946.

W. Karush. Minima of functions of several variables with inequalities as side constraints. Master's thesis, Dept. of Mathematics, Univ. of Chicago, 1939.

M. J. Kearns, R. E. Schapire, and L. M. Sellie. Toward efficient agnostic learning. *Machine Learning*, 17(2):115–141, 1994.

M. Kennel, R. Brown, and H. D. I. Abarbanel. Determining embedding dimension for phase-space reconstruction using a geometrical construction. *Phys. Rev. A.*, 45:3403–3411, 1992.

G. Kimeldorf and G. Wahba. A correspondence between Bayesian estimation of stochastic processes and smoothing by splines. *Ann. Math. Statist.*, 41:495–502, 1970.

G. Kimeldorf and G. Wahba. Some results on Tchebycheffian spline functions. *J. Math. Anal. Applic.*, 33:82–95, 1971.

M. Kirby and L. Sirovich. Application of the Karhunen-Loève procedure for the characterization of human faces. *IEEE Transactions on Pattern Analysis and Machine Intelligence*, 12(1):103–108, 1990.

J. Kohlmorgen, K.-R. Müller, and K. Pawelzik. Analysis of drifting dynamics with neural network hidden markov models. In M. Jordan, M. Kearns, and S. Solla, editors, *Advances in Neural Information Processing Systems 10*, Cambridge, MA, 1998. MIT Press.

T. Kohonen. Self-organized formation of topologically correct feature maps. *Biological Cybernetics*, 43:59 – 69, 1982.

A. N. Kolmogorov and S. V. Fomin. *Introductory Real Analysis.* Prentice-Hall, Inc., 1970.

H. König. *Eigenvalue Distribution of Compact Operators.* Birkhäuser, Basel, 1986.

U. Kreßel. The impact of the learning–set size in handwritten–digit recognition. In T. Kohonen et al., editor, *Artificial Neural Networks — ICANN'91*, pages 1685 – 1689, Amsterdam, 1991. North–Holland.

U. Kreßel. Polynomial classifiers and support vector machines. In W. Gerstner et al., editor, *Artificial Neural Networks — ICANN'97*, pages 397 – 402, Berlin, 1997. Springer Lecture Notes in Computer Science, Vol. 1327.

U. Kreßel and J. Schürmann. Pattern classification techniques based on function approximation. In H. Bunke and P.S.P. Wang, editors, *Handbook on Optical Character Recognition and Document Analysis*, pages 49 – 78. World Scientific Publishing Company, Singapore, 1997.

H. W. Kuhn and A. W. Tucker. Nonlinear programming. In *Proc.* 2nd *Berkeley Symposium on Mathematical Statistics and Probabilistics*, pages 481–492, Berkeley, 1951. University of California Press.

Y. LeCun, B. Boser, J. S. Denker, D. Henderson, R. E. Howard, W. Hubbard, and L. J. Jackel. Backpropagation applied to handwritten zip code recognition. *Neural Computation*, 1:541 – 551, 1989.

Y. LeCun, L. D. Jackel, L. Bottou, A. Brunot, C. Cortes, J. S. Denker, H. Drucker, I. Guyon, U. A. Müller, E. Säckinger, P. Simard, and V. Vapnik. Comparison of learning algorithms for handwritten digit recognition. In F. Fogelman-Soulié and P. Gallinari, editors, *Proceedings ICANN'95 — International Conference on Artificial Neural Networks*, volume II, pages 53 – 60, Nanterre, France, 1995. EC2. The MNIST benchmark data is available from http://www.research.att.com/~yann/ocr/mnist/.

W. S. Lee, P. L. Bartlett, and R. C. Williamson. The importance of convexity in learning with squared loss. *IEEE Transactions on Information Theory*, 1998. to appear.

K. C. Li. Asymptotic optimality of C_L and generalized cross validation in ridge regression with application to spline smoothing. *Ann. Statist.*, 14:1101–1112, 1986.

W. Liebert, K. Pawelzik, and H. G. Schuster. Optimal embeddings of chaotic attractors from topological considerations. *Europhys. Lett.*, 14:521 – 526, 1991.

B. Lillekjendlie, D. Kugiumtzis, and N. Christophersen. Chaotic time series: Part ii. system identification and prediction. *Modeling, Identification and Control*, 15 (4):225–243, 1994.

N. Littlestone and M. Warmuth. Relating data compression and learnability. Technical report, University of California Santa Cruz, 1986.

E. N. Lorenz. Deterministic nonperiodic flow. *J. Atmos. Sci.*, 20:130–141, 1963.

G. Loy and P. L. Bartlett. Generalization and the size of the weights: an experimental study. In *Proceedings of the Eighth Australian Conference on Neural Networks*, pages 60–64, 1997.

D. J. C. MacKay. The evidence framework applied to classification networks. *Neural Computation*, 4:720–736, 1992a.

D. J. C. MacKay. A practical Bayesian framework for backprop networks. *Neural Computation*, 4:448–472, 1992b.

M. C. Mackey and L. Glass. Oscillation and chaos in physiological control systems. *Science*, 197:287–289, 1977.

S. Mallat. *A Wavelet Tour of Signal Processing.* Academic Press, 1998.

O. L. Mangasarian. Multi-surface method of pattern separation. *IEEE Transactions on Information Theory*, IT-14:801–807, 1968.

O. L. Mangasarian. Misclassification minimization. *J. Global Optimization*, 5:309–323, 1994.

O. L. Mangasarian. Mathematical programming in data mining. *Data Mining and Knowledge Discovery*, 42(1):183–201, 1997.

O. L. Mangasarian and R. Meyer. Nonlinear perturbations of linear programs. *SIAM Journal on Control and Optimization*, 17(6):745–752, 1979.

O. L. Mangasarian, R. Setiono, and W. H. Wolberg. Pattern recognition via linear programming: Theory and application to medical diagnosis. In *Proceedings of the Workshop on Large-Scale Numerical Optimization, 1989*, pages 22–31, Philadelphia, Pennsylvania, 1990. SIAM.

O. L. Mangasiarian. Linear and nonlinear separation of patterns by linear programming. *Operations Research*, 13:444–452, 1965.

J. Mercer. Functions of positive and negative type and their connection with the theory of integral equations. *Philos. Trans. Roy. Soc. London*, A 209:415–446, 1909.

C. J. Merz and P. M. Murphy. UCI repository of machine learning databases, 1998. [http://www.ics.uci.edu/~mlearn/MLRepository.html]. Irvine, CA: University of California, Department of Information and Computer Science.

C. A. Micchelli. Interpolation of scattered data: distance matrices and conditionally positive definite functions. *Constructive Approximation*, 2:11–22, 1986.

J. Moody and C. Darken. Fast learning in networks of locally-tuned processing units. *Neural Computation*, 1(2):281–294, 1989.

S. Mukherjee, E. Osuna, and F. Girosi. Nonlinear prediction of chaotic time series using a support vector machine. In J. Principe, L. Gile, N. Morgan, and E. Wilson, editors, *Neural Networks for Signal Processing VII — Proceedings of the 1997 IEEE Workshop*, pages 511 – 520, New York, 1997. IEEE.

B. Müller and J. Reinhardt. *Neural Networks: An Introduction.* Springer Verlag, 1990.

K.-R. Müller, J. Kohlmorgen, and K. Pawelzik. Analysis of switching dynamics with competing neural networks. *IEICE Transactions on Fundamentals of Electronics, Communications and Computer Sciences*, E78–A(10):1306–1315, 1995.

K.-R. Müller, A. Smola, G. Rätsch, B. Schölkopf, J. Kohlmorgen, and V. Vapnik. Predicting time series with support vector machines. In W. Gerstner, A. Germond, M. Hasler, and J.-D. Nicoud, editors, *Artificial Neural Networks — ICANN'97*, pages 999 – 1004, Berlin, 1997. Springer Lecture Notes in Computer Science, Vol. 1327.

P.M. Murphy and D.W. Aha. UCI repository of machine learning databases. Department of Information and Computer Science, University of California, Irvine, California, 1992.

B. A. Murtagh and M. A. Saunders. MINOS 5.4 user's guide. Technical Report SOL 83.20, Stanford University, 1993.

K. G. Murthy. *Linear Programming.* John Wiley & Sons, New York, New York, 1983.

S. Murthy, S. Kasif, and S. Salzberg. A system for induction of oblique decision trees. *Journal of Artificial Intelligence Research*, 2:1–32, 1994.

I. Nagayama and N. Akamatsu. Approximation of chaotic behavior by using neural network. *IEICE Trans. Inf. & Syst.*, E77-D(4), 1994.

J. Nash. The embedding problem for riemannian manifolds. *Annals of Mathematics*, 63:20 – 63, 1956.

R. Neal. Priors for infinite networks. Technical Report CRG-TR-94-1, Dept. of Computer Science, University of Toronto, 1994.

R. Neal. *Bayesian Learning in Neural Networks.* Springer Verlag, 1996.

N. J. Nilsson. *Learning machines: Foundations of Trainable Pattern Classifying Systems.* McGraw-Hill, 1965.

E. Oja. A simplified neuron model as a principal component analyzer. *J. Math. Biology*, 15:267 – 273, 1982.

P. J. Olver. *Applications of Lie Groups to Differential Equations.* Springer-Verlag, 1986.

M. Opper. Learning in neural networks: Solvable dynamics. *Europhysics Letters*, 8 (4):389–392, 1989.

M. Opper and W. Kinzel. Physics of generalization. In E. Domany J.L. van Hemmen and K. Schulten, editors, *Physics of Neural Networks III.* Springer Verlag, New York, 1996.

M. Opper, P. Kuhlmann, and A. Mietzner. Convexity, internal representations and the statistical mechanics of neural networks. *Europhysics Letters*, 37(1):31–36, 1997.

M. Oren, C. Papageorgiou, P. Sinha, E. Osuna, and T. Poggio. Pedestrian detection using wavelet templates. In *Proc. Computer Vision and Pattern Recognition*, pages 193–199, Puerto Rico, 1997.

E. Osuna, R. Freund, and F. Girosi. An improved training algorithm for support vector machines. In J. Principe, L. Gile, N. Morgan, and E. Wilson, editors, *Neural Networks for Signal Processing VII — Proceedings of the 1997 IEEE Workshop*, pages 276 – 285, New York, 1997a. IEEE.

E. Osuna, R. Freund, and F. Girosi. Support vector machines: Training and applications. AI Memo 1602, Massachusetts Institute of Technology, 1997b.

E. Osuna, R. Freund, and F. Girosi. Training support vector machines: An application to face detection. In *Proc. Computer Vision and Pattern Recognition '97*, pages 130–136, 1997c.

N. H. Packard, J. P. Crutchfield, J. D. Farmer, and R. S. Shaw. Geometry from a time series. *Phys. Rev. Lett.*, 45:712–716, 1980.

E. Parzen. An approach to time series analysis. *Ann. Math. Statist.*, 32:951–989, 1962.

E. Parzen. Statistical inference on time series by rkhs methods. In R. Pyke, editor, *Proceedings 12th Biennial Seminar*, Montreal, 1970. Canadian Mathematical Congress. 1-37.

K. Pawelzik, J. Kohlmorgen, and K.-R. Müller. Annealed competition of experts for a segmentation and classification of switching dynamics. *Neural Computation*, 8 (2):342–358, 1996a.

K. Pawelzik, K.-R. Müller, and J. Kohlmorgen. Prediction of mixtures. In C. von der Malsburg, W. von Seelen, J. C. Vorbrüggen, and B. Sendhoff, editors, *Artificial Neural Networks — ICANN'96*, pages 127–133, Berlin, 1996b. Springer Lecture Notes in Computer Science, Vol. 1112.

K. Pearson. On lines and planes of closest fit to points in space. *Philosophical Magazine*, 2 (sixth series):559–572, 1901.

J. C. Platt. A resource-allocating network for function interpolation. *Neural Computation*, 3(2):213–225, 1991.

J. C. Platt. Sequential minimal optimization: A fast algorithm for training support vector machines. Technical Report MSR-TR-98-14, Microsoft Research, 1998.

T. Poggio. On optimal nonlinear associative recall. *Biological Cybernetics*, 19: 201–209, 1975.

T. Poggio and F. Girosi. Networks for approximation and learning. *Proceedings of the IEEE*, 78(9), 1990a.

T. Poggio and F. Girosi. Regularization algorithms for learning that are equivalent to multilayer networks. *Science*, 247:978–982, 1990b.

M. Pontil and A. Verri. Properties of support vector machines. *Neural Computation*, 10:955 – 974, 1997.

M. J. D. Powell. Radial basis functions for multivariable interpolation: A review. In *Algorithms for Approximation, J.C. Mason and M.G. Cox (Eds.)*, pages 143–167. Oxford Clarendon Press, 1987.

W. H. Press, S. A. Teukolsky, W. T. Vetterling, and B. P. Flannery. *Numerical Recipes in C: The Art of Scientific Computing (2nd ed.)*. Cambridge University Press, Cambridge, 1992.

J. C. Principe and J. M. Kuo. Dynamic modeling of chaotic time series with neural networks. In J. D. Cowan, G. Tesauro, and J. Alspector, editors, *Advances in Neural Information Precessing Systems 7*, San Mateo, CA, 1995. Morgan Kaufmann Publishers.

R.T. Prosser. The ε–Entropy and ε–Capacity of Certain Time–Varying Channels. *Journal of Mathematical Analysis and Applications*, 16:553–573, 1966.

J. R. Quinlan. *C4.5: Programs for Machine Learning.* Morgan Kaufmann, 1993.

C. Rasmussen. *Evaluation of Gaussian Processes and Other Methods for Non-Linear Regression.* PhD thesis, Department of Computer Science, University of Toronto, 1996. ftp://ftp.cs.toronto.edu/pub/carl/thesis.ps.gz.

H. J. Ritter, T. M. Martinetz, and K. J. Schulten. *Neuronale Netze: Eine Einführung in die Neuroinformatik selbstorganisierender Abbildungen.* Addison-Wesley, Munich, Germany, 1990.

A. Roy, S. Govil, and R. Miranda. An algorithm to generate radial basis function (RBF)-like nets for classification problems. *Neural Networks*, 8(2):179–202, 1995.

A. Roy, L. S. Kim, and S. Mukhopadhyay. A polynomial time algorithm for the construction and training of a class of multilayer perceptrons. *Neural Networks*, 6:535–545, 1993.

A. Roy and S. Mukhopadhyay. Iterative generation of higher-order nets in polynomial time using linear programming. *IEEE Transactions on Neural Networks*, 8 (2):402–412, 1997.

M. A. Saunders S. S. Chen, D. L. Donoho. Atomic decomposition by basis pursuit. Technical Report Dept. of Statistics Technical Report, Stanford University, 1996.

S. Saitoh. *Theory of Reproducing Kernels and its Applications.* Longman Scientific & Technical, Harlow, England, 1988.

T. D. Sanger. Optimal unsupervised learning in a single-layer linear feedforward network. *Neural Networks*, 2:459–473, 1989.

T. Sauer, J. A. Yorke, and M. Casdagli. Embedology. *J. Stat. Phys.*, 65:579–616, 1991.

C. Saunders, M. O. Stitson, J. Weston, L. Bottou, B. Schölkopf, and A. Smola. Support vector machine - reference manual. Technical Report CSD-TR-98-03, Department of Computer Science, Royal Holloway, University of London, Egham, TW20 0EX, UK, 1998. TR available as http://www.dcs.rhbnc.ac.uk/research/compint/areas/comp_learn/sv/pub/report98-03.ps; SVM available at http://svm.dcs.rhbnc.ac.uk/.

R. J. Schalkoff. *Digital Image Processing and Computer Vision.* John Wiley and Sons, Inc., 1989.

R. Schapire, Y. Freund, P. Bartlett, and W. Sun Lee. Boosting the margin: A new explanation for the effectiveness of voting methods. *Annals of Statistics*, 1998. (To appear. An earlier version appeared in: D.H. Fisher, Jr. (ed.), Proceedings ICML97, Morgan Kaufmann.).

M. Schmidt and H. Gish. Speaker identification via support vector classifiers. In *Proc. ICASSP '96*, pages 105–108, Atlanta, GA, 1996.

I. Schoenberg. Positive definite functions on spheres. *Duke Math. J.*, 9:96–108, 1942.

B. Schölkopf, C. Burges, and V. Vapnik. Extracting support data for a given task. In U. M. Fayyad and R. Uthurusamy, editors, *Proceedings, First International Conference on Knowledge Discovery & Data Mining.* AAAI Press, Menlo Park,

CA, 1995.

B. Schölkopf. *Support Vector Learning.* R. Oldenbourg Verlag, Munich, 1997.

B. Schölkopf, P. Bartlett, A. Smola, and R. Williamson. Support vector regression with automatic accuracy control. In L. Niklasson, M. Bodén, and T. Ziemke, editors, *Proceedings of the 8th International Conference on Artificial Neural Networks*, Perspectives in Neural Computing, Berlin, 1998a. Springer Verlag. In press.

B. Schölkopf, C. Burges, and V. Vapnik. Incorporating invariances in support vector learning machines. In C. von der Malsburg, W. von Seelen, J. C. Vorbrüggen, and B. Sendhoff, editors, *Artificial Neural Networks — ICANN'96*, pages 47 – 52, Berlin, 1996a. Springer Lecture Notes in Computer Science, Vol. 1112.

B. Schölkopf, P. Knirsch, A. Smola, and C. Burges. Fast approximation of support vector kernel expansions, and an interpretation of clustering as approximation in feature spaces. In *20. DAGM Symposium Mustererkennung*, Lecture Notes in Computer Science, Berlin, 1998b. Springer. To appear.

B. Schölkopf, S. Mika, A. Smola, G. Rätsch, and K.-R. Müller. Kernel PCA pattern reconstruction *via* approximate pre-images. In L. Niklasson, M. Bodén, and T. Ziemke, editors, *Proceedings of the 8th International Conference on Artificial Neural Networks*, Perspectives in Neural Computing, Berlin, 1998c. Springer Verlag. In press.

B. Schölkopf, P. Simard, A. Smola, and V. Vapnik. Prior knowledge in support vector kernels. In M. Jordan, M. Kearns, and S. Solla, editors, *Advances in Neural Information Processing Systems 10*, Cambridge, MA, 1998d. MIT Press.

B. Schölkopf, A. Smola, and K.-R. Müller. Nonlinear component analysis as a kernel eigenvalue problem. Technical Report 44, Max-Planck-Institut für biologische Kybernetik, 1996b.

B. Schölkopf, A. Smola, and K.-R. Müller. Kernel principal component analysis. In W. Gerstner, A. Germond, M. Hasler, and J.-D. Nicoud, editors, *Artificial Neural Networks — ICANN'97*, pages 583 – 588, Berlin, 1997a. Springer Lecture Notes in Computer Science, Vol. 1327.

B. Schölkopf, A. Smola, and K.-R. Müller. Nonlinear component analysis as a kernel eigenvalue problem. *Neural Computation*, 10:1299 – 1319, 1998e.

B. Schölkopf, A. Smola, K.-R. Müller, C. Burges, and V. Vapnik. Support vector methods in learning and feature extraction. In T. Downs, M. Frean, and M. Gallagher, editors, *Proceedings of the Ninth Australian Conference on Neural Networks*, pages 72 – 78, Brisbane, Australia, 1998f. University of Queensland.

B. Schölkopf, K. Sung, C. Burges, F. Girosi, P. Niyogi, T. Poggio, and V. Vapnik. Comparing support vector machines with gaussian kernels to radial basis function classifiers. *IEEE Trans. Sign. Processing*, 45:2758 – 2765, 1997b.

J. C. Schouten, F. Takens, and C. M. van den Bleek. Estimation of the dimension of a noisy attractor. *Physical Review E*, 50(3):1851–1860, 1994.

J. Schürmann. *Pattern Classification: a unified view of statistical and neural approaches.* Wiley, New York, 1996.

D.W Scott. *Multivariate Density Estimation.* Wiley-Interscience, New York, 1992.

H. S. Seung, H. Sompolinsky, and N. Tishby. Statistical mechanics of learning from examples. *Physical Review A*, 45(8):6056–6091, 1992.

J. Shawe-Taylor, P. Bartlett, R. Williamson, and M. Anthony. A framework for structural risk minimization. In *COLT*, 1996.

J. Shawe-Taylor, P. L. Bartlett, R. C. Williamson, and M. Anthony. Structural risk minimization over data-dependent hierarchies. *IEEE Transactions on Information Theory*, 1998. To appear. Also: NeuroCOLT Technical Report NC-TR-96-053, 1996, ftp://ftp.dcs.rhbnc.ac.uk/pub/neurocolt/tech_reports.

J. Shawe-Taylor and N. Cristianini. Data-dependent structural risk minimisation for perceptron decision trees. In *Advances in Neural Information Processing Systems 10*, 1998.

P. Simard, Y. LeCun, and J. Denker. Efficient pattern recognition using a new transformation distance. In S. J. Hanson, J. D. Cowan, and C. L. Giles, editors, *Advances in Neural Information Processing Systems 5*, pages 50–58, San Mateo, CA, 1993. Morgan Kaufmann.

A. Skorokhod and M. Yadrenko. On absolute continuity of measures corresponding to homogeneous Gaussian fields. *Theory of Probability and its Applications*, XVIII:27–40, 1973.

F. W. Smith. Pattern classifier design by linear programming. *IEEE Transactions on Computers*, C-17:367–372, 1968.

A. Smola and B. Schölkopf. From regularization operators to support vector kernels. In M. Jordan, M. Kearns, and S. Solla, editors, *Advances in Neural Information Processing Systems 10*, Cambridge, MA, 1998a. MIT Press.

A. Smola and B. Schölkopf. On a kernel-based method for pattern recognition, regression, approximation and operator inversion. *Algorithmica*, 1998b. In press.

A. Smola, B. Schölkopf, and K.-R. Müller. The connection between regularization operators and support vector kernels. *Neural Networks*, 11:637–649, 1998a.

A. Smola, B. Schölkopf, and K.-R. Müller. Convex cost functions for support vector regression. In L. Niklasson, M. Bodén, and T. Ziemke, editors, *Proceedings of the 8th International Conference on Artificial Neural Networks*, Perspectives in Neural Computing, Berlin, 1998b. Springer Verlag. In press.

A. Smola, B. Schölkopf, and K.-R. Müller. General cost functions for support vector regression. In T. Downs, M. Frean, and M. Gallagher, editors, *Proc. of the Ninth Australian Conf. on Neural Networks*, pages 79 – 83, Brisbane, Australia, 1998c. University of Queensland.

J. Stewart. Positive definite funcions and generalizations, an historical survey. *Rocky Mountain Journal of Mathematics*, 6(3):409–434, 1978.

M. Stitson, A. Gammerman, V. Vapnik, V. Vovk, C. Watkins, and J. Weston. Support vector regression with ANOVA decomposition kernels. Technical Report CSD-TR-97-22, Royal Holloway, University of London, 1997.

F. Takens. Detecting strange attractors in fluid turbulence. In D. Rand and L.S. Young, editors, *Dynamical Systems and Turbulence*, pages 366–381. Springer-Verlag, Berlin, 1981.

M. Talagrand. The Glivenko–Cantelli problem, ten years later. *Journal of Theoretical Probability*, 9(2):371–384, 1996.

W. Thomas. Database marketing: Dual approach outdoes response modeling. *Database Marketing News*, page 26, 1996.

R. Vanderbei. Loqo: An interior point code for quadratic programming. Technical Report SOR 94-15, Princeton University, 1994.

R. J. Vanderbei. LOQO user's manual – version 3.10. Technical Report SOR-97-08, Princeton University, Statistics and Operations Research, 1997. Code available at http://www.princeton.edu/~rvdb/.

V. Vapnik. *Estimation of Dependences Based on Empirical Data [in Russian]*. Nauka, Moscow, 1979. (English translation: Springer Verlag, New York, 1982).

V. Vapnik. *The Nature of Statistical Learning Theory.* Springer Verlag, New York, 1995.

V. Vapnik. Structure of statistical learning theory. In A. Gammerman, editor, *Computational and Probabalistic Reasoning*, chapter 1. Wiley, Chichester, 1996.

V. Vapnik. *Statistical Learning Theory.* Wiley, New York, 1998. forthcoming.

V. Vapnik and A. Chervonenkis. A note on one class of perceptrons. *Automation and Remote Control*, 25, 1964.

V. Vapnik and A. Chervonenkis. Uniform convergence of frequencies of occurence of events to their probabilities. *Dokl. Akad. Nauk SSSR*, 181:915 – 918, 1968.

V. Vapnik and A. Chervonenkis. On the uniform convergence of relative frequencies of events to their probabilities. *Theory of Probability and its Applications*, 16(2): 264–280, 1971.

V. Vapnik and A. Chervonenkis. *Theory of Pattern Recognition [in Russian]*. Nauka, Moscow, 1974. (German Translation: W. Wapnik & A. Tscherwonenkis, *Theorie der Zeichenerkennung*, Akademie-Verlag, Berlin, 1979).

V. Vapnik and A. Chervonenkis. Necessary and sufficient conditions for the uniform convergence of means to their expectations. *Theory of Probability and its Applications*, 26(3):532–553, 1981.

V. Vapnik, S. Golowich, and A. Smola. Support vector method for function approximation, regression estimation, and signal processing. In M. Mozer, M. Jordan, and T. Petsche, editors, *Advances in Neural Information Processing Systems 9*, pages 281–287, Cambridge, MA, 1997. MIT Press.

V. Vapnik and A. Lerner. Pattern recognition using generalized portrait method.

Automation and Remote Control, 24, 1963.

V. Vapnik, E. Levin, and Y. Le Cun. Measuring the VC-dimension of a learning machine. *Neural Computation*, 6(5):851–876, 1994.

N. Ya. Vilenkin. *Special Functions and the Theory of Group Representations*, volume 22 of *Translations of Mathematical Monographs*. American Mathematical Society Press, Providence, NY, 1968.

M. Villalobos and G. Wahba. Inequality constrained multivariate smoothing splines with application to the estimation of posterior probabilities. *J. Am. Statist. Assoc.*, 82:239–248, 1987.

G. Wahba. Convergence rates of certain approximate solutions to Fredholm integral equations of the first kind. *Journal of Approximation Theory*, 7:167 – 185, 1973.

G. Wahba. Improper priors, spline smoothing and the problem of guarding against model errors in regression. *J. Roy. Stat. Soc. Ser. B*, 40:364–372, 1978.

G. Wahba. Spline interpolation and smoothing on the sphere. *SIAM J. Sci. Stat. Comput.*, 2:5–16, 1981.

G. Wahba. Constrained regularization for ill posed linear operator equations, with applications in meteorology and medicine. In S. Gupta and J. Berger, editors, *Statistical Decision Theory and Related Topics, III, Vol.2*, pages 383–418. Academic Press, 1982a.

G. Wahba. Erratum: Spline interpolation and smoothing on the sphere. *SIAM J. Sci. Stat. Comput.*, 3:385–386, 1982b.

G. Wahba. A comparison of GCV and GML for choosing the smoothing parameter in the generalized spline smoothing problem. *Ann. Statist.*, 13:1378–1402, 1985a.

G. Wahba. Multivariate thin plate spline smoothing with positivity and other linear inequality constraints. In E. Wegman and D. dePriest, editors, *Statistical Image Processing and Graphics*, pages 275–290. Marcel Dekker, 1985b.

G. Wahba. *Spline Models for Observational Data*, volume 59 of *CBMS-NSF Regional Conference Series in Applied Mathematics*. SIAM, Philadelphia, 1990.

G. Wahba. Multivariate function and operator estimation, based on smoothing splines and reproducing kernels. In M. Casdagli and S. Eubank, editors, *Nonlinear Modeling and Forecasting, SFI Studies in the Sciences of Complexity, Proc. Vol XII*, pages 95–112. Addison-Wesley, 1992.

G. Wahba, D. Johnson, F. Gao, and J. Gong. Adaptive tuning of numerical weather prediction models: randomized GCV in three and four dimensional data assimilation. *Mon. Wea. Rev.*, 123:3358–3369, 1995a.

G. Wahba, Y. Wang, C. Gu, R. Klein, and B. Klein. Structured machine learning for 'soft' classification with smoothing spline ANOVA and stacked tuning, testing and evaluation. In J. Cowan, G. Tesauro, and J. Alspector, editors, *Advances in Neural Information Processing Systems 6*, pages 415–422. Morgan Kauffman, 1994.

G. Wahba, Y. Wang, C. Gu, R. Klein, and B. Klein. Smoothing spline ANOVA for exponential families, with application to the Wisconsin Epidemiological Study of Diabetic Retinopathy. *Ann. Statist.*, 23:1865–1895, 1995b.

T. L. H. Watkin, A. Rau, and M. Biehl. The statistical mechanics of learning a rule. *Reviews of Modern Physics*, 65:499–556, 1993.

A. S. Weigend and N. A. Gershenfeld (Eds.). *Time Series Prediction: Forecasting the Future and Understanding the Past.* Addison-Wesley, 1994. Santa Fe Institute Studies in the Sciences of Complexity.

P. Werbos. *Beyond Regression: New Tools for Prediction and Analysis in the Behavioral Sciences.* PhD thesis, Harvard, 1974.

J. Werner. *Optimization - Theory and Applications.* Vieweg, 1984.

J. Weston and C. Watkins. Multi-class support vector machines. Technical Report CSD-TR-98-04, Department of Computer Science, Royal Holloway, University of London, Egham, TW20 0EX, UK, 1998.

H. Widom. Asymptotic behaviour of eigenvalues of certain integral operators. *Archive for Rational Mechanics and Analysis*, 17:215–229, 1964.

R. A. Wilkinson, J. Geist, S. Janet, P. J. Grother, C. J. C. Burges, R. Creecy, B. Hammond, J. J. Hull, N. J. Larsen, T. P. Vogl, and C. L. Wilson. The first census optical character recognition system conference. Technical Report NISTIR 4912, National Institute of Standards and Technology (NIST), Gaithersburg, 1992.

C. K. I. Williams. Computation with infinite networks. In M. Mozer, M. Jordan, and T. Petsche, editors, *Advances in Neural Information Processing Systems 9*, Cambridge, MA, 1997. MIT Press.

C. K. I. Williams. Prediction with gaussian processes: From linear regression to linear prediction and beyond. In M. I. Jordan, editor, *Learning and Inference in Graphical Models.* Kluwer, 1998. To appear. Also: Technical Report NCRG/97/012, Aston University.

R. C. Williamson, A. J. Smola, and B. Schölkopf. Generalization performance of regularization networks and support vector machines via entropy numbers of compact operators. Technical Report NC-TR-98-019, Royal Holloway College, University of London, UK, 1998a.

R. C. Williamson, A. J. Smola, and B. Schölkopf. A Maximum Margin Miscellany. Typescript, 1998b.

W. H. Wolberg and O. L. Mangasarian. Multisurface method of pattern separation for medical diagnosis applied to breast cytology. *Proceedings of the National Academy of Sciences, U.S.A.*, 87:9193–9196, 1990.

A. Wolf, J. B. Swift, H. L. Swinney, and J. A. Vastano. Determining lyapunov exponents from a time series. *Physica D*, 16:285–317, 1985.

D. Xiang. *Model Fitting and Testing for Non-Gaussian Data with a Large Data Set.* PhD thesis, Technical Report 957, University of Wisconsin-Madison, Madison

WI, 1996.

D. Xiang and G. Wahba. A generalized approximate cross validation for smoothing splines with non-Gaussian data. *Statistica Sinica*, 6:675–692, 1996.

D. Xiang and G. Wahba. Approximate smoothing spline methods for large data sets in the binary case. Technical Report 982, Department of Statistics, University of Wisconsin, Madison WI, 1997. To appear in the Proceedings of the 1997 ASA Joint Statistical Meetings, Biometrics Section, pp 94-98 (1998).

P. V. Yee. *Regularized Radial Basis Function Netowrks: Theory and Applications to Probability Estimation, Classification, and Time Series Prediction.* PhD thesis, Dept. of ECE, McMaster University, Hamilton, Canada, 1998.

E. C. Zachmanoglou and Dale W. Thoe. *Introduction to Partial Differential Equations with Applications.* Dover, Mineola, N.Y., 1986.

X. Zhang and J. Hutchinson. Simple architectures on fast machines: practical issues in nonlinear time series prediction. In A. S. Weigend and N. A. Gershenfeld, editors, *Time Series Prediction: Forecasting the Future and Understanding the Past.* Santa Fe Institute, Addison-Wesley, 1994.

G. Zoutendijk. *Methods of Feasible Directions: a Study in Linear and Non-line ar Programming.* Elsevier, 1970.

Index

adaptive RBF networks, 248
annealed VC entropy, 118
ANOVA, 73, 74

basis pursuit de-noising, 279
Bayes' rule, 57
Bayesian posterior classifier, 52
boosting, 51, 55
Bregman methods, 197
Bunch-Kaufman algorithm, 154

capacity, 2, 125
central moments, 113
chaotic system, 214
choice of parameters, 225, 249
Christoffel symbols, 95
chunking, 158, 159, 177, 187
classification
    multi-class, 255
    multicategory, 317
    pairwise, 255
    soft, 75
complete set of equations, 106
compression, 275
conditional density estimation, 40
conditional probability estimation, 38
conjugate gradient, 154, 155, 198
covariance, 74
covariance matrix, 328
covering number, 130
cross kernel, 296
    Gaussian-like, 299
    spline, 297

data
    test, 1
    training, 1
    validation, 249, 289
data set
    Boston housing, 288
    Daimler-Benz OCR, 261
    electrons, 282
    face detection, 275
    Mackey Glass, 250
    MNIST, 148, 201, 264
    MPI chair recognition, 340
    NIST, *see* MNIST
    noisy Lorenz, 230
    people detection, 275
    pure Lorenz, 229
    Ripley, 278, 282
    Santa Fe Competition, 251
    skin, 282
    UCI Adult, 200
    USPS, 150, 321, 342
    web categorization, 201
decision function, 8
decision tree, 313
decision variables, 120
decomposition algorithm, 13
density estimation, 293
    spline, 296
determinant, 122
dichotomies, 118
dictionary of kernels, 299, 300
differential operator, 72
dimensionality reduction, 335
distribution
    posterior, 57
    prior, 57
dynamical reconstruction, 215

embedding, 249
empirical risk minimization, 217

entropy number, 130

fat-shattering dimension, 47, 58, 117
feature, 328
  extraction, 331
  space, 5, 29, 273, 329, 345

GACV, 69, 78
Gaussian process, 74
GCKL, 78, 79
generalization bound, 2, 43, 132
generalization
    bound, 33
Generalized Portrait, 3
geodesic, 101
Green's function, 14, 72
group
  generators, 108
  infinitesimal, 108
Growth function, 2, 130

Hessian, 84
Hilbert space, 74
hyperplane
  canonical, 3, 31, 32
  optimal, 3, 27, 28
  separating, 27
  soft margin, 9

image recognition, 181
interior point optimizer, 149
invariance
  additive, 109
  local, 104
  no-go theorem, 110

Karush-Kuhn-Tucker conditions, 4, 152, 153, 171, 186
kernel, 6, 350
  ANOVA, 285, 287
  constant spline, 296
  cross, *see* cross kernel
  dictionary, 299
  Gaussian, 142, 225, 249
  Gaussian-like, 299
  indefinite, 350
  Laplacian, 142
  Mercer, 6, 7, 30
  multiplicative, 286
  Non-Mercer, 298, 350
  polynomial, 6, 274, 333, 349
  positive semidefinite, 91
  radial basis function, 7
  reproducing, 7, 71, 74
  sigmoid, 7, 98, 299
  spline, 286, 291
  trick, 25, 328, 346
  unitary invariant, 333
KKT, *see* Karush-Kuhn-Tucker
Kullback-Leibler distance, 76, 79

Lagrange multipliers, 4, 171
Lagrangian, 4
learning from examples, 1, 25
likelihood, 88
logit, 70, 75
Lorenz system, 228
Lorenz time-series, 229
loss function, 10, 11, 133
  ε-insensitive, 10, 245
  Huber, 223, 246
  squared, 300

main effects spaces, 74
manifold, 91
margin, 32, 35, 45, 55, 117, 126
Maurey's theorem, 138
Mercer's condition, 90
metric, 92
  Riemannian, 92
Moore-Aronszajn Theorem, 71
Multisurface method of pattern recognition, 309

Nash's theorem, 99
noisy data, 230
nonlinear reconstruction, 214
nonparametric regression, 69
notation, 15

odds ratio, 75
operator equation, 38, 40, 295
operators, 129
  complete system of, 106
optical character recognition, 13, 200, 261, 321, 341
optimization, *see* programming problem

PAC bounds, 44
Parzen's windows, 301
PCA, *see* principal component analysis
perceptron, 33, 118
  relaxation rule, 198
polynomial classifier, 264
positive definite function, 100
principal component analysis, 264, 327
  kernel, 331
  linear, 328
  nonlinear, 329, 336
programming problem
  dual, 5, 8, 11, 221
  linear, 298, 310
  primal, 4, 9, 10, 219, 280
  quadratic, 169
projected conjugate gradient, 198
pseudoinverse, 248

quadratic programming, 147, 148, 169, 185

randomization, 80
randomized trace, 84
reduced set method, 13, 273, 334
regression, 11
  dictionary of kernels, 299, 300
  linear programming, 298
  squared loss, 300
regularization, 14, 345
  L_1, 298, 300
regularization network, 128
regularized RBF, 224
representer of evaluation, 71
representer theorem, 71
Resource Allocating Network, 198
risk
  actual, 1
  empirical, 1
  regularized, 14
risk factor, 78
row-action methods, 197

saddlepoint, 122
scalar curvature, 96
Sequential Minimal Optimization, 177, 178, 185
  benchmarking, 198
  code optimization, 193
  experimental results, 201
  pseudo-code, 195
sigmoid neural networks, 52
slack variables, 9, 15, 28
SMO, *see* Sequential Minimal Optimization
sparse data, 185
sparse dot product, 194
spherical distribution, 119
spherical Gaussian distribution, 126
spline, 72
state space, 249
statistical mechanics, 118
stopping criteria, 199
structural risk minimisation, 46
structural risk minimization, 26, 143, 217
  data dependent, 47
support vector, 4, 27, 29
  decision trees, 313
  density estimation, 40, 295
  essential, 32
  expansion, 4, 14, 271
  mechanical interpretation, 5
  pattern recognition, 8
  regression, 10, 244, 279
  set, 13
  virtual, 13
SVM

fixed-threshold, 197
implementation, 147, 169, 185, 224
nonlinear reconstruction, 228
semi-supervised, 323
training, 147, 169, 185
decomposition algorithm, 171, 187
Osuna's method, *see* decomposition algorithm
SVM^{light}, 169
symbols, 15

Takens theorem, 214
Tchebychev system, 72
tensor
metric, 93
Ricci, 96
Riemann, 95
text categorization, 179, 201
thermodynamic limit, 120
thin plate spline, 74
threshold, 10, 246
time series, 211, 244
noisy, 250
non-stationary, 251
prediction, 211, 248
transduction, 35, 323

VC dimension, 2, 26, 32, 44, 58, 120, 131
volume element, 97

working set, 172, 197